Children in Police Custody

CLARENDON STUDIES IN CRIMINOLOGY

Published under the auspices of the Institute of Criminology, University of Cambridge; the Mannheim Centre, London School of Economics; and the Centre for Criminology, University of Oxford.

General Editors:
Mary Bosworth and Carolyn Hoyle
(*University of Oxford*)

Editors:
Alison Liebling, Paolo Campana, Loraine Gelsthorpe, and Kyle Treiber
(*University of Cambridge*)
Tim Newburn, Jill Peay, Coretta Phillips, and Peter Ramsay
(*London School of Economics*)
Ian Loader and Lucia Zedner
(*University of Oxford*)

RECENT TITLES IN THIS SERIES:
Rethinking Drug Laws: Theory, History, Politics
Seddon

A Precarious Life: Community and Conflict in a Deindustrialized Town
Willis

From Conflict to Modern Slavery: The Drivers and the Deterrents
Heys

Exporting the UK Policing Brand 1989-2021
Sinclair

Penality in the Underground: The IRA's Pursuit of Informers
Dudai

Assessing the Harms of Crime: A New Framework for Criminal Policy
Greenfield and Paoli

Power and Pain in the Modern Prison: The Society of Captives Revisited
Crewe, Goldsmith, and *Halsey*

Armed Robbers: Identity and Cultural Mythscapes in the Lucky Country
Taylor

Crime, Justice, and Social Order: Essays in Honour of A. E. Bottoms
Liebling, Shapland, Sparks, and *Tankebe*

Policing Human Rights
Martin

Children in Police Custody

Adversity and Adversariality Behind Closed Doors

Miranda Bevan

Great Clarendon Street, Oxford, OX2 6DP,
United Kingdom

Oxford University Press is a department of the University of Oxford.
It furthers the University's objective of excellence in research, scholarship,
and education by publishing worldwide. Oxford is a registered trade mark of
Oxford University Press in the UK and in certain other countries

© Miranda Bevan 2024

The moral rights of the author have been asserted

First Edition published in 2024

All rights reserved. No part of this publication may be reproduced, stored in
a retrieval system, or transmitted, in any form or by any means, without the
prior permission in writing of Oxford University Press, or as expressly permitted
by law, by licence or under terms agreed with the appropriate reprographics
rights organization. Enquiries concerning reproduction outside the scope of the
above should be sent to the Rights Department, Oxford University Press, at the
address above

You must not circulate this work in any other form
and you must impose this same condition on any acquirer

Public sector information reproduced under Open Government Licence v3.0
(http://www.nationalarchives.gov.uk/doc/open-government-licence/open-government-licence.htm)

Published in the United States of America by Oxford University Press
198 Madison Avenue, New York, NY 10016, United States of America

British Library Cataloguing in Publication Data

Data available

Library of Congress Control Number: 2023946427

ISBN 978-0-19-285549-7

DOI: 10.1093/oso/9780192855497.001.0001

Printed and bound by
CPI Group (UK) Ltd, Croydon, CR0 4YY

Links to third party websites are provided by Oxford in good faith and
for information only. Oxford disclaims any responsibility for the materials
contained in any third party website referenced in this work.

General Editors' Introduction

The *Clarendon Studies in Criminology series* aims to provide a forum for outstanding theoretical and empirical work in all aspects of criminology and criminal justice, broadly understood. The Editors welcome submissions from established scholars as well as manuscripts based on excellent PhD dissertations. The series was inaugurated in 1994, with Roger Hood as its first General Editor, following discussions between OUP and Oxford's then Centre for Criminological Research. These days, it is edited under the auspices of three centres: the Centre for Criminology at the University of Oxford, the Institute of Criminology at the University of Cambridge, and the Mannheim Centre for Criminology at the London School of Economics. Each institution supplies members of the Editorial Board and, in turn, the Series General Editor or Editors.

Children in Police Custody: Adversity and Adversariality behind Closed Doors by Miranda Bevan provides a detailed, theoretically informed, empirical analysis of children's experiences of youth justice as suspects. We know very little about this population or their treatment, and so this careful study offers much-needed original evidence. In it, Bevan draws on interviews with children and young people with recent experience of police custody in England and Wales, as well as with a range of practitioners. She also presents material drawn from extensive periods of observation conducted in police custody blocks.

From that range of empirical evidence, Bevan crafts a detailed, moving account of the system, revealing multiple failures and challenges from the start. Children thus describe being restrained inappropriately by the police and not knowing what will happen to them following arrest. Their understanding of their legal rights is often poor and they do not seem to receive age-appropriate information or treatment.

While she documents that the police's communication about their rights has improved, the children are not always able to understand what they are told. In practical terms, this means that child suspects sometimes decline a solicitor, despite this potentially adversely affecting their case.

The figure of an 'appropriate adult' (AA), whose role is to assist children in custody is also shown to be lacking. Not only do they often arrive some time after the child is detained, but also their access to the child is often severely curtailed. Bevan is firm: 'too often the role serves more to legitimize the process than to protect and enable the child suspect', she writes. Together, such matters have an inevitable effect. Despite the statutory duty of the police to safeguard and protect children in their care, detention is harmful and, Bevan concludes, 'exacerbates and entrenches disadvantage'.

While most of the book documents the problems children face, in the conclusion, Bevan offers some solutions. Most obviously, she notes, detention should be used as sparingly as possible. More generally, as the title of the book suggests, Bevan argues that the adversarial nature of the criminal process makes it hard to discern the children's vulnerability. A better system, she suggests, would centre children's rights and their care, as it does for child victims.

This is a nuanced account of a difficult and understudied part of the criminal justice system. While the barriers to reform are clearly high, Bevan makes a persuasive case for change. We think that this book has the potential for policy impact and we welcome it to the series.

Mary Bosworth and Carolyn Hoyle
General Editors
Centre for Criminology, University of Oxford
July 2023

Preface

In November 1975, the Court of Appeal quashed the convictions of three teenagers for offences relating to the murder of Maxwell Confait and the subsequent fire at his home in April 1972.[1] Ahmet Salih and Ronald Leighton were children at the time of the incident, aged fourteen and fifteen years, respectively; Colin Lattimore was eighteen years old but had been identified in the police station as having 'the mental age of a boy of 14 years'.[2] The subsequent inquiry into the investigation, led by Sir Henry Fisher, had called into question the reliability of confessions made by the boys in their interviews conducted in police custody, on which the prosecutions had exclusively relied. The inquiry identified that each had been interviewed by the police in the absence of a parent or independent adult and that there had been other breaches of the Judges' Rules and Administrative Directions that then governed the detention and questioning of suspects, including failures to inform the boys of their legal rights and the oppressive and unfair questioning of Colin Lattimore in particular.[3] The 'disquiet' caused by the *Confait* case, and the 'serious questions' concerning the treatment of young suspects raised by the Fisher Inquiry, were a significant factor in the setting up of the Royal Commission on Criminal Procedure in 1977,[4] which, in turn, led to the passing of the Police and Criminal Evidence Act 1984 (PACE), the legislation that still governs the treatment and questioning of suspects in the police station today.

Given this history, it has almost become an expectation, when writing about the treatment of child suspects,[5] to refer to the *Confait* case, and with

---

[1] For full detail, see Sir Henry Fisher, 'Report of an Inquiry by the Hon. Sir Henry Fisher into the Circumstances Leading to the Trial of Three Persons on Charges Arising Out of the Death of Maxwell Confait and the Fire at 27 Doggett Road, London SE6' (His Majesty's Stationery Office (HMSO) 1977).
[2] ibid 11.
[3] ibid.
[4] Royal Commission on Criminal Procedure (RCCP), 'Report (Cmnd 8092)' (HMSO 1981) 3.
[5] I use the phrase 'child suspect' and 'young suspect' to refer to ten-to-seventeen-year-olds detained by the police for investigation following arrest on suspicion of a criminal offence, in preference to the term 'juvenile' used in PACE.

good reason. It illustrates starkly the serious injustice that can occur when reliance is placed on evidence elicited from children[6] in the police station when the protections they should enjoy have not been afforded to them. What is said, or not said, by a suspect in police interview is 'of fundamental importance for the development and the outcome of the case';[7] indeed, often it is determinative of it.[8] This is particularly the case for child suspects since admissions made in police interview are more likely, than for an adult to result in diversion from the criminal process by the offering of an out-of-court disposal[9] or the imposition of a referral order following a guilty plea.[10] Thus, the child is formally sanctioned but without their treatment in police custody being scrutinized by a court.

However, the *Confait* case should not just stand as a cautionary reminder of these dangers. Rather, reflecting on the case raises for me a clear question: are we satisfied that the sort of injustice experienced by Colin Lattimore, Ronald Leighton, and Ahmet Salih is not being repeated for child suspects today? The surprising answer is that for decades we have not been able to say. Indeed, the question has barely been considered. It is fifty years since the *Confait* suspects were in the police station, and it is over thirty-five years since Parliament responded to those 'serious concerns' raised in the Fisher Inquiry with fundamental legislative change to the way police powers are governed, through the passing of PACE and its attendant Codes of Practice.[11] A child suspect in police custody today is under the care of an officer independent of the investigation, the custody officer (CO), whose role is to ensure that the requirements of PACE and *Code C* are observed.[12] An 'appropriate adult' (AA), most often a parent or carer, must be present for key parts of the investigation process, including the police

---

[6] I use the terms 'child' and 'children' to refer to ten-to-seventeen-year-olds. The choice of term is a conscious one, designed to emphasize their rights and their entitlement to distinctive treatment under the United Nations Convention on the Rights of the Child, although I am conscious that some teenagers may not ordinarily welcome the application of the term to them. I address this and other compromises in the methodological discussion in Chapter 1.
[7] Edward Cape, Jacqueline Hodgson, and Taru Spronken, *Suspects in Europe* (Intersentia 2007) 19–20.
[8] Frank P Belloni, *Criminal Injustice: An Evaluation of the Criminal Justice Process in Britain* (Macmillan 2000).
[9] Crime and Disorder Act 1998, s 66ZA and 66ZB.
[10] Powers of Criminal Courts (Sentencing) Act 2000, s 16-28.
[11] In particular, *Code C: Revised Code of Practice for the Detention, Treatment and Questioning of Persons by Police Officers*, updated 4 November 2020 (in force at time of writing) (*Code C*). Any relevant variance with the version in force at the time of fieldwork, published May 2014, will be noted as it arises.
[12] PACE, s 37.

interview,[13] and has the duty of safeguarding the child's rights, entitlements, and welfare.[14] The child, and their AA, must be informed of their legal rights and offered free and independent legal advice.[15] Yet, we have hitherto had very limited insight into how those protections are implemented today and whether, taken together, they provide effective protection for young suspects. The young suspect's experience of the police custody process, in particular, is rarely explored. Brookman and Pierpoint wrote, in 2003, that young suspects were 'all but invisible in the criminal justice literature',[16] and they have largely remained so. Research, which has included suspects' views and experiences alongside other observational or quantitative work, is itself limited. In the past thirty years, there have only been four empirical studies in England and Wales which have examined the custody process as a whole and sought to incorporate the views of suspects,[17] but they have focused almost exclusively on adult experiences.[18] The voices of children and young people with experience of police custody are rarely heard, both in England and Wales and internationally,[19] and where children have participated in

[13] *Code C* (n 11) 11.15ff. AA support is also required for adults identified as 'vulnerable'; see *Code C* para 1.13(d) and Annex E.
[14] Crime and Disorder Act 1998, s 38(4)(a) and *Code C* (n 11) para 1.7A. *Code C* para 1.7A, added in the July 2018 edition of *Code C*, postdates the fieldwork period, but it has clarified, rather than changed significantly, the content of the AA's role.
[15] *Code C* (n 11) paras 6.1 and 6.5A.
[16] Fiona Brookman and Harriet Pierpoint, 'Access to Legal Advice for Young Suspects and Remand Prisoners' (2003) 42 Howard Journal of Criminal Justice 452, 453.
[17] Satnam Choongh, *Policing as Social Discipline* (Clarendon Press 1997); Tim Newburn and Stephanie Hayman, *Policing, Surveillance and Social Control: CCTV and Police Monitoring of Suspects* (Willan Publishing 2002); Layla Skinns, *Police Custody: Governance, Legitimacy and Reform in the Criminal Justice Process* (Willan Publishing 2011); Layla Skinns and Andrew Wooff, 'Pain in Police Detention: A Critical Point in the "Penal Painscape"?' (2020) Policing & Society 1; Layla Skinns, Andrew Wooff, and Amy Sprawson, 'Preliminary Findings on Police Custody Delivery in the Twenty-First Century: Is It "Good" Enough?' (2017) 27 Policing & Society 358.
[18] Choongh (n 17) involved the largest number of child suspects (eight), although it is important to note that all of these studies predated the inclusion of seventeen-year-olds within the 'juvenile' category. As a result, some studies, such as Newburn and Heyman's *Policing, Surveillance and Social Control* (n 17), included seventeen-year-olds, but they would not have experienced the protections afforded to 'juveniles'. At the time of writing, an ongoing study was engaging with children in police custody but had not yet reported: Vicky Kemp and others, *Examining the Impact of PACE on the Detention and Questioning of Child Suspects by the Police in England and Wales* (Nuffield Foundation, 25 May 2023) <https://www.nuffieldfoundation.org/project/impact-of-pace-on-the-detention-and-questioning-of-young-suspects> accessed 10 October 2023.
[19] For notable exceptions, see Vicky Kemp and Dawn Watkins, 'Exploring Children's Understanding of the Legal Rights of Suspects in England and Wales' (2022) 22(3) Youth Justice 320; re Northern Ireland, Katie Quinn and John Jackson, 'The Detention and Questioning of Young Persons by the Police in Northern Ireland', Northern Ireland Office Research & Statistical Series: Report No. 9 (2003) and re Israel, Nadera Shalhoub-Kevorkian

research projects in this area, the numbers involved have tended to be very modest.[20] The invisibility of child suspects in research to date is a particular cause of concern for two reasons. First, the indications that we have from the wider research on the implementation of protections in police custody suggest that the problems identified by Fisher continue to be repeated, with the key supports introduced for children in the wake of the *Confait* case being neither implemented consistently nor functioning effectively. For example, quantitative research into the uptake of legal advice by young suspects in England and Wales found that 43% of children who went on to be charged did not request to see a solicitor, and that ten-to-thirteen-year olds were the least likely age group to request and receive legal advice.[21] Equally, police interview analysis has revealed that oppressive and unfair questioning techniques have persisted, against which the almost invariable presence of an AA has proved an inadequate protection.[22] The independent role of the CO has, it seems, also proved ineffective in securing key procedural rights—for example, authorisation of detention has been observed often to amount to little more than a rubber-stamping exercise,[23] time spent in police custody by children has lengthened considerably,[24] and those who are not bailed are almost always detained post-charge in police custody in infringement of their statutory rights.[25] Without insights from child suspects themselves, it is not possible to

---

and Bella Kovner, 'Child Arrest, Settler Colonialism, and the Israeli Juvenile System: A Case Study of Occupied East Jerusalem' (2018) 58 British Journal of Criminology 709.

[20] See eg Vicky Kemp and Jacqueline Hodgson, 'Chapter 4. England and Wales Empirical Findings' in Miet Vanderhallen and others (eds), *Interrogating Young Suspects: Procedural Safeguards from an Empirical Perspective*, Vol 2 (Intersentia 2016), which involved a single focus group with five young people.

[21] Vicky Kemp, Pascoe Pleasence, and Nigel J Balmer, 'Children, Young People and Requests for Police Station Legal Advice: 25 Years On from PACE' (2011) 11 Youth Justice 28.

[22] Roger Evans, 'The Conduct of Police Interviews with Juveniles', Royal Commission on Criminal Justice, Research Study No 8 (HMSO 1993); Sarah Medford, Gisli H Gudjonsson, and John Pearse, 'The Efficacy of the Appropriate Adult Safeguard during Police Interviewing' (2003) 8 Legal and Criminological Psychology 253; Kemp and Hodgson (n 20).

[23] Roxanna Dehaghani, 'Automatic Authorisation: An Exploration of the Decision to Detain in Police Custody' (2017) Criminal Law Review 187.

[24] Extending for children from an average of five hours in the late 1990s (Coretta Phillips and David C Brown, 'Entry into the Criminal Justice System: A Survey of Police Arrests and Their Outcome', Home Office Research Study 185 (Home Office 1998)) to just under eleven hours in 2015 (HM Inspectorate of Constabulary (HMIC), *The Welfare of Vulnerable People in Custody* (HMIC 2015). See also Vicky Kemp, Nigel Balmer, and Pascoe Pleasence, 'Whose Time Is It Anyway? Factors Associated with Duration in Police Custody' (2012) Criminal Law Review 736.

[25] PACE, s 38(6); see Layla Skinns, *Overnight Detention of Children in Police Cells* (Howard League for Penal Reform 2011).

identify fully the barriers they face in engaging with the intended protections or to understand the implications of implementation failures on their experience of custody, their ability to engage with the legal demands made on them in that setting, and their enjoyment of their wider rights, particularly those guaranteed by the European Convention on Human Rights and the United Nations Convention on the Rights of the Child.

Second, for most children who find themselves in conflict with the law, a period in police custody after arrest is their only substantive experience of the criminal justice system. Although there has been a welcome reduction in recent years, there were still, in the year to March 2022, just under 53,000 arrests of children (aged 10–17) for notifiable offences.[26] These numbers dwarf those children who were proceeded with at court (17,200) and those receiving community (7,700) and custodial sentences (550).[27] It seems extraordinary that we should previously have known so little about this most common of sustained youth justice experiences. This is particularly concerning since the limited insights hitherto available reveal that, for children, police detention is often experienced as frightening,[28] disempowering,[29] and punitive.[30] North American research has amply illustrated the likely negative impact of punitive police experiences on young people's development as citizens,[31] and procedural justice scholars have established the significance of fair decision-making and respectful treatment in the maintenance of police legitimacy.[32] Understanding children's responses to police detention experiences, and identifying how and why those responses are triggered, is key. This is particularly important because arrests are a site of significant racial disproportionality—arrests of Black children, for example, accounted for 13% of all children arrested in the year

---

[26] Youth Justice Board/Ministry of Justice (YJB/MoJ), *Youth Justice Statistics 2021–22, England and Wales* (National Statistics 2023) 1.2.
[27] ibid 5.1, 5.3.
[28] All-Party Parliamentary Group for Children, '"It's All about Trust": Building Good Relationships between Children and the Police, Report of the inquiry held by the All-Party Parliamentary Group for Children, 2013–2014' (National Children's Bureau 2014); HMIC (n 24).
[29] Choongh (n 17).
[30] Neal Hazel, Ann Hagell, and Laura Brazier, *Young Offenders' Perceptions of Their Experiences in the Criminal Justice System. Summary and Full Report of Research Activities and Results* (Economic and Social Research Council 2003).
[31] See eg Benjamin Justice and Tracey L Meares, 'How the Criminal Justice System Educates Citizens' (2014) 651 Annals of the American Academy of Political and Social Science 159.
[32] Tom R Tyler, *Why People Obey the Law* (Yale UP 1990); Tom R Tyler and Yuen J Huo, *Trust in the Law: Encouraging Public Cooperation with the Police and Courts* (Russell Sage Foundation 2002).

to March 2022, despite Black children making up only 4% of the general ten-to-seventeen-year-old population.[33]

In response to the invisibility of child suspects, this book illuminates the hidden experiences of children in police detention, drawing on the first substantial qualitative study in England and Wales to assess the custody process as a whole from the perspective of the child suspect. It provides, for the first time, a comprehensive empirical account of the experience of children in police custody in England and Wales. The chapters trace the child's journey through a detention episode, creating a rich, multidimensional picture of the child's experience of police custody, the extent to which they engage the rights and protections that should be afforded to them, and the impact of their detention on their participation in the process.

With the two identified areas of concern squarely in mind, the analysis aims to answer two central questions. First, adopting a rights-based approach, I investigate whether the legal framework now in place provides effective protection from injustice for child suspects today. From the detailed insights provided by young participants in the research, I map the complex challenges posed for children's legal agency in the adversarial setting of the custody block and evaluate the capacity of the available protections to enable truly effective participation within the constraints of police custody. Second, a parallel criminological exploration of the detention experience enables me to examine the impact of police detention on the very many children who experience it every year in England and Wales. I develop a picture of the intersecting adversities experienced by child suspects, and the complex power dynamics that they must navigate in police custody, to arrive at an understanding of the particular pains of police detention for children and their impact.

Broadening the argument from police custody to the wider youth justice system, the book contributes to contemporary debates about the experience and conceptualization of suspect and defendant 'vulnerability' and reflects on the challenges of affording effective support to enable all participants to exercise their rights in an adversarial criminal justice process. Drawing on approaches in other jurisdictions, I call for a retrenchment in the use of police custody for children suspected of offending and a reappraisal of how those who must be detained should be supported to enable their effective participation in the criminal justice process in custody and beyond.

---

[33] YJB/MoJ, *Youth Justice Statistics, 2021–22* (n 26), 1.4. For the most recent relative rate index of arrests of children, see YJB/MoJ, *Youth Justice Statistics 2018–19, England and Wales* (National Statistics 2020) 8.

Acknowledgements

I would like to thank, first and foremost, all the young people who spoke to me during the course of this research, both those who I met in police stations and those who I interviewed. Without them, plainly, there would be no study, and I am hugely grateful to them for giving up their time to talk to me. Telling me about their experiences was not always easy, and I hope that I have done justice to their accounts. My thanks also to the family members and carers who supported the young people to take part in this study and to those parents who gave up their own time to be interviewed by me.

This study could not have been completed without the very dedicated support of the gatekeepers through whom I recruited those young people and the gatekeepers who supported the project to get off the ground. I am acutely aware of, and extremely grateful for, the time and energy many people dedicated to arranging the interviews. I am sorry that anonymity requirements prevent me from naming them because their commitment and hard work deserves to be recognized.

I also owe a huge debt to the three police forces with whom I conducted observations. From vetting through to arranging my access to the suites themselves, it was a substantial undertaking. I am really grateful to everyone that I encountered on observations. I was made to feel very welcome. Thank you for talking to the researcher with the racing pen, for fielding endless questions, and making me many cups of tea. I am grateful also to all the detainees who, in difficult circumstances, were willing to allow me to track their experiences. My thanks, too, to all the professionals and volunteers who I interviewed, both as part of the main study and during my scoping exercise. Your insights were invaluable.

I will be forever indebted to my PhD supervisors, Tim Newburn and Coretta Phillips, whose support and patience was unwavering. I feel very privileged to have worked with them—they are an inspiration. I am very grateful to the London School of Economic and Political Science (LSE) for supporting the research with a studentship, which made this whole endeavour possible. I am also grateful to the Economic and Social Research Council for the assistance of a Post-Doctoral Fellowship (Reference ES/

V007084/1), which enabled me to convert my thesis into this book, and the support of Leo Cheliotis and Peter Ramsay during my year back at LSE. I would also like to thank the anonymous reviewers whose comments were of considerable assistance in refining earlier drafts.

Last, but not least, special thanks to my wonderful family, my husband Andy, and our children, whose love keeps me going.

Miranda Bevan
15 May 2023

Contents

Table of Case Law   xix
Table of Legislation   xxiii
List of Abbreviations   xxvii

1. Bringing Child Suspects into the Light   1
    Introduction   1
    Who Is a 'Child' Suspect in England and Wales?   1
    The Ramifications of Natural Developmental Immaturity in Custody   5
    What Do We Know about the Children Who Find Themselves in
      Police Custody?   6
    Invisibility of Child Suspects in Legislation and Policy   13
    Invisibility in the Courts and Other Accountability Mechanisms   18
    Invisibility in Previous Research   21
    Theoretical Underpinning of Research Methods   25
    Research Methods   37
    The Structure of the Book   46

2. The Early Stages: Adversity and Adversariality in Collision   49
    Introduction   49
    Immediate Situational Adversity   53
    The Early Custody Journey: Procedure and Existing Literature   59
    The Early Custody Journey: Child Suspect Experiences   60
    Authorisation of Detention: Procedure and Existing Literature   71
    Authorisation of Detention: Child Suspect Experiences   73
    Risk Assessment: Procedure and Existing Literature   78
    Risk Assessment: Child Suspect Experiences   80
    Search and Seizure of Belongings: Procedure and Existing
      Literature   83
    Search and Seizure of Belongings: Child Suspect Experiences   87
    Conclusion   90

**3. The Child as Legal Actor: Understanding and Exercising
    Rights**   98
    Introduction   98
    Communicating Legal Rights: Procedure and Existing Literature   103
    Communicating Legal Rights: Child Suspect Experiences   105

Exercising the Right to Legal Advice: Procedure and Existing
   Literature   112
Exercising the Right to Legal Advice: Child Suspect Experiences   118
Benefiting from Legal Rights   132
Conclusion   145

4. Making Good the Imbalance? Examining the Appropriate Adult Role   153

Introduction   153
The AA Role: Procedure and Existing Literature   157
The Role in Practice: Child Suspect Experiences   168
Support and Welfare   177
Facilitating Rights: Understanding   183
Facilitating Rights: Supporting the Child to Exercise Their
   Legal Rights   185
Assisting with Communication   188
Guardian of Due Process   191
Conclusion   195

5. In the Cell: The Process Is the Punishment   204

Introduction   204
Being in the Cell: Child Suspect Experiences of Detention   207
Limiting Detention Periods: Procedure and Existing Literature   213
Limiting Detention Periods: Child Suspect Experiences   216
Adjustments to Detention Conditions: Procedure and Existing
   Literature   220
Adjustments to Detention Conditions: Child Suspect Experiences   222
Barriers to Child Friendly Detention   235
Exclusionary Effects   247
Conclusion   255

6. Police Interview: A Counterproductive Process?   258

Introduction   258
Fitness to Be Interviewed: Procedure and Existing Literature   262
Fitness to Be Interviewed: Child Suspect Experiences   266
Questioning in Interview: Procedure and Existing Literature   276
Questioning in Interview: Child Suspect Experiences   282
Maintaining 'No Comment': Procedure and Existing Literature   293
Maintaining 'No Comment': Child Suspect Experiences   294
Interview Protections: Procedure and Existing Literature   297
Interview Protections: Child Suspect Experiences   299
Conclusion   303

7. Conclusion: Rethinking the Use of Police Custody for Children — 308
How Far Have We Really Come Since *Confait*? — 308
Turning Youth Justice on Its Head: The 'Pains' of Police Custody — 314
Why Has So Little Progress Been Made? — 318
Reform: Retrenchment — 331
Reform: Achieving Child First Police Custody — 337
Implications for the Wider Youth Justice System — 342

Appendix A: Schedule of Young Participant Interviews — 347
Appendix B: Schedule of Police Station Observations — 351
Bibliography — 355
Index — 381

Table of Case Law

Al-Fayed v Commissioner of the Police of the Metropolis [2004]
EWCA Civ 1579, (2004) 148 SJLB 1405............................72n.75
Attorney-General's Reference (No 2 of 2001) [2003] UKHL 68,
[2004] 2 AC 72 ....35n.225

Cadder v HM Advocate [2010] UKSC 43,
[2010] 1 WLR 2601 .... 35n.226, 35n.228, 112n.62
C (A minor) v Director of Public Prosecutions (1996) AC 1 ....344n.117
C (A minor) v Sevenoaks Magistrates' Court [2009] EWHC 3088
(Admin), [2010] 1 All ER 735...................................14n.88
Commissioner of the Police for the Metropolis v MR [2019]
EWHC 888 (QB)..72n.70

D v Chief Constable of Merseyside Police [2015] EWCA Civ 114,
[2015] Crim LR 539................... 84n.119, 84n.121, 90n.143, 233n.98
Director of Public Prosecutions v L [1998] 12 WLUK 285,
[1999] Crim LR 752..72n.70

Gillick v West Norfolk and Wisbech Area Health Authority and
Department of Health and Social Security [1984] QB 581 (QBD)......44n.256

H and M v Director of Public Prosecutions [1997] 12 WLUK 189,
(1998) Crim LR 653................................. 19n.123, 165n.97
Hanningfield v Chief Constable of Essex [2013] EWHC 243 (QB),
[2013] 1 WLR 3632 ....72n.75
Hayes v Chief Constable of Merseyside [2011] EWCA Civ 911,
[2012] 1 WLR 517..72n.75

Local Authority v B [2008] EWHC 1017 (Fam), [2009] 1 FLR 289..........162n.72

Owens v Chief Constable of Merseyside Police [2021] EWHC 3119 (QB)....84n.122

R v Abdurahman (Ismail) [2019] EWCA Crim 2239, [2020] 4 WLR 6......35n.230
R v Blake 1989 1 WLR 432, (1989) 89 Cr App R 179.....................164n.88
R v Dean Thomas [2020] EWCA Crim 117, [2020] 4 WLR 66 ....14n.88
R v Lubemba [2014] EWCA Crim 2064,
[2015] 1 WLR 1579 .... 14n.85, 279n.83, 308n.2
R v Grant Murray [2017] EWCA Crim 1228, CA, [2018]
Crim LR 71 .... 14n.86, 279n.84

xx Table of Case Law

R v *Gunning* (1980) 98 Cr App R 303 .... 321n.41
R v *Jefferson (Andrew Steven)* [1994] 1 All ER 270 (CA (Crim Div)) 164n.90
R v *Jogee* [2016] UKSC 8, [2017] AC 387 .... 122n.123
R v *Morse and Others* [1990] 11 WLUK 237,
 [1991] Crim LR 195 .... 19n.122, 165n.93
R v *Nottle* [2004] EWCA Crim 599 .... 114n.83
R v *Petkar* [2003] EWCA Crim 2668, [2004] 1 Cr App R 22 .... 286n.120
R v *Palmer* (Acton Crown Court), 17 October 1991 .... 164n.89
R v *Pritchard* (1836) Eng R 540, (1836) 7 C & P 303; 173 ER 135 .... 101n.11
R v *Roble* [1997] 1 WLUK 233, [1997] Crim LR 449 .... 114n.83
R v *Samuel* [1988] Q.B. 615 (CA) 112n.61, 148n.175
R v *W* [1994] 1 WLUK 214, [1994] Crim LR 130
 (CA (Crim Div)) 19n.122, 165n.94
R v *Walsh* [1989] 7 WLUK 174, (1990) 91 Cr App R 161 .... 148n.176
R v *Ward* [2018] EWCA Crim 1464 .... 162n.71
R (*Alconbury Developments Ltd*) v *Secretary of State for the Environment,
 Transport and the Regions* [2001] UKHL 23, [2003] 2 AC 295 .... 35n.231
R (*AR (a child)*) v *Waltham Forest LBC* [2021] EWCA Civ 1185, [2021] PTSR
 1777 .... 236n.104
R (*AS*) v *Great Yarmouth Youth Court* [2011] EWHC 2059 (Admin),
 [2012] Crim LR 478 and Crim PD 3F.12ff 14n.88
R (*BG*) v *Chief Constable of the West Midlands* [2014] EWHC 4374
 (Admin), (2015) 179 JP 93 .... 15n.96
R (*Hallam and Nealon*) v *SoS for Justice* [2019] UKSC 2, [2020] AC 279 .... 35n.230
R (*HC (a child by his litigation friend CC)*) v *Secretary of State for
 the Home Department* [2013] EWHC 982 (Admin),
 [2014] 1 WLR 1234 (HC) 4n.20, 34, 153n.2, 158n.28, 199n.160, 304n.166
R (*Kaiyam*) v *SOS for Justice* [2014] UKSC 66, [2015] AC 1344 .... 35n.230
R (*Prudential plc*) v *Special Commissioner of Income Tax (Institute of
 Chartered Accountants in England and Wales intervening)* [2010]
 EWCA Civ 1094, [2011] QB 669 .... 202n.165
R (*R*) v *Durham Constabulary* [2005] UKHL 21, [2005] 1 WLR 1184 ...... 35n.224
R (*T*) v *Secretary of Justice for Justice* [2013] EWHC 1119 (Admin),
 [2013] ACD 88 .... 15n.95
Re *Gallagher's Application for Judicial Review* [2019] UKSC 3,
 [2020] AC 18 .... 132n.147
Reeves v *Commissioner of Police of the Metropolis* [2000] 1 AC 360 (HL),
 [1999] 3 WLR 363 .... 84n.120
Richardson v *Chief Constable of West Midlands Police* [2011]
 EWHC 773 (QB), [2011] 2 Cr App R 1 .... 72n.75

ST v *Chief Constable of Nottinghamshire Police* [2022]
 EWHC 1280 (QB) 72n.76, 75n.84, 217n.59, 332, 334n.89

TI v *Bromley Youth Court* [2020] EWHC 1204, [2020]
 2 Cr App R 22 (Admin) 14n.88

NEW ZEALAND

Police v FG [2020] NZYC 328 (29 June 2020) 196n.155

UNITED STATES

Commonwealth v Smith 472 Pa 492 (1977) 149n.188
Fare v Michael C 442 US 707 (1979) 100n.9, 101n.12, 148n.177
In Re Gault 387 US 1 (1967). 100n.9
Miranda v Arizona 384 US 436 (1966) 100n.9
West v United States 399 F2d 467 (1968) 101n.13

EUROPEAN COURT OF JUSTICE

Adamkiewicz v Poland 54729/00, 2 March 2010 .... 35n.222
Blokhin v Russsia App no 47152/06, 23 March 2016 .... 35n.222
Dvorski v Croatia App no 25703/11, 20 October 2015 .... 35n.222
Edwards and Lewis v United Kingdom App nos 39647/98 and
    40461/98, 27 October 2004 .... 32n.207
Ibrahim and Others v UK App nos 50541/08, 50571/08, 50573/08, and
    40351/09, 13 September 2016 .... 112n.62
Kress v France App no 39594/98, 7 June 2001 .... 32n.208
Murray v UK App no 18731/91, 8 February 1996; 22 EHRR 29 .... 112n.62
Panovits v Cyprus App no 4268/04, 11 March 2009, (2008)
    27 BHRC 464 .... 34, 34n.221, 93n.150, 99n.3, 101n.15, 111n.59,
                                        122n.124, 132n.146, 263n.32, 283n.115,
                                                          304n.166, 313n.16
Regner v Czech Republic App no 35289/11, 19 September 2017 .... 32n.207
Salduz v Turkey App no 36391/02, 27 November 2008,
    (2009) 49 EHRR 19. .... 35n.227, 112n.62
SC v United Kingdom App No 60958/00, 10 November 2004,
    (2005) 40 EHRR 10. .... 14n.82, 34n.220, 308n.1
Stanford v UK App no 16757/90 ECHR, 23 February 1994 .... 34n.218
T v United Kingdom App no 24724/94, 16 December 1999 and
   V v United Kingdom App no 24888/94, 16 December 1999,
    (2000) 30 EHRR 121 .... 14n.81, 33n.211, 34n.219, 308n.1

Table of Legislation

PRIMARY LEGISLATION

Age of Criminal Responsibility
  (Scotland) Act 2019 1–4
Bail Act 1976 .... 15n.96
  s 7 .... 219n.65
Children Act 2004 78–80
  s 11 ... 13, 72n.76, 91n.146, 93n.153,
            94–95, 213n.38,
            220n.66, 334n.87
Children and Young Persons
  Act 1933
  Pt III 13
  s 31 ..... 14n.79, 15n.95, 60n.46, 61,
            220n.74, 228n.94, 315n.22
  s 34A 14n.80
  s 41 .... 15n.94
  s 44 .... 13n.74
  s 45 .... 13n.78
  s 47 .... 13n.77
  s 50 .... 2n.5, 98n.1
  s 53 .... 343n.113
Children and Young Persons
  Act 1969 1–4
Children's Hearings (Scotland)
  Act 2011 .... 3n.11
Coroners and Justice Act 2009
  s 104 .... 14n.87
Crime and Disorder
  Act 1998 ...... 2n.4, 3n.12, 162–63
  Pt III 315n.23
  s 34 .... 343n.116
  s 37 .... 13n.73
  s 38 .... 159n.41, 160n.46
  s 38(4)(a) ixn.14, 157n.25
  s 66ZA viiin.9, 113n.71
  s 66ZA(1)(b) 260n.17
  s 66ZB viiin.9, 113n.71
  s 66B(3) 260n.17

Criminal Justice and Courts
  Act 2015
  s 17(3) 333n.85
  s 42 1–2
Criminal Justice and Public
  Order Act 1994 111
Criminal Justice (Scotland)
  Act 2016
  s 9 339–40
  s 11(2)(a)(ii) 340n.105
  s 51(2) 334n.88
Criminal Procedure and
  Investigations Act 1996 ... 19n.119
Equality Act 2010
  s 2 .... 304n.163
Human Rights Act 1998 .... 30–31, 308
  s 2 .... 35n.231
Legal Aid Sentencing and
  Punishment of Offenders
  Act 2012 18–21
  Sch 1 Pt I, paras 21–22 ...... 20n.126
Magistrates' Courts Act 1980
  s 13 .... 219n.65
Modern Slavery Act 2015
  s 49 .... 213n.35
Police and Criminal Evidence
  Act 1984 .... vii, viin.5, 1–2, 13,
         14–15, 46–47, 50, 70, 92, 100–2,
            100–1n.10, 103, 111, 130,
            153–57, 160, 175–76,
            204–6, 208n.22,
            216–18, 308
  s 18 .... 71n.64, 76n.85
  s 30A 71n.65
  s 32 .... 71n.64, 76n.85
  ss 36–37 .... 321n.42
  s 36(5) 30n.192, 70
  s 37 ...... viiin.12, 17n.111, 28n.180,
            71–72, 90–91, 216n.56

xxiv Table of Legislation

s 37(3) 30n.193, 70, 258n.1, 332
s 37(7) 71n.62, 217n.61
s 38(6) xn.25, 15–16nn.96–97,
214n.43, 335–36
s 39 . . . . .78n.91
s 40 . . . . .214n.41
s 40(12) 218n.62
s 41 . . . . .214n.39
s 54 . . . . .83n.108, 83n.112
s 54(9) 83n.109
s 57 13
s 58(1) 113n.70
s 65 . . . . .106n.44
ss 76–78 . . . . .260n.21
s 76 . . . . 17, 147, 193n.149
s 77 . . . . 148n.174
s 77(1)(b)(ii) 148n.174
s 78 . . . . 17, 147, 193n.149
s 82 147
Powers of Criminal Courts
(Sentencing) Act 2000
ss 16–28 . . . . .viiin.10, 18n.116,
261n.24
s 91 . . . . .13n.75
Youth Justice and Criminal
Evidence Act 1999 . . . . .2n.4
Pt II. 50n.3
Ch 1 .51n.10

SECONDARY LEGISLATION

Criminal Procedure Rules
2020/759 . . . . . . 13, 14–15, 308n.2
Pt 18 .308n.2
r 3.8(3)(b) 14n.83
National Police Records
(Recordable Offences)
Regulations 2000/1139 . . .106n.43
Rights of Children and Young Persons
(Wales) Measure 2011 c.02
s 1 . . . . .17n.112
The Police Act 1997 (Criminal
Record Certificates: Relevant
Matters) (Amendment)
(England and Wales)
Order 2020/1364 . . . . . . 132n.147

The Rehabilitation of Offenders
Act 1974 (Exceptions)
Order 1975 (Amendment)
(England and Wales)
Order 2020/1373 . . . . . . 132n.147

INTERNATIONAL

European Convention on Human
Rights . . . . viii–x, 30–31, 308
Art 3 . . . . 30–31, 36
Art 5 30–31
Art 6 . . . . 30–31, 32–36, 274
Art 6(1) 30–31
Art 6(3)(c) 111
Art 8 30–31
Art 12 . . . . 31, 36
Art 37 . . . . 31, 36
Art 37(b) 31, 339–40
Art 37(c) 31
Art 40 . . . . 31, 36
Art 40(1) 31
Art 40(2) 31
Art 40(2)(b)(ii) 112n.63
General Comment No 10 (2007)
on children's rights in the
child justice system
(CRC/C/GC/10) 2n.8, 59n.37,
99n.4, 205n.5
General Comment No 24 (2019)
on children's rights in the
child justice system
(CRC/C/GC/24) 71n.66,
112n.64, 213n.37, 304n.167
para 22 . . . . 2n.8, 99n.4, 343n.114
paras 38–53 . . . . .33n.214
para 39 . . . . .59n.38
para 41 . . . . .33n.212
para 45 . . . . .36n.233
paras 46– 47 . . . . .115n.85
para 46 . . . . 36n.233, 59n.37,
90n.145, 205n.5
para 55 .99n.5
para 59 . . . . .277n.67
Guidelines of the Committee of
Ministers of the Council

of Europe on child friendly justice
(adopted by the Committee of
Ministers on 17 November
2010 at the 1098th meeting
of the Ministers'
Deputies)...............32n.210
UN Standard Minimum Rule for the
Administration of Juvenile
Justice (adopted on 10 December
1985 at the 40th Session of the
General Assembly)
para 14.2 ....59n.37
United Nations Convention on
the Rights of Person with
Disabilities............. 333–34
United Nations Convention on
the Rights of the Child ..... viii–x,
viiin.6, 1–2, 31, 34, 36,
57–58, 70, 89–90,
111, 213, 308
Art 1......................4n.19
Art 12........ 93n.154, 274, 291–93
Art 37............ 71n.66, 93n.154,
313–14
Art 37(b) 205n.3, 213, 334n.90
Art 37(c) 205n.4, 255n.151
Art 37(d) 111
Art 40............ 93n.154, 291–93
Art 40(1) 205n.4, 255n.151,
322n.44

Italy

Criminal Code
Arts 97–98..................3n.10

Netherlands

Ambtsinstructie politie
Art 27.................. 200n.163

New Zealand

Oranga Tamariki Act 1989 333–34
s 5(1)(b)(i)................334n.91
s 222.................... 200n.161
s 226.................... 202n.166
s 236.....................337n.98

Table of Legislation xxv

OTHER LEGISLATION

Codes

Code of Criminal Procedure
Art 490................. 200n.163
Art 489(1) 152n.196
PACE Code of Practice... 1, 13–14, 118
Code A................84, 85n.130
Code C........ viiin.11, ixn.14, 1–2,
1–2n.1, 14–15, 16n.103,
17–18, 25n.160, 50, 60n.47,
61, 70, 71–72, 78n.92, 83–86,
85n.130, 87–90, 102–3, 105–6,
113–14, 118–32, 137, 145–46,
147, 154–55, 155n.13, 157–67,
158n.26, 159n.42, 162n.70,
172–77, 178, 196, 208n.22,
220, 220n.71, 222, 226–28,
226n.89, 229, 239–41, 258,
263, 276, 296–97, 320–28
Pt 5.................. 342n.110
para 1.1 ....214n.40
para 1.3 ....263n.34
para 1.4 ....53n.21
para 1.7 .... 159n.40, 172–77
para 1.7(b).......17n.108, 52n.20
para 1.7A........ixn.14, 17n.107,
151n.192, 158n.26,
173–74, 191–92
para 1.13(d) ixn.13, 52n.20,
265n.45
para 1.17A..... 157–67, 174n.126
para 2.4 ....159n.33
para 3.1 ....103nn.21–22, 309n.8,
339n.101
para 3.2 ....103n.28, 104n.29
para 3.2A...............104n.30
para 3.3A.......... 104n.35, 109
para 3.8A......138n.154, 173–74,
273n.60
para 3.12 ....53n.23
para 3.13 ...... 103n.23, 168, 199
para 3.15...16n.103, 103nn.24–25,
106n.48, 158nn.29–30,
174n.126, 174n.127,
227n.92

para 3.17 ...... 16n.104, 104n.33, 158n.27, 159n.34
para 3.18 ..... 174n.126, 220n.72, 226n.90
para 4.1 ....83n.109
para 4.5 ....83n.113
para 5.1 ....106n.49
para 5.5 ....322n.46
para 5.6 .... 103n.27, 220n.71, 226n.89, 239–41, 322n.45
para 5.7 ....227n.91
para 6.1 .... ixn.15, 114n.76
para 6.4 .... 114n.77, 125
para 6.5 .... 114nn.78–79, 125
para 6.5A ixn.15, 114n.80, 129, 147–48, 150, 159n.32, 339n.102
para 8.4 .... 240n.115
para 8.7 ....240n.114, 322n.47
para 8.8 .... 17n.109, 62n.50, 220, 220n.67, 222n.80, 223n.84, 329n.73
para 8.10 ....220n.68
para 9.3 ....220n.70
para 11.1A..............114n.83
para 11.15 ..... 16n.106, 159n.36, 277n.71
para 11.17 .... 159n.39, 174, 278n.72
para 11.17A........... 174n.124, 278n.73
para 11.18 ....159n.36
para 12.3 .....100–1n.10, 262–65, 263n.36, 265n.44, 270
para 12.5 274–76
para 15.3 .... 177n.133
Annex A 16n.105, 85n.126
para 5................159n.35
para 10...............84n.118
para 11(c) 159n.35, 159n.36
para 11(d).........84n.123, 88
Annex B.........103n.27, 105–6, 114n.76, 226n.89

Annex 2B...............85n.126
Annex E................. ixn.13
Annex G 100–2, 100–1n.10, 262, 263, 268–70, 274, 303, 312n.14, 320–21
para 1................263n.35
paras 2–3.............263n.31
para 2.................... 262
para 3.................... 262
para 3(a) 101n.14, 266–76
para 3(b) 266–76
para 4................264n.41
para 5................265n.46
para 6................264n.42
para 8.......202n.167, 263–64, 273–74
Notes for Guidance 14–15
NFG 1B............. 159n.42, 172–77, 196
NFG 1D 312n.15
NFG 1E.............. 161–62
NFG 1G...............53n.22
NFG 1K..............162n.70
NFG 5E..............226n.89
NFG 6ZA 125
NFG 8D 208n.22
NFG 9B....... 14–15, 220n.70
NFG 11C......14–15, 259n.13, 276, 303–7
NFG 16C.............159n.37
Code G
para 2.8 333

Practice Direction

Criminal Practice Directions—
October 2015 as amended April 2016, November 2016, January 2017, April 2018, October 2018, April 2019, October 2019, May 2020, and October 2020 (Crim PD), 3D.2 ....14–15, 14n.84, 308n.2

List of Abbreviations

AA	appropriate adult
ABE	Achieving Best Evidence
ABH	actual bodily harm
ACPO	Association of Chief Police Officers
ADHD	attention deficit hyperactivity disorder
AO	arresting officer
APP(DC)	Authorised Professional Practice (Detention and Custody)
APP(DC)(CRS)	Authorsied Professional Practice (Detention and Custody) (Control, Restraint and Searches)
APP(DC)(CYP)	Authorised Professional Practice (Detention and Custody) (Children and Young Persons)
APP(DC)(RA)	Authorised Professional Practice (Detention and Custody) (Risk Assessment)
APPGC	All-Party Parliamentary Group for Children
APP(I)(II)	Authorised Professional Practice (Investigation) (Investigative Interviewing)
ASC	autism spectrum condition
ASD	autism spectrum disorder
BAME	Black, Asian or ethnic minority
CA	custody assistant
CAMHS	Child and Adolescent Mental Health Services
CDA 1998	Crime and Disorder Act 1998
CJJI	Criminal Justice Joint Inspection
CO	custody officer
CPN	community psychiatric nurse
Crim PD	Criminal Practice Directions
Crim PR	Criminal Procedure Rules 2020/759
CSI	crime scene investigation
CYPA 1933	Children and Young Persons Act 1933
DCI	Defence for Children International
ECHR	European Convention on Human Rights
ECtHR	European Court of Human Rights
EHRC	Equality and Human Rights Commission
ESRC	Economic and Social Research Council

FAA	familial appropriate adult
FI	fitness to be interviewed
FME	forensic medical examiner
FMHP	forensic mental health practitioner
FNP	forensic nurse practitioner
HCP	health-care professional
HMIC	His Majesty's Inspectorate of Constabulary
HMICFRS	His Majesty's Inspectorate of Constabulary, Fire and Rescue Services
HMIP	His Majesty's Inspectorate of Prisons
HMI Probation	His Majesty's Inspectorate of Probation
HMSO	His Majesty's Stationery Office
HO	Home Office
ICV	independent custody visitor
Ins	(Police) Inspector
IO	investigating officer
i/v	interview
JDR	juvenile detention room
LA	local authority
LD	learning disability
L&D	Liaison and Diversion services
LSE	London School of Economics and Political Sciences
MACR	minimum age of criminal responsibility
MoJ	Ministry of Justice
NAAN	National Appropriate Adult Network
NFG	Notes for Guidance
NGO	non-governmental organization
NPCC	National Police Chiefs' Council
PAA	paid appropriate adult
PACE	Police and Criminal Evidence Act 1984
PCC	Police and Crime Commissioner
PEACE	model of interviewing (Perception and planning; Engage and explain; Account, clarification, challenge; Closure; Evaluation)
PFI	private finance initiative
PNC	police national computer
PRT	Prison Reform Trust
ProfAA	professional appropriate adult
PTSD	post-traumatic stress disorder
PYO	persistent young offender
RCCJ	Royal Commission on Criminal Justice
RCCP	Royal Commission on Criminal Procedure

List of Abbreviations

RHAA	residential home appropriate adult
RI schemes	Northern Ireland registered intermediary schemes
Sol	solicitor
SQIFA	screening questionnaire interview for adolescents
UN Committee	United Nations Committee on the Rights of the Child
UNCRC	United Nations Convention on the Rights of the Child
VAA	volunteer appropriate adult
YJB/MoJ	Youth Justice Board/Ministry of Justice
YJCEA	Youth Justice and Criminal Evidence Act 1999
YJS	youth justice system
YOT	youth offending team
YOTAA	youth offending team appropriate adult
YP	young person
YS	young suspect (tracked during fieldwork)

1
Bringing Child Suspects into the Light

Introduction

This introductory chapter explores in greater depth the invisibility of child suspects in several arenas: in legislation and policy, in the courts and accountability mechanisms, and in academic consideration. It introduces the theoretical framework within which the experiences of children in police detention will be evaluated and describes the research methods employed in the empirical work to explore the custody process from a child suspect perspective. The chapter closes by setting out the framework of the book and the progression of the chapters through the child's police custody journey.

Who Is a 'Child' Suspect in England and Wales?

Before turning to legislation and policy, it is important to consider what is meant by a 'child' in the context of police custody in England and Wales and what we know about the children likely to find themselves in police custody. How a 'child' is defined in the youth justice system (YJS), and in policing in particular, reveals much about the prevailing attitudes that lie behind the legislation and policy framework. The choice of terminology is informative and potentially influential. The Police and Criminal Evidence Act 1984 (PACE) section 37(15) defines an arrested person who 'appears to be under the age of 18' as a 'juvenile', and this is the term predominantly used for children in PACE *Code C*, the Code of Practice which governs their treatment in police custody.[1] The term 'juvenile' is not neutral but bears

---

[1] *Code C: Revised Code of Practice for the Detention, Treatment and Questioning of Persons by Police Officers* (updated 4 November 2020). (In force at the time of writing. Any relevant

overtones of immature transgression and risk, derived from its long linkage with the concept of 'juvenile delinquency'.[2] Additionally, in contrast to the term 'child', 'juvenile' defines by reference to what the individual is not (an adult) rather than emphasizing their distinctive needs and rights.[3] The College of Policing has, in preference, adopted the language of 'children and young persons' in their guidance, and the wider YJS has long since moved away from the terminology of 'juveniles'.[4] However, the term lingers stubbornly in the police custody context, not only in PACE and the *Code C* but also in the day-to-day language of custody blocks. Child suspects in detention are typically referred to as 'juveniles', or sometimes more affectionately as 'juvies', almost never as children, even those at the younger end of the age bracket. Indeed, my references to young suspects as 'children' during observations often raised eyebrows, even prompting the occasional dig at my supposed naivety: 'They're not all little cherubs' (custody officer (CO) 25).

Notably, a child facing criminal investigation in police custody in England and Wales may be strikingly young in comparison with the youngest suspects in Europe and comparable liberal democracies. For the purposes of arrest and detention, the lower age threshold for criminal investigation is determined by the minimum age of criminal responsibility (MACR), set in England and Wales at ten years.[5] This is amongst the very lowest MACRs in Europe,[6] and internationally,[7] and substantially below the minimum age of 'at least 14 years of age' urged by the United Nations Committee on the Rights of the Child (the UN Committee).[8] Additionally, many countries which have

---

variance with the version in force at the time of fieldwork, published May 2014, will be noted as it arises.)

[2] The phrase crystallized in the early nineteenth century; see for discussion Susan Magarey, 'The Invention of Juvenile Delinquency in Early Nineteenth-Century England' (1978) 34 Labour History (Canberra) 11; Peter King, 'The Rise of Juvenile Delinquency in England 1780–1840: Changing Patterns of Perception and Prosecution' (1998) Past & Present 116.

[3] Jens Qvortrup, *Childhood Matters: Social Theory, Practice and Politics* (Avebury 1994).

[4] See eg in the Crime and Disorder Act 1998 and the Youth Justice and Criminal Evidence Act 1999.

[5] Children and Young Persons Act 1933, s 50.

[6] Alongside Northern Ireland, which also has a MACR of 10. See for discussion Barry Goldson, 'COUNTERBLAST: "Difficult to Understand or Defend": A Reasoned Case for Raising the Age of Criminal Responsibility' (2009) 48 Howard Journal of Criminal Justice 514.

[7] See information on MACRs internationally collated by the Child Rights International Network available at <https://archive.crin.org/en/home/ages/europe.html> accessed 10 October 2023.

[8] General Comment No 24 (2019) on children's rights in the child justice system (CRC/C/GC/24), para 22. (General Comment No 24 replaces General Comment No 10 (2007) (CRC/C/GC/10) extant at the time of fieldwork. Any relevant variance will be noted as it arises.)

a low MACR often have secondary higher thresholds of criminal responsibility for less serious offences[9] or an additional age bracket within which an individual child's competence must be established or their presumed incompetence rebutted—known as *doli incapax* provisions.[10] Equally, some jurisdictions with a low MACR, such as France and Greece, limit sanctions for the youngest children to educational measures imposed in family and youth courts.[11] In England and Wales, there is no such stepped approach to criminal responsibility, nor *doli incapax* provision,[12] and, whilst most children who are prosecuted will appear in the specialized youth court, the youngest children arrested and detained in police custody still face adversarial proceedings, a finding of full criminal responsibility, and the prospect of punitive sanctions. In this regard, England and Wales is truly an outlier; described by Barry Goldson as 'manifestly out of sync with the norms of European youth justice law, policy and practice'.[13]

Provisions to raise the MACR in England and Wales to sixteen were passed into law in the Children and Young Persons Act 1969 but never brought into force. The hardening of attitudes to children in conflict with the law in the 1990s, cemented in the aftermath of the tragic murder of Jamie Bulger by two ten-year-olds, has all but extinguished any lingering political will to raise the MACR.[14] Over the past ten years, Liberal Democrat Peer Lord Dholakia has repeatedly introduced Private Member's Bills seeking to raise the MACR to twelve years for England and Wales.[15] The Coalition and

---

[9] See eg New Zealand, where a ten-or eleven-year-old can only be prosecuted for murder or manslaughter.
[10] See eg Italy, Criminal Code, Articles 97–98.
[11] Frieder Dunkel, 'Juvenile Justice Systems in Europe—Reform Developments between Justice, Welfare and "New Punitiveness"' (2014) 1 Kriminologijos Studijos 31, 43–44. See for similar specialized proceedings the Scottish Children's Hearings system, governed by the Children's Hearings (Scotland) Act 2011 and for comparison with other youth justice approachesMichael Cavadino, *Penal Systems: A Comparative Approach* (Sage 2006) ch 13.
[12] *Doli incapax* provisions were abolished in England and Wales by the Crime and Disorder Act 1998.
[13] Goldson (n 6) 517. See also Neal Hazel, 'Cross-National Comparison of Youth Justice (Youth Justice Board (YJB) 2008) <https://dera.ioe.ac.uk/7996/1/Cross_national_final.pdf> accessed 14 August 2023.
[14] Recent youth justice reviews have shied away from firm recommendations. See Lord Carlile, 'Independent Parliamentarians' Inquiry into the Operation and Effectiveness of the Youth Court' (June 2014) <http://michaelsieff-foundation.org.uk/content/inquiry_into_the_operation_and_effectiveness_of_the_youth_court-uk-carlile-inquiry.pdf> accessed 14 August 2023 and Charlie Taylor, *Review of the Youth Justice System in England and Wales* (Ministry of Justice (MoJ) 2016).
[15] Lord Dholakia's most recent Age of Criminal Responsibility Bill (2021 HL Bill 31) received its first reading on 15 June 2021 but fell with the prorogation of Parliament. For discussion of Lord Dholakia's initiatives see Harriet Wishart, 'Young Minds, Old Legal Problems: Can

Conservative governments have consistently stated that they do not support raising the MACR,[16] and none of Lord Dholakia's Bills have ever progressed beyond the first reading in the House of Commons.[17] By contrast, the MACR in Scotland was recently raised from eight to twelve years with the passing of the Age of Criminal Responsibility (Scotland) Act 2019. The punitive turn in youth justice[18] continues to exert its influence on policy-making for children in England and Wales and to shape attitudes towards young suspects and defendants.

In respect of the point at which age-related protections cease in police custody, England and Wales is now in line with international approaches. The upper threshold of eighteen, applicable in policing and wider youth justice legislation, accords with international human rights approaches and the United Nations Convention on the Rights of the Child (UNCRC), which defines as a child 'every human being below the age of 18 years'.[19] However, in terms of police custody, this has not long been the position. Contrary to the approach taken elsewhere in the YJS, seventeen-year-olds were, until the October 2013 revision of *Code C*, treated as adults in police custody. The raising of the threshold for a 'juvenile' to eighteen was only achieved following tireless campaigning by the families of Kesia Leatherbarrow, Joe Lawton, and Eddie Thornber—three seventeen-year-olds who took their own lives following detention in police custody as an adult—and a successful judicial review of the Home Secretary's previous refusal to amend *Code C* accordingly.[20] PACE itself was only amended in this regard when the Criminal Justice and Courts Act 2015 section 42 came into force on 26 October 2015.

Neuroscience Fill the Void? Young Offenders & the Age of Criminal Responsibility Bill— Promise and Perils' (2018) 82(4) Journal of Criminal Law 311

[16] See eg HL Deb 20 December 2010 cc815-7, HC Deb 20 July 2011 c1107-8W, HC Deb 11 August 2011 c108, and HL Deb 29 January 2016 c1574-5.
[17] Lord Dholakia's Age of Criminal Responsibility Bill (2019 HL Bill 405) progressed the furthest but fell awaiting its second reading in the House of Commons.
[18] See for discussion John Muncie, 'The Globalization of Crime Control—The Case of Youth and Juvenile Justice: Neo-liberalism, Policy Convergence and International Conventions' (2005) 9 Theoretical Criminology 35.
[19] Adopted and opened for signature, ratification, and accession by General Assembly Resolution 44/25 of 20 November 1989, entered into force 2 September 1990, Article 1.
[20] *R (HC) v Secretary of State for the Home Department and Another* [2013] EWHC 982 (Admin), [2014] 1 WLR 1234 (*HC*).

The Ramifications of Natural Developmental Immaturity in Custody

Whilst the stance of politicians may not have softened, clinical understanding of the implications of young age for participation in criminal justice processes has deepened considerably since the late 1990s. The past twenty years have seen real progress in our understanding of child development and our knowledge of the maturation of the teenage brain in particular.[21] Whilst the cognitive competence of an individual will generally be well developed by age sixteen, the social and emotional capacities required in decision-making continue to develop into the early twenties.[22] Adolescents can exert adult-like control over their behaviour, but their ability to perform optimally is less consistent than adults.[23] Risk-taking, reduced future-orientation, and impulsivity, along with reckless and experimenting behaviours, are now understood to be normal, adaptive features of adolescent behaviour and more likely to be engaged in, and influenced by, the presence of peers.[24]

These aspects of natural developmental immaturity have particular ramifications for young suspects. Research has explored the effects of developmental immaturity on children's ability to engage in legal processes. Increasingly, findings confirm that children aged under sixteen demonstrate inadequate functional and decision-making abilities that are capable of compromising their capacity for participating effectively in criminal proceedings.[25] Indeed, Thomas Grisso and colleagues' research in the United States revealed that adolescents aged eleven to thirteen were three times as

---

[21] Richard J Bonnie and Elizabeth S Scott, 'The Teenage Brain: Adolescent Brain Research and the Law' (2013) 22 Current Directions in Psychological Science 158.

[22] Kathryn L Mills and others, 'Developmental Changes in the Structure of the Social Brain in Late Childhood and Adolescence' (2014) 9 Social Cognitive and Affective Neuroscience 123; BJ Casey, Sarah Getz, and Adriana Galvan, 'The Adolescent Brain' (2008) 28 Developmental Review 62; Elizabeth Cauffman and Laurence Steinberg, 'Emerging Findings from Research on Adolescent Development and Juvenile Justice' (2012) 7 Victims & Offenders 428.

[23] Beatriz Luna and others, 'The Teenage Brain: Cognitive Control and Motivation' (2013) 22 Current Directions in Psychological Science 94.

[24] Sarah-Jayne Blakemore, 'Avoiding Social Risk in Adolescence' (2018) 27 Current Directions in Psychological Science 116; Laurence Steinberg and others, 'Around the World, Adolescence Is a Time of Heightened Sensation Seeking and Immature Self-Regulation' (2018) 21 Developmental Science 12532.

[25] Michael E Lamb and others, 'Developmental Factors Affecting Children in Legal Contexts' (2013) 13 Youth Justice 131; Alexandra O Cohen and others, 'When Is an Adolescent an Adult? Assessing Cognitive Control in Emotional and Nonemotional Contexts' (2016) 27 Psychological Science 549.

likely as young adults (aged eighteen to twenty-four) to be 'seriously impaired' on legal abilities, and adolescents aged fourteen to fifteen were twice as likely to be impaired.[26] His work has also identified that children tend to view rights as conditional, considering that they can be withdrawn by authorities and that they are unlikely to have the capacity to appreciate the implications of waiving rights.[27] Of concern, in addition, children are more vulnerable to interrogative pressure, and, under pressure, they are more likely to confess, and to confess falsely, than older individuals.[28]

However, such challenges will not always be readily apparent. Qualitative work in England and Wales[29] and overseas[30] suggests that, for some older adolescents, their physical maturity and apparent familiarity with criminal justice processes can mask their social and emotional immaturity in this context. In particular, repeat experience of the YJS has not been shown to result in greater understanding of legal concepts, trial processes, or rights.[31] Indeed, studies of young people repeatedly involved in the legal system in the United States have, in fact, demonstrated poorer understanding of legal concepts than those with no such experience.[32]

What Do We Know about the Children Who Find Themselves in Police Custody?

Such difficulties are related to normal development. However, research over the past twenty years has also seen a growing appreciation that, as a group,

---

[26] Thomas Grisso and others, 'Juveniles' Competence to Stand Trial: A Comparison of Adolescents' and Adults' Capacities as Trial Defendants' (2003) 27 Law & Human Behaviour 333.
[27] Thomas Grisso, 'The Competence of Adolescents as Trial Defendants' (1997) 3 Psychology, Public Policy, and Law 3.
[28] Saul Kassin and others, 'Police-Induced Confessions: Risk Factors and Recommendations' (2010) 34 Law & Human Behaviour 3; Allison Redlich and Gail Goodman, 'Taking Responsibility for an Act Not Committed: The Influence of Age and Suggestibility' (2003) 27 Law & Human Behaviour 141.
[29] Joyce Plotnikoff and Richard Woolfson, 'Young Defendants Pack: Scoping Study' (YJB 2002) <https://vdocuments.site/young-defendants-pack-scoping-study-lexicon-limited-young-defendants-pack-scoping.html> accessed 14 August 2023.
[30] Michele Peterson-Badali and Rona Abramovitch, 'Children's Knowledge of the Legal System: Are They Competent to Instruct Legal Counsel?' (1992) Canadian Journal of Criminology 130; Karen Saywitz, Carol Jaenicke, and Lorinda Camparo, 'Children's Knowledge of Legal Terminology' (1990) 14 Law & Human Behaviour 523.
[31] Plotnikoff and Woolfson (n 29); Peterson-Badali and Abramovitch (n 30).
[32] See eg Karen Saywitz and Carol Jaenicke, 'Children's Understanding of Legal Terminology' (Annual Meeting of the Society for Research on Child Development, Baltimore 1987).

children in trouble with the law 'are seriously disadvantaged on a number of important social, educational and health indicators'.[33]

Dispositional Vulnerabilities

There has been no clinical study examining the frequency of intellectual and developmental disabilities or mental health disorders amongst child suspects in England and Wales.[34] In relation to adults, the evidence base is limited but indicates significantly raised prevalence of such conditions amongst adult detainees and problems arising from co-morbidity.[35] The most recent study, conducted in a South London police station, found that, of 134 adults interviewed, 29% had a current mental illness (with 40% having a lifetime diagnosis), 8% met the threshold for post-traumatic stress disorder, 21% screened positive for a personality disorder, 11% for attention deficit hyperactivity disorder (ADHD), and 4% for an intellectual disability.[36]

Clinical research in the United Kingdom and internationally, conducted with children and young people in the criminal justice system, predominantly in secure settings, suggests that child suspects may also have similarly raised prevalence of a number of neuro-disabilities, cognitive disabilities, and developmental disorders.[37] In particular, there is a noted over-representation amongst young people who have offended of learning

---

[33] Jessica Jacobson and others, *Punishing Disadvantage: A Profile of Children in Custody* (Prison Reform Trust (PRT) 2010).

[34] Nor is there much evidence internationally. Although see for a Dutch study of autism spectrum conditions in child arrestees Charlotte AML Geluk and others, 'Autistic Symptoms in Childhood Arrestees: Longitudinal Association with Delinquent Behavior' (2012) 53 Journal of Child Psychology & Psychiatry 160 and more general health assessment of French child arrestees: Cassandre Coudert and others, 'Adolescent Arrestees Detained in Police Cells: An Observational Study in the Paris, France, Area' (2019) 133 International Journal of Legal Medicine 1251.

[35] Iain G McKinnon and others, 'Police Custody Health Care: A Review of Health Morbidity, Models of Care and Innovations within Police Custody in the UK, with International Comparisons' (2016) 9 Risk Management & Healthcare Policy 213; Jason J Payne-James and others, 'Healthcare Issues of Detainees in Police Custody in London, UK' (2010) 17 Journal of Forensic & Legal Medicine 11; Susan Young and others, 'The Effectiveness of Police Custody Assessments in Identifying Suspects with Intellectual Disabilities and Attention Deficit Hyperactivity Disorder' (2013) 11 BioMed Centre Medicine 248.

[36] Chiara Samele and others, 'The Prevalence of Mental Illness and Unmet Needs of Police Custody Detainees' (2021) 31(2) Criminal Behaviour & Mental Health 80.

[37] See for discussion Carlile (n 14); Nancy Loucks, *No One Knows: Offenders with Learning Difficulties and Learning Disabilities—A Review of Prevalence and Associated Needs* (PRT 2007).

disability (a reported prevalence of 23–32% in comparison with 2–4% in the general child population),[38] although the prevalence rate has been identified to be lower amongst girls.[39] Additionally, the prevalence of autism spectrum conditions amongst this group is also particularly marked (a reported prevalence rate of 15% in comparison with 0.6–1.2% in the general child population),[40] as is the incidence of ADHD (a reported prevalence rate of 12% in comparison with 1.7–9% in the general child population).[41] Studies have also noted the frequent co-occurrence of neuro-developmental disorders with traumatic brain injury amongst children and young people in contact with the YJS.[42] Most strikingly, communication disorders appear to be concerningly high amongst young people who offend (a reported prevalence rate of 60–90% in comparison with 5–7% in the general child population).[43] The frequency of co-occurrence of these conditions has also been noted amongst children.[44] Research using Office for National Statistics data has identified that children and young people with a learning disability were six times more likely than their peers to have a psychiatric

---

[38] Nathan Hughes, *Nobody Made the Connection: The Prevalence of Neurodisability in Young People Who Offend* (Office of the Children's Commissioner 2012) 9; Richard Harrington and Sue Bailey, *Mental Health Needs and Effectiveness of Provision for Young Offenders in Custody and in the Community* (YJB 2005); Leo Kroll and others, 'Mental Health Needs of Boys in Secure Care for Serious or Persistent Offending: A Prospective, Longitudinal Study' (2002) 359 The Lancet 1975.

[39] Prathiba Chitsabesan and others, 'Learning Disabilities and Educational Needs of Juvenile Offenders' (2007) 2 Journal of Children's Services 4.

[40] Hughes (n 38) 10; Henrik Anckarsäter and others, 'Autism Spectrum Disorders in Institutionalized Subjects' (2008) 62 Nordic Journal of Psychiatry 160; Henrik Anckarsäter and others, 'Prevalences and Configurations of Mental Disorders among Institutionalized Adolescents' (2007) 10 Developmental Neurorehabilitation 57; Marc Woodbury-Smith, 'Conceptualising Social and Communication Vulnerabilities among Detainees in the Criminal Justice System' (2020) 100 Research in Developmental Disabilities 103611. For child arrestees in a Dutch study see Geluk and others (n 34).

[41] Hughes (n 38) 10; Anckarsäter and others, 'Prevalences and Configurations' (n 40).

[42] Prathiba Chitsabesan and others (2015) 'Traumatic Brain Injury in Juvenile Offenders', (2015) 30(2) Journal of Head Trauma Rehabilitation 106; Hope Kent and Huw Williams, *Traumatic Brain Injury* (His Majesty's Inspectorate of Probation (HMI Probation) 2021).

[43] Karen Bryan, Jackie Freer, and Cheryl Furlong, 'Language and Communication Difficulties in Juvenile Offenders' (2007) 42 International Journal of Language & Communication Disorders 505; Juliette Gregory and Karen Bryan, 'Speech and Language Therapy Intervention with a Group of Persistent and Prolific Young Offenders in a Non-custodial Setting with Previously Un-diagnosed Speech, Language and Communication Difficulties' (2011) International Journal of Language & Communication Disorders 202; Pamela C Snow, 'Speech–Language Pathology and the Youth Offender: Epidemiological Overview and Roadmap for Future Speech–Language Pathology Research and Scope of Practice' (2019) 50 Language, Speech & Hearing Services in Schools 324.

[44] Amanda Kirby, *Neurodiversity—A Whole-Child Approach for Youth Justice* (2021) (HMIP).

or neuro-developmental disorder.[45] Reduced intellectual functioning, in particular, will not only challenge a child's ability to engage with the significant cognitive demands of the custody process but has also been linked to increased suggestibility, acquiescence, and compliance in interview,[46] and thus to false confession (as was considered to have occurred in the case of Colin Lattimore in the *Confait* case).[47]

Children experiencing mental health issues are also substantially more likely than their peers to find themselves in conflict with the law.[48] Although the rates of severe mental health disorders, such as schizophrenia, may not be high amongst young defendants and suspects, many are likely to present with severe childhood-onset conduct disorders,[49] anxiety and mood disorders (which peak in adolescence),[50] and post-traumatic stress disorder.[51] However, a significant challenge for the YJS, and particularly for professionals within the custody suite, is that many lifelong mental illnesses begin in adolescence, and so a child suspect's condition may be as yet undiagnosed or untreated.[52] Thus, research suggests that many child suspects face the double challenge of navigating a process, demanding even for adults,

---

[45] Eric Emerson and Chris Hatton, 'The Mental Health of Children and Adolescents with Learning Disabilities in Britain' (2007) 1(3) Advances in Mental Health and Learning Disabilities 62.

[46] Rebecca Milne, Isabel CH Clare, and Ray Bull, 'Using the Cognitive Interview with Adults with Mild Learning Disabilities' (1999) 5 Psychology, Crime & Law 81; Gisli H Gudjonsson, *The Psychology of Interrogations and Confessions: A Handbook* (Wiley 2003); Isabel CH Clare and Gisli H Gudjonsson, 'Interrogative Suggestibility, Confabulation, and Acquiescence in People with Mild Learning Disabilities (Mental Handicap): Implications for Reliability during Police Interrogations' (1993) 32 British Journal of Clinical Psychology 295.

[47] Sir Henry Fisher, 'Report of an Inquiry by the Hon. Sir Henry Fisher into the Circumstances Leading to the Trial of Three Persons on Charges Arising Out of the Death of Maxwell Confait and the Fire at 27 Doggett Road, London SE6' (Her Majesty's Stationery Office (HMSO) 1977).

[48] Martin Knapp and others, *Youth Mental Health: New Economic Evidence* (Personal Social Sciences Research Unit, London School of Economics and Political Science 2016).

[49] Eileen Vizard, 'Child Defendants: Occasional Paper 56' (Royal College of Psychiatrists 2006)').

[50] Ronald C Kessler and others, 'Lifetime Prevalence and Age-of-Onset Distributions of DSM-IV Disorders in the National Comorbidity Survey Replication' (2005) Archives of General Psychiatry 593; Kathleen R Merikangas and others, 'Lifetime Prevalence of Mental Disorders in U.S. Adolescents: Results from the National Comorbidity Survey Replication—Adolescent Supplement (NCS—A)' (2010) Journal of the American Academy of Child and Adolescent Psychiatry 980.

[51] Hans Steiner, Ivan G Garcia, and Zakee Mathews, 'Post Traumatic Stress Disorder in Incarcerated Juvenile Delinquents' (1997) Journal of the American Academy of Child Psychology and Psychiatry 357.

[52] Knapp and others (n 48).

with the additional strain of managing a further dispositional condition, indeed, often several co-morbidities.

Childhood Adversities and Structural Disadvantage

However, many children coming into contact with the police are likely to experience a third intersecting level of difficulty, arising from adverse life experiences or other childhood disadvantages. There are clear links between offending behaviour and psychosocial adversity,[53] and child suspects have a significantly raised likelihood of having suffered childhood trauma, including childhood abuse (sexual, physical, or emotional), familial violence, traumatic brain injury, and bereavement.[54] For example, research with young people in the secure estate reveals high rates of bereavement, including traumatic and multiple bereavements,[55] and parental absence,[56] whilst experience of family violence, for example, has been consistently associated with offending,[57] particularly violence[58] and child-to-parent assault.[59] Children who have been excluded from school are over-represented in secure institutions in England and Wales,[60] as are those who have been

---

[53] See eg Jessica M Craig and others, 'A Little Early Risk Goes a Long Bad Way: Adverse Childhood Experiences and Life-Course Offending in the Cambridge Study' (2017) 53 Journal of Criminal Justice 34; Bryanna Hahn Fox and others, 'Trauma Changes Everything: Examining the Relationship between Adverse Childhood Experiences and Serious, Violent and Chronic Juvenile Offenders' (2015) 46 Child Abuse & Neglect 163.

[54] Mark Liddle and others, *Trauma and Young Offenders: A Review of the Research and Practice Literature* (Beyond Youth Custody 2016); Jacobson and others (n 33); Ingrid Obsuth and others, 'Violent Poly-Victimization: The Longitudinal Patterns of Physical and Emotional Victimization throughout Adolescence (11–17 Years)' (2018) 28 Journal of Research on Adolescence 786.

[55] Nina Vaswani, 'The Ripples of Death: Exploring the Bereavement Experiences and Mental Health of Young Men in Custody' (2014) 53 Howard Journal of Criminal Justice 341.

[56] Jacobson and others (n 33) 51.

[57] Marian Stuart and Catherine Baines, *Safeguards for Vulnerable Children: Three Studies on Abusers, Disabled Children and Children in Prison* (Joseph Rowntree Foundation 2004); Wesley G Jennings, Alex R Piquero, and Jennifer M Reingle, 'On the Overlap between Victimization and Offending: A Review of the Literature' (2011) 17 Aggression & Violent Behavior 16.

[58] Mackenzie Kushner, 'Betrayal Trauma and Gender: An Examination of the Victim-Offender Overlap' (2020) Journal of Interpersonal Violence NP3750.

[59] Sam Lewis and Amanda Holt, 'Constituting Child-to-Parent Violence: Lessons from England and Wales' (2021) 61(3) British Journal of Criminology 792; Melanie Simmons and others, 'Sixty Years of Child-to-Parent Abuse Research: What We Know and Where to Go' (2018) 38 Aggression & Violent Behavior 31.

[60] Taylor (n 14).

'looked after' by a local authority.[61] Although accounting for less than 1% of the total child population,[62] children who were, or had a history of being, 'looked after' accounted for 59% of the children in the youth secure estate in 2021–22.[63]

The drivers of this disproportionate representation of children with adverse childhood experiences within the YJS are complex. However, it appears that the police may themselves contribute to their numbers by selecting for adversarial engagement children from less advantaged backgrounds, constructing a group of young people who 'become the objects of continual scrutiny'.[64] At the same time, research into 'county lines' drug supply has uncovered how children with such adversities in their backgrounds are increasingly being targeted for criminal exploitation. County lines offenders were identified as recruiting children who had experienced social services intervention, who were 'looked after', were frequently 'missing' from care settings, had behavioural or developmental disorders, or had been excluded from school.[65]

Advances in developmental neuroscience reveal that significant childhood adversity can have a negative physical effect on the developing brain, including areas of the brain which control planning, emotional regulation, and perspective-taking[66]—all capacities required to successfully navigate a period in police custody. Deficits caused by developmental adversity can also result in a range of behavioural difficulties (including raised impulsivity, volatile and hostile behaviour, and cognitive deficiencies

---

[61] Howard League for Penal Reform, *Criminal Care: Children's Homes and Criminalising Children* (Howard League 2016); Jo Staines, *Risk, Adverse Influence and Criminalisation. Understanding the Over-Representation of Looked After Children in the Youth Justice System* (PRT 2016).
[62] Department for Education, 'Children Looked After in England Including Adoptions' (updated 5 April 2022) <https://explore-education-statistics.service.gov.uk/find-statistics/children-looked-after-in-england-including-adoptions/2021> accessed 14 August 2023.
[63] HMIP, *Children in Custody 2021–22* (HMIP 2023) 7.
[64] Lesley McAra and Susan McVie, 'The Usual Suspects?: Street-Life, Young People and the Police' (2005) 5 Criminal Justice 5, 28.
[65] National Crime Agency, 'County Lines Drugs Supply, Vulnerability and Harm 2018', NAC(19)095, (2019) <https://nationalcrimeagency.gov.uk/who-we-are/publications/257-county-lines-drug-supply-vulnerability-and-harm-2018/file> accessed 14 August 2023, para 21; Alexandra Turner, Lucy Belcher, and Iryna Pona, 'Counting Lives: Responding to Children Who Are Criminally Exploited' (Children's Society 1 July 2019) 28ff <www.childrenssociety.org.uk/information/professionals/resources/counting-lives> accessed 14 August 2023.
[66] Eamon McCrory and Essi Viding, 'The Neurobiology of Maltreatment and Adolescent Violence' (2010) 375 The Lancet 1856; Essi Viding, Nathalie MG Fontaine, and Eamon J McCrory, 'Antisocial Behaviour in Children With and Without Callous-Unemotional Traits' (2012) 105 Journal of the Royal Society of Medicine 195.

such as reductions in IQ), working memory, and attention capacities.[67] Additionally, adverse histories can make an individual more susceptible to providing misleading information in interview.[68] Thus, it is important to maintain an appreciation not only of the significant likelihood that child arrestees are, or have been, themselves victims but also that they are likely to be functionally disadvantaged in the custodial episode as a result of the trauma they have experienced.

Additionally, young people from Black, Asian and minority ethnic backgrounds have long been identified as over-represented in the YJS.[69] Black boys in particular are consistently over-represented at arrest and, thus, in police custody. In the year to March 2022, Black children accounted for 13% of child arrests—two percentage points higher than the figure ten years previously, although down from 17% in the year to March 2020.[70] Investigation into disproportionality throughout the criminal justice process suggests that Black, Asian, and ethnic minority child suspects may be disadvantaged in engaging with support and decision-making in police custody as a result of the impact of racism experienced by them or their communities. Specifically, long-standing distrust of the criminal justice system within their communities may mean that Black, Asian, and ethnic minority children are less likely to engage and trust legal advice and to answer questions in interview.[71] At the same time, Black children, in particular, have been identified as being 'adultified' by professionals, ascribed adult-like characteristics which undermine recognition of their developmental immaturity and result in them being viewed as more culpable than their peers.[72]

---

[67] Craig A McEwen and Bruce S McEwen, 'Social Structure, Adversity, Toxic Stress, and Intergenerational Poverty: An Early Childhood Model' (2017) 43 Annual Review of Sociology 445.

[68] Kim E Drake, Ray Bull, and Julian CW Boon, 'Interrogative Suggestibility, Self-Esteem, and the Influence of Negative Life-Events' (2008) 13 Law & Criminological Psychology 299.

[69] David Lammy, 'The Lammy Review. An Independent Review into the Treatment of, and Outcomes for, Black, Asian and Minority Ethnic Individuals in the Criminal Justice System (Ministry of Justice (MoJ) 2017).

[70] YJB/MoJ, *Youth Justice Statistics 2021-22, England and Wales* (National Statistics 2023), para 1.4.

[71] Phil Bowen, *Building Trust: How Our Courts Can Improve the Criminal Court Experience for Black, Asian, and Minority Ethnic Defendants* (Centre for Justice Innovation 2017); Lammy (n 69).

[72] Jahnine Davis and Nicholas Marsh, 'Boys to Men: The Cost of "Adultification" in Safeguarding Responses to Black Boys' (2020) 8 Critical and Radical Social Work 255; Phillip Atiba Goff and others, 'The Essence of Innocence: Consequences of Dehumanizing Black Children' (2014) 106 Journal of Personality & Social Psychology 526.

Immediate Situational Adversity

Finally, this complex and multifaceted disadvantage experienced by child suspects intersects with the immediate situational adversity every detainee experiences by virtue of their detention. However, the power differential experienced by the child suspect, alone and in the total control of adult police officers, is inevitably more extreme than that faced by an adult suspect. The importance of adjusting the custody process to accommodate the particular needs and capacities of child suspects could not be more plain or more urgent. However, as I explore in the following sections, the child suspect is all but invisible in a number of important respects.

Invisibility of Child Suspects in Legislation and Policy

In England and Wales, the need for children to be treated differently from adults finds expression in the distinctive aims and principles which govern the YJS. The primary aim of the YJS in England and Wales is to 'prevent offending by children and young persons',[73] and the police and the courts also have a duty under the Children Act 2004, section 11 to 'safeguard and promote the welfare of children and young people' (known as the 'welfare principle').[74] However, in comparison to the provisions for child defendants post-charge, child suspects are largely overlooked in the domestic legal framework and their needs minimally catered for.

In keeping with this distinct orientation of the YJS, for the vast majority of child defendants, the legal framework provides for a court experience which is designed to be very different from that of an adult defendant. Save for 'grave' crimes[75] and in other limited circumstances,[76] children are tried in the youth court, which is adapted to meet their needs (Children and Young Persons Act 1933 (CYPA 1933), Part III). There is no public access to the court,[77] modified language and different modes of address are used, and judges and magistrates are required to have special training.[78] Children

---

[73] Crime and Disorder Act 1998, s 37.
[74] See also duty on the courts to have regard for the 'welfare' of children appearing before them: CYPA 1933, s 44.
[75] Powers of Criminal Courts (Sentencing) Act 2000, s 91.
[76] Where the child is charged with homicide or jointly charged with an adult.
[77] CYPA 1933, s 47.
[78] ibid, s 45.

waiting for their hearings are accommodated separately from adult defendants,[79] and the Court should require the attendance of a parent or guardian for those under sixteen.[80] Following *T v UK: V v UK*[81] and *SC v UK*,[82] the Criminal Procedure Rules[83] (and accompanying Criminal Practice Direction)[84] require 'every reasonable step' to be taken to facilitate the participation of young and vulnerable defendants. Case law also continues to break new ground, particularly in respect of the questioning of witnesses, including child defendants. The courts now require advocates to adapt their questioning to the child witness, rather than the child having to contend with adult phrasing,[85] and specific training to equip advocates for that task is expected.[86] Whilst there is no statutory right in force,[87] an intermediary (a specialist communication supporter) can be granted to a child defendant, for the whole trial if necessary.[88] There are different, shorter, timescales for the completion of youth court proceedings, and sentencing hearings are attended by specialist youth offending team (YOT) representatives and lead to a different regime of disposals.

Undeniably, there remains a stubborn inequity between protections for child defendants and those available to child witnesses.[89] The adultification and responsibilization of child defendants[90] has hardened even as our understanding of the challenges children experience in participating in

---

[79] ibid, s 31.
[80] ibid, s 34A, unless to do so would be 'unreasonable'.
[81] *T v United Kingdom* App no 24724/94, 16 December 1999 and *V v United Kingdom* App no 24888/94, 16 December 1999, reported as a joint decision in (2000) 30 EHRR 121.
[82] *SC v United Kingdom* App no 60958/00, 10 November 2004, (2005) 40 EHRR 10.
[83] Criminal Procedure Rules 2020/759 (Crim PR) r 3.8(3)(b).
[84] Criminal Practice Directions—October 2015 as amended April 2016, November 2016, January 2017, April 2018, October 2018, April 2019, October 2019, May 2020, and October 2020 (Crim PD), 3D.2.
[85] *R v Lubemba* [2014] EWCA Crim 2064, [2015] 1 WLR 1579, [45].
[86] *R v Grant Murray* [2017] EWCA Crim 1228, CA, [2018] Crim LR 71.
[87] Coroners and Justice Act 2009, s 104, which provides for intermediary support for a defendant who gives evidence, has not yet been brought into force.
[88] *C v Sevenoaks Magistrates' Court* [2009] EWHC 3088 (Admin), [2010] 1 All ER 735; *R (AS) v Great Yarmouth Youth Court* [2011] EWHC 2059 (Admin), [2012] Crim LR 478 and Crim PD 3F.12ff. See most recently *R v Dean Thomas* [2020] EWCA Crim 117, [2020] 4 WLR 66 and *TI v Bromley Youth Court* [2020] EWHC 1204, [2020] 2 Cr App R 22 (Admin).
[89] Penny Cooper and David Wurtzel, 'A Day Late and a Dollar Short: In Search of an Intermediary Scheme for Vulnerable Defendants in England and Wales' (2013) Criminal Law Review 4; Laura CH Hoyano, 'Coroners and Justice Act 2009—Special Measures Directions Take Two: Entrenching Unequal Access to Justice?' (2010) Criminal Law Review 345; Vizard (n 49).
[90] Barry Goldson and John Muncie, *Youth, Crime and Justice: Critical Issues* (Sage 2006); John Muncie, 'Institutionalized Intolerance: Youth Justice and the 1998 Crime and Disorder Act' (1999) 19 Critical Social Policy 147.

trial processes has grown.[91] Equally, there is mounting evidence that trial protections for children do not function in practice as the law in the books proposes. Reviews of youth court processes have consistently identified shortcomings in the training of advocates the inaccessibility of the proceedings and failures to address the participation needs of child defendants and to capitalize on opportunities for diversion.[92] Too often, children find themselves appearing in adult courts before benches or judges not trained to accommodate their needs and with insufficient specialist support, and there are increasingly lengthy delays in their cases being concluded.[93] Nonetheless, whilst not as extensive or consistently implemented as would be preferable, there is, at least for the child defendant, a statutory framework and supporting case law which marks out a significantly differentiated process.

By contrast, the process for children in police detention in England and Wales is much more minimally adjusted. A child detained by the police after arrest experiences essentially the same process, in the same environment, as an adult suspect. In contrast to the child appearing in the youth court, a child in police custody is not dealt with by staff with specialist youth training in fully separate facilities or subject to different timescales in terms of their detention.[94] Age-differentiated protection in primary legislation is extremely limited. The statutory prohibition against contact between children and adults in the criminal process barely bites in custody because it is limited to adults who have been 'charged',[95] thus excluding the majority of adult detainees. There is no requirement to remove a child to more suitable local authority accommodation pre-charge or where a child is detained for a suspected breach of bail conditions.[96] For the few children who are remanded after charge, subject to very limited exceptions, there is a statutory

---

[91] Grisso (n 27) 3; Lamb and others (n 25); Plotnikoff and Woolfson (n 29).
[92] Carlile (n 14); Taylor (n 14).
[93] Tim Bateman, 'The State of Youth Justice' (National Association for Youth Justice 2020) 87ff <https://thenayj.org.uk/cmsAdmin/uploads/state-of-youth-justice-2020-final-sep20.pdf and https://justiceinnovation.org/publications/time-get-it-right-enhancing-problem-solving-practice-youth-court> accessed 14 August 2023; Gillian Hunter and others, 'Time to Get It Right: Enhancing Problem-Solving Practice in the Youth Court' (Centre for Justice Innovation 2020) <CJI-TIME-TO-GET-IT-RIGHT.pdf (justiceinnovation.org)> accessed 13 August 2023.
[94] A twenty-four-hour time limit in the first instance: PACE, s 41.
[95] CYPA 1933, s 31 applies in court cells and for those attending court on bail: *R (T) v Secretary of State for Justice* [2013] EWHC 1119 (Admin), [2013] ACD 88.
[96] The Bail Act 1976 includes no requirement, as under PACE, s 38(6), to transfer to local authority accommodation (see eg *R(BG) v Chief Constable of the West Midlands* [2014] EWHC 4374 (Admin), (2015) 179 JP 93.

requirement that they be transferred to local authority accommodation until their appearance in court.[97] However, this statutory duty is honoured more in the breach, with the transfer of child remandees vanishingly rare,[98] despite the introduction of a Concordat to increase compliance.[99] The only two substantive statutory adjustments for a child suspect pre-charge are that a parent or other person responsible for the child's welfare must be informed 'as soon as is practicable' (PACE, section 57) and, if the child suspect is a girl, that she must also be 'under the care of' a female officer during her detention (CYPA 1933, section 31).[100] If, as Andrew Ashworth has observed, there is a 'symbolic importance' in the placing of certain standards in primary legislation,[101] then the invisibility of child suspects in PACE and related legislation is a striking indicator of the system's disregard for them.

What other protections there are exist predominantly in secondary legislation, notably the PACE Codes of Practice (especially *Code C*) and in guidance prepared by the College of Policing in the form of 'Authorised Professional Practice (Detention and Custody)' (APP(DC)).[102] Here too, the adjustments are modest—the major provision being the support of an appropriate adult (AA). The AA is required to attend the police station[103] and must be present with the child for significant events in their detention, such as for the explanation of legal rights,[104] for strip and intimate searching,[105] and for interview.[106] A wide range of supportive duties are

---

[97] PACE, s 38(6).
[98] For example, in 2020, HM Inspectorate of Constabulary, Fire and Rescue Services (HMICFRS) (formerly HMIC) published five custody inspection reports, for: Leicestershire, Sussex, Bedfordshire, Northumbria, and British Transport Police. Across those five forces, in the year preceding inspection only six children had been transferred. The reports are accessible at <https://hmicfrs.justiceinspectorates.gov.uk/our-work/article/criminal-justice-joint-inspection/joint-inspection-of-police-custody-facilities/#reports> accessed 14 August 2023.
[99] Home Office, 'Concordat on Children in Custody' (2017) <https://assets.publishing.serv ice.gov.uk/government/uploads/system/uploads/attachment_data/file/655222/Concordat_on_Children_in_Custody_ISBN_Accessible.pdf> accessed 14 August 2023.
[100] Although this does not require constant attention by a female officer.
[101] Andrew Ashworth, *The Criminal Process: An Evaluative Study* (1st edn, OUP 1994) 299.
[102] First published 23 October 2013, last modified 2 May 2023 <https://www.college.pol ice.uk/app/detention-and-custody> accessed 14 August 2023. (Any variance with the version (modified March 2016) in force at the time of the fieldwork will be noted as it arises.) The College of Policing makes clear that this is guidance only: 'Police officers and staff are expected to have regard to APP in discharging their responsibilities. There may, however, be circumstances when it is perfectly legitimate to deviate from APP, provided there is clear rationale for doing so.' See the College of Policing website <www.app.college.police.uk/about-app> accessed 14 August 2023.
[103] *Code C* (n 1), para 3.15.
[104] ibid, para 3.17.
[105] ibid, Annex A.
[106] ibid, para 11.15.

Invisibility of Child Suspects in Legislation and Policy   17

ascribed to the AA, including providing advice and assistance, ensuring due process, assisting understanding and exercise of their rights, and enabling communication.[107] However, despite the significance and complexity of the role, it is primarily fulfilled by a parent or guardian,[108] inevitably untrained and provided with minimal information about the role, or by lay volunteers (see Chapter 4 for a full discussion).

Otherwise, in terms of child-specific protections, there is simply a prohibition on a child being detained with an adult in a cell and not in an adult cell at all unless no other 'secure' or 'more comfortable' accommodation is available.[109] In *Code C's* accompanying 'Notes for Guidance' (NFG), there is the additional requirement that the child should be checked on in their cell 'more frequently' whilst detained (NFG, 9B). In all other regards, APP(DC) and *Code C* simply counsel that 'special care' should be taken (eg when questioning a child (NFG, 11C)) and efforts made to ensure that procedures are strictly followed and detention times are kept to a minimum, avoiding, in particular, detention overnight.[110] Responsibility for ensuring that these exhortations are heeded lies with the CO, who has a role independent of the investigation and is responsible for the welfare and proper processing of all detainees.[111] However, in contrast to the duties imposed on the judge by the Criminal Procedure Rules (Crim PR) and Criminal Practice Directions (Crim PD), PACE and *Code C* place no onus on the CO or investigating officers to enable the effective participation of a child suspect. Nor does the relevant legislation make direct reference to a child's other rights under the UNCRC.[112]

The implications of the relative invisibility of the child suspect in the legal framework are profound. This comparative review of the differentiation in pre- and post-charge settings reveals that the specialization of the custody experience to accommodate the child suspect is of a different order entirely to the specialization of the youth court. Adjustments in police

---

[107] ibid, para 1.7A.
[108] ibid, para 1.7(b).
[109] ibid, para 8.8.
[110] See eg APP(DC)(Children and Young Persons) (first published 23 October 2013, updated 2 May 2023) 2 <https://www.college.police.uk/app/detention-and-custody/detainee-care/children-and-young-persons> accessed 15 August 2023 (APP(DC)(CYP)). (Any variance with the version in force at the time of fieldwork (modified 28 July 2015) will be noted as it arises.)
[111] PACE, s 37.
[112] Although the College of Policing's guidance (APP(DC)(CYP) 1 (n 110)) and the National Police Chiefs' Council *National Strategy for the Policing of Children and Young People* do. See also in Wales the Rights of Children and Young Persons (Wales) Measure 2011 c.02, s 1.

custody are additions to the process, or (more limited) restrictions of it, requiring specific application by the police officers involved rather than a separate scheme designed specifically to accommodate the child or young person. This is a particular cause for concern given the adversarial context of the pre-charge process for child suspects, which I discuss in detail in Chapter 2.[113] But the overarching issue, relevant here, is the lack of an independent arbiter at the investigation stage, who can ensure fairness between the parties and the meaningful implementation of supportive adjustments to the process. The absence of such oversight is critical for children in police custody, where the power differential between the CO (and investigating officers) and the child suspect is inevitably extreme.

Invisibility in the Courts and Other Accountability Mechanisms

In an adversarial system, such as that in place in England and Wales, fairness is ultimately secured by the presence of the judge (or magistrates) at trial. As far as the criminal case is concerned, the remedy for breaches of *Code C*, and the failure to implement adjustments required in the guidance, is the exclusion at trial of improperly obtained evidence, under PACE, sections 76 and 78. However, this remedy is less likely to be available to child suspects than to adult suspects as a result of their relative invisibility in the later stages of the criminal justice process as well. As Roger Evans observed in 1994, the prevalence of out-of-court disposals means that the majority of children are 'dealt with without recourse to the courts ... Since pre-court decisions by the police take place behind closed doors there is little or no opportunity to ascertain how the interview has been conducted or to test the reliability of any confession.'[114] Although the proportion continues to fall, in the year to March 2022, 52% of first-time entrants into the YJS received a youth caution.[115] For those who are prosecuted, the mandating of a referral order for a first guilty plea[116]—a disposal considered

---

[113] Including contested notions of 'adversarial' and 'inquisitorial systems': see Mirjan Damaška, 'Evidentiary Barriers to Conviction and Two Models of Criminal Procedure: A Comparative Study' (1973) 121 University of Pennsylvania Law Review 506.

[114] Roger Evans, 'Police Interrogations and the Royal Commission on Criminal Justice' (1994) 4 Policing & Society 73, 74.

[115] YJB/MoJ (n 70), para 2.1.

[116] Save where a custodial sentence is required: Powers of Criminal Courts (Sentencing) Act 2000, s 16-28.

Invisibility in the Courts and Other Accountability Mechanisms 19

to be advantageous for young defendants—means that significantly fewer cases proceed to trial in the youth court. Whilst diversion in all its forms is generally to be welcomed, it has the unintended effect of removing opportunity for the criminal courts to scrutinize the treatment of children in police custody.

Even where there is a trial, the child's experience as a suspect is rarely examined and is generally relevant only where an issue is raised as to the admissibility of the police interview. In this regard, the courts place heavy reliance on summarized records of interview,[117] which are often incomplete[118] and less likely than a full transcript to reveal undue pressure being imposed or to provide insight into the impact of troubling treatment in advance of the interview. In addition, the majority of children are prosecuted in the youth court, which has a less onerous scheme of prosecution disclosure than the Crown Court,[119] and swifter summary procedures[120] not well suited to the revelation and investigation of pre-charge issues. There have been few reported cases challenging the admissibility of evidence arising from alleged breaches of *Code C* in relation to child suspects.[121] But, whilst not particularly consistent,[122] the higher courts have generally taken a relatively permissive approach.[123] This may hardly be surprising, given the closed nature of the police custody process and the lack of available information about the impact of the process on child suspect participation. As Simon Pemberton has observed, there is 'an inherent danger of moral indifference to actions that fall outside people's sphere of experience'.[124]

Young suspects are also under-represented in engaging other accountability mechanisms. Children are the least likely group to make a formal

---

[117] John Baldwin, 'Preparing Records of Taped Interview' and 'The Role of Legal Representatives at the Police Station' and 'Supervision of Police Investigation in Serious Criminal Cases' (HMSO 1992); Michael Zander and P Henderson, 'Crown Court Study', Royal Commission on Criminal Justice Research Study 19 (HMSO 1993); Fiona Brookman and Harriet Pierpoint, 'Access to Legal Advice for Young Suspects and Remand Prisoners' (2003) 42 Howard Journal of Criminal Justice 452.
[118] John Baldwin, 'Summarising Tape Recordings of Police Interviews' (1991) Criminal Law Review 671.
[119] Criminal Procedure and Investigations Act 1996.
[120] See eg initiatives such as Department of Constitutional Affairs, 'Delivering Simple, Speedy, Summary Justice', July 2006, DCA 37/06.
[121] Discussed in more detail in Chapter 4.
[122] See eg R v *Morse and Others* [1990] 11 WLUK 237, (1991) Crim LR 195; cf R v W [1994] 1 WLUK 214, (1994) Crim LR 130.
[123] See eg *H and M v DPP* [1997] 12 WLUK 189, (1998) Crim LR 653.
[124] Simon Pemberton, 'A Theory of Moral Indifference: Understanding the Production of Har by Capitalist Society' in Paddy Hillyard and others (eds), *Beyond Criminology: Taking Harm Seriously* (Pluto Press 2004) 78.

complaint about police conduct. Those aged seventeen or under made up only 1% of complaints made against the police in 2021–22.[125] Nor are many children and their families likely to have the financial means to pursue a civil action against the police, a situation exacerbated by the reduction in legal aid for such litigation under the Legal Aid Sentencing and Punishment of Offenders Act 2012.[126] This is particularly worrying since there are concerns about the effectiveness of oversight mechanisms generally in police custody,[127] which are arguably compounded by the invisibility of child suspects in official data. In 2015, His Majesty's Inspectorate of Constabulary (HMIC) (now His Majesty's Inspectorate of Constabulary, Fire and Rescue Services, HMICFRS) published a thematic inspection, *The Welfare of Vulnerable People in Police Custody*, which raised concerns about quality assurance mechanisms within forces to ensure that College of Policing and similar guidance was being implemented for children.[128] In particular, HMIC noted a lack of management information about child suspects and inadequate monitoring of issues such as the throughput of children in police custody, use of force, requests for local authority accommodation, and delays associated with AA attendance.[129]

Whilst there is evidence that internal monitoring within forces has improved, official data on child suspects remains scarce. Until recently, HMIC's specific recommendations for monitoring and data collection had not been substantively acted upon.[130] However, progress is being made. In November 2022, the Home Office published—for the first time—experimental statistics for police custody.[131] These included the number of detentions in police custody; age group, sex, and ethnicity of detainees;

[125] Independent Office for Police Conduct, 'Police Complaints: Statistics for England and Wales 2021/22', Table 10 <https://view.officeapps.live.com/op/view.aspx?src=https%3A%2F%2Fwww.policeconduct.gov.uk%2Fsites%2Fdefault%2Ffiles%2Fdocuments%2F202122-Data-tables-FINAL.ods&wdOrigin=BROWSELINK> and <https://www.policeconduct.gov.uk/publications/police-complaints-statistics-england-and-wales-report-202122> accessed 15 August 2023.
[126] Legal Aid Sentencing and Punishment of Offenders Act 2012, Sch 1 Pt I, paras 21–22.
[127] See eg in respect of Independent Custody Visitors John Kendall, *Regulating Police Detention, Voices behind Closed Doors* (Policy Press 2018).
[128] HMIC, *The Welfare of Vulnerable People in Police Custody* (HMIC 2015).
[129] ibid 109ff.
[130] ibid 124. See Penelope Gibbs and Fionnuala Radcliffe, '24 Hours in Police Custody—Is Police Detention Overused?' (Transform Justice 2020) <https://www.transformjustice.org.uk/publication/24-hours-in-police-custody-is-police-detention-overused/> accessed 15 August 2023.
[131] Home Office, 'Police Powers and Procedures: Other PACE Powers, England and Wales, Year Ending 31 March 2022' (National Statistics 2022) <Police use of force statistics, England and Wales: April 2021 to March 2022-GOV.UK (www.gov.uk)> accessed 13 August 2023.

whether a child was detained overnight; whether an appropriate adult was called; and details of strip searches carried out. Yet, there is still some way to go. Data on police custody could only be provided by twenty-six of the forty-three forces (and by twenty-eight of the forty-three forces in relation to strip search), and the published statistics still do not address key measures recommended by HMIC, such as length of detention, transfer to local authority accommodation, and delays in appropriate adult attendance.

Invisibility in Previous Research

Despite the significance of the custody process for criminal justice outcomes, and youth justice outcomes in particular, the experience of the child as suspect has barely registered in the academic consciousness. As outlined in the preface, researchers rarely venture into the closed world of the custody block. However, when they have sought to explore the suspect experience, adult suspects have tended to be the focus of their attention. Of the four 'post-PACE' custody studies which sought suspect views of the whole custody process, only Satnam Choongh's 1992 fieldwork in two police stations involved child participants in any number. Yet, Choongh interviewed just eight 'juveniles' within the eighty interviews he conducted with suspects exploring their views of the fairness of their detention and interrogation experience and their understanding and engagement of their rights.[132] The three subsequent studies taking a suspect perspective engaged adult suspects almost exclusively,[133] although it is important to note that the earlier two of these studies pre-dated the inclusion of seventeen-year-olds within the 'juvenile' category. As a result, Newburn and Heyman's study, for example, included some seventeen-year-olds,[134] but they would not have experienced the protections which should be afforded to 'juveniles'.

Looking beyond 'whole-process' studies, more focused research into particular aspects of the process (such as the police interview, the uptake of legal advice, or the efficacy of AAs) has tended to analyse police

---

[132] Satnam Choongh, *Policing as Social Discipline* (Clarendon Press 1997).
[133] The earlier two concerned adult suspects only: Tim Newburn and Stephanie Hayman, *Policing, Surveillance and Social Control: CCTV and Police Monitoring of Suspects* (Willan Publishing 2002); Layla Skinns, *Police Custody: Governance, Legitimacy and Reform in the Criminal Justice Process* (Willan Publishing 2011). One young suspect participated in Layla Skinns and colleagues' later study: Layla Skinns and Andrew Wooff, 'Pain in Police Detention: A Critical Point in the "Penal Painscape"?' (2020) Policing & Society 1.
[134] Newburn and Hayman (n 133).

interviews[135] or custody records,[136] or engage with adult participants,[137] rather than with child suspects themselves. Vicky Kemp and Jacqueline Hodgson's study investigating procedural safeguards for juvenile suspects during pre-trial interrogation is a notable exception. However, their research was part of a comparative European study and, as a result, their engagement with young suspects is modest in scale. They conducted a single focus group with five children and young people with experience of police interrogation, alongside separate focus groups with police, lawyers, and AAs and the analysis of twelve young suspect interview recordings.[138] More recently, Kemp and Watkins have explored children's understanding of their legal rights in police custody with a diverse group of children, both with and without experience of police custody.[139] For further academic insights into the child suspect experience, one must cast the net wider still to more general research initiatives which have sought children and young people's views about, and experiences within, the criminal justice system as a whole. Such studies have revealed scattered insights into children's experiences in police custody. Most useful amongst these are the thirty-seven interviews of thirteen-to-seventeen-year-olds conducted by Neal Hazel, Ann Hagell, and Laura Brazier;[140] interviews with sixty-five young defendants by Joyce Plotnikoff and Richard Woolfson;[141] and Home Office research with young people in the secure estate.[142]

---

[135] See eg Sarah Medford, Gisli H Gudjonsson, and John Pearse, 'The Efficacy of the Appropriate Adult Safeguard during Police Interviewing' (2003) 8 Law and Criminological Psychology 253.
[136] See eg Vicky Kemp, Pascoe Pleasence, and Nigel J Balmer, 'Children, Young People and Requests for Police Station Legal Advice: 25 Years On from PACE' (2011) 11 Youth Justice 28.
[137] See eg Harriet Pierpoint, 'A Survey of Volunteer Appropriate Adult Services in England and Wales' (2004) 4 Youth Justice 32.
[138] Vicky Kemp and Jacqueline Hodgson, 'Chapter 4. England and Wales Empirical Findings' in Miet Vanderhallen and others (eds), *Interrogating Young Suspects: Procedural Safeguards from an Empirical Perspective*, Vol 2 (Intersentia 2016). At the time of writing, an ongoing study was engaging with children in police custody but had not yet reported: Vicky Kemp and others, *Examining the Impact of PACE on the Detention and Questioning of Child Suspects by the Police in England and Wales* (Nuffield Foundation, 25 May 2023) <https://www.nuffieldfoundation.org/project/impact-of-pace-on-the-detention-and-questioning-of-young-suspects> accessed 10 October 2023.
[139] Vicky Kemp and Dawn Watkins, 'Exploring Children's Understanding of the Legal Rights of Suspects in England and Wales' (2022) 22(3) Youth Justice 320.
[140] Neal Hazel, Ann Hagell, and Laura Brazier, *Young Offenders' Perceptions of Their Experiences in the Criminal Justice System* (Economic and Social Research Council 2003).
[141] Plotnikoff and Woolfson (n 29).
[142] Juliet Lyon, Catherine Dennison, and Anita Wilson, ' "Tell Them So They Listen": Messages from Young People in Custody', Home Office Research Study 201 (Home Office 2000).

Nor is the invisibility of child suspects in academic consideration unique to this jurisdiction. Research in other jurisdictions is equally sparse, and the very few studies conducted have, again, involved small numbers of young suspects. Of most relevance is Katie Quinn and John Jackson's mixed-methods study looking specifically at the experience of young suspects in police custody in Northern Ireland. This included custody record analysis; observational case studies based on the police interviews of twelve young suspects; and follow-up interviews, where practicable, with young people and those supporting them. Nine young suspects were spoken to in total, although the material from young people themselves appears to be very limited.[143] Research conducted with children in police detention in Israel, although relating experiences in a very different context and lasting significantly longer than in England and Wales, also offers useful insights, particularly into the impact of police detention on plea decision-making.[144]

Child suspects are more visible in the grey literature in this area, although their voices are few. HMIC's thematic inspection included interviews with nine children who had had experience of police custody,[145] whilst a study of non-familial AA provision for children in police custody by the Children's Commissioner's garnered the views of a further four children.[146] Finally, two young people gave evidence about their experiences in police custody as part of the All-Party Parliamentary Group for Children's (APPGC) inquiry into the relationships between children and the police.[147]

There can be no doubt that the methodological and ethical challenges posed by research with young suspects, as described later in this chapter, have played a significant part in their invisibility in previous research. However, the limited material that has hitherto been available underlines how important it is to hear from children with experience of police custody.

---

[143] Katie Quinn and John Jackson, 'The Detention and Questioning of Young Persons by the Police in Northern Ireland', Northern Ireland Office Research & Statistical Series: Report No 9 (Northern Ireland Office 2003).

[144] Catherine Cook, *Stolen Youth: The Politics of Israel's Detention of Palestinian Children* (Pluto Press in association with Defence for Children International (DCI), Palestine section 2004); Nadera Shalhoub-Kevorkian and Bella Kovner, 'Child Arrest, Settler Colonialism, and the Israeli Juvenile System: A Case Study of Occupied East Jerusalem' (2018) 58 British Journal of Criminology 709.

[145] HMIC (n 128) Annex F.

[146] Tim Bateman, 'A Night in the Cells: Children in Police Custody and the Provision of Non Familial Appropriate Adults' (Office of the Children's Commissioner 2017) <www.childrenscommissioner.gov.uk/wp-content/uploads/2018/06/A-Night-in-the-Cells.pdf> accessed 16 August 2023.

[147] APPGC, 'Children and the Police Inquiry: Oral Evidence Session 2: The Detention of Young People in Police Custody' (National Children's Bureau 2014).

I explore the material in detail in the empirical chapters that follow, but the insights that we do have reveal a detention experience which is marked by fear and anxiety[148] and a sense of anger and powerlessness.[149] Young people spoke of the boredom and distress of being confined in cells,[150] and detention was widely experienced as coercive and punitive.[151] Lack of trust and humiliation characterized children's recollections of their dealings with officers,[152] whilst there were clear indications that young people did not understand, or feel able to engage, their rights.[153] These insights find some reflection in studies involving young adults in pre-trial detention settings[154] and international research with young people with experience of police custody[155] but also reveal experiences particular to children, and particular to this jurisdiction, which require further investigation.

In addition, the material available from more discrete studies, focused on particular protections, suggests that the limited framework of protections for child suspects is rarely fully implemented or, where in place, often does not function effectively. For example, in respect of the AA safeguard, analysis of police interviews with young suspects by Evans[156] and Medford, Gudjonsson, and Pearse[157] has revealed significant concerns about the effectiveness of the AA safeguard during questioning, particularly in light of the passivity of AAs and the tendency of family members to intervene in ways which could be unhelpful or unsupportive of the young person. More recently, a Criminal Justice Joint Inspection (CJJI) produced a thematic review of the provision of AAs for young suspects.[158] This raised concerns that the role has become focused on fulfilling the requirements of the process rather than on safeguarding the young person and meeting their

---

[148] ibid; HMIC (n 128).
[149] Choongh (n 132); Hazel and others (n 140); Kemp and Watkins (n 139).
[150] HMIC (n 128); Quinn and Jackson (n 143).
[151] Hazel and others (n 140).
[152] HMIC (n 128); APPGC (n 147).
[153] Plotnikoff and Woolfson (n 29); Choongh (n 132).
[154] Helen Jones, 'The Pains of Custody: Young Men's Experiences of Pre-prison Custodial Settings' (2011) Prison Service Journal 20.
[155] See eg Canadian research Christine Goodwin-De Faria and Voula Marinos, 'Youth Understanding & Assertion of Legal Rights: Examining the Roles of Age and Power' (2012) 20 International Journal of Children's Rights 343.
[156] Roger Evans, 'The Conduct of Police Interviews with Juveniles', Royal Commission on Criminal Justice, Research Study No 8 (HMSO 1993).
[157] Medford, Gudjonsson, and Pearce (n 135).
[158] Criminal Justice Joint Inspection (CJJI), 'Who's Looking Out for the Children? A Joint Inspection of Appropriate Adult Provision and Children in Detention after Charge' (CJJI 2011).

welfare needs in custody, noting, as other commentators have, the need for clarity around the role of the AA.[159] Although some progress has been made in this latter regard,[160] as I explore in Chapter 4, a number of significant contradictions and incoherences continue to challenge effective implementation of the AA safeguard. Other protections identified as functioning problematically for children in more focused research studies include concerns around the low uptake of legal advice by young suspects[161] and the detention of children and young people in the police station overnight, especially after charge.[162]

The research on which this book draws responds to these troubling glimpses of young suspect experiences and the shortcomings of the protections which should mitigate the police custody process for them. It aims to bring child suspects into the light in order to begin to address the gaps in our knowledge of their experiences. In so doing, the book also reviews the implications for the child suspect of the limited legal framework of protections and the lack of oversight by the courts and through other accountability mechanisms.

Theoretical Underpinning of Research Methods

Before addressing the methods employed in the research, I turn first to the theoretical framework which informs the study. Commentators in the criminal process arena have frequently employed Herbert Packer's normative models of 'crime control' and 'due process',[163] which compete for priority in the functioning of criminal justice processes.[164] Packer's 'crime

---

[159] See Brian Littlechild, 'Reassessing the Role of the "Appropriate Adult"' (1995) Criminal Law Review 540; Harriet Pierpoint, 'Extending and Professionalising the Role of the Appropriate Adult' (2011) 33 Journal of Social Welfare and Family Law 139.
[160] By virtue of the statement of the AA role introduced in the July 2018 revision of *Code C* (n 1).
[161] Brookman and Pierpoint (n 117); Kemp, Pleasence, and Balmer (n 136); Layla Skinns, '"Let's Get It Over With": Early Findings on the Factors Affecting Detainees' Access to Custodial Legal Advice' (2009) 19 Policing & Society 58.
[162] CJJI (n 158); Layla Skinns, *Overnight Detention of Children in Police Cells* (Howard League for Penal Reform 2011); Augusta Itua, '"It's Horrible When They Keep You in There at Night." Ending the Overnight Detention of Children in Police Custody' (Just for Kids Law 2022).
[163] Herbert L Packer, 'Two Models of the Criminal Process' (1964) 113 University of Pennsylvania Law Review 1.
[164] See for example Andrew Sanders, *Criminal justice* (4th edn, OUP 2010).

control' model prioritizes the 'repression of criminal conduct', aiming to produce a 'high rate of apprehension and conviction',[165] processing an endless stream of cases as if on an 'assembly line or conveyor belt'.[166] By contrast, the 'due process' model has a different, competing emphasis, although Packer is clear that the one is not the converse of the other. Conscious of the 'stigma and loss of liberty' which the criminal justice system may impose, the due process model favours 'controls and safeguards' and provides the maximum protection to the innocent, operating in the manner of an 'obstacle course'.[167]

Of the many critiques of Packer's models,[168] perhaps the most apposite for this study, and that which identifies why Packer's models remain relevant but cannot provide a comprehensive framework for this analysis, is that advanced by John Griffiths.[169] Griffiths identifies that the scope of Packer's models is restricted in particular by a 'limited conception of the function of criminal law', namely, 'detection, apprehension, prosecution and punishment of offenders'. Packer's portrayal of the criminal process, Griffiths argues, is reduced to a struggle between 'two contending forces whose interests are implacably hostile': the individual, who is advantaged by the due process model, and the state, which is advantaged by the crime control model. Yet, Griffiths points to the wider impact of the criminal justice process, observing, 'Children, defendants, and everyone else, learn both from the *objective* of a process they participate in and from the *nature* of the process'. As Feeley has argued, any process analysis must address and account for the 'strong competing norms and incentives which act at cross-purposes to the system's formal goals and norms'.[170] Such competing incentives in the police custody phase include administrative convenience,[171] organizational risk management, and the impact of resourcing constraints[172] (particularly temporal limitations) and sway not just police

---

[165] Packer (n 163) 9–10.
[166] ibid 10–11.
[167] ibid 16, 13.
[168] See eg Doreen J McBarnet, 'Pre-Trial Procedures and the Construction of Conviction' (1975) 23 Sociological Review (Keele) 172; Damaška (n 113).
[169] John Griffiths, 'Ideology in Criminal Procedure or A Third "Model" of the Criminal Process' (1970) 79 Yale Law Journal 359.
[170] Malcolm Feeley, 'Two Models of the Criminal Justice System: An Organizational Perspective' (1973) 7 Law & Society Review 407.
[171] Jerome H Skolnick, *Justice without Trial: Law Enforcement in Democratic Society* (Wiley 1966).
[172] Ashworth (n 101), although Ashworth acknowledges that this element may have 'assumed greater significance since Packer wrote', 28.

actors but all parties, including those acting for, and supporting, a suspect. Packer's models do not adequately account for these factors. Nor do they accommodate consideration of the wider obligations of the youth justice process to have regard to the 'best interests' and welfare of the child—the emphasis on rehabilitation rather than punishment.

Whilst the adversarial struggle between the child and the state in respect of the allegation is hugely significant in the custody process, as I discuss in greater detail in Chapter 2, by no means does it provide either a comprehensive explanation of a child's treatment in police custody or a suitable lens through which to consider all of its implications.[173] Instead, in seeking a theoretical framework that can respond to the complexity of the issues and the breadth of the enquiry, I turn to the evaluative approach conceived initially by Ashworth,[174] and developed with Mike Redmayne and, more recently, Liz Campbell, in their book *The Criminal Process*.[175] Inevitably, their theory traverses some common ground with Packer's models, but it offers a more nuanced and complex normative framework against which to understand and evaluate the custody process in the round. They argue that the criminal process should have two co-existing goals: 'of regulating procedures for bringing suspected offenders to trial so as to produce accurate determinations, and of ensuring that fundamental rights are protected in those processes'.[176] Thus, their approach addresses not only the product of the process, the evidence gathered, and the legal outcome (and its ramifications) but also the impact of the process itself on the individual and their enjoyment of a broader spectrum of rights.

Internal Values

In developing their framework, Campbell, Ashworth, and Redmayne sketch out, first of all, the 'internal values' which should shape the criminal process in the pursuit of those twin aims. They identify the importance of procedures which 'serve the rule of law, by making decisions more consistent,

---

[173] Commentators have developed, and built on, Packer's models, including as issues such as the victim's position in the criminal process have come to the fore (see eg Roach Kent, 'Four Models of the Criminal Process' (1999) 89 Journal of Criminal Law & Criminology 671).
[174] Ashworth (n 101).
[175] Liz Campbell, Andrew Ashworth, and Mike Redmayne, *The Criminal Process* (5th edn, OUP 2019).
[176] ibid 55.

more predictable and less arbitrary' and which regulate the gathering of evidence within the investigation stage. Central to the endeavour of the investigative stage in particular is the obtaining of reliable evidence which can 'form the basis of an effective and legitimate trial'.[177] Thus, a 'primary function' of criminal procedure is to 'provide safeguards against unreliable forms of evidence'.[178]

In his original formulation of the framework, Ashworth stressed the importance of the principle described by Jeremy Bentham as 'rectitude'—the 'need to ensure evidence is as reliable and accurate as possible'.[179] This is of particular salience to the custody process since its primary, statutory purpose is the obtaining of evidence.[180] As miscarriages of justice, such as the *Confait* case, have illustrated, a focus on rectitude is critical in police custody, given the fallibility of certain forms of evidence (particularly confession evidence) generated in that setting, the impact of police and other professional occupational cultures, and the difficulty of detecting false confessions at trial. Where the suspect is a child, safeguards to ensure that the evidence obtained is reliable are, I suggest, all the more important, given the extreme imbalance in power between officer and child and the likely impact of developmental factors on the child's ability to withstand the pressures of interview.

Campbell and colleagues acknowledge that, in reality, few allegations result in a trial, and indeed, as discussed in the preface, this is particularly the case for children, who are more likely to be diverted without charge or plead guilty at first appearance. However, the lack of a contested trial does not undermine the importance of a criminal process which produces reliable evidence on which accurate determinations, including decisions to offer an out-of-court disposal or to take no further action, can be made. Indeed, the fact that a judge will rarely, in reality, scrutinize the fairness of the procedures which led to a guilty plea or the acceptance of an out-of-court disposal makes the importance of a properly regulated, fair, and rights-respecting criminal investigation all the greater.

To achieve not only effectiveness but also legitimacy in determinations, the police (and later the courts) must, in exercising their coercive powers, treat the suspect (later the defendant) with dignity and respect. Campbell

---

[177] ibid 26.
[178] ibid 26.
[179] Ashworth (n 101) 29.
[180] PACE, s 37.

and colleagues argue that the criminal process, in reflecting the values of a liberal state and a retributive rationale for punishment, should be underpinned by respect for the individual suspect, or defendant, as a rational rights-bearing subject and by the principle of proportionality.[181] They acknowledge that the 'central dilemma of criminal procedure' is to 'reconcile a process which will bring cases to effective trial with the protection of human rights, including the requirement of a fair trial'.[182] As Ashworth asserts, prior to conviction, the criminal process should impose the 'minimum burdens' on those subject to it on the basis that, in accordance with the right to liberty, there should be 'no punitive action' before conviction: 'The greater the burdens and deprivations imposed at the pre-trial stage, the stronger the justifications needed to uphold them.'[183] The assessment of what restrictions might be a proportionate response—in terms of investigative needs and public protection requirements—to the alleged offending of a child is, as we shall see, critical. This is especially the case where the allegation is likely to be at the lower end of the seriousness scale but the impact of detention, and other pre-conviction processes, is liable to be substantial. The stakes are high, not only in terms of achieving a fair outcome in an individual child's case but also in terms of their ongoing relationship with the police and authority more generally. Research underlines that unfair and coercive treatment of those in contact with the police can have lasting negative effects.[184] Campbell and colleagues stress, in this regard, the importance of diversion in the criminal process, where the seriousness of the allegation does not warrant the stress of the full criminal procedure, in order to spare such individuals from the fallible and 'unpredictable' trial process.[185]

Legitimate determinations require that those fair procedures are also fairly implemented. Ashworth argues that this requires special protection for children and for those who may be especially vulnerable: 'favourable discrimination—as by the provision of extra advice, support or protection'. In this regard, Ashworth stresses the importance of effective provision and communication of information to enable enjoyment of that additional protection.[186] In terms of ensuring equal enjoyment of rights and

[181] Campbell, Ashworth, and Redmayne (n 175) 23.
[182] ibid 25.
[183] Ashworth (n 101) 31.
[184] Benjamin Justice and Tracey L Meares, 'How the Criminal Justice System Educates Citizens' (2014) 651 Annals of the American Academy of Political & Social Science 159.
[185] Campbell, Ashworth, and Redmayne (n 175) 25.
[186] Ashworth (n 101).

non-discrimination, the findings of the Lammy Review,[187] particularly around low levels of trust in the police and criminal justice professionals, underline the barriers to full enjoyment of legal protections by Black, Asian, and minority ethnic suspects and defendants and indicate the need for particular care to be taken in ensuring that rights are fully and accessibly explained for all.

Fair implementation also demands integrity on the part of officers and those exercising coercive power over suspects and defendants; that the investigation of crime should not itself involve the breaching of rules, nor should the courts condone such methods or the taking of any advantage as a result of such breaches.[188] This is of critical importance in achieving fairness in a prosecution system where there is such inequality between the power of the state and the individual—an imbalance which is particularly marked for the child in police custody. Campbell and others observe that, if the trial is to function as a communicative process, as Anthony Duff and others contend,[189] then 'the state must also establish the legitimacy of its own claim to hold the defendant to account'.[190] Integrity is particularly important in the closed confines of police custody, where the adjustment of the procedure to the needs of a child suspect depends substantially on the exercise of discretion and where ethnographic research into police behaviour has consistently identified 'cop cultures' which may work against such accommodations.[191] In particular, despite the distancing of COs from investigating officers,[192] the existence of internal solidarity between both groups, and its impact on decisions such as authorisation of detention,[193] has been identified as problematic in repeated custody studies.[194] Police tendencies towards cynicism[195] and suspicion[196] have been observed to result in problematic characterization or stereotyping of certain groups and contempt for

---

[187] Lammy (n 69).
[188] Ashworth (n 101).
[189] Antony Duff and others, *The Trial on Trial. Vol 3, Towards a Normative Theory of the Criminal Trial* (Hart Publishing 2007) 288.
[190] Campbell, Ashworth, and Redmayne (n 175) 27.
[191] See for general discussion Benjamin Bowling, Robert Reiner, and James Sheptycki, *The Politics of the Police* (5th edn, OUP 2019).
[192] PACE, s 36(5).
[193] PACE, s 37(3).
[194] Choongh (n 132); Roxanna Dehaghani, 'Automatic Authorisation: An Exploration of the Decision to Detain in Police Custody' (2017) 3 Criminal Law Review 187; Michael McConville, Andrew Sanders, and Robert Leng, *The Case for the Prosecution* (Routledge 1991).
[195] See eg Sarah Charman, *Police Socialisation, Identity and Culture: Becoming Blue* (Palgrave Macmillan 2017).
[196] Simon Holdaway, *Inside the British Police: A Force at Work* (Blackwell 1983).

groups seen as undeserving.[197] Young people have been included amongst those identified as 'police property',[198] being suitable for control and order maintenance policing,[199] whilst those who might undermine police control in custody, particularly legal representatives, may be seen as unwelcome 'challengers' whose presence is to be minimized and capacity to intrude reduced.[200] Finally, there remains the constant potential for suspects' rights and needs to be overlooked in the interests of achieving results, as notable miscarriages of justice illustrate,[201] whether driven by what might be described as 'noble-cause' corruption[202] (sometimes combined with the view that the legal framework unnecessarily hampers the police and/or favours the defence),[203] or the constant need to appear 'efficient',[204] or a combination of these factors.

Systems of accountability are, as Ashworth observes, key in terms of securing principled exercise of discretion.[205] As already identified, there is a range of measures by which police and criminal justice practitioners may be held accountable (including oversight by more senior police officers, inspections by Independent Custody Visitors and the due process role of the AA), in addition to intervention by the courts. It is critically important that these systems ensure meaningful oversight of day-to-day practice, and their efficacy in achieving appropriate adjustment of the processes for children, and the honouring of their rights in custody, will be reviewed as the process unfolds.

---

[197] Bethany Loftus, 'Policing the "Irrelevant": Class, Diversity and Contemporary Police Culture' in Megan O'Neill, Monique Marks, and Anne-Marie Singh (eds), *Police Occupational Cultures* (JAI Press 2007); David J Smith and Jeremy Gray, 'Police and People in London: The Police in Action' (Policy Study Institute 1983).

[198] John Lee, 'Some Structural Aspects of Police Deviance in Relations with Minority Groups' in Clifford Shearing (ed), *Organizational Police Deviance* (Butterworth 1981) 53–54.

[199] Choongh (n 132); Didier Fassin, *Enforcing Order: An Ethnography of Urban Policing* (English edn, Polity 2013).

[200] Holdaway (n 196) 71–77. In relation to reducing the presence of lawyers in particular see McConville, Sanders, and Leng (n 194); Andrew Sanders, Lee Bridges, and Adele Mulvaney, *Advice and Assistance at Police Stations and the 24 Hour Duty Solicitor Scheme* (Lord Chancellor's Department 1989).

[201] Ashworth (n 101) 10ff for discussion.

[202] Carl B Klockars, 'The Dirty Harry Problem' (1980) 452 Annals of the American Academy of Political & Social Science 33.

[203] As acknowledged in Royal Commission on Criminal Justice (RCCJ), 'Report (Cmnd 2263)' (HMSO 1991), ch 1, para 24.

[204] Skolnick (n 171) 44.

[205] Ashworth (n 101).

External Values: Child Rights

This theoretical framework, and the internal values identified, emphasizes the importance of rights, but, beyond specific procedural rights, the content of those rights is largely externally determined. In relation to suspects generally, the primary source of rights is the European Convention on Human Rights (ECHR), incorporated domestically by the Human Rights Act 1998. Of particular relevance for the suspect are the prohibition on torture and inhuman and degrading treatment (Article 3), the right to liberty and security of the person (Article 5), and the right to private and family life (Article 8). However, fair trial rights (Article 6) are of central salience for the suspect and the evaluative theory developed here. Ashworth calls for a 'greater emphasis' pre-trial on the principle of equality of arms and on the 'quality of legal advice available to defendants when they make what turn out to be crucial choices'.[206] Equality of arms is a fundamental component of a 'fair hearing' within the meaning of Article 6(1) of the ECHR.[207] The Grand Chamber has repeatedly reaffirmed that equality of arms requires a 'fair balance' between the parties, each being afforded a 'reasonable opportunity to present his case under conditions that do not place him at a substantial disadvantage vis-à-vis his opponent'.[208] As the RCCJ observed, 'the fairer the treatment which all parties receive at the hands of the system, the more likely it is the jury's verdict ... will be correct'.[209] This is a key concern in the case of child suspects, where the power imbalance between the detained child and the adult investigating officer is extreme. Issues of disclosure of information relating to the allegation, meaningful access to legal advice, and opportunity to give a good account of oneself in police interview will be relevant to consideration of this principle.

However, identification as a child should trigger a specific range of rights guaranteed by the UNCRC and related instruments,[210] which set out minimum standards for the protection of children in conflict with the law.

---

[206] Ashworth (n 101).
[207] *Regner v Czech Republic* App No 35289/11, 19 September 2017, [146]. See also *Edwards and Lewis v United Kingdom* App nos 39647/98 and 40461/98, 27 October 2004.
[208] See eg *Kress v France* App no 39594/98, 7 June 2001, [72].
[209] RCCJ (n 203) ch 1, para 27.
[210] Particularly the UN Standard Minimum Rules for the Administration of Juvenile Justice (adopted on 10 December 1985 at the 40th Session of the General Assembly) (Beijing Rules). See also the Guidelines of the Committee of Ministers of the Council of Europe on child friendly justice (adopted by the Committee of Ministers on 17 November 2010 at the 1098th meeting of the Ministers' Deputies).

Where a child is concerned, rights under the ECHR must be interpreted in line with the UNCRC.[211] Two of the general principles which underpin the Convention are of special relevance for child suspects: that the 'best interests of the child' must be a 'primary consideration' in all actions undertaken by authorities (including the courts) (Article 3) and the child's right to be heard and listened to in all matters affecting them (Article 12). In relation to more specific rights, Article 37 (which prohibits inhumane treatment and limits detention) and Article 40 (which sets out the child's rights in child justice processes) are of particular importance. That Article 40 rights extend to the investigatory phase is clear, Article 40(2) being applicable to 'every child alleged as, accused of having infringed the penal law'. The UN Committee also stresses the requirement to safeguard children's fair trial rights (Article 40(2)) 'from the moment of contact with the system, including at the stopping, warning or arrest stage, while in custody of the police or other enforcement agencies'.[212] Pre-trial detention plainly engages Article 37, which requires that any deprivation of liberty, including arrest and detention, must be used 'only as a measure of last resort and for the shortest appropriate period'(37(b)) and that any child deprived of their liberty must be 'treated with humanity and respect … and in a manner which takes into account the needs of persons of his or her age' (37(c)). Additionally, Article 40(1) sets out the right of any child alleged to have committed an offence to be 'treated in a manner consistent with the promotion of the child's sense of dignity and worth'. The UN Committee stresses the importance of 'child-friendly' provision and the need to conduct proceedings in an 'atmosphere of understanding to allow the child to fully participate'.[213] Such adjustments in police custody may include the use of 'child-friendly language at all stages, child-friendly layouts of interviewing spaces' and 'support by appropriate adults'.[214] Domestically, the National Police Chiefs' Council (NPCC) has stated its ambition that all children should be treated as 'children first' in 'all encounters' with the police.[215]

This requirement for child friendly justice feeds into the broader right of effective participation, first formally acknowledged for children in 1985 in

---

[211] *T v UK; V v UK* (n 81).
[212] General Comment No 24 (n 8), para 41.
[213] ibid, para 46. See for discussion Stephen Case and Ann Browning, *Child First Justice: The Research Evidence-Base* (Loughborough University 2021).
[214] General Comment No 24 (n 8), paras 38–53.
[215] National Police Chiefs' Council (NPCC), *National Strategy for the Policing of Children and Young People* (NPCC 2016) 8.

the Beijing Rules.[216] The right of effective participation has also been recognized as an implied right under Article 6 of the ECHR.[217] In *Stanford v UK*, the European Court of Human Rights (ECtHR) held that Article 6 'read as a whole, guarantees the right of an accused to participate effectively in a criminal trial'.[218] The ECtHR was first asked to consider the right in relation to children in *T v UK; V v UK*,[219] T and V being eleven years old at the time of their trial for the murder of James Bulger. In finding the right applicable to children, the Court stressed at [84] the importance of adjustment to facilitate effective participation:

> it is essential that a child charged with an offence is dealt with in a manner which takes full account of his age, level of maturity and intellectual and emotional capacities, and that steps are taken to promote his ability to understand and participate in the proceedings.

The fullest explanation of the right to participate effectively, and duties to facilitate the same, was provided in the subsequent case of *SC v UK*, another case involving a child aged eleven at trial.[220] The reasoning of the court in *SC v UK* was closely modelled by the ECtHR when asked to consider whether the right applied to the investigatory stage in *Panovits v Cyprus*,[221] where the applicant was seventeen years old at the time of his arrest and detention by the police. The Court observed at [67]:

> The right of an accused minor to effective participation in his or her criminal trial requires that he be dealt with with due regard to his vulnerability and capacities from the first stages of his involvement in a criminal investigation and, in particular, during any questioning by the police. The authorities must take steps to reduce as far as possible his feelings of intimidation and inhibition ... and ensure that the accused minor has a broad understanding of the nature of the investigation, of what is at stake for him or her, including the significance of any penalty which may be imposed as well as of his rights of defence and, in particular, of his right to remain silent ... It means that he or she, if

---

[216] Beijing Rules (n 210), para 14.2.
[217] Entered into force on 21 September 1970.
[218] *Stanford v UK* App no 16757/90 ECHR, 23 February 1994, [26].
[219] *T v UK; V v UK* (n 81).
[220] *SC v UK* (n 82), [86].
[221] *Panovits v Cyprus* App no 4268/04, 11 March 2009, (2008) 27 BHRC 464, [67].

necessary with the assistance of, for example, an interpreter, lawyer, social worker or friend, should be able to understand the general thrust of what is said by the arresting officer and during his questioning by the police.

The principle in *Panovits v Cyprus* has been confirmed in subsequent judgments of the ECtHR,[222] but it has not been applied directly at domestic level in England and Wales. The case was referred to, obiter, with approval in *HC*.[223] Moses LJ, whilst not required to determine the applicability of the principle, observed that the police interview was an 'important part of the preparatory and preliminary process' of the determination of a criminal charge, distinguishing that position from the circumstances in *R(R) v Durham Constabulary*,[224] in which Article 6 was held not to be engaged in relation to a decision to warn a child in police custody.[225] Moses LJ's reasoning must be correct. The Supreme Court in *Cadder v HM Advocate*[226] held that Article 6 guarantees pertained in the police station in relation to legal advice, following *Salduz v Turkey*,[227] a unanimous decision of the Grand Chamber and one which Hope LJ held had given rise to a 'clear and constant jurisprudence'—one with which the Court concluded that the decision in *Panovits v Cyprus* was 'entirely consistent'.[228] Notwithstanding the emergence of a 'looser approach'[229] taken more recently to the application of Strasbourg jurisprudence,[230] it is highly likely that the principle would be followed domestically.[231]

The principle of effective participation has received limited examination, particularly with regard to how it might be conceived for the child

---

[222] See eg *Blokhin v Russsia* App no 47152/06, 23 March 2016, [195]; *Dvorski v Croatia* App no 25703/11, 20 October 2015, [80]; *Adamkiewicz v Poland* 54729/00, 2 March 2010, [85].

[223] See n 20.

[224] [2005] UKHL 21, [2005] 1 WLR 1184.

[225] ibid, [91–93], on the basis that once prosecution had been ruled out, the decision did not involve 'the determination of a criminal charge against him' (following Attorney-General's Reference (No 2 of 2001) [2003] UKHL 68, [2004] 2 AC 72).

[226] [2010] UKSC 43, [2010] 1 WLR 2601 (*Cadder*).

[227] App no 36391/02, 27 November 2008, (2009) 49 EHRR 19.

[228] *Cadder* (n 226), [46–47].

[229] Lewis Graham, '"Fair Trial", Case Commentary' (2020) 5 Criminal Law Review 453, 455–56.

[230] See eg R v *Abdurahman (Ismail)* [2019] EWCA Crim 2239, [2020] 4 WLR 6; *R (Kaiyam) v SOS for Justice* [2014] UKSC 66, [2015] AC 1344; *R (Hallam and Nealon) v SoS for Justice* [2019] UKSC 2, [2020] AC 279.

[231] Human Rights Act 1998, s 2; *R (Alconbury Developments Ltd) v Secretary of State for the Environment, Transport and the Regions* [2001] UKHL 23, [2003] 2 AC 295.

suspect.[232] Following *Panovits v Cyprus*, enabling a child to participate effectively in proceedings might be understood to comprise three key elements—first, the need for adjusted treatment which takes account of both the child's inherent need for special care and protection and their situational adversity; secondly, the fostering of the child's understanding of their legal jeopardy and an informed appreciation of their options (vis a vis the allegation) and their defence rights; and thirdly, the enabling of their general comprehension of the processes and questioning, with assistance as required, so that they can engage directly with them. I will examine more closely the details of this right as the empirical findings unfold. Suffice it to say, at this stage, that the emphasis in both the ECtHR case law and the UNCRC (and related instruments) is on the child as a competent legal actor, achieving full and active participation with assistance and adjustment of the proceedings as necessary.[233]

In addition to these rights, guaranteed in international law, Campbell and colleagues also identify several jurisdictionally specific external values which shape the criminal process and the way the twin aims of the process are achieved. These include the use of lay fact-finders and adversarialism. Although of critical significance for the later process, the involvement of lay fact-finders has limited influence on the custody process itself. But adversarialism, as we shall see, has a profound impact on both the demands made of the child in the custody process and the efficacy with which the protections which should be afforded to them function. I explore this aspect in detail in Chapter 3.

Theoretical Framework for Evaluating the Process for Child Suspects

Drawing, therefore, on the evaluative framework developed by Andrew Ashworth, with Liz Campbell and Mike Redmayne, I propose to assess the police custody process for children by reference to two co-existing aims: the production of accurate determinations and the use of fair procedures which

---

[232] Abenaa Owusu-Bempah, 'Understanding the Barriers to Defendant Participation in Criminal Proceedings in England and Wales' (2020) 40(4) *Legal Studies* 1; but see for conceptualizations derived from court practitioners' perspectives: Jessica Jacobson and Penny Cooper, *Participation in Courts and Tribunals: Concepts, Realities and Aspirations* (Bristol UP 2020).

[233] See in particular General Comment No 24 (n 8), paras 45, 46.

protect the child's fundamental rights. In respect of the former aim, the production of accurate determinations, I focus in particular on the generation of evidence which is as reliable and accurate as possible, this being the primary focus of the custody process. In exploring how fully such 'rectitude' is achieved, I will evaluate whether the procedures are effective in regulating the investigation and safeguarding against unreliable forms of evidence and whether they enable, as a result, consistent and non-arbitrary decision-making.

With regard to 'fair procedures', I will consider whether child suspects are treated with dignity and respect for them as rational rights-holders. Proportionality is a key component of fairness in this context, and I will evaluate whether the process imposes only the 'minimum burdens' on the individual suspect, with suitable diversionary action where that is appropriate. Procedures will only be fair in practice where fairly implemented, which, in relation to the child suspect, will require a consideration of whether special adjustment and additional support is provided, in accordance with legislation and guidance, to enable them to enjoy their rights in the custody setting. Finally, I will also consider whether officers and other staff implement the process and respond to the child suspect with integrity sufficient to establish the legitimacy of the pre-charge procedure and whether accountability mechanisms are effective in identifying where rules are breached and guidance not heeded. This framework is shaped by, and the process in practice will be evaluated with reference to, the rights of the child suspect, guaranteed by the UNCRC (particularly Articles 3, 12, 37, and 40) and the ECHR, particularly Article 6. I will focus on the child's right to be detained only as a last resort, to experience child friendly processes, and to participate effectively in the procedures.

Research Methods

With this theoretical framework in mind, I turn then to the methods employed in gathering the data on which this book draws. I outline here in brief the approach adopted and the scope of the data collected. At every turn, the design and implementation of this study raised challenges and required compromises. There are a number of parallels between the efforts of a researcher keen to hear a child suspect's perspective and understand their reflections on their experience and the task of a police officer investigating a child's response to an allegation, particularly what was in his or her mind at the time of an alleged offence. In light of this, I also address, in this section, some of the challenges encountered in planning and conducting the research because, in themselves, they illuminate some of the tensions at the heart of the treatment of children who find themselves detained in the police station and provide an introduction to the issues which run through this book.

Methods Overview

The central aim of the study was to hear the voices of child suspects. To that end, I interviewed forty-one children and young people with recent experience of police custody as in England and Wales, referred to here collectively as 'young participants' and individually by pseudonym to retain anonymity. The interviews were conducted between January and September 2017. The sample group covered a range of ages at the time of interview: ten to fourteen years (n = 5), fifteen to sixteen years (n = 19), seventeen to eighteen years (n = 15), and over eighteen years (n = 2), including eight girls and fourteen young people who identified themselves as Black, Asian, or of minority ethnic status. Young participants had varying levels of police custody experience—some had only one detention experience (n = 6), some several (two to four episodes, n = 18), whilst others had been detained more frequently (more than five episodes, n = 17). A table setting out the anonymized details of the young participants is included in Appendix A. They were accessed through gatekeepers, predominantly YOTs and defence solicitors. Semi-structured interviews were conducted in a range of settings, including YOT offices, education settings, and home settings, with a preference, where practicable, for a location of the participant's choosing. Fully informed consent was provided by all young participants and by an adult with parental responsibility where the child was under sixteen. The average length of the interviews was just over forty-three minutes. In keeping with the approach taken in similar research with young people[234] (and in accordance with YOT gatekeeper arrangements for their own user research), a £15 'thank you' in the form of a gift voucher was provided to each young participant.

---

[234] See eg HMIC (n 128) 210.

Young participant interviews were informed by 192 hours of observations conducted in 6 police custody blocks[235] across 3 force areas between July and November 2016.[236] The forces comprised a major regional metropolitan force (F3) and two county forces: one serving a mixed rural and urban catchment (F1), the other with more substantial areas of significant urban deprivation (F2). The custody blocks observed varied in terms of facilities (older and newer blocks, larger and smaller facilities) and differing arrangements for health care (including Liaison and Diversion Services) and AA provision (where a familial AA (FAA) or the employee of a residential home where relevant (RHAA)) could not attend). This included YOT workers (YOTAA), volunteer AAs (VAA) (co-ordinated by YOTs, by Police and Crime Commissioners, and through private providers), and paid AAs (PAA) co-ordinated by private providers.

The police custody observations involved tracking all young suspects passing through the block (n = 47, referred to in the text as YS1–YS47), observing processes and conditions within the block, and holding face-to-face conversations with police officers and staff (n = 96), health-care professionals (n = 14), solicitors[237] (Sol)(n = 9), independent custody visitors (ICV) (n = 3), and AAs (n = 11). These conversations took the form of discussions with all available staff and other adults working on the shift, as duties allowed, in interview rooms, consultation rooms, or waiting areas. They were informed by a separate topic guide for each role and were supplemented by shorter conversations during the shifts, responding to events as they unfolded. In addition, further semi-structured interviews were carried out, away from the police station, with additional AAs (n = 11), solicitors (n = 4), and ICVs (n = 3). This sample included professionals and volunteers encountered on observation but where there was not time for discussion and AAs who had supported young participants and were willing to be interview (FAAs interviewed away from the police station were also offered the £15 'thank-you' voucher).

All the interviews and fieldnotes were transcribed in full and subjected to thematic analysis.[238] The material was coded (using NVivo 11.4.1)

---

[235] Referred to variously by participants as custody 'suites', 'the cells', or, more generically, 'the police station'.
[236] Role abbreviations and numerical signifiers are used for all young suspects, forces, custody blocks, and adult participants to preserve their anonymity.
[237] Those providing legal advice are referred to throughout as solicitors for ease, although the group also includes Accredited and Probationary Police Station Representatives.
[238] Virginia Braun and Victoria Clarke, 'Using Thematic Analysis in Psychology' (2006) 3 Qualitative Research in Psychology 77.

using a hybrid approach,[239] combining both deductive[240] and inductive[241] methods. The initial coding framework was formulated using the structural elements of the custody process. It was additionally informed (as were the interview topic guides) by themes arising out of a 'scoping study' conducted between mid-2015 and early 2016, in which I conducted informal interviews with sixteen experts in the area: professionals working in police custody, police, academics, and non-governmental organization (NGO) stakeholders. Separate nodes were added as themes emerged from repeated review and constant cross-comparison of the data.[242]

Methodological Reflections

Visibility and Protection

Research involving vulnerable participants and sensitive topics, such as in this study, rightly involves significant scrutiny as part of the academic ethical approval process. In addition, securing gatekeeper engagement and access through police forces demanded an iterative process of addressing safeguarding and related ethical issues, undergoing vetting by police forces, and securing other authorizations as required by local authorities. I made the decision not to seek to interview children during their time in police custody out of concern for the voluntariness of any participation and an anxiety not to overburden or confuse them during the process or delay their release from custody. This limited my ability to capture their immediate reactions to detention as it was unfolding. But it does, instead, allow me to review their more considered reflections on release. However, this approach meant that I faced the challenge of recruiting participants after the event through gatekeepers. This proved problematic, not least because gatekeeper organizations were generally working within such budgetary constraints[243]

---

[239] Jennifer Fereday and Eimear Muir-Cochrane, 'Demonstrating Rigor Using Thematic Analysis: A Hybrid Approach of Inductive and Deductive Coding and Theme Development' (2006) 5 International Journal of Qualitative Methods 80.
[240] Benjamin F Crabtree and William F Miller, 'A Template Approach to Text Analysis: Developing and Using Codebooks' in David Silverman (ed), *Doing Qualitative Research* (Sage 1992).
[241] Richard E Boyatzis, *Transforming Qualitative Information: Thematic Analysis and Code Development* (Sage 1998).
[242] Sheila M Fram, 'The Constant Comparative Analysis Method Outside of Grounded Theory' (2013) 18 Qualitative Report 1.
[243] The annual grant for YOTs in 2016–17 during the fieldwork period was £67 million, a reduction of £9.1 million on the previous year's grant.

that supporting research often required individuals within the organization to commit their own time to support the work. But progress was slow also because gatekeepers had their own concerns, being hesitant to exhaust young people's application to the ongoing court process or compliance with a current court order by introducing an additional research interview. However, once prosecution was concluded, or a court order nearly completed, gatekeepers were sometimes then reluctant to involve young people in the research for fear of retraumatizing or labelling them or more generally wanting to avoid the criminogenic effects of ongoing contact with criminal justice agencies.[244]

Undoubtedly, such checks and approvals are necessary and more general protective approaches wholly appropriate. Nonetheless, the challenges encountered in obtaining approval and securing access to young participants shed light on the striking lack of qualitative research with children about their experiences with the criminal justice system. There can be no doubt that our collective concerns significantly limit children's potential to participate in research.[245] There is also a certain irony that such protections are applied to children as research participants, yet, although police and other adult interactions with child suspects are governed by a range of professional and safeguarding duties, in practice, children in police custody are frequently required to reveal deeply personal information in an often public and intimidating setting, including relating experiences of self-harm, and they are asked to make crucial legal decisions often in the absence of any significant parental or carer input. The protective approach taken in research thus provides a useful backdrop against which to consider the manner in which unconvicted children in police custody are protected and their well-being assured.

Consent and Stamina

Vulnerable participants may experience research as coercive or violent,[246] and the need for special care when seeking consent from children is well

---

[244] Lesley McAra and Susan McVie, 'Youth Crime and Justice: Key Messages from the Edinburgh Study of Youth Transitions and Crime' (2010) 10 Criminology & Criminal Justice 179.
[245] As others have also observed: Michael A Grodin and Leonard H Glantz, *Children as Research Subjects: Science, Ethics and Law* (OUP 1994); Pranee Liamputtong, *Researching the Vulnerable: A Guide to Sensitive Research Methods* (Sage 2007).
[246] Gayatri Chakravorty Spivak, 'Can the Subaltern Speak?' in Cary Nelson and Lawrence Grossberg (eds), *Marxism and the Interpretation of Culture* (University of Illinois Press 1988).

established.[247] It was essential to ensure that free and informed consent was obtained from every participant before any interview was conducted and that every participant understood, and could exercise, the right to withdraw at any time.[248] Accessible information sheets were produced for child participants on all aspects of the project—including issues such as anonymity, confidentiality (and its limitations), and the use to be made of the data. These were reviewed with each participant in advance of the interview, using tailored examples and seeking out young participants' own understandings to ensure comprehension. Obtaining consent cannot be rushed. Yet, whilst for some the process was engaging and sparked discussion which led well into the research interview, for others, the process demanded a level of concentration which meant that their energy and focus were significantly depleted before the research issues could be addressed.

This is a challenge all research with children must navigate, but in the context of this study, it usefully highlights the varying capabilities amongst comparably aged children and offers a backdrop against which to reflect on the capacity of child suspects to participate effectively in a police interview. The repeated questionings to which a child is subjected before police interview begins—in booking-in, risk assessment, health examination, and providing instructions to a lawyer where requested—far outweigh the preliminary demands of research participation. Just as with the consent process, each is a necessary prerequisite for fair treatment. But, as will become apparent, coping with the demands of even the protective aspects of the custody process, and managing desperation to get it all over and 'get out', are key themes which echo throughout the custody process and impinge on engagement at every stage.

Autonomy and Compromise

I approached young participants as engaged social actors, with different rather than lesser competencies,[249] capable of being reliable and competent research participants.[250] In my prior professional experience, as a barrister

---

[247] See for discussion Virginia Morrow and Martin Richards, 'The Ethics of Social Research with Children: An Overview' (1996) 10 Children & Society 90.
[248] See for discussion of consent as an ongoing state Les Back, *The Art of Listening* (Berg 2007); David Buckingham, 'What Are Words Worth? Interpreting Children's Talk about Television' (1991) 5 Cultural Studies 228.
[249] Martin Woodhead and Dorothy Faulkner, 'Subjects, Objects or Participants? Dilemmas of Psychological Research with Children' in Pia Monrad Christensen and Allison James (eds), *Research with Children: Perspectives and Practices* (2nd edn, Routledge 2008).
[250] Alan France, 'Young People' in Sandy Fraser and others (eds), *Doing Research with Children and Young People* (Sage 2007).

representing young defendants at court, I had found that child defendants often, spontaneously and at some length, spoke about their treatment in police custody, having had no other opportunity to voice, or make sense of, those experiences. I wanted to give the young participants in this study as much scope as possible to explore their experiences and to focus on those aspects that they considered particularly important. However, the method chosen also had to be a highly effective use of the limited time available. Not only was I conscious of stamina issues, but I also had to be aware of likely constraints arising in respect of parent and carer convenience (where relevant), as well as venue availability, especially where YOT premises were used after school hours.

The interview format offered the facility to engage with a young person immediately, with the minimum of preamble beyond the informed consent process. But I was concerned that the very adult mode of the research interview would too closely mirror the police interview and would therefore accentuate the power imbalance, present in much research, that I was keen to neutralize.[251] Peer-to-peer research and other participatory approaches plainly lend themselves to engaging young people on difficult issues on a more level footing.[252] However, given the scarcity of prior information in respect of young suspect experiences, the breadth of the process that I hoped to cover, and my desire not to underscore young participants' criminal justice experiences with protracted engagement with the research,[253] I concluded that predominantly participatory approaches were unsuitable for this study. Nonetheless, I was able to retain a considerable degree of autonomy for young participants by positioning them in the interview as 'experts by experience',[254] an approach adopted with significant success in other research with children in this area.[255] Thus, they could take the lead in identifying areas of importance, and in shaping the discussion, whilst feeling as if they were partners in, rather than objects of, the research. The

---

[251] See for discussion Berry Mayall, 'Conversations with Children: Working with Generational Issues' in Christensen and James (n 249).
[252] See eg Helen Beckett and Camille Warrington, 'Making Justice Work: Experiences of Criminal Justice for Children and Young People Affected by Sexual Exploitation as Victims and Witnesses' (University of Bedfordshire 2015); Carlie Goldsmith, '"It Just Feels Like It's Always Us": Young People, Peer Bereavement and Community Safety' (2012) 15 Journal of Youth Studies 657.
[253] Mindful as YOT workers were of the criminogenic effects of prolonging contact with the criminal justice system and agents connected with it: McAra and McVie, 'Key Messages' (n 244).
[254] Louis Cohen, *Research Methods in Education* (5th edn, RoutledgeFalmer 2000).
[255] Beckett and Warrington (n 252); Hazel and others (n 140).

effect was striking, with young people speaking eloquently about their experiences and showing real enthusiasm and insight, identifying challenges, and offering options for reform.

The decision to seek additional adult consent in addition for under sixteens involved a similar trade-off. I was mindful of the 'Gillick-competency' framework[256] and reluctant to undermine young participants' agency. However, a combination of practical considerations (particularly the traumatic nature of some material likely to be discussed and concerns about the fragmented support structures around some young people) and pragmatism (acquiescing to YOTs' general approach that any such user research with under-sixteens should involve parental consent) drove my decision-making. However, by incorporating parental consent forms into information leaflets, and with the extra effort of gatekeepers maintaining communication with young participants and their families, no interview was cancelled for want of parental consent, nor was I aware of any gatekeeper encountering a young person who was keen to be involved but who could not engage because of a lack of parental support for the project.

Such autonomy/protection dilemmas do not permit of easy answers. Nor do I suggest that my methodological compromises will have avoided exclusion and promoted full participation in every case. However, the challenges encountered in the research provide an introduction to similar, but more significant, tensions between autonomy and protection in police custody and within more demanding resource constraints. These particularly arise with regard to the implementation of the AA protection and the accessing of legal advice. In respect of both supports, balancing autonomy rights (such as the right to refuse legal advice) with fair trial rights, particularly the right to effective participation, requires a similar trade-off to be made.

A Reflexive Approach

I have sought throughout to take a reflexive approach to the research. Although an 'indispensable ingredient of rigorous investigation',[257] as Coretta Phillips and Rod Earle have identified, reflexivity is not always unproblematically employed.[258] I have tried, in the narrative that I construct

---

[256] To assess a young person's competence to give consent based on their 'maturity and understanding and the nature of the consent required' (*Gillick v West Norfolk and Wisbech Area Health Authority and Department of Health and Social Security* [1984] QB 581 (QBD)).

[257] Loic Wacquant, 'From "Public Criminology" to the Reflexive Sociology of Criminological Production and Consumption' (2011) 51 British Journal of Criminology 438, 439.

[258] Coretta Phillips and Rod Earle, 'Reading Difference Differently?' (2010) 50 British Journal of Criminology 360.

from the data, to be mindful of my multiple, intersecting identities (which include mature, white, middle-class, graduate, parent, and legal professional) and how my positionality has shaped my approach to the research, the data that I have elicited, and how I interpret it.

By way of example, it is notable that very few young participants recounted instances in which they felt that they had been discriminated against on the basis of their ethnicity in the police station. On first assessment, this is welcome, and it may represent the factual infrequency of such incidents. But it is important, in analysing this feature of the data, to be clear about what can reliably be understood by it. In doing so, I bear in mind the potential effect that my ethnicity might have had on the discussion generated. As a white, adult researcher, young Black, Asian, and minority ethnic participants may well have felt inhibited from raising incidents of a racist nature.[259] Equally, some young participants' natural immaturity and difficulty in coping with the custody experience may provide another explanation of that deficit, namely, that the relative absence of accounts of racial discrimination in the custody suite, contrasted with the slightly higher rate of accounts of such discrimination at the point of arrest, reveals instead that the overwhelming challenges of the custody suite for some young people, particularly the desire to 'get out', may drown out the occurrence of other concerns, such as racial discrimination, in that setting.

In a not dissimilar way, the CO, and other adults, encountering a child in police custody, must construct their own narrative of a child suspect: their understanding, their attitude towards those dealing with him or her, their ability to participate, their need for support, and the veracity of any account they might advance in interview. The data COs rely on is, as is mine, varied and incomplete, constructed from the child's immediate presentation, often hard-to-verify historic information, snippets of behaviour, instinctive reactions, and partial responses to questioning. They, as I, bring to their understandings a range of intersecting perspectives: as professional, member of the community, parent, agent of law enforcement, or protective presence. As the chapters unfold, the enormity of their challenge comes into focus, as does the importance of the accuracy of their assessment in mitigating the harms of police custody and avoiding the sort of injustice experienced by the teenagers in the *Confait* case.

---

[259] See for discussion ibid and Paul Connolly, 'Race, Gender and Critical Reflexivity in Research with Young Children' in Christensen and James (n 249).

The Structure of the Book

Having set out the theoretical and methodological approaches taken in this study, I close this chapter with an overview of how the child suspect's experience in police custody unfolds throughout the book. The empirical exploration begins in Chapter 2, which focuses on the earliest stages of police detention—the child's arrest, their arrival in detention, and the 'booking-in' process, in which the child arrestee is presented to the CO for their detention to be authorized. The discussion will explore young participants' responses to these early phases of custody—the hostile intensity of their arrest, the shock and anxiety of arriving in detention, and the often alien demands of the booking-in and risk assessment processes. I focus in particular on child suspect reactions to the CO, and vice versa, introducing two key aspects in tension throughout the custody process—the implications of the various adversities experienced by the child and the adversarial nature of the detention experience.

Chapter 3 considers the child as legal actor in custody, beginning with the delivery of rights information as part of the booking-in process. I explore, in particular, young participant understandings of their legal rights and the barriers they experience in taking up the offer of legal advice—the challenges of engaging with complex rights information in the emotional turmoil of custody and the misconceptions and misunderstandings that hamper their decision-making. The discussion situates the research findings on these issues in the context of previous research internationally, particularly in North America. For those who do request legal advice, the analysis then explores young participant accounts of the challenges of engaging with their representative and of navigating the complex loyalties at play in providing instructions and making the decisions required of them. The chapter closes with a call for mandatory legal advice for children in police custody.

In Chapter 4, I turn from the legal rights enjoyed by all to the particular rights of children in detention to be treated in an age-appropriate fashion. The chapter focuses on the provision of the AA. The analysis considers, in particular, the efficacy and coherence of the AA role in securing child friendly treatment, exploring the tensions between welfare and justice, and privacy and lack of privilege, which the AA must navigate. The conflicted position of the CO as gateway to the protection, the power dynamics between the AA and other protagonists, and the resource constraints within which both custody teams and AAs operate are also implicated. The conclusion considers how the AA role might be reconceptualized to better meet the needs of the child suspect.

Chapter 5 explores the impact of detention itself and its accompanying deprivations on child suspects. Focusing on experiences in the cell, young participant reflections provide a rich account of an oppressive and minimally adjusted experience, revealing, in stark contrast to the 'minimum burdens' principle, a process often experienced as deeply punitive, recalling Malcolm Feeley's assessment of lower criminal court proceedings that 'the process itself is the punishment'.[260] The discussion considers the drivers for the minimal adjustment of the detention conditions for young suspects, acknowledging risk and resourcing but also exploring the power dynamics of police–suspect relations and the extra-legal purposes of detention. In closing, I explore the ramifications of punitive custody processes for children through a procedural justice lens and consider the exclusionary impacts of such punitive experiences.

The final empirical chapter, Chapter 6, addresses the culmination of the custody process—the police interview—and evaluates the outcomes of police detention against the theoretical framework. I review the challenges of assessing fitness for interview in the custody block and the inadequacies of the current arrangements. In relation to the obtaining of accurate and reliable evidence, the analysis explores the cumulative impact of the child's custody experience on their ability to cope with interview and to give a good account of themselves when questioned. I focus, in particular, on the counterproductive impact of coercive interviewing tactics, which are liable to confuse and frustrate rather than to foster effective participation and elicit reliable evidence. I argue, in the conclusion, for a recognition that, in most cases, the investigation, and the wider purposes of the youth justice process, are not best served by interviewing a child in detention.

Young participant accounts underline, in rich and concerning detail, their need for protection and support to exercise their rights effectively in the critical legal moment which is police custody. Yet, reviewing the process in its entirety reveals clearly that, in police detention, the very factors which demand additional supports to enable effective participation—the intersecting challenges experienced by the child, the adverse circumstances in which they find themselves, and the adversarial framing of the process—are those factors which tend to frustrate the effective implementation of the

---

[260] Malcolm M Feeley, *The Process Is the Punishment: Handling Cases in a Lower Criminal Court* (1st edn, Russell Sage Foundation 1979) 30.

protections they should enjoy. The closing chapter, Chapter 7, in reflecting on these findings, returns to the questions posed in the preface—whether the provisions now enshrined in PACE and the broader legal framework provide effective protection from injustice for children today. I conclude with a call for widescale retrenchment of the use of police custody for children, proposing a framework for 'child first' police custody[261] for those few who must be detained, and consider the ramifications of the findings for youth justice processes more generally.

---

[261] Case and Browning (n 213).

2
The Early Stages
Adversity and Adversariality in Collision

> So they've took me out to the main reception, that's when I've seen people coming in and out of their cells. So I'm lookin' at people and they're lookin' at me and I'm just starin' at them, like, scared, but tryin' to act not scared...so I'm starin' at them thinkin', 'Who's this?' and, 'Who's that? Which one of these is gonna be the one to hurt me or kill me?
>
> (Elijah)

Introduction

This first empirical chapter traces the child suspect's experiences in the initial stages of their custody journey. It charts their arrival in detention, the wait to be booked in, and the demands of engaging with the Custody Officer (CO) for the authorisation of their detention, the risk assessment, and the search. This period can last a matter of fifteen or twenty minutes or can extend to over an hour or more. Often immediately following arrest, this can be a time of high emotion and uncertainty for a child, particularly if they have never been in police custody before, as Elijah's reflections in the epigraph illustrate. For the vast majority of child suspects, they are entirely on their own during this critical period. The cast of supporting adults and professionals—solicitors, appropriate adults (AAs), healthcare professionals—are not yet within their reach. More often than not, they are handcuffed, and surrounded by officers and, frequently, other, generally older, suspects. What happens to a child, and how they react during this opening phase, can have a fundamental effect on their custody experience: how they are treated, what support they may be afforded, and how they experience and cope with the process. In seeking to understand these interactions, this chapter explores two key issues in tension throughout the custody process which challenge the rights of children in custody, shape the application of adjustments, and undermine their efficacy in securing fair outcomes: the implications of the multifaceted adversity experienced by the child suspect and the adversarial nature of the custody process.

Adversity and Vulnerability

The opening phases of the police custody process are focused on ensuring that the child's rights are observed—particularly their right not to be detained unless strictly necessary—and that their needs are identified. As outlined in Chapter 1, the adversities experienced by many child suspects are likely to be multiple and intersecting. All child suspects are naturally developmentally immature by virtue of their young age.[1] However, many are also likely to experience particular psychosocial disadvantages (developmental or behavioural disorders, learning disability, and communication difficulties), as well as adverse childhood experiences, such as being in local authority care or having suffered abuse or bereavement.[2] These challenges for the child are further magnified by the situational adversity in which they find themselves on arrest and in detention.

As explored in Chapter 1, the child should, on paper at least, enjoy a range of protections as a result of their youth, but what of adjustment to accommodate the other challenges that they experience and the intersection of those adversities with their developmental immaturity? How do COs and other adults in the detention setting identify and address their complex needs at this early stage? Criminal justice legislation and practice typically ascribes the term 'vulnerable' to designate those participants who, as a result of these and similar adversities, are entitled to adjusted treatment within the process.[3] The term is widely used in the discourse of

---

[1] Michael E Lamb and others, 'Developmental Factors Affecting Children in Legal Contexts' (2013) 13 Youth Justice 131.
[2] Jessica Jacobson and others, *Punishing Disadvantage: A Profile of Children in Custody* (Prison Reform Trust 2010).
[3] See eg Youth Justice and Criminal Evidence Act 1999 (YJCEA 1999), Part II.

police custody in this same sense[4] and, as we shall see, in discussions in the custody blocks observed. Long ascribed to children,[5] vulnerability became a pervasive theme in social welfare and youth justice discourse under New Labour.[6] However, as a concept it is deeply contested, subjective, and highly malleable,[7] and this is particularly the case for child suspects. There are several aspects of the concept of vulnerability, as applied to children in conflict with the law, which merit brief identification before turning to the empirical material. First is the association of vulnerability with 'weakness and frailty' and 'deservingness'.[8] It is linked, in particular, with victimhood, a connection which reaches back to the roots of the word itself. 'Vulnerable' derives from the latin verb 'vulnerare' meaning 'to wound, hurt or damage',[9] thus vulnerability means literally 'an openness to harm'. In criminal justice policy especially, the term is much more closely associated with the victim as 'vulnerable witness' than it is comfortably ascribed to suspects and defendants.[10]

Second, there is also the close linkage between vulnerability and 'risk',[11] the two concepts being, as Beck described it, 'two sides of the same coin'.[12] An identification of vulnerability has come to encompass not only risk of harm to the child but also often a risk of harm by the child as well. As a result, a child who fails to conform to expectations of how the vulnerable should behave, who does not adequately 'perform' their vulnerability by

---

[4] See eg Roxanna Dehaghani, '"Vulnerable by Law (But Not by Nature)": Examining Perceptions of Youth and Childhood "Vulnerability" in the Context of Police Custody' (2017) 39 Journal of Social Welfare and Family Law 454; Roxanna Dehaghani, *Vulnerability in Police Custody: Police Decision-Making and the Appropriate Adult Safeguard* (Routledge 2019); Layla Skinns, *Police Powers and Citizens' Rights: Discretionary Decision-Making in Police Detention* (Routledge 2019) ch 8.
[5] Harry Hendrick, 'Constructions and Reconstructions of Childhood: An Interpretative Survey, 1800 to the Present' in Allison James and Alan Prout (eds), *Constructing and Reconstructing Childhood: Contemporary Issues in the Sociological Study of Childhood* (Taylor and Francis 2003).
[6] See for discussion Kate Brown, 'Re-moralising "Vulnerability"' (2012) 6 People, Place & Policy Online 41.
[7] See for discussion Kate Brown, *Vulnerability and Young People: Care and Social Control in Policy and Practice* (Policy Press 2015).
[8] ibid 32; see also Robert EE Goodin, *Protecting the Vulnerable: A Re-analysis of Our Social Responsibilities* (University of Chicago Press 1985).
[9] Douglas A Kidd, *Collins Gem Latin Dictionary* (Collins 1957).
[10] See eg in the YJCEA 1999, Part II ch 1, 'Special Measures Directions in Case of Vulnerable and Intimidated Witnesses' excludes the accused.
[11] Brown, *Vulnerability and Young People* (n 7) 183.
[12] Ulrich Beck, *World at Risk* (English edn, Polity Press 2009) 178. See for discussion Kate Brown, 'Questioning the Vulnerability Zeitgeist: Care and Control Practices with "Vulnerable" Young People' (2014) 13 Social Policy & Society 371, 372.

behaving in a problematic or non-compliant way,[13] is liable to be subject to a control response as a 'young offender' rather than a care response as a 'child in need'.[14] Yet, such dichotomous approaches to concerning youth behaviour fail to appreciate the complexities of navigating adversity as a child, that signalling vulnerability, for example, may be associated with leaving oneself open to victimization.[15] Finally, but perhaps most importantly, young people enmeshed in criminal justice processes not infrequently reject the application of the term 'vulnerable' to themselves,[16] particularly because the paternalistic implications of the concept undermine their sense of agency and of having survived the challenges that they have navigated.[17] In this sense, vulnerability as an overarching concept downplays the structural adversity experienced by many children in conflict with the law[18] and tends to stigmatize what might be considered individual 'deficits'. As Edstrom notes, vulnerability tends to 'force the analysis back to individuals and their bodies ... at the expense of power relations, accountability, structures and dynamics'.[19]

Vulnerability is thus a shifting, often complicating, concept when applied to children, and that lack of clarity is also reflected, unhelpfully, in the legal framework in police custody. In the Police and Criminal Evidence Act 1984 (PACE), *Code C*, child suspects are not explicitly identified, by virtue of their youth, as being 'vulnerable'. A 'vulnerable' person in police custody is defined as anyone who 'because of a mental health condition or mental disorder' is liable to be at risk in interview of providing unreliable answers.[20]

---

[13] Dehaghani, '"Vulnerable by Law"' (n 4) 463.
[14] Barry Goldson, 'Children in Need or Young Offenders? Hardening Ideology, Organizational Change and New Challenges for Social Work with Children in Trouble' (2000) 5 Child & Family Social Work 255.
[15] James A Densley, *How Gangs Work: An Ethnography of Youth Violence* (Palgrave Macmillan in association with St Antony's College 2013); James Windle, Leah Moyle, and Ross Coomber, '"Vulnerable" Kids Going Country: Children and Young People's Involvement in County Lines Drug Dealing' (2020) 20 Youth Justice 64.
[16] See eg Brown, *Vulnerability and Young People* (n 7).
[17] See eg Katie Ellis, 'Contested Vulnerability: A Case Study of Girls in Secure Care' (2018) 88 Children and Youth Services Review 156.
[18] See eg Windle, Moyle, and Coomber (n 15).
[19] Jerker Edström, 'Time to Call the Bluff: (De)-constructing "Women's Vulnerability", HIV and Sexual Health' (2010) 53 HIV and Sexual Health Development 215, 217.
[20] *Code C: Revised Code of Practice for the Detention, Treatment and Questioning of Persons by Police Officers* (updated 4 November 2020), para 1.13(d), (In force at time of writing. Any relevant variance with the version in force at time of fieldwork, published May 2014, will be noted as it arises.) In the 2014 version of *Code C* in force at the time of fieldwork, the 'vulnerable suspect' was defined as a 'person who is mentally disordered or mentally vulnerable' (para 1.7(b)).

A person of any age may be 'vulnerable' in the terms of the *Code*,[21] and indeed, somewhat contradictorily, it would appear that having no diagnosed mental health condition does not prevent a person being so designated.[22] Nonetheless, although both groups might enjoy similar protections, 'juveniles' are distinguished from 'vulnerable' persons—they are two separate 'special groups'.[23] Thus, although common discourse in police custody may recognize 'vulnerable suspects' as encompassing all those who merit special adjustment, paradoxically, within the legal framework, child suspects are not automatically recognized as falling within that group.

In consideration of the problematic notion of vulnerability, I favour the use of 'adversity' as an overarching term to encompass those features and experiences, whether inherent or situational, which intersect to make the custody process more difficult or challenging for children. Established in child development literature, and often employed alongside the discussion of resilience,[24] the term situates these difficulties as issues with which the child contends rather than features for which the child may be considered responsible. Nonetheless, the discourse of vulnerability remains a feature of the custody block, as will become apparent as the chapter unfolds, with problematic consequences for the child suspect.

Immediate Situational Adversity

With these observations in mind, I address in turn each of the substantive stages of the custody process, placing the procedure in the context of what is known from the existing literature before exploring young participant experiences. However, before embarking on this analysis, I consider, first of all, the state of mind of the child suspect as they arrive in police custody. Understanding the challenges of police custody for children requires us to start by stepping outside the custody block. Every detainee experiences what might be described as immediate situational adversity in police custody by virtue of their detention in the total control of the police. However,

---

[21] *Code C* (n 20), para 1.4.
[22] ibid, 'Note for Guidance' (NFG), 1G.
[23] ibid, para 3.12.
[24] See eg Robbie Gilligan, 'Adversity, Resilience and Young People: The Protective Value of Positive School and Spare Time Experiences' (2000) 14 Children & Society 37; Judith Rumgay, 'Scripts for Safer Survival: Pathways Out of Female Crime' (2004) 43 Howard Journal of Criminal Justice 405.

the child's experience of this state is arguably more acute, given the more extreme power asymmetry between them as lone child arrestee and multiple adult officers. Young participants related two particular features which tended to magnify this experience for them and set the tone for their detention experience: the circumstances of their arrest and their lack of knowledge about what to expect in police custody.

The Impact of Arrest: 'The police officers, they just don't care'

The moment of arrest emerged as key to understanding the custody experience for children. Although young participants appreciated that my focus was on the police station, many were keen to discuss their arrest. Approximately half described arrests that were heavy-handed, some involving allegations of significant violence and assault, mirroring the accounts of children almost twenty years earlier.[25] Handcuffs were frequently the source of complaint, especially when young participants felt they had been used, or kept on, without justification. On observations, I often noted children brought into the booking-in area in handcuffs, often after a considerable, and apparently wholly compliant, wait.[26]

Excessively coercive experiences on arrest were commonly triggered by restraint approaches which were not adapted to children. Several young participants told me that they could slip off handcuffs, and would 'squirm' their way out of physical restraint (Aaron). Officers, too, noted that children could be 'harder to restrain—their arms come back. Like a cat or a snake—they turn in on themselves' (CO10). At the same time, officers reported that their restraint training is 'not juvenile specific' (CO15) (you just have to 'use your common sense' (CA21))[27] and that the handcuffs used are of an adult

---

[25] Juliet Lyon, Catherine Dennison, and Anita Wilson, '"Tell Them So They Listen": Messages from Young People in Custody', Home Office Research Study 201 (Home Office 2000).

[26] The routine production of arrestees for booking-in in handcuffs is commonly noted in His Majesty's Inspectorate of Constabulary, Fire and Rescue Services (HMICFRS) reports. See eg HMICFRS, 'Report on an Unannounced Inspection Visit to Police Custody Suites in Gloucestershire' (1 June 2022) <www.justiceinspectorates.gov.uk/hmicfrs/publication-html/report-on-an-unannounced-inspection-visit-to-police-custody-suites-in-gloucestershire> accessed 15 August 2023.

[27] By contrast, the lack of child-specific restraint training for officers in the secure estate has been the subject of successful legal challenge: see R (on the application of ZY) (by his litigation friend BA) v Secretary of State for Justice (unreported, 5 September 2018).

size and weight. As a result, younger, often smaller, arrestees tended to experience harsher restraint as cuffs were tightened to prevent escape: 'bare (too) tight so it cut your wrists' (Jamal). Such behaviour was seen as petty, and sometimes deliberately punitive ('when you say, "Can you take it out, it hurts", they do it up tighter' (Will)) and emblematic of the police's lack of concern for their welfare: 'They don't loosen them, just silly things like that. The police officers they just don't care' (Carter).

More serious allegations of inappropriate use of force often arose in respect of arrest experiences exacerbated by immaturity. Young participants frequently described arrest following a chase. Sometimes, this was sought out and thrilling: 'boom, you bolt off and the police would jump after you, the sirens, the flashlights out, you're hiding in the bushes and everyone's heart's racing and it's literally like an adrenalin rush' (Simon). Cultural criminologists have long identified the sheer pleasure of transgression as a motivating factor for young people[28] and the capacity of such expressive behaviour to break the monotony of their young lives.[29] For others, running away was more a function of their fear, as fourteen-year-old Michael explained: 'Cos I got scared and when I get scared I run fast. Like I go. And then all I want to do is just run home.' Such behaviour might be easily anticipated, but police responses, untailored to accommodate youthful behaviours, often resulted in greater use of force. For example, Michael had been knocked off his bike by a police van in pursuit, Luke had been tasered, and Jake's co-arrestee and Jamal had been bitten by police dogs. The use of greater numbers of officers, even for minor arrests, could enflame the situation further, as Avery describes: 'But you're just winding me up more by having seven officers jumping me and nicking me like.' For those experiencing mental health difficulties, arrest could be particularly distressing. Sandor explained, 'I was really, really anxious. I was paranoid and almost got an anxiety attack, because I've also got mental health problems, so that didn't help.' The combination of physical and cognitive demands could be exhausting as well: 'it's a lot to take in when you're getting nicked' (Alex).

Black, Asian, and minority ethnic participants were represented amongst those who were vocal about mistreatment by street officers, but not disproportionately so, and they did not generally express more negative

---

[28] Jack Katz, *Seductions of Crime* (Basic Books 1988).
[29] Pat O'Malley and Stephen Mugford, 'Crime, Excitement and Modernity' in Gregg Barak (ed), *Varieties of Criminology* (Praegar 1994); Mike Presdee, *Cultural Criminology and the Carnival of Crime* (Routledge 2000).

views than White participants, contrasting with previous research[30] and the disproportionality literature.[31] One such young participant, Carter, explained, 'There are certain police officers that won't, how do I say it, won't be racist in front of everyone, but they will be racist to you on the sly, if you understand what I mean?', but more commonly young participants did not identify ethnicity as a factor in adverse experiences on arrest. The exception to this general position was the single young participant who was an Irish traveller who complained of discrimination by officers both on the street and in custody, the harshness of his experiences prompting the reflection, 'we're not dogs, we're humans'. However, as discussed at the conclusion of Chapter 1, I approach these observations from young participants with some care, conscious that my ethnicity may have inhibited young participants in raising issues of race. Each Black, Asian, or ethnic minority young participant who complained of mistreatment on arrest had experienced several, and often regular, arrest and detention experiences. As a result, the data does not lend itself well to exploring in more depth how their experiences in the police station following a specific incident of mistreatment, the support of AAs, or solicitors, for example, mitigated (or magnified) their responses. Each young participant in this group had legal advice on at least one occasion, and the majority experienced support by AAs known to them (familial AAs) as well as volunteer or paid AAs (non-familial AAs) on different occasions.

The prominence of these problematic arrest accounts in young participant interviews, and the palpable emotion with which they were recounted, gives some indication of the profound feelings they engendered at the time. This intensity of emotion tended to magnify the hostile control responses of adult officers in young participant minds such that they were overwhelmingly experienced as punitive, and for some, deliberately provocative. Shows of police force were liable to elicit fear and distress, which could, in turn, trigger a more aggressive response. This feeling, that it was necessary to respond in kind to force as a form of self-defence, was more commonly described by Black, Asian, and minority ethnic young participants.

---

[30] Lyon, Dennison, and Wilson (n 25); Ben Bowling and Coretta Phillips, 'Policing Ethnic Minority Communities' in Tim Newburn (ed), *Handbook of Policing* (Willan 2003); Phil Bowen, *Building Trust: How Our Courts Can Improve the Criminal Court Experience for Black, Asian, and Minority Ethnic Defendants* (Centre for Justice Innovation 2017).

[31] See eg David Lammy, 'The Lammy Review. An Independent Review into the Treatment of, and Outcomes for, Black, Asian and Minority Ethnic Individuals in the Criminal Justice System' (Ministry of Justice (MoJ) 2017); Amnesty International, *Trapped in the Matrix: Secrecy, Stigma and Bias in the Met's Gangs Database* (Amnesty International 2018).

As Alex, a Black young participant, explained, 'There's times when it's too much. And I feel like I have to fight back and let them know that I'm not scared.'

Such a response has a compounding effect. It crystallizes (if not present before) an oppositional approach to the police in the mind of the child. Likewise, from a police perspective, problematic behaviour on arrest seemed to cement the child's conversion from vulnerable young citizen to suspect and likely perpetrator—a transformation which has significant repercussions as the process unfolds. Even if calm on presentation, as part of the booking-in process, the CO would be informed of any restraint used on arrest: 'If the officer says "He's been bad, he's been that. He's done this, he did this." Then they all get angry at you' (Rezar). Often the desk would be notified ahead of arrival if the arrestee was a 'fighter'. Sometimes, a problematic young arrestee would be held 'on the van' to calm down before they were brought into the block or would be taken straight into the cells without being booked-in and informed of their rights and entitlements. Thus, whilst young participants may rarely identify a discriminatory element to their treatment on arrest, there are indications in the data that the experiences of Black, Asian, and ethnic minority suspects on arrest may entrench negative experiences later in the police custody process.

There was also a longer-term attitudinal impact of these encounters which affected how young participants reacted to future custody episodes and the wider justice system. For some, this was straightforwardly negative, such as for Carter, who concluded, 'most police officers, they're just dickheads'. For others, the unnecessary and punitive nature of the arrest resulted, over time, in a form of detachment, even a sense that the process was farcical. Harper explained, 'I find the situation completely hilarious as to why I've been arrested.' This was particularly the case where the young person felt that their arrest had been petty and unjustified. Elijah described how 'These lot are just takin' the piss now. They're just arrestin' me to take the mick. Like, they're tryin' to do it to annoy me.' Harper explained how damaging this realization could be: 'I think the police now have got that reputation in the sense of they can't be trusted because of the system as a whole is just corrupt.'

Lack of Knowledge: 'The first time I was so scared'

Young participant accounts suggest that their level of understanding about what would happen to them in police detention could contribute substantially to this situational adversity in custody. Children in the general population often have very little understanding of what to expect following an arrest,[32] and this can be a source of anxiety for them when arrested.[33] Indeed, fear of the unknown is prominent in the few accounts previously available of children's[34] and young adults'[35] experiences of police detention.

Echoing these findings, a substantial number of young participants explained that they had had very little idea of what would happen following arrest. For some, like Elijah above, this was a source of fear and real anxiety: 'The first time I was so scared, like ... I didn't know where I was going, what was gonna happen, if I was gonna get fed, you know what I mean, I was just worried' (Aidan). Fear could be magnified when combined with very limited knowledge of the wider criminal justice process. Kate explained, 'I thought I was gonna get sent to jail 'cause they were right going on, "It'll go to court" and all this and that, and I'm thinking, "Oh my God, what have I done to my future now? What's going on?" It was scary.' In the absence of better information, young participants relied on what they had learned from listening 'to tracks, like music' (Hudson), watching television, or from peers with experience of arrest. However, the inaccuracy of these sources was liable to cause greater anxiety, particularly around the nature of the cell. Avery was concerned about other arrestees, thinking that custody might be 'like America sometimes when you see them in films they're all in a big cage together'. Those with friends or relatives with police custody experience tended to be better informed, although the picture that young participants got from friends tended to be very negative, adding to their disquiet: 'I just got told it's dirty, not nice an' it's cold' (Riley). Reliance by children on peer and popular culture information for knowledge about the police and criminal justice process has been long identified[36] but not successfully addressed, with—as we see here—problematic results.

---

[32] Miranda Bevan, 'Investigating Young People's Awareness and Understanding of the Criminal Justice System: An Exploratory Study' (Howard League for Penal Reform 2016) <https://howardleague.org/wp-content/uploads/2016/06/Investigating-young-people%E2%80%99s-awareness-and-understanding-of-the-criminal-justice-system.pdf> accessed 15 August 2023.

[33] Neal Hazel, Ann Hagell, and Laura Brazier, *Young Offenders' Perceptions of Their Experiences in the Criminal Justice System* (Economic and Social Research Council 2003).

[34] HM Inspectorate of Constabulary (HMIC) (now HMICFRS), *The Welfare of Vulnerable People in Police Custody* (HMIC 2015) 6.

[35] Helen Louise Jones, 'The Pains of Custody: How Young Men Cope through the Criminal Justice System' (DPhil thesis, University of Hull 2007).

[36] See eg similar Ian Loader, *Youth, Policing and Democracy* (Macmillan 1996); Robert McAuley, *Out of Sight: Crime, Youth and Exclusion* (Willan 2007); Vicky Kemp and Dawn Watkins, 'Exploring Children's Understanding of the Legal Rights of Suspects in England and Wales' (2022) 22(3) Youth Justice 320.

The Early Custody Journey: Procedure and Existing Literature

In light of these observations, I turn now to consider how the procedures should be adjusted in this early phase of the custody process. The first component of the right to effective participation, the need for adjusted treatment which takes account of both the child's inherent need for special care and protection and their situational adversity, is plainly key. In this regard, the UN Committee on the Rights of the Child (the UN Committee) has identified that proceedings should be conducted in 'an atmosphere of understanding'[37] by professionals who are 'well-informed about the physical, psychological and social development of children and adolescents, as well as about the special needs of the most marginalized children'.[38] The UN Committee also emphasizes the importance of gender-sensitivity and appropriate adjustments for children with disabilities both in terms of physical accommodations and as 'support with psychosocial disabilities, assistance with communication and the reading of documents'.[39] Children should not be held in police cells 'except as a measure of last resort and for the shortest period of time' and 'mechanisms for swift release to parents or appropriate adults should be prioritized'.[40] The importance of separation from adults is stressed, 'including in police cells', and the Committee emphasizes the need for 'separate facilities for children deprived of their liberty that are staffed by appropriately trained personnel and that operate according to child-friendly policies and practices'.[41]

How is this reflected in domestic provisions? As discussed in Chapter 1, legislative requirements to adjust the procedures for children are extremely limited. However, the College of Policing's guidance, 'Authorised Professional Practice (Detention and Custody)' (APP(DC))[42] requires that COs should 'prioritise and triage vulnerable detainees', including

---

[37] General Comment No 24 (2019) on children's rights in the child justice system (CRC/C/GC/24), para 46. (General Comment No 24 replaces General Comment No 10 (2007) (CRC/C/GC/10), extant at the time of fieldwork. Any relevant variance will be noted as it arises.) See also UN Standard Minimum Rule for the Administration of Juvenile Justice (adopted on 10 December 1985 at the 40th Session of the General Assembly) (Beijing Rules), para 14.2.
[38] General Comment No 24 (n 37), para 39.
[39] ibid, para 40.
[40] ibid, para 85. See also para 88.
[41] ibid 92.
[42] (First published 23 October 2013, last modified 2 May 2023) <http://Detention and custody | College of Policing> accessed 15 August 2023. (Any variance with the version (modified March 2016) in force at the time of the fieldwork will be noted as it arises.)

young suspects, as part of the booking-in process; indeed, the custody team[43] should be notified in advance of their arrival 'where practicable'.[44] Otherwise, there is simply a requirement for all arrestees to be brought before the CO 'as soon as practicable' after arrival at the station and that those awaiting being booked-in should be supervised in a holding cell or another 'suitable and safe area', and 'where practicable', not in a police vehicle.[45] There is no statutory requirement for children to be separated from adult arrestees at this initial stage since the latter have generally not yet been 'charged with an offence'.[46] The only separation required in *Code C* is that a child may not be 'placed in a cell with a detained adult'.[47]

The Early Custody Journey: Child Suspect Experiences

Waiting to Be Booked-In

Prioritization: 'Just put me in my cell'

Despite the requirement in the APP to 'prioritise' child arrestees, the data suggests that this rarely occurs. Young participants often described lengthy waits to be booked-in, spending 'an hour or two' in a holding cell (Azade) or 'over an hour in the van' (Zoe). Only in Force Area 1 (F1) was the custody team notified in advance of child suspects being brought in. During busy periods on observation, I could discern no systematic prioritization of young suspects in terms of booking-in. Some COs suggested that they would 'bring them (juveniles) through or might deal with them first' (CO22), others only if there was a 'medical issue' (CO32), whilst some were plain that they would not prioritize a child. I observed several young suspects made to wait for lengthy periods including, for example, YS29, who I watched wait an hour and forty-five minutes, sitting with adult arrestees in the holding area, whilst older arrestees were booked-in before him.[48]

---

[43] COs and custody assistants (CAs, sometimes referred to as designated detention officers) manning the custody block or suite.
[44] APP(DC) (n 42) (Response, Arrest and Detention) (first published 23 October 2013, updated 28 October 2022) 6 <https://www.college.police.uk/app/detention-and-custody/response-arrest-and-detention> accessed 15 August 2023.
[45] ibid.
[46] Children and Young Persons Act 1933, s 31.
[47] *Code C* (n 20), para 8.8.
[48] See for similar observations HMIC (n 34).

Not only does lack of prioritization extend the period of initial uncertainty and distress for child suspects, but it can also present further difficulties. Sometimes, swift processing of an arrestee can be a critical factor in the overall length of detention. For example, YS31, a fourteen-year-old, arrived at the police station at 11.25am, having been arrested on a warrant, requiring production to the next available court. Timely booking-in would likely have enabled his production to court that afternoon, but by the time he was booked-in, approximately two hours later, that was no longer possible,[49] necessitating the child's detention overnight. Most straightforwardly, children lack the stamina to cope with lengthy, boring delays:

> You're sitting, you're sitting, you're sitting. Plus, you've waited an extra twenty minutes outside in the hallway, to wait for everyone else to get booked-in, so that you can go in and get booked-in ... Then, you're waiting another half an hour on your feet. Your feet are starting to hurt. Your wrists were hurting for that half an hour, or hour and a half, of handcuffs ... Then, at the book-in, they take it off. Then, you're there. Then, another person will come to get booked-in. He will probably be drunk or something. So, he's there screaming down the hallways. Then, it ge ts too much. You just want to go. You just say, 'Just put me in my cell.'
>
> (Rezar)

As an investigating officer (IO) observed, 'It's a very long dragged-out process to have a juvenile in it—it's wrong' (IO4). For a child of school age, a wait of even forty minutes without distraction could be unfamiliar and hard to deal with and could adversely affect their ability to engage with the risk assessment and rights process which follows. Some custody staff did not seem to appreciate the challenges of delays, complaining of young arrestees lacking patience ('They want everything now' (CA27)), whilst young participants spoke of wrestling with the urge to 'kick off' (Tom).

Separation: 'They looked scary'

Perhaps the greatest difficulty arising from lack of prioritization, however, is the contact with arrested adults that this often produces. Unsurprisingly, given the lack of requirement in the Children and Young Persons Act 1933, section 31 and *Code C*, the data suggests that separation is not routinely

---

[49] The problem of courts closing their lists for the day early—at 1 or 2pm—has been the subject of concern raised elsewhere; see ibid.

attempted, save with regard to cell occupation,[50] and infrequently achieved. One young participant had noted that officers 'don't like kids being near other people coming in' (Jake), and several professionals suggested that officers worked hard to keep young suspects separate from older detainees, but this was not borne out on observation or in the majority of young participants' accounts.

In some areas, waiting arrestees are placed in holding cells outside the booking-in area. This achieves some measure of separation. However, often holding cells have glass doors, meaning that, whilst physically separate, a young arrestee can still see, and be seen by, older arrestees. Azade recalled of such an arrangement: 'it was just like everyone was looking at everyone'. This could be distressing for those unfamiliar with the process. Michael, for example, described 'crying a lot' in the holding cells: 'The people who was arrested in the other holding cells ... They looked scary ... I was just breaking down—I thought I was gonna go in the same cell as them.' The common fear was that they might be hurt by the other arrestees: 'you're sat there thinking "What have they done? Has he killed someone? Has he done something serious? Am I gonna be sat with him in the cell?"' (Simon). This was particularly associated with arrests when very young, or inexperienced in custody, as we see with Elijah, in the epigraph.

The unpredictability of the situation was also a concern. Luke explained that older arrestees could be, 'like scary. Cos you don't know what they're gonna do ... do you know what I mean?' He described being detained, handcuffed, in a holding cell with a drunk adult man. Fearing that he was going to be attacked, Luke had kicked the man and had been threatened by officers with an assault charge as a result. Worryingly, he was not alone in being involved in a physical confrontation with an adult detainee. Evan described his first experience in custody: 'Somehow, I got into a fight with a thirty-year-old man that had just been brought in for ABH [actual bodily harm] ... And then police dragged me away like it's my fault ... I went, "I'm nine years old, I want my mum." They went, "No".' These incidents are shocking, not only because of the gross failure in the police's duty of care but also because they provide a stark insight into the confrontational, often punitive, response of some staff to children in custody, even at the very beginning of the process. The effects of such incidents can be far-reaching. Evan reflected, 'To be honest, after that one night, I did not care. I've been

---

[50] *Code C* (n 20), para 8.8 is invariably observed.

the same way every day.' For Luke, his experience had significantly reduced the legitimacy of the police in his eyes, as might be anticipated by procedural justice scholars.[51] He recalled his response to the threat of prosecution, 'I said whatever and started laughing at him.'

By contrast, some young participants related striking up conversations with adult detainees whilst waiting in open holding areas. I observed this occurring in F2 (block 3), where the holding area was visible from the custody desk, enabling me to watch a child arrestee (YS29) in lengthy conversation with an adult arrested for possession with intent to supply. In the harsh surrounds of the custody block, such conversations could be welcome. Kate described how an older arrestee, whom she had met in holding, had helped her during booking-in: 'My mind-set was scream and shout at first, and then seeing him all calm and just collected and be like, "Don't worry (Kate) you'll be out of here in a bit", it calmed me down a bit.' Luke also described how an older arrestee could be reassuring: 'he's there as well, like you're there, you've both done wrong and you're in it together'. It is plainly concerning that the process enables young people to associate with more serious offenders and particularly worrying that they might be cast as a supportive presence, potentially normalizing more serious offending.

I saw nothing to suggest that prioritization of child suspects and separation of them from adults during holding is not achievable. In each area, arresting officers (AOs) could call ahead to notify the custody team of impending arrivals, and all the blocks that I observed had unglazed holding rooms, secure waiting areas, or cell capacity in which a child suspect could wait. Indeed, where the preservation of evidence requires it, separation is achieved and sometimes rigorously enforced. For example, in the case of multi-handed arrests, co-suspects are often kept apart, as Hussain described: 'you're not allowed to look at each other, you're not allowed to talk to each other, you're not allowed to make gestures or anything'. Sometimes, staff were extremely pressurized, but often failure to separate seemed to arise from a lack of appreciation or inclination to accommodate rather than impracticability. Indeed, some staff could not see the need for separation: 'They don't need to be segregated—it doesn't make a difference. The ones that are new here aren't here for long and the regulars have seen it all before anyway' (CO36).

---

[51] Tom R Tyler, *Why People Obey the Law* (Yale UP 1990).

At the Desk

Once the custody team are ready to book-in the child, they are brought before the CO, generally seated behind a high desk, in the booking-in area. These areas can vary hugely, depending on their physical arrangement, how busy they are, and the behaviour of any arrestees present. A solicitor during my initial scoping interviews encapsulated the more problematic end of the spectrum in describing her local station, an older, smaller block, as

> a really frightening place. It's always overflowing—they're queuing to book them in. There are drunk, violent people, people being sick. The lighting is bad. The atmosphere is confrontational and aggressive ... I'd be petrified if I was there as a detainee as an adult—let alone as a child or someone with mental health difficulties.[52]

By contrast, in my fieldnotes, I described the booking-in area in block 1 (F1) as 'really well-lit (with high windows) ... bright and generally clean ... no obvious smell'. Nor are booking-in areas always busy with officers or ringing with the shouts of detainees. They can be eerily quiet when at low occupation, especially in blocks where the cells are some distance from the desk itself. However, what is common to all booking-in areas is the sense of institutional control embodied in the chest-high desk behind which the CO sits, elevated above the AO and arrestee, and reinforced by notices threatening prosecution for misbehaviour. They also feel very public arenas, with the constant reminder of ongoing surveillance in the presence of cameras and CCTV recording notices.

Adult participants, both lay and professional, tended to be very negative about the suitability of custody blocks as environments for children, particularly in respect of the noise. For example, a familial appropriate adult (FAA1) recalled 'hearing people banging on doors, head butting the doors ... It's horrible. It is horrible', whilst one custody assistant (CA13) reflected that ten-to-thirteen-year-olds in particular should not be subjected to the 'screaming, banging, abusive language and violence' of the custody block. On observation, young arrestees at the desk would often be distracted by shouting coming from the cells or other detainees who were

---

[52] Telephone conversation with specialist defence solicitor (scoping study), 10 June 2015.

being abusive to the custody staff, glancing warily towards the source of the noise.

'You've just gotta stay calm'

Young participants tended not to refer to the physical features of the space, and rarely did they make specific reference to the noise at booking-in. Rather, they often spoke eloquently of the effect of the coercive nature of the setting, describing their behaviour in terms of resigned compliance.[53] For some young participants, this sense of powerlessness arose from the presence of lots of officers. Rezar explained: 'like it's all of them against you. It's just you there, you're basically in their house ... You feel like you can't say nothing to do anything. You feel annoyed and angry, but at the same time, you feel like you've got nothing to say.'[54] A number of young participants acknowledged the sheer futility of 'kicking off' in the police station, emphasizing the importance of not reacting: 'you've just gotta stay calm' (Aidan), 'just try and keep it in' (Dexter).

Echoing adult suspect reflections,[55] some young participants expressed a strong sense of reciprocity in behavioural terms between staff and detainees, considering that aggressive or abusive behaviour would be repaid in some way by officers. Robert explained, 'they just get you back. They just come in (to the cell), like pretend that they're doing something like a job and then they'll just come and hit ya.' I saw no evidence of physical assault on observation, although I bear in mind the impact of my presence as observer. However, there was a degree of confirmation from some staff that they would not particularly temper their response to a difficult young suspect or make allowance for their natural developmental immaturity: 'I treat them all the same. If they start being idiots I'm not going to hold back because of their age. At the end of the day they're in here for a reason' (CA3).

Commonly, young participants described moderating their behaviour for fear of an outburst prolonging their detention: 'If you start kicking off with the police, you're just gonna be in there longer, aren't you?' (Riley). I bear in mind that young participants may not have felt comfortable endorsing

---

[53] See for corresponding experiences Hazel, Hagell, and Brazier (n 33).
[54] See for similar experiences recounted by adult detainees Layla Skinns, *Police Custody: Governance, Legitimacy and Reform in the Criminal Justice Process* (Willan Publishing 2011).
[55] Layla Skinns, Andrew Wooff, and Amy Sprawson, 'Preliminary Findings on Police Custody Delivery in the Twenty-First Century: Is It "Good" Enough?' (2017) 27 Policing & Society 358.

violent behaviour for a range of reasons, including their engagement with, or presence at the premises of, the youth offending team. However, their accounts fit with my observations. Most commonly, young arrestees presented at the desk in a subdued state; some appearing to be frightened or nervy but more often they were silent or sullenly uncooperative.

Staying calm in this situation is challenging, and several young participants explained that they would let out their emotions once in the cell. Dexter, for example, explained, 'I just try and keep it in. But ... when I get angry and that, when I go in the cell I just bang the door and start booting it.' This was also noted by COs: 'Juveniles are very agitated when they first come in. The majority are hard to talk to. Half an hour in and they're trashing everything, banging in the cell, ordering lots of food and drinks' (CO24). Interestingly, Andrew Wooff and Layla Skinns have described a different approach taken by adults detainees, who tended towards 'emotional outpourings and aggression' at the desk, followed by more 'self-reflection and privacy of emotions' in the cell.[56] The contrast suggests the greater power imbalance between officer and child, and the child's habituation to submission before authority figures.

Acting Up, Acting Tough

A minority of young participants described behaving problematically towards COs. For a small number of young participants, antagonizing or being abusive to custody staff could be a 'thrill' (Luke) or 'part of the game' (Avery). They tended to be those with regular experience of custody, and it was notable that they had identified (contrary to the assumptions of the majority above) that there was, in fact, little comeback for such behaviour. Luke explained, 'it's funny, because they [COs] get annoyed and they can't do nothing about it ... (laughs) ... You can abuse them and they can't say nothing to you.' Aaron had spotted that 'There's always someone different on (duty at the desk) by the time I get out.' Staff variously complained that young people who get booked-in with their friends might laugh and joke around together as if it were a 'day out at the police station' (CA18). Indeed, several young participants talked animatedly about being arrested with friends: 'it's just funny ... We just look at each other and laugh' (Robert).

---

[56] Andrew Wooff and Layla Skinns, 'The Role of Emotion, Space and Place in Police Custody in England: Towards a Geography of Police Custody' (2018) 20 Punishment & Society 562, 576.

Whilst I do not seek to excuse such behaviour, it is possible to identify a range of telling triggers for it. Patent in much of this behaviour is straightforward immaturity. Additionally, sometimes, this behaviour was a response to the coercive environment of the custody block, particularly where young participants felt that the force used was excessive or their treatment disrespectful. Aidan described how he had 'flipped once' during booking-in when he was arrested with an ex-girlfriend, 'and they wasn't being nice to her, you know what I mean, like they weren't treating her well', whilst others, in the face of the total control of the officers, exercised any form of agency they could. Jayden, for example, had identified that he could annoy COs if he took a long time in answering straightforward questions or asking for a glass of water: 'I just long it out, it gets them.'

An AA from a residential home (RHAA3) observed of young suspects, 'They are intimidated by the system and embarrassed. They don't want to admit that they're vulnerable ... You know that the cockiness or rudeness sometimes hides vulnerability and insecurity.' Her assessment is largely borne out in the data in that those who behaved problematically tended to be disadvantaged in one or more respects. Notably, girls were disproportionately represented in the group of those who reported being abusive towards COs or were disruptive during observations. A number emphasized the importance of not showing fear or weakness. Azade, aged fourteen, for example, reflected on being worried about her Mum but countered, 'well obviously I don't show that, innit'. Rather, she described being verbally abusive to COs: 'If I go in there (the custody block), the police officer I'll get rude to him and I'll say go eat your donuts or something.' Similarly Black, Asian, and minority ethnic young participants were more likely than their White counterparts to emphasize the importance of being assertive to avoid being manipulated by the police. Alex, for example, explained, 'I feel like, police officers, if they think you're weak they will try and like, I don't know, target you', whilst young participants who reported being more disruptive were also more likely to have disclosed a mental health issue or a developmental or behavioural disorder.

A few COs made the link between problematic behaviour and vulnerability: 'Juveniles are very rarely violent—the violent ones tend to be the ones with mental health issues' (CO15). However, generally, I was conscious of a fairly widespread lack of sympathy across custody blocks for child suspects but especially those who were regularly arrested and behaved abusively or showed 'attitude' (CO35). A number of officers, in different roles, described child suspects in very pejorative terms as, for example, 'feral' (IO7) or 'Mr Obnoxious Bastard' (CO23). They had, in effect, lost the right, in officers' minds, to be treated as children in need and became characterized as offenders. One CA observed, with some resentment, 'we have to treat them as if they were vulnerable' (CA18).[57] As CO21 identified, 'the problem is they (young suspects) are rude to the staff here and so they can be overlooked—their vulnerability'.

In discussion, it was clear that many COs relied on outward signs of what they considered to be vulnerability, drawing on notions of frailty and weakness, an approach observed in other jurisdictions as well.[58] Thus, the CO booking in YS26, a sixteen-year-old first-time arrestee, explained, 'If he was very vulnerable I would be happy to go into a room with a young person (for booking-in). You can tell looking at them waiting in the corridor if they're really frightened.' It was frustrating during fieldwork to receive confirmation of the continued absence of suitable training, as indicated in earlier reviews.[59] No CO participant had received specific training on engaging with children, on child development, or on prevalent childhood health and well-being issues. CO7's response to such an enquiry was typical: 'I have had no youth specific training as a custody sergeant. You use your life experience, experience of your own children and everything.' Such an approach is not a reliable basis for identifying needs and adjusting appropriately since child suspects are likely to experience a range of intersecting adversities of a different order to those of the children of COs and staff.

Custody Officers and Staff

Young participant accounts reveal that the way that a CO or CA interacts with a child suspect in these early stages can have a huge impact on not only the child's initial impressions but also their whole experience of the custody suite. Asked what they valued in the attitudes of COs and staff, young participant responses revealed two significant themes.

---

[57] Echoing findings in: Dehaghani, '"Vulnerable by Law"' (n 4).
[58] Skinns, *Police Powers* (n 4).
[59] All-Party Parliamentary Group for Children (APPGC), 'Children and the Police Inquiry: Oral Evidence Session 2: The Detention of Young People in Police Custody (National Children's Bureau 2014); HMIC (n 34) 7.

Respectful Treatment: 'Proper polite and cheerful'

Consistent with observations of young people in respect of street officers,[60] a number of young participants identified COs as 'good' if they were 'friendly' (Sadie), 'proper polite and cheerful' (Riley), and did not seek, or manage, to provoke them. As Evan explained, this did not mean over-friendliness but merely basic courtesy and respect. Indeed, often expectations were fairly low. Rezar described the 'best' CO as one who 'proper treats you like normal. Not like an animal.'[61] A number of young participants talked positively about COs who could 'joke around with you' (Jo) or have a 'bit of banter' (Luke). I saw humour used in each force area to very good effect to defuse situations and to engage and relax young suspects.

Conversely, some young participants complained about what they perceived to be rudeness or grumpiness and being sworn at by COs. In particular, they objected to what they considered to be arrogance on the part of COs, especially when issuing instructions. Riley provided an example. Instead of asking, 'Will you take your laces out, please?', such a CO would instead say something like, 'You've gotta take your laces out, don't think you're goin' anywhere with them in.' On observation, it was generally the case that officers who sought to anticipate and defuse exchanges that might be upsetting or aggravating prompted calmer and more cooperative interactions. Unnecessary intolerance on the part of an officer was liable to be reciprocated, as Avery explained: 'I said it to the one officer before, I was like when you're treating me with respect I'm gonna treat you with respect but if you treat me like a piece of shite I'm going to speak to you like a piece of shite. So it swings both ways.' As with arrest, some young participants felt deliberately goaded by officers, who would 'try and wind you up, ... push you to do or say stuff that can get you put into the cell longer' (Will). Although I did not observe verbally abusive behaviour towards young detainees, I did see several instances of this sort of unnecessary exchange. For example, the CO booking-in a fifteen-year-old (YS34) who had been arrested shortly after an unconnected court appearance observed, for no reason, 'So you lasted

---

[60] Loader (n 36) 137, 140.
[61] See for similar in relation to adults and its prominence in the conceptualization of 'dignity' in detention Layla Skinns, Angela Sorsby, and Lindsey Rice, '"Treat Them as a Human Being": Dignity in Police Detention and Its Implications for "Good" Police Custody' (2020) 60(6) British Journal of Criminology 1667.

just over an hour before you were locked up.' When YP34 then started to express concern about disruption likely to be caused by the search of his mother's address, the arresting officer aggravated the situation further by responding, 'If no-one's home they'll just put the door in', prompting YS34 to remonstrate.

Humane Approaches: Officers who 'actually care'

Young participants also particularly welcomed COs who were not judgemental: 'not like criticizing you because you're in there' (Sadie). Conversely, they were vocal in their dislike and resentment of officers who they felt treated them as 'criminals', who 'look at you as if you're not a real human like if you've committed an offence' (Zayn). Closely allied to this was a sense of frustration at officers who seemed to 'stereotype' or 'categorize' them as criminals just because they are young. Harper felt that this prevented officers from seeking to understand fully 'why people do what they do ... they don't have like two minutes to kind of stop and kind of look at a person'.

Young participants particularly appreciated a CO who they felt was not just doing a job. Elijah explained that good COs, 'They don't just act like they care, they don't just say things like, "Oh, yeah, yeah, if you need anythin', we're here", and then, when you ask for things, they ignore ya. They actually care.' Interestingly, a number of young participants spoke positively about COs who tried to give them advice, to warn them off going down a path of offending. CO43 described giving such advice:

> Maybe if I can make a kid see how Mum feels by their actions—then I'll say something. Then I would try—maybe when releasing them or cautioning them. I do think it's part of my role to say something in that situation, to try to prevent future offending.

Jo, for example, responded positively to receiving this sort of advice: 'you can see that they are trying to help you out. They don't want you to be in this situation.' Such an approach could have a profound effect. Avery spoke movingly about the interest shown in her by one officer which enabled her to turn her very chaotic life around. However, not all young participants appreciated such advice. Aidan and Luke in particular both resented being given what they considered to be 'a lecture'.

Authorisation of Detention: Procedure and Existing Literature

The first substantive act in custody is the authorisation of detention. The CO, independent of the investigation (PACE, section 36(5)) hears the grounds for the arrest from the AO and can only authorize detention in order to 'secure or preserve evidence' or to 'obtain such evidence by questioning' (PACE, section 37(3)).[62] The test is strictly one of 'necessity'; the APP stresses that COs should authorize detention 'only when it is **necessary** to detain rather than when it is convenient or expedient' (bold in the original).[63] It is important to note that there is no requirement for an arrested person to be detained at a police station in order for them or their home address to be searched and for items such as a phone to be seized from them[64] or for them to be required to attend for interview under caution.[65] Despite the more rigorous approach for young arrestees required under Article 37 of the United Nations Convention on the Rights of the Child (UNCRC),[66] PACE and *Code C* provide no specific adjustment to the authorization process to take account of children's right to be detained only as a measure of 'last resort'. However, the APP exhorts officers to take particular care to ensure that the provisions of PACE have been 'strictly applied' to avoid lengthy detention for children.[67]

The wording of the APP reflects longstanding concerns about the unnecessary detention of arrestees addressed in the Royal Commission on Criminal Procedure[68] and debated during the passage of PACE through Parliament.[69] Douglas Hurd, then Home Office Minister, stressed the importance of a strict

---

[62] Where there is sufficient evidence to charge, then the arrestee's detention may be authorized to obtain advice on charge from the Crown Prosecution Service (PACE, s 37(7)).

[63] APP(DC) (n 42) (Response, Arrest and Detention) (n 44) 7.

[64] Power to search premises of an arrestee: PACE, s 18. Power to search the defendant on arrest and any premises he or she was in at the time of arrest or immediately before arrest: PACE, s 32.

[65] An individual can be de-arrested or arrested and released on bail (including with certain bail conditions) to attend the police station under PACE, s 30A without first being taken to the police station.

[66] The UNCRC Committee urges states to ensure that 'the law places clear obligations on law enforcement officers to apply Article 37 in the context of arrest' and recommends that no child be deprived of liberty unless they are sixteen or older and there are 'genuine public safety or public health concerns' (General Comment No 24 (n 37) 85–89).

[67] APP(DC) (n 42) (Children and Young Persons) (first published 23 October 2013, updated 2 May 2023) 2 <https://www.college.police.uk/app/detention-and-custody/detainee-care/children-and-young-persons> accessed 16 August 2023 (APP(DC)(CYP)).

[68] Royal Commission on Criminal Procedure (RCCP), 'Report (Cmnd 8092)' (Her Majesty's Stationery Office (HMSO) 1981).

[69] Hansard, HC, Vol 60, cols 378–415, 1984.

application of the test, memorably glossing the term 'necessary—not desirable, convenient or a good idea but necessary'.[70] However, research has consistently identified what has been described as a 'rubber-stamping' approach taken by COs,[71] with near-blanket approaches taken to authorization. The ability of the CO to operate independently of the investigation in this decision (as required by PACE, section 36(5)) to 'stand back from their institutional and collegial ties' with fellow police officers has been called into question.[72] Indeed, far from the CO acting as the 'bulwark' between investigating officer and suspect, McConville and others observed that police culture, particularly group solidarity, tended to 'dictate mutual reinforcement of authority' so that the legal requirement to authorise detention had become a 'working rule' that arrestees should be detained.[73] There has been no previous study of the particular application of the test in respect of young arrestees, nor of young people's awareness of this critical decision.

The courts, too, have effectively endorsed routine authorisation of detention by COs, holding that the CO is entitled to assume that the arrest was lawful[74] and declining to interfere with CO decision-making.[75] Although in a recent, and trenchant, judgment, in which the decision to arrest and detain a fourteen-year-old of good character was described as 'reprehensible and lamentable', Cotter J emphasized the importance of officers placing 'front and centre' their duty 'to consider the best interests, safeguarding and promotion of the welfare of children' when making such decisions.[76]

---

[70] Hansard, HC, Standing Committee E, col 1229, 1984, quoted in Andrew Sanders, *Criminal Justice* (4th edn, OUP 2010). See also *Commissioner of the Police for the Metropolis v MR* [2019] EWHC 888 (QB).

[71] Roxanna Dehaghani, 'Automatic Authorisation: An Exploration of the Decision to Detain in Police Custody' (2017) 3 Criminal Law Review 187, 190. See also Tom Bucke and David Brown, 'In Police Custody: Police Powers and Suspects' Rights under the Revised PACE Codes of Practice', Home Office Research Study 174 (Home Office 1997); Michael McConville, Andrew Sanders, and Robert Leng, *The Case for the Prosecution* (Routledge 1991); Ian K McKenzie, 'Helping the Police with Their Inquiries: The Necessity Principle and Voluntary Attendance at the Police Station' (1990) Criminal Law Review 22; Coretta Phillips and David C Brown, 'Entry into the Criminal Justice System: A Survey of Police Arrests and Their Outcomes', Home Office Research Study 185 (Home Office 1998) 49.

[72] McConville, Sanders, and Leng (n 71) 42.

[73] ibid 43. See also McKenzie (n 71) 22, 24.

[74] *DPP v L* [1998] 12 WLUK 285, [1999] Crim LR 752.

[75] *Al-Fayed v Commissioner of the Police of the Metropolis* [2004] EWCA Civ 1579, (2004) 148 SJLB 1405; *Richardson v Chief Constable of West Midlands Police* [2011] EWHC 773 (QB), [2011] 2 Cr App R 1; *Hayes v Chief Constable of Merseyside* [2011] EWCA Civ 911, [2012] 1 WLR 517; *Hanningfield v Chief Constable of Essex* [2013] EWHC 243 (QB), [2013] 1 WLR 3632. See Dehaghani, 'Automatic Authorisation' (n 71) for discussion.

[76] *ST v Chief Constable of Nottinghamshire Police* [2022] EWHC 1280 (QB), [99] and [149]; Children Act 2004, s 11.

Authorisation of Detention: Child Suspect Experiences

The decision to authorize the child's detention is arguably the most important moment in the custody process. The requirement for the identification of 'necessity' grounds (PACE, section 37) before their detention can be authorized is the provision which has the greatest protective power for a young suspect. Given the critical nature of this decision, it was extraordinary to observe how it functions in practice. What is most striking is that the young suspect is invariably entirely alone, with no solicitor or AA to protect their interests or inform the decision-making process. On observation, there was routinely no explanation that the CO had to decide whether detention was 'necessary'. If the CO provided any explanation at all, they tended to say, 'I'm going to hear now about the circumstances of your arrest' or similar. Unsurprisingly, only one young participant, Logan, showed a good understanding of this point in the process. No other young participant appeared to understand even that a decision had been made by the CO rather than the AO simply informing the CO of the grounds for arrest and the basis for detention. Whilst *Code C* requires the CO to 'note' but not 'invite' comment from the arrestee at this stage (*Code C*, 3.4(a)), the decision to authorize detention is one which, arguably, a young arrestee might participate usefully in, given the opportunity, in terms of providing information about adults into whose care they could be bailed or offering information to satisfy the officer of their return on bail.

A 'sea change' underway?

One CO in Dehaghani's empirical research observed that there may be 'the beginning of a sea change' moving towards a true examination of the question 'Is it necessary to detain?'[77] Although the fieldwork in this study was conducted less than two years after Dehaghani's, it appears, at least in the way COs discussed the issue, that the sea change was underway. In all three areas, COs and solicitors talked about, and many welcomed, a changing approach to detaining children. Although this manifested itself not in increased refusals to authorize detention—I saw only one refusal (YS37)

---

[77] Dehaghani, 'Automatic Authorisation' (n 71) 202.

and one young participant described an instance (Logan). Rather, fewer children, it seemed, were being brought into custody, that 'the message has got out', that COs had 'started giving bobbies (street officers) a hard time' (CO26) and 'stupid arrests' had therefore stopped (CO24). However, as CO26 noted, whilst local officers had got the message, detectives from specialist divisions still 'look at you if you ask for necessity grounds'.

Although the impact of custody on a child was referenced in discussions, where COs described having refused to authorize detention, the issue of 'risk' appeared to be their primary motivation. Discussions often focused on the prevalence of self-harm and the potential for a police contact death if a child is detained. As COs 37 and 38 remarked, 'we are petrified of juveniles coming in'. Contrary to the COs in Dehaghani's research,[78] who felt pressurized by senior officers to authorize detention, COs in the force areas that I observed were more likely to feel pressure to refuse for fear of criticism from senior officers. COs in F3 complained about receiving 'the usual email' (CO34) or 'getting into trouble' (CO43) for detaining a child overnight. My data does not reveal the particular motivations of more senior officers, although there was some suggestion that this may be a result of the more rigorous recording of overnight detention figures.[79]

Independence Issues: 'If she's arrested you, we 'ave to take you'

Despite protestations about giving AOs a 'hard time', my observations suggest that it is still difficult for COs to put aside their collegial solidarity with fellow officers.[80] As CO32 explained, 'I have refused detention—I don't like to because the officer has felt it is the best course of action.' Similarly, Logan recounted being told by a CO when he complained about the basis for his detention, 'if she's arrested you, we 'ave to take you'. Several officers remarked that prior notification of a 'juvenile' coming in was welcome because they could avoid the awkwardness of face-to-face refusal: 'they [AOs] get criticism if I refuse at the desk' (CO35).[81] There was also some

---

[78] ibid.
[79] Following Layla Skinns, *Overnight Detention of Children in Police Cells* (Howard League for Penal Reform 2011).
[80] McConville, Sanders, and Leng (n 71).
[81] See for similar Dehaghani, 'Automatic Authorisation' (n 71).

concern that refusing to authorize detention might undermine operational effectiveness.

Few young participants appreciated the significance of the CO's distinctive white shirt, meant to distinguish them from street officers, or understood their intended independence from AOs and investigating teams. Those who were aware did not consider the separation to function meaningfully: 'Yeah but the way they speak to each other from what I've known, from my experience, they seem like they are all cool with each other' (Hussain). Indeed, Malik recalled a CO offering to help an AO to construct her grounds for detention, ' "We can go to the back if you want to talk about it" ... I still remember what he said.'[82]

Investigative Convenience: 'What do you need to keep me for?'

Amongst the young suspects that I tracked, there was a significant number of detentions for which it was doubtful that necessity grounds were made out. In particular, a number of detentions related to multi-handed arrests in respect of which the sort of 'routine' authorization noted by previous commentators still appears to occur.[83] For example, YS14 and 15 were both sixteen-year-old boys who had been arrested in the early hours for non-dwelling burglary and theft arising from their presence in an unoccupied commercial building. Neither of them had a previous record; both had engaged parents. The grounds for detention, to 'obtain evidence by questioning' (YS14) and to 'detain for interview' (YS15), plainly reflected case-construction convenience, particularly to encourage admissions, but not 'necessity'.[84] I did see one example of a multi-handed arrest where detention was plainly necessary (five-handed arrest for violent disorder leading to a stabbing, YS45–47), but this was something of an exception. The majority of child detentions tracked on observation arose in respect of low-level allegations: common assault, low-value theft, criminal damage, and taking without consent.

---

[82] See for a similar instance ibid.
[83] McConville, Sanders, and Leng (n 71) 43.
[84] Such a routine decision to detain without substantive consideration of whether there is any real risk of collusion or the disposal of outstanding property should, in future, be challengeable following *ST v CC of Notts* (n 76): see para [143].

There were also several detentions said to be necessary to enable search or seizure of items, especially mobile phones. For example, the grounds for detention in the case of YS34 were given as 'to search home address', prompting even YS34 himself to ask: 'What do you need to keep me for?' As identified above, the powers to search and seize do not require custodial arrest.[85] For some officers, the 'necessity' requirement was overridden because it was considered 'in the interests' of the young suspect for them to be detained. For example, the CO dealing with YS34 explained, 'it's in his interests too—to stay here and to be interviewed, following strip search and home search—it's not good for him to send him home and then say come back another day'. Undeniably, voluntary attendance processes can extend timescales, if only minimally, but this seemed rather to be about police convenience, voluntary attendance being viewed by some as 'hard work' and 'much more hassle' (CO41).

Extra-PACE Objectives: 'Show them what is done when you've done something wrong'

Benefit to the young person and the community was also used to justify detentions which had an incapacitative or social disciplinary aspect. CO34 described keeping a young suspect overnight: 'It sends a message and keeps the community safe. I really had to write up my rationale. It was partly for his own protection and family members—someone had given him an alternative address and it was my decision to keep him in.' Little consideration was given to the possibility of negative repercussions: 'if they're out and about at night, being in a cell for a few hours. I don't see anything wrong with it. It won't do them any harm—especially if they know they've been up to something' (CA33). Some officers emphasized the perceived deterrent value of custody: 'What is the harm in coming here—cooling off, shouting in the cell? We don't care if they kick off here. I think it is a bit of a deterrent' (CO43). Such observations echo Choongh's finding that police custody was used as a form of control and social discipline[86] and situate these child suspects squarely within the category of 'police property'.[87]

---

[85] PACE, ss 18, 32.
[86] Satnam Choongh, *Policing as Social Discipline* (Clarendon Press 1997).
[87] John Lee, 'Some Structural Aspects of Police Deviance in Relations with Minority Groups' in Clifford Shearing (ed), *Organizational Police Deviance* (Butterworth 1981) 53–54.

Indeed, there was a sense for some staff that, precisely because of their youth, the didactic or deterrent effect of the custody suite is particularly important. COs and CAs in all areas expressed the belief that maintaining a harsh custody experience is important for young people in order to 'show them what is done when you've done something wrong' (CA21), and that 'we're still in charge' (CO29); indeed, for a number, there was a 'need to change the style of policing—it's too friendly, we need to make it less comfortable for them here' (CO15), that custody should be 'harder—not traumatic but tougher' (CO12) to achieve that end.

Detention as 'safeguarding'

Detention following arrest for domestic assaults was very common on observations (ten instances in the young suspect (YS) sample of forty-seven) and often in circumstances which called into question necessity grounds. The most prominent factor driving these detentions was the failure of other resource-stretched services in the community, such as Child and Adolescent Mental Health Services (CAMHS) and social care.[88] Not infrequently, the AOs and CO had little option practically, and detention was authorized on a 'safeguarding' basis. For example, eleven-year-old YS5, who had an autism spectrum condition (ASC) diagnosis, was detained for over eight hours following his arrest for common assault on family members one Sunday afternoon. Officers had been called out several times over the weekend. His mother, being unable to cope, had sought help from the local authority but had been told to try to manage until Monday. The CO observed, 'What can we do? We can't keep him here.' Formally, his detention was authorized, but it was implicitly accepted that the necessity grounds for investigation and interview were not made out. The officer in the case reflected, 'Whatever he says (in interview) we're going to go for avoiding caution and prosecution. We'll refer to YOT [the youth offending team] for intervention and try to get some services engaged ... We don't want to criminalize them this young.' His view aligns with that of IO4 in F2: 'Juveniles are generally here for low-level offences. They're normally having other problems. Crime is often not the central feature—the problem is with drugs or at home.' There were four other similar cases of children with emerging

---

[88] For the devastating effect of austerity measures on services for young people, particularly CAMHS, see House of Commons, 'Health Committee, Children's and Adolescents' Mental Health and CAMHS, Third Report of Session 2014–15' (HMSO 2014) 3ff <https://publications.parliament.uk/pa/cm201415/cmselect/cmhealth/342/342.pdf> accessed 16 August 2023.

mental health conditions or developmental disorders (attention deficit hyperactivity disorder (ADHD), ASC, or learning disability) who had been arrested for assault on a family member: (YS1, YS13, YS22, YS28—all aged fourteen). Whilst to an extent understandable, given the lack of available alternatives, it is a somewhat perverse conclusion that the detention of these children is desirable from a safeguarding perspective.

Likewise, in F2, there were a substantial number of residential homes and officers commented that their residents were disproportionately represented amongst young detainees: 'Otherwise juveniles are being diverted from custody. Just care homes—we don't see many other juveniles' (CO20). In that force area, I tracked nineteen young suspects, of which seven were 'looked after' by the local authority and one more was a 'child at risk'.[89] Four individual episodes involved arrests arising out of young people involved in assault or damage in their children's home (YS17, YS26, YS27, YS30). Each of those young people contended with further adversities in addition to their 'looked after' status, including self-harm, ADHD, anxiety and depression, and mental illness. Whilst there has been a sustained and welcome fall in child arrest numbers nationally,[90] it is plain that the children who are still being detained tend to be those who are the most disadvantaged and for whom the adversities they experience are likely to render the detention episode seriously punitive.

Risk Assessment: Procedure and Existing Literature

COs have the essential job of ensuring the safety and welfare of the detainee whilst in police custody and keeping a record of their detention.[91] The CO must conduct a risk assessment (RA) of the arrestee to identify whether they present any specific risks to staff, others, or themselves in custody. This is initiated as part of the booking-in process but ongoing throughout their detention.[92] APP(DC)(Risk Assessment) (APP(DC)(RA)) provides guidance

---

[89] Although the true figure may well have been higher—there was no specific question asked during booking-in, which meant that 'looked after' status would be routinely identified.
[90] Howard League for Penal Reform, 'Child Arrests in England and Wales 2020' (Howard League 2021) <https://howardleague.org/publications/child-arrests-in-england-and-wales-2020> accessed 16 August 2023.
[91] PACE, s 39.
[92] *Code C* (n 20), para 3.6.

on the process to be adopted, including a checklist of questions,[93] but there is no standardized RA tool, and despite the guidance, there is substantial variance between forces in terms of content of the RA and its delivery.[94]

Clinical research has examined the efficacy of RA processes generally, consistently noting under-identification of suspects with mental health issues, learning disability, and developmental disorders, both in England and Wales[95] and internationally.[96] McKinnon and Finch have identified a number of factors which may undermine effective assessment by the CO.[97] These include environmental and resourcing issues (particularly pressure to process detainees quickly), IT limitations (especially with regard to data sharing of patient records), and the availability of mental health services in the custody block and in the community. They also noted police cultural factors which could affect assessment, such as cynicism in relation to the truthfulness of detainee disclosures and a tendency towards risk aversion arising from what some COs described as a 'blame culture' within police custody, as well as an 'apparent lack of trust' amongst detainees as to how sensitive information would be handled.[98]

In relation to children specifically, the APP(DC) acknowledges the police's duty under the Children Act 2004 to have regard for the need to safeguard and promote the welfare of child suspects and recognizes the raised prevalence of dispositional vulnerabilities and adverse childhood experiences within the child suspect population. It also stresses the importance of a wide-ranging and thorough RA and counsels against relying on chronological age or physical maturity in evaluating ability to engage with the assessment process.[99] Concerns have been raised that the language used

---

[93] APP(DC)(RA) (first published 23 October 2013, updated 20 July 2023) 2 <https://www.college.police.uk/app/detention-and-custody/detention-and-custody-risk-assessment> accessed 16 August 2023.
[94] Melanie-Jane Stoneman and others, 'Variation in Detainee Risk Assessment within Police Custody across England and Wales' (2018) 29 Policing & Society 951.
[95] Iain G McKinnon and Don Grubin, 'Health Screening in Police Custody' (2010) 17 Journal of Forensic & Legal Medicine 209; Iain G McKinnon, Julie Thorp, and Don Grubin, 'Improving the Detection of Detainees with Suspected Intellectual Disability in Police Custody' (2015) 9 Advances in Mental Health and Intellectual Disabilities 174; Iain G McKinnon and Don Grubin, 'Health Screening of People in Police Custody—Evaluation of Current Police Screening Procedures in London, UK' (2013) 23 European Journal of Public Health 399.
[96] Iain G McKinnon and others, 'Police Custody Health Care: A Review of Health Morbidity, Models of Care and Innovations within Police Custody in the UK, with International Comparisons' (2016) 9 Risk Management & Healthcare Policy 213.
[97] Iain McKinnon and Tracy Finch, 'Contextualising Health Screening Risk Assessments in Police Custody Suites—Qualitative Evaluation from the HELP–PC Study in London, UK' (2018) 18 BioMed Central Public Health 393.
[98] ibid 402.
[99] APP(DC)(CYP) (n 67) 3–4.

in RAs, the sometimes less-than-helpful manner of the CO asking the questions, and the physical environment of the booking-in area, particularly its public nature, are not conducive to child suspects disclosing relevant information.[100] However, in 2015, His Majesty's Inspectorate of Constabulary (HMIC) found that no force inspected had an RA format specifically designed to be used for child suspects.[101] In addition, COs receive extremely limited training in respect of child development, disorders commonly affecting children, and child protection[102] and would welcome more training in relation to mental health and related conditions more generally.[103]

Risk Assessment: Child Suspect Experiences

Although RA formats varied across areas, a number of common issues emerged which reduced the effectiveness of the RA process for children. Most critically, in no area was the RA format tailored for young suspects[104] to reflect their better physical health, in general, than adults and the raised prevalence of developmental disorders, learning disability, and mental health concerns amongst young people in contact with the criminal justice system. Across the forces observed, the RA questions concentrate on physical health and risk of self-harm—the clear focus being to prevent a detainee coming to physical harm in the cell rather than considering the child's emotional and wider well-being in detention and identifying challenges to their effective participation in the process. Some COs were concerned that young suspects did not understand the questions, particularly that a single question asking about their 'mental health' would not prompt relevant disclosure about ADHD, ASC, or learning disability, for example. Notably, questions which might trigger useful information, such as whether they are 'looked after' or have special help at school, were not routinely asked, nor were RAs often repeated in the presence of the AA. Although some COs

---

[100] Criminal Justice Joint Inspection (CJJI), 'Who's Looking Out for the Children? A Joint Inspection of Appropriate Adult Provision and Children in Detention after Charge' (CJJI 2011) 28ff; HMIC (n 34) 85.
[101] HMIC (n 34) 85.
[102] APPGC (n 59); HMIC (n 34) 7.
[103] Amy Wainwright and Dara Mojtahedi, 'An Examination of Stigmatising Attributions about Mental Illness amongst Police Custody Staff' (2020) 68 International Journal of Law & Psychiatry 101522; Maggie Leese and Sean Russell, 'Mental Health, Vulnerability and Risk in Police Custody' (2017) 19 Journal of Adult Protection 274.
[104] In line with observations in HMIC (n 34).

adjusted their approach ad hoc for children, others reported that they did not 'treat juveniles any differently' (CO31). The motivation for sticking to script tended to be risk aversion. COs were desperately conscious of the risk burden that they carried ('if anyone dies it's our fault' (CO26)) and were reluctant to miss out questions 'in case something were to happen' (CO29); as an Inspector observed, 'We're very, very risk averse—we know no other way' (Ins2).

Explanation for child suspects about the purpose of the RA was often limited, and young participants explained how this could affect disclosure: 'I could've told them that I've got an EHC plan[105] ... I could've told them that I've been in hospital, but I didn't really wanna 'cause I didn't see the point in them knowing anything like that' (Kate). Staff and professionals suggested that some young suspects were simply disinclined to raise issues: 'It's not in their nature to say that they have ADHD or dyslexia or to complain' (Sol8). The adversarial nature of the investigatory process, and the custody experience more generally, also inhibited responses. Sandor, for example, explained, 'I was really concerned about just the fact that I'm anxious or depressed, are they going to use it in a way so that I'd say everything that happened?'[106] Some young participants decided against disclosures because they felt that the police did not have the 'right to know' (Will) or it was 'none of their business' (Carter). Conversely, Logan suggested that he might actively mislead by saying that he had a particular difficulty requiring constant observation just to inconvenience the officers: 'you're wasting their time, they got to stand there all night ... it's just something to agg [aggravate] 'em by ... I just laugh at them all night.'

Many young participants complained about the length of the RA, that COs ask, 'long, bare, unnecessary things' (Jayden). There was variation across sites, but in F3, for example, the full risk assessment contained dozens of questions and it could take twenty minutes to complete 'for a competent adult' (CO41). This was particularly difficult for participants in the younger age group (ten-to-fourteen-year-olds), some of whom described being bored and tired and becoming abusive during lengthy RAs or disruptive afterwards as a result. Regular attendees particularly objected to the repetition of the same questions week after week, perceiving it to delay interview and release—'just long out the process even more' (Harper).

---

[105] An Education, Health and Care Plan is put in place for young people needing more support than is available through special educational needs support in school.
[106] See for similar distrust experienced by adults McKinnon and Finch (n 97).

Logan suggested that 'They should ask you "Has anything changed since the last time you came here?"', and where, occasionally, COs did take such an approach, this was appreciated by young participants.

A significant number of young participants referred to the presence of other arrestees during their RA, which tended to inhibit their responses, particularly if the people were known to them, were local offenders, or (for girls) members of the opposite sex. COs themselves raised concerns about the 'very intrusive, very personal' (CO39) nature of questions concerning self-harm which, where answered positively, would routinely involve questions about most recent episodes, methods, and triggers. This could be very upsetting for young participants: 'you're kind of bringing back kind of emotions that necessarily you might of, you might of like passed for that time being' (Harper). Others responded more angrily:

> If they ask about it, I just go, 'Yes, but I don't do it no more.' And then they start goin' into more about it, 'Oh, when did you do it?' And I'm like, 'Just shut the fuck up.' Oh, it pisses me off, innit.
>
> (Aaron)[107]

Particularly concerning was the suggestion that a young suspect might be unwilling to disclose a vulnerability because of the harsh response likely to follow. Harper explained that she had learnt to deny a history of suicidal ideation: 'I didn't tell them nothing. Cos then I feel that it's gonna be used against me. Then like all your clothes get taken and they think you're gonna commit suicide in your cell and it's just daunting like.'

Given these difficulties, it is frustrating that the response to positive disclosures during RA is extraordinarily limited. As CO23 recounted, 'It's a monster—to write all the info down but then I only do one of three things: send them to hospital, to see the nurse or to the cell.' As I discuss in Chapter 5, positive disclosures rarely triggered adjustments to the detention conditions for young suspects beyond greater surveillance. The RA process should be a key moment in gathering information which can be used to reduce the impact of detention on young suspects and to ensure that they are in a fit state for interview. However, the data suggests that it tends, instead, to be a source of distress for young suspects: at best, it is long and

---

[107] See for similar distress reported by young people in custodial institutions Paul Gray, '"I Hate Talking About It": Identifying and Supporting Traumatised Young People in Custody' (2015) 54 Howard Journal of Criminal Justice 434.

tiring; at worst it can trigger adverse responses and be traumatic in itself. Such intrusive and public questioning would never be deemed an acceptable approach to a child in a health-care setting or, indeed, to a child witness. The constraints within which custody teams operate are undeniably significant, but they cannot justify such disregard for child suspects and their needs. It could not realistically be argued, on this data, that child suspects are treated as 'children first' in respect of risk assessment.

Search and Seizure of Belongings: Procedure and Existing Literature

The booking-in process also requires officers to conduct an initial search of every suspect to 'ascertain ... everything' they have with them.[108] Here, too, there is no adjustment for children. However, all searches must be conducted by a member of the 'same sex' as the person being searched[109] and APP(DC) (Control, Restraint and Searches) (APP(DC)(CRS)) emphasizes that they should be performed with 'respect and dignity' and in an area where the individual 'can neither be seen by anyone who does not need to be present nor by a member of the opposite sex'.[110] Although the CO can retain a suspect's clothing and personal effects, this must follow individual risk assessment balancing the need to 'protect the right to life' with respect for the detainee's dignity.[111] The power to retain items is restricted to a limited number of bases, including where the CO believes the person may use the item to harm themselves or another or to damage property.[112] The reasons for retention must be recorded,[113] and the importance of explaining the reasons for search and for retaining items is underlined.[114]

Concerns about the potential for searches of this sort to be humiliating and upsetting have long been raised, including by the Royal Commission on Criminal Procedure (RCCP).[115] The Commission considered that

---

[108] PACE, s 54.
[109] PACE, s 54(9); *Code C* (n 20), para 4.1.
[110] APP(DC) (n 42) (Control, Restraint and Searches) (first published 23 October 2013, updated 2 September 2021) 14 <https://www.college.police.uk/app/detention-and-custody/control-restraint-and-searches> accessed 16 August 2023 (APP(DC)(CRS)).
[111] ibid 15.
[112] PACE, s 54.
[113] *Code C* (n 20), para 4.5.
[114] APP(DC)(CRS) (n 110) 13.
[115] RCCP (n 68), para 3.116.

officers should use their discretion 'sensibly' in deciding what should be retained by the police and suggested that a watch, for example, should only be removed 'in exceptional cases', given the proposed introduction of time limits on detention.[116] Successive studies have noted that suspects routinely have all their personal property removed without explanation and by force where necessary—a process that 'strips the suspect of his personal identity and brings home to him the extent to which he has lost control of his world'.[117]

A strip search in police custody, involving the 'removal of more than outer clothing', is only legitimate where the officer thinks it is necessary to remove something which may be concealed and which the detainee would not be allowed to keep. But such searches should not be conducted routinely if there is no reason to consider that articles are concealed.[118] The removal of an item of clothing to prevent self-harm can constitute a strip search.[119] Whilst the police in custody have a duty to take reasonable care to prevent a person self-harming,[120] officers should consider 'alternative and less invasive measures' when seeking to prevent self-harm.[121] An intimate search involves a physical examination of a person's body orifices other than the mouth.[122] *Code C* rightly draws attention to the 'intrusive nature' of searches of this sort, cautions against underestimating the risks involved, and requires that these searches be conducted 'with proper regard to the sensitivity and vulnerability' of the individual.[123]

There is adjustment for the strip and intimate searching of child arrestees. Save in cases of urgency (where there is a risk of serious harm to the detainee), an AA must be present when a child or young person is strip searched, although the young suspect can ask that the AA not observe the search itself.[124] Before an intimate search can be conducted, the AA must be present for the young person to be informed of the authorization and

---

[116] ibid, para 3.117.
[117] Choongh (n 86) 87–88; see also Skinns, *Police Custody* (n 54) 77.
[118] *Code C* (n 20), Annex A, para 10.
[119] *D v Chief Constable of Merseyside Police* [2015] EWCA Civ 114, [2015] Crim LR 539.
[120] *Reeves v Commissioner of Police of the Metropolis* [2000] 1 AC 360 (HL), [1999] 3 WLR 363.
[121] Obiter comments of Pitchford LJ in the case of *D* (n 119) at [44].
[122] Although what constitutes an intimate search has been complicated by the case of *Owens v Chief Constable of Merseyside Police* [2021] EWHC 3119 (QB).
[123] *Code C* (n 20), Annex A, para 11(d).
[124] ibid, para 11(c).

Search and Seizure of Belongings: Procedure and Existing Literature   85

grounds for the search,[125] and consent is required to be given where the intimate search is a drugs search.[126]

There is very limited previous literature on the searching of young suspects by police or their experiences of it.[127] Children in HMIC's user-voice study indicated a 'strong view that strip searches were undignified and degrading'.[128] In their thematic inspection, HMIC encountered some efforts to consider alternatives to strip search but had also observed strip searching in the absence of an AA and in circumstances that breached privacy requirements and seemed unnecessary. Although her case represents a particularly shocking example, Child Q's account of her strip search at her school in 2020 is important in underlining how traumatic strip search can be, particularly in the absence of an AA, and the lasting impact of such an experience.[129] Child Q's experiences prompted the Children's Commissioner to conduct an investigation into strip search of children by police in England and Wales under PACE, *Code A*.[130] The report contains two case studies from young people with experience of strip search as a child which underline not only the traumatizing and degrading experience of the search itself but also its potentially damaging effects for the child in the longer term.[131]

The subsequent review of Child Q's case found that 'racism (whether deliberate or not) was likely to have been an influencing factor in the decision

---

[125] ibid, para 2A.
[126] Consent must be sought from the child or young person (where he or she is fourteen or over) and their AA. Where the child is under fourteen, only the AA's consent is sought (*Code C* (n 20), Annex A, 2B).
[127] See in relation to the secure estate Lord Carlile, 'An Independent Inquiry into the Use of Physical Restraint, Solitary Confinement and Forcible Strip Searching of Children in Prisons, Secure Training Centres and Local Authority Secure Children's Homes' (Howard League 2006); Howard League for Penal Reform, *The Carlile Inquiry 10 Years On: The Use of Restraint, Solitary Confinement and Strip Searching on Children* (Howard League 2016).
[128] HMIC (n 34) 89–90.
[129] Jim Gamble and Rory McCallum, 'Local Child Safeguarding Practice Review: Child Q' (City & Hackney Safeguarding Children Partnership March 2022) <https://chscp.org.uk/wp-content/uploads/2022/03/Child-Q-PUBLISHED-14-March-22.pdf> accessed 16 August 2023.
[130] Children's Commissioner, 'Strip Search of Children in England and Wales—Analysis by the Children's Commissioner for England' (Children's Commissioner 2023). The search of Child Q was conducted under the police's powers contained within PACE *Code A* (in exercise of their statutory powers to stop and search) rather than under *Code C* (n 20) (in exercise of their statutory powers to detain). For the different powers of the police under *Codes A* and *C*, see Chris Bath, *Police Searches of People—A Review of PACE Powers* (National Appropriate Adult Network 2022).
[131] Children's Commissioner (n 130) 26ff.

to undertake a strip search.'[132] Sadly, this is not a new finding. Newburn and colleagues' study of the use of strip search in a North London police station revealed striking ethnic disproportionality, with detainees of African-Caribbean heritage being slightly more than twice as likely as White European detainees to be strip searched.[133] This disproportionality was reflected in HMIC's thematic investigation[134] and is even more starkly illustrated in the Children's Commissioner's recent research. She found that Black children in England and Wales were over six times more likely to be strip searched (under *Code A*) compared to national population figures, while White children were disproportionately less likely to be strip searched (around half as likely compared to national population figures).[135] The Home Office's partial data for strip search in police custody (from a subset of twenty-six forces) for the year to March 2022 indicates that 19% of detained children identifying as Black or Black British were strip searched in comparison to only 6% of White child detainees.[136]

Choongh has observed the communicative power of strip search, particularly where conducted in public or humiliating circumstances: 'Nothing could be more effective in driving home to the suspect the completeness of his defeat.'[137] That effect is starkly illustrated in the account of Dr Koshka Duff. An academic, she was arrested in 2013 by the Metropolitan Police when she sought to inform a child, who was subject to stop and search, of his legal rights. She felt that her strip search, which was accompanied by derogatory and insulting behaviour, had been calculated to intimidate and punish her for her intervention.[138]

---

[132] Gamble and McCallum (n 129) 32.
[133] Tim Newburn, Michael Shiner, and Stephanie Hayman, 'Race, Crime and Injustice? Strip Search and the Treatment of Suspects in Custody' (2004) 44 British Journal of Criminology 677.
[134] HMIC (n 34).
[135] Obtained by way of Freedom of Information Act requests, Children's Commissioner (n 130) 35.
[136] Home Office, 'Police Powers and Procedures: Other PACE Powers, England and Wales, Year Ending 31 March 2022' (National Statistics 2022) 2.4 <https://www.gov.uk/government/statistics/police-powers-and-procedures-other-pace-powers-england-and-wales-year-ending-31-march-2022/police-powers-and-procedures-other-pace-powers-england-and-wales-year-ending-31-march-2022> accessed 16 August 2023.
[137] Choongh (n 86) 102.
[138] BBC, Woman's Hour (26 January 2022) <www.bbc.co.uk/programmes/m0013rb0> accessed 16 August 2023. More recently, an inspection of Metropolitan Police custody suites found that 'not all strip searches were warranted or properly justified': HMICFRS, 'Report on an Unannounced Inspection Visit to Police Custody Suites in Metropolitan Police Service, 9–20 July 2018' (HMICFRS 2018) 10, 32 <www.justiceinspectorates.gov.uk/hmicfrs/publications/metropolitan-joint-inspection-of-police-custody> accessed 16 August 2023.

Search and Seizure of Belongings: Child Suspect Experiences

Initial Search and Seizure: 'I felt harassed'

Although pat-down searching is increasingly commonplace in our everyday lives, it is important to approach initial searching in custody in the context of the powerlessness young participants described experiencing during booking-in. Some child suspects, particularly those in the younger age group, found even this level of searching upsetting in the intimidating and adult setting of the custody block: 'I felt harassed—does that make sense?' (Azade). Nor did it always mitigate the experience to be searched by someone of the child's own gender. Thirteen-year-old Kaiden lived in a female-headed household and recounted being afraid and objecting to being searched by an unknown male officer. Some officers appreciated that a more delicate approach to searching may be appropriate for young people, but they also identified the tension between more sympathetic approaches and the need for effectiveness. A young suspect found to have in the cell an item of contraband missed in a search might lead to their police national computer ('PNC') entry being flagged with a marker indicating a history of concealing items, which can trigger regular strip searching on future occasions.

It was routine, on observation, for all the personal effects of child suspects, including outer jackets and watches, to be seized. I only observed one young suspect allowed to retain a non-clothing item: in that case, a book. As with the RA, the overriding consideration for COs is physical risk; the emotional welfare of the child is not obviously a consideration. The routinized nature of these seizures involved no apparent assessment of the actual risk presented by the individual child suspect. Property seized in this way was invariably recorded in the custody record and signed for, but I did not observe anything more than the most cursory explanation about seizing personal items, certainly nothing which amounted to the sort of explanation or justification required in *Code C*, 4.5 or the APP (APP(CRS), 6.2). Inspecting a child's personal possessions also has the potential to be significantly humiliating. For example, in F3, I observed a male CO pick over the contents of a young girl's bag, including tampons and make-up, in the presence of male arresting officers (re YS42). There was no prospect that she would be allowed to retain the bag or that items involved in relation to the allegation would be discovered in her possession, the proceeds of her alleged theft having been recovered at the scene.

The major point of contention for many young participants was the taking of laces and cords from their clothing, ostensibly to prevent them being used for self-harm. The data suggests that there is a near-blanket approach to the taking of these in some areas; as one Inspector observed to me in F2, 'You'd have to be Mother Mary to be allowed to keep your cords in this place.' Young participants generally understood why laces and cords were taken, and a reasonable number did not object, although not all of those considered that the measure was justifiable. However, this was a source of real anger and resentment for a number of participants. There was particular frustration when the cords were cut out ('I go mad when they cut 'em, me' (Dexter)) or when it was not possible to put laces or cords back in: 'it does my head … it's like you're just ruining my clothes' (Sadie).

Risk aversion seems to overwhelm any appreciation officers may have of how much a hoodie or pair of shoes may be valued by a young person, particularly those whose backgrounds are significantly disadvantaged. Or it obscures the understanding that walking home without laces in one's shoes can be embarrassing, potentially notifying the observant of your arrest (Malik). Not only does this approach tend to cause outbursts in the custody suite ('The only time we get kicking off is taking laces or cords' (CO24)), but it also has the capacity to undermine the legitimacy of the police. Several young participants found police attitudes to laces and cords laughable. Will retorted, 'I normally just sit there and think to myself—what are you doing? I just laugh at them. I just use them as a laughing stock—that's what they are.'

Strip Search: 'Like a violation'

Discussion of strip search prompted emotional accounts from young participants. Whilst a necessary tool, the data reveals how problematic strip search can be. On observation, strip searching was almost exclusively conducted with a view to preventing self-harm and predominantly involved girl suspects. Girls were over-represented amongst young participants who spoke of strip search, but boys also spoke of the intrusive and humiliating effects of the practice. For Carter, for example, who had been strip searched eleven times, the experience felt 'like a violation.'[139] Whilst Carter was in the group of Black, Asian, and minority ethnic participants, this group was not disproportionately represented amongst those who reported being strip

---

[139] Echoing similar accounts in HMIC (n 34).

searched, in contrast to the statistical findings reviewed.[140] However, the sample group was small and so it is not possible to draw any conclusions in this regard.

Several young participants complained about being required to remove all of their clothes at once, contrary to the guidance in *Code C*, Annex A 11(d)). Sadie found having to do so as 'weird' and 'uncomfortable'. Aaron described how he had responded to being made to take off all his clothes in the absence of an AA, only to be given them back ten minutes later: 'I started goin' mad, innit? I went, 'You fuckin' paedo ... I were goin' sick, me.' One can appreciate how exposed a child might feel in such a situation, the more so for a young person with a history of abuse at the hands of an adult.

Most concerning were the accounts of repeat strip searches where a child has a 'warning marker' on the PNC or force custody system for 'conceals blades' or similar, often associated with a girl hiding razor blades in a bra or using the underwiring in a bra to self-harm. Avery described how these 'markers' operate. On one occasion, in custody, she had been found to have an unauthorized item with her in the cell (following an inadequate search, she suggested), resulting in a forcible strip search. After that first occasion, 'they like just put my name in the system then for some reason it used to come up with that—snuck something into the cells before so they used to always do it (strip search)'. Strip searching, she explained, feels 'like they've taken all your dignity', and she would routinely respond violently when it was proposed. When Avery challenged the CO, the response would be, ''Cos you've done it in the past', and indeed, custody staff on observation acknowledged that this did occur: 'We tell them this is what happens every time you come in here—we can't leave you' (CA40). Abigail, who had had similar experiences, felt that such an approach was unjustified: 'the excuse that they use is that I used to self-harm and so they need to check me. That's the excuse that they use innit.'

Strip Search: 'You're damned if you do, damned if you don't'

Officers in all three areas expressed genuine concern about the traumatizing effect of strip searching children: 'No-one wants to do it—strip search—but

---

[140] See Home Office, 'Police Powers and Procedures' (n 136).

sometimes it's got to be done' (CO10). Mindful of best practice guidance, staff discussed using constant watch[141] as an alternative to strip search. However, as CO10 observed, constant watch is demanding and can be risky: 'if they're not fully searched and if you nod off—a few seconds that's enough (for self-harm to occur) and it could happen'. It is also hugely resource intensive and, for some COs, it was not seen as an option for long periods. CO31 explained that he had used handcuffs to prevent self-harm but that this would not be an option for a smaller child, who could slip out of the cuffs. Difficulties securing AAs were also raised,[142] and several officers recounted urgent strip searches conducted on children with markers who were also displaying or reporting an intention to harm themselves, which had become really problematic. I heard accounts of young female suspects resisting violently, requiring other, often male, officers to intervene. Such instances tended to be recounted with real anguish as officers wrestled to reconcile balancing the need to keep a child safe against the traumatizing effects of the search. As CA40 explained, 'You're damned if you do, damned if you don't.' However, there did not seem to be much consideration of 'alternative and less invasive measures'.[143] Ultimately, the need to address risk overshadowed concerns about the emotional effects on these most vulnerable of child suspects, and coercive approaches tended to predominate. As CO31 explained, 'It all comes down to justification. I'd rather rationalize to a disciplinary hearing than to the coroner's court.'

Conclusion

The picture which emerges from these early stages of police detention is one of a process largely unadjusted to account for young suspects. The data indicates limited separation between adult and child suspects, almost no prioritization, and scant adjustment to accommodate the child suspect. Seen through the eyes of young participants, it is clear that aspirations for 'child first'[144] or 'child friendly'[145] treatment are rarely being realized at this stage

---

[141] Where the suspect is watched in the cell, either through an open door or through CCTV monitoring.
[142] I address the particular role of AAs during strip/intimate search in Chapter 4.
[143] Pitchford LJ in *D* (n 119) at [44].
[144] National Police Chiefs' Council (NPCC), 'National Strategy for the Policing of Children and Young People' (NPCC 2016) 8. <https://www.npcc.police.uk/SysSiteAssets/media/downloads/publications/publications-log/local-policing-coordination-committee/national-strategy-for-the-policing-of-children-young-people.pdf> accessed 16 August 2023.
[145] General Comment No 24 (n 37) 46.

of the process. Duties to 'safeguard and promote the welfare of children and young people'[146] and wider international obligations under the UNCRC appear, frequently, to be overridden or narrowly construed to reflect physical safety alone, whilst the varied adversities children face are too often not addressed. In practice, as well as on paper, there is little evidence of the special protection Campbell and others identified as a necessary component in achieving fairness for a child in the criminal justice process.[147] Treatment with dignity and respect is commonly trumped by routinized risk aversion without particular consideration of the individual child's position, whilst problematic linkages of the notion of vulnerability with victimhood, frailty, and risk colour the approach of COs and staff, with negative outcomes for child suspects which resonate throughout the process.

The Impact of Failures to Respond to Adversity

The impact of the failure to accommodate a child suspect's natural developmental immaturity is felt from the very outset. Participants' youthful reactions to arrest and, for some, their diminutive stature, often resulted in arrest experiences which had an oppressive, punitive, character. On arrival in the custody block, their heightened emotional state, combined with a lack of physical stamina and patience, and their limited knowledge and understanding of what would occur, often caused significant anxiety, frustration, or anger. As the booking-in process unfolds, young participant experiences reveal how the contingent nature of the custody process meant that such emotional responses could have a negative impact on their relations with COs and thus the support provided to them. Non-compliance on arrest or an outburst at booking-in, for example, might disincline a CO to approach the young suspect as a child first or undermine the child's own capacity to engage with the risk assessment process.

For some child suspects, their dispositional vulnerabilities can be identified as a factor in their arrest and the CO's conclusion that authorisation of detention is unavoidable, often outside the narrow grounds stipulated in PACE, section 37. In addition, the prevalence of behavioural and

---

[146] Children Act 2004, s 11.
[147] Liz Campbell, Andrew Ashworth, and Mike Redmayne, *The Criminal Process* (5th edn, OUP 2019).

developmental disorders and mental health conditions amongst those who responded aggressively to the booking-in process provides an early glimpse of the profound difficulty the detention experience itself presents for this group and for custody teams tasked to care for them. Equally, other childhood adversities can be seen to exacerbate the challenges for child suspects in these early stages—whether that is in heightening anxiety about the impact of arrest on precarious living arrangements or where coping strategies such as self-harm trigger more coercive responses, such as strip search. Of particular concern also is the indication that Black, Asian, and minority ethnic children may, through fear, resort to defensive defiance on arrest more readily than their White peers, often tainting how they are approached by staff in the custody block.

The data presents a picture of child suspects who, in line with the prevalence research, experience multiple, intersecting adversities. These challenges have, in turn, a cumulatively negative impact, in a variety of ways, on their ability to cope with detention and to engage effectively with the demands of the process. This multifaceted interaction of different adversities reflects observations of the 'cascading and interactive' operation of social disadvantage in other spheres.[148] It is plain, even at this early stage, that for many children, a detention episode imposes burdens, and involves deprivations, more severe than can be justified by their alleged misconduct or the demands of the criminal justice process. In this sense, their treatment could not sensibly be described as a proportionate response or in keeping with the 'minimum burdens' principle advanced by Ashworth.[149] Humiliating and demeaning treatment at the outset lent the whole custody episode a gratuitous and punitive aspect for many young participants.

We shall see, as the process unfolds, the impact of disproportionately harsh treatment on the quality of the evidence produced, 'rectitude', and the fairness of the overall justice process. In particular, the first element of enabling effective participation in the processes, adjusted treatment which takes account both of the child's inherent needs and their situational adversity, appears not to be frequently achieved. Indeed, far from effective steps being taken to reduce the child's 'feelings of intimidation and inhibition' to

---

[148] Madison Powers and Ruth R Faden, *Social Justice: The Moral Foundations of Public Health and Health Policy* (OUP 2006) 69. See also Evelyne Durocher and others, 'Understanding and Addressing Vulnerability Following the 2010 Haiti Earthquake: Applying a Feminist Lens to Examine Perspectives of Haitian and Expatriate Health Care Providers and Decision-Makers' (2016) 8 Journal of Human Rights Practice 219.

[149] Andrew Ashworth, *The Criminal Process: An Evaluative Study* (1st edn, OUP 1994) 31.

enable their effective participation,[150] the booking-in process, particularly RA and search, tends to operate to cement such feelings. Despite the fact that these early stages of the process are intended to ensure the protection of fundamental rights and that needs are identified and addressed, they are experienced, rather, as being punitive in themselves. Indeed, young participants' recollections echo the systematic mortification experienced by prisoners and inmates in Goffman's seminal study, *Asylums*.[151]

Adversariality in Police Custody

I turn then to consider what indications there are, in this early stage of the custody process, to explain why there is such limited adjustment for children in police custody. The psycho-social adversity experienced by young suspects and the prevalence of dispositional vulnerabilities within the suspect population is well documented, including in custody guidance.[152] Equally, the statutory duties to safeguard children and promote their welfare[153] and the international obligations to adjust processes to afford children special protections are long-standing.[154] Why, then, is police custody so poorly adjusted, both on paper and in practice, to accommodate the needs of child suspects? Undeniably, there are institutional constraints on what can be achieved for children in detention. In particular, the physical limitations of the custody suite and the time limits imposed by PACE challenge the thorough assessment of the child suspect and the provision of less coercive responses. There are structural factors, too, which contribute to harsh or unnecessary detention experiences, particularly failures in local authority provision and community health care. The 'punitive turn' in youth justice,[155] for example, has stalled consideration of raising the age of criminal responsibility, which would remove the youngest of child suspects

---

[150] *Panovits v Cyprus* App no 4268/04, 11 March 2009, (2008) 27 BHRC 464, [67].
[151] Erving Goffman, *Asylums: Essays on the Social Situation of Mental Patients and Other Inmates* (Penguin Books 1968) 24.
[152] See APP(DC)(CYP) (n 67) 3–4.
[153] See eg the Children Act 2004, s 11.
[154] See eg UNCRC Articles 12, 37, and 40; the 'Beijing Rules' (n 37)); Guidelines of the Committee of Ministers of the Council of Europe on child friendly justice (adopted by the Committee of Ministers on 17 November 2010 at the 1098th meeting of the Ministers' Deputies).
[155] John Muncie, 'The "Punitive Turn" in Juvenile Justice: Cultures of Control and Rights Compliance in Western Europe and the USA' (2008) 8 Youth Justice 107.

from police custody altogether. Arguably, legislators and policymakers are also implicated. The category of 'juvenile' has been rendered almost meaningless by the lack of statutory adjustment to accommodate youth. As we shall see in Chapter 4, obligations to address the child's needs and accommodate their immaturity are deflected to the AA—the mandatory and catch-all answer to the challenges custody presents for children. However, none of these factors account adequately for the failure to respect rights and implement protections which are not frustrated by these constraints. They do not explain, for example, why child suspects are not prioritized or why efforts are not made more frequently to conduct a risk assessment in a manner which is effective in ensuring the child's welfare and maintains a child's privacy and dignity.

The matrix of factors, as we will explore throughout the coming chapters, is complex, but these opening phases of the custody process provide some indications of one aspect which might be driving such an approach, namely, the adversarial nature of the custody process. In this regard, I adopt a broad definition of 'adversarial' to encompass not only the role of police detention as part of the wider adversary criminal justice process but also the generally oppositional relationship between the child and the CO and custody staff, which challenges the imposition of protections and suitable adjustment.

By adversary criminal justice process, I have in mind the common law Anglo-American system of adjudication in which the procedural action is controlled by the parties and in which the adjudicator is engaged only at the trial stage and in an essentially 'passive' role.[156] The criminal justice process in England and Wales might now be described as closer to a 'mixed' adversarial/inquisitorial process, given the judge's pre-trial case management role and the relative rarity of a fully contested trial. Nonetheless, as Jacqueline Hodgson has observed, the process can still be described as 'broadly adversarial', particularly in regard to the continuing 'police monopoly on carrying out the investigation that will form the prosecution case, unsupervised by any central judicial authority'.[157] As the NPCCs 'National Strategy for Police Custody' makes plain, the 'primary purpose' of police

---

[156] Mirjan R Damaška, *Evidence Law Adrift* (Yale UP 1997) 74.
[157] Jacqueline S Hodgson, *The Metamorphosis of Criminal Justice: A Comparative Account* (OUP 2020) 7.

custody is to render a suspect 'amenable to the investigation of a criminal offence'.[158]

The role of the CO in having particular responsibility for the welfare and protection of the child suspect is fundamentally challenged by this focus. Placing control of the support to be provided to one party into the hands of, effectively, the other party is 'theoretically unsound', as Lord Devlin has noted in respect of similar expectations placed on the police in the wider investigation: 'There is a great difference between playing fair with an opponent, which the police are rightly required to do, and holding the balance between him and yourself.'[159] This is particularly the case where the CO, and their supporting staff, are functioning under significant resource pressures and strong institutional motivation to reduce organizational risk. McConville and colleagues, in 1991,[160] detailed persuasively the central importance of the police custody process in case construction, and the data in this study suggests the continuation of this approach. We will see this play out as the chapters unfold, but the impact of the adversarial imperative in this early stage is evident in the willingness to separate co-suspects but not to keep children apart from older arrestees and in the automatic approach to authorisation of detention. Entering the custody block from a police van in handcuffs, the child arrestee is rarely approached as a child first, for whom all alternatives to custody must be rigorously considered, but rather as a 'suspect' present for the obtaining of evidence by questioning.

This adversarial stance is also reflected in, and facilitated by, police cultural behaviours, which entrench the more generalized oppositional nature of the custody process. In these early stages, we can already see the impact of the collegiality between officers, which eases authorisation of detention,[161] and the inclination towards suspicion and cynicism[162] observable in the manner in which some staff approached child suspects. Similarly, despite the CO's intended independence from the investigation, some displayed

---

[158] NPCC, 'National Custody Strategy' (NPCC 2017) 3 <https://www.npcc.police.uk/SysSiteAssets/media/downloads/publications/publications-log/local-policing-coordination-committee/national-strategy-for-the-policing-of-children-young-people.pdf> accessed 16 August 2023.
[159] Patrick D Devlin, *The Judge* (OUP 1979) 71.
[160] McConville, Sanders, and Leng (n 71) 42.
[161] ibid.
[162] See eg Simon Holdaway, *Inside the British Police: A Force at Work* (Blackwell 1983) and more recently Sarah Charman, *Police Socialisation, Identity and Culture: Becoming Blue* (Palgrave Macmillan 2017); Bethan Loftus, 'Policing the "Irrelevant": Class, Diversity and Contemporary Police Culture' in Megan O'Neill, Monique Marks, and Anne-Marie Singh (eds), *Police Occupational Cultures* (JAI Press 2007).

a distinctly 'crime-control' mindset,[163] prioritizing the routinized processing of child suspects that were assumed to be perpetrators, apparently unconcerned by the stigmatizing experience of RA and search. This was perhaps most marked where detention was authorized for social disciplinary purposes[164]—where the child suspect was positioned in opposition to the community or the victim. Here, we also glimpse the impact of an increasingly prevalent theme in police culture: the 'predominance of a public service motivation'[165] and particularly a more victim-orientated focus.[166] Whilst this reorientation is largely to be welcomed, the focus on the victim can have an adverse effect on the treatment of the alleged offender. David Garland has observed the 'zero sum relationship that is assumed to hold between the one and the other' as stifling concern and respect for the offender, or here the suspect, on the basis that it undermines concern and respect for the victim.[167] This victim-orientation intersects with the concept of vulnerability, and its association with victimhood, to the exclusion of the child suspect. Thus, child suspects become identified not as vulnerable and in need of care but as perpetrators for whom a softened approach is not appropriate, especially where they are regular attendees. Such approaches serve to 'other' child suspects, enabling officers to treat them in a way that they would not entertain for a child witness, for example. Equally, the child suspect who behaves problematically because of immaturity or a history of trauma, who fails to conform to notions of vulnerability as frailty and weakness, is not recognized as deserving of support.

Institutional and individual preoccupations with managing the risk presented by a child suspect also introduce an oppositional aspect to the interaction between officer and child. COs' consciousness of the risk of the child coming to physical harm in the cells, and the impact in disciplinary terms of such an event, casts the child as a potential threat and reframes displays of vulnerability and need, especially with regard to self-harm, as risks to be neutralized. It is perhaps unsurprising that this is the outcome, given the

---

[163] Herbert L Packer, 'Two Models of the Criminal Process' (1964) 113 University of Pennsylvania Law Review 1, discussed in detail in Chapter 1.
[164] Choongh (n 86).
[165] Nick Caveney and others, 'Police Reform, Austerity and "Cop Culture": Time to Change the Record?' (2020) 30 Policing & Society 1210, 1222
[166] Sarah Charman, 'Making Sense of Policing Identities: The "Deserving" and the "Undeserving" in Policing Accounts of Victimisation' (2020) 30 Policing & Society 81.
[167] David Garland, *The Culture of Control: Crime and Social Order in Contemporary Society* (Clarendon Press 2001) 143.

framing of the process—as an assessment of 'risk'. The police's duty under the Children Act 2004, section 11 not only to keep the child safe but also to 'promote' their 'welfare' is lost. It is equally unsurprising that the response mechanisms tend towards surveillance, strip search, and the removal of personal items rather than focusing on means by which well-being can be promoted and the detention experience mitigated for the child. The problematic linkage of vulnerability with risk in this assessment drowns out the need of the child for age-appropriate, child friendly support. That COs regularly feel obliged to require a young child to undergo the humiliating and degrading experience of strip search in the name of safeguarding points to the fundamental unsuitability of police custody, as currently implemented, for children. Such a procedure is damaging and distressing not only for the child but also for the adults involved.

This oppositional approach is not, however, unilateral, and it is apparent, even in these early stages, that child suspects also engage in adversarial behaviour, often for a combination of reasons. As Waddington has observed, the officer–child relationship is inevitably 'structurally adversarial' as the police use their coercive powers to 'maintain adherence to adult conceptions of appropriate behaviour', expecting and demanding deference as they do so.[168] The coercive nature of the arrest process sets the tone of the custody experience for some, whilst for others, a hostile approach may already be engrained behaviour, or an instinctive response to unadjusted police treatment, or the confrontational situation in which they find themselves. Whatever the motivation, we shall see, as the custody process unfolds, that such adversarial attitudes, whilst often entirely understandable, tend not to serve child suspects well—both in hardening CO attitudes further and in acting as a barrier to engaging with the support available. I turn, in Chapter 3, to consider the first of those supports, the provision of legal advice.

---

[168] Peter AJ Waddington, *Policing Citizens: Authority and Rights* (UCL Press 1999) 47. See also Loader (n 36).

3
The Child as Legal Actor
Understanding and Exercising Rights

> Just do without [a solicitor] ... I don't need one. They just long it out ... They just say everything that you could say yourself really.
>
> **(Jamal)**

Introduction

I turn, in this second empirical chapter, to explore whether child suspects are enabled to function effectively as legal actors in the police custody process. In fixing the minimum age of criminal responsibility (MACR) in England and Wales at ten,[1] the criminal law lays claim to a child's capacity to bear responsibility for their actions from that age. But the extent to which those children are able to act as autonomous legal actors (and to exercise, in police custody, the rights which balance that responsibility) has not been widely considered. A child's ability, with assistance, to engage with their legal rights in an informed, rational, and voluntary fashion is assumed by the criminal process and central to its fair operation—the production of reliable evidence and the avoidance of wrongful convictions of the sort experienced by the *Confait* suspects. Conversely, proceeding against a child, or any individual, who is not able to engage competently with the criminal process undermines its communicative effect and the dignity of the process itself.[2]

---

[1] Children and Young Persons Act 1933, s 50.
[2] See for discussion Richard J Bonnie, 'The Competence of Criminal Defendants: A Theoretical Reformulation' (1992) 10 Behavioral Sciences & the Law 291.

Introduction

The concept of effective participation, as delineated in *Panovits v Cyprus*[3] and elaborated upon by the Committee on the Rights of the Child (the UNCRC Committee),[4] situates the child suspect at the centre of the investigatory process. The approach blends autonomy and protection—the child having both a right to fully participate and to be heard directly, 'not only through a representative'[5] but also to be enabled to do so by child friendly measures and by support where necessary. However, identifying how the balance should be struck, particularly with regard to the provision of legal advice, is not always easy.[6] As Jamal's reflections in the epigraph indicate, there is a range of issues which makes the exercise of rights and legal decision-making more difficult for young suspects, in particular a general lack of appreciation of the nature and content of their rights and their desperation to leave custody.

This chapter reviews the extent to which children are supported to understand and exercise their legal rights in police custody, including making the key decisions required of them—whether to request legal advice and how to respond to police questioning. The opening section considers valid decision-making in police custody. I review its importance and set out how it is conceptualized in the chapter and applied in the analysis which follows. I also address, briefly, some of the issues which may make decision-making more challenging for child suspects. The empirical discussion is then broken down into three sections. In order to exercise rights, the suspect must first be made aware of them. With this in mind, the first section picks up the booking-in process where Chapter 2 left off and considers how effectively the child is informed of their rights and entitlements by the custody officer (CO). I then turn to consider the extent to which child suspects are enabled to exercise their legal rights, focusing on the uptake, or waiver, of legal advice. In the third empirical section, I reflect on whether the child in detention is, in practice, able to benefit from the rights they seek to exercise. In this section, I consider the challenges the child suspect encounters in engaging with their legal representative and how effectively they are able to make use of legal advice in deciding whether to answer

---

[3] *Panovits v Cyprus* App no 4268/04, 11 March 2009, (2008) 27 BHRC 464, [67].
[4] General Comment No 24 (2019) on children's rights in the child justice system (CRC/C/GC/24), para 22. (General Comment No 24 replaces General Comment No 10 (2007) (CRC/C/GC/10) extant at the time of fieldwork. Any relevant variance will be noted as it arises.)
[5] General Comment No 24 (n 4), para 55.
[6] Ton Liefaard and Yannick van den Brink, 'Juveniles' Right to Counsel during Police Interrogations: An Interdisciplinary Analysis of a Youth-Specific Approach, with a Particular Focus on the Netherlands' (2014) 7 Erasmus Law Review 206.

questions in interview. In closing, I reflect on the challenges for children in exercising their rights in detention and conclude that the provision of expert and properly resourced legal advice is critically important in enabling the child as legal actor. Finally, I consider options for reform of the requirement for children to opt into legal advice, drawing on developments in comparable adversarial jurisdictions in North America.

Legal Autonomy in Police Custody: Essential But Challenged

The suspect's ability to participate as an autonomous legal actor in the investigative process is of fundamental importance in an adversarial process. In a predominantly inquisitorial system, responsibility for the fairness and effectiveness of the investigation process largely rests with the authorities, demanding little of the suspect, who features mainly as the subject of the investigation. But a predominantly adversarial process, of the sort operated in England and Wales, relies, for its integrity, in large part on the competent engagement of the suspect (and later defendant) since the parties bear responsibility for the procedural action.[7]

Central to the concept of legal autonomy is the individual's competence to make the decisions required of them,[8] particularly with regard to the exercise of their legal rights. Despite its importance, how decisional competence in this regard should be understood in the criminal process in England and Wales has not been significantly developed. There is no specific requirement for courts to consider whether any waiver of rights has been competently made, as there is, for example, in US jurisdictions.[9] In police custody, consideration of the suspect's participatory abilities is confined to the assessment of their fitness to be interviewed, which focuses specifically on their ability to answer questions in interview.[10] Nor, indeed, has

---

[7] Mirjan Damaška, 'Evidentiary Barriers to Conviction and Two Models of Criminal Procedure: A Comparative Study' (1973) 121 University of Pennsylvania Law Review 506.

[8] Richard Bonnie, 'Fitness for Criminal Adjudication: The Emerging Significance of Decisional Competence in the United States' in Ronnie Mackay and Warren Brookbanks (eds), *Fitness to Plead: International and Comparative Perspectives* (OUP 2018).

[9] Following *In Re Gault* 387 US 1 (1967) and *Fare v Michael C* 442 US 707 (1979), 'Miranda' warnings (*Miranda v Arizona* 384 US 436 (1966)) are generally considered to be applicable in 'juvenile proceedings' in US jurisdictions.

[10] Police and Criminal Evidence Act 1984 (PACE), *Code C: Revised Code of Practice for the Detention, Treatment and Questioning of Persons by Police Officers* (updated 4 November

the concept of decisional competence in trial proceedings more generally been substantially developed, largely as a result of the stagnation of the law of unfitness to plead and the retention of the outdated '*Pritchard* Test'.[11]

How, then, should a child's ability to make valid decisions about the exercise of their legal rights be conceptualized? In US jurisdictions, before accepting a child's waiver of their Fifth Amendment rights, which include the right to legal advice and the right to silence, the court must be satisfied that they made a 'knowing, intelligent, and voluntary' waiver under the 'totality of the circumstances'.[12] A valid waiver requires the child to understand the basic meaning of their rights, appreciate the consequences of waiving them, and give their waiver free from coercion by the police. The 'totality of the circumstances' has been held to encompass (amongst other factors) age, education, knowledge of the charge and the relevant rights, the circumstances surrounding the interrogation, and the individual's previous experience of the justice system.[13] This test largely reflects the approach in the fitness-assessment of fitness to be interviewed in PACE, *Code C*, Annex G, which considers the individual's ability to 'understand the nature and purpose' of the interview, to 'comprehend' the questioning, 'appreciate the significance of any answers given, and make 'rational decisions' about whether to answer (paragraph 3(a)).[14] This emphasis on ensuring 'understanding' and appreciation of the 'significance' of different outcomes is also echoed in the broader concept of effective participation.[15]

Drawing on these frameworks, in the analysis that follows, I look for four elements in assessing whether child suspects are supported to engage in valid decision-making with regard to rights: a factual understanding of

---

2020) para 12.3 and Annex G. (In force at time of writing. Any relevant variance with the version in force at time of fieldwork, published May 2014, will be noted as it arises.)

[11] *R v Pritchard* (1836) Eng R 540, (1836) 7 C & P 303, 173 ER 135. See for discussion Miranda Bevan and David Ormerod, 'Chapter 4: Reforming the Law of Unfitness to Plead in England and Wales: A Recent History' in Mackay and Brookbanks (n 8). Indeed, the situation for child defendants is even less well developed since the *Pritchard* test has no application in the youth court. See for discussion Miranda Bevan, 'Effective Participation in the Youth Court', Howard League What is Justice? Working Papers 21/2016 <https://howardleague.org/wp-content/uploads/2016/04/HLWP_21_16.pdf#:~:text=Effective%20participation%20in%20the%20youth%20court%20Miranda%20Bevan,than%20adults%20when%20they%20face%20a%20criminal%20allegation> accessed 16 August 2023.

[12] *Fare* (n 9) 717.
[13] ibid 725; *West v United States*, 399 F2d 467 (1968).
[14] *Code C* (n 10), Annex G, para 3(a). The Annex G framing of fitness for interview itself reflects formulations of more general decisional competence developed in the United States; see eg Bonnie, 'Competence' (n 2).
[15] *Panovits v Cyprus* (n 3), [67].

the information relevant to the decision, an appreciation of the nature and consequences of the decision, the capacity to reason logically using this information, and an ability to make and communicate the decision free from coercion. I bear in mind that all such decisions are highly contextualized. In keeping with the concept of the 'totality of the circumstances', I take into account the range of relevant factors affecting the individual decision made, including the demands of the environment; the child's prior understanding and previous experience; and their ethnicity, gender, and relative youth.

Autonomous decision-making is likely to be particularly challenging for child suspects. As discussed in Chapter 1, children, especially those aged under sixteen, have been found to demonstrate inadequate functional and decision-making capacity.[16] Younger adolescents, in particular, are less likely, or less able, to assess the risks and longer-term consequences of legal decisions.[17] Even older adolescents and young adults may show impaired judgement, having a reduced ability to regulate their behaviour and to make decisions in a manner in keeping with their cognitive capacities.[18] For child suspects, such capacities are likely to be challenged not only by their natural developmental immaturity but also by its combination with other adversities.[19] The impulsiveness associated with attention deficit hyperactivity disorder (ADHD), for example, can hamper careful selection of an appropriate course of action, whilst exposure to trauma and other childhood adversities can give rise to deficits in problem-solving and self-regulation which reduce decision-making competency.[20]

---

[16] Alexandra O Cohen and others, 'When Is an Adolescent an Adult? Assessing Cognitive Control in Emotional and Non-emotional Contexts' (2016) 27(4) Psychological Science 549; Michael E Lamb and Megan PY Sim, 'Developmental Factors Affecting Children in Legal Contexts' (2013) 13(2) Youth Justice 131.

[17] Thomas Grisso and others, 'Juveniles' Competence to Stand Trial: A Comparison of Adolescents' and Adults' Capacities as Trial Defendants' (2003) 27 Law & Human Behaviour 333, 357.

[18] ibid; Elizabeth Cauffman and Laurence Steinberg, 'Emerging Findings from Research on Adolescent Development and Juvenile Justice' (2012) 7 Victims & Offenders 428.

[19] Christine Schnyder Pierce and Stanley L Brodsky, 'Trust and Understanding in the Attorney–Juvenile Relationship' (2002) 20 Behavioral Sciences & Law 89, 103.

[20] Alan E Kazdin, 'Adolescent Development, Mental Disorders, and Decision Making of Delinquent Youths' in Thomas Grisso and Robert G Schwartz (eds), *Youth on Trial: A Developmental Perspective on Juvenile Justice* (University of Chicago Press 2000).

Communicating Legal Rights: Procedure and Existing Literature

Before considering how child suspects approach their legal rights, it is important to understand what those rights are, how they are communicated, and what level of basic awareness is achieved. Rights communication generally occurs at the conclusion of the booking-in process. First, the CO must tell the suspect 'clearly' about their 'continuing rights', which they can exercise at any stage.[21] These are the right to 'free and independent' legal advice, the right to have someone told of their arrest, the right to consult the Codes of Practice, and the right to be 'informed about the offence ... and why they have been arrested and detained'.[22] The CO must also inform an adult responsible for the child's welfare and the appropriate adult (AA) (often, but not always, the same individual) of the arrest[23] and ask the AA to come to the station.[24] There is no requirement to involve the child in this process, although they must also be told about the AA's role and that they can 'consult privately' with the AA 'at any time'.[25]

Otherwise, *Code C* makes surprisingly scant provision to ensure that a suspect, including a child, is informed of, and can understand, their rights. Beyond these 'continuing rights', no other rights or entitlements are required to be relayed orally to a suspect of any age or capacity. For example, child suspects have the important right, common to all suspects, not to be held 'incommunicado'.[26] This includes being 'allowed to telephone one person for a reasonable time'.[27] However, there is no requirement in *Code C* for the CO to inform the suspect orally of these incommunicado rights. Nor must they be included in the 'written notice' which must be given to every suspect.[28] This document must repeat the 'continuing rights' and inform the suspects of other rights, including their right to remain silent; their right to medical assistance; and their entitlement to, amongst other things,

---

[21] *Code C* (n 10), para 3.1.
[22] And, where applicable, their right to interpretation and translation and to communicate with their High Commission, Consulate, or Embassy (ibid, para 3.1).
[23] ibid, para 3.13.
[24] ibid, para 3.15.
[25] ibid, para 3.15.
[26] ibid, para 5ff.
[27] ibid, para 5.6. This is additional to the informing of the AA and adult responsible for their welfare. An inspector, or more senior officer, can delay or deny either privilege if the child is held for an indictable offence and there are reasonable grounds for believing that the exercise will interfere with the investigation or lead to physical harm (*Code C*, Annex B).
[28] *Code C* (n 10), para 3.2.

food and drink, access to washing facilities, and exercise 'where practicable' ('the Notice').[29] However, again, there is no requirement for the CO to outline for the suspect the contents of the notice or why it might be worth reading, although the suspect must be given an 'opportunity' to read it and sign to acknowledge receipt of it.[30] Concerns about the accessibility of this notice have long been raised,[31] including with regard to children.[32]

The child's continuing rights must be delivered or repeated in the presence of the AA.[33] Yet, strikingly, beyond this, *Code C* includes no provision to adjust the process to ensure child friendly rights delivery—even the requirement that an 'easyread'[34] version of the rights notice 'should also be provided if available' does not specify that a 'juvenile' should receive it.[35] However, the College of Policing's guidance 'Authorised Professional Practice (Detention and Custody)(Children and Young Persons)' (APP(DC)(CYP))[36] reminds COs that children may be 'less aware of their rights and entitlements than adults' and of the need to tailor communication to meet 'any speech, language or communication needs'.[37] Particular stress is placed on the importance of ensuring that children are aware of the role of the AA and their right to legal representation. The importance of children being told how to complain is also underlined, although, perhaps surprisingly, there is no corresponding requirement in *Code C* for the CO to inform a suspect of this right.

Doubts have been raised in several studies about the extent to which young people are fully informed of, and enabled to appreciate, their rights

---

[29] ibid, para 3.2.
[30] ibid, para 3.2A.
[31] Isabel CH Clare, 'Devising and Piloting an Experimental Version of the "Notice to Detained Persons"', Royal Commission on Criminal Justice Research Study No 7 (Her Majesty's Stationery Office (HMSO) 1992); Sarah Parsons and Gina Sherwood, 'Vulnerability in Custody: Perceptions and Practices of Police Officers and Criminal Justice Professionals in Meeting the Communication Needs of Offenders with Learning Disabilities and Learning Difficulties' (2016) 31 Disability & Society 553.
[32] Criminal Justice Joint Inspection (CJJI), 'Who's Looking Out for the Children? A Joint Inspection of Appropriate Adult Provision and Children in Detention after Charge' (CJJI 2011).
[33] *Code C* (n 10), para 3.17.
[34] A format designed to be accessible and easy to understand, often involving the use of pictures and icons.
[35] *Code C* (n 10), para 3.3A.
[36] APP(DC) (Children and Young Persons) (first published 23 October 2013, updated 2 May 2023) <https://www.college.police.uk/app/detention-and-custody/detainee-care/children-and-young-persons> accessed 16 August 2023 (APP(DC)(CYP)). (Any variance with the version in force at the time of fieldwork (modified 28 July 2015) will be noted as it arises.)
[37] ibid 5.

in the custody suite.[38] Layla Skinns has observed that rights are often delivered in a 'routinized' way, with officers paying only 'lip service' to PACE and *Code C*.[39] This echoes long-standing concerns surrounding the inadequate, or high-paced, cautioning of children in interview.[40] No research in this jurisdiction has previously considered in detail how rights information is delivered to children in police custody.

Communicating Legal Rights: Child Suspect Experiences

Tailored Delivery? 'I do pretty much the same spiel with everyone'

Despite the emphasis in APP(DC)(CYP) on delivering tailored and intelligible rights information to children, on observation, the communication of this key information to child suspects was very variable. Some COs clearly appreciated the comprehension challenges for children and were careful to deliver the material in an accessible manner. However, I also observed COs provide the information to children at pace and in an almost robotic fashion, with no effort made to adjust the process to engage with the young person or check their understanding.[41] Here, the emphasis was on moving through the procedure efficiently and on ensuring that any evidence gathered was not rendered inadmissible through a procedural irregularity rather than on enabling participation: 'I do pretty much the same spiel with everyone—so that I know it's been done' (CO43).[42] The wording of much of what is said during the process is reasonably straightforward, or is habitually simplified by custody staff; for example, the 'Codes of Practice' are typically referred to as 'the rulebook'. However, there was also widespread

---

[38] See eg Satnam Choongh, *Policing as Social Discipline* (Clarendon Press 1997) 143.
[39] Layla Skinns, *Police Custody: Governance, Legitimacy and Reform in the Criminal Justice Process* (Willan Publishing 2011) 129.
[40] Roger Evans, 'The Conduct of Police Interviews with Juveniles', Royal Commission on Criminal Justice, Research Study No 8 (HMSO 1993); more recently, Megan PY Sim and Michael E Lamb, 'An Analysis of How the Police "Caution" Is Presented to Juvenile Suspects in England' (2018) 24(8) Psychology, Crime & Law 851–72.
[41] As also observed in Skinns, *Police Custody* (n 39).
[42] See for similar Vicky Kemp, Nigel Balmer, and Pascoe Pleasence, '"Whose Time Is It Anyway?" Factors Associated with Duration in Police Custody' (2012) Criminal Law Review 736; Jodie Blackstock and others, *Inside Police Custody: An Empirical Account of Suspects' Rights in Four Jurisdictions* (Intersentia 2013).

use, without any explanation, of terms that plainly meant little to the child hearing them, for example, 'recordable offence',[43] 'speculative search',[44] and 'PNC'.[45]

Conditions such as developmental disorders and learning disability could exacerbate comprehension difficulties significantly. The need for delivery which is adjusted to take account of child suspects' particular needs was plain. Evan, for example, explained that he had trouble holding lengthy or complex information in his head when younger: 'I'd have to read it to myself because, while they're talking, it's like, when they get to the end of the sentence, I can't even remember the start of the sentence.' Asked if he could get help with comprehension, he responded, 'If it were a good one [CO], then yeah. If not, then no.' Evan's experience illustrates how a sense of powerlessness in engaging with criminal justice professionals and youthful disinclination to ask for help or challenge a failure to assist[46] can interact problematically with additional adversities, here learning disability, to exacerbate difficulties further. We see repeatedly that the demands of the custody process serve to magnify the impact of pre-existing and intersecting adversities.

A Pared-Down Approach

There were also several surprising omissions in the communication of rights. Significantly, first, despite the requirement in *Code C*, paragraph 3.15 and the emphasis in the APP(DC)(CYP) on explaining the role,[47] I never saw a child told of their right to speak to the AA privately 'at any time'.[48] Second, in no booking in was a young person told of their right not to be held incommunicado.[49] Whilst *Code C* does not strictly require this, one might reasonably expect that a child friendly approach would encompass

---

[43] Essentially an offence punishable by imprisonment, National Police Records (Recordable Offences) Regulations 2000/1139.
[44] Checking a suspect's fingerprints or samples for a match in the police database (PACE, s 65).
[45] Police national computer.
[46] A common feature: Thomas Grisso, *Juveniles' Waiver of Rights: Legal and Psychological Competence* (Plenum Press 1981); Christine Goodwin-De Faria and Voula Marinos, 'Youth Understanding & Assertion of Legal Rights: Examining the Roles of Age and Power' (2012) 20 International Journal of Children's Rights 343.
[47] APP(DC)(CYP) (n 36) 5.
[48] *Code C* (n 10), para 3.15.
[49] ibid, para 5.1.

notification of these straightforwardly humane measures, especially where a child may be detained without any external assistance for many hours and where family members may be unable to attend as AA (as frequently occurred). I observed one young suspect (YS34) ask for a phone call on booking in. The CO refused ('I can't let you speak to just anyone') without any effort to explain or follow the process required in *Code C*, Annex B for an inspector's authorisation of refusal. Finally, I also observed no CO make any reference to a suspect's right to complain, again, despite the emphasis on doing so in the APP(DC)(CYP).[50]

There are three features common to these omissions: first, they are liable to increase demands on, or scrutiny of, custody staff if detainees are aware of the right; second, they are capable of mitigating the harshness of the experience; and third, there is no requirement for the detainee to sign the record to confirm that they have been informed. It was apparent that the rights process is too often pared down to the bare minimum required to ensure the admissibility of evidence were the process to be scrutinized at court. For many COs, concerns to ensure the participation and emotional welfare of the young suspect appeared to be overridden by practical constraints and institutional motivations. This is, to a degree, understandable, given the varied pressures under which COs frequently operate, but nonetheless problematic from a rights perspective.

Presumed Familiarity: Using 'the right words'

On observation, booking in was almost invariably preceded by the CO asking, 'Have you been here before?' or 'Have you been arrested before?' A positive answer generally triggered an even briefer recitation of their rights on the clear assumption that a child who has been in custody is already familiar with their rights and entitlements. This was reinforced by a general presumption in custody that young suspects who used the 'the right words: bail condition, CPS for decision' could be relied upon to 'understand the system' (PAA1). The repetitive nature of repeated bookings in could also reinforce this approach. Avery described trying to limit the rights process out of frustration: 'in the end and that I was just like "Yeah, I know it all, I know it all" before they've even finished their questions'. Indeed, regular

---

[50] APP(DC)(CYP) (n 36) 5.

detainees could be prey to the same assumptions as COs. Luke explained, 'I know the ins and outs of everything now because I've been in there so many times that—so it's just, I know everything.' However, young participants with regular experience of custody, including those who used 'the right words', often displayed very limited awareness of their rights, revealing how problematic reliance on evidence of previous experience could be.[51] Luke, for example, despite his confidence, had very patchy understanding of his rights, with no appreciation of critical features, such as the independence of the solicitor.

Repetition of Rights in the Presence of the AA: Unintended Consequences

The AA's presence could have a positive effect on understanding. Aidan described asking his Mum to explain any words that he did not understand during the process, whilst Tom simply found it easier to take the information in when he was told for the second time. Although routinely complied with (only Jake complained that the process was not repeated), this protection relies, for its effectiveness, on the AA arriving in good time and being able themselves to support the young person's understanding.[52] But the protection could have an unanticipated, negative effect on the most vulnerable of young suspects. Mindful of the requirement, some COs took the view that, in the absence of the AA, rights information may not be understandable at all by a particularly young suspect or one with significant dispositional vulnerabilities. Although motivated by an acknowledgement of participation concerns, this could mean that the child suspects in the greatest adversity had almost no information at all about their rights, sometimes for several hours where the attendance of the AA was delayed. For example, the CO who booked in, otherwise very sympathetically, fourteen-year-old YS28 explained, 'I made perfectly clear we won't be having him long. He's autistic as well so I haven't done rights or anything.' In fact, no AA

---

[51] As also observed in Karen Barnes and J Clare Wilson, 'Young People's Knowledge of the UK Criminal Justice System and Their Human Rights' (2008) 10 International Journal of Police Science & Management 214; Grisso, *Juveniles' Waiver of Rights* (n 46); Vicky Kemp and Dawn Watkins, 'Exploring Children's Understanding of the Legal Rights of Suspects in England and Wales' (2022) 22(3) Youth Justice 320.

[52] Discussed in detail in Chapter 4. See for similar Hillary B Farber, 'The Role of the Parent/Guardian in Juvenile Custodial Interrogations: Friend or Foe?' (2004) 41 American Criminal Law Review 1277.

was available and YS28 spent seven hours in the cell, without any attempt to explain his rights and entitlements, before being bailed.

The Notice of Rights and Entitlements: The 'long, boring piece of paper'

During observations, the notice was routinely 'provided', either being handed to the suspect or pointed out as available on the booking-in desk. However, it was notable that, frequently, young suspects did not even glance at the paper. Even where it was handed to the young person, they almost invariably left it on the custody desk, an approach confirmed by the majority of young participants. Rarely did the CO encourage the young suspect to take it with them; indeed, often there was a discouraging accompanying comment: 'That long boring piece of paper outlines your rights' (CA to YS27), 'You'll probably rip it up but I've got to give it to you' (CO to YS43). COs seemed generally unconcerned by neglect of the notice: 'it's very, very rare that they take the rights and entitlements notice—they're not interested' (CO25).

Some COs expressed an assumption that the AA would read through the notice with a child, although only Tyler, of the young participants, could recall this having occurred. Other COs suggested that they would 'go over it' with the young suspect themselves to check their understanding (eg CO29), although I did not observe this occurring either. Commonly, a CO might mention the availability of bedding and food and drink, perhaps reading material, but it was rare for young participants to suggest that they had been given an explanation of the notice. Unusually, Riley described having been given time to read the notice: 'They just pass you the paper and say, "Read it." ... At the end of it, they turn around and go, "Did you understand all that or do you want me to go into any further detail?"' His response was fairly predictable: 'You just say you understand it ... Even if I don't understand, I'd say I understand ... Just to skip time.'

The notices encountered on observations were in a format jointly approved by the Home Office, the Legal Aid Agency, and the Law Society.[53]

---

[53] Either the ten-page June 2014 version (F1 and 2) or the October 2014 version, which condenses the same information into four close-typed pages (F3). The most recent version is similar, <https://www.gov.uk/government/publications/notice-of-rights-and-entitlements-english/notice-of-rights-and-entitlements-english> accessed 16 August 2023.

Although somewhat lacking in respect of the AA role, the notices otherwise generally included all the required information. It is their accessibility which is of greatest concern. The longer, ten-page June 2014 version resembled a GCSE exam paper in format. The shorter, four-page October 2014 version was dauntingly close-typed. Unsurprisingly, most young participants suggested that, even if they picked it up, they did not read the notice: 'it confuses' (Logan), contains 'all big words' (Luke), or was just 'boring' (Aaron). Some simply were not in a state of mind to read a long and complex document; others were more creative: 'I just make paper aeroplanes' (Rezar).[54]

In 2011, the CJJI recommended that an 'age-appropriate' version of the notice be introduced.[55] No age-appropriate versions were in regular use in the custody suites observed in 2016,[56] although I encountered ample supplies of two 'easyread' formulations of the notice during observations.[57] Despite the stipulation in *Code C*, para 3.3A, I did not observe either 'easyread' notice being provided to a child suspect. Indeed, staff responses to easyread versions were very striking. Some officers confidently asserted that an easyread version was not available, despite (in one block) there being boxes of the document stacked around the booking-in desk. Others were simply dismissive of the document, one referring to it as 'The Beano' (CO23), whilst the approach of some others seemed to stem from a reluctance to acknowledge young suspects' particular needs, easyread being 'really geared towards vulnerable adults' (CO41) ('I don't routinely give it to juveniles—it's for those with ADHD, LD [learning disability], Autism,

---

[54] See for similar indifference Vicky Kemp and Jacqueline Hodgson, 'Chapter 4. England and Wales Empirical Findings' in Miet Vanderhallen and others (eds), *Interrogating Young Suspects: Procedural Safeguards from an Empirical Perspective*, Vol 2 (Intersentia 2016).

[55] CJJI (n 32) 33.

[56] There is now at least one nationally available age-appropriate notice: 'So You've Been Arrested: A Guide to Custody for Young People' (2017) <https://www.gov.uk/government/publications/notice-of-rights-and-entitlements-easy-read> accessed 16 August 2023. At the time of writing, video information is now available and is starting to be used in some force areas: National County Lines Coordination Centre, 'Rights and Entitlements in Police Custody Video—England and Wales' <https://www.youtube.com/watch?v=3oKMWe-_fXc&t=27s> accessed 16 August 2023. However, its use is not widespread or mandated, and more recent fieldwork in 2020–21 suggests that the printed notice remains in general use: Vicky Kemp and others, *Examining the Impact of PACE on the Detention and Questioning of Child Suspects by the Police in England and Wales* (Nuffield Foundation, 25 May 2023) <https://www.nuffieldfoundation.org/project/impact-of-pace-on-the-detention-and-questioning-of-young-suspects> accessed 3 October 2023.

[57] One forty-four-page version produced by Hertfordshire Police and another ten-sided A5 leaflet entitled, 'You Have Been Arrested—This Will Tell You What Will Happen'. The latter covered slightly different information to the approved notice.

Down Syndrome' (CO30)), despite the frequent disclosure during risk assessments of such conditions by young suspects.

However, in this reluctance to provide an easyread version, it is possible to glimpse signs of a more concerning motivation. Previous research has suggested that inaccessible communication of rights may be a 'ploy' to prevent take-up of those rights, particularly the right to legal advice.[58] Whilst mindful of the limtiations on what a busy CO can effectively convey to a child suspect in the circumstances, there are some indications that staff may not be particularly proactive in promoting rights awareness because ignorance of rights suits them. As CO41 observed in rejecting the easyread version, 'it's too prescriptive—it raises expectations and probably we can't meet them'. CA1 described the irritation of an engaged suspect making demands from the notice: 'I find it quite annoying. "But it says here" ... they (suspects) go on and on.' Not infrequently, young suspects who made no demands on staff were described as 'good as gold' whilst those who pushed for their entitlements tended to be framed as 'demanding' (CA26).

This analysis of the communication of legal rights reveals a range of issues which undermine its effectiveness and challenge young suspect rights awareness, particularly the failure to adjust the process to accommodate the child's youth and capabilities and an undue readiness to assume familiarity. The importance for effective participation of officers showing 'due regard' for the child's 'vulnerabilities and capacities' and reducing 'feelings of intimidation and inhibition', as identified in *Panovits v Cyprus*,[59] is amply illustrated. However, two features emerge as preventing child friendly approaches. In the first place, the legal framework is arguably inadequate in failing to differentiate effectively between the approach required for children and that for adults. Limiting adjustment to the simple presence of an AA for rights delivery is liable to be ineffective, as I explore in more detail in Chapter 4. Second, within such a scant legal framework, where time is scarce and resources limited, we see that the rights process is liable to become pared down, reduced to a routinized exercise focused on shoring up any evidence which may be obtained rather than on the child's welfare and participation.

Unsurprisingly, given these findings, very few young participants had an awareness of their rights and entitlements beyond the 'continuing rights'.

---

[58] Blackstock and others (n 42); Kemp, Balmer, and Pleasence, '"Whose Time Is It Anyway?"' (n 42).
[59] *Panovits v Cyprus* (n 3), [67].

No young participant was aware of the right to consult privately with an AA at any time, whilst the ability to make a phone call, to have time in the exercise yard, or take a shower were appreciated by few participants and engaged by even fewer. (I address the uptake of these rights and entitlements in detail in Chapter 5.) However, awareness of rights is only part of the picture, a necessary but insufficient pre-requisite for active engagement of those rights.[60] I turn now to explore the child suspects' exercise of their legal rights in greater depth in relation to the uptake of legal advice.

Exercising the Right to Legal Advice: Procedure and Existing Literature

The right to legal assistance in navigating the investigatory stage is 'fundamental'[61] and an essential element of fair trial guarantees under Article 6(3)(C) of the European Convention on Human Rights (ECHR), applicable in the pre-charge detention period by virtue of what is now an established line of authority.[62] Article 37(d) of the UNCRC similarly requires every detained child to have 'prompt access to legal and other appropriate assistance',[63] and the UNCRC Committee has made clear that the child must have 'access to legal or other appropriate assistance' from the 'outset of the proceedings'[64] and 'during questioning', in addition to a 'parent, legal guardian or other appropriate adult'.[65] A person purporting to provide 'other appropriate assistance' must have 'sufficient knowledge of the legal aspects of the child justice process and receive appropriate training'.[66] Initially recommended in police custody as a counterweight to the increase of police powers enshrined by PACE,[67] domestically, the right has assumed even greater importance since

---

[60] Goodwin-De Faria and Marinos (n 46).
[61] *R v Samuel* [1988] QB 615 (CA), [627].
[62] *Murray v UK* App no 18731/91, 8 February 1996, 22 EHRR 29; *Salduz v Turkey* App no 36391/02, 27 November 2008, (2009) 49 EHRR 19; *Cadder v HM Advocate* [2010] UKSC 43, [2010] 1 WLR 2601. Although for a degree of retreat see *Ibrahim and Others v UK* App nos 50541/08, 50571/08, 50573/08, and 40351/09, 13 September 2016.
[63] See also ECHR, Art 40(2)(b)(ii).
[64] General Comment No 24 (n 4) 49.
[65] ibid 60.
[66] ibid 52.
[67] Hannah Quirk, *The Rise and Fall of the Right of Silence* (Routledge 2017); Royal Commission on Criminal Procedure (RCCP), 'Report (Cmnd 8092)' (HMSO 1981). There had been a common law right to legal advice under the Judge's Rules, but it was rarely exercised and infrequently facilitated.

the introduction of adverse inferences from silence in the Criminal Justice and Public Order Act 1994. This development renders decision-making around the right of silence more difficult,[68] especially for children and other vulnerable suspects.[69]

In England and Wales, all suspects have the right to free legal advice before and during police interview, but it must be requested, even by a child as young as ten.[70] This is a challenging decision for a child requiring a base-level understanding of their legal jeopardy, the demands that will be made of them in the process, and the role of the legal representative. The child's ability to engage meaningfully with the offer of legal advice is of particular importance given the emphasis on diversion for children and the imposition of out-of-court disposals (OOCD) (including community resolutions).[71] This has three specific repercussions for child suspects. First, in most cases, in order to receive an OOCD, the child is required to make an admission, generally in police interview, as to their commission of an offence.[72] Although an investigating officer might make this plain in advance of interview, this is not inevitable, and such a requirement is unlikely to be apparent to the child or a family member acting as AA (a 'familial AA'). Thus legal advice is key in terms of enabling a child to access all disposal options. Second, resolving the case by way of an OOCD is desirable from a police perspective because it involves less paperwork than compiling a file for prosecution. This incentivizes the use of pressurizing tactics on child suspects. Yet, because children are likely to be arrested for less serious offences, they are more likely to be interviewed by officers without advanced interview training, which would balance such institutional motivations and enable the more careful approach required to support the child's vulnerabilities.[73] Third, because of the prevalence of OOCDs and the high rate of guilty pleas to obtain referral orders,[74] there is less chance that the interview

---

[68] Blackstock and others (n 42).
[69] Quirk (n 67); Isabel CH Clare, Gisli H Gudjonsson, and Philippe M Harari, 'Understanding of the Current Police Caution (England and Wales)' (1998) 8 Journal of Community & Applied Social Psychology 323.
[70] PACE, s 58(1).
[71] Crime and Disorder Act 1998, s 66ZA and 66ZB.
[72] With the exception of 'Outcome 22'—a form of no further action not requiring an admission.
[73] Mandatory interview training (PIP1) does not address the specific needs of child suspects. See Kate Gooch and Piers von Berg, 'What Happens in the Beginning, Matters in the End: Achieving Best Evidence with Child Suspects in the Police Station' (2019) 19(2) Youth Justice 85.
[74] Discussed in the preface.

itself will be scrutinized by a court. The importance of the child having access to a solicitor[75] in police custody, available to address and prevent coercion when it arises, could not be plainer.

What, then, is the procedure to enable the child to engage legal advice? Every suspect must be explicitly informed of the availability of 'free independent legal advice',[76] and COs must not do or say anything 'with the intention of dissuading' them from taking legal advice.[77] Where legal advice is declined, the officer should request, and record, the reason for refusal and 'should point out that the right includes the right to speak with a solicitor on the telephone'.[78] The suspect should also be reminded that they can speak to a solicitor on the telephone, that the right to legal advice is 'continuing', and that they can change their mind at any time.[79]

Policy acknowledges that young suspects might find making a decision about legal advice challenging. Thus, the AA can request legal advice, even where the child has refused, although the child can still choose not to consult with the solicitor who attends.[80] Additionally, the APP emphasizes the importance of ensuring that children are aware of their right to legal representation[81] and requires COs to be trained to enable them to ensure that young suspects and their AA 'fully comprehend the possible benefits and importance of seeking legal advice'.[82]

However, *Code C* places no duty on COs or arresting officers (AOs) to provide fuller information about the allegation or the available evidence at this stage to enable them to make an informed assessment about exercising the right. If the suspect opts for legal advice, then the solicitor, generally in a 'pre-interview briefing', must be provided with 'sufficient information' to enable them to understand the nature of the allegation and why the child is suspected of having committed it.[83] But notably, where the child is unrepresented, APP advises, 'Investigators should not normally provide

---

[75] Representation is often provided by accredited police station representatives rather than qualified solicitors, but for ease, the terms 'solicitor' or 'legal representative' are used interchangeably.
[76] *Code C* (n 10), para 6.1. This can be delayed in certain circumstances; see *Code C*, Annex B.
[77] ibid, para 6.4.
[78] ibid, para 6.5.
[79] ibid, para 6.5.
[80] ibid, para 6.5A.
[81] APP(DC)(CYP) (n 36) 5.
[82] ibid 5.
[83] *Code C* (n 10), para 11.1A. See also PACE, *Code G*, 'Notes for Guidance' (NFG) 3; *R v Roble* [1997] 1 WLUK 233, [1997] Crim LR 449; *R v Nottle* [2004] EWCA Crim 599.

self-represented suspects with material prior to interview as they may not, without context, fully appreciate the evidential value of the material provided.'[84] This is somewhat at odds with the approach urged by the UNCRC Committee, which stresses the need for 'all practitioners' to support children to 'comprehend the charges and possible consequences and options', including children who are to be diverted.[85]

Quantitative research has revealed strikingly low uptake of legal advice amongst child suspects in England and Wales. Kemp and others, analysing custody record data from 2009, found that 43% of children who went on to be charged did not request to see a solicitor and that ten-to-thirteen-year-olds were the least likely of all age groups to request and receive legal advice.[86] More recent data is not currently available for child suspects, but a slow increase in legal advice request rates for adults has been observed lately.[87] Earlier research provides some insights into the potential drivers of low uptake amongst children. Phillips and Brown's Home Office survey found that the strongest single predictor of uptake of legal advice was offence type, with low 'juvenile'[88] uptake (in 33% of cases compared with 39% for adults) being associated with their arrest for less serious offences in comparison to adults.[89] The presence of a familial AA has also been linked to refusal,[90] particularly when combined with assurances of swift release.[91] Indeed, Medford and colleagues' police interview study revealed that, in

---

[84] APP (Investigation) (Investigative Interviewing) (first published 23 October 2013, updated 26 October 2022) 24 <www.college.police.uk/app/investigation/investigative-interviewing/investigative-interviewing> accessed 16 August 2023 (APP(I)(II)).

[85] General Comment No 24 (n 4) 46–47.

[86] Vicky Kemp, Pascoe Pleasence, and Nigel J Balmer, 'Children, Young People and Requests for Police Station Legal Advice: 25 Years On from PACE' (2011) 11 Youth Justice 28.

[87] Vicky Kemp, 'Digital Legal Rights: Exploring Detainees' Understanding of the Right to a Lawyer and Potential Barriers to Accessing Legal Advice' (2020) 2 Criminal Law Review 129, finding an average of 56% of detainees requesting legal advice based on review of 88,304 custody records from a 7-month period in 2017.

[88] This research, and that of Sarah Medford, Gisli H Gudjonsson, and John Pearse, 'The Efficacy of the Appropriate Adult Safeguard during Police Interviewing' (2003) 8 Law and Criminological Psychology 253, was conducted before the raising of the upper age limit in PACE of a 'juvenile' from sixteen to seventeen.

[89] Coretta Phillips and David C Brown, 'Entry into the Criminal Justice System: A Survey of Police Arrests and Their Outcomes', Home Office Research Study 185 (Home Office 1998). For offence seriousness, and strength of the case, as factors in adult waiver see Layla Skinns, ' "Let's Get It Over With": Early Findings on the Factors Affecting Detainees' Access to Custodial Legal Advice' (2009) 19(1) Policing & Society 58; Kemp, 'Digital Legal Rights' (n 87).

[90] Phillips and Brown (n 89); Tom Bucke and David Brown, 'In Police Custody: Police Powers and Suspects' Rights under the Revised PACE Codes of Practice', Home Office Research Study 174 (Home Office 1997).

[91] Kemp, Pleasence, and Balmer, '25 Years On' (n 86).

contrast to the position for adults, the presence of an AA for a child did not increase the likelihood of a solicitor being present.[92]

In adult suspect accounts, concerns about delay caused by obtaining legal advice are prominent,[93] and indeed, the data, to an extent, bears out their concerns.[94] Lack of appreciation of the benefits of legal advice, particularly misconceptions about the need for a solicitor for a suspect who is innocent, also feature in adult accounts of waiver.[95] Existing evidence on how children understand the offer of legal advice in police custody in England and Wales is very limited, tending to involve very few child participants[96] or to have had a very much wider frame of reference.[97] Kemp and Watkins' study is a welcome exception. Their young participants, including children and young people with and without experience of police custody, displayed shortcomings in their understanding of the value of legal advice similar to those of adult suspects, although they were also concerned about the cost of legal advice and tended not to appreciate the 'fundamental and inalienable' nature of their legal rights.[98] There is, however, a wealth of North American psychological research in this area. This suggests that, while most children might understand the straightforward notion that lawyers are present as 'helpers',[99] many may not consider that someone would be available to speak for them personally.[100] In particular, appreciation of the concept of adviser/client privilege appeared generally not to be well developed amongst children, particularly younger children,[101] who were less

---

[92] Medford, Gudjonsson, and Pearse (n 88) 262.
[93] See Choongh (n 38); Bucke and Brown (n 90); Skinns, '"Let's Get It Over With"' (n 89); Kemp, 'Digital Legal Rights' (n 87).
[94] Kemp, Balmer, and Pleasence, '"Whose Time Is It Anyway?"' (n 42). Extended detention periods associated with legal advice were also observed in Phillips and Brown (n 89) and Layla Skinns, '"I'm a Detainee; Get Me Out of Here": Predictors of Access to Custodial Legal Advice in Public and Privatized Police Custody Areas in England and Wales' (2009) 49 British Journal of Criminology 399.
[95] Skinns, '"Let's Get It Over With"' (n 89); Vicky Kemp and Nigel Balmer, 'Criminal Defence Services: Users' Perspectives: Interim Report' (Nottingham Legal Services Research Centre 2008); Kemp, 'Digital Legal Rights' (n 87).
[96] See eg Kemp and Hodgson (n 54), which included a focus group involving only five young people.
[97] Neal Hazel, Ann Hagell, and Laura Brazier, *Young Offenders' Perceptions of Their Experiences in the Criminal Justice System* (Economic and Social Research Council 2003).
[98] Kemp and Watkins (n 51) 326.
[99] Michele Peterson-Badali and Rona Abramovitch, 'Children's Knowledge of the Legal System: Are They Competent to Instruct Legal Counsel?' (1992) Canadian Journal of Criminology 130.
[100] Thomas Grisso, 'The Competence of Adolescents as Trial Defendants' (1997) 3 Psychology, Public Policy, & Law 3.
[101] Peterson-Badali and Abramovitch (n 99).

likely to understand that privilege prevents disclosure to parents,[102] the police, or judges.[103] As with the exercising of rights more generally, children experiencing additional adversities have been observed to be more likely to waive their right to legal advice, particularly children with attention deficit and hyperactivity issues.[104]

Ethnicity has also been identified as a factor in both understanding the role of, and trust in, a legal adviser. In a US context, Pierce and Brodsky found that Black children demonstrated poorer understanding of the role of their legal representative, even when accounting for differences in intellectual functioning and understanding. Black, Asian, and minority ethnic children were less likely to have sufficient trust in their representative to disclose information to them, whilst high-functioning Black children showed particularly depleted levels of trust.[105] Similar depletion of trust in legal professionals has been noted in Black, Asian, and minority ethnic adults in England and Wales.[106]

Finally, there are indications of a police cultural angle to low uptake. Holdaway found that solicitors were included within the group of unwelcome 'challengers' in the police station.[107] Early research post PACE suggested that the police may prefer suspects not to have legal advice[108] and that solicitors were considered to interfere with case construction objectives.[109] There are also long-standing concerns about police 'ploys' to discourage uptake by suspects generally by delivering oral rights information incomprehensibly or unduly quickly or through more explicit efforts to dissuade.[110]

---

[102] Pierce and Brodsky (n 19).

[103] Michele Peterson-Badali and others, 'Young People's Experience of the Canadian Youth Justice System: Interacting with Police and Legal Counsel' (1999) 17(4) Behavioral Sciences & Law 455.

[104] Jodi L Viljoen, Jessica Klaver, and Ronald Roesch, 'Legal Decisions of Preadolescent and Adolescent Defendants: Predictors of Confessions, Pleas, Communication with Attorneys, and Appeals' (2005) 29 Law & Human Behavior 253.

[105] ibid; Pierce and Brodsky (n 19).

[106] David Lammy, 'The Lammy Review. An Independent Review into the Treatment of, and Outcomes for, Black, Asian and Minority Ethnic Individuals in the Criminal Justice System' (Ministry of Justice (MoJ) 2017); Phil Bowen, *Building Trust: How Our Courts Can Improve the Criminal Court Experience for Black, Asian, and Minority Ethnic Defendants* (Centre for Justice Innovation 2017).

[107] Simon Holdaway, *Inside the British Police: A Force at Work* (Blackwell 1983) 71–77.

[108] See eg Andrew Sanders, Lee Bridges, and Adele Mulvaney, *Advice and Assistance at Police Stations and the 24 Hour Duty Solicitor Scheme* (Lord Chancellor's Department 1989).

[109] Michael McConville, Andrew Sanders, and Robert Leng, *The Case for the Prosecution* (Routledge 1991).

[110] See eg Lee Bridges and Andrew Sanders, 'Access to Legal Advice and Police Malpractice' [1990] Criminal Law Review 494. See also Kemp, Balmer, and Pleasence, '"Whose Time Is It Anyway?"' (n 42); Vicky Kemp, 'Effective Police Station Legal Advice, Country Report 2: England and Wales' (University of Nottingham 2018).

Indeed, solicitors giving evidence to the All Party Parliamentary Group for Children (APPGC) described how police had 'actively encouraged children to cede their rights when in custody, telling the child that they would be released far more quickly if they did not ask for legal representation'.[111]

Exercising the Right to Legal Advice: Child Suspect Experiences

Uptake of legal advice within the young participant group, and those young suspects tracked on observation, was broadly in line with Kemp's 2009 findings. Nearly half of young participants reported never having requested a solicitor or having waived legal advice on one or more occasions. Girls were marginally more likely than boys to have declined (five out of eight waiving the right), and young Black, Asian, and minority ethnic participants were also somewhat more likely than their White peers to have refused legal advice (eight out of fourteen refusing the right).[112] Younger participants were also less likely to opt for advice: seven out of twelve ten-to-fifteen-year-olds had waived legal advice on at least one occasion. Of the forty-three young suspects tracked on observations who were interviewed by the police (or for whom an interview was planned), twenty-four refused initially (with eight of those accepting legal advice only when it was requested as part of a blanket requirement by non-familial AAs, that is, those attending as part of a local scheme where a familial AA was unavailable.

Understanding the Right: 'I didn't even know what really a solicitor is'

The inadequacies of the process by which children are informed of their rights are heavily implicated in the limited exercise of legal rights and particularly in low uptake of legal advice. The vast majority of young participants remembered having been asked if they wanted a solicitor or legal

---

[111] All Party Parliamentary Group for Children (APPGC), '"It's All about Trust": Building Good Relationships between Children and the Police. Report of the Inquiry Held by the All Party Parliamentary Group for Children, 2013–2014 (National Children's Bureau 2014) 14. See for similar concerns Kemp and Hodgson (n 54).
[112] Echoing findings in Vicky Kemp, *Transforming Legal Aid: Access to Criminal Defence Services* (Legal Services Commission 2010).

advice at booking in, and certainly every rights process that I observed included the offer of legal advice in some form—sometimes in language close to that in *Code C*, referencing 'free and independent legal advice', sometimes a simple enquiry as to whether the child would like a 'solicitor'. For some, the use of 'jargon' (Harper) could be a barrier to rights comprehension and exercise. A small number of young participants simply struggled to understand the terminology—the words 'solicitor' and 'legal advice' used without clarification could cause difficulty, especially when employed separately. Or they found the offer just too alien to engage with: 'at first I said no innit 'cos I didn't know what to say' (Azade).[113]

However, more commonly, it was clear that whilst young participants were generally able follow the syntax of the rights recitation and comprehend the sense of most of the words used, they were often unable to engage with the meaning and significance of their rights and entitlements. For example, young participants might understand that they were entitled to look at the 'rulebook' (the Codes of Practice), but they often did not appreciate why they may wish to do so, or how that information might be of use, or have any belief that they could effectively challenge their treatment. Jake encapsulated this difficulty, describing his grasp as 'not really' understanding. Kyle, for example, explained his decision to decline legal advice: 'I didn't even know what really a solicitor is ... I knew like they try and help you but I didn't really know like the whole gist of it.' CO29 similarly reflected on the rights process: 'They understand it—but I don't think they understand the importance of it.' This accords with a developmental psychological appreciation that immaturity may affect decision-making, not by reason of cognitive deficiency but through immature judgement and reasoning.[114]

Natural developmental immaturity played a further role in challenging a deeper appreciation of legal rights. Not only could the exhaustion and frustration of the drawn-out waiting process and the lengthy risk assessment (RA) significantly undermine the child's ability to focus on, and take in, the rights and entitlements information, but also, commonly, young participants said that they avoided asking questions or revealing a lack of understanding because this would simply prolong the process and might delay release. Malik described the frustration that builds up: 'Yeah, so they're asking me these fucked up questions man. Just do the thing, take me in the

---

[113] See for similar in all-ages research ibid; Kemp and Balmer (n 95).
[114] Elizabeth Scott and Thomas Grisso, 'The Evolution of Adolescence: A Developmental Perspective on Juvenile Justice Reform' (1997) 88 Journal of Criminal Law & Criminology 137.

cell, interview me, let me out. Why take so long?' Here, youthful impatience is exacerbated by lack of knowledge; few young participants appreciated the separation of the CO from the investigation process and that the length of the booking-in process has little bearing, if any, on the timing of their release.

Limited Appreciation of the Nature and Purpose of Legal Advice: 'I don't need one'

In particular, the majority of young participants displayed a very limited appreciation of the nature and purpose of legal advice, and this was a significant driver of refusal. As observed in North American research,[115] young participants had a minimal understanding of solicitors as capable of helping but little more. This frequently proved insufficient to enable them to make an informed choice about exercising the right. As a result, young participants often failed to appreciate the consequences of the decision to waive legal advice, to understand what they were passing up, and thus a prevalent reason given by young participants for declining advice was 'I don't need one' (Riley).[116] Indeed, several COs described this as the most frequently expressed reason for refusal, and it was regularly repeated by young suspects on observation, often linked to concerns about delay or advanced as an additional explanation for waiver on that basis.

For a significant number of young participants, this assessment rested on a judgement about the seriousness of the allegation, on the premise that a trivial allegation does not justify the delay a solicitor will cause:

> Nothing's gonna come of it. It's gonna be either a fine or a slap on the wrist. I knew that, so there's no point getting that whole ... If you ask for a solicitor, you've gotta wait for one to come available—back to your cell.
> (Simon)

This explains, to an extent, the association of waiver with low seriousness noted in previous studies.[117] Other misconceptions feeding into this line of

---

[115] Peterson-Badali and Abramovitch (n 99).
[116] See for similar in respect of adults Kemp, 'Digital Legal Rights' (n 87).
[117] Phillips and Brown (n 89); Bucke and Brown (n 90). See also Kemp and Watkins (n 51).

refusal included that legal advice was not required if you were 'guilty' or intended to make admissions: 'it's just a waste of time, especially if I'm admitting to it anyway ... I don't think it's needed really' (Hudson).[118] Whilst, by contrast, some others took the view that a solicitor was not necessary if you were 'innocent'. This was noted by COs to be a particularly common reason for declining. Young participants tended to reject the idea that lawyers could play a part in protecting the innocent, often advancing a concerning, but age-consistent, sense of invulnerability.[119] Riley's rejection of the need for a solicitor when wrongly arrested was fairly typical: 'No. I wouldn't have been arsed 'cause you're not provin' it was me 'cause it wasn't me'. As the *Confait* case so starkly illustrates, the integrity of pre-charge procedures is key to avoiding miscarriages of justice.[120] For the innocent and the guilty, the solicitor can play a key role in securing the right outcome.

An Appreciation of the Consequences of Waiving Legal Advice?

However, a child cannot sensibly pursue any of these lines of reasoning, assessing seriousness or likely guilt or innocence, without a reasonable understanding of their legal jeopardy. To be able to identify one's innocence or guilt reliably, the child must have a basic understanding of what behaviour is criminal. However, in line with research findings indicating significant misunderstandings about common offences,[121] young participants often failed to grasp their liability arising from less obvious offences, such as handling, whilst more technically worded offences, such as 'being on enclosed premises' (Jake) or public order offences—'the sections' (Rezar)—remained thoroughly obscure. Issues of secondary liability, commonly encountered by child suspects, who are more likely than adults to

---

[118] See for similar Kemp and Hodgson (n 54).
[119] Cauffman and Steinberg (n 18); Sarah-Jayne Blakemore, 'Avoiding Social Risk in Adolescence' (2018) 27 Current Directions in Psychological Science 116; Sean M Kassin, 'On the Psychology of Confessions: Does *Innocence* Put *Innocents* at Risk?' (2005) American Psychologist 215.
[120] Roger Evans, 'Police Interrogations and the Royal Commission on Criminal Justice' (1994) 4 Policing & Society 73.
[121] Miranda Bevan, 'Investigating Young People's Awareness and Understanding of the Criminal Justice System: An Exploratory Study' (Howard League for Penal Reform 2016) <https://howardleague.org/wp-content/uploads/2016/06/Investigating-young-people%E2%80%99s-awareness-and-understanding-of-the-criminal-justice-system.pdf> accessed 16 August 2023.

be arrested in relation to group activity,[122] could be particularly challenging. Although the case of *R v Jogee*[123] has simplified the law of joint enterprise, young participant accounts suggest (unsurprisingly) that secondary liability arising out of involvement as one of a group is not widely understood by children. Elijah, for example, described an occasion when he had declined legal advice: 'Like, when I was in trouble for bein' with my mates, I was thinkin', "Why do I need a solicitor for this?" It's my mate's problem, not mine. All I'm bein' asked is why was I with him.' Refusal of legal advice on such a basis is deeply troubling.

Unsurprisingly, given the limited legal requirements, information provided to child suspects about the offence for which they had been arrested tended to be very brief. Invariably, the name of the offence would be given, typically in legal terms; for example, 'You've been arrested on suspicion of common assault' (YS1). But frequently, no further explanation was provided about the nature or severity of the allegation or the strength of the evidence against the child. Frequently, a nod or mumbled 'yes' to the question, 'Do you know why you've been arrested?' appeared to shortcut the process even further. Inevitably, it is unlikely that the CO would be appraised of the details of the investigation, but AOs and investigating officers (IOs) tended not to be much more forthcoming. At the time of making the decision about legal advice, I did not observe children being provided with any explanation which might enable the child to have a meaningful appreciation, as proposed in *Panovits v Cyprus*, of 'the nature of the investigation' or of 'what is at stake for him or her, including the significance of any penalty which may be imposed'.[124] In line with the APP,[125] on observation, IOs did not routinely provide unrepresented suspects pre-interview disclosure or any indication of the likely penalties and their ramifications.[126]

The lack of information is problematic for the child's ability to engage with the offer of legal advice. Frequently, without the support of their AA at the initial booking in, young participants described how they reached their own conclusions about the nature and strength of the investigation to inform their decision. These conclusions were based on a range of

---

[122] Asha Goldweber and others, 'The Development of Criminal Style in Adolescence and Young Adulthood: Separating the Lemmings from the Loners' (2011) 40 Journal of Youth and Adolescence 332.
[123] [2016] UKSC 8, [2017] AC 387.
[124] *Panovits v Cyprus* (n 3), [67].
[125] APP(I)(II) (n 84).
[126] See for similar Kemp and Hodgson (n 54).

assumptions, such as how long it took for them to be arrested or the outcome they had received in respect of a previous, but often wholly dissimilar, allegation. Their assessments of any penalty likely to be imposed were often similarly uninformed. Kyle, for example, summarized his assessment of one previous arrest: 'I knew it was a serious thing but it's not like I were gonna get locked up or anything.' The allegation transpired to relate to an assault in the street with a claw hammer which, depending on previous convictions, might easily have resulted in a custodial sentence.

Being Able to Reason Logically about the Options: The Impact of the Process

A number of young participants described not engaging in any meaningful way with the offer of legal advice. For some, anxiety about bigger issues, such as the impact of the arrest on family relations or future prospects, overwhelmed their attention, drowning out concerns about the legal process. Some others were simply not in a frame of mind to give any sensible consideration to the offer. Often, they were still in a highly emotional state as a result of the arrest experience or struggling to contain their anxiety about what the detention process would involve. Even as early as their arrival at the booking-in desk, some young people were too exhausted to engage, sometimes having spent an hour or more waiting to be processed. Worryingly, a small group of young participants did not consider the offer at all because they simply did not care about the legal outcome. Elijah, for example, considered legal advice 'just extra oxygen wasted': 'Like, as soon as I'm in there, I'm in there. I wish they would let me get on with my time and give me my punishment and then we get it done and they leave it. I don't really care 'bout the legal advice.'

A Choice Free from Coercion? 'I just wanted to get out'

The punitive experience of arrest, the distress of the early custody process, and, for more experienced young participants, the anticipation of harsh detention conditions (discussed in detail in Chapter 6) created in many young participants a desperation to leave the custody block. In combination with young participants' naturally developmentally immature judgement, particularly their inability to defer gratification or to assess long-term effects,[127] this desperation had an overwhelming impact on their decision-making such that it could not sensibly be described as free or voluntary. By far the most significant factor in declining legal advice was the delay which a solicitor was considered inevitably to cause: 'I didn't want one … I just wanted to get out' (Alex). This accords with findings in all-ages and adult research,[128] but it is the extremely limited tolerance for even a modest delay amongst young participants that was most striking. Hudson's reasoning was not unusual: 'they take too long. It's just an extra like hour, 45 minutes that I'm gonna be in there so.' Rebecca Helm has noted similarly powerful incentives to plead guilty created by the chance to get out of custody and to avoid the lengthy and expensive criminal trial process. As she observes, circumstances can 'subvert the voluntary nature of a decision, particularly for those who are vulnerable and therefore lack choice in a meaningful way'.[129]

Steering

The CO is plainly in a powerful position when it comes to steering a child towards, or away from, taking legal advice since they control the information provided to the child, at least in advance of the AA's arrival. In contrast to suggestions of the use of deliberate ploys in earlier literature, there was, in this study, very limited evidence of explicit attempts to dissuade young suspects from taking legal advice.[130] Nonetheless, there are two regards in which COs might be said to steer the child towards waiver: by implicit dissuasion and by a notable disinclination to encourage children to opt into legal advice. In respect of the latter, despite the requirement in APP(CYP) 3.3, I did not observe COs ensuring that child suspects fully understood the 'possible benefits and importance of seeking legal advice'. Whilst CO approaches varied, generally any explanation of the role for child suspects tended to be brief. YS43, for example, asked the CO what a solicitor was, and the CO responded briefly, 'Gives you legal advice'. Unilluminated, YS43 declined. In respect of implicit dissuasion, it was notable how often a child's

---

[127] Lawrence Steinberg and others, 'Around the World, Adolescence Is a Time of Heightened Sensation Seeking and Immature Self-Regulation' (2018) 21(2) Developmental Science e12532.
[128] Choongh (n 38); Kemp, 'Digital Legal Rights' (n 87).
[129] Rebecca K Helm, 'Conviction by Consent? Vulnerability, Autonomy and Conviction by Guilty Plea' (2019) 83 Journal of Criminal Law (Hertford) 161, 165.
[130] For discussion see Miranda Bevan, 'Young Suspect Perspectives: An Exploration of the Factors Affecting the Uptake of Legal Advice by Children in Police Custody' (2020) 8 Criminal Law Review 686, 695.

reasons for refusing legal advice prompted no further advice or challenge. The following exchange was typical:

CO: You're entitled to a solicitor—free and independent legal advice. Do you know what that is?
YS19: Yeah.
CO: Do you know what they do? You understand about legal advice?
YS19: They just make everything longer.
CO: I can't comment on it. We'll put you down 'no' for now and you can go through it again with your Mum.

Opting for legal advice can extend detention periods significantly. However, on observation, this was rare,[131] and generally the detention times of the young suspects that I tracked were not significantly extended, if at all, as a result of a request for legal advice. COs readily acknowledged that lengthy delays before interview were frequently caused by issues with the investigation rather than the attendance of the solicitor—something long appreciated.[132] Yet, a CO would rarely challenge delay as a reason for refusal or explain about likely investigation timescales. For those who were regularly detained, the notion that delay was caused by solicitors was often reinforced by a subsequent lack of explanation about the true reasons for lengthy detention periods.

When I questioned this approach, several COs explained that they are prohibited by *Code C* from advising suspects to take legal advice or, indeed, making any overtly positive observations about such support. CO41 explained, 'If the young person was here for rape, first time in the police station—I can't advise. I'll just repeat again—"It's free and it's independent".' *Code C*, paragraph 6.4 (and 'Notes for Guidance' (NFG) 6ZA) certainly prevent the CO from doing or saying anything which might dissuade a suspect from taking legal advice, and *Code C*, paragraph 6.5 prohibits the CO pressing a suspect, who has clearly refused advice, on their reasons for waiver. However, neither provision prevents the CO fostering understanding or facilitating uptake as the APP(CYP) requires. Nor is the suggestion that COs are hidebound by the language of *Code C* sustainable, given

---

[131] Often caused by duty solicitors taking on multiple cases at once—'case-stacking': see Kemp, 'Effective Police Station Legal Advice' (n 110).
[132] See Vicky Kemp, '"No Time for a Solicitor": Implications for Delays on the Take-Up of Legal Advice' 2013 (3) Criminal Law Review 184.

that, despite the requirement in *Code C*, paragraph 6.5, I did not hear any CO explain to a detainee who was refusing advice that they could speak to a solicitor on the telephone.[133]

It would be difficult to identify that such failures were necessarily deliberate ploys to prevent children receiving legal advice.[134] There are undeniably a number of factors at play in these interchanges, not least the volume of information which must be imparted at booking in and the time pressure under which COs operate. Nonetheless, the data suggest that the CO's independent role as guardian of the suspect's rights can be difficult to maintain when it seems to conflict with institutional objectives and the interests of investigating colleagues.[135] It was common in all force areas for COs to complain about certain solicitors who always advised clients to go 'no comment', and few expressed any appreciation that the presence of the solicitor protects the prosecution as well as the defence. It seems that emphasizing the importance of getting legal advice to a child suspect was, for some, a step too far in fulfilling their role.

Adversarial Approaches

However, perhaps more concerning was the way in which the adversarial framing of the process distorted children's approach to the issue of legal advice. Several young participants aged under fourteen suggested that they would prefer not to have a solicitor because it would make them look guilty. Kaiden asked me:

> But if I get a solicitor, does that not mean that I done something wrong? ... Because the people that get solicitors—don't they think that they've done something bad for them actually to get a solicitor? ... Be dead guilty—that's what I think.

Some COs noted this issue ('I think they feel it implies guilt' (CO38)) but without suggesting that they would disabuse a child of this misconception. It is unsurprising that a child might reach this view, given their lack of understanding of the process more generally and the tendency for

---

[133] For previous observations of failures to offer telephone advice see Kemp, 'Digital Legal Rights' (n 87).
[134] A conclusion that Dixon arrived at on similar evidence: David Dixon, 'Legal Regulation and Policing Practice' (1992) 1 Social & Legal Studies 515.
[135] As observed in Choongh (n 38); McConville, Sanders, and Leng (n 109).

television, particularly US dramas, to provide much-needed information. As Sol6 observed,

> In films and TV series the person says 'I want my lawyer now', after they've admitted something. Juveniles think if you ask for a lawyer you're admitting something—that you are guilty. They don't appreciate that the court takes no notice of that.

For many older participants, the adversarial nature of the setting triggered a deep distrust which drove them to waive advice. Despite the relatively routine inclusion of a reference to the solicitor being 'independent', a significant number of young participants said that they had refused legal advice because of doubts about the independence of the solicitor, particularly of the 'duty' solicitor.[136] Harper, for example, explained that she would 'never get a solicitor from custody, like one of their solicitors' because 'it's just that they're attached kind of thing, if you get what I mean. I just think they're too like involved with the police.' Psychological research suggests that this may, in part, be an issue of legal competence—that children may fundamentally fail to understand issues of solicitor independence and legal professional privilege.[137] However, as Harper's phrase 'one of their solicitors' makes clear, there is, as Kemp[138] has noted, a difficulty with the positioning of the CO as the conduit of the offer. Since the offer is made by an officer, it is understandable that a child assumes that the solicitor will be working for the police. For some young people, a positive experience of legal advice had reduced this distrust. But for others, this scepticism could be lasting and might be reinforced, or initiated, by family members as well. Cole, for example, explained, 'My mum's always told me never just get a lawyer from the police station, I don't know why.'

In this adversarial setting, the power imbalance between child and officers also distorted young participants' capacity to choose freely. Many young participants were extremely conscious that they were in the total control of the CO and often felt that the CO would be inclined to act against their interests. As a result, some young participants felt that opting for legal advice introduced scope for officers to deliberately delay release. Luke, for

---

[136] A solicitor arranged by the police through the Criminal Defence Service. Adults, albeit those who opted for such assistance, expressed similar concerns about the independence of duty solicitors in Kemp and Balmer (n 95) 44.
[137] Grisso, 'Competence of Adolescents' (n 100); Peterson-Badali and Abramovitch (n 99).
[138] Kemp, *Transforming Legal Aid* (n 112) 92.

example, suggested that requesting a solicitor gave the police the opportunity to drag detention out: 'Police don't rush doing things. If you ask them for a solicitor they'll do it an hour later.'

Protections against Poor Decision-Making

There are several protections designed to act as a potential brake on flawed decision-making. First, the right to legal advice is one of the suspect's 'continuing' rights, meaning that they can engage the right at any time, including following initial refusal. More often than not, on observation, child suspects were informed that their right to legal advice was 'ongoing' and that they could change their mind. However, I did not observe any instances of a delayed request for advice by a young suspect following initial refusal, and only one young participant related having reversed a legal advice decision having refused a solicitor initially, whilst drunk (Tom). The major barrier to this provision enabling take-up following further reflection is the harshness of the custody process, combined with a developmentally natural predisposition to favour the short-term benefit of release from custody. Young participants' accounts indicate that the longer a child has been in the cell, the less likely they are to change their mind and engage a protection perceived to add to that delay: 'when you go into a cell all you want is just get out of there' (Hussain).[139]

This issue has a bearing on the second, and arguably key, protection against poor-decision-making: the AA's right to override a young suspect's refusal of advice (*Code C*, 6.5A). Familial AAs experienced many of the same challenges to their decision-making as the children that they supported.[140] In the vast majority of cases, the child is without independent adult support when first offered legal advice—with young suspects commonly waiting five or more hours before first contact.[141] Arriving late in the process, a familial AA was often distressed and anxious to secure the child's release, as well as sometimes being concerned about a lengthy delay

---

[139] See for similar observations David Dixon, 'Juvenile Suspects and the Police and Criminal Evidence Act' in David AC Freestone and Hugh Keith Bevan (eds), *Children and the Law: Essays in Honour of Professor HK Bevan* (Hull University Press 1990).

[140] I discuss the AA role in more detail in Chapter 4.

[141] More recent examination has revealed even longer delays. See Tim Bateman, 'A Night in the Cells: Children in Police Custody and the Provision of Non-familial Appropriate Adults' (Office of the Children's Commissioner 2017) <www.childrenscommissioner.gov.uk/wp-content/uploads/2018/06/A-Night-in-the-Cells.pdf> accessed 16 August 2023.

conflicting with their own caring or employment responsibilities. They were therefore highly unlikely to override a child's waiver and themselves request legal advice, with the inevitable delay that would then be occasioned. FAA4, for example, decided not to require legal advice for her daughter: 'she'd be stuck in there til they [the solicitor] come ... So I didn't want that, I didn't wanna be sat around waiting ... she wanted to get it over and done with and just get interviewed and get out.' Putting down a child as a 'no for now' is thus highly problematic and provides some explanation of why the presence of a familial AA has been associated with low uptake.[142]

Like the children they were present to support, familial AAs were often hampered by gaps in their own knowledge and appreciation of the right to legal advice. On observation, they were not routinely made aware of their own right to request legal advice for the child. Indeed, other untrained AAs from residential care homes (RHAA1 and 2) and even the youth offending service (YOTAA1) were not always clear either about the existence of this power. Even where aware, familial AAs often displayed the same lack of appreciation of the role of the solicitor as child suspects. FAA5 explained about declining to override her child's refusal of a solicitor:

> I'd not been in that situation before so I just went along with everything, you know ... and thought 'Do I need a solicitor?' I don't know. So, I'm not really clued up with it all, you know what I mean, but I just said no.

Familial AA decisions to decline legal advice were also particularly influenced by the CO or investigating officer making reference to the minor nature of the allegation or the relatively benign sanction which might follow.[143] The suggestion that her child would receive a caution had been a significant contributory factor in FAA5's decision to decline advice. Even non-familial AAs could be swayed by this reasoning. PAA4, for example, explained that where she considered that a child 'is going to get a simple caution or a YOT referral' and a 'solicitor won't make any difference', she would not override refusal.

Non-familial AAs attending to support older or more experienced child suspects raised a further issue not previously identified in research—a reluctance to undermine the agency of the child by overriding their decision to decline advice. As CO38 explained, 'It winds them [child suspects] up

---

[142] See n 90.
[143] As identified in Kemp, Pleasence, and Balmer, '25 Years On' (n 86).

because they feel the decision has been taken out of their hands. A lot of the time we want them in the driving seat.' Some non-familial AAs were also concerned that overriding the child's wishes would undermine the difficult process of building rapport with an unknown child suspect. The AA, particularly an AA not previously familiar with the child, is placed in an invidious position by virtue of *Code C*'s ambivalent approach to the child suspect's decision-making around legal advice. At one and the same time, the AA is required to enable the child as an autonomous legal actor but is also expected to decide when their special need for protection requires that autonomy to be overridden. What approach should the AA take? Kaiden, for example, was angry that he had had his refusal of legal advice overridden and would have much preferred to make up his own mind. But he was also one of the young participants who believed that having a solicitor would make him look guilty. An AA favouring the autonomy of a young suspect runs the risk of neutering essential protections intended to be in place for a child like Kaiden.

As a result of these issues, the protection in *Code C*, 6.5A appears rarely to be effective save, as related above, where a local AA scheme providing non-familial AAs took a blanket approach requiring a solicitor to attend for all child suspects. This resulted in F1 in a significant boost in the rates of uptake of legal advice—a child's initial refusal, in cases where a non-familial AA would be attending, would be met with an explanation that a solicitor would be required in any event, and the request was automatically made on their behalf. Whilst the child retains the right to refuse to meet the solicitor who attends, no child refused advice once the solicitor arrived at the station.

Not Enabled in Practice

The picture which emerges in relation to the exercise of legal rights is worrying in the extreme. Busy COs too often deliver a pared-down version of the rights information, paying lip service to *Code C* but failing to provide the level of explanation required to enable children to engage meaningfully with their rights. Despite the emphasis in the APP, it seems that rarely is effort made to ensure the child's full comprehension of their rights, particularly 'the possible benefit and importance of seeking legal advice'[144] to

---

[144] APP(DC)(CYP) (n 36) 5.

equip them to make an informed and reasoned choice. The child generally receives minimal information about the alleged offence for which they have been arrested and is not supported at this stage to appreciate, even in broad-brush terms, what is at stake for them. In addition, the protections intended to support greater awareness of rights and entitlements, and to mitigate poor decision-making (particularly repetition of rights in the presence of the AA and their power to override the child's decision) operate inconsistently and present practical problems of their own. The results are unsurprising. Thus, although, in contrast to the young suspects in the *Confait* case, today's child suspects in England and Wales are invariably informed of their right to legal advice, they are not effectively enabled to appreciate and engage that right. As a result, a significant proportion continue to decline legal advice, in line with earlier quantitative research,[145] rendering them no better protected than Colin Lattimore, Ronald Leighton, and Ahmet Salih.

A now familiar blend of issues emerges to explain the inadequacy of the rights process. There are structural as well as institutional failings in the way the process is conceived. *Code C* itself contains no provisions requiring child friendly communication of information to children, nor does it stipulate the provision of sufficient information about the child's legal jeopardy and the benefits of legal advice to enable the child, and their AA, to make an informed and reasoned choice about uptake. Additionally, the rights delivery process brings into sharp focus the conflicted position of the CO role created by PACE—aligned with the prosecution but the guardian of defence rights in an adversarial process. Thus, what limited guidance there is to ensure child friendly provision, particularly in the APP(CYP), is not routinely followed, and the AA is neither speedily secured nor sufficiently supported to perform their role.

In relation to engaging their right to legal advice, young participants themselves described a range of factors similar to those identified as associated with adult decisions to decline legal advice. However, it is the magnification of those factors for children that is striking—their desperation to avoid even a forty-five-minute delay, the pervasive nature of their distrust, and the depth of their lack of appreciation of their own legal jeopardy and the criminal justice process more generally. Their decision-making capacity, already compromised by virtue of their youth (and sometimes further depleted by pre-existing conditions such as learning disability), is often

---

[145] Kemp, Pleasence, and Balmer, '25 Years On' (n 86).

critically undermined by the tension between the distress they experience, or anticipate, in detention and the prospect of swift release. The contingency of the custody process comes into sharp focus as the failure to reduce child suspects' feelings of 'intimidation and inhibition' in the initial phases[146] (as discussed in Chapter 2) combines with their mounting desire to 'get out', to challenge their capacity to identify and understand relevant information, reason logically, and make decisions in their best legal interests. In effect, it is the very reasons which make legal advice so critical for child suspects— their compromised legal competence, their situational vulnerability in the adversarial custody process, and the emphasis on out-of-court disposals— which are revealed as driving low uptake of this key right. The evidence lays bare how frankly unrealistic it is to expect a child as young as ten in police custody to engage in an informed and reasoned fashion with this key legal decision.

Benefiting from Legal Rights

Having reviewed the child's ability to exercise their legal rights, with a particular focus on legal advice, I turn now to consider the extent to which they are able to enjoy the benefits of those rights, even when they are activated. I assess, first of all, the challenges for a child in engaging with the solicitor once they attend, and then review, in light of legal advice, how young participants approached the other key decision required of them in custody, whether to answer questions in police interview.[147]

---

[146] *Panovits v Cyprus* (n 3), [67].

[147] In addition to deciding whether to answer questions in interview, a child in detention may also be faced with the issue of whether to accept an out-of-court disposal (although these are more commonly referred for consideration at an appointment with youth offending services). This, too, is a key legal question and presented several challenges for young participants and familial AAs, including appreciating the legal ramifications of acceptance and weighing the offer rationally when desperate to leave the custody block. The implications of accepting a caution or conditional caution have changed substantially since the fieldwork in light of the change in disclosure regime in 2020 following the Supreme Court's ruling in *Re Gallagher's Application for Judicial Review* [2019] UKSC 3, [2020] AC 18, effected by The Rehabilitation of Offenders Act 1974 (Exceptions) Order 1975 (Amendment) (England and Wales) Order 2020/1373 and The Police Act 1997 (Criminal Record Certificates: Relevant Matters) (amendment) (England and Wales) Order 2020/1364. As a result, I do not address this legal decision in detail in this chapter.

Engaging with the Solicitor

For those who do not waive legal advice, positive interactions with solicitors could transform a child's ability to act as an autonomous legal agent. Practical, not sugar-coated, advice about 'what's going on' (Sadie) was really valued, particularly where it enabled young people to exercise some control. For some, this arose from feeling that they were able to make choices, as Luke explained: 'Yeah I've got a really good solicitor, he's brilliant like. He'll listen to me and then like he'll ask me what I wanna do.' For others, simple strategies to counteract the power imbalance in custody were particularly welcomed: 'He (the solicitor) was like, "If they ask you a silly question, just tap with the paper and just end the interview." I was alright then' (Jo). Simon described the effect of this sort of advice: 'it felt like we was in control, and it wasn't the policeman in control'. However, not everyone who opted for legal advice was able to engage effectively with their representative or felt that they had benefited from the interaction. Young participants revealed a striking number of barriers which hampered them in providing full instructions and then receiving comprehensive, and comprehensible, advice.

Trust: 'I don't trust no one in there'

Feeling able to trust the solicitor was key to engagement for many young participants. Nathan, for example, explained that a solicitor is good if 'they're on your side all the way innit', and to a degree, this could be easily conveyed: 'they tell you in the meeting none of this is going to be going back to the police innit—this like … what we're saying stays between us'. A number of young people described how, once they found a solicitor they trusted, they would use them again and again. Indeed, for several young people, particularly those who had experienced residential care, a longstanding relationship with a solicitor was a source of constancy and support and avoided the distressing need to explain one's background history repeatedly. Conversely, the ethnicity of the solicitor tended not to be a significant feature. The young Irish traveller participant linked his trust in his solicitor to their cultural affinity with him and his family. However, no other Black, Asian, or minority ethnic young participant expressed a similar preference.

However, for many young participants, lack of trust was a prevalent issue. As with the decision to request advice, the independence of the solicitor was an issue, regardless of what the CO had said during the rights process. As Aaron explained, 'I don't trust no one in there ... If you're part of the feds, you're part of the feds.' Several young participants believed that solicitors, duty or otherwise, were not only linked to the police but also actively engaged in furthering police objectives. For example, Aidan felt that duty solicitors were 'sent' to 'get information' out of him, whilst Carter explained that solicitors generally were 'just there to get you to admit things so that the police can bring up evidence'. Conversely, Will was concerned that 'no comment' advice was part of a strategy:

> Like they just see, they just wanna know if you done it and the best way to do it is to go to court and go to trial. So I think they, I think they try and make you go to trial so then they can actually find out if ... to prove you're guilty or not guilty.

Such vigilance to issues of independence is understandable in the hostile environment of custody. Likewise, young participants' limited appreciation of, and confidence in, the concept of legal professional privilege is in keeping with the North American research into children's abilities to engage with lawyers.[148] In line with the findings of Pierce and Brodsky,[149] although numbers are small, those who expressed particular difficulties engaging with and trusting solicitors tended to be ethnically diverse young participants or those with additional vulnerabilities, such as ADHD or a learning disability. As Malik, a young Asian participant, explained, 'I know, whatever you say to them is private and confidential and whatever, but ... Fuck 'em, still can't trust 'em man. I don't know, I can't.'

Young participants often described mitigating perceived risks by restricting what they divulged to their solicitor. Nathan, for example, explained that he held back some information, 'Just in case like ... if they actually did go and tell.' Such an approach could be catastrophic in terms of enabling the solicitor to give reliable advice. As with waiver, young participants' decision-making in this regard tended to be guided by their own, often uninformed, assessment of their situation. For example, Jo was prepared to provide a full account to his solicitor because the allegation was a 'big deal'; conversely, Hussain felt that it was alright to provide a full account precisely because the allegation he faced was not that serious.

---

[148] See eg Peterson-Badali and others (n 103).
[149] Pierce and Brodsky (n 19).

Withheld material commonly related to the involvement of others in the alleged offending: 'I wouldn't mention anything anyone else did, 'cos that's just like the code, you know what I mean, you don't do that to your mates' (Aidan). Concerns not to be a 'grass' or a 'snitch' were prevalent. This is unsurprising since group offending is more common amongst children than adults, and concerns about grassing have long been noted in young people's relations with the police.[150] But it is also problematic since it elevates the importance of a child providing full instructions in respect of their own and others' activity, whilst also introducing a layer of difficulty into young people's decision-making in the police station, with which many older suspects do not have to contend. Luke, for example, believed that if the solicitor understood that others were involved, he or she would 'try and force' him into telling the police. He felt that a duty solicitor, in particular, would advise: 'if you tell the police it was them and not you, then you'll be able to get out. That's what they want you to do, they want you to grass 'em up.' Navigating such tensions makes serious demands of the child's legal capabilities as well as their emotional maturity. The child must understand not only something of case construction in an adversarial process but also have a good working appreciation of the solicitor's role—what use can, and cannot, be made of the instructions provided and that the solicitor's role is to advise, not to direct them, on their options. Such an understanding requires both a good adviser and trust and maturity on the part of the client. As a result, it is unsurprising that children may struggle to understand the relationship and experience advice as pressure, prompting further distrust and isolation.

Competence and Engagement: 'He just didn't say anything'

Young participants spoke approvingly about solicitors who managed to convey to them that they were not just 'doing a job' but who 'actually seem like they wanna help you and they're interested … someone that genuinely doesn't want you to come back' (Alex). Being able to show kindness and understanding, even when a young person may be talking about offending behaviour, was particularly appreciated: 'like she was even um she was nice like even when I was telling her my story, I felt that I could be fully truthful to her' (Hussain). By contrast, several young people spoke with real distress and anger about those who made clear that they were not interested. Riley,

---

[150] Ian Loader, *Youth, Policing and Democracy* (Macmillan 1996).

for example, described a solicitor who had spent their entire consultation, and apparently parts of the interview, on his mobile: 'So I reckon he didn't give a shit, 'cause he didn't care... He just didn't say anything.'

Some young participants, particularly Black, Asian, and minority ethnic participants, described holding back information, or rejecting advice, on the basis of previous poor experiences of legal advice. However, assessing the competence of a solicitor can be extremely difficult, particularly for a child who may not fully understand the role or appreciate the unpredictable nature of an adversarial process. Indeed, research indicates a developmental component to children's negative experiences of lawyers.[151] Some young participants were frustrated by, and disinclined to trust, a solicitor who would not give a firm prediction: 'she wasn't telling me what they'd give me. She just saying, we'll see what they give you' (Malik). Hussain expressed a similar lack of confidence in a solicitor who could not provide a firm prediction of outcome: 'he's not even that smart so I didn't really ask him too much after that'. Conversely, several young participants were very critical of solicitors whose advice had not resulted in the outcome anticipated, especially when firm advice to make 'no comment' in interview had not prevented prosecution. Kaiden, for example, objected, 'They all put you in a direction. Because one solicitor they told me to do this (make no comment), and I still got in trouble.'

Delay: 'You bastard, why did you come so late?'

Delay in the attendance of the solicitor also emerged as a further barrier to positive engagement. This could easily breed resentment: 'You bastard why did you come so late?' (Malik). Unless the solicitor explains to their client the cause of the delay, there is inevitably the danger that the child will consider the solicitor to be at fault. Causes of delayed access to legal advice are a complex interaction of police occupational cultures and solicitor working practices. In one sense, access to the young suspect is wholly controlled by the CO, who, on observation, would generally set in motion the request for advice swiftly but would ask the solicitor to attend only when required for interview. To a degree, this is driven by practical considerations, including a lack of waiting and conferencing space in some blocks. But there are shades of police occupational and adversarial inclinations to keep solicitors,

---

[151] Ann Tobey, Thomas Grisso, and Robert Schwartz, 'Youth's Trial Participation as Seen by Youths and Their Attorneys: An Exploration of Competence-Based Issues' in Grisso and Schwartz (n 20).

potentially challenging 'outsiders',[152] out of the custody suite and away from their clients. In some observation venues, solicitors were required to wait outside the block in a separate section entirely. Once present, I observed solicitors waiting, often in frustration, for access to their client. SO18 complained that COs working at their computers are 'desperately trying not to catch your eye. They say they're busy when you want to get a prisoner out of their cell or the like.' Solicitor participants explained that they may have a phone call with a detainee in advance of arrival. But generally, they did not rely on this being confidential since, commonly, the call might occur in earshot of custody staff or be put through to the cell on a five-minute timer, preventing the taking of instructions or the provision of substantive advice.

However, solicitors' own working practices could contribute to delayed access, not least because the low level of the fixed single attendance fee means that attendance long in advance of, or following, interview is financially unsustainable.[153] That low fee could have more problematic repercussions. In all three areas, AAs and officers complained of duty solicitors taking on numerous cases, leading to lengthy delays. PAA4 complained about one duty solicitor who did this frequently, 'On one occasion he (the solicitor) had nine cases—took them all on without asking for help. I asked why and he said he wouldn't get paid if he passed any on to a colleague.' COs felt powerless to intervene: 'you can be waiting three to four hours for duty solicitor to be available ... you can call the centre and ask for a second duty solicitor to come down but sometimes they refuse' (CO17).

The Toll of the Process: 'I couldn't be bothered telling them nothing'

Such delays could have a knock-on effect in terms of the child's ability to engage. After six or eight hours in a cell, a child may well be in a wholly unsuitable frame of mind for talk with with their solicitor. As Malik explained, 'They don't give a fuck. I couldn't be bothered telling them nothing. I just wanted to get out of there. I was just doing nothing but chatting shit.' The simple burden of having to answer yet more questions could also trigger withdrawal. By the time a solicitor arrives, a child will already have fielded the CO's lengthy questions at booking in and RA, and they may also have

---

[152] Holdaway (n 107).
[153] Sir Christopher Bellamy, 'Independent Review of Criminal Legal Aid' (29 November 2021) 69 <https://www.gov.uk/government/groups/independent-review-of-criminal-legal-aid#final-report> accessed 16 August 2023.

been asked questions by a non-familial AA and a health-care professional as well. Although focused on assisting the young person, such questioning can be exhausting and oppressive for a child, particularly where difficult issues such as self-harm have been addressed. Aaron described how this could lead to shut-down with his solicitor: 'It pisses me off, innit, 'cause they all—every fuckin' person asking me what happened. I'm just like, "Shut your fuckin' mouth".'

This particular difficulty is sometimes exacerbated by the provisions of *Code C* and police interpretations of them. Solicitors are entitled to review the custody record; however, the RA and medical information is 'not required to be shown or provided' to the solicitor or AA unless withholding it may 'put that person at risk'.[154] Often, this material may include useful information to support communication and the solicitor's assessment of their client's fitness for interview. On observation, COs tended not to disclose such material—as the CO dealing with YS29 explained 'you've got to weigh it up—it's personal info, we don't reveal unless it's necessary', overlooking— the very public way in which RA information is often obtained. There were indications of an adversarial cast to the narrow construction of the provision. CO26, for example, felt that solicitors ask for the custody record to 'put you on the back foot'. However, this adversarial approach means that the AA and solicitor may have to repeat questions about communication difficulties or the client's mental state, adding to the demands made of the child and potentially contributing to the sort of shut-down described by Aaron.

Deciding Whether to Answer Questions in Police Interview

In light of these challenges, I turn, then, in this final empirical section, to review the extent to which children in detention were able to engage with their right to silence and, in particular, to benefit from the assistance of a solicitor when deciding whether to answer questions in interview. Concerns about the comprehensibility of the caution have been raised repeatedly[155] and addressed in separate, focused studies.[156] But the difficulties which arise for

---

[154] *Code C* (n 10), para 3.8A.
[155] Quirk (n 67).
[156] Susanne Fenner, Gisli H Gudjonsson, and Issabel CH Clare, 'Understanding of the Current Police Caution (England and Wales) among Suspects in Police Detention' (2002) 12 Journal of Community and Applied Social Psychology 83; Sim and Lamb (n 40).

children in understanding and using legal advice in this regard in police custody have not been explored in detail in this jurisdiction. Research in England and Wales into children's experiences at court,[157] and of the criminal justice system more generally,[158] suggests that children may frequently be confused about criminal justice processes, struggle to engage with justice system actors, and labour under significant misunderstandings about legal concepts but may often be reluctant to raise their difficulties. Interestingly, young participants in Kemp and Watkins' study appeared to express a degree of confidence, and a sense of agency, in exercising their right to silence. However, Kemp was sceptical that children's decision-making in that regard was truly voluntary and based on genuine understanding such that they were able to make decisions in their own best interests.[159]

Factual Understanding and Appreciation of the Consequences of Silence: 'It'll just go against you'

Whilst a very small group of young participants showed an impressive degree of understanding about their legal position and their options in interview, this was unusual. A number of young participants, particularly those who were under fifteen and relatively inexperienced, were plain that they had not fully comprehended the advice they had been given. For example, Jake, aged thirteen at the time of his detention, explained, 'I understand bits of it, but I didn't *understand* like' (emphasis in the original speech).

Strikingly, although the general level of comprehension amongst interviewees was poor, approximately one-third of young participants were confident that they had been able to understand the advice that they had received about answering questions in interview. Yet, on probing, this confidence was frequently found to be misplaced. In this regard, I am conscious of the lapse of time between custody episode and research interview and the inevitable memory deterioration. I therefore focus only on specific misconceptions rather than where recollection was hazy. However, even on this measure, a significant number of those who had been confident about advice on 'no comment' displayed specific and significant misconceptions

---

[157] Joyce Plotnikoff and Richard Woolfson, 'Young Defendants Pack: Scoping Study' (Youth Justice Board (YJB) 2002) <https://vdocuments.site/young-defendants-pack-scoping-study-lexicon-limited-young-defendants-pack-scoping.html> accessed 16 August 2023; Jessica Jacobson and Jenny Talbot, *Vulnerable Defendants in the Criminal Courts: A Review of Provision for Adults and Children* (Prison Reform Trust 2009).
[158] Hazel, Hagell, and Brazier (n 97).
[159] Kemp and Watkins (n 51) 331ff.

about the ramifications of taking that course. For example, young participants related believing that it makes no difference at court if you are silent in interview (Cole), that making no comment in interview obliges you to give evidence at a trial (Hussain) or would lead to them being called back into custody (Kaiden). Perhaps a reflection of the adversarial setting of the police interview, their appreciation of the ramifications of silence in interview tended to be unduly negative, and there was a strong sense that an adverse inference, however that was conceived by the young participant, would almost inevitably be drawn: 'it'll just go against you, say if it does go to court and you start explainin' yourself' (Aaron). Similarly, the lack of appreciation of the interview as an opportunity for the young participant to give their account of the allegation was striking. Only one young person (Logan) volunteered this viewpoint. Rather, a number of young participants suggested that whatever you said in interview would be 'used against you': 'everything they asked or anything like that, I just felt like it was against me' (Sandor).

This misplaced confidence in understanding the right of silence accords with Kemp and Watkins's concerns and is reflected in focused research on caution comprehension in adults and children.[160] Its causes are hard to discern, but the practical effects are plain and worrying. Not only do these young participants' misconceptions fundamentally undermine their ability to make informed choices, but also their undue confidence in their comprehension makes detection of those deficits by solicitors very difficult. Whilst generally mindful of the volume and complexity of the information which has to be conveyed to a child in police custody, the majority of solicitors (and AAs) nonetheless displayed a significant degree of confidence generally in young people's abilities to understand and make use of legal advice. As Sol3 put it, 'understanding problems are the exception rather than the rule', that difficulties arose 'not because they are a youth, but because they have ancillary medical problems'. Indeed, contrary to research findings identifying children's limited legal competence, two solicitors suggested that children fared no worse than adults or, indeed, might even do better in comprehending legal advice 'because they are in the learning phase of their lives' (Sol6).

The reluctance of young participants to seek clarifications for fear of prolonging the process clearly exacerbates this issue. As Sandor described, 'I

---

[160] ibid 331ff and see n 156.

just wanted to get through everything as quickly and as smoothly as possible and just leave.' There is also the related difficulty, linked to the time pressures associated with advising in custody, that solicitors, like COs, commonly explained that they would check whether a client had previous experience of custody and would adjust the pace and depth of explanation accordingly. They operated on the assumption that, as Sol3 described it, 'they've been here so many times they speak as adults do because clearly they know what's going on'. As we saw in Chapter 2, this rarely proves to be a reliable indicator of rational understanding.

One concerning solution to this difficulty, adopted by some solicitors, appears to be to circumvent the process of advising almost entirely. When asked about what advice she had received about answering questions in interview, Kate, for example, explained of the solicitor, 'He didn't really explain it to me 'cause he went, "If it comes to trial, then I'll talk to ya." He said, "It won't come to trial. It's pointless."' Several young participants described how the solicitor always advised 'no comment': 'No matter what, every single time he (the solicitor) just says "no comment"' (Will). This was also noted by officers, who, on observation, in each area complained of certain solicitors who always advised 'no comment'.

On one view, to direct a young client without providing any meaningful advice is to fundamentally undermine that young person's right to participate effectively in the legal process. However, it is important to assess this approach in context. Young suspects are in the midst of an exhausting process and facing the imminent demands of the police interview. To burden a young person with complex advice which may not, in fact, be engaged may seem counterproductive. Equally, for a young person facing an allegation which is not suitable for an OOCD, if the young person has any cognitive or communication difficulties, a sensible solicitor may well conclude that an adverse inference would not be drawn and that 'no comment' is indeed the best approach, in any event. Thus, these findings, whilst they may indicate, in one sense, a failure in terms of traditional legal advice, more urgently highlight the constraints on advising children in the custody setting and the fundamental challenge of conveying complex legal information to young suspects whose natural psycho-social immaturity makes the processing of such material in that setting extraordinarily difficult.

Rational Decision-Making? Just getting it 'over and done with'

As with the question of waiver, some young participants seemed not to engage in the legal decision-making process in a meaningful way at all.

Frequently, young participants decided to make no comment in response to the toll of the process without real engagement with legal advice or weighing the ramifications of their choice. Some described deciding on silence against legal advice because they were hungry or 'too tired, too knackered with everything' (Rezar). Delay could also prompt silence, either in order to get out more quickly ('if you stick to "no comment" you just get it over and done with, don't ya?'(Aidan)) or because of frustration: 'if they've took forever you just wanna go "no comment"' (Logan). Some young participants used silence as a form of resistance strategy, having identified that 'the only power you've got is when you go into the interview room' (Hussain) and that 'they (the police) hate it when you go "no comment"' (Jayden). Elisabeth Carter has also observed this isolated moment of control,[161] and, indeed, the use of silence in interview as a form of resistance to institutional authority had been long observed.[162] These tended to be ethnically diverse young participants, providing a potential factor in disproportionality in later stages of the youth justice process, although the numbers are too small to draw firm conclusions about the role of ethnicity in this regard. For others, the adversarial setting intruded on decision-making and brought concerns about independence to the fore. Will, for example, was concerned that 'no comment' advice given by his solicitor was part of a strategy:

> Like they just see, they just wanna know if you done it and the best way to do it is to go to court and go to trial. So I think they, I think they try and make you go to trial so then they can actually find out if ... to prove you're guilty or not guilty.

Against the harshly punitive experience of the custody block, we should not be surprised by deep distrust and the prioritizing of immediate situational concerns over longer-term prospects and legal advice. Reduced capacity for future orientation and heightened reward sensitivity are natural features of adolescent psycho-social development.[163] However, it should be a cause of significant concern that we expect young suspects to make legal decisions which may have a lasting effect on their life chances in such circumstances.

---

[161] Elisabeth Carter, *Analysing Police Interviews: Laughter, Confessions and the Tape* (Bloomsbury 2011).
[162] Quirk (n 67); Daniel Kurzon, 'The Right of Silence: A Socio-pragmatic Model of Interpretation' (1995) 23(1) Journal of Pragmatics 55.
[163] Cauffman and Steinberg (n 18).

Free from Coercion? Juggling Competing Obligations

The reflections of those who did engage more meaningfully in the decision-making process uncover a knot of tensions arising from the presence of several different authority figures, especially where they may be in conflict. A number of young participants revealed an age-consistent deference to adults and authority which constrained their decision-making. Some felt obliged to comply with police demands in interview. One participant explained, 'I just feel like if I say, "No comment", then I'd be holding them back, not working with them (the police), not being polite' (Sandor). As one solicitor observed, 'They're incredibly honest—children—that's the problem ... I think they're socialized into that position—teachers asking them questions' (Sol1). Sandor's desire to assist, for example, led him to make very extensive admissions ('I was as open as I could have been'), which went beyond the police's allegations and aggravated his sentence.

For some, the solicitor also commanded authority, and it was common for young participants to describe feeling bound to follow legal advice, that they had been 'told' to go 'no comment' (Jo) and could not demur.[164] Azade, for example, complained about being given 'no comment' advice: 'I wanted them to know my side didn't I, but whatever the lawyer says, innit, so.' Staff too noted this: 'lots of them think they have to do exactly what the solicitor tells them' (CA28). The presence of a familial AA sometimes added a third competing authority figure to the often conflicting demands of the police and the solicitor. Although several young participants welcomed the presence of a parent, their 'support' could be more prescriptive than enabling. As explored in Chapter 5, this could be problematic, particularly where a familial AA pressurized a young suspect to 'just tell the truth' (Sol2) in contradiction to the solicitor's advice.

An additional tension which young participants had to grapple with in considering advice and making decisions arose from the involvement of their peers in the alleged offending. Maintaining loyalty to peers could severely strain young suspects' ability to make decisions in their own legal best interests. Protecting friends and avoiding being trapped into being a 'grass' were significant drivers of 'no comment' interviews, including against advice:

---

[164] Also observed in Kate Johnston and others, 'Assessing Effective Participation in Vulnerable Juvenile Defendants' (2016) 27 Journal of Forensic Psychiatry & Psychology 802; and in respect of plea decisions Michael McConville, *Standing Accused: The Organisation and Practices of Criminal Defence Lawyers in Britain* (Clarendon Press 1994).

The amount of times I've gotten arrested for what my friends have done, and I'll do a 'no comment' because I know they could, if I was to speak in an interview with them, I know they (the police) could get it out of me because that's how clever they are.

(Alex)

The Importance of Expert, Appropriately Resourced, and In-Person Legal Advice

Young participant accounts of engaging with solicitors and using legal advice to make decisions in custody underline how vital good-quality representation is for children in police custody. Advising a child in detention is extraordinarily demanding. The adviser must have the 'soft skills' to establish rapport with them, often in a very short space of time. They must be able to identify any participatory difficulties a child may have, including where the child does not wish to reveal their lack of comprehension, and be capable of engaging empathetically with them when they are liable to be exhausted, distressed, and distrusting. The volume and complexity of the information which a child must be able to assimilate in adverse and time-pressured circumstances is extreme. The fair functioning of the process demands that they grasp legal professional privilege, the role of the lawyer, their right of silence and its ramifications alongside offence-specific and sentencing information, where relevant. Young participant accounts reveal that failure to grasp any one of these aspects can be fatal to their engagement with the solicitor and their legal decision-making and can damage trust for future interactions. It is plain that timely access to a legal representative with specialist training in youth justice processes and advising young suspects is essential.

The arrangements for police station legal advice during the COVID-19 pandemic raise the prospect of the wider use of remote legal representation (virtual and audio only), both for legal consultation and in interview. Remote legal advice was in use for child suspects in police custody, albeit with restrictions, between April 2020 and 1 May 2021.[165] A nationwide survey of AAs with experience of the COVID arrangements has raised

---

[165] NPCC and others, 'COVID Joint Interim Interview Protocol Version 2' (in force to 1 May 2021) <https://www.cps.gov.uk/sites/default/files/documents/legal_guidance/National-Interview-Protocol-COVID19-v2.pdf> accessed 16 August 2023.

significant concerns around the use of remote legal advice for child and vulnerable suspects.[166] In particular, AAs felt that remote provision had a negative impact on a suspect's ability to engage with legal advice in a number of critical respects, particularly their ability to receive and understand advice and to raise issues of comprehension.[167] They considered that without a solicitor present physically in interview, the suspect was less able to follow legal advice during questioning and to participate effectively in the process.[168] At the same time, AAs also noted that solicitors seemed more passive when engaging remotely in the interview and were less likely to intervene.[169] Whilst no young participants had experience of remote legal advice, the fieldwork pre-dating the pandemic, their difficulties engaging with legal advice outlined in this chapter correspond closely with those aspects which were considered to be even more challenging with remote legal advice. This study provides compelling evidence that remote legal advice is fundamentally unsuitable for children in police custody. Whilst the latest protocol reverts to the default position of advice in person for children, save in limited and exceptional circumstances,[170] the wider use of remote legal advice in police custody as a future cost-saving measure remains a concerning possibility. Although the government has indicated its view that 'children should be prioritised for in-person legal advice',[171] the evidence of this study underlines the importance of remaining vigilant against any erosion of the right for children to receive legal advice in person in police custody.

Conclusion

Young participants' accounts of their understanding and exercise of legal rights make sobering reading. Considering the four components of valid

---

[166] Transform Justice, National Appropriate Adult Network, and Fair trials, National Appropriate Adult Network and Fair Trials, 'Not Remotely Fair? Access to a Lawyer in the Police Station during the COVID-19 Pandemic' <https://www.transformjustice.org.uk/publication/not-remotely-fair-access-to-a-lawyer-in-the-police-station-during-the-covid-19-pandemic/> accessed 16 August 2023.

[167] ibid 20–21.

[168] ibid 21–22.

[169] ibid 22–23.

[170] NPCC and others, 'Covid Joint Interim Interview Protocol, Version 4—October 2021' <www.cps.gov.uk/sites/default/files/documents/publications/National-Interview-Protocol-COVID19-Version-4-4-Oct-2021.pdf> accessed 16 August 2023.

[171] HC Deb 28 June 2022, Vol 717, col 66WH.

decision-making set out in opening, it is clear that, frequently, child suspects are not enabled to act as autonomous legal actors and to effectively engage their legal rights in police custody. The findings suggest that child suspects are commonly not appraised of the existence of the full range of their rights and are insufficiently supported to achieve a meaningful factual understanding of the content of their key legal rights, particularly the right to legal advice. The factual content required to make important decisions, especially in relation to representation and silence in interview, is complex and, for many children, unfamiliar. Child suspects are also not enabled to appreciate the nature and consequences of the decisions they must make. The impact of the process, its emotional and physical toll, combined with the child's naturally compromised decision-making capacity, not only disinclines the child from raising comprehension difficulties but also fundamentally undermines their ability to identify relevant information and reason logically about their options. For children who are particularly young (under fifteen), coping with mental health issues or other neurodivergence, or who are in a marginalized group by virtue of their ethnicity or gender, the challenge could be even greater. In terms of coercion, the child's desperation to 'get out' of custody, and the need to navigate the tensions of competing authority figures (officers, familial AAs, and solicitors), and peer loyalties, compromise their ability to make truly free decisions in custody. At the same time, the adversarial backdrop of the process brings distrust into play from the child's perspective and foregrounds institutional motivations for COs.

This analysis raises fundamental questions which lie beyond the narrow confines of the custody block. It exposes the inadequacy of arguments which support the maintenance of a strikingly low MACR on the basis that the child at ten is capable of understanding right from wrong. As Crofts has forcefully argued, such common-sense appeals are 'a gross simplification of the issue'.[172] These findings underline the very real challenges involved for a child, particularly if they are under fifteen, in engaging the rights which balance those responsibilities applied to them with such ease by policymakers. More research is required to investigate these issues, but this study identifies the real risk of unfairness where the child's rights cannot be engaged

---

[172] Thomas Crofts, 'Catching Up with Europe: Taking the Age of Criminal Responsibility Seriously in England' (2009) 17 European Journal of Crime, Criminal Law, and Criminal Justice 267, 285.

effectively in a justice-focused process. I address these issues in more detail in Chapter 7.

Returning to the custody block, it was plain that, for many young participants, the toll of the process, and their response to the adversarial nature of the setting, fundamentally undermined their ability in custody to engage in valid decision-making, even with legal advice. Their experiences make a strong case for children receiving legal advice and preparing for interview on bail rather than in detention, where they have the time and emotional space to engage with the legal process. Interview in custody should be limited to circumstances where the allegation is serious and the demands of the investigation genuinely require detention or where the child is likely to be remanded in custody and public protection requires their immediate containment.

For those who must experience custodial interview, it is clear that the current arrangements are inadequate to enable child suspects to function as autonomous legal actors. Certainly, strengthening *Code C* requirements for notification of rights, and the guidance in the APP, would be beneficial in improving the rights process, as would better training for COs and custody staff in communicating with children and adjusting their practice to accommodate common dispositional vulnerabilities. Equally, whilst I review the AA role in detail in Chapter 4, it is clear that reducing delays in AA attendance and more accessible resources to enable familial AAs to fulfil the role would also be likely to improve comprehension of legal rights and increase uptake of legal advice. However, the extent of the challenges identified in this chapter, the demands made of the child and their AA, and the conceptual difficulties presented by the CO's conflicted position as gatekeeper of the child's rights indicate that, in practice, more fundamental reform is required. Young participant accounts suggest that expert and well-resourced legal support is essential to enable the child to understand and engage their rights in a meaningful fashion. Even with such assistance, decision-making may be difficult, but without it, there is a real risk that the child's fair trial rights, and thus the integrity of the whole process, are undermined. The evidence suggests an urgent need to reconsider the requirement for a child suspect to request legal advice.

Waiver and Competence to Waive

In this regard, the 2016 Taylor Review of the Youth Justice System proposed 'a presumption that a solicitor is called and legal advice is provided, unless the child expressly asks not to'.[173] On one view, any proposal to enhance the regime for children engaging legal advice is to be welcomed, and for some child suspects who are unsure, the hurdle of rejecting a standardized position may be sufficient to dissuade them from refusing legal advice, particularly if the solicitor was immediately available. However, the strength of feeling expressed by young participants around issues of delay suggests that many would have few qualms about opting out. Equally, the existence of a presumption is likely to do little to overcome concerns about the independence of solicitors or to address misconceptions about the benefit and value of legal advice. Such a reform runs the risk of a change of emphasis, from request to waiver, but little improvement in practice.

One potential additional protection, were waiver introduced, would be to include a requirement to establish competence to waive before a court could receive in evidence any admissions made in interview or an out-of-court disposal be offered on the basis of the same. As discussed, such a requirement does not currently exist. An application may be made at trial to exclude any confession, under PACE, section 76 or 78 (or under the common law power preserved by section 82).[174] However, section 76 focuses on 'oppression' or the actions of individuals other than the suspect, whilst, although not requiring impropriety,[175] an application under section 78 is unlikely to succeed in the absence of 'significant and substantial' breaches of *Code C*.[176] Neither section easily accommodates excluding a confession on the basis that the child was not able validly to refuse their right to legal advice, particularly where an AA is present.

On first consideration, the introduction in England and Wales of a competence-to-waive test (such as that in US jurisdictions, which requires 'knowing, intelligent, and voluntary' waiver under the 'totality of the circumstances')[177] might be considered an improvement, given the lack of scope for addressing this issue currently at trial. However, in practice, in the United States, the test has been revealed to function

---

[173] Charlie Taylor, *Review of the Youth Justice System in England and Wales* (MoJ 2016) 22.
[174] PACE, s 77 (Confessions by mentally handicapped persons) will not be relevant, given the requirement for the absence of an 'independent person' (s 77(1)(b)(ii))—the AA will invariably be present in interview.
[175] *Samuel* (n 61).
[176] See eg *R v Walsh* [1989] 7 WLUK 174, (1990) 91 Cr App R 161, 163.
[177] *Fare* (n 9) 717.

problematically for children,[178] with commentators raising a number of issues, including that it fails to capture youth-specific capacity issues[179] and that the range of factors which have been included within the test has resulted in a judicial discretion which is 'virtually unlimited and unreviewable'.[180] Research continues to reveal complexities in understanding and appreciating the different aspects of the warnings, as well as a need for further refinement of the 'totality of the circumstances' factors.[181] Commentators have, as a result, argued that Miranda safeguards are 'dead'[182] or have been effectively 'gutted' by police practices, with 'little hope of meaningful repair'.[183]

In light of these difficulties, in some North American jurisdictions, there is, in addition, a 'per se' exclusionary approach, which requires the child to be assisted by an 'interested adult', occasionally a lawyer[184] but more generally a parent,[185] to validly waive their rights in relation to certain offences or for certain age groups.[186] However, parental 'per se' requirements have, unsurprisingly, been associated with some of the shortcomings identified in this study with regard to *Code C*, paragraph 6.5A, particularly parents' interests conflicting with children's legal interests and parents themselves lacking an appreciation of the value and benefit of legal advice.[187] In some cases, the courts mitigate such deficits by assessing whether the adult was, indeed, 'interested' in the sense of being concerned for the child, had themselves comprehended the rights, and had enough time to confer with the child.[188] However, despite these protections, and efforts to improve the

---

[178] Barry C Feld, 'Juveniles' Competence to Exercise Miranda Rights: An Empirical Study of Policy and Practice' (2006) 91 Minnesota Law Review 26.
[179] Grisso, *Juveniles' Waiver of Rights* (n 46).
[180] Barry C Feld, 'Juveniles' Waiver of Legal Rights: Confessions, *Miranda*, and the Right to Counsel' in Grisso and Schwartz (n 20) 113.
[181] See eg Heather Zelle, Christina L Riggs Romaine, and Naomi ES Goldstein, 'Juveniles' Miranda Comprehension: Understanding, Appreciation, and Totality of Circumstances Factors' (2015) 39 Law & Human Behavior 281.
[182] Alfredo Garcia, 'Is Miranda Dead, Was It Overruled, or Is It Irrelevant?' (1998) 10 St Thomas Law Review 461.
[183] Charles D Weisselberg, 'Mourning Miranda' (2008) 96 California Law Review 1519, 1521, and 1524
[184] See eg Illinois.
[185] See eg Massachusetts for children under fourteen years.
[186] See for discussion of the two approaches Thomas Grisso, 'Juveniles' Capacities to Waive Miranda Rights: An Empirical Analysis' (1980) 68 California Law Review 1134; Feld, 'Juveniles' Competence to Exercise Miranda Rights' (n 178).
[187] Feld, Juveniles' Waiver of Legal Rights' (n 180).
[188] See eg *Commonwealth v Smith*, 472 Pa 492 (1977), 500; Farber (n 52).

delivery of rights information,[189] children in US jurisdictions continue to waive their Miranda rights at extraordinarily high rates.[190]

Whilst there is not room here to analyse in detail the intricacies of the various US approaches, this brief comparison suggests both that difficulties experienced by children in appreciating and exercising legal rights are prominent and similar in US jurisdictions and that mitigating those difficulties in adversarial settings is unlikely to be adequately achieved by a requirement to waive (rather than opt in) or a test of competence to waive, including with the requirement for parental decision-making support. Additionally, and importantly, a retrospective assessment of competence to waive applied at trial cannot hope to remedy an inability to access legal rights by those who are diverted or plead guilty.

Striking the Right Balance between Autonomy and Protection

In my view, the findings make a compelling case for mandatory legal advice, both prior to and during interview. In advancing this proposition, I bear in mind that young participant accounts reveal that autonomy and control are cherished but scarce commodities in police custody. However, asking the child to opt for, or waive, legal advice preserves their autonomy in a superficial sense, but fatally undermines it in practical effect. The evidence suggests that a curtailment of this limited freedom is necessary to make possible their meaningful engagement as a legal actor in the critical decisions required of them in police custody, particularly whether to answer questions in interview. These latter decisions are those for which their autonomy is crucial—decisions which are informed and enabled, not limited, by legal advice. How the child chooses to respond to the advice provided remains, of course, their prerogative. As Sanders and Young memorably observed,

> If they can be held in stinking conditions against their will, their mouths and hair invaded against their will, and questioned against their will why

---

[189] There are hundreds of juvenile Miranda warning formulations in use in US jurisdictions. For analysis of 293 such formulations Richard Rogers and others, 'Juvenile Miranda Warnings: Perfunctory Rituals or Procedural Safeguards?' (2012) 39 Criminal Justice and Behavior 229.
[190] Feld, 'Juveniles' Competence to Exercise Miranda Rights' (n 178).

shouldn't they be given something that does them good against their will?[191]

In the case of child suspects, the argument is more compelling. They are required to submit to the presence of an AA to 'support, advise and assist them'[192] at various stages of the process; why should they not also be required to receive legal advice as well and have their interests protected in interview?

As a less favourable alternative, the child's autonomy in relation to legal advice could be preserved to a degree by enabling them to waive representation only once they have received advice from the solicitor in respect of their role, the purpose of legal advice, and the consequences of waiver. The evidence in this study strongly supports Feld's assertion that only someone with legal training can adequately explain to a child what is at stake for them; the seriousness and ramifications of their legal position; and, indeed, how legal advice can support them.[193] This alternative is not ideal since the child would not then receive advice on how to answer questions in interview or have their interests protected in that setting. However, it is arguably preferable to the other available compromise, which I have previously identified,[194] that some autonomy could be preserved by empowering the child to decline to consult at all with a solicitor who attends having been mandatorily called, reflecting a similar power in *Code C*, paragraph 6.5A, where the AA overrides the child's waiver. This latter option is even less desirable because it leaves open the prospect of the child proceeding without any expert advice at all. There are also indications that this degree of autonomy is not particularly favoured. COs and AAs observed during fieldwork that, where an AA overrode a child's waiver, it was very unusual for the child to refuse to consult with the solicitor once they had attended.

The call for mandatory legal advice is not new[195] or without precedent. In the European Union, legal advice for detained child suspects is often mandatory and cannot be waived (eg in Belgium, France, Spain, Sweden, and Portugal) or only following an initial legal consultation (eg in the

---

[191] Andrew Sanders, *Criminal Justice* (2nd edn, OUP 2000) 242.
[192] *Code C* (n 10), para 1.7A.
[193] Feld, 'Juveniles' Waiver of Legal Rights' (n 180).
[194] Bevan, 'Young Suspect Perspectives' (n 130) 701.
[195] Fiona Brookman and Harriet Pierpoint, 'Access to Legal Advice for Young Suspects and Remand Prisoners' (2003) 42 Howard Journal of Criminal Justice 452.

Netherlands).[196] Nor is such a proposal without its challenges. For mandatory legal advice to be effective and not a source of additional delay, it must be properly resourced and provided by practitioners with child-specific training and youth justice expertise.[197] This study underlines the findings of the Independent Review of Criminal Legal Aid that current levels of remuneration for police station work are insufficient.[198] Better funding is required so that representatives can engage with child suspects earlier in the detention process to afford them sufficient time to establish rapport and to enable their young clients to understand and utilize their advice. In Chapter 4, I turn from professional advice to lay support to consider in detail the other key protection for children in police custody: the appropriate adult safeguard.

---

[196] Code of Criminal Procedure, Art 489, para 1. See for details of nation states Defence for Children, Belgium, 'Mapping of Youth Lawyers Systems in the European Union, Country Overviews of 18 European Member States 2017' <https://lachild.eu/database/> accessed 16 August 2023.

[197] For a similar focus on youth justice expertise for mandatory advice in Belgium see Hanne Schoovaerts, Miet Vanderhallen, and Sara-Jane McIntyre, 'Lawyers and Children: Is There a Need for Mandatory Legal Assistance in Suspect Interviews?' (2021) 23 International Journal of Police Science & Management 55.

[198] Bellamy (n 153).

4
Making Good the Imbalance?
Examining the Appropriate Adult Role

> It was awful, absolutely awful. I'm absolutely petrified because ... I've never been in a police station in my life ... I didn't have a clue ... what I feel now after coming out, reading everything that should have happened, I feel like I really let [my son] down by not knowing.
>
> (FAA2)

Introduction

This chapter turns from legal rights applicable to all suspects to the particular support that children in police custody in England and Wales should be afforded: the presence of an appropriate adult (AA). The AA has been described as the child suspect's 'principal protection'.[1] Indeed, it is, in effect, the only substantive age-specific adjustment guaranteed to a child in police detention. As Moses LJ observed in the case of *HC*, the AA safeguard is 'critical because it provides a gateway to a young person's access to justice',[2] necessary to make good the 'imbalance' between the young suspect and the prosecution in police custody.[3] The AA role is multifaceted, designed not only to safeguard the child's welfare and provide emotional support and assistance but also to aid communication and oversee due process, including enabling the child to understand their rights. Although a 'crucial'[4]

---

[1] David C Brown, 'PACE Ten Years On: A Review of the Research', Home Office Research Study 155 (Home Office 1997) 187.

[2] *R on the Application of HC (a child by his litigation friend CC) v Secretary of State for the Home Department* (*HC*) [2013] EWHC 982 (Admin), [2014] 1 WLR 1234 [63].

[3] ibid, Moses LJ [58].

[4] Criminal Justice Joint Inspection (CJJI), 'Who's Looking Out for the Children? A Joint Inspection of Appropriate Adult Provision and Children in Detention after Charge' (CJJI 2011) 13.

and demanding protection, the AA is a non-professional role, fulfilled most often by untrained family members or lay individuals with a limited level of training. As one mother's reflection in the epigraph on her experience acting as an AA for her son illustrates, family members in particular may be ill equipped to perform this vital function, with profound ramifications for the child's ability to participate effectively in the custody process.

How effective are AAs in making good that 'imbalance'? In his review of the Youth Justice System in 2016, Charlie Taylor observed that the AA role for children is 'ill understood and variably exercised'.[5] Indeed, empirical research into the functioning of the protection for children is very limited. Three large-scale studies, which analysed tape-recorded police interviews with young suspects,[6] have considered the contributions of AAs during the questioning of children but are all now of some age.[7] More recent studies touching on AA input in young suspect interviews have tended to be on a smaller scale[8] or in a different jurisdiction.[9] What scrutiny there has been of the role for children has tended to focus on the provision of AAs where family members cannot attend.[10] The effectiveness, and experience of, family members and other untrained individuals fulfilling the AA role in this jurisdiction for children has not been researched

---

[5] Charlie Taylor, *Review of the Youth Justice System in England and Wales* (Ministry of Justice (MoJ) 2016) 20.

[6] Roger Evans, 'The Conduct of Police Interviews with Juveniles', Royal Commission on Criminal Justice, Research Study No 8 (Her Majesty's Stationery Office (HMSO) 1993); Sarah Medford, Gisli H Gudjonsson, and John Pearse, 'The Efficacy of the Appropriate Adult Safeguard during Police Interviewing' (2003) 8 Law & Criminological Psychology 253; Stephen Moston and Terry Engelberg, 'Police Questioning Techniques in Tape Recorded Interviews with Criminal suspects' (1993) 3 Policing & Society 223.

[7] In particular, the research considered by the Royal Commission on Criminal Procedure Paul Softley and others, 'Police Interrogation: An Observational Study in Four Police Stations', Home Office Research Study No 4 (HMSO 1980).

[8] Vicky Kemp and Jacqueline Hodgson, 'Chapter 4. England and Wales Empirical Findings' in Miet Vanderhallen and others (eds), *Interrogating Young Suspects: Procedural Safeguards from an Empirical Perspective*, Vol 2 (Intersentia 2016)).

[9] See in respect of Northern Ireland Katie Quinn and John Jackson, 'Of Rights and Roles' (2007) 47 British Journal of Criminology 234; and Scotland Lindsay DG Thomson, V Galt, and Raj Darjee, 'Professionalizing the Role of Appropriate Adults' (2007) 18 Journal of Forensic Psychiatry & Psychology 99.

[10] Harriet Pierpoint, 'A Survey of Volunteer Appropriate Adult Services in England and Wales' (2004) 4 Youth Justice 32; Harriet Pierpoint, 'Quickening the PACE? The Use of Volunteers as Appropriate Adults in England and Wales' (2008) 18 International Journal of Research & Policy 397; Tim Bateman, 'A Night in the Cells: Children in Police Custody and the Provision of Non Familial Appropriate Adults' (Office of the Children's Commissioner 2017) <www.childrenscommissioner.gov.uk/wp-content/uploads/2018/06/A-Night-in-the-Cells.pdf> accessed 17 August 2023.

in any focused fashion. But most strikingly, the voices of children themselves are rarely heard, and their experiences of AA support have not previously been explored empirically in detail. Nor, indeed, is there much evidence from children of their experience of comparable protections in other jurisdictions.[11] The very limited research involving children with experience of the AA protection in this jurisdiction has tended to engage very small groups of children.[12] This chapter, for the first time, draws on the views of a sizeable number of children with experience of AA support and interviews with a variety of adults who have fulfilled the role to investigate how effectively the needs of children in police custody are met by this key provision.

I begin by setting out the circumstances in which the role was initially created and thereafter outline how the AA protection is currently formulated within the Police and Criminal Evidence Act 1984 (PACE) *Code C*[13] and related guidance. I then review in more detail the issues arising in respect of the role from the existing literature, before turning to the empirical data itself. I analyse the implementation and experience of the role with regard to each of the aspects identified in *Code C* as well as considering overarching issues which constrain the operation of the protection. In the ensuing discussion, I consider the tensions and shortcomings of the role identified in the empirical analysis before concluding with a consideration of options for reform of the protection, with reference to approaches adopted in other jurisdictions.

---

[11] See by way of an exception Quinn and Jackson (n 9).
[12] For example, nine children (the largest group) were interviewed in His Majesty's Inspectorate of Constabulary (HMIC) (now His Majesty's Inspectorate of Constabulary, Fire and Rescue Services, HMICFRS), *The Welfare of Vulnerable People in Police Custody* (HMIC 2015), representing the largest group, whilst only four children were interviewed for Bateman, 'A Night in the Cells' (n 10). At the time of writing, an ongoing study was engaging with children in police custody but had not yet reported: Vicky Kemp and others, *Examining the Impact of PACE on the Detention and Questioning of Child Suspects by the Police in England and Wales* (Nuffield Foundation, 25 May 2023) <https://www.nuffieldfoundation.org/project/impact-of-pace-on-the-detention-and-questioning-of-young-suspects> accessed 10 October 2023.
[13] *Code C: Revised Code of Practice for the Detention, Treatment and Questioning of Persons by Police Officers* (updated 4 November 2020). (In force at time of writing. Any relevant variance with the version in force at time of fieldwork, published May 2014, will be noted as it arises.)

A Lack of Clarity at the Inception of the Role

The formalization of the appropriate adult role in England and Wales finds its roots in the *Confait* case, which turned the spotlight on children's needs in police custody as never before. The case illustrated vividly how variously disadvantaged children are as suspects in police detention, requiring assistance not just to ensure that their rights are respected and due process observed but also to provide them with the emotional reassurance and support to mitigate the inevitable intimidation and inhibition likely to arise in the coercive setting of the police station. However, whilst acknowledging the complex nature of the support required, in his review of the case, Sir Henry Fisher did not grapple with how the child's different needs might most appropriately be met.[14] At the time of the *Confait* case, the Judge's Rules and Administrative Directions required that, 'as far as practicable', a child should only be interviewed in the presence of a parent or guardian or, in their absence, 'some other person who is not a police officer' and was of the same sex as the child.[15] None of the young *Confait* suspects had had independent adult support when they made their initial confessions. However, both Colin Lattimore's father and Ronald Leighton's mother had subsequently signed statements confirming that they were 'perfectly satisfied' with the way officers had taken the statements in which the boys had confirmed those confessions.[16] In reviewing the operation of the protection, Sir Henry Fisher noted the evidence given by Barrie Irving and Professor Morris to the Inquiry that parents may be 'unable or unwilling to stand up for their children and that the children themselves would not expect their parents to do so and would gain no comfort and support from their presence', but he nonetheless recommended simply that the Administrative Directions be strengthened.[17] The Royal Commission on Criminal Procedure (RCCP) followed suit, despite also recognizing that 'parents may not always act in a supportive way and that their presence may

---

[14] Sir Henry Fisher, 'Report of an Inquiry by the Hon. Sir Henry Fisher into the Circumstances Leading to the Trial of Three Persons on Charges Arising Out of the Death of Maxwell Confait and the Fire at 27 Doggett Road, London SE6' (HMSO 1977).

[15] Home Office, 'Judges' Rules and Administrative Directions to the Police' (HMSO 1964). Initially, a 'child' for these purposes was under fourteen, but in 1968 this was raised to under seventeen by Home Office, Administrative Direction 4, Home Office Circular of 31 May 1968 (HMSO 1968).

[16] Christopher Price and Jonathan Caplan, *The Confait Confessions* (Marion Boyars 1977) 35.

[17] Fisher (n 14), para 16.27ff.

not necessarily solve the problem of the juvenile's suggestibility'.[18] However, they concluded that parents should have an 'opportunity to be present when their child is in trouble' without addressing how the shortcomings parents may display in fulfilling the role might be mitigated.[19] Thus, when the AA role was first introduced in *Code C* in 1985, it reflected the recommendations of the RCCP in simply strengthening the Administrative Directions.

This lack of clarity at the outset about the nature of the protection required, and the attributes necessary to provide that support, has dogged the protection ever since. The operation of the AA role for children has been considered in a number of subsequent reviews, in particular by the Royal Commission on Criminal Justice (RCCJ),[20] the Home Office's Appropriate Adult Review Group,[21] and, more recently, in two thematic inspections, a Criminal Justice Joint Inspection (CJJI)[22] and one by HM Inspectorate of Constabulary (HMIC).[23] Each time, the issues identified by Sir Henry Fisher and the RCCP have surfaced and further challenges besides, especially frequent and lengthy delays to the arrival of the AA and problems arising from the AA's lack of legal privilege.[24] However, whilst the scope of the role has been better delineated in subsequent revisions of *Code C*, the underlying approach of relying predominantly on untrained, familial support has persisted.

The AA Role: Procedure and Existing Literature

The Role as Currently Formulated

The only definition of the role in primary legislation states simply that the purpose of the AA is to 'safeguard the interests of children and young persons detained or questioned by the police'.[25] *Code C*, paragraph 1.7A clarifies that the AA's role is to 'safeguard the rights, entitlements and welfare' of

---

[18] RCCP, 'Report (Cmnd 8092)' (HMSO 1981), para 4.103.
[19] ibid, para 4.103.
[20] RCCJ, 'Report (Cmnd 2263)' (HMSO 1991).
[21] Home Office, 'Appropriate Adults: Report of Review Group' (Home Office 1995).
[22] CJJI, 'Who's Looking Out?' (n 4).
[23] HMIC, *Welfare of Vulnerable People* (n 4).
[24] See for discussion Richard Gwynedd Parry, 'Protecting the Juvenile Suspect: What Exactly Is the Appropriate Adult Supposed to Do?' (2006) 18 Child and Family Law Quarterly 373.
[25] Crime and Disorder Act 1998, s 38(4)(a).

the suspect and sets out four specific functions which they are expected to fulfil, 'amongst other things'. In the first instance, the AA has a supportive role. The AA must 'support, advise and assist' the child when giving or providing information, or participating in any procedure, but not give legal advice. Second, the AA has a due process function; they must 'observe whether the police are acting properly and fairly' with respect to the child's rights and entitlements and should bring any concerns to the attention of a senior officer (of Inspector rank or above). Third, the AA plays a part in enabling communication. The AA is required to assist the child to 'communicate with the police' (whilst respecting their right of silence). Finally, the AA has a role in rights facilitation. The AA is required to help the child to 'understand their rights' and 'ensure those rights are protected and respected'.[26] To enable this function, the AA should be given a copy of the Notice of Rights and Entitlements ('the Notice').[27] Having in mind the right of the child to 'participate effectively' in the proceedings, I interpret this facilitation role, read alongside the AA's role to 'advise and assist', to encompass not only enabling the child to understand their rights but also supporting the child in exercising those rights. It is in this regard that the AA might properly be described as the 'a gateway to a young person's access to justice'.[28]

As part of the booking-in process, the custody officer (CO) must, 'as soon as practicable', contact the AA, inform them of the child's whereabouts and of the grounds for their detention, and ensure that the AA's attendance at the station is 'secured'.[29] The child must also be told, at that stage, of the AA's duties, as set out in *Code C*, paragraph 1.17A, and that they can 'consult privately with their AA 'at any time'.[30] The duties, set out in *Code C*, paragraph 1.17A, should be repeated to the AA on their arrival. They should also be provided with the guidance prepared by the Home Office, in conjunction with the National Appropriate Adult Network (HO/NAAN) Guide.[31] The AA has the right to

---

[26] Paragraph 1.7A was inserted into *Code C* (n 13) in July 2018. At the time of the fieldwork, the role was instead clarified in various guidance documents, primarily that prepared by the Home Office and the National Appropriate Adults Network (HO/NAAN), 'Guide for Appropriate Adults' (2011) <https://assets.publishing.service.gov.uk/government/uploads/system/uploads/attachment_data/file/117682/appropriate-adults-guide.pdf> accessed 17 August 2023. The role as described in this guide, still required to be provided to AAs on arrival in custody, is substantially in keeping with the inserted para 1.7A, if slightly broader in framing.
[27] *Code C* (n 13), para 3.17.
[28] HC (n 2), [63].
[29] *Code C* (n 13), para 3.15.
[30] ibid, para 3.15.
[31] HO/NAAN (n 26). College of Policing, 'Authorised Professional Practice (Detention and Custody)(Children and Young Persons)' (first published 23 October 2013, updated 2 May

request legal advice for the child (if they have declined)[32] and to inspect the custody record,[33] although there is no duty in *Code C* for the CO to inform the AA of this. The AA must be present when the young suspect is told his or her rights (or the rights must be repeated in the AA's presence on their arrival),[34] for intimate or strip searches,[35] in interview,[36] and for charge,[37] or where an out-of-court disposal is to be imposed.[38] Further guidance about how to fulfil the various duties is not required to be given orally, save in respect of interview, where the AA should be told that they are 'not expected to act simply as an observer' and that the purpose of their presence is to 'advise' the child, 'observe' whether the interview is being 'conducted properly and fairly', and to 'facilitate communication' with the child.[39]

The role should be fulfilled by a parent or guardian in the first instance (familial AA or FAA) or a representative of a local authority where the child is in care. Failing that, a 'non-familial' AA may be a 'social worker' of the local authority or, as a last resort, any 'responsible adult aged 18 or over' who is not a police officer or employed by the police in any way.[40] Local authorities have a statutory duty to provide AA services for young suspects whose family members cannot act.[41] This may be covered in-house but is often fulfilled using external 'schemes' which arrange for trained lay adults, either paid AAs ('PAA') or volunteers ('VAA') to attend. However, an individual cannot act as AA if they are suspected of involvement in the offence, the victim or a witness of the allegation, involved in its investigation, or have previously received admissions about the allegations from the young person.[42]

2023) 11 <http://Children and young persons | College of Policing> accessed 17 August 2023 (APP(DC)(CYP)). (Any variance with the version in force at the time of fieldwork (modified 28 July 2015) will be noted as it arises.)

[32] *Code C* (n 13), para 6.5A (although the child cannot be required to speak to the solicitor on arrival).
[33] ibid, para 2.4.
[34] ibid, para 3.17.
[35] ibid, Annex A, paras 5 and 11(c), unless urgent.
[36] ibid, para 11.15. Although there is provision for strip searches and interview to occur in the absence of the AA where urgently required (see *Code C* (n 13), Annex para 11(c) and para 11.18, respectively).
[37] ibid, para 16.1, 'if they are present at the time' ('Notes for Guidance' (NFG), 16C).
[38] See Miranda Bevan, 'Vulnerable Suspects: The Investigation Stage' in Penny Cooper and HHJ Heather Norton (eds), *Vulnerable People and the Criminal Justice System* (1st edn, OUP 2017) for the full scope of these requirements.
[39] *Code C* (n 13), para 11.17.
[40] ibid, para 1.7.
[41] Crime and Disorder Act 1998 (CDA 1998), s 38.
[42] *Code C* (n 13), NFG 1B.

Issues Raised in the Existing Literature

Delays

Since their formal introduction, there have been concerns about delays in securing the attendance of AAs, both familial[43] and non-familial.[44] In 1992, Brown and others found that young suspects spent approximately 60% of their time in custody waiting for the AA to arrive.[45] However, the introduction of the statutory duty on local authorities to provide AAs where family members cannot act[46] seems not to have reduced delays significantly. In 2015, HMIC identified, from custody-record analysis, young suspects waiting on average five-and-a-half hours for their AA,[47] whilst in 2017, the Children's Commissioner reported children experiencing an average wait of more than nine hours between arrest and the arrival of a non-familial AA.[48]

Various reasons have been observed for these delays, including the arrest of a young suspect late at night[49] and other work commitments on the part of volunteer AAs.[50] However, significant delays appear to arise also because of call-outs being delayed for the obtaining of further evidence[51] and to coincide with points in the custody process,[52] particularly interview.[53] Indeed, none of the young participants in HMIC's thematic inspection could recall the AA being present, save immediately prior to interview.[54]

---

[43] Brian Littlechild, 'An End to "Inappropriate Adults"?' (1998) Childright 8; Harriet Pierpoint, 'Reconstructing the Role of the Appropriate Adult in England and Wales' (2006) 6 Criminology and Criminal Justice 219; Tim Newburn and Stephanie Hayman, *Policing, Surveillance and Social Control: CCTV and Police Monitoring of Suspects* (Willan Publishing 2002).

[44] David C Brown, Tom Ellis, and Karen Larcombe, 'Changing the Code: Police Detention under the Revised PACE Codes of Practice', Home Office Research Study No 129 (HMSO 1992); Pierpoint, 'Quickening the PACE?' (n 10); Bateman, 'A Night in the Cells' (n 10).

[45] Brown, Ellis, and Larcombe (n 44), predating the CDA 1998 (n 41).

[46] CDA 1998 (n 41), s 38.

[47] HMIC, *Welfare of Vulnerable People* (n 12).

[48] Bateman, 'A Night in the Cells' (n 10) 6.

[49] HMIC, *Welfare of Vulnerable People* (n 12); Pierpoint, 'Quickening the PACE?' (n 10).

[50] Teresa Nemitz and Philip Bean, 'The Effectiveness of a Volunteer Appropriate Adult Scheme' (1998) 38 Medicine, Science & the Law 251; Harriet Pierpoint, 'How Appropriate Are Volunteers as "Appropriate Adults" for Young Suspects? The "Appropriate Adult" System and Human Rights' (2000) 22 Journal of Social Welfare and Family Law 383.

[51] Pierpoint, 'Quickening the PACE?' (n 10).

[52] Layla Skinns, *Police Custody: Governance, Legitimacy and Reform in the Criminal Justice Process* (Willan Publishing 2011).

[53] CJJI, 'Who's Looking Out?' (n 4); HMIC, *Welfare of Vulnerable People* (n 12).

[54] HMIC, *Welfare of Vulnerable People* (n 12) 186.

As to effect, some studies have suggested that such delays result in longer overall detention times for young suspects,[55] although a direct causal link has not been clearly established.[56] David Dixon posited that delays in AA attendance might induce false confessions,[57] although Phillips and Brown found no evidence to support this contention.[58] However, plainly, as the CJJI have suggested,[59] operating within a more limited timescale as a result of delayed arrival is likely to make fulfilling the role more challenging.

The Complexity of the Role

Such time constraints are particularly concerning because of the multi-faceted nature of the role. This has long been identified as problematic:[60] 'ambiguous and contradictory'[61] and 'complex and demanding'.[62] In recommending its codification, the RCCP apparently appreciated that the role was 'not as easy as it was to describe' but opted for a 'practical solution' rather than engaging with the legal challenges thrown up by the support required.[63] There have been repeated calls for clarity in terms of the scope and focus of the role,[64] arguably inadequately addressed by the most recent clarification in *Code C*, paragraph 1.7A. In particular, there is a tension between the welfare aspects of the role and the AA's duty to ensure

---

[55] CJJI, 'Who's Looking Out?' (n 4); Vicky Kemp, Nigel Balmer, and Pascoe Pleasence, 'Whose Time Is It Anyway? Factors Associated with Duration in Police Custody' (2012) Criminal Law Review 736; Skinns, *Police Custody* (n 52).

[56] Layla Skinns, 'Stop the Clock? Predictors of Detention without Charge in Police Custody Areas' (2010) 10 Criminology & Criminal Justice 303.

[57] David Dixon, 'Juvenile Suspects and the Police and Criminal Evidence Act' in David AC Freestone and Hugh K Bevan (eds), *Children and the Law: Essays in Honour of Professor HK Bevan* (Hull University Press 1990).

[58] Coretta Phillips and David C Brown, 'Entry into the Criminal Justice System: A Survey of Police Arrests and Their Outcomes', Home Office Research Study 185 (Home Office 1998) 54.

[59] CJJI, 'Who's Looking Out?' (n 4), para 3.39.

[60] Pierpoint, 'Volunteer Survey' (n 10); Quinn and Jackson (n 9); Roxanna Dehaghani, 'Interpreting and Reframing the Appropriate Adult Safeguard' (2022) 42(1) Oxford Journal of Legal Studies 187.

[61] Pierpoint, 'Quickening the PACE?' (n 10) 399.

[62] Ian Cummins, "'The Other Side of Silence': The Role of the Appropriate Adult Post-Bradley' (2011) 5 Ethics & Social Welfare 306, 308.

[63] Observations of Barrie Irving in an unpublished conference paper, referenced in Teresa Nemitz and Philip Bean, 'Protecting the Rights of the Mentally Disordered in Police Stations: The Use of the Appropriate Adult in England and Wales' (2001) 24 International Journal of Law & Psychiatry 595 600–02.

[64] Fiona Brookman and Harriet Pierpoint, 'Access to Legal Advice for Young Suspects and Remand Prisoners' (2003) 42 Howard Journal of Criminal Justice 452; Pierpoint, 'Volunteer Survey' (n 10); Evans (n 6); C Palmer, 'The Appropriate Adult' (1996) Legal Action 6; Ciaran White, 'Re-assessing the Social Worker's Role as an Appropriate Adult' (2002) 24 Journal of Social Welfare & Family Law 55.

due process;[65] what Cummins describes as a crossing of the 'welfare and justice axis'.[66] Research to date, whilst identifying this tension, has not explored how this plays out for young suspects. Pierpoint's survey research with AA scheme coordinators identified what she describes as 'role-creep' towards welfare-orientated functions,[67] whilst, by contrast, volunteer AAs supporting vulnerable adults viewed their role primarily as ensuring due process.[68] Concerns have also been raised that the AA has become simply another part of the custody process, an administrative role focusing 'on complying with PACE 1984 rather than safeguarding and promoting the welfare of children and young people'.[69]

Lack of Legal Privilege

Just as problematic is the question of what duty of confidentiality, if any, the AA owes to the child (or vulnerable suspect). *Code C*, NFG 1E answers the question in the negative: 'An appropriate adult is not subject to legal privilege.'[70] This has been confirmed in the case of *R v Ward*,[71] where admissions made to an AA by an adult suspect who was 'very shaken' and 'in a bad way of anxiety' were held to be admissible at trial. This is the more troubling because there is no duty on the CO to inform an untrained AA, or a child, of this lack of privilege. Indeed, the suspect's right to talk 'privately' to the AA 'at any time' might be taken as an endorsement that they may speak freely in that discussion to the AA, present for their support and guidance. *Code C*, NFG 1E is also problematic because it does not, in fact, set out the whole picture. The presence of an AA at a conversation which would otherwise attract legal privilege (ie in a consultation with a legal adviser) does not destroy that privilege, at least.[72] However, this is not appreciated by all legal

---

[65] Nemitz and Bean, 'Protecting the Rights' (n 63).
[66] Cummins, 'AA Post-Bradley' (n 62) 308.
[67] Harriet Pierpoint, 'Extending and Professionalising the Role of the Appropriate Adult' (2011) 33 Journal of Social Welfare & Family Law 139, 150–51.
[68] Tricia Jessiman and Ailsa Cameron, 'The Role of the Appropriate Adult in Supporting Vulnerable Adults in Custody: Comparing the Perspectives of Service Users and Service Providers' (2017) 45 British Journal of Learning Disabilities 246.
[69] CJJI, 'Who's Looking Out?' (n 4) 7. See also Medford, Gudjonnson, and Pearse (n 6); Ian Cummins, 'A Path Not Taken? Mentally Disordered Offenders and the Criminal Justice System' (2007) 28 Journal of Social Welfare & Family Law 267.
[70] See also *Code C* (n 13), NFG 1K.
[71] [2018] EWCA Crim 1464, [5].
[72] *Local Authority v B* [2008] EWHC 1017 (Fam), [2009] 1 FLR 289, see for discussion Chris Bath, 'Legal Privilege and Appropriate Adults' (2014) 178 Criminal Law & Justice Weekly 404.

representatives, many of whom routinely refuse to allow AAs to be present for legal consultation for fear of them destroying their privilege.[73]

This lack of privilege has long been identified as problematic. The RCCJ felt that it potentially 'undermines the whole purpose of the role',[74] and the Appropriate Adult Review Group, which reviewed the protection at the Commission's instigation, recommended, in 1995, that privilege should apply to the AA's discussions with the suspect, but this has never been adopted.[75] Concerns have continued to be raised by commentators in this regard,[76] but there has been no previous investigation of the extent to which child suspects, and their familial AAs, appreciate that lack of privilege and whether it affects the operation of the protection.

Concerns about the Suitability and Effectiveness of Familial AAs

Whilst there is no available official data, research suggests that the majority of young suspects continue to be supported by familial AAs,[77] even following the enactment of the CDA 1998.[78] Echoing the reservations expressed by Sir Henry Fisher and the RCCP, in 1991, the RCCJ acknowledged that 'parents may find it difficult to remain objective' and may assist the police or, indeed, be 'too defensive', concluding that a 'more systematic approach' was needed to both suitability and training of the AA.[79] No more systematic approach has emerged with regard to familial AAs. Subsequent research has repeatedly observed family members showing distress or hostility towards young suspects;[80] a response that Quinn and Jackson observed officers found 'useful' for their purposes.[81] Roger Evans's 1993 analysis of 160 'juvenile' interviews, for example, revealed that parents (and other non-professionals) acted as AAs in 80% of the cases examined, but

---

[73] Nick Dent and Sean O'Beirne, 'Inappropriate Adults? A Review of the Current Use of Appropriate Adults in the Criminal Justice System' (2021) 85 Journal of Criminal Law (Hertford) 44.
[74] RCCJ (n 20) 44, para 87.
[75] Home Office, 'Report of Review Group' (n 21).
[76] Gwynedd Parry (n 24); Nemitz and Bean, 'Protecting the Rights' (n 63).
[77] Tom Bucke and David Brown, 'In Police Custody: Police Powers and Suspects' Rights under the Revised PACE Codes of Practice', Home Office Research Study 174 (Home Office 1997); Phillips and Brown (n 58).
[78] Kemp and Hodgson (n 8).
[79] RCCJ (n 20) 43–44.
[80] See eg Bucke and Brown (n 77); Roxanna Dehaghani, *Vulnerability in Police Custody: Police Decision-Making and the Appropriate Adult Safeguard* (Routledge 2019).
[81] Quinn and Jackson (n 9) 245.

in three quarters of these, the AA did not intervene, and when they did so, they were as likely to be unsupportive as supportive.[82] In a US study, parents who had had a negative relationship with their child in advance of the arrest tended to overreact to the arrest and respond in harsher and more negative ways to their children.[83]

A sense of this parental hostility emerges from accounts provided by young people in Hazel and colleagues' study of experiences of the youth justice system.[84] However, the very limited evidence from children themselves tends to focus more firmly on feeling inhibited from speaking openly in front of family members in interview,[85] echoing similar observations made by vulnerable adults.[86] The courts have not provided much clarity on when the attitude of a non-familial AA will render them unsuitable to act. In keeping with the importance ascribed by the RCCP to the AA being someone in whom the child 'has confidence',[87] in *R v Blake*, an estranged father who showed 'no empathy' was held to be unsuitable as AA.[88] However, in *R v Palmer*,[89] the court focused, by contrast, on the importance of the AA having 'authority' over the young person.[90] Conversely, whilst the ability of a familial AA to provide reassurance is glimpsed in some research studies, more often as a general acknowledgment[91] or as the observation of officers,[92] there is little evidence from children themselves about this aspect of support.

The ability of a familial AA to perform the range of tasks required of them has not been considered empirically in any depth, nor how, if at all, the CO assesses their capacity for the role. The courts appear to have taken a somewhat inconsistent approach to an AA's capacity. In *R v Morse*

---

[82] Evans (n 6) 39.
[83] Wesley T Church II and others, '"What Do You Mean My Child Is in Custody?" A Qualitative Study of Parental Response to the Detention of Their Child' (2009) 12 Journal of Family Social Work 9.
[84] Neal Hazel, Ann Hagell, and Laura Brazier, *Young Offenders' Perceptions of Their Experiences in the Criminal Justice System* (Economic and Social Research Council 2003).
[85] HMIC, *Welfare of Vulnerable People* (n 12) 186.
[86] Jessiman and Cameron (n 68).
[87] RCCP (n 18), 4.103.
[88] 1989 1 WLR 432, 440.
[89] (Acton Crown Court), 17 October 1991.
[90] See also *R v Jefferson (Andrew Steven)* [1994] 1 All ER 270 (CA(Crim Div)), in which a father who criticized his fifteen-year-old son in interview, intervening to question him or challenge his exculpatory statements, was deemed to be an appropriate AA.
[91] Chris Bath and others, *There to Help: Ensuring Provision of Appropriate Adults for Mentally Vulnerable Adults Detained or Interviewed by the Police* (National Appropriate Adult Network 2015) 12.
[92] Quinn and Jackson (n 9) 244.

and Others,⁹³ excluding evidence of a confession obtained from a child in presence of his father as AA (having an IQ under seventy, being virtually illiterate, and probably incapable of appreciating the gravity of his son's situation), Beezley J held that a person unable to discharge any or all of the AA's responsibilities is an inappropriate choice. He gave as an 'extreme example' of an inappropriate AA a parent who spoke little English who would 'nullify' the purpose of the code, being a 'mere token presence' in interview. However, by contrast, in *R v W*,⁹⁴ a woman who was psychotic and suffering paranoid delusions at the time of the interview of her thirteen-year-old child was a suitable AA since her psychosis was considered to be confined to a dispute with a neighbour and she was capable of dealing rationally with current events.

Commentators have raised concerns more generally about family members' lack of training and knowledge of the role itself and their awareness of the custody process and criminal justice system.⁹⁵ Indeed, research in the United States with 170 English-speaking parent–child pairs identified that 'a sizeable subset of parents may not have the requisite practical understanding of police practices and youth rights within the context of interrogation to protect children's legal interests as the law presumes'.⁹⁶ There is no reason to consider that parents in England and Wales are any better informed. The permissive approach taken by the courts to the obligation to inform (see *H and M v Director of Public Prosecutions*)⁹⁷ is unlikely to have encouraged rigorous efforts on the part of COs, although it has been suggested that the role is, in any event, 'too complex for cursory explanation' by a CO in a busy custody suite.⁹⁸

How does this manifest itself in familial AA performance of their due process role? Brown identified that family members could be unduly compliant in the face of police requests and were intimidated and confused by the experience.⁹⁹ By way of illustration, when asked by Thames Television

---

⁹³ [1990] 11 WLUK 237, [1991] Crim LR 195.
⁹⁴ [1994] Crim LR 130, [1994] 1 WLUK 214 (CA (Crim Div)).
⁹⁵ Bath, *There to Help* (n 91); HMIC, *Welfare of Vulnerable People* (n 12); John Williams, 'The Inappropriate Adult' (2000) 22 Journal of Social Welfare & Family Law 43.
⁹⁶ Jennifer Woolard and others, 'Examining Adolescents' and Their Parents' Conceptual and Practical Knowledge of Police Interrogation: A Family Dyad Approach' (2008) 37 Journal of Youth & Adolescence 685, 696.
⁹⁷ [1997] 12 WLUK 189, (1998) Crim LR 653.
⁹⁸ Williams (n 95) 44.
⁹⁹ Brown (n 1). See for similar in a US context Church II and others (n 83).

why she had made her statement approving the taking of her son's confession statement, Mrs Leighton reflected:

> I can't explain it really, they just say 'sign'. I mean when you've got a room full of detectives and you know they look at you and they say 'sign', you naturally sign. I mean, I was just as scared as what Ronnie was.[100]

Similarly passive roles have been identified by comparable supporting adults in other jurisdictions, including in Australia[101] and Ireland.[102] Conversely, Kemp and Hodgson identified that some parents may pursue goals which are inconsistent with the child's best legal interests.[103] But exactly how familial AAs understand and engage with this complex role has not been explored in any detail.

Concerns about the Suitability and Effectiveness of Non-familial AAs

The performance of non-familial AAs has also raised concerns. Pierpoint posits that scheme AAs, by virtue of their likely age and social status, may hold unduly positive attitudes towards the police, which may reduce their effectiveness in pursuing their role robustly.[104] It has also been suggested that scheme AAs may take a paternalistic approach to young suspects[105] or discriminate against young Black, Asian, or minority ethnic suspects.[106] Young people spoken to as part of inspections were 'ambivalent' about non-familial AAs and consistently felt that family had played a more significant part in interview.[107]

Commentators have also expressed doubts about the effectiveness of social workers acting as AAs,[108] especially where a conflict of interest may

---

[100] Reported in Price and Caplan (n 16) 35.
[101] Layla Skinns, *Police Powers and Citizens' Rights: Discretionary Decision-Making in Police Detention* (Routledge 2019) 170–71; re New South Wales David Dixon and Gail Travis, *Interrogating images: audio-visually recorded police questioning of suspects* (University of Sydney 1990).
[102] Skinns, *Police Powers* (n 101); Louise Forde, 'Realising the Right of the Child to Participate in the Criminal Process' (2018) 18 Youth Justice 265.
[103] Kemp and Hodgson (n 8).
[104] Pierpoint, 'How Appropriate Are Volunteers?' (n 50). Although see HMIC, *Welfare of Vulnerable People* (n 12) for examples of robust challenge by non-familial AAs.
[105] Pierpoint, 'How Appropriate Are Volunteers?' (n 50).
[106] Littlechild, 'An End to "Inappropriate Adults"?' (n 43).
[107] CJJI, 'Who's Looking Out?' (n 4) 34.
[108] Jacqueline Hodgson, 'Vulnerable Suspects and the Appropriate Adult' (1997) Criminal Law Review 785.

arise from their previous engagement with, or authority over, the child.[109] In particular, social workers might have conflicting duties of confidentiality and disclosure[110] or be biased towards the police.[111] Equally, there is potential for conflict between the social worker's therapeutic and pastoral role (making them liable to encourage admissions) and the legal best interests of the suspect.[112] Finally, there are long-standing concerns about the lack of training for the role received by social worker AAs.[113]

The Scope of the Empirical Data

Of the forty-one young participants interviewed in this study, thirty-nine spoke of their experiences of having an AA, with many describing AA assistance in respect of a number of different custody episodes. In addition, I spoke to twenty-two AAs across the observations and separate adult interviews. This includes eleven semi-structured interviews with people who have acted as AAs (FAA1-7, RHAA1-2 (residential care home employees regularly acting as an AA), YOTAA (a youth offending team (YOT) employee who regularly acts as an AA), and ProfAA (an experienced, paid AA also coordinating AA services for a national provider). In observation areas, there was a good variation of AA provision, where familial AAs (or representatives of the child's accommodation provider) could not act, enabling me to hold informal interviews with eleven further AAs acting in different capacities (VAA-4, PAA1-5, RHAA3-4). These discussions tended to last twenty to forty minutes and generally took place in a separate room. As a qualitative study, this research is unable to identify the frequency of different types of support. Nonetheless, in keeping with previous observations, the majority of young participants in this study had been supported by family members: eighteen had only experienced familial AA support, fourteen had experienced both familial and non-familial support, and only seven young participants had been supported exclusively by non-familial AAs.

---

[109] Quinn and Jackson (n 9); White (n 64); Dent and O'Beirne (n 73).
[110] Brian Littlechild, 'Reassessing the Role of the "Appropriate Adult"' (1995) Criminal Law Review 540.
[111] Bucke and Brown (n 77).
[112] Hannah Quirk, *The Rise and Fall of the Right of Silence* (Routledge 2017); John Pearse and Gisli H Gudjonsson, 'Police Interviewing Techniques at Two South London Police Stations' (1997) 3 Psychology, Crime & Law 63; Quinn and Jackson (n 9).
[113] Ibid; Bucke and Brown (n 77); White (n 64).

The Role in Practice: Child Suspect Experiences

I turn now to examine the functioning of the AA support in practice. I focus on the four aspects of the role previously identified: support, rights facilitation, due process, and communication.[114] As will become apparent, very different issues arise in each regard, depending on the nature of the AA, and so I address each aspect in relation to familial and non-familial AAs separately. However, before I embark on that analysis, I consider, first of all, several overarching aspects which fundamentally reduce the scope of the protection for both groups.

Delay: 'We're not going to get an AA just down for rights'

The most striking finding in relation to the AA role in practice is their conspicuous absence for substantial swathes of the detention episode. Although not a quantitative study, the accounts of young participants, and the average time lapse between booking in and AA arrival on observation, indicate delays broadly in line with the average waiting time of five-and-a-half hours observed by HMIC.[115] Approximately half of those young suspects tracked on observation for whom data is available waited over five hours to see an AA, including some very much longer delays, with familial AA delays broadly comparable with scheme AA delays within the sample. Of those young people that I interviewed, whilst young participants in the ten-to-fourteen-year age bracket were more likely to relate a much shorter waiting time, this was not the case for all of that group, and many young participants (particularly those detained at age sixteen and seventeen) complained of very much longer waits, often overnight.

Where an arrest is unplanned, some delays are inevitable. Family members described various difficulties, such as work commitments, having to make childcare arrangements, or being asked to attend a distant custody block whilst relying on public transport. In a geographically spread force (such as F3), the nearest custody block could be thirty or forty miles from the AA's home address. RHAA1 and 2 described how securing an AA from

---

[114] The AA's role in interview is dealt with in more detail in chapter 6.
[115] HMIC, *Welfare of Vulnerable People* (n 12) 92.

a residential home might mean waiting for additional staff to come on shift. Likewise, AA schemes could also struggle to fill the request swiftly. In F2 and F3, COs complained of real problems securing a non-familial AA, particularly where a child was arrested after 9pm, sometimes resulting in children being detained overnight.[116] In discussions with both COs and scheme AAs, overnight delays were often justified on the basis that the young person was unlikely to be interviewed, in any event, at that time, overlooking the AA's significant role outside interview. Even during working hours, attendance might be difficult to secure. Where the scheme relied on volunteers, this could be a problem. ICV2 (F2) explained that it would not be 'unusual' for someone to be in custody at midday but not see an AA until the evening: 'they're waiting for an AA to finish their work and have something to eat and come in at 8pm at night. Because they're volunteers they can't drop everything and run.' Jurisdictional issues could also cause delays where local social services departments refused to arrange an AA because the young suspect was arrested out of their home area (eg YS45).[117]

However, in very many cases, on observation, COs and interviewing officers deliberately delayed the attendance of the AA for young suspects to coincide with stages in the process, particularly interview, as previous research has noted.[118] In F2 and F3, deliberate delay of the AA to coincide with interview was routine. Indeed, so fixed is this approach in some areas (such as F2) that the task of coordinating AA attendance was no longer retained by the CO but consigned to officers involved in the investigation instead. The AA's attendance would be arranged when 'we've got a timescale for interview' (CA43) or when 'we're ready to deal with them' (CO24). CO27's observation—'we're not going to get an AA just down for rights'—represented a fairly standard approach. In F1, there was more of a culture of calling the AA (whether family or scheme) down for rights and entitlements to be explained to the child, but then sending them away. To a degree, scheme AAs seemed to be complicit in this. For example, VAA2 explained, 'Normally I come down for rights and entitlements and interview all at once ... If I know it's just for rights I wouldn't accept the call.' Likewise, PAA5 could see no sense in being called out for a young suspect late at night

---

[116] See for similar Kemp, Balmer, and Pleasence (n 55); Layla Skinns, *Overnight Detention of Children in Police Cells* (Howard League 2011).
[117] Although refusal on this basis was prohibited in the Youth Justice Board (YJB), 'Case Management Guidance 2014' (YJB 2014), s 3, para 1.3, which was then applicable.
[118] See for similar findings in previous research nn 52–53.

because they were not going to be interviewed. ProfAA confirmed this approach: 'They aim to do it all in one hit. That's really because of budgetary constraints. LAs [local authorities] and YOTs don't want to pay for us to come down twice', although there was, she said, increasing area variation, with YOTs in some areas insisting on young suspects going no more than two hours at a time without seeing an AA.

Family members related often being informed speedily of the arrest (as required in *Code C*, 3.13) but frequently having their attendance delayed, including overnight. FAA1, for example, described being informed one night of her son's arrest in F2. She was told to telephone at 8am the following morning, when she was asked to come in at 10am, but then waited two-and-a-half hours in reception before seeing her son. These observations were borne out by young participants, a number of whom recalled seeing AAs only just before interview and that, if arrested at night, they would generally see their family member in the morning. Rezar explained, 'Yeah, literally, when they say, "We're interviewing you now." You walk out and you see your mum, or whoever. Then, they tell you, "Do you want five minutes to talk to them?"'. Unfortunately, it seemed that independent custody visitors (ICVs) had little purchase on this approach to delay. Although one ICV had raised concerns (ICV2), their standard questionnaire does not touch on this issue—typically enquiring whether an AA has been notified rather than checking the timing of their attendance.

Effects of Delay

As the evidence of intimidation and inhibition reviewed in Chapter 2 makes plain, the early hours of police detention are a critical period, particularly for those in detention for the first time. Many young suspects are in desperate need of support and advice and for contact with someone not connected to the police. It is very troubling, therefore, that AAs, the central protection provided to children in custody, are regularly not seeing young suspects until five hours or longer into their detention experiences. Indeed, awaiting the arrival of the AA was, in itself, a source of anxiety for some young suspects. For a very young suspect, the need for personal support in those early hours is frankly obvious, as L&D5 explained:

> The youngest person I've seen was eleven-to-twelve years old. He was in a cell on his own. He'd broken up a polystyrene cup and was putting bits into his mouth. I think he's too young to be locked in a cell... The fact that the door's locked and he's got nobody at that age—it's not appropriate

in my view. From the moment they get here an AA should be with them all the time. They shouldn't just turn up for rights and interview.

Quite apart from the young suspect missing the personal reassurance of a familiar, or at least friendly, adult to help manage their emotions and expectations, the child has no independent support to understand what is happening, to engage their rights and entitlements during this phase, and to enable them to provide key information to facilitate their safe detention. Indeed, as identified in Chapter 3, the reading of the young person's rights and entitlements may have been delayed entirely to await the AA's attendance.

Delayed arrival hampers the familial AA's ability to perform the role. If asked to attend to coincide with interview, their opportunity to familiarize themselves with any information provided about their role, and about rights and entitlements, is substantially reduced. Young participants complained of the opportunity for only brief discussions with familial AAs, or no discussion at all (Megan), before being required for legal consultation and then interview, something confirmed on observation. Different challenges arise for non-familial AAs. Delayed arrival places significant pressure on tasks which may take some time, particularly rapport-building, assessing fitness for interview, and checking understanding. In addition, where the young person then consulted alone with a solicitor,[119] AAs found that there might not be time before interview for a further consultation with the young person to check understanding of any legal advice and support their decision-making.

As a result, such delays can fundamentally undermine the AA's ability to support the young suspect in ways critical to enabling their effective participation in the process, particularly their decision-making in interview. Whilst the question of whether such delays can induce false confessions[120] would be impossible to answer using qualitative data, in light of the myriad factors affecting such a course, the evidence certainly indicates routes by which delay may contribute to that outcome. Was there evidence to support previous findings that AA delay may add to the total length of time a young person is in police custody?[121] This was certainly the impression that

---

[119] Not uncommon. The AA does not have the right to insist on being present for legal conference.
[120] See nn 57–58.
[121] See eg Kemp, Balmer, and Pleasance (n 55).

some young participants had, particularly where they could compare their experience with adult co-arrestees. Officers also expressed concerns about the impact on overall detention periods, given the difficulties securing attendance. CO27 reflected for example, 'I do think being a juvenile can keep people in custody an extra four to five hours.' Likewise, solicitors provided examples of situations where delays identifying an AA, or coordinating their attendance, had led to a young person being detained overnight, for example, Sol3. On observation, there were occasional instances where the delayed arrival of an AA clearly extended detention. For example, fourteen-year-old YS28 was detained for over seven hours without an AA becoming available before being bailed to return for interview when an AA could be arranged. Otherwise, it was generally difficult to separate delays arising due to the timing of the AA's attendance from delays caused by, for example, the investigation, coordination of the parties for interview, or avoiding interviewing a young suspect during the night.

CO Control: 'As long as it supports the police'

The support that a young suspect can enjoy from the AA is also wholly managed—and often further significantly curtailed—by the CO, in addition to their control over the timing of their arrival. This occurs in the following three different ways.

Suitability

The CO controls who is able to fulfil this vital protection. Despite the importance of the role, beyond the hierarchy set out in *Code C*, paragraph 1.7 and the case-specific exclusions in NFG 1B, neither *Code C* nor APP(DC) provide any guidance as to how to address issues of suitability for the role—whether in terms of cognitive capacity, awareness of the role and processes, or attitude towards the police and the criminal justice system. Although of importance, given the roles' demands, the cognitive capacity of an AA to fulfil the role and their own ability to understand the process and communicate effectively was not systematically considered on observation.[122] COs explained that a potential AA might be rejected for being drunk. Likewise, I was told of two episodes where, by chance, it was spotted that a parent

---

[122] Beyond where English was obviously not the familial AA's first language, in which case an interpreter was likely to be offered.

attending as AA had previously required an AA themselves (CO20, Sol11). Indeed, I observed a familial AA struggling to grasp information on charge being given to her son, prompting him to respond, 'Mum I know what I'm doing, shut up.' The CO observed to me after their departure, 'which one needs the AA—that's what you need to ask yourself'. He had clearly identified that the AA was incapable of fulfilling the role satisfactorily, but did not act to engage further help. Such indifference is perhaps not surprising—there is no requirement to consider the issue and little at stake, given the low likelihood of scrutiny in court and the permissive approach taken in case law. Even if minded to, it could be very difficult for a CO to investigate the capacity of a familial AA in brief exchanges in the custody suite. AAs may not wish, or be embarrassed, to reveal linguistic or cognitive problems. Nor are many solicitors likely to be concerned. As Sol2 put it, 'Family appropriate adults are OK if they keep their mouths shut.' An AA confused into silence would be unlikely to be an issue.

Although I did not myself observe any acts of aggression or hostility by familial AAs towards child suspects, nonetheless, this was identified as an issue by some COs. Familial AAs could be 'livid' (CO41), whilst CA2 observed that 'most of the time when parents come in you hear shouting', reflecting previous research findings.[123] Some COs described how they would work to avoid such conflict, for example, by trying to persuade an overwrought parent to step aside and allow someone less close to the suspect to be AA: 'sometimes a step-parent is better' (CO6). But more commonly, officers seemed to consider that parents being suitably angry with their child in custody was to be welcomed as long as it did not go too far: 'The right amount of giving a juvenile a hard time is OK—as long as it supports the police. When it gets in the way it's not good' (CO9). The informal social control capacity of the parent can thus be harnessed for police objectives.

By contrast, COs did not show such a high threshold for antagonism towards themselves and fellow officers. CO7 described how he had refused to allow one parent to act as AA: 'she's a teacher but her attitude is so anti-police I've declined to use her as AA ... she's biased so I can't use her in my view.' CO21 expressed a similar view: 'if the AA is antagonistic—I would deem them not appropriate and say so'. Such an approach reveals the fragility of the protection and the ease with which a CO may undermine it. The familial AA who is, for example, 'insistent that their children have been

---

[123] See eg Nemitz and Bean, 'Effectiveness of a VAA Scheme' (n 50).

assaulted' (CO26), may be raising valid concerns. Plainly, an antagonistic parent should not be allowed to frustrate the process, but it is problematic that the process allows a CO to remove a parent who may be simply, if forcefully, fulfilling their role.[124]

Although research has long identified the potential for conflicts of interest to arise where social workers and YOT workers are involved, there was limited awareness amongst COs of such issues. By way of example, although the Youth Justice Board Case Management Guidance 2014 (in force during fieldwork) prohibited a staff member from a residential care home attending as AA in relation to an incident occurring within the home,[125] the accounts of young participants, RHAA1 and 2, and one observed case (YS30) suggest that this may not always be observed.

Enabling the AA

The effectiveness of an AA in large part depends on what the child suspect and the AA understand the role to consist of. What the CO is required to tell the child and AA about the role has been enhanced since the fieldwork, with the introduction of the role description in *Code C*, 1.7A. Nonetheless, during observation, I did not observe a single young suspect receive the full information, then prescribed by *Code C*, paragraph 3.18, that the AA's duties 'include giving advice and assistance and that they can consult privately with them at any time'.[126] Some young suspects whose booking in I observed, particularly those who had been arrested a number of times before, received no information at all about the role. Where the information was given, it tended to be less than informative. For example, YS4, in custody for the first time, was told that the AA's role was 'basically to sit in a room with you'.

On no occasion did I observe a child suspect being told they could 'consult privately' with their AA 'at any time',[127] nor was any young participant aware of this right. This is arguably a significant omission on the part of COs since the provision has the capacity to transform the experiences of young suspects in custody. To be able to speak privately, on demand, with

---

[124] Removal of an AA from interview requires authorization from a senior officer (*Code C* (n 13), para 11.17A), but there is no clear restriction on the CO's capacity to refuse to allow an AA to act at the outset.

[125] YJB (n 117), s 3, para 1.3.

[126] *Code C* (n 13) (May 2014), para 3.18. See for current requirements *Code C* (n 13) (4 November 2020), paras 1.7A and 3.15, and for similar observations: Brown, Ellis, and Larcombe (n 44).

[127] *Code C* (n 13), para 3.15 (both at the time of fieldwork and at the time of writing).

someone trusted, even if only on the telephone, could be a huge relief, given the uncertainty and anxiety recounted by young participants. Many young participants were clear that they would have welcomed the chance to speak to a familial AA earlier in their detention experience. Some COs were apparently unaware of the requirement. Others noted that requests for contact would be hard to meet in the current circumstances, which is undeniably true, especially where a scheme AA was required. ProfAA acknowledged that contracts with YOTs to provide AAs rarely allowed for such a facility. Like the requirement not to detain in a cell, it appears not to figure in the institutional consciousness. This entitlement is not included in the Notice, nor referred to in the APP (although it is mentioned in the HO/NAAN Guide).[128]

Unsurprisingly, young participants had very varied understandings of the support they could expect from an AA. Some, particularly those who had been supported by familial AAs exclusively, had no real idea at all about the AA's purpose, and no young participant, whatever their experience, had grasped the full extent of the role. This lack of awareness may be mitigated if the AA is clearly informed of their role. However, despite the requirements in *Code C* and the APP(DC)(CYP), familial AAs also tended to be provided with fairly limited information. The explanation was often very brief, typically along the lines of informing the AA that they were present 'to make sure the young person is cared for—so that they understand fully what is going on' (CO38). Experienced familial AAs might receive even less information, as CO6 explained: 'You can see on the custody record if they've been in before—so you can tailor the message.' Non-familial AAs with a professional background, received no information at all. This, too, could be problematic—for example, I encountered three who were apparently unaware of their right to request legal advice for the young suspect (RHAA1, RHAA2, and YOTAA).

Nor was the printed HO/NAAN guidance invariably provided as required.[129] In F1, no printed guidance was provided, whilst in F2, the AA was required to sign a sheet which repeated the AA role in interview (as set out in *Code C*, paragraph 11.17). In F3, the HO/NAAN Guide was routinely given out to familial AAs, although I did not see any officer explain the relevance of the document. FAA3, who had acted as AA in F3, explained that 'when I got there they did give me all these papers to read', but she had

---

[128] HO/NAAN (n 26).
[129] APP(DC)(CYP) (n 31) 11.

not taken in their contents and 'just signed away'. On observation, COs never went beyond what was required in *Code C* in supporting the AA and rarely achieved what was set out there. I saw no familial AA being offered the custody record to look at, being invited to go through the Notice with the young person and informed how to make a complaint or of the young suspect's rights to speak to them at any time. As a result, familial AAs described very limited understandings of the role, as FAA2 relates in the epigraph. Despite the general lack of information, some familial AAs felt able to engage with the role. FAA4, for example, felt confident that she would be able to complain 'to the head sergeant' if she needed to. But others revealed how the combination of the wholly unfamiliar and ill explained, with the extreme stress of the episode, meant that they lapsed into passivity.[130]

Access

Finally, simple access to the young suspect is also heavily controlled by the CO once the AA attends. On observation, AAs were frequently only present with the young suspect when they were required by *Code C* to legitimize 'set-piece' elements of the process: repetition of rights and entitlements, strip search (where required), the taking of photographs and biometric data, interview and charge. Some familial AAs were allowed to sit out with the young suspect, particularly after police interview, but this was not routine: 'The only time you see your kids is if you go into interview … I can hear (my son) breaking his heart crying and they wouldn't let him come out' (FAA7). Where there was a delay in the process, familial AAs were routinely told to go home, wait in their car or a nearby cafe, or in the public waiting section of the station. However, the situation is little better for non-familial AAs. YOTAA explained that he was allowed to sit out with young suspects because of his security clearance. But the approach was more variable for scheme AAs, with some suggesting that they could only exceptionally sit with a young suspect, for example, if they were 'very upset' (PAA5). AAs attending from a residential care home similarly explained: 'most of the time the young person goes back in the cell and we wait upstairs' (RHAA1).

There is a degree to which this is a resourcing issue. In all blocks observed, there was very limited space for AAs to wait within the custody suite, with or without the young suspect. But commonly, police cultural and institutional drivers could be identified. Like lawyers and other 'challengers',[131]

---

[130] As observed in Bucke and Brown (n 77).
[131] Simon Holdaway, *Inside the British Police: A Force at Work* (Blackwell 1983), 71-7.

the intrusive presence of an AA, including a scheme AA, their potential to challenge and interfere with police control, was not always welcome. Not infrequently, parents in particular were approached with suspicion, their presence perceived as a risk rather than a key welfare aid: 'Generally speaking we don't let parents sit in the cell with them because parents put cigarettes in crisp packets' (CO27).[132] As a result, not only was the AA's ability to provide ongoing support dramatically reduced but also their due process role was severely restricted by being removed from the custody suite. An AA would be unlikely to be 'available'[133] to make representations where detention is being reviewed or to identify if rights and entitlements are being afforded. As previous commentators have long noted,[134] in many cases, the AA role for young suspects had indeed become process-driven, focused on compliance with PACE rather than on the welfare of young suspects.

Support and Welfare

Familial AAs: 'She helps me and she makes me feel safe'

Turning to the four specified aspects of the role, I consider first the extent to which familial AAs are able to 'support, advise and assist' children in police custody and ensure their welfare in custody. For some young participants, the presence of a parent, in particular, did not reassure at all. As Azade explained of her mother, 'basically we don't have a relationship like that'. But strikingly, just over half of the thirty-nine young participants who spoke of their AA experience described feeling reassurance from having a family member or other familiar adult with them. This was particularly the case for younger participants, for whom presence alone was comforting. Tyler, arrested at age twelve, explained of his Mum, 'she helps me and she makes me feel safe'. Likewise Michael, who was thirteen on arrest, explained: 'Just to have my Mum there—it means a lot to me.' But seventeen- and eighteen-year-olds also related feeling supported by family members, even those not

---

[132] See for similar suspicion in relation to other volunteers Nadia J Britton, 'Race and Policing: A Study of Police Custody' (2000) 40 British Journal of Criminology 639, 650.
[133] *Code C* (n 13), para 15.3.
[134] CJJI, 'Who's Looking Out?' (n 4); Cummins, 'A Path Not Taken?' (n 69).

describing first-time experiences. For one young suspect, the strength of the familial bond appeared to override what might be more current difficulties: YS19, who was seventeen, told the CO he was 'in care but I want my mum to come down'. But such reassurance was not restricted to family members. Harper described a foster carer acting as AA as a, 'safe haven ... by her being there it kind of kept me calm'.

The nature of the support described varied. Young participants valued familial AAs for their capacity to make them feel calm and to reduce their anxiety and distress. For others, the familial AA was someone they could trust or 'rely on' (Luke) in the hostile and unpredictable world of custody. A familial AAs' inability to explain the process did not appear to entirely undermine their capacity to reassure—the relief of familiar support after the traumatic experience of arrest and detention seemed to override concerns about the criminal justice process. Nonetheless, where a familial AA could also explain the process or advocate for the child, this was particularly appreciated.[135] Aidan preferred his Mum as AA: 'she knows what she's doing as well, you know what I mean, like she's a bit smart'. Whilst Mums were more frequently referred to in terms of reassurance, male family members were often favoured in this regard where they had familiarity arising from their own experiences with the criminal justice system.

Officers and professionals also acknowledged this important reassurance role. Sol11 observed:

> some clients really, really calm down once their parents are there ... their parents are going, you know, 'Don't worry, it's OK I still love you.' That sort of conversation can make them go 'phew'.[136]

Familial AAs, too, described how important this role was for them. FAA1 and 2, for example, were tearful in describing their anxiety to be able to support their child in custody. FAA4 thought that if she could not be there with her child she would 'be going round the twist'.

The strength of this reassurance reveals starkly the contradictory nature of the denial of legal privilege—that for a young suspect detained in a harsh, adversarial setting, the only adult who appears to be 'on their side'

---

[135] Also recounted by young participants in HMIC, *Welfare of Vulnerable People* (n 12).
[136] See for similar in a court setting Ali Wigzell, Amy Kirby, and Jessica Jacobson, *Youth Proceedings Advocacy Review: Final Report* (Institute for Criminal Policy Research 2015) <https://cilexregulation.org.uk/wp-content/uploads/2019/02/Youth-proceedings-advocacy-review-report.pdf> accessed 17 August 2023.

is not someone in whom they can safely confide. Granted, investigating officers may rarely exploit the lack of privilege where parents are involved. However, young participants described a range of familiar adults in the role, including brothers, uncles, grandparents, and family friends, who could be treated differently. This unfairness is compounded by no warning being given to the young person of this position. No suspect, or AA, was told of the lack of privilege on observation, nor does it feature in the Notice. This is not a breach of *Code C*—there is no requirement to inform; rather, the unfairness is fixed at an institutional level. Unsurprisingly, only one young participant (Harper) displayed any understanding of the potential duties to disclose information that the AA might be under, whilst no lay familial AA was aware of the position.

Whilst parental anger features heavily in previous literature, interestingly, this was not a significant feature of young participants' accounts. This may result from their loyalty towards family members or their preoccupation in the research interview with communicating their greater antipathy towards officers. Equally, the lack of references may arise from the inevitable fact of parental displeasure. Those few who did raise the issue tended to be accepting of it: 'to be honest it's all expected, to be honest I don't really mind' (Hussain). Parental anger at least demonstrates that the person cares about the young suspect, a gesture otherwise rarely experienced by children in custody.

Notably, those few who referred to familial anger in custody tended to relate that parents were cross when they were initially produced: 'when you go come out your cell, they are always angry, looking at you. You're just there, like, "Oh"' (Rezar). Often, on observation, the child was brought to meet the AA at the desk and the CO immediately detailed the grounds of arrest and began to repeat the rights before the child and the AA have had a chance to talk together. This could be challenging for both parties. Emotions run high. Jake described how his mother's anger at being told the allegation led him to feel that he had to 'defend himself' against the allegations in front of the CO. This not only has legal implications for the young person but also lends a tone to the AA–child relationship at that point which can be challenging, particularly if, as commonly occurred, there is little time for discussion before the interview process begins. Such difficulties could plainly be mitigated by the CO providing the AA and the child an opportunity to talk privately before the formal repetition of grounds and rights at the desk. That this does not generally occur may simply reflect a lack of thought, but it may reflect the police's view that a suitable level of parental anger can be 'useful'.[137]

More commonly, young participants described feeling a burden to family members attending as AAs, whether because their parent was unwell (eg Kate), had to look after younger siblings (eg Jo), or was coming from work (eg Jayden). Several young people described the positive effects of such emotion as a catalyst for desistance: 'the last time, when I saw her come in, I thought, "Nah, this can't happen again. I can't let this happen again"' (Elijah). However, the heartfelt concern that many expressed clearly weighed on them in custody and was another challenge to cope with. Young people described feeling a 'disappointment' (Tyler), 'like a dickhead' (Malik), that it was 'embarrassing' that the familial AA had to 'waste' their time attending (Harper).[138] Sometimes, young participants worried in the cell about whether their parent would come at all, adding to the general uncertainty of their detention, or they experienced the familial AA's inability to attend as a form of rejection (Cole). Indeed, the pressures of the process weighed on both parties. FAA3 described being challenged ('Why didn't you come for me?') when she could not attend due to childcare issues.

Parental distress in custody was particularly hard for young people to deal with. Michael said that seeing his mother cry 'makes you feel you wanna break down', whilst Alex described reacting to his mother's tears more problematically by 'annoying the police officer' for the 'rest of the day'. For some, particularly suspects under fifteen, these difficulties did not outweigh the benefits of having a parent present. But Sandor, for example, seventeen at the time of arrest, whose mother's tears had made him cry, felt that 'it would have been way easier and much, much, better, if I didn't have to deal with her being there'.

---

[137] Quinn and Jackson (n 9) 245.
[138] A sentiment not restricted to England and Wales. See for similar in Canada Julia Miriam Christina Broeking, 'Parents' Involvement in Youth Justice Proceedings from the Perspective of Youth: A Pilot Study' (MA thesis, University of Toronto 2003) and China: Yu Mou, 'The Transplanted Appropriate Adult Scheme in China' (2021) 60 Howard Journal of Crime and Justice 25.

Non-familial AAs: 'A complete stranger, I just don't want her'

By contrast, very few young participants described experiencing emotional support from non-familial AAs. Those who did tended to be referring to AAs with whom they already had some relationship, either as a long-standing social worker ('they're basically my Mum and Dad' (Evan)) or as a staff member in a residential home. RHAA 1 and 2 certainly felt that, since they worked with their residents on a daily basis, they were able to provide familiarity and reassurance. YS36, for example, was anxious to make contact with carers at her placement on arrest and had an obvious rapport with the staff member who attended.

However, such relationships could also introduce conflicts of interest,[139] undermining the AA's capacity to reassure and the young participant's willingness to engage emotionally. Abigail, for example, found AAs from her residential home 'sometimes helpful, sometimes not'. Such ambivalence may be unsurprising, especially given the relationship of control that such an AA may have with a young resident and the relative frequency of some children in residential care being arrested for disturbances within the home.[140] A similar position arose in respect of YOT workers. For example, in F3, YOTAA explained that he acted as AA for those children who were 'known' to the YOT through criminal justice disposals: 'they're our kids and we know them better than anyone'. This undeniably led to a degree of familiarity, and, indeed, YOTAA was well liked by some young participants from F3. However, even so, YOTAA appreciated that they saw him primarily in his role working with them as 'young offenders'. His capacity to provide unconditional emotional support is fundamentally challenged by his position.

Young participant accounts, however, reveal a range of obstacles for building rapport where there is no previous relationship. First, making a connection could be challenging where the AA was of a different gender, ethnicity, generation, or class. Matching attributes, given AA availability and custody timescales, is rarely possible, but young participants were voluble about the barriers this may present: 'I just remember her being old and I just didn't pay much attention to her … a complete stranger, I just don't want her' (Cole). Zayn, a young Black participant recalled, 'they brought

---

[139] As observed by White (n 64).
[140] Howard League for Penal Reform, 'Ending the Criminalisation of Children in Residential Care. Briefing One' (Howard League 2017).

someone, some next White guy I don't even know who he was, I'm not going to feel comfortable around him, he felt like a police officer himself'.

Second, lowering one's guard could be difficult in police custody, whatever the skills or attributes of the AA. Zayn explained that the AA might act 'like they really care' but his reaction was 'just do your job man—not in the mood. They try to make it something it isn't.' Yemi's position was equally understandable: 'I'm the type of person to just keep myself to myself really, especially somebody that I've never seen before. Then I wouldn't really want to tell them about my emotions.' For some young participants, their focus remained on getting out, and the non-familial AA's role in that process was their most important attribute: 'He just sort of was there. He did his thing, he got me out of there—that's what I'm happy about to be honest with you' (Malik). Such connection may be made even more difficult by the adversity experienced by the young person to be supported. Officers and solicitors described non-familial AAs being 'abused' (CO26) and told to 'fuck off' (Sol6) by child suspects. However, the fact that mental health conditions, developmental disorders, and previous trauma may sometimes contribute to problematic behaviour was not always understood. Some AAs appreciated that challenging behaviour of this sort may just be a 'coping mechanism' (VAA4), but others considered some child suspects to be 'just angry' (PAA1). Third, delayed arrival could add to these pressures: 'you need to be able to get that rapport built in five to six minutes of meeting somebody' (ProfAA). Solicitors and COs could often identify one particular scheme AA working locally who was very good, but too often, the evidence suggests, such rapport could not be established in the time allowed.

Even where rapport could be achieved, trust issues may remain, particularly because of the adversarial context. Non-familial AA approaches to this challenge differ. For example, VAA2 explained that they always stressed 'I'm a volunteer—totally independent', whilst YOTAA demonstrated commitment by organizing for the young suspect to make a phone call to a friend or relative. But such efforts may not allay fears. Harper was generally sceptical: 'How do I know they're not gonna kind of go back and tell the officers or kind of go against me?' She was particularly conscious of social workers' safeguarding duties ('they're obliged to say something'), reflecting concerns about confidentiality expressed by vulnerable adults.[141] As identified in Chapter 3, scheme AAs explained that building trust could be particularly

---

[141] Jessiman and Cameron (n 68).

difficult, ironically, if, acting in the young suspect's best interests, they overrode a child's refusal of legal advice.

Where this connection could not be established, young participants reported that non-familial AAs 'can't do much' (Jamal), they 'just sit there ... you don't want one' (Cole).[142] At best, chatting to the AA generally might help to 'get your mind off' the present difficulties (Jo) and had the potential benefit of 'being just something to do, chatted to him for as long as I could so I didn't have to go back in the cell' (Tom). But, more concerningly, some complained about the burden of having to cope with a plethora of personal questions from unknown AAs for no perceived benefit. For some, this was 'just like family stuff that he [the AA] didn't really need to know' (Tom). But the questions could be really onerous, particularly considering the number of the other questions asked of young suspects, especially during risk assessment (RA). I felt exhausted myself as PAA5, for example, recounted the areas she would cover with a child suspect: home life, education, employment, mental and physical health, alcohol, drugs, self-harm, anger management issues, hospital appointments, Child and Adolescent Mental Health Services, and social worker contact, in addition to issues of self-esteem, empathy for the victim, and explanation for the offending, addressed after the interview. As PAA1 acknowledged, much of this information is simply 'for the record ... it goes into my report' but does not trigger further referrals or support. One can appreciate Harper's view of this sort of questioning ('now that's another person knowing your business ... that's another person that you've gotta talk to') or the adverse response of some young participants, exhausted by repeated questionings.

Facilitating Rights: Understanding

Familial AAs: 'I'm not really clued up with it all'

The limited understanding of their rights, the uncertainty and confusion, that many young participants displayed (discussed in detail in Chapter 3) underlines how important this aspect of the AA role is. However, plainly, in order to support the child's understanding of their rights, the AA must

---

[142] CJJI, 'Who's Looking Out?' (n 4).

themselves have a reasonable appreciation of the child's rights in custody and during interview. Some familial AAs, through personal experience themselves in custody or previous experience as an AA, had developed a working understanding of the process and suspect rights. Hussain, for example, was positive about the expertise of his mother, who had acted for older siblings: 'I think she gets it.' However, the data suggests that the understanding of even experienced familial AAs could be incomplete and sometimes inaccurate.

More commonly, young participants identified that familial AAs, particularly those who had not attended custody before, entirely lacked previous knowledge of the system and of the child's rights—a position acknowledged by familial AAs themselves. Such deficits could be fundamental. CO24 commented, 'Sometimes parents say they don't know what a solicitor is.' FAA5's response was fairly typical of the position suggested by many young participants:

> I'd not been in that situation before so I just went along with everything, you know, what they did and they have to do and thought 'Do I need a solicitor?' I don't know. So, I'm not really clued up with it all, you know what I mean?

Of course, if APP(DC)(CYP) is followed correctly, the familial AA should be provided with the HO/NAAN Guidance, and encouraged to read the Notice of Rights and Entitlements. As discussed, on observation, the former did not always happen, and the latter never occurred. However, even assuming that this does occur and, further, that the AA has time to review the material and it is in a language and format that they can understand, the evidence suggests that the AA may not be in a state of mind to access the information. FAAs described custody suites as 'horrible' (FAA1), 'daunting . .. frightening, a bit scary' (FAA5). A first experience could be quite overwhelming. Several young participants observed that, in this intimidating atmosphere, a confused familial AA tends not to seek help; 'they just don't talk about it' (Sadie).

Non-familial AAs: A Better But Varied Picture

The picture in terms of knowledge is generally very different for non-familial AAs. Training delivered by organized AA schemes, such as that delivered by ProfAA, and through the National Appropriate Adult Network generally includes ample information on the process and the child suspect's rights. The challenge for scheme AAs in terms of facilitating rights understanding lay more in whether they had established sufficient rapport with the child to enable engaged discussion. However, not all non-familial AAs that I encountered had been trained and there were some significant gaps in their knowledge. For example, RHAA1 and 2, who had both fulfilled the role many times, had had no training and were not aware that they were entitled to information about the grounds of arrest and detention, to look at the custody record, or to require a solicitor to attend if a child declines advice. Even those who had received some training revealed some interesting deficits in understanding of the process and its protections. I was not convinced that YOTAA, for example, appreciated his right to require the attendance of a solicitor where the child refuses: 'So I can't say look I'm not listening to what you're saying—I will get you a solicitor whether you like it or not. I don't think I've got that role.'

Facilitating Rights: Supporting the Child to Exercise Their Legal Rights

Familial AAs: '(Mum) didn't really get the whole "no comment" thing'

The AA is a critical support in enabling the child not only to understand but also to exercise their legal rights. As explored in Chapter 3, engaging with the complex and demanding custody process is challenging for children. Real assistance is required to address the power imbalance in police custody between child and officer. Whilst the AA is not present to give legal advice, they could play a key role in advising and assisting a young suspect in their decision-making in custody. However, the AA's ability to support decision-making around the uptake of legal advice is challenged by their late arrival, their own limited appreciation of the role, and their prioritization of welfare issues over legal interests.

For a child, the issue with which the most support is, arguably, required, and the critical question in terms of prosecution, is whether to exercise their right of silence. A few young participants clearly felt that their parent supported them well in this regard. Aidan, for example, explained, 'she helps me through it, you know what I mean? Like before we go into an interview she tells me what to do... and things like that, she helps me a lot, my mum.' This tended to arise where the parent was experienced in, or knowledgeable about, the criminal justice system, although, inevitably, the young suspect is not in a position to judge the quality of this advice. Approximately one-third of young participants said that they had spoken to a solicitor in the presence of a family member, and such support could work well alongside legal advice—as Luke described: 'we're a team'.

However, more commonly, the familial AA's presence in consultation with the solicitor did not make a positive difference to the child, and some young participants were emphatic that decisions around answering questions were not for parents to be involved in: 'sometimes there's things to sort out that are not for them' (Kaiden). Jo explained that such decisions are 'just for me and the solicitor because I think no-one else should know about it'.

This latter position appears to arise from two separate, but related, issues. The first is that a significant minority of young participants were reluctant to reveal offending behaviour in front of a family member (as I discuss in more detail in respect of communication beneath). Second, FAAs did not always understand or welcome the legal advice a young person might receive. In particular, some parents could be 'outraged about 'no comment' advice' (Sol3). This could arise in part out of unfamiliarity with the system. Alex explained that, at first, his Mum 'didn't really get the whole "No comment" thing', and he had had to explain, 'Sometimes you just don't wanna give them (the police) information.' But more consistently, the 'outrage' arose from a paternalistic, welfare orientation that the evidence suggests tends to dominate the approach of some familial AAs. Solicitors in all areas raised concerns about the tension between their advice, pursuing the best legal interests of the suspect, and the tendency of the familial AA to want the child to admit, to 'just tell the truth' (Sol2). Solicitors found that 'no comment' advice could be hard to explain to a parent. Sol12 recounted that a parent might typically respond, 'I've worked for fifteen years with my son teaching him integrity and honesty and you've come in, in one fell swoop, and ruined that.' Solicitors detailed how this could lead to parents pressurizing a child to respond to questioning against their legal interests. Carter was clear that he preferred a non-familial AA because 'they can't tell me what to do' in this way. Solicitors also suggested that this could cause animosity and loss of confidence between the adviser and AA and could result in parents making admissions on behalf of a child in interview, contrary to the child's decision, following legal advice, to decline to answer questions.

Non-familial AAs: 'Have you understood what the solicitor said to you?'

Several young participants valued the advice of non-familial AAs. Jo appreciated AAs who were 'trying to help you out ... Sometimes they tell you, "Oh, don't do that" because it is not good for you, and that.' But many more young participants felt that non-familial AAs had not supported them in terms of advice. The data reveals quite clearly that the lack of legal privilege is a major factor in this ineffectiveness. It operates in two particular ways. First, non-familial AAs are, as a result, trained to avoid discussing the details of the allegation with the young suspect. Although AAs are not present to give legal advice, this means that a young suspect who refuses legal advice is likely to have no adult with whom they can talk over the allegation and consider their options. Second, because of the lack of privilege, solicitors said that, almost without exception, they would avoid having non-familial AAs (particularly social worker AAs) in their consultation with the child. As a result, the AA is unable to support communication between suspect and adviser and cannot effectively check the child's understanding or support their decision-making in respect of any advice given. Trained AAs explained that they would try to check understanding of advice by asking 'Have you understood what the solicitor said to you? Are you happy with the advice?' (ProfAA, VAA1). Such questions, whilst well intentioned, are unlikely to be a reliable identifier of comprehension difficulties. Nor, non-familial AAs suggested (eg YOTAA, PAA1), do the police always allow time for them to speak with the young suspect after legal consultation and before interview. As a result, many are not in a position to mitigate the effects of a young suspect's decisional immaturity, nor can they balance the power differential between young suspect and legal adviser. Additionally, there are indications in the data that non-familial AAs who do give advice are not immune to the paternalistic approach commonly adopted by familial AAs.[143] As RHAA2 explained, 'I tell them the easiest way to do this is to be honest.'

---

[143] See Pierpoint, 'How Appropriate Are Volunteers?' (n 50).

Assisting with Communication

Familial AAs: 'You're just gonna make yourself lie just cos your mum's there'

In a straightforward sense, it was apparent that the role of communication enabler can work well for a young suspect where the AA is known to them. As FAA1 described, 'there've been times when the officer's said something to (my son) and he doesn't understand it. So therefore I just step in and I interpret it my way ... And then (he) understands it straight away.' Sol4 explained that, despite some parents being 'very upset and excited', on 'the communication side they are obviously better'. However, this depends on the AA's own ability to understand. Kyle described struggling to understand some of what officers were saying, and when I asked whether his Mum, acting as AA, was able to help him, he laughed in response, retorting, 'I don't think she understood it at all!'

I discuss the AA's engagement in interview in more detail in Chapter 7. However, there are three particular issues which arise in respect of communication more generally which I address here. First, for familial AAs who have a child with a significant communication difficulty, the burden placed on a familial AA is arguably too great. They may be experienced in supporting their child's communication in everyday life. However, enabling their child's effective engagement in questioning in an adversarial setting can be much more demanding, requiring questioners to adjust their interrogation technique, in addition to supporting comprehension. I made a point of asking COs and solicitors whether they had experience of using an intermediary[144] as an additional adjustment for a young suspect. None had such experience, and COs generally responded with some surprise to the suggestion. No Liaison and Diversion specialist spoken to within the custody suite had proposed any additional support for a young suspect of this sort.

Second, a familial AA's ability to support communication may be considerably hampered by their own linguistic difficulties. Four young participants raised issues in respect of their familial AA's difficulties with understanding English. This can be addressed by the use of an interpreter,

---

[144] An intermediary is a communication specialist, often a qualified speech and language therapist or a psychologist, specially trained to facilitate communication within a criminal justice setting.

as Azade had experienced for her mother, although the AA's ability then to support the child's communication in English with the officer or solicitor will inevitably be dramatically reduced. However, more concerning still is the suggestion that this assistance might be declined, as Sandor had, or not identified as required. Jo recounted, 'I have to explain it to my mum because like she doesn't really understand that much ... because of her English.' He described how this had made his custody experience more difficult 'because like what they tell me, and then my mum goes, "Oh, tell me what they said." And then I need to tell her, and then they are saying something else and I have to tell her again.'

Third, there were numerous instances of the presence of a family member in fact inhibiting communication with solicitors and officers. Young participants described their reluctance to talk about their involvement in offending in front of family. Their motivations were not limited to avoiding getting into trouble at home. Aidan, for example, described his shame:

> cause I have done a lot of bad things, you know what I mean, and when you admit it in front of my Nan she like, she looks shocked, and like she's not happy with me ... cause I want my Nan to be proud of me, you know what I mean, and I don't want her to be thinking what an idiot I am.

For Hussain, there was a more instrumental aspect—he tried to avoid his Mum concluding that his friends were a bad influence and restricting their association.

For some, revealing everything in front of parents simply had to be endured: 'Like she needs to know everything doesn't she' (Jackson). But others suggested that they might deliberately falsify their account as a result. Sadie, for example, distinguished between the presence of her solicitor ('you tell them the actual truth don't ya') and her parents: 'Cos obviously you tell your Mum a different story don't ya ... "Mum, I didn't do anything" [laughs] ... And you're just gonna make yourself lie just cos your Mum's there—do you know what I mean?' Some young people try to avoid the issue entirely, either by giving a false name during arrest, which can necessitate detention and have ramifications for their case later on, or, as CO1 noted, 'You hear juveniles saying "Don't contact Mum" or "Can't I have YOT?"'

Solicitors widely acknowledged the difficulty of getting young suspects to talk in front of family members. Sol12 found, as Sadie suggested, that 'accounts usually differ' between that given in consultation alone and that in interview with parents, giving rise to the potential for professional embarrassment. We see, in these insights, how damaging to their effective participation it can be, and harmful to their legal interests more generally, where the parents' relationship of control with the young suspect comes to the fore. The police may consider it supportive of their objectives to engage parents' capacity for informal social control of the young person,[145] but in reality it is likely to produce negative outcomes.

Non-familial AAs: Sufficient Expertise and Knowledge?

Different challenges may arise for non-familial AAs, namely, the identification, and support, of more significant communication needs. In respect of identification, COs and staff variously expressed their confidence that, if not raised or identified during RA, the AA will spot any particular communication difficulty a young suspect may have. A non-familial AA who knows a young suspect in a professional capacity may, indeed, be aware of such a problem. However, this does not always mean that officers will act on their information. RHAA1 expressed her frustration that in supporting as AA a young resident with Asperger's, although raised 'at the very beginning', this 'didn't seem to make a blind bit of difference' to their communication with him.

For a non-familial AA who does not know the young person, identification may be extremely difficult. Psychologists have long noted the challenge for health-care professionals (HCPs) in identifying such conditions in custody.[146] On observations, scheme AAs had no access to medical or social-care records, and they generally relied on a brief consultation with the young suspect immediately before interview.[147] The chances of an AA without information identifying such conditions will be limited, particularly since scheme AAs reported varying levels of training in communication with children and in the presentation of common conditions (eg attention deficit hyperactivity disorder (ADHD), learning disabilities

---

[145] See Quinn and Jackson (n 9).
[146] Gisli H Gudjonsson, Gwilym D Hayes, and Paul Rowlands, 'Fitness to Be Interviewed and Psychological Vulnerability: The Views of Doctors, Lawyers and Police Officers' (2000) 11 Journal of Forensic Psychology 74.
[147] See for similar Kemp and Hodgson (n 8). Although ProfAA stated that in some areas contractual arrangements allow scheme AAs to have access to local authority records.

(LDs), and autism spectrum condition (ASC)), including some reporting no specific training in these aspects at all, for example VAA3. Turning to their capacity to support a significant communication difficulty, none of the scheme AAs that I encountered had a specialist background in mental health, or LD, or supporting communication difficulties. Likewise, ProfAA stated that her organization did not have any AAs with such specialist skills. Where, as was often the case, the call-out specified a child suspect with an LD or an ASC, she would simply make sure that someone 'good' and 'experienced' was allotted. Clearly, for those with significant communication needs, this protection is liable to be inadequate.

Guardian of Due Process

Familial AAs: 'You've just gotta go along with 'em cos it's the police'

Successful fulfilment of the due process role by a familial AA requires a number of pre-requisites. First, the individual must be aware that their role encompasses this aspect. As discussed, the AA's due process duties were not consistently communicated on observation. Second, the AA must be able to identify unfairness and a failure to respect the young person's rights. Whilst a lay person might have a basic understanding of unfairness, as FAA4 explained ('if I thought it weren't right, that wouldn't be fair'), meaningful due process protection requires the AA to have some underlying appreciation of the basic details of the custody process and the young suspect's rights in that regard. As already identified, this was was often patchy and very limited.

On observation, AAs were invariably present at set-piece events in the custody process—including for strip searches and the taking of fingerprints and biometric data. However, observations revealed the very real danger that the AA's presence becomes simply process-serving. Familial AAs, lacking the knowledge required to scrutinize the process, tended to report being passive observers of these set pieces. Indeed, for some, the experience as a result was more profoundly negative. Several FAAs made reference to this aspect of the role as humiliating. YS10's familial AA described it as 'demeaning'; FAA3 was 'mortified to be there'. Indeed, observing a parent standing mutely by as their child's photograph, prints, and DNA were taken, I was struck by the extent to which, rather than being a protective presence, it seemed that the AA was there to receive a very visual display of the control the police had over her child.

Third, and most importantly perhaps, where an AA has concerns, they must feel confident to raise a challenge. Where the AA is a family member, the power differential between them and the CO is marked and highly unlikely to foster effective challenge. For some parents, there was a sense of trust in the police, an assumption that what they experience is how it should be and cannot be questioned: 'you've just gotta go along with 'em cos it's the police' (FAA5). For some familial AAs, challenging an officer goes against everyday instincts: 'Like I said, the only thing I could ever think of when I'm in trouble is to call the police. I can't do that 'cause these are the police and I am more intimidated than I've ever been in my life' (FAA2). Raising an issue about proper police conduct with a police officer in a police station, especially where that officer controls the release of one's child, would require an unusual degree of confidence for a family member. Zayn's observation typifies the difficult situation a familial AA faces: 'My Mum's not really good at all that law stuff, so she just keeps quiet.'

Where an AA does raise an issue, the manner of their doing so could also be a factor in dictating how effective it is. Reciprocity in terms of behaviour has been observed previously in police custody,[148] and the data suggests that this extends to AAs as well. A polite request, it seemed, was more likely to be accommodated. CO13 commented in respect of YS10: 'his father understands and is pretty supportive of us so we're happy. Some of them are perfectly polite with us. It's one of those things—how you treat people affects how they treat you back.' But not infrequently, a familial AA may raise an issue in a more confrontational manner, whether because of distress, distrust, or dislike of the police or because of their lack of familiarity with that context. Those who described advocating forcefully for their child often suggested that their complaints had been ignored. FAA1 explained, 'I've had one sergeant and I told him, basically, what I felt. Why I felt like it and he just stood there and went, "That's your opinion."' She reflected, 'they don't like it because I don't pussy foot around them'. FAA7, who had gone to some length to explain about her child's medical condition, complained: 'They don't listen to you at all ... I said like "I've showed you the medical report, I've showed you everything and I've showed you

---

[148] Layla Skinns, Andrew Wooff, and Amy Sprawson, 'Preliminary Findings on Police Custody Delivery in the Twenty-First Century: Is It "Good" enough?' (2017) 27 Policing & Society 358.

medication. I'm not hiding anything and still this is the way you're treating me kids."' Sadie, for example, had no confidence in her mother's power to ensure her good care: 'Like say if you say, "Oh, Mum I've not been fed", your Mum can't do nothing.'

Sometimes, the police response could be more aggressive. FAA2, who had become quite distressed in custody, described the CO shouting at her when she asked why they were taking fingerprints and DNA. The experience was, she said, 'really intimidating'. I did not observe any familial AAs acting in an antagonistic manner, but a number of officers referred to families who were perceived to be unnecessarily interventionist or combative in very negative terms: they were 'feral' (IO2), 'anti-police' (CO26), or 'obstructive' (CO32). Such familial AAs were clearly not perceived to be fulfilling a due process role. Rather, they were viewed through an adversarial lens and treated with the same suspicion as might be accorded to the suspect they supported. Ultimately, a parent forcefully demanding due process rights could be silenced by simply being required to wait outside the suite or (in extreme cases) being removed from their role as AA altogether. There is now the right of the AA to 'inform' an Inspector, or more senior officer, of due process concerns (*Code C*, 1.7A), although whether this power will be widely understood and used, and what should occur once an Inspector is 'informed', remains unclear. Otherwise, the familial AA's power in this aspect of the role is limited, particularly at the time of the detention episode. Their remonstrations might be captured on CCTV footage (and in the custody record, should the CO choose to record them) and could become relevant in the unlikely event that the child is prosecuted and applies to exclude evidence obtained in interview.[149] Otherwise, they may lodge a complaint after the event or bring a civil action against the police, although, as discussed in Chapter 1, such occurrences are vanishingly rare.

The evidence reveals, however, another more intrinsic challenge in the effective performance of this aspect of the role. Where a familial AA identified a due process concern, there was often a danger that their focus on accelerating their child's release might prevent them pursuing those concerns. FAA2, for example, reported an exchange with a CO over signing documents:

---

[149] PACE, s 76 or 78.

I had said to him at the very last second, 'What is it that I'm actually signing though? Because I can't see what is it that you're asking me to sign.' He said, 'Well, you want to take your son home, don't you?' And so at that point obviously there's no ifs or buts, I just need to sign. I want to get him home.

Non-familial AAs: Lack of Challenge

Non-familial AAs' knowledge of, and confidence in, the due process role was generally very different. However, they, too, could be acquiescent when they identified breaches, but often for rather different reasons. Pierpoint[150] has raised concerns that non-familial AAs may hold positive attitudes towards the police which may disincline them to challenge police misconduct robustly or may foster anti-suspect sentiment. In contrast to observations by HMIC inspectors of volunteer AAs challenging unprofessional conduct,[151] I did not see a single non-familial AA challenge custody staff about the treatment of a young suspect. Of course, no challenge could be expected where due process is followed, but this was not always the case. For example, YS5, an eleven-year-old boy with an ASC, was detained for nearly eleven hours. VAA1, who attended, observed to me, 'I couldn't understand why it took so long' but raised no issues about delay with the CO.

There would appear to be two potential causes of this passivity. First, in each area, I noticed a familiarity between some of the non-familial AAs and the custody staff. Inevitably, working alongside each other is bound to breed some collegiate relations. ProfAA explained that she had had to correct an officer who referred to her as his 'colleague' in front of a suspect she was supporting. Similar issues have been observed in respect of ICVs.[152] Second, there was a sense in which some non-familial AAs took an administrative, and pared down, approach to the role, not engaging particularly with COs in respect of young suspects' rights and welfare.[153] In F3, CO41 observed of the local AA provision, 'the scheme sees the case not the child', whilst CO26 felt that scheme AAs asked for the custody record simply 'so they can tick a box. They never ask anything about it.' As identified above,

---

[150] Pierpoint, 'How Appropriate Are Volunteers?' (n 50).
[151] HMIC, *Welfare of Vulnerable People* (n 12).
[152] See John Kendall, *Regulating Police Detention, Voices behind Closed Doors* (Policy Press 2018).
[153] See for similar CJJI, 'Who's Looking Out?' (n 4).

there was certainly, for some scheme AAs, a conflict between wanting to fulfil the role and the constraints of the contractual arrangements with the YOT.

Non-familial AAs were also not entirely immune to the tensions between welfare concerns and legal best interests experienced by familial AAs. For example, during a 'fitness for interview' assessment, YS28 was asked whether he felt fit and ready for interview and whether he wanted to eat something beforehand. When he said he wanted to eat something, but hesitated to clarify what, the scheme AA intervened to say, 'If you want something hot it will hold things up', at which point, the child indicated that he would go ahead with the interview without food. The AA's concern to hasten the process was understandable from a welfare perspective but arguably jeopardized his due process rights in prompting him to proceed to interview when he may not have felt up to questioning.

Conclusion

A Composite and Conflicted Role

This comprehensive review of the AA protection makes plain the significance of each aspect of the support intended to be provided by the AA. In particular, many children's need for reassurance and the value many young participants placed on contact with a familiar and trusted adult are among the most striking findings of this study. However, the evidence makes equally plain that requiring a single individual to fulfil all elements of the role for a child is, in practice, wholly unrealistic. The role's four aspects require particular attributes and skills, which are highly unlikely to be found in, and utilized effectively by, a single individual. A familial AA, as we have seen, may be able to provide reassurance but is likely to lack the knowledge to be able effectively to monitor the appropriateness of the process or support rights realization. A non-familial AA is more likely to be able to identify failings in due process, or where rights have been neglected, but will rarely be able to establish a sufficient degree of rapport to reassure. Equally, whilst familial AAs may be more attuned to the young suspect's difficulties, and more motivated to raise issues, their emotional state, and distrust on the part of the police, mean that their concerns may not be acted on. Conversely, whilst more likely to be listened to, the detachment of a non-familial AA, and their familiarity with custody routines in practice and individual custody officers and staff in particular, may disincline them from raising an issue. The identification of such challenges reflects concerns raised in other jurisdictions where a similar supporting adult role exists.[154] By way of recent example in New Zealand, where a single adult, nominated by the child suspect, is required to perform a comparable array of tasks, the role's demands have been similarly criticized:

> It is unrealistic to expect that a parent can adequately perform both the role of providing psychological and emotional assistance and also ensuring the young person understands their legal rights.[155]

However, as well as the unrealistic demands of the role, its composite nature also produces unhelpful contradictions in its performance. In particular, the welfare-focused aspects of the supporter role are revealed often to come into conflict with the AA's rights-facilitation and due process responsibilities, particularly for the familial AA. The study provides striking illumination, in the child suspect context, of a tension previously identified as being at the heart of the AA role for vulnerable adults, that the role crosses the 'justice and welfare axis'.[156] Legal advisers in police custody have the clear remit of protecting the legal best interests of a child suspect, appropriate to the 'justice' context of the custody suite. By contrast, the AA's remit is complex and multifaceted. In such circumstances, the familial AA's paternalistic approach is understandable. After all, this is not only the primary mode of their relationship with the child but also, unlike the complexities of custodial rights, a realm of operating with which they are familiar. Although the tension between welfare and justice rationales reverberates throughout the youth justice process, it is the ascribing of responsibility in both spheres simultaneously within the AA role which engages that conflict in a particularly challenging way and with potentially profound implications for young suspects' due process rights.

In addition, the overarching issues identified reveal that the complex demands of the role can be heightened by other constraints on its effective performance. Such constraints are varied, including the challenges for familial AAs attending under pressure of work or family commitments, for non-familial AAs providing the full service within limiting contractual

---

[154] See eg in a US context Woolard and others (n 96).
[155] *Police v FG* [2020] NZYC 328 (29 June 2020), [172].
[156] Nemitz and Bean, 'Protecting the Rights' (n 63); Cummins, 'AA Post-Bradley' (n 62).

arrangements, and for COs balancing suspect rights with institutional concerns about detention times. However, the evidence illustrates clearly that inadequate or problematic performance of the AA role can, in fact, exacerbate, rather than mitigate, the challenges of the custody process for children by extending detention periods, raising anxiety levels, undermining legal advice, and hampering participation. Whilst, for some children, familial reassurance was key, for others, the presence of an AA with whom they are closely attached, or who has a substantial measure of control over them, could make the custody process more difficult—whether this arose from the burden of coping with the AA's distress, inconvenience, or anger or the inhibitory effect of their presence in terms of revealing involvement in offending behaviour. The operation of informal social control and attachment on the behaviour of young people—in terms of their desistance or offending—is complex and age-dependent.[157] Such dynamics will almost inevitably be engaged in the aftermath of the custody episode. But what young participant accounts reveal clearly is how problematic it can be to complicate the demands of the legal process by introducing into the custody suite itself, and the decisions to be made there, a familial AA's informal social control function (or, in the case of a YOT worker, social worker, or RHAA, their more formal control capacity and disclosure duties). Whilst some officers appeared to view the presence of angry parents and carers as supportive of their concerns, the evidence suggests that their presence could have a very negative impact for the child.

Conceptual Issues

Beyond its composite and conflicted nature, the findings lay bare a number of additional shortcomings in the way that the role is conceived. First, whilst the role is of critical importance, as the only substantive child-specific protection for a young suspect, there is no systematic method of assessing the suitability of the individual AA to perform it—a concern raised as long ago as 1991 by the RCCJ.[158] The exclusions provided in *Code C*, NFG 1B are designed to ensure that evidence in interview is not tainted, but they offer

---

[157] See eg Machteld Hoeve and others, 'A Meta-Analysis of Attachment to Parents and Delinquency' (2012) 40 Journal of Abnormal Child Psychology 771; Robert J Sampson, *Crime in the Making: Pathways and Turning Points through Life* (Harvard UP 1993).

[158] RCCJ (n 20) 43–44.

little guide as to the capabilities required to fulfil the role, and the courts have provided minimal further clarity. It is concerning but not, as a result, unsurprising to have encountered in this study familial AAs who lack the cognitive capacity to fulfil their support function, sufficient appreciation of the custody and criminal justice processes to discharge their due process role, or adequate English to engage with the process themselves, let alone to support communication in interview. In particular, to be able to identify, and then support in an interrogation setting, a communication difficulty of any severity is a highly specialist task. That the AA, particularly a familial AA, should be assumed to be equipped for that task, in circumstances where the CO may have no guidance or scope to scrutinize their suitability, makes a nonsense of the protection.

Second, the findings confirm the RCCJ's concerns that the AA's lack of privilege is capable of undermining the 'whole purpose of the role'. We see that lack of privilege can result in non-familial AAs, and sometimes familial AAs, being effectively prevented from supporting child suspect decision-making and facilitating their understanding of their legal jeopardy, any legal advice they may have received, and the options open to them. That young suspects and familial AAs were, almost without exception, unaware of this lack of privilege reveals a gross unfairness at the heart of the role—that a lone child should be provided with an adult who seems to be on their side, to whom they should be told that they can speak 'privately' at any time, but who, unknown to the child, may yet be required to divulge the contents of their discussions to the police and the courts.

Third, and perhaps most substantially, the data reveals the fundamental incoherence that lies at the heart of the role—the CO's control of the AA function. The CO dictates who is suitable to act, when the AA is asked to attend, when they might be allowed into the custody area, what they know of the role (where the AA is not trained), and the access they have to the young person. Even the AA's avenues for immediate redress—escalation to a senior officer, lodging a complaint, recording their concerns on the custody record—rely, to an extent, on explanation from, and the cooperation of, the CO. The AA is structurally stymied, and their capacity to provide due process oversight of the CO and fellow officers is largely neutered by the CO's control. The evidence demonstrates vividly that there is a fundamental problem within an adversarial context with providing a vital protection for one party which is wholly controlled by the other party, particularly where the power differential between the parties is so extreme. The institutional motivations of the CO—case construction, crime control, and risk management—are liable to predominate at the expense of the due process rights of the young suspect.

Avenues for Reform

In 2006, Richard Gwynedd Parry observed that 'it is difficult to avoid the conclusion that the appropriate adult is currently no more than a succour to demonstrate a nominal recognition of the need to protect the juvenile'.[159] The findings in this study tend to support the drawing of that conclusion. The *Confait* case revealed the urgent need for emotional support and due process protections for children, and vulnerable adults, in police custody. But the Fisher Report, and subsequent Commissions and reviews, failed to address with any clarity how the welfare and legal needs of child suspects can adequately be addressed. Although the intervening years have seen some clarification of the needs of young suspects, and the areas in which support is required, the format of a single lay supporting adult has been retained, despite long-standing, and repeated, recognition of its inadequacy.

This study identifies that expecting a single individual to act as a panacea for the adversities experienced by a child in police detention is unrealistic, and at times counter-productive, particularly where that individual is an untrained family member grappling with their own response to the child's detention. The AA is revealed frequently to be unable to foster the effective participation of the child in the custody process and to make good the 'imbalance' between the child suspect and the prosecution.[160] More problematic still, the shortcomings of the role are likely to be felt most significantly by those with the most pronounced needs, and those, particularly Black, Asian and minority ethnic young suspects, whose trust in the process and its players is likely already to be significantly depleted. As a result, the child in custody today is often little better protected from wrongful conviction than the young *Confait* suspects. The role is liable to mask failings in the integrity of the process rather than to reveal them. The AA's presence serves to legitimize the process more than it enables the young suspect.

Young participant perspectives indicate that a fundamental review of the AA protection is required, with a clear emphasis on identifying how the needs of the child might best be addressed in police custody. Whilst further

---

[159] Gwynedd Parry (n 24) 394.
[160] *HC* (n 2), Moses LJ, [58].

focused research is plainly required, drawing on the experiences of young participants in this study, and on the approaches taken in other jurisdictions, several avenues for reform clearly present themselves. In the first instance, the evidence supports the separation of the welfare and emotional support functions from the AA's other duties. Young participant accounts underline the importance of these functions and suggest that they should, where possible, be fulfilled by someone known to, and trusted by, the child. Whilst this individual may frequently be a parent or carer, it is apparent that this would not be the choice of every child suspect and that parental presence can exacerbate the challenges of custody. The evidence illustrates the importance of uncoupling the parents' right to be notified of, and to have contact with, their child in detention (prioritized by the RCCP) from the presence of a trusted adult to reassure and support the child during the process.

In this regard, a review of the AA safeguard might consider the approach taken in New Zealand, for example, which empowers the child to choose a supporting adult. The child 'nominates' the person to fulfil the supporting adult role (subject to reasonable objection by the police).[161] Similarly, in the Netherlands, the supporting adult is conceived as a 'trusted person', an adult from the child's inner circle, but not necessarily a close relative.[162] Since the trusted person would not be required to oversee due process, the child could choose whether they want them to be present in interview or not, as they do in the Netherlands, circumventing the inhibitory aspects of a familiar adult's presence. Where a child nominates an adult who does not have parental responsibility, this need not undermine the parent's right to be notified of the arrest, its grounds, and the child's whereabouts, as currently preserved by *Code C*, paragraph 3.13. Nor need this necessarily prevent the parent or guardian visiting the child in custody, should they so wish. In the Netherlands, for example, in addition to securing a 'trusted person', the police are also obligated to inform the parents or legal guardian of the child of the arrest and their right to visit the child in custody.[163]

---

[161] Oranga Tamariki Act 1989, s 222.

[162] Staatscourant 2010, 4003. See for discussion Marc van Oosterhout and Dorris de Vocht, 'Chapter 5: Protecting Juvenile Suspects in a Pedagogical But Punitive Context. Country Report the Netherlands' in Michele Panzavolta and others (eds), *Interrogating Young Suspects: Procedural Safeguards from a Legal Perspective* (Intersentia 2015) 285ff.

[163] Ambtsinstructie politie, Art 27; Code for Criminal Procedure, Art 490. For discussion see van Oosterhout and de Vocht (n 162) 285–86.

Conclusion 201

Second, the evidence underlines the critical importance of the remaining aspects of the AA role, particularly due process oversight and rights facilitation, from the earliest stages of the process. Given the demands of these functions, and the difficulties identified in challenging the police and other actors in professional roles, it is apparent that having a lay person in the role, particularly where they are wholly untrained, undermines this key protection. Were mandatory legal advice to be introduced, as proposed in Chapter 3, the review could consider incorporating the due process and rights-facilitation protections into the legal adviser role. The legal adviser could certainly fulfil due process oversight during interview. However, given the inevitable limitations on legal aid funding, it is unlikely that the solicitor would be available to oversee due process and support rights understanding and exercise in the earliest stages of the custody process. Additionally, they would not be able, of course, to support the child to make independent decisions around whether to follow legal advice.

More realistically, the remaining appropriate adult functions would still require separate fulfilment. The findings suggest that this (non-legal) advisory and facilitation role, a sort of 'custody navigator', should be paid and, if not fully professional, should be performed by a youth specialist, with training beyond that which is currently required of a scheme AA. The training should encompass youth justice processes, common conditions prevalent amongst young people and effective communication with children. The evidence indicates the importance of the individual being asked to attend as soon as a child is arrested so that they are with the child from the very earliest stage in the custody process, and in particular for authorisation of detention, risk assessment, and the initial rights process. They would also be able to support any 'trusted person' identified by the child and, if necessary (although this is obviously undesirable), fulfil that support role where no such individual is available. This study suggests that there would be advantage in this custody navigator having direct contact with Children's Services and being able to access any existing social services files on the child. The role could sit within the YOT, but the individual ought not also to be engaged in supervising children under court orders or as part of a referral order. Vetting by the force may also prevent there being any objection to them remaining with the child in detention, where necessary. Recruitment strategies ought to focus on attracting younger adults and Black, Asian, and ethnic minority applicants. Individuals with a background in youth work, youth mentoring, and teaching would potentially be well suited to the role.

There remains the issue of privilege in relation to private consultation with the child for any individual attending as a trusted adult or a custody navigator. The findings merely add empirical weight to long-standing calls for reform in this regard.[164] The complexity of legal privilege, its association with professional status,[165] and the added complication of the disclosure duties of social workers and other professionals performing the role have previously operated as barriers to the introduction of privilege for AAs. There is, nonetheless, precedent for a more straightforward provision which might address the issue and merit exploration as part of a review. In New Zealand, evidence of 'any communication' between the 'nominated person' in the supporting adult role and the child in consultation prior to interview (with or without their lawyer) is inadmissible in any proceedings for an offence.[166]

A final area for review is the provision of intermediary support in interview for a child with profound communication needs. Whilst intermediary support is not excluded under current arrangements,[167] and might occasionally be achieved for a child interviewed on bail or on a voluntary basis, it would appear to be extraordinarily unusual, if ever achieved, for children in detention under current arrangements. Nonetheless, for some child suspects, just as for some child defendants, an intermediary will very occasionally be required. Any review should also consider introducing provision for intermediary assistance for child and other vulnerable suspects where that is required to enable them to participate effectively in the interview process. The Northern Ireland registered intermediary schemes (RI schemes), piloted in 2013 and subsequently rolled out in 2017, demonstrate that assessment and access to intermediary support can be achieved for a suspect, even where they are detained prior to interview.[168] Evaluation of those RI schemes reveals very positive responses from both police and family members.[169] Whilst the larger jurisdiction of England and Wales would

---

[164] Home Office, 'Review of Review Group' (n 21); Gwynedd Parry (n 24).
[165] See with regard to legal advice privilege *R v (Prudential plc) v Special Commissioner of Income Tax (Institute of Chartered Accountants in England and Wales intervening)* [2010] EWCA Civ 1094, [2011] QB 669.
[166] Oranga Tamariki 1989, s 226.
[167] See *Code C* (n 13), Annex G, para 8.
[168] John Taggart, '"I Am Not Beholden to Anyone … I Consider Myself to Be an Officer of the Court": A Comparison of the Intermediary Role in England and Wales and Northern Ireland' (2021) 25 International Journal of Evidence & Proof 141.
[169] Department of Justice, 'Northern Ireland Registered Intermediaries Schemes Pilot Project Phase II Review' (July 2016) <www.justice-ni.gov.uk/publications/northern-ireland-registered-intermediaries-schemes-pilot-project> accessed 17 August 2023.

inevitably present greater logistical problems, the arguments for introducing such a scheme are persuasive, both from an equality-of-arms perspective and in consideration of the extreme demands of police interview for detained young suspects with specific communication difficulties. Demand for such support would likely be very low were a specialist custody navigator introduced, who could facilitate communication for those who have less profound communication needs.

The additional supportive arrangements considered in this conclusion, and in Chapter 3, would inevitably require much greater resource to be applied per case. However, as I discuss in the chapters which follow, this study reveals the importance of reducing the number of children detained in police custody very substantially, such that these proposals ought to be manageable within current resourcing. I turn next to the heart of the custody process from the child's perspective: the cell and the more general punitive impact of police detention.

5
In the Cell

The Process Is the Punishment

EVAN: Basically, police just think it's fun and games. So, like, 'cause it's innocent until proven guilty?
MB: Yeah.
EVAN: No it's not. It's completely not. 'Cause you get accused of somethin', straight away you've done it. You've done it, and you get punished for it.

Introduction

This chapter explores young suspects' experiences of being detained in the police station. For the majority of young participants, what it was like 'in the cell' was what they remembered most vividly and reacted to most forcefully about custody episodes. Remarkably consistent in their overwhelmingly negative response to the conditions in which they were detained, many described the cell or detention room in similar terms, as 'terrible' or 'horrible'. Frequently lasting ten hours or more, detention was, at best, boring and stressful, at worst close to intolerable, engendering widespread anger and resentment. Far from being atypical, Evan's conclusion, in the epigraph above, that police detention is a form of punishment, was widely reflected amongst fellow young participants and, indeed, is echoed in the very limited literature which has previously captured children's police custody experiences.[1]

However, the police station is not intended to be a site of punishment. Pre-charge detention ought, in principle, to impose the 'minimum burdens' on the unconvicted. The suspect should undergo only such deprivations and restrictions of liberty as represent a proportionate response to the necessities of investigation and public protection.[2] Every suspect should be

---

[1] Neal Hazel, Ann Hagell, and Laura Brazier, *Young Offenders' Perceptions of Their Experiences in the Criminal Justice System* (Economic and Social Research Council 2003) 23; Satnam Choongh, *Policing as Social Discipline* (Clarendon Press 1997); Juliet Lyon, Catherine Dennison, and Anita Wilson, '"Tell Them So They Listen": Messages from Young People in Custody', Home Office Research Study 201 (Home Office 2000).
[2] Andrew Ashworth, *The Criminal Process: An Evaluative Study* (1st edn, OUP 1994) 31.

treated with dignity and with respect for them as rights-holders. But the child suspect in particular, as I argued in Chapter 1, should be afforded special adjustment and additional support to enable them to engage their rights. They should be detained only as 'a measure of last resort', and for the 'shortest appropriate period',[3] and in conditions appropriate to their needs and consistent with the promotion of their 'sense of dignity and worth'.[4] In short, police detention should, as far as possible, be managed in a way which treats child suspects in a 'child friendly' way, as the UN Committee on the Rights of the Child (the UN Committee)[5] and domestic guidance[6] envisage.

The child as detainee has only previously been glimpsed in all-ages police custody research[7] or makes a brief appearance in studies examining children's responses to the youth justice system as a whole[8] or policing more generally.[9] The only other research to touch on children's experiences in the cell, and that briefly, is Kemp and Watkins's exploration of children's understanding of the legal rights of suspects,[10] and Kemp and others' ongoing research study which examines the impact of the Police and Criminal Evidence Act 1984 (PACE) on children's detention and questioning.[11]

Despite the aspirations of domestic and international legal frameworks, these scattered accounts reveal that, for a child, police detention could be 'frightening and daunting'[12] and that the boredom they experienced, arising from a near-total lack of stimulus, was a pervasive source of

---

[3] UN Convention on the Rights of the Child (UNCRC), adopted and opened for signature, ratification and accession by General Assembly Resolution 44/25 of 20 November 1989, entered into force 2 September 1990, Art 37(b).
[4] UNCRC (n 3), Arts 37(c) and 40(1).
[5] General Comment No 24 (2019) on children's rights in the child justice system (CRC/C/GC/24), para 46. (General Comment No 24 replaces General Comment No 10 (2007) (CRC/C/GC/10) extant at the time of fieldwork. Any relevant variance will be noted as it arises).
[6] National Police Chiefs' Council (NPCC), 'National Strategy for the Policing of Children and Young People' (NPCC 2016) 8 <national-strategy-for-the-policing-of-children-young-people.pdf (npcc.police.uk) > accessed 17 August 2023.
[7] Choongh (n 1), for example, included interviews with only eight 'juveniles'.
[8] See eg Hazel, Hagell, and Brazier (n 1); Lyon, Dennison, and Wilson (n 1).
[9] All Party Parliamentary Group for Children (APPGC), '"It's All about Trust": Building Good Relationships between Children and the Police. Report of the inquiry held by the All Party Parliamentary Group for Children, 2013–2014' (National Children's Bureau 2014).
[10] Vicky Kemp and Dawn Watkins, 'Exploring Children's Understanding of the Legal Rights of Suspects in England and Wales' (2022) 22(3) Youth Justice 320.
[11] Vicky Kemp and others, *Examining the Impact of PACE on the Detention and Questioning of Child Suspects by the Police in England and Wales* (Nuffield Foundation, 25 May 2023) <https://www.nuffieldfoundation.org/project/impact-of-pace-on-the-detention-and-questioning-of-young-suspects> accessed 3 October 2023, 55-57.
[12] APPGC (n 9) 13.

distress.[13] These isolated voices recount lengthy detention episodes which were often disorientating and stressful and could emotionally destabilize a young detainee. As one young witness told the All Party Parliamentary Group for Children (APPGC), being in a cell can 'mess with your head'.[14] Anger and frustration are also recurrent themes, arising as a result of unexplained delays and the sense of utter powerlessness experienced in detention.[15] More detailed consideration of the experiences of young adults detained in the early stages of the criminal process has identified the experience of 'entry shock', where feelings of distress and fear are more acute in the early phases of detention.[16] This accords with increased levels of suicide and self-harm identified amongst adult detainees during the early hours of custody.[17]

This study allows a deeper exploration of the impact of detention on child suspects in police custody, enabling a fuller explanation of what it is that triggers these very negative experiences. Thus, in the first part of this chapter, I review young participants' responses to their detention and the conditions in which they were held and explore what, for them, made custody so punitive. I then turn, in the second part of the chapter, to investigate why, in light of the protections which should be in place, such negative experiences persist. I examine the domestic protections on paper and reflect on the extent to which they are, in practice, implemented. Finally, I explore some of the barriers to the implementation of those protections and to the achieving of child friendly custody. In light of young participant experiences and this picture of the partial and ineffective implementation of the intended protections, the chapter closes with a consideration of whether the normative requirements of the criminal process are met for children in police detention—whether the custody process could be said to impose the 'minimum burdens' on the child suspect.

---

[13] Hazel, Hagell, and Brazier (n 1); Kemp and others, *Examining the Impact of PACE* (n 11) 56.
[14] APPGC (n 9) 13. See also Kemp and Watkins (n 10) 329.
[15] Hazel, Hagell, and Brazier (n 1).
[16] Helen Louise Jones, 'The Pains of Custody: How Young Men Cope through the Criminal Justice System' (DPhil thesis, University of Hull 2007) 174.
[17] Ian Cummins, 'A Place of Safety? Self-Harming Behaviour in Police Custody' (2008) 10(1) Journal of Adult Protection 36.

Being in the Cell: Child Suspect Experiences of Detention

Conditions in Detention: 'Just horrible'

Sadie's summary of detention conditions was fairly typical: 'It's just horrible—it's just four walls innit ... it's freezing. It smells, it's just not a nice place to be.' The absence of a window was considered a particular deprivation ('there's nothing, it's just a wall' (Luke)), drawing unfavourable comparisons with a prison cell from those with experience. Almost one-quarter of young participants used the motif of being 'thrown' into the cell, seemingly to emphasize what they perceived to be harsh or neglectful treatment. A number found their feelings hard to verbalize: 'I just don't like it—going in them walls ... I don't know, I can't explain' (Jayden).

The majority complained about the harsh conditions in the cell—of the 'hard' bench ('I call 'em trays, me. They're not beds, they're trays' (Evan)), blankets like 'you would put on top of a horse', and the thin plastic-covered mattresses 'like what you got in PE' (Zayn). Some were denied a pillow (Elijah), blankets, or a mattress (Malik). Whilst some had found the cells clean, particularly in more modern blocks, others complained of unsanitary conditions, especially when arrested late at night: 'it was just dirty, like all the walls just dirty ... I couldn't really sleep in there' (Jayden). Kate described being detained in a cell occupied immediately before her by 'an addict' who had been sick in the toilet and on the floor: 'I was like, "Surely my human rights make me have a better cell than this?"' Indeed, a significant number of young people described officers as 'taking the mick' or 'taking the piss' out of them by the conditions in which they were held. Animal motifs were also commonly used by young participants to underline what they considered to be degrading treatment. Harper, for example, reflected of the food provided that "I wouldn't give it to the dog', an assessment echoed by CO33: 'The food here is awful—you wouldn't serve it to animals.'[18]

Indeed, food was a central focus of complaint, and the overwhelming majority of young participants were very vocal in their disgust at what was provided. They commonly described the food as 'shit', 'horrible', and 'disgusting'. Some complained that it was 'cold', even 'frozen still inside' (Aaron), when they received it,[19] whilst others felt provoked by its poor

---

[18] See for similar Kemp and others, *Examining the Impact of PACE* (n 11) 55–57.
[19] Recalling similar complaints in Layla Skinns, *Police Custody: Governance, Legitimacy and Reform in the Criminal Justice Process* (Willan Publishing 2011).

quality. Harper felt that the food was 'adding more like flames to the fire' for a young person coming into custody in an angry state. Staff at all sites generally agreed that the food they served was pretty unpalatable, being largely microwave meals not requiring refrigerated storage. Drink options for children, who often did not drink the tea or coffee routinely offered, were limited. Many favoured hot chocolate, although this had unhelpfully been discontinued in some areas (eg F3), reducing the choice to cartons of orange juice or water. The prominence of eating and drinking in participants' accounts is unsurprising, reflecting similar significance accorded to food in previous studies.[20] For some, the stark contrast between home-cooked food, 'a big scran at home', and 'a fucking little microwave meal' in custody (Aaron) was emblematic of the staff's uncaring—even insulting—treatment.

Toilet issues were a particular source of humiliation and distress. For a number, the presence of an open toilet in the cell was disturbing, especially when it had not been flushed. Having to request toilet paper was 'bad' (Carter) and 'embarrassing' (Logan), and several participants felt that staff deliberately delayed responding to such requests. But young participants' greatest anxiety related to whether staff conducting visits, or observing them on CCTV, might see them using the in-cell toilet.[21] Striking in this regard was the very limited information or reassurance with which young participants seem to have been provided: 'The person who took me to the cell just ... pointed me to the camera. "There's a camera there" and then that was it really' (Elijah). A number were annoyed that they had not been told about pixilation of toilet areas on CCTV viewing screens,[22] while others

---

[20] Hazel, Hagell, and Brazier (n 1); HM Inspectorate of Constabulary (HMIC) (now His Majesty's Inspectorate of Constabulary, Fire and Rescue Services, HMICFRS), *The Welfare of Vulnerable People in Police Custody* (HMIC 2015); Tricia Jessiman and Ailsa Cameron, 'The Role of the Appropriate Adult in Supporting Vulnerable Adults in Custody: Comparing the Perspectives of Service Users and Service Providers' (2017) 45 British Journal of Learning Disabilities 246; Jones (n 16).

[21] See for similar Tim Newburn and Stephanie Hayman, *Policing, Surveillance and Social Control: CCTV and Police Monitoring of Suspects* (Willan Publishing 2002), although in contrast to their findings, there was no discernible difference between genders or ethnicities in young participant responses.

[22] Despite the requirement for all detainees to be made aware of pixilation arrangements: Police and Criminal Evidence Act 1984 (PACE) *Code C: Revised Code of Practice for the Detention, Treatment and Questioning of Persons by Police Officers* (updated 4 November 2020). (In force at time of writing. Any relevant variance with the version in force at time of fieldwork, published May 2014, will be noted as it arises.) Notes for Guidance (NFG), 8D. Only in F2 was a written notice given to detainees about CCTV and pixilation. In all three areas, verbal information about CCTV coverage was rarely given.

were doubtful about its implementation. For some young participants, these oversights were a source of significant discomfort as they would attempt to 'hold it' until release.

Coping with Confinement: 'Trapped in a room'

For many young participants, the oppressive isolation of police custody could be difficult to manage. First, the sudden and total nature of their isolation could be deeply painful, with the instant severing of lines of contact with the outside world:

> it's horrible, it's just out of the comfort zone. Like, you're always texting someone, you've always got someone to talk to, and then all of a sudden you're just shoved in like a cage sort of like room and then you've got nothing to do, doing nothing, you've just gotta wait. You've just gotta wait—and you dunno how long it's gonna be.
>
> (Will)

Second, the sense of containment could be oppressive and particularly distressing for some. Young participants' accounts were often dominated by the blank, pressing presence of the walls: 'you're just in a square box, aren't you, it's concrete all around you' (Aidan). As Will above, several young participants referred to feeling that they were stuck in a cage or trapped in the space:

> It's just being trapped in a room. I was literally, I felt like I wanted to kill myself. I was just locked in a room. It's horrible. It is one of the worst experiences you can ever have, I think.
>
> (Tom)

For others, it was the sense of separation that was really difficult, often exacerbated by uncertainty about when they would be released: 'It's cruel to be honest' (Hussain). Tyler described how, although the space was 'open ... it felt small because you were on your own and there was no-one around'. RHAA4 observed that this aspect could be particularly difficult for those in residential care: 'it forces you to think in a tiny space ... usually a child in care doesn't spend much time alone'. Closely allied with, and feeding into, this sense of isolated containment is the pain many children experienced as a result of feeling stripped of their personal possessions. Echoing similar complaints made by adult detainees,[23] the sense of 'having nothing' was prominent and, as discussed in Chapter 3, the removal of all their belongings, beyond their immediate clothing, was a source of particular distress and resentment.

Coping with the Lack of Stimulation: 'It's bare long'

Megan's description captures the response of many to this confinement without stimulation: 'It's boring. It does your head in. There's nothing to do.' Indeed, 'boring' was the most commonly used descriptor as it is in the few accounts we have from other children and young people with experience of police custody.[24] However, this study enables a deeper understanding of what was meant by this seemingly simple term. For a significant number of young participants, 'boring' was used straightforwardly to encapsulate the relentlessly blank environment of the cell: 'looking at four walls. Every two seconds going round and round' (Simon). A number of young participants, particularly those with regular experience of custody, described habitual mechanisms that they employed to cope. Almost half of young participants explained that they would try to sleep as a means of managing the tedium of the cell: 'just get your head down 'cos there's literally nothing to do in there' (Dexter). Others were more resourceful. Will, for example, explained that he liked to do complex arithmetical calculations in his head, whilst some took a more strategic approach, with several using the space to think about how they might respond to police interview questions. However, more commonly, activities to pass the time tended to be repetitive actions as a means of simply getting through the waiting, for example, counting tiles, walking around in circles, fashioning makeshift balls out of clothing, or ripping up packaging into missiles to throw at cups or the sink. Several young people (generally, but not exclusively, boys) described exercising: doing sit ups or using the mattress for punching practice. As Rezar explained, 'You just do anything to get you unfocused for a bit.'

However, these methods were not always effective, and a number of young participants struggled to cope with the boredom: 'it's right hard' (Nathan). It was widely acknowledged across custody staff, health-care

---

[23] Layla Skinns and Andrew Wooff, 'Pain in Police Detention: A Critical Point in the "Penal Painscape"?' (2020) 1 Policing & Society 251.

[24] Jones (n 16); Hazel, Hagell, and Brazier (n 1) 193.

professionals (HCPs) and appropriate adults (AAs) that the lack of stimulus could be 'really difficult' (L&D3). Thus, for some young participants, the initial descriptor 'boring' in fact related to periods of confinement that were close to intolerable for them. As Tom explained, aged eighteen at the time of his research interview, 'I mean it would be bad for an hour but the length I was in there, it was terrible ... I think if I had to go in now I'd cry. I would actually cry'. Some recalled feelings of serious agitation and emotional anguish echoing individual accounts provided to His Majesty's Inspectorate of Constabulary (HMIC)[25] and the APPGC[26] and the experiences of children enduring longer periods in solitary or cellular confinement.[27] Zoe's description as 'bugging out like, I was actually going crazy. I can't be in a small room for too long' mirrors strikingly the experiences of young people held in solitary confinement in the United States: 'since it's a small room it makes you think crazy',[28] 'It can make you go crazy'.[29] Although these accounts are associated with much longer-term or 'supermax' confinement, the experiences recounted by young participants (including loss of control, self-harm, and suicidal ideation) have long been identified as associated with solitary confinement, defined by the UN Standard Minimum Rules for the Treatment of Prisoners custody ('Mandela Rules') as less than two hours of meaningful contact with others daily.[30] The Mandela Rules prohibit solitary confinement for any young person—a prohibition which is urged upon the UK government by both the Equality and Human Rights Commission (EHRC)[31] and medical experts.[32]

---

[25] HMIC (n 20) 189.
[26] APPGC (n 9) 13.
[27] See eg Kate Gooch, 'A Childhood Cut Short: Child Deaths in Penal Custody and the Pains of Child Imprisonment' (2016) 55 Howard Journal of Crime and Justice 278, 281–82.
[28] Alysia Santo '"Sometimes You Gotta Go in the Shower and Go Knife-to-Knife, Right?"' (Marshall Project & New York Magazine 2015) <www.themarshallproject.org/2015/06/28/this-is-rikers> accessed 17 August 2023.
[29] Bronx Defenders, 'Voices from the Box: Solitary confinement at Rikers Island (Bronx Defenders 2014) <www.bronxdefenders.org/wp-content/uploads/2014/09/Voices-From-the-Box.pdf> accessed 17 August 2023.
[30] UN Standard Minimum Rules for the Treatment of Prisoners, adopted at the First UN Congress on Crime Prevention and Criminal Justice, Geneva 1955.
[31] EHRC, 'Protecting Human Rights: Key Challenges for the UK's Third Universal Periodic Review' (EHRC) 2016<www.equalityhumanrights.com/sites/default/files/protecting-human-rights-uk-third-universal-periodic-review-december-2016.pdf>, accessed 17 August 2023.
[32] British Medical Association, Royal College of Paediatrics and Child Health, and Royal College of Psychiatrists, 'Joint Position Statement on Solitary Confinement of Children and Young People' (2018) <www.rcpch.ac.uk/sites/default/files/2018-04/solitary_confinement_position_statement.pdf> accessed 17 August 2023.

HCPs also commented about young detainees being 'visibly distressed' (L&D2), at times 'too distressed to talk about it' (L&D7), and incidents of self-harm, or attempted self-harm, were not uncommon. This extreme distress was an issue raised across the age range. Nor, for young people, did confinement need to be lengthy to be hard. As Zoe explained, 'It's bare long. Honestly every minute feels like ten minutes.' Even detention in a cell for two or three hours could be extremely difficult for a child.

Managing Uncertainty: 'What's going on? It was scary'

Adult detainees have described experiencing a sense of 'uncertainty' and 'liminality' in police custody.[33] However, for child suspects, uncertainty appeared to have an altogether more destabilizing and intense aspect.[34] Some young participants described an almost vertiginous anxiety, unable to fall back on wider life experience, in the dark about likely outcomes, and preoccupied by the potential loss of youthful promise and opportunity:

> I thought I was gonna get sent to jail 'cos they were right going on, 'It'll go to court' and all this and that, and I'm thinking, "Oh my God, what have I done to my future now. What's going on?' It was scary.
>
> (Kate)

For some, the fear was about the process itself: 'the worst bit was that I knew I was gonna have an interview, like straight after I get out of this cell, so the whole time I was like a bit paranoid in the head I was thinking right what am I gonna say, what are they gonna ask me?' (Hussain). Young participants also frequently made reference to anxiety in custody about whether they would be pressurized to 'grass' (inform) on associates. Often, this was confined to concerns about peers, but several were contending with what might be considered exploitation circumstances with very serious

---

[33] Skinns and Wooff (n 23) 253.
[34] A similar response has also been observed in young remand prisoners: Sinead Freeman and Mairead Seymour, '"Just Waiting": The Nature and Effect of Uncertainty on Young People in Remand Custody in Ireland' (2010) 10 Youth Justice 126; Joel Harvey, *Young Men in Prison: Surviving and Adapting to Life Inside* (Willan Publishing 2007).

repercussions: 'Literally you're putting your life at risk, or your loved ones at risk' (Zayn).[35]

Nor were process-specific anxieties restricted to first-timers. Not knowing what was happening in their case, particularly when or whether they might be released, could be a source of considerable frustration and distress even for experienced young suspects. Regular attendee Jo explained, 'Well, sometimes you just like want to know, isn't it? You're like "Ahhhh". Sometimes, I just get pissed off over it ... and I get stressed out too quick. I don't even know why', whilst for Tom, it was 'just horrible' and for Will, 'probably like the worst bit'. As is frequently the case in this study, the distress was often magnified for those who experienced greater adversity and for whom life outside was less settled. Yemi was worried, for example, about the effect of arrest on his placement in residential care. As Sadie explained, 'All your problems come to mind and then more problems come to your mind because you're in there. And then it's just stress.'[36]

Limiting Detention Periods: Procedure and Existing Literature

These young participant reflections make difficult reading. They paint a picture of an unduly harsh process and one which is barely adjusted to take account of children's needs and capacities. Yet, as I outlined in the introduction, this ought not to be the position for any child in pre-charge detention. International obligations stress that detention periods should be restricted to the 'shortest appropriate period' and emphasize the importance of 'child friendly' provision for children in police detention.[37] Domestically, the police have a general statutory duty to 'safeguard and promote the welfare of children' in their care.[38] However, the domestic legal framework of child-specific adjustments to detention conditions for young suspects is extremely limited.

---

[35] None of the young participants whose arrests were potentially identifiable as resulting from criminal exploitation had been referred through the National Referral Mechanism (Modern Slavery Act 2015, s 49), nor was that referral route volunteered by any officers encountered during fieldwork where children were arrested out of area or in circumstances suggestive of exploitation.

[36] The emergence of thoughts about aspects of their lives that young people would rather not revisit has been noted in other custodial settings: Diana Medlicott, *Surviving the Prison Place: Narratives of Suicidal Prisoners* (Ashgate 2001); Paul Gray, ' "I Hate Talking about It": Identifying and Supporting Traumatised Young People in Custody' (2015) 54 Howard Journal of Criminal Justice 434.

[37] General Comment No 24 (n 19), para 46ff.

[38] Children Act 2004, s 11.

Time limits on the detention of children in police custody are the same as for adults, and there is no statutory recognition of their rights under the UNCRC Article 37(b) to detention 'only as a last resort' and for the 'shortest appropriate period'. In the first instance, a suspect must not be detained for more than twenty-four hours,[39] and all detainees must be dealt with 'expeditiously and released as soon as the need for detention no longer applies'.[40] There is no shorter timescale for child suspects. Nor is there any differentiation between child and adult in terms of reviews of detention, when the necessity of continued detention is scrutinized, which, for all detainees, must occur after six hours and then at nine-hourly intervals.[41] In respect of children detained pre-charge, the only distinction lies in the College of Policing's Authorised Professional Practice guidance, which requires senior officers to apply the provisions of PACE 'strictly' to prevent children being detained 'any longer than necessary, both pre and post-charge'.[42] The police are, however, statutorily required to transfer a child who has been refused bail after charge to local authority accommodation, pending his or her appearance in court (whether this is overnight or during the day).[43] However, this does not apply to detention pre-charge or to those arrested for suspected breach of bail conditions.

The very limited quantitative data available indicates that these scant protections are failing to prevent children from enduring lengthy periods in police custody. Indeed, despite significant reductions in the numbers of child arrests,[44] detention periods appear to be extending unchecked. In the mid-1990s, young suspects were found to be detained on average for five hours when arriving with an AA and over seven hours if an AA had to be called, in comparison to an adult average of six hours and forty minutes.[45] Subsequent research suggests that detention times across all ages groups

---

[39] PACE, s 41.
[40] *Code C* (n 22), para 1.1.
[41] PACE, s 40.
[42] Authorised Professional Practice (Detention and Custody)(Children and Young Persons) (APP(DC)(CYP) (first published 23 October 2013, last updated 2 May 2023) 2 <https://www.college.police.uk/app/detention-and-custody/detainee-care/children-and-young-persons> accessed 17 August 2023. (Any relevant variance between the current APP versions and versions in force at the time of the fieldwork will be noted as it arises.)
[43] PACE, s 38(6), subject to extremely limited exceptions.
[44] Howard League for Penal Reform, 'Child Arrests in England and Wales 2020' (Howard League 2021) <https://howardleague.org/publications/child-arrests-in-england-and-wales-2020> accessed 17 August 2023.
[45] Coretta Phillips and David C Brown, 'Entry into the Criminal Justice System: A Survey of Police Arrests and Their Outcomes', Home Office Research Study 185 (Home Office 1998) 110.

have continued to rise,[46] with HMIC finding, in 2015, an all-age average detention time across inspected forces of just under eleven hours.[47] Most recently, analysis of 3,722 electronic custody records for child detainees collected from 8 forces (for periods in 2019, 2020, and 2021) identified an average detention duration of eleven hours and thirty-six minutes.[48]

The detention of children overnight, in particular, is a long-standing problem. Research in 2011 suggested that overnight detention was routine, both pre- and post-charge, with over 53,000 under-16-year-olds detained overnight across 24 police forces in 2008–09.[49] Various factors were identified, including the nature of the offence and the timing of the arrest, delays caused by the attendance of AAs and solicitors, and difficulties in the referral process between police and local authorities.[50] At the time of the fieldwork, forces were looking forward to the introduction of concordat arrangements intended to improve post-charge referral processes.[51] Regrettably, not all forces and local authorities have signed the Concordat on Children in Custody,[52] and, although there have been some improvements following its introduction, overnight detention remains a significant issue.[53] Indeed, experimental Home Office data on overnight detentions of children, published for the first time in November 2022 and providing only a snapshot of twenty-six forces, revealed that just under half (45%) of children taken into custody were detained overnight.[54] More worrying

---

[46] Vicky Kemp, Nigel Balmer, and Pascoe Pleasence, '"Whose Time Is It Anyway?": Factors Associated with Duration in Police Custody' (2012) Criminal Law Review 736.
[47] HMIC (n 20) 83, although these figures include some individuals remanded after charge.
[48] Kemp and others, *Examining the Impact of PACE* (n 11) 68.
[49] Layla Skinns, *Overnight Detention of Children in Police Cells* (Howard League 2011), 'overnight' meaning the child spent more than four hours in custody between midnight and 8 am (27).
[50] ibid.
[51] Home Office, 'Concordat on Children in Custody' (Home Office 2017<www.gov.uk/government/publications/concordat-on-children-in-custody> accessed 17 August 2023).
[52] Only 27 of 39 forces and 88 of 333 local authorities: see ibid.
[53] Augusta Itua, '"It's Horrible When They Keep You in There at Night." Ending the Overnight Detention of Children in Police Custody' (Just for Kids Law 2022) <https://www.justforkidslaw.org/sites/default/files/upload/J4KL_Detention%20briefing%202022_0.pdf> accessed 17 August 2023.
[54] Home Office, 'Police Powers and Procedures: Other PACE Powers, England and Wales, Year Ending 31 March 2022' (National Statistics 2022) <https://www.gov.uk/government/statistics/police-powers-and-procedures-other-pace-powers-england-and-wales-year-ending-31-march-2022/police-powers-and-procedures-other-pace-powers-england-and-wales-year-ending-31-march-2022> accessed 17 August 2023. Overnight detention is defined as where a child spends at least four hours in custody and that at least part of this period must be between midnight and 4 am.

still, overnight detention is a site of striking racial disparity—in the experimental data, 21% of children detained overnight were Black or Black British.[55]

Limiting Detention Periods: Child Suspect Experiences

No Longer Than 'necessary'?

The need to avoid keeping a child in detention any longer than absolutely necessary, especially overnight, was frequently referred to by custody officers (COs) and other adults on observation. Yet, although I did observe instances of officers deciding to bail a young suspect where it was apparent that no progress could be made,[56] there were still many cases where children were detained for extremely long periods. During fieldwork, it was only possible to obtain the complete times for thirty-three of the forty-nine separate custody episodes tracked. However, the average (mean) pre-charge detention time of these thirty-three episodes was eleven hours and forty-five minutes, with eighteen being detained pre-charge for over ten hours. Young participants reported similar experiences. Almost three-quarters described detention episodes which lasted more than ten hours.

What is continuing to drive these long periods in detention for children? In keeping with earlier all-ages examinations,[57] arrests late in the evening or in the early hours were a feature in a significant number of those longer detention periods (twelve of the eighteen episodes over ten hours). As noted in Chapter 4, the unavailability of AAs in such cases was also implicated, especially where local schemes did not provide an 'out-of-hours' service. But delays in these circumstances tended to arise more from the decision to delay interview until morning, on the basis that questioning a child at night was neither desirable nor fair, rather than difficulty sourcing an AA to attend.[58] Whilst, in terms of enabling effective participation, a reluctance to

---

[55] ibid, table 2.4.
[56] Although calling into question the 'necessity' of their detention in the first instance: PACE s 37.
[57] Kemp, Balmer, and Pleasence, '"Whose Time Is It Anyway?"' (n 46).
[58] See for similar Vicky Kemp and Jacqueline Hodgson, 'Chapter 4. England and Wales Empirical Findings' in Miet Vanderhallen and others (eds), *Interrogating Young Suspects: Procedural Safeguards from an Empirical Perspective*, Vol 2 (Intersentia 2016).

interview at night is to be applauded, where a CO was unwilling or unable to bail a young suspect, this adjustment to accommodate the child's needs could have the unfortunate effect of prolonging detention, often without AA support. In some cases, it was plain that more careful consideration of the timing of arrest could have avoided lengthy detention.[59]

Most commonly, investigative delay extended detention periods, officers frequently citing reduced resources as the root cause (especially in F2). This was particularly associated with multi-handed arrests—a more common occurrence for children than adults.[60] Solicitors complained that delays occurred because the police favoured interviewing all co-suspects before a decision on charge and bail could be made—prioritizing the interests of case construction over the needs of child suspects. Conversely, conflicts of interests arising where a single duty solicitor represented several young suspects arrested together could also contribute to delays—an issue beyond the control of the CO. Additionally, young participants and solicitors complained of lengthy post-interview detention while the police awaited advice from the Crown Prosecution Service: 'it's really dreadful. It can extend things by hours' (Sol11). Such delays particularly irked young participants. Although legitimated by PACE,[61] it is questionable how often detention in these circumstances will be necessary, given the high threshold for remanding children into custody. Some COs suggested that prolonged detention was more convenient for young suspects since being bailed to await advice could extend the charge decision by several weeks, although several solicitors considered that any convenience benefited the police rather than the child. Unsurprisingly, young participants tended to suggest that they would prefer release and extended uncertainty to lengthy delays in detention.

Additionally, detention reviews during observation appeared to have little direct effect in reducing detention periods for children. Those reviews that I observed tended to be perfunctory and somewhat formulaic, often conducted over the phone. I did not get the impression in any case that the inspector was seriously weighing the question of further detention, nor did I encounter a young suspect being released as a result of a review. Young participants seemed to view such reviews as (sometimes unwelcome) updates, when they 'tell you you're going to be there for longer' (Sadie), rather

---

[59] It is to be hoped that the judgment in *ST v Chief Constable of Nottinghamshire Police* [2022] EWHC 1280 (QB) will encourage more responsible decision-making around the timing of arrest in future.
[60] Where more than one person is arrested as part of the same incident/allegation.
[61] PACE, s 37(7).

than opportunities to make representations. Their greatest impact appeared indirect, in the sense that COs often referred to the need to justify continuing detention at reviews, and an upcoming review might prompt an enquiry with the investigating officers as to progress with a child's case. Rarely were AAs or solicitors 'available' in the block to make representations at reviews[62]—working practices and CO orchestration resulting in their attendance generally just before interview. Sol11 (working in F2) suggested that COs would ask 'whether we want to be involved in the normal reviews, and usually we aren't'. Unsurprisingly, therefore, I did not encounter representations being made by an AA or solicitor for any review of detention that I tracked (although I did not observe reviews in every case), nor were any representations noted on custody records that I reviewed. It is frustrating to note the inefficacy of the review process as a check on lengthy detention periods, given that this problem has been identified since the late 1990s.[63]

Longer Detention for Those Experiencing Greater Adversity

More concerning still is that those young suspects experiencing prolonged detention tended to be those who had a mental health issue, or some form of neurodivergence, or who experienced other additional adversity in their lives. On observation, every one of the young suspects who spent more than twenty hours in custody pre-charge was in the care of the local authority. Girls, and Black, Asian, and ethnic minority young suspects were also over-represented in the group of young suspects experiencing longer detention times. Identifiable factors in respect of their prolonged detention periods included structural challenges, especially finding appropriate accommodation and mental health support to enable safe release, and administrative difficulties arising from children living in placements out of their home area, although it was notable, on observation, that a social worker or carer attending as AA with particular knowledge of the child in question could have a really positive impact in terms of securing bail or an appropriate

---

[62] ibid, s 40(12).
[63] See David C Brown, 'PACE Ten Years On: A Review of the Research', Home Office Research Study 155 (Home Office 1997); Skinns, *Police Custody* (n 19).

placement (as in the case of YS26 and 27) or finding secure accommodation after charge (YS13).[64]

There were, however, indications of cultural attitudes within custody teams and among legal advisers which meant that those with more adverse childhood experiences, or greater experience of police custody, might not be treated with the same urgency as other young suspects. It was suggested by some that the harsh experience of the custody suite had less effect on them: 'They get better looked after here than at home' (CO34). As one legal adviser noted, 'There is probably a hardening to frequent attendees—by the custody sergeant and probably by me as well. Certain people are more used to being here and the impact is not so great.' For example, YS20, a fourteen-year-old girl with substantial experience of police custody, was in custody over eighteen hours, arrested for common assault on a security guard. She requested legal advice, but the solicitor did not attend until approximately sixteen hours had passed and was not involved in any review of detention. Her continued detention was approved twice by the Inspector, despite the glacially slow pace of the investigation and the fact that YS20 spent significant periods in distress and on constant watch.

The evidence also reveals a concerning picture of very lengthy detentions for young people arrested for breach of bail or wanted on warrant. These children are required by statute to be detained by the police and produced to the next available court.[65] Staff and young participants gave accounts of children detained for whole weekends waiting to be produced to court. Eleven young participants recounted custody periods of over thirty hours on at least one occasion following arrest for breach of bail, generally involving detention over a weekend. Again, those longer detentions often involved young people in residential care, commonly where breaches related to a breakdown in a particular placement.

---

[64] Two of the three young suspects remanded after charge were 'looked-after' (YS13 and YS20), with only YS13 being found secure accommodation. All three had significant dispositional vulnerabilities.
[65] Bail Act 1976, s 7; Magistrates' Courts Act 1980, s 13.

Adjustments to Detention Conditions: Procedure and Existing Literature

Child-specific adjustments to detention conditions within the legal framework are similarly meagre. Despite the police's overarching statutory duty to 'safeguard and promote the welfare of children and young people',[66] the translation of this duty into specific provisions for their care in custody is minimal, to say the least. Aside from the provision of an appropriate adult (addressed in Chapter 4), the most significant protection is that a child must not be placed in a cell with a 'detained adult' and not held in a police cell at all unless there is 'no other secure accommodation' and the CO considers that it is 'not practicable to supervise them if they are not placed in a cell'.[67] Where a child is kept in a cell, a reason must be recorded.[68] APP(DC)(CYP) makes reference to a recommendation made by the APPGC that new custody facilities should provide a 'separate area' for young detainees, 'even for short term detention', although no specifics are provided.[69]

Young detainees should, 'whenever possible', be visited in the cell 'more frequently' than the standard hourly requirement for adults.[70] This protection seems designed, in light of the low frequency of significant illness or issues arising from substance dependency amongst children, to mitigate the impact of isolation and to address their distinct welfare needs when detained in police custody. In this regard, a child has the same rights as an adult not to be held incommunicado (particularly the entitlement to make a phone call for a reasonable period),[71] but this is supplemented, on paper at least, by the right to speak to their AA 'at any time'[72] and by the possibility of family or friends being allowed to visit them whilst in custody.[73]

Turning to adjustments for particular groups of children, a girl suspect must be under the care of a female officer or staff member.[74] However,

---

[66] Children Act 2004, s 11.
[67] *Code C* (n 22), para 8.8 or in the (presumably highly unlikely event) that other secure accommodation is less 'comfortable'.
[68] *Code C* (n 22), para 8.10.
[69] APP(DC)(CYP) (n 42), 6.
[70] *Code C* (n 22), para 9.3, NFG 9B.
[71] ibid, para 5.6. This is additional to the right to have someone informed of their arrest (*Code C* (n 22), NFG 5E) and can only be delayed or denied on the written authority of an Inspector (or more senior officer) (*Code C* (n 22), para 5.6, Annex B) and only where the suspect is detained in respect of an indictable offence.
[72] ibid, para 3.18.
[73] Discretionary under ibid, para 5.4.
[74] Children and Young Persons Act 1933 (CYPA 1933), s 31.

APP(DC)(CYP) clarifies that, subject to risk assessment, the carer 'need not be physically present and with the detainee at all times, but must be readily available and assigned to the detainee throughout the period of detention' and that she 'should visit the detainee and check on her welfare needs'. The detainee herself must be told that 'she can ask to see the carer at any time'.[75] Additionally, a substantial section within APP(DC)(CYP)[76] details the raised prevalence of characteristics or 'difficult life events' amongst young detainees, which are likely to increase risks to their safety and well-being in custody. The extensive list of eighteen bullet points includes physical and mental health problems; history of self-harm; developmental disorders such as attention deficit hyperactivity disorder (ADHD); being in the care of the local authority; having experienced abuse, neglect, or trauma; and being physically or emotionally immature. APP(DC)(CYP) requires officers to 'carefully consider these when planning how to support, observe and care for children' who may have such vulnerabilities, although, unhelpfully given the lack of specialist training of many staff,[77] APP(DC)(CYP) provides no indication of what such adjustments might be.

From the very limited material that we have in respect of child suspects, there are indications that these scant protections are not consistently implemented. HMIC's thematic study of the welfare of vulnerable people in custody, for example, noted 'few instances where they [children] were allowed to wait in interview rooms instead of in a cell'.[78] Kemp and others' more recent study identifies shortcomings both in the *Code C* provisions and their implementation.[79] However, previous research has not examined the full range of child-specific protections, the factors associated with non-implementation, or the effectiveness of the protections.

---

[75] APP(DC)(CYP) (n 42), 9.
[76] ibid 3–4.
[77] See in respect of autism spectrum disorder (ASD) Nick Chown, '"Do You Have Any Difficulties That I May Not Be Aware Of?" A Study of Autism Awareness and Understanding in the UK Police Service' (2010) 12 International Journal of Police Science & Management 256; in respect of learning disability Richard Cant and Penny Standen, 'What Professionals Think about Offenders with Learning Disabilities in the Criminal Justice System' (2007) 35 British Journal of Learning Disabilities 174; more generally Skinns, *Police Custody* (n 19).
[78] HMIC (n 20) 77.
[79] Kemp and others, *Examining the Impact of PACE* (n 11) 93.

Adjustments to Detention Conditions: Child Suspect Experiences

Routine Use of Adult Cells

Despite the prohibition,[80] in all three observation areas, placing a child in an adult cell was routine and unremarkable and not generally noted on the custody record.[81] Likewise, all but one young participant recounted being detained in a room which they described in terms conforming internally to a standard adult cell. The accounts that the majority provided of the hard bench, the blue mattress, open toilet, and door with a hatch and spyhole suggest that they were held in accommodation that was, or was very similar to, an adult cell.

This key protection in *Code C*, 8.8 has been rendered effectively meaningless, but how and why? In the first instance, this is a physical resourcing issue. In the six suites that I visited, there were very limited alternatives to adult cell accommodation. In each suite, there were designated 'juvenile detention rooms' (JDRs) (or, in one block, a 'vulnerable' section (F2/3)). However, those rooms were, without exception, internally identical to the adult cells in the block in terms of dimension, lighting, and 'furniture'. On observation, the only physical difference, where there was any, between accommodation for young suspects and adult police cells related to the height of the bench[82] or the nature of the door. In one suite (F2/3), 'vulnerable' cells had a glass panel (approximately one-quarter of the door's width running floor to ceiling); in two other suites, JDRs had neither a hatch nor a glass panel (F3/5 and F3/6). A CO explained that this latter adjustment made the room 'not a cell' because of the need to open the door, therefore, to see or speak to the detainee. In other suites, the difference between a JDR and a cell was limited to its designation or signage. One young participant described, with approval, being in a cell with an entirely glass door, the opacity of which could be adjusted from outside (Tom). However, otherwise, the oppressive nature of the cell in young participant accounts related to its scale and the harshness of its 'furniture'—the nature of the door or the height of the bench largely went unremarked.

---

[80] *Code C* (n 22), para 8.8.
[81] In line with findings in HMIC (n 20).
[82] In some 'vulnerable' cells, the bench is lower to prevent injury from falling off it.

Perhaps unsurprisingly, custody staff showed limited commitment to the use of JDRs and did not always place children in them when available. Often, there were suitability concerns—in F1/2, the JDRs were very close to the booking-in desk and therefore extremely noisy, whilst in F2, the perspex doors prompted concerns about exposure to vulnerable adults in facing cells. Institutional concerns also sometimes overrode the use of JDRs. Young co-suspects were often placed in cells that ensured the greatest distance from each other to protect against collusion, regardless of whether they were accommodated in JDRs or not. In only two of the six blocks visited (F1/1 and F3/6) was there any alternative, roomier secure accommodation—in each case, a single secure waiting room in sight of the custody desk, significantly larger than a cell with a sizeable window, looking onto the booking-in area. In both blocks, these were used sometimes for child suspects as a form of respite, generally for short time periods ('half an hour to an hour' (CO10)), but not routinely for a whole detention episode, in part because of concerns about additional exposure to adult detainees in the booking-in area.

Such a dearth of more child friendly accommodation is enabled by the permissive language of *Code C*. The prohibition on the use of an adult cell is fundamentally undermined by the practicability exemption. In addition, *Code C* provides no positive statement of what suitable 'juvenile' accommodation might be, enabling a semantic nod to compliance by the relabelling of an adult cell as a JDR. This institutional indifference is manifest in APP(DC)(CYP),[83] which notes that new custody facilities are 'usually built to the Lambeth design, which is unisex and suitable for children and young people'. The Lambeth design cell is 7 m squared by area (sufficient for a 2.5 × 2.8 m cell).

Enduring Adult Distress

On observation, no cells were shared, whether by adults or children, meeting the requirement for separation from 'detained adults' in the cell.[84] Nonetheless, commonly, children were exposed to significant levels of noise from adults in neighbouring cells: 'if it's a weekend, Friday or Saturday,

---

[83] APP(DC)(CYP) (n 42) 5.
[84] *Code C* (n 22), para 8.8, although Luke described being placed in a holding cell with an adult (see Chapter 2).

you've got all the drunk people in there. It's always loud. They're always screaming, they're always doing something' (Rezar). Hussain, for example, recounted listening to a drunk man: 'he just made so much noise, he wanted to get out of his cell, or he said "I'm gonna cut myself. I'm gonna do this, I'm gonna do that."' On observations, whilst some blocks could be eerily quiet, I found the frequent, and often sustained, anguished adult screaming and shouting hard to deal with, even just being present as a researcher. COs and AAs in various suites described noise levels as 'awful' (CO34), 'horrific' (CO40), or 'like bedlam' (VAA2).[85]

Once alone in the cell, concerns about violence at the hands of other detainees, raised in Chapter 2, might subside, but hearing others in distress could trigger new security fears. Jayden recalled how unsettling it was to listen to 'a woman just screaming for like three hours straight, just screaming' (Jayden). Jake explained, 'for someone's first time in the cell it can be quite frightening ... all these people around you acting all crazy'. Hearing other detainees apparently in need and not attended to could understandably trigger doubts about one's own safety and the care that one might receive. As Alison Liebling has observed, 'what makes a prison feel safe—the most important determinant of distress—is responsive, approachable and respectful staff'.[86] Adults working in custody were often conscious of the unsettling, even damaging, effects for a child of 'Sitting in the cell when terrified, not understanding the process and having people screaming and shouting' (L&D3). As Sol7 explained, 'They [child suspects] talk about people they can hear in the cell next door, someone screaming. They laugh it off sometimes, but you can tell they're affected by it.'

The requirement for accommodation separation in APP(DC)(CYP) appeared to have had some impact, and efforts had been made to separate JDRs from adult accommodation in all blocks.[87] However, this was frequently poorly implemented so as to be wholly ineffective. For example, in F1/1 and F3/4, separation was attempted by a lockable grilled gate, whilst in F3/5, a solid door had been installed but was rarely closed, being considered generally ineffective in shielding young suspects from seeing or hearing adult detainees. This is disappointing since those few young participants

---

[85] See for similar Kemp and Hodgson (n 58).
[86] Alison Liebling, 'Moral Performance, Inhuman and Degrading Treatment and Prison Pain' (2011) 13 Punishment & Society 530, 535; see also Joel Harvey, 'Crossing the Boundary: The Transition of Young Adults into Prison' in Alison Liebling and Shadd Maruna (eds), *The Effects of Imprisonment* (Willan 2013).
[87] As required by APP(DC)(CYP) (n 42), 6.

who had experienced being detained away from the intrusion of adult noise spoke of its positive effects.

When a 'Visit' Is Not a Visit

In all three forces, children were consistently visited half-hourly by custody assistants (CAs); however, the general approach to visiting surprised me. To the uninitiated, the notion of a 'visit' suggests, at the very least, an interaction in the same room as the child. I anticipated efforts to engage with young suspects, to provide reassurance and support. Undoubtedly, this does sometimes occur. Kate, for example, described 'giggling' with a CA who had told her of her own life, 'how she used to be a right little tearaway'. A number of CAs suggested that they did treat children differently to adult detainees: 'I spend more time in cells with juveniles than I do with an adult' (CA2); 'I do try to get to know them. If they're in school, what their interests are—to make the process not as scary as it seems' (CA18). However, I was disturbed to discover, on observation, that generally, a 'visit', including for a young suspect, simply involves the officer looking through a spyhole or lifting the hatch in the door to check that the detainee is breathing, accompanied by a perfunctory enquiry: 'You OK? Need a drink?' (eg F3 observation CA39). Young participants confirmed this very minimal interaction, generally recalling checks being conducted through the 'spyhole' (Aaron): 'they open the flap and close it' (Carter). Jake described the effect of such a 'visit': 'I could only see their eyes.'

Undeniably, this is, in part, driven by resourcing issues. Staff described how the pressures on them reduced their ability to adopt more sympathetic approaches: 'We don't really treat them much differently (to adults)—we don't have the time to sit with them' (CA11); 'there's absolutely no time any more to talk to anyone. Staffing levels are down and they fill us up more' (CA42). The challenges of the situation also hamper children benefiting from support when offered. Young participants often did not feel in the right state of mind to engage with staff. Harper described feeling, in the cell, that 'if somebody comes like and speaks to me now, like, I'm just gonna go mad at them'. Some young suspects took a more adversarial approach, suggesting that they would reject the offer to talk to staff in any event, ''cos they've arrested me' (Michael) or, more generally, because of their confrontational relationship with the police: 'I prefer not to, I don't really like get on wiv police' (Aidan). Several custody staff stated that they would be more likely to approach sympathetically a child who is 'upset and tearful' (CA11) or 'If they're sat in a cell—timid—then I talk to them' (CA29). As CA31 explained, for those who are behaving problematically or 'sulking ... sometimes it's better not talk to talk to them because it gets them all irate'. Whilst an understandable approach, this is not a reliable way of identifying young suspects in need of reassurance and underlines the need for better training for custody staff.

Thus, the protection of frequent visiting was routinely reduced, effectively, to a tick-box exercise—a presentational implementation of custody requirements—as has also been observed in relation to adult detainees.[88] The check can be evidenced if required at trial, and the physical safety of the child is confirmed, but their wider welfare is not addressed. Indeed, as implemented, the half-hourly visiting requirement could be counterproductive. Conducting and recording even the minimal interactions routinely observed was highly resource-intensive, whilst for some young suspects, visit rounds simply exacerbated their frustrations. Hudson explained, 'it sounds like they're coming to the door and 'cause you can hear the keys ... you think, "Yes 'I'm getting out, I'm getting out." And all they do is that little flap, just move the flap and then just go ... that is the worst thing.' For others, the noise of the hatch being opened disturbed their sleep: 'It's well annoying because it's dead loud' (Sadie).

Minimal Contact with the AA and Family Members

The child suspect's rights to have contact with sympathetic adults, particularly the entitlement to make a phone call for a reasonable period[89] and the right to speak to the AA 'at any time',[90] are capable of dramatically improving their experience in detention. Contact with someone close to a young suspect could be transformative. Michael, who is asthmatic, spoke

---

[83] C Adams, 'Suspect Data: Arresting Research' in Roy D. King and Emma Wincup (eds), *Doing Research on Crime and Justice* (OUP 2000); Layla Skinns, *Police Powers and Citizens' Rights: Discretionary Decision-Making in Police Detention* (Routledge 2019).

[89] *Code C* (n 22), para 5.6, additional to the right to have someone informed of their arrest (*Code C*, NFG 5E). This can only be delayed or denied on the written authority of an inspector (or more senior officer) (*Code C*, para 5.6, Annex B) and only where the suspect is detained in respect of an indictable (ie non-summary only) offence and where the inspector reasonably believes that such contact will have certain specified negative impacts on the investigation.

[90] ibid, para 3.18.

emotionally about talking to his mum through the cell intercom. It made him feel 'calm and relaxed' and slowed his breathing: 'It makes me imagine she's there with me.' For others, the agency which such entitlements enabled was really important. A phone call allowed Jayden to contact his familial AA to reassure himself that they were on their way. Similarly, Kate really appreciated being able to speak to her mum to break the news of her arrest and ease the worry for them both: 'My mum is not well personally. She's disabled. I said to her, "Please don't come. You don't need the stress."' In the context of the strain a custodial episode might place on a young person's relationship with their family, this could be very beneficial.

Given the lack of reference to these contact rights and entitlements on observation (see Chapter 3), I was unsurprised to hear from many young participants that they had no understanding of them: 'I thought that was just CSI [crime scene investigation] and that' (Riley). For those in the know, these entitlements were 'sometimes' granted (Dexter), especially if they were in for a long period of time: 'like two days ... so I got to speak to my Mum on the phone' (Alex). Some others were aware of the entitlement to a phone call but unclear how to exercise it: 'But they've never said how I could do it, during when I was in the cell or anything like that' (Hussain). However, a number of young participants described asking to make a phone call and being refused, including very young participants: 'sometimes they say you can't call her' (Kaiden). Will recalled challenging a CA, having read the notice, and being fobbed off: 'I said to him, "Look mate I'm allowed a call. It says in the rules I'm allowed, legally allowed to make a call mate".... And he was like, "No you're not ... you tell us who to call and then we ring 'em."' Logan recounted with frustration being told, '"Oh, we can't. We're too busy." That's always the answer.' CA38 confirmed that resourcing was certainly an issue in F3: 'If they ask they can have one [a phone call] when it's quiet. We can't do it when it's busy.'

Even where phone contacts were allowed, there were further issues around the privacy of the call itself. The phone call to which a suspect is entitled under *Code C*, 5 is not private; indeed, suspects should be told that their call may be 'listened to and given in evidence'.[91] However, the right to speak to an AA 'at any time' is a right to speak 'privately'.[92] There is a grey area where young suspects speak on the phone to family members who subsequently attend as AAs. Generally, the approach of staff was adversarial in

---

[91] ibid, para 5.7.
[92] ibid, para 3.15.

stance, to 'monitor the call' (CO38), often requiring the young person to talk to parents on speakerphone at the desk and insisting that they speak in English: 'we need to be able to hear what they're saying' (CA25). Young suspects' rights to private support from AAs are plainly not fully realized in this way, although it was not clear to me that staff were necessarily aware either of a child's right to private consultation or that their incommunicado rights are additional to intimation and AA contact requirements. Likewise, the idea of a visit from family or friends was not realistically contemplated in any block: 'generally juvenile or otherwise they don't get visits—not even at Christmas' (CO23).

As discussed in Chapter 4, AA presence in person was frequently substantially delayed and, once in the block, their contact with a young suspect was heavily controlled. COs in all areas generally rejected the option of allowing child suspects to wait for long periods in an interview room, or similar waiting area, with a familial AA,[93] and even non-familial AAs often complained about being required to wait outside the block. Suspicion of the motives of non-familial AAs was an issue, but the lack of appropriate accommodation for AA and child to wait together was also a factor, with COs sometimes understandably reluctant to allow a child to sit out with their AA in the general booking-in area to avoid further exposure to adult detainees.

Support for Girls

As with AA and family contacts, the requirement that a girl be under the care of a female officer[94] has the potential to be a powerful emotional support, particularly in the significantly male environment of the custody suite. However, the snapshot provided by this data suggests that it, too, may have become more presentational, even vestigial, in its practical implementation. Of the eight girls tracked on observation, none took up the offer to speak to a female officer, and their custody records did not indicate a specified female 'carer' being allocated, nor were there specific female welfare checks made. Similarly, of the eight girls in the young participant group,

---

[93] An issue also identified in Kate Gendle and Jessica Woodhams, 'Suspects Who Have a Learning Disability: Police Perceptions toward the Client Group and Their Knowledge about Learning Disabilities' (2005) 9 Journal of Intellectual Disabilities 70.
[94] CYPA 1933, s 31.

several did not recall being asked if they wanted to speak to a female officer. Of those who did, none had opted to speak to a female officer or recalled having one specifically allocated to them.

Several issues emerged as driving this. In the first instance, whilst, on observation, girls were almost invariably offered the assistance of a female officer, the timing and manner of the offer was crucial. The question tended to be asked later in the booking-in process at the end of the risk assessment (RA), when patience was often strained, and alongside the offer of sanitary protection. For example, YS20 was told, 'You can talk to a female member of staff—if you need a sanitary towel or anything like that just let us know, OK?' The implicit linkage between the two entitlements narrows the assumed scope of the support and renders the offer one most girls would rather pass over as quickly as possible. For example, when I asked Sadie if she had spoken to a female officer, she was quick to say that she had refused, explaining, 'It's just embarrassing, you don't wanna talk about that do you?'

Second, the familiar issue of the adversarial nature of the relationship between young people and the police is also implicated. Avery reflected on the offer, 'It don't make a difference 'cos, as far as I was concerned, they were all authority. They also do the same job. So it's them against me. So it ain't really gonna help.' Finally, there is the issue of availability. Whilst, on observation, custody teams were generally mixed gender, this was not always the case. Officers in F3 observed, 'There is not always a female [CA] on duty. You can call one up but in the middle of the night it can be difficult to get someone down' (CO23). This could be particularly problematic where a girl had to be prevented physically from self-harming: 'then you have to send a male officer in to untangle the shirt and bra' (CO23).

General Welfare Support

Before turning to adaptations for those experiencing additional adversities, and to place those observations in context, it is helpful to consider what the data suggests was the approach taken to supporting the welfare of those not considered especially vulnerable. On observation, a child suspect's need for support to cope with detention was often painfully obvious. Officers and staff in all areas acknowledged the difficulty that children had coping with the lack of stimulation and that this could trigger problematic responses: 'boredom is the issue for juveniles—creates the "behaviour"' (CO33). It was equally acknowledged, that 'happy people are quiet people' (CO27). However, although several COs were consistent in offering, even recommending, books to children, I saw little effort made more widely to provide age-appropriate distractions for young suspects. Even the available reading material tended not to be suitable for children. In each of the observation sites, there were book and magazine selections, but staff acknowledged, often without particular concern, that the range of material for children was very limited: 'There is no reading material specifically for youngsters—it's just donated or what officers leave behind' (CO27). Young participant accounts supported this picture. Whilst reading was not for everyone, a significant number of young participants said that they found reading helped to pass the time in custody or that they would like to have read a book or magazine if one had been offered. However, some, including regular attendees, said they had never been offered a book or were unaware of their availability, and others reported being told nothing was available or only being offered *Code C* or a bible.

The lack of prominence given to supporting emotional welfare and providing age-appropriate adjustments to cell conditions was striking, given that many young suspects are in custody in excess of ten hours. Risk of self-harm was the predominant reason advanced, with damage to the cell also a prominent reason for refusal. Undoubtedly, the CO's primary role is to prevent the child coming to physical harm in the cell. However, there seemed to be little appetite for tailored or dynamic assessment to balance risk and welfare considerations, with the blanket position being that the child entered the cell with no possessions or distraction items beyond the occasional book or magazine, unless issues arose or a request was made. To a degree, this is driven by time pressures on COs and staff in custody, although the blocks that I observed were not always busy. But there was also a degree of both institutional and individual indifference to the experience of children in the cell. In none of the blocks observed was there any provision of alternative materials, generally cheap and widely available, to support children deemed to be at greater risk in the cell, for example, crayons or foam balls, nor, as with the reading matter, was much concern expressed about this lack of child friendly resources. The child in custody was, in this regard, very much approached as a suspect in the first instance, and their needs as a child, facing long hours in confinement, seemed rarely to be prioritized.

Adapting for Additional Adversities

The young participants and suspects engaged in this study bore out the concerns in the APP, showing high levels of adverse life experiences and a prevalence of diagnoses of developmental disorders and mental health issues. However, despite the exhortation in APP(DC)(CYP) to 'carefully consider these when planning how to support, observe and care for children',[95] very few adjustments were made by COs in response to positive disclosures of dispositional vulnerabilities during the RA. Almost invariably, young people with additional vulnerabilities experienced the cell unadjusted, with their conditions triggering simply a different level of surveillance: regular rousing, detention in a CCTV cell, constant monitoring by CCTV, or being on 'constant observation' with an officer sitting in the open doorway of the cell. The focus of the RA is squarely on physical risk to life and limb and the consequential risk (to the force and the individual officer) of such an eventuality rather than risk to emotional well-being or, as I discuss in Chapter 6, unfitness for interview.

Beyond increased surveillance, removal of clothing, and the sparing use of a secure waiting area, I did not observe any COs suggesting particular adjustment to a young person's detention conditions as a result of the RA. Sol8, who specializes in representing young people with dispositional vulnerabilities, could only recall a single instance of a client being provided with a specific adjustment—the retention of a comfort item. On observation, no questions were asked those disclosing an ASC, for example, about any sensory issues they may have or other information which might support their care. One officer with a family member who has an ASC observed, 'I despair of how we [the police] deal with special needs' (IO2).

Considering the conditions, and average length of detention, for child suspects, this lack of adjustment is truly shocking. However, one can trace a range of factors driving it. Training for officers on mental health and related issues, although varying by area, was generally extremely limited and often conducted through NCAL packages (digital click-through programmes). In response to my queries about particular vulnerabilities, staff typically observed, 'there's not a lot we can do with our powers' (CA10). Whilst, in the circumstances, this rings rather hollow, there is some basis for their position. As identified, in all blocks observed, there was limited alternative

---

[95] APP(DC)(CYP) (n 42) 3–4.

accommodation available, and the time pressure on all officers does mean that deeper consideration, or more complex risk assessment to enable a young suspect to retain personal items, for example, is unlikely to occur.

There were HCPs available to all blocks and generally on site. Sometimes, a disclosure would trigger a CO to put a young suspect down to see the nurse, although this was not routinely the case for non-acute complaints, and there could be a very long wait to be seen. HCPs sometimes provided medication, such as Ritalin for those with ADHD, but could do so generally only after a six-hour delay following arrival to avoid dangers of overdosing. There was also the suggestion that frequent attenders were less likely to be referred, as Forensic Nurse Practitioner (FNP) 4 explained: 'There's a certain group of children who are here regularly—they are quite used to the way things are, and unless they have particular complaints we don't get to see them.' Even where Liaison and Diversion services[96] (L&D) were in place, with the expectation that all young suspects would be seen, this did not always occur: 'we try our best to get through them but it's highly pressurized in here and acutely unwell people need to come above them in the list' (L&D6).

However, there was also a range of factors limiting the effectiveness of HCPs. First, they too were restricted, to an extent, by a lack of expertise. Many were experienced in emergency medicine, but they were very rarely child and adolescent specialists, nor expert in developmental disorders or learning disability. Second, recommending adjustments to account for vulnerabilities was not considered core to their role, even for L&D specialists. HCP approaches tended to reflect the COs' focus on physical risk: 'we're primarily here to make sure they're fit and safe' (FNP6); 'it's about blame culture—we're here to prevent deaths in custody' (FNP5). L&D5 encapsulated the general approach of HCPs: 'developmental issues—autism, asperger's ... family issues—we're not equipped to deal with that in this sort of place'.

HCPs were perhaps most effective when used as a calming device by COs or to provide reassurance. However, this tended to be on a reactive basis, often in response to apparent deterioration or threatened self-harm in the cell. Sandor, for example, who had provided custody staff with a medical

---

[96] In 2014, following recommendations in Lord Keith Bradley, 'The Bradley Report, Lord Bradley's Review of People with Mental Health Problems or Learning Disabilities in the Criminal Justice System' (Department of Health 2009), the government funded, through NHS England, a scheme for forensic mental health practitioners to be available in police stations and courts in ten areas across England, rolling provision out nationally in 2017.

letter about receiving therapy for anxiety, described himself as having 'got lucky', even though he was placed initially with no additional support in an adult cell and without seeing the nurse. He explained, 'I was in there for about thirty to forty-five minutes and in that time I started talking to myself and therefore they sent the nurse in ... we were just talking and at some point I forgot that I was in a police station.' Several other young participants spoke positively about chatting to nurses, even if only for the time out of the cell that this enabled. However, again, the adversarial context could intrude, and several young suspects described distrusting and refusing to see HCPs, an issue that I noted on observation and was raised by a number of COs as well. As with cell visits, several young people simply did not want to talk to a stranger: 'I just say fuck off, don't wanna talk to you' (Luke).

Self-Harm

Of particular concern was the response in custody to threats of, or attempts to, self-harm. Several HCPs described young suspects struggling to cope with extreme distress, resulting in 'a lot of panic attacks' (FNP5) and attempts to self-harm. Resorting to self-harm in response to situations that feel intolerable has been noted in previous research with young adult offenders in custody[97] and was a phenomenon that I observed myself in respect of several young suspects, particularly those experiencing additional adversities. Officers, too, described young suspects struggling with lengthy detention: 'If they're here five to six hours they can cope—after that they start to do stupid things' (CO27).

Despite the long-standing identification of this issue, the range of options for officers to prevent self-harm was surprisingly limited. As described above, HCPs could be used for calming, but only where available and where the young person is willing to engage. Otherwise, prevention measures tended to be rather more blunt. One common approach was simply to remove any clothing or bedding which might be used for that purpose. Whilst this may be effective in neutralizing physical risk, it can be extremely traumatic, and automatic resort to this approach is not recommended.[98] Avery

---

[97] See eg Heather Inch, Paul Rowlands, and Ahmed Soliman, 'Deliberate Self-Harm in a Young Offenders' Institution' (1995) Journal of Forensic Psychiatry & Psychology 161.
[98] See obiter comments of Pitchford LJ in *D v Chief Constable of Merseyside Police* [2015] EWCA Civ 114, [44].

described what happened when she had tied her jumper around her neck in the cell:

> I wouldn't let go. Took my jumper off me and then cos I was cold I went and hid under like, underneath the blanket and underneath the mattress. They took all that away and then they said that they're gonna like strip me down, I just like be in a cell with nothing on so I can't cause myself any harm.

Often, the only perceived alternative approach is to place the suspect on constant watch, a device I saw used in respect of six young suspect detentions (YS18, 20, 24, 27 (via CCTV), 29, and 30). Apart from being extraordinarily resource-intensive, it is not necessarily effective. HCPs acknowledged that, whilst for some, constant watch might be comforting, for others, the experience itself could be 'a bit threatening—a big person there watching you' (L&D3), could 'escalate matters' (L&D4), or be 'very intrusive and difficult to handle' (L&D7).

However, most concerning is the response by staff when these measures are ineffective or where there is an acute threat of self-harm. For example, I observed YS24 having to be physically restrained by a number of officers when his behaviour, eight hours into a custody episode, deteriorated suddenly from banging on the cell door and buzzing to tying his t-shirt around his neck. When officers tried to remove the t-shirt, he became violent, shouting and struggling. A number of officers were involved and eventually managed to control him, initially face down on the floor, cuffed to the rear and with two sets of Velcro straps on his legs. The efforts of a nurse and a very sympathetic CO got him calmed and sitting up quite quickly, although his handcuffs were only removed and his t-shirt returned two hours later. This sort of episode, whilst not commonplace, is not particularly unusual. I tracked another young suspect physically restrained to prevent self-harm on two separate occasions (as YS18 and YS30) and officers described to me having physically to restrain other young suspects in like circumstances. Several young participants, all girls, also described being restrained by multiple officers to prevent self-harm. As with YS24, the numbers often engaged meant that this could be a mixed-gender group, which was also problematic, as Sadie noted: 'I don't like when it's men though—when they're grabbing me. Like women that's fine. But men I don't like it.'

Although the use of force in this way is distressing to watch, and arguably seriously dangerous, staff have little option. They are ill equipped to respond in a child-centred fashion when faced with such behaviour, and their primary concern is understandably risk of physical harm, both to themselves and to the young suspect. However, the child and their vulnerability can easily be overlooked in the response, as CO9's description reveals:

> You have to deal with the threat as opposed to the person or your perception. You deal with what you're faced with. My personal experience, you're almost dealing with a caged animal—in a secure environment that becomes their domain. When you open the door what they are going to do is governed by them—you need to be mindful of that when you go in.

Barriers to Child Friendly Detention

This review of the domestic protections makes bleak reading. The data indicate that the protections, arguably inadequate on paper, are, in practice, rarely implemented in full, and where they are in place, they are often ineffective. Children generally undergo essentially the same detention experience, in the same conditions, as adult suspects—frequently subjected to lengthy detention and in conditions which are rarely adjusted to be child friendly. Facilities for detaining children are, from their perspective, virtually indistinguishable from adult cells, and the treatment of young detainees by the majority of custody staff is minimally adjusted to take account of their youth and any additional vulnerabilities they may have, if adjusted at all. Although there are more positive accounts, most young participants described very limited efforts to provide distraction or support for them during the waiting process. The research data suggests that police custody is, as a result, far from being a child friendly experience.

In significant respects, the evidence confirms the scattered insights into the child's experiences in police custody that emerge from previous and more recent research.[99] However, the number and breadth of young participant accounts in this study, and the other contextual material, has enabled a much richer picture of their experiences to be constructed and allows insights into why these issues have persisted. Superficially, the most easily identifiable issue is the constraints imposed by a lack of

---

[99] Kemp and others, *Examining the Impact of PACE* (n 11).

police resources, not only with regard to physical facilities and equipment but also in terms of time, manpower, and training. The impact of structural factors is also felt, particularly in failures of third-party provision in the community, including the inadequacy of residential care provision for 'looked-after' children and the underfunding of Child and Adolescent Mental Health Services in the community. Resourcing issues are, to varying degrees, relatively easily remediable. Indeed, at the time of writing, there are scattered initiatives across different forces to train officers with regard to the impact of adversity and trauma[100] and to ensure that there is more provision to support children whilst in the cell, with distraction boxes (containing foam balls, wobble cushions, and the like) and murals in JDRs.[101] However, addressing the issues with third-party agencies which impact on police custody is more challenging. Despite the efforts of the Custody Concordat initiative,[102] it is still the case that very few children remanded after charge are being transferred out of the custody block,[103] largely as a result of underfunding of secure accommodation by central government.[104] However, there are initiatives in some areas to work more closely with third parties to improve the support for child suspects and to reduce detention periods.[105]

Yet, the research also enables identification of those less obvious features of the custody process which drive the failings in child friendly provision. The data reveals a complex of situational and police cultural issues which present a more intractable barrier to the improvement of detention experiences for children. Most prominent amongst these are the following four factors.

---

[100] For example, the work of Barnardo's with West Midlands Police, West Midlands Violence Reduction Partnership, 'Trauma Informed' <https://westmidlands-vrp.org/about/trauma-informed> accessed 18 August 2023.

[101] For example, the work of Inspector Gary Mckenzie of Police Scotland in adapting a custody block in Glasgow to be child friendly.

[102] See n 51.

[103] Itua (n 53).

[104] See for discussion *R (on the application of AR (A Child)) v Waltham Forest LBC* [2021] EWCA Civ 1185, [2021] PTSR 1777.

[105] For example, the Northamptonshire Police TICTAC initiative <https://www.northants.police.uk/news/northants/news/news/2022/april/northamptonshire-police-introduce-trauma-informed-custody-for-detained-children/> accessed 18 August 2023.

Pedagogical and Social Disciplinary Approaches

Despite being unconvicted, often, young suspects were approached by those responsible for their care as offenders first, 'here for a reason' (CA3, CA42), rather than children first. Equally, often, where sympathy was expressed for young suspects or difficulties in their lives acknowledged, this tended to focus on poor parenting or discipline at home: children who have been 'pulled up', not 'brought up' (CA10), 'degenerate' families (CA16) with parents who 'don't give a damn', or where the mother and grandmother are 'on the game' (CA13). They were, in this way, identified as products of those parts of society that have been described as 'police property'.[106] These observations often fed into corresponding statements about the benefit of an episode in custody in response to a lack of discipline at home, that it might 'do the trick' (CA10) in terms of preventing offending. CO34 articulated the thinking: 'I like to think some good can come—I think sometimes it's in their best interests—they might not have enjoyed it but it can set them on the right path.' A similar 'pedagogical' approach has also been observed in street policing of children and young people.[107]

Sometimes, more explicitly, social disciplinary motivations, emphasizing the deterrent and incapacitative benefits of a night in the cells, were revealed.[108] As CA21 observed, 'This is probably not the best place to be but I think it is good to have this here to show them what is done when you've done something wrong.' This attitude also drew on the view of some COs that the courts were too lenient, undermining the work of the police and the youth justice system more generally: 'Stick them in a cell—time passes slowly ... They see it as a punishment—more than what happens at youth court.' As CO12 commented, 'The only real penalty is a period in a cell—it's like the naughty step.' CO43 displayed similar thinking:

> I agree it should be a last resort, but I think [detaining in the custody suite] is a power we need and should have ... They get lots of chances before prosecution—even before a referral. There's a real contrast with

---

[106] John Lee, 'Some Structural Aspects of Police Deviance in Relations with Minority Groups' in Clifford Shearing (ed), *Organizational Police Deviance* (Butterworth 1981) 53–54; Benjamin Bowling, Robert Reiner, and James Sheptycki, *The Politics of the Police* (5th edn, OUP 2019) 174–75.
[107] Ian Loader, *Youth, Policing and Democracy* (Macmillan 1996).
[108] Choongh (n 1); also Roger Evans, 'The Conduct of Police Interviews with Juveniles', Royal Commission on Criminal Justice, Research Study No 8 (HMSO 1993).

the rest of the youth justice system—I don't mind remotely being the big bad wolf in it all.

This attitude was not limited to police officers and staff. ICV3, for example, commented that young people were there to 'learn a lesson' and, as such, 'It isn't a hotel and we don't want to give young, old or vulnerable the wrong impression—the wrong reason as to why they're there in the first place.'

These adversarial approaches, particularly the interest in deterrence, inevitably undermine a welfare approach, producing an embedded sense of 'less eligibility'—that for detention to have a deterrent effect, the treatment of the individual must not be superior to the minimum standard outside,[109] reducing the implementation of the protections. There was a sense that efforts to adjust the process would undermine its vital effect, even that the process at present is too 'warm and fluffy' (CO12) or that young suspects are 'mollycoddled' (CA23). Some custody staff suggested, with regret, that police custody is no longer a 'fearful place' (CO24) and that young suspects viewed it as a 'kind of day out' (CA23). Such attitudes tend to undermine the more child friendly approaches of others. Several of the more humane custody staff made reference to being accused of, or feeling as if they were, too 'soft' (CA 40) with detainees ('If they're awake I'll speak to them and ask them if they want a drink. People will say "What are you doing talking to them?"' (CA41)), whilst sympathetic approaches by particular officers, or during particular episodes, could easily be undone by isolated harsh experiences:

> It depends on the police officers that you have 'cause like there was one time ... when I went in there was one really nice police officer that helped me and was like, 'Do you want a blanket? Do you want something to eat?' There was just one that gave me attitude all the time, 'You're not having a blanket. You don't deserve it. You're a criminal', this and that, and I'm like, 'Alright.' But it was *really* scary to think how long I'm going to be in here.
>
> (Kate) (italic emphasizes stress in the original speech)

---

[109] Georg Rusche, *Punishment and Social Structure* (Columbia University Press 1939)

An Extraordinary Imbalance of Power

The unique power dynamic of the custody block is also implicated. The suspect in the cell is wholly reliant on custody staff for their every need, including to know what time it is,[110] to have a drink of water, and, in some blocks, to get toilet paper. Every adjustment provided, virtually every right exercised whilst in the cell, is dependent upon the good will of the custody staff. This places the burden on busy custody staff to tend to what may be repeated requests, often made, or followed up, using the buzzer, the call button situated in all cells. Where the suspect is a child, the power dynamic between young detainee and adult captor is even more extreme, and the demands they make may be greater, given their natural immaturity, particularly their unfamiliarity with the system, their uncertainty, and difficulty coping with detention. Additionally, clinical research also suggests that prevalent dispositional vulnerabilities, such as ADHD, may prompt more frequent buzzer usage.[111]

On observation, some staff were very patient in answering calls, acknowledging the challenges for young suspects: 'they want to know what's happening now. They don't feel in control—don't quite understand what's happening' (CO38). But, as Skinns has also noted, the buzzer could be a particular source of resentment and friction,[112] and it was easy for even a relatively compliant child suspect to behave in a way considered unacceptable to some custody staff. Some CAs, particularly those of a social disciplinary cast of mind, appeared to resent being required to tend to young suspects' non-essential needs, considering requests for reading material, additional food, or exercise presumptuous. For example, when YS11 requested a magazine on being taken a drink, the CA responded, 'He'll be putting in his milk order next!'. Some took particular exception to repeat attenders who were persistent in asserting their rights. CA32, for example, spoke of regular detainees who would 'demand phone calls. They're always being arrested—but they insist on it', drawing a contrast between this 'very, very demanding' behaviour and 'model prisoners', who made no such requests.[113]

---

[110] Watches are routinely removed.
[111] Susan J Young and others, 'The Effectiveness of Police Custody Assessments in Identifying Suspects with Intellectual Disabilities and Attention Deficit Hyperactivity Aisorder' (2013) 11 BioMed Centre Medicine 248
[112] Skinns, *Police Custody* (n 19).
[113] Similar distinctions have been noted by Choongh (n 1) 83.

This problematic power dynamic had two particular effects on the implementation of protections and the enabling of child suspect rights. First, one obvious means of reducing demand is not to advertise too widely those rights and supports that the child can request. As noted in Chapter 2, staff rarely spelt out rights and entitlements beyond the 'continuing rights', and so young participants often had only a partial appreciation of the services and protections to which they were entitled. Few young participants had been in an exercise yard[114] or had a shower,[115] and many, including some with significant and sometimes prolonged experience in custody, had no idea that such facilities were available. For example, Luke, who had been in custody a number of times, was confident: 'No, no, there's no showers in the police station.' As an independent custody visitor (ICV) explained with regard to juvenile detainees, 'You say to them, "Do you know, if you want to have a walk around an exercise yard there is one? If you want to stretch your legs." And invariably they haven't been told that', whilst questions about showers often evinced 'blank looks' (ICV2). Similarly, in relation to items to occupy children within the cell, several staff made reference, in discussions with me, to the availability of a pen and paper (to which every suspect is entitled under *Code C*, 5.6), which could be used for drawing. However, this was not routinely offered; rather, it was available 'if they know the process' (CO38). However, incommunicado rights were never given verbally on booking in, and only one young participant (Elijah) was aware of this entitlement.

Second, some staff took a highly selective approach where rights requests were made. On fieldwork, sometimes young suspects' buzzers would be left to ring and ring unanswered, turned down or switched off for a limited period if buzzing was considered to be 'repeated or abusive' (CA1).[116] On observation, staff were often very busy, but not invariably so. Indeed, a number of officers made plain that a refusal to afford a young suspect a requested entitlement did not always arise as a result of practicability issues. Some staff took the approach that entitlements, particularly phone calls, and exercise or shower facilities, were a measure for those who were 'not coping well' (CA8, CA24) or for children experiencing a particularly long detention period, such as over a weekend (as Alex related above), rather than as an entitlement to be considered, and acceded to where practicable,

---

[114] This should be offered daily if practicable: *Code C* (n 22), para 8.7.
[115] ibid, para 8.4 stipulates: 'Access to toilet and washing facilities must be provided.'
[116] See for similar, Skinns, *Police Custody* (n 19).

in respect of any child suspect. Some other officers took a more manipulative approach, using access to comforts and entitlements as a form of management tool, rewarding good behaviour by granting requests and refusing entitlements where behaviour was considered unacceptable.

> Like a parent I work with a reward system. You've done as you're told, as I asked you to, then you can have X. Now when they come in, they treat me decent and don't cause issues, they're fine. If you let people get away with murder you make a rod for your own back.
>
> (CO41)

Such variable approaches to the enabling of rights triggered in many young participants a sense of being neglected whilst in the cell, that their needs did not consistently entitle them to reasonable assistance. As Malik complained, 'They don't offer you nothing in there man. What they tell you lot and what they do to us is two different things.' As a result, many young participants felt that their treatment during detention was unnecessarily unpleasant and disrespectful: 'It's just like they don't care, they're not bothered' (Logan). The switching off, or turning down, of the buzzer, in particular tended to exacerbate difficulties coping ('imagine if I'm ill or have a heart attack or something … you turn a bit panicky' (Rezar)) and was experienced as particularly punitive.

Resignation and Resistance: A Vicious Cycle

Young participants commonly described one of two responses to this neglect of, or inconsistent response to, their rights and entitlement requests. Both such reactions tend to further undermine the implementation of protections. For some, this treatment resulted in a pervasive sense of disempowerment and utter helplessness, with profound implications for young suspects' understanding and engagement of their rights. Unsurprisingly, many young participants in this study, as in Choongh's, displayed 'extreme scepticism about the utility of rights',[117] having learnt that rights are only patchily, or even conditionally, honoured: 'so there's no point in ringing the

---

[117] Choongh (n 1) 177.

bell, they're just gonna waste your time' (Hussain).[118] Equally, a number of young participants took the view that there was no point in complaining about harsh or inconsistent treatment: 'you can't do nowt about it' (Cole). In particular, a formal complaint was considered to be pointless since the police would always believe officers over suspects,[119] echoing young people's experiences within the wider youth justice system.[120] For the many young participants who were familiar with having to be resilient in the face of adversity in their lives outside, this loss of autonomy, their total reliance on the officers and staff, could be frustrating and was a source of pain in and of itself: 'you feel like you can't say nothing to do anything. You feel annoyed and angry, but at the same time, you feel like you've got nothing to say' (Rezar).

A smaller group of children responded by taking any opportunity to wrest back some sense of control. There was little scope for 'backstage forms of resistance',[121] given the near panoptical supervision of detainees, especially in the more modern blocks. As in early childhood, one of the few ways in which young suspects could exercise control is in relation to food consumption.[122] Prison literature, too, identifies food and eating as a site of resistance and identity work.[123] Although the scope for identity work in police custody is limited, ordering food and then refusing to eat was relatively common on observation and in young participant accounts. Some young participants described more openly defiant responses, particularly in the form of throwing food around the cell: 'that'll give 'em something to tidy up' (Luke). Other behaviours of this sort described by young participants included shouting or banging repeatedly on the cell door and flooding the cell.

For some young participants, defiant or disruptive behaviour was simply a desperate attempt to get the attention of unresponsive custody staff. Abigail explained, 'when I'm pressing the bell and they're not answering

---

[118] Also observed in clinical research: Thomas Grisso, *Juveniles' Waiver of Rights: Legal and Psychological Competence* (Plenum Press 1981).

[119] Also observed in Deena Haydon, Siobhán McAlister, and Phil Scraton, 'Young People, Conflict and Regulation' (2012) 51 Howard Journal of Criminal Justice 503; Lyon, Dennison, and Wilson (n 1).

[120] Hazel, Hagell, and Brazier (n 1); APPGC (n 9);. Harvey, *Young Men in Prison* (n 34).

[121] Ben Crewe, *The Prisoner Society: Power, Adaptation, and Social Life in an English Prison* (OUP 2009).

[122] For a discussion of food and control: Carole Marie Counihan and Steven L Kaplan, *Food and Gender: Identity and Power* (Harwood Academic Publishers 1998).

[123] Thomas Ugelvik, 'The Hidden Food: Mealtime Resistance and Identity Work in a Norwegian Prison' (2011) 13 Punishment & Society 47; Crewe (n 121).

I just boot the door'. More commonly, it was a way of processing strong emotions, particularly anger, frustration or anxiety: 'They wouldn't get hold of my mum, they were saying apparently that they'd rung her and they tried everything they can, but they weren't doing anything. So I started kicking off, that's only because they weren't helping me, innit' (Cole). Harper described destructive behaviour as a necessary coping mechanism: 'Unless I like emotionally drain myself—when I feel so angry I just drain myself. That's the only time I can sleep.' Problematic and destructive behaviours were particularly common amongst much younger participants and those who were managing additional adversities, such as adverse childhood experiences or neuro-developmental disorders. Kaiden, one of the youngest participants, explained, 'I don't like behaving because there's no fun in that.' His account of his motivation for messing up his cell reveals the sharply adversarial nature of these interactions: 'Well one of the police officer made me angry, so one police officer has to clean it up. So one for one ... So basically it was like a game, he had 1-nil, I had 1-nil.'

These more problematic responses trigger a sort of vicious cycle. Defiant or destructive behaviour only served to exacerbate the harshness of the custody experience and consolidate punitive or disciplinary attitudes on the part of staff. Efforts to prevent self-harm often involved restraint and the removal of clothing, whilst disruptive behaviour could be exhausting, sometimes triggering a spiral of yet harsher treatment and more entrenched resentment. As CO21 observed, 'the problem is they [young suspects] are rude to the staff here and so they can be overlooked—their vulnerability'. Sometimes, staff would resort to threatening a problematic child suspect. Sometimes, the threat was to delay their release: 'some of them will be like "You're just gonna be staying in for longer if you don't calm down"' (Nathan). Such a threat may be effective, but young suspects tended to conclude that their period in detention was therefore deliberately manipulated for punitive purposes by the custody staff. A number of suspects suggested that staff deliberately 'long it out' (Jamal) to punish them. The other threat particularly complained of by young participants was that of a criminal damage charge. Undeniably, there are occasions where young suspects cause considerable damage to their cell. However, in some situations, the use of this threat seemed heavy-handed and emblematic of the failure by staff to take a welfare approach to young suspects. For example, YS17, a seventeen-year-old boy in residential care with markers for self harm, had been in custody for approximately twenty hours when the custody record records that he was spotted 'scratching the wall' in his cell. The staff response was not to address his need for distraction but to warn him for criminal damage. The custody record shows that, moments later, he was discovered to have been sharpening a plastic spoon, which he had pressed in half to make the shape of a knife.

This spiral is also self-perpetuating in the sense that more punitive responses are undoubtedly enabled by staff becoming inured to the plight of the people in their cells. Seeing detainees in a state of extreme distress is not uncommon in the custody suite. CO23 commented to me, 'I think all cops get some sort of PTSD [post-traumatic stress disorder]—I don't think they really realize. If I talk to someone in a pub I know that I have an entirely different outlook... Sometimes I wonder why I have no empathy.' I observed this for myself. My fieldnotes for F2 have the following entry:

> 8.10 pm—A man screaming at the top of his voice—several times—really raw and disturbing to listen to. No one seems to notice. A sergeant comments to no one in particular, 'I hope if I start screaming like that someone will take notice of me.' No action was taken.

Low Visibility of Detention Conditions

The low visibility of the custody block, and thus the lack of repercussions for those who overstep the mark, whether suspect or staff, also has an effect on the treatment of detainees. The low visibility of police work generally is well documented in the literature,[124] but oversight of conditions in the custody block is particularly limited, as discussed in Chapter 1. This is especially so for child suspects, whose treatment is less likely than that of adults to be scrutinized by a court as a result of the (otherwise) welcome focus on diversion of young suspects out of the criminal justice system. Even where they are prosecuted, judges and lawyers operating within the adversarial system are focused on the circumstances of the allegation, not on the conditions of detention, save in those few cases where these may found an argument to exclude the evidence from the interview at trial.[125] CCTV footage of the custody suite will rarely be examined and can prove extremely difficult to

---

[124] See eg Joseph Goldstein, 'Police Discretion Not to Invoke the Criminal Process: Low-Visibility Decisions in the Administration of Justice' (1960) 69 Yale Law Journal 543.
[125] Lesley McAra, 'Models of Youth Justice' in David J Smith (ed), *A New Response to Youth Crime* (Willian 2010).

access.[126] In addition, young suspects are unlikely themselves to make a formal complaint and rarely will they have the financial support to pursue a civil claim.

As we have seen, the CO's role as guardian of child's welfare and rights is fundamentally challenged by their own institutional and adversarial motivations. Their decision-making is dominated by the very substantial risk burden they bear, tending to result in indications of vulnerability, especially with regard to self-harm, being approached as physical risks to be neutralized rather than welfare needs to be addressed. Supporting adults rarely observe first hand the conditions of detention. Lawyers do not typically see the child in the cell, and the capacity of familial AAs to challenge detention conditions is very limited. For example, no information about the requirement for alternative accommodation is contained in the notice provided at booking in, and familial AAs rarely see the space in which their child is detained. Of those participating, only FAA7 had seen the accommodation in which her child (then a thirteen-year-old) was detained. She was appalled ('They put him in a proper adult man's cell—I seen it myself as I was passing by. I've seen them taking [him] out of it and I thought it was totally, completely unbelievable') but unable effectively to challenge his treatment. The efficacy of independent oversight is also questionable. Recent research into ICVs concluded that they were 'likely to be ineffective' and 'made no impact on how the police ran custody'.[127] My own discussions with ICVs tend to support that view. ICV participants were generally aware of the limited non-cell accommodation, for example, but did not express distinct concern, identifying resource and operational constraints on officers as justifications. Although one did note that 'some of the ICVs think that the cells are too harsh for younger people' (ICV3).

Nor is scrutiny by HMIC/His Majesty's Inspectorate of Constabulary, Fire and Rescue Services (HMICFRS) particularly effective with regard to detention conditions. Inspections routinely appear to condone the use of JDRs that are internally identical to adult cells. For example, in the three forces observed, the inspection reports immediately preceding or post-dating my observations contain no recommendations relating to the provision of roomier or more sympathetic 'juvenile' accommodation. As noted

---

[126] See eg the two years it took Dr Koshka Duff to obtain CCTV footage of her police detention, recounted on BBC, Woman's Hour (26 January 2022) <www.bbc.co.uk/sounds/play/m0013rb0> accessed 18 August 2023.
[127] John Kendall, *Regulating Police Detention, Voices behind Closed Doors* (Policy Press 2018) 118.

in their own thematic inspection, their work is also hampered by limited custody data collection in many force areas.[128] Although, at the time of writing, matters are improving,[129] there was, during fieldwork, very little collection of data about the use of force or constant watch, for example, and some apparent resistance to it. In F3, for example, CO25 exclaimed, 'If I submitted a form for every time we hustled someone back to their cell or every time someone takes their t-shirt off!' as if this would be an impossible task.

This low visibility is plainly of serious concern. Not only does it enable the widespread failures in implementation observed, but also more abusive treatment may be going unchecked. Several young participants reported staff being verbally or physically abusive to them. At its most serious, Avery complained of an officer who had hit her head repeatedly against a cell wall, causing a cut across her forehead. Such accounts are deeply shocking. However, low visibility works in other ways as well. Several young people told me that they felt they could, in effect, behave as they liked in custody because there was no comeback. Staff, as well, were aware of, and resented, this lack of oversight. CO33 commented 'they don't see at court what they [child suspects] were like—they never get to know'.

Examining these four factors reveals the depth of the challenge for making police custody child friendly and reducing the punitive nature of the process. Mutually reinforcing and self-perpetuating, these four factors, unless addressed, threaten to undermine any efforts to reform the detention experience and, arguably, explain the lack of progress in reducing the punitive impact of police custody. At the heart of the punitive nature of the custody process is the fundamental unsuitability of the police custody setting for children as currently implemented. The combination of the extreme adversity experienced by the child—both situational and emotional—and the adversarial attitudes of those in whose total and unchecked control they find themselves is, quite simply, inimical to a child friendly detention experience. Whilst this problematic state of affairs was acknowledged by some COs, HCPs in particular were vocal about the unsuitability of the custody environment:

> In my view children shouldn't be in custody. I don't think it's the right place for them ... There should be a dedicated room not in custody but

[128] HMIC (n 20).
[129] See for discussion Chapter 1 (n 130–31).

in the police station, where social services come down. Bringing a child in and putting them in a cell is not healthy. I wouldn't like to see my kids brought in here.

(L&D5)

Exclusionary Effects

But what are the impacts of such punitive detention experiences? The observation that criminal procedure can be experienced as punishment in and of itself is not new. Indeed, the findings in this research strongly echo those of Malcolm Feeley in his late 1970s study of the processing of cases in a lower criminal court in the United States. He noted that where the burdens of the pre-trial experience outweigh the anticipated consequences of the criminal sanction, 'the process itself becomes the punishment'.[130] Importantly, he also observed that such an imbalance had concerning implications for the individual's access to justice and, ultimately, the fairness of the criminal process as a whole. In Chapter 6, I consider the implications of punitive detention experiences for children's engagement in the immediate criminal process but address here the wider impact of these punitive processes on children's ongoing attitudes towards the police and youth justice system.

The arrest and detention of a child is a critical moment for the criminal justice system's relationship with them and for the child's legal socialization. In discussing legal socialization, I draw on Tyler and Fagan's definition of it as the 'developmental process by which individuals internalize the norms of the law through their direct and vicarious interactions with law and legal actors'.[131] As with adults, research in the United States and the United Kingdom has shown that when adolescents experience their interactions with police, and other legal authorities as procedurally fair, this reinforces their views of the legitimacy of the law and shapes their law-related

---

[130] Malcolm M Feeley, *The Process Is the Punishment: Handling Cases in a Lower Criminal court* (1st pbk edn, Russell Sage Foundation 1979) 201.
[131] Tom R Tyler, Jeffrey Fagan, and Amanda Geller, 'Street Stops and Police Legitimacy: Teachable Moments in Young Urban Men's Legal Socialization: Street Stops and Police Legitimacy' (2014) 11 Journal of Empirical Legal Studies 751 757; Jeffrey Fagan and Tom R Tyler, 'Legal Socialization of Children and Adolescents' (2005) 18 Social Justice Research 217.

behaviour positively, contributing to future compliance and desistance.[132] Judgements about the fairness of treatment by legal agents have been consistently identified as being more influential in shaping evaluations of legal authority than judgements about the fairness or favourableness of the specific criminal justice outcome.[133] By contrast, treatment by legal actors that is experienced as unjust, unfair, and disproportionately punitive has been found to result in legal cynicism and can perpetuate criminal activity.[134] As Tyler and colleagues have observed, 'legitimacy matters', and 'legitimacy deficits are real in their consequences for public safety'.[135] Legitimacy thus accumulates, but can also be eroded, through complex social interactions with legal actors, not only those directly experienced by the child but also those experienced vicariously through friends, family, and others in the community.[136]

Procedural Injustice Undermining Perceptions of Police Legitimacy

The majority of research on these issues with children and young people has focused on police activity in the community, stop and search, and its equivalent in the United States. Whilst this study provides only a snapshot of young people's views, young participants' reflections on their experiences in police custody suggest that, in broad terms, previous research findings on legal socialization and procedural justice also hold true for longer and more complex interactions in the police custody context. Young participants very rarely expressed negative attitudes towards the police and legal authorities arising from the outcomes of a detention episode—whether they were charged, prosecuted, or received a particular level of sanction. Likewise, those few who reported generally respectful treatment were more

---

[132] Ben Bradford, 'Policing and Social Identity: Procedural Justice, Inclusion and Cooperation between Police and Public' (2014) 24 Policing & Society 22; Jeffrey Fagan and Alex R Piquero, 'Rational Choice and Developmental Influences on Recidivism among Adolescent Felony Offenders' (2007) 4 Journal of Empirical Legal Studies 715.
[133] Tom R Tyler and Yuen J Huo, *Trust in the Law: Encouraging Public Cooperation with the Police and Courts* (Russell Sage Foundation 2002).
[134] See eg Robert J Sampson and Dawn J Bartusch, 'Legal Cynicism and (Subcultural?) Tolerance of Deviance: The Neighborhood Context of Racial Differences' (1998) 32 Law & Society Review 777.
[135] Tyler, Fagan, and Geller (n 131) 775.
[136] Rod K Brunson and Ronald Weitzer, 'Police Relations with Black and White Youths in Different Urban Neighborhoods' (2009) 44 Urban Affairs Review 858.

likely to hold positive views about the police and legal authorities. However, those who related what they considered to be unfair treatment in police detention often described holding extremely negative views of the police as a result: 'due to my experiences (in police custody) I can tell ya, I don't like the police' (Luke). In particular, episodes of unjustified detention or gratuitously harsh treatment were notable in accounts of negative ongoing attitudes to the police and reduced perceptions of their legitimacy. Alex, for example, described how, 'When I go there for no reason, that's what really makes me look at them a different way and it just brings on hatred.' Tom, reflecting on almost twenty hours in custody, concluded, 'I just don't have a really good opinion, like a good view on them [the police] anymore.' The APPGC received similar accounts from young people of experiences with the police which were 'both negative and long-lasting, cementing hostile and distrustful views of the police for years to come'.[137]

Perhaps unsurprisingly, given the power asymmetry in custody and the child's total reliance on COs and staff, unfair interpersonal treatment that was experienced as an abuse of power or a manipulation was particularly identifiable as reducing the moral authority of the police in the eyes of young participants. A number of young people were angered by what they perceived to be the police exploiting their symbolic authority: 'they just piss me off because they think they can throw their weight around because they've got a police badge on' (Robert). In line with procedural justice research, young participant experiences underline how interactions which displayed a lack of care or benevolent motive could be particularly damaging to perceptions of police legitimacy. Will described how he had come to think of the police as 'piggy scum' following difficult experiences in custody, explaining, 'they're meant to be there to help, do you know what I mean, not to make things worse for you'. Young participants complained that, far from acting in a neutral and consistent way, the police discriminated against them, that officers saw them not as people but, as Luke explained, 'They think "criminal, criminal". That's what they think.' Young participants felt that they experienced differential treatment for a range of different reasons, including being 'a young person' (Kate), having family members with a criminal history (Abigail), and being Black, Asian, or

---

[137] APPGC (n 9) 9. See also Carlie Goldsmith, ' "It Just Feels Like It's Always Us": Young People, Safety and Community' (DPhil thesis, University of Brighton 2011); Steve Rogowski, 'Young Offenders: Their Experience of Offending and the Youth Justice System' (2000) 70 Youth and Policy 52.

minority ethnic (Jo). Those who had been arrested on more than one occasion felt particularly discriminated against:

> We get treated like we're just a criminal, if you know what I mean. As soon as you've gone through the police doors, the police cells, and you've got a record, you get classed as something you're not, innit?
>
> (Aaron)

Such discriminatory treatment understandably triggered anger and resentment and fostered a lack of trust in the police and authorities. This accords with similar observations by Young Advocates for Youth Justice:

> Policing was the area young people felt stereotyping is seen the most. They felt that stereotyping by police has created a lack of trust which has spread throughout the whole system, resulting in an unwillingness of young people to listen at school or elsewhere. Frightening and frustrating police interactions can also cause fear and anger from children and young people that has short- and long-term impacts.[138]

Indeed, some young participants made clear that discriminatory behaviour undermined the moral authority of the police and the criminal justice process to such a degree that they considered the system to be 'stupid' (Cole), 'corrupt' (Harper), or 'a joke' (Elijah). As Will explained, 'I just think to myself they're idiots, just pure idiots mate ... I just use them as a laughing stock—that's what they are.'

Negative views of the police following custodial encounters were disproportionately expressed by those who were regularly detained. This may be a function of the 'spiralling effect' noted by Tyler, in which pre-existing views as to the legitimacy, or lack of legitimacy, of a legal authority (here, the police) taint (or enhance) subsequent individual contacts such that 'it is progressively more or less likely that authorities will be able to gain deference through the use of fair procedures'.[139] As Zoe explained, 'I always hated the

---

[138] Millie Hall, 'Young Advocates for Youth Justice: A Youth-Led Report from Children and Young People with Experience of the System' (Alliance for Youth Justice/Leaders Unlocked 2022) 17 <www.ayj.org.uk/news-content/young-advocates-report-publication> accessed 18 August 2023.

[139] Tom R Tyler, 'Procedural Justice, Legitimacy, and the Effective Rule of Law' (2003) 30 Crime & Justice 283.

police, but ever since then [being in police custody] I'll never ever like a police officer. Like never.' However, in contrast to research in the United States into anticipatory injustice, the expectation of unfair or discriminatory treatment in the legal system,[140] Black, Asian, and minority ethnic young people, whilst present in this group, were not over-represented, although, notably, the very small group of those who expressed positive views about the police subsequent to a custodial experience was disproportionately comprised of White young people who had had only one experience in police custody.

Impact on Compliance and Cooperation

As observed in the legal socialization literature, the research findings suggest that the reduction in police legitimacy triggered by the custody process could have an effect on both compliance with the law and cooperation with legal authorities. In contrast to the belief of some officers that a harsh custody experience might 'set them on the right path' (CO34), such unnecessarily punitive experiences, and the concomitant reduction in police legitimacy, could have the opposite effect:

> by putting you in a room, making you sit by yourself, it's not going to make you accept, reflect on the thing you've done. It's going to make you think like, 'You lot treat me like shit.' I might as well do worse things in there. I don't know, it makes you entirely a bit different ... Basically, if I get treated like this, what's the point? The police officer don't see criminals as equals to them, they see 'em as people that are just ... I don't know, they're less anyway so.
>
> (Carter)

Carter's reactions recall Lawrence Sherman's defiance theory.[141] Alienated from the police, experiencing detention as an unfair, stigmatizing response to him as an individual, rather than to the behaviour for which he was arrested, Carter rejects, by his defiance, the shame he has been made to feel.

---

[140] Jennifer L Woolard, Samantha Harvell, and Sandra Graham, 'Anticipatory Injustice among Adolescents: Age and Racial/Ethnic Differences in Perceived Unfairness of the Justice System' (2008) 26 Behavioral Sciences & Law 207.
[141] Lawrence W Sherman, 'Defiance, Deterrence, and Irrelevance: A Theory of the Criminal Sanction' (1993) 30 Journal of Research in Crime and Delinquency 445.

Sherman's formulation also provides insights into the ramifications of such treatment. According to defiance theory, the alienated individual is then predisposed to repeat the offending behaviour since he has symbolically labelled the sanction (detention) and the sanctioner (the police) as deserving of punishment, not the original behaviour which led to the arrest. Some other young participants described attitudes to the police following detention that would be likely to exacerbate future encounters and potentially lead to further arrests. For example, Avery explained, 'I hated the police beforehand like I'd never really speak to 'em, but then [following police detention] like my anger just grew on and like I didn't really care, like wouldn't listen to 'em. Every time I see 'em I used to run away.'

Impact on Reporting Crime and Seeking Help

Of concern, in addition to this hostility, were the observations of several young participants that, as a result of their experiences in the custody block, they would not trust the police or go to them for assistance in future. Tom explained his reservations:

> it's the sort of thing where if I needed them I wouldn't even bother... I just wouldn't wanna call 'em, just because I don't think they're that nice people. Since I was in there for so long and they were useless when I was in there, I just don't really think they're that trustworthy.

Sadie expressed a different sort of reluctance, stemming from the feeling of being labelled as a criminal. Although generally still well disposed to the police for their work in dealing with the 'horrible people out there', she said that she would not feel comfortable going to them or confident that they would help her because, as she put it, 'I'm a criminal as well.' Given the high levels of victimization amongst young people who find themselves in conflict with the law,[142] this position is extremely concerning. This is particularly so because research has identified links between procedural injustice, reductions in police legitimacy, and increased approval of—even

---

[142] Frederick P Rivara and others, 'Victim as Offender in Youth Violence' (1995) 26 Annals of Emergency Medicine 609; David J Smith and Russell Ecob, 'An Investigation into Causal Links between Victimization and Offending in Adolescents' (2007) 58 British Journal of Sociology 633.

reliance on—self-help behaviours, particularly amongst Black, Asian, and ethnic minority young people living in high-crime neighbourhoods.[143] In a US context, Gau and Brunson found that these behaviours (eg navigating their home areas in groups of peers or family) could result in further police scrutiny from officers who struggled to distinguish such self-help responses from gang activity,[144] whilst research in the United Kingdom has identified reduced confidence in the police as a driver of street gang affiliation and youth violence[145] and as being associated with increased approval of private violence and vigilantism.[146]

Vicarious Effects

There was also evidence within this study of the vicarious impact of policing interactions perceived as unfair and illegitimate on peers and other members of the community.[147] The hostility to the police generated by a custody encounter was not restricted to the individual child suspect involved but fed into, and perpetuated, pre-existing youth and community hostility towards the police. As noted in Chapter 2, young participants finding themselves in custody for the first time commonly arrived with negative understandings of police treatment in custody received from peers and family members who had prior experience. For example, Sandor described how his peers' previous negative experiences of the police, both in custody and on the street, had given him the understanding that 'police officers just enjoy power over youth and like to take out their problems on them'. A considerable number of young participants related an antipathy towards the police which pre-dated their custody experiences ('I just don't

---

[143] Jacinta M Gau and Rod K Brunson, 'Procedural Injustice, Lost Legitimacy, and Self-Help: Young Males 19 Adaptations to Perceived Unfairness in Urban Policing Tactics' (2015) 31 Journal of Contemporary Criminal Justice 132.
[144] ibid 145.
[145] Louis Gladstone Annan and others, 'What Makes Young People Get Involved with Street Gangs in London? A Study of the Perceived Risk Factors' (2021) 50(5) Journal of Community Psychology 2198; Keir Irwin-Rogers, Abhinay Muthoo, and Luke Billingham, 'Youth Violence Commission: Final Report' (London Youth 16 July 2020) <https://londonyouth.org/youth-violence-commission-final-report> accessed 18 August 2023.
[146] Nicole E Haas, Jan W de Keijser, and Gerben JN Bruinsma, 'Public Support for Vigilantism, Confidence in Police and Police Responsiveness' (2014) 24 Policing & Society 224; Jonathan Jackson and others, 'Monopolizing Force? Police Legitimacy and Public Attitudes toward the Acceptability of Violence' (2013) 19 Psychology, Public Policy, and Law 479.
[147] Brunson and Weitzer (n 136).

like the police full stop, or any of them' (Nathan)) and which was simply reinforced by their experiences in custody. Nathan's more generalized sense of alienation recalls research in the United States context which suggests that punitive experiences with the police can negatively shape the formation of young people's wider 'civic identity'[148] as part of a 'hidden curriculum' of 'anticitizenry' education by the state through which young people are

> bombarded with messages that they are not citizens belonging to the group of the whole in charge of governing, but are a class of problem people to be excluded, monitored, and surveilled, treated harshly and punished arbitrarily.[149]

Particularly striking was the capacity of custody processes perceived as procedurally unjust to alienate not only the young suspects themselves but also, crucially, family members, on whom the criminal justice system relies to support desistance. FAA/1 described how she and her partner had experienced disrespectful and aggressive treatment when acting as AAs for their children. Her attitude to the police as a result was stark: 'I hate 'em, I hate 'em.' There was some evidence that pre-existing positive attitudes towards the police might protect against a reduction in perceptions of police legitimacy amongst this group. FAA5, whose experience in custody had been, on her own account, 'not too bad', had retained her trust in the police, explaining, 'I've always liked the police anyway—at the end of the day they do a good job.' However, FAA2, who had been distressed and intimidated by the harsh treatment she and her son experienced in custody, was clear about the effect for her:

> I really have no faith, and that's the one thing I've always had faith in, the police. Yeah, respect for them doing their job and all that, but obviously the way they treated a child that had never even spoken to a police officer, and me, I just think they're worse than some criminals really.

---

[148] Vesla M Weaver and Amy E Lerman, 'Political Consequences of the Carceral State' (2010) 104 American Political Science Review 817, 819.

[149] Benjamin Justice and Tracey L Meares, 'How the Criminal Justice System Educates Citizens' (2014) 651 Annals of American Academy Political & Social Science 159, 167. See also Maria José Bernuz Beneitez and Els Dumortier, 'Why Children Obey the Law: Rethinking Juvenile Justice and Children's Rights in Europe through Procedural Justice' (2018) 18 Youth Justice 34.

Conclusion

In concluding this chapter, I return to the evaluative framework outlined in Chapter 1 and ask whether police custody for children could be said to conform with Campbell and others' 'minimum burdens' thesis. This thesis is predicated on the principles that, in accordance with the individual's right to liberty, there should be 'no punitive action before conviction' and that suspects should be treated with dignity and respect as rational, rights-bearing subjects.[150] It is bolstered, in the case of children, by the UNCRC requirements that their particular needs should be met by adjusted conditions which promote their 'sense of dignity and worth' and that detention should be a measure of 'last resort' and for the 'shortest appropriate period'.[151] The data reviewed in this chapter suggests that the reality of police custody for children is commonly the antithesis of these aspirations—that it is, rather, a deeply punitive experience and one which can have a lasting impact. Far from feeling that they were accorded dignity and respect, their accounts reverberate with the sense of being treated in a degrading and inhumane fashion, that their rights were neglected or even deliberately frustrated. Confined in what were widely considered to be 'horrible' conditions, child suspects struggled to cope with oppressive isolation and lack of stimulation during protracted periods in largely unadjusted adult cells. Lapsing into resignation or defiantly resisting this unnecessarily harsh treatment, they routinely failed to engage their full rights and entitlements. As a result, many, like Evan, whose observations opened the chapter, experienced police custody as a form of punishment. Far from setting children on the 'right path' (CO34), we see how damaging and excluding such experiences can be, not only for the young suspects themselves but also for their families and wider community.

The fundamental challenge of criminal procedure is to strike a balance between the individual's right to liberty and the needs of the investigation and the protection of the public. Here, the question of proportionality comes into play. As Ashworth has argued, 'The greater the burdens and deprivations imposed at the pre-trial stage, the stronger the justifications needed to uphold them.'[152] Even where the suspect is a child, there will

---

[150] Liz Campbell, Andrew Ashworth, and Mike Redmayne, *The Criminal Process* (5th edn, OUP 2019) 23.
[151] UNCRC (n 3), Arts 37(c) and 40(1).
[152] Ashworth (n 2) 31.

sometimes be necessary encroachments on their liberty. The offence(s) they are alleged to have committed may be so serious, the obtaining of forensic evidence so urgent, or the threat posed to the investigation were the child to be at liberty so great as to demand immediate detention. However, such circumstances are—and were, in this study—rare. Indeed, the question of proportionality seemed rarely to be considered. Of the forty-seven child suspects tracked on observation, only five were obviously arrests which required police detention, and all of those young suspects were sixteen or seventeen years of age. Two suspects (YS32 and 33) were arrested out of their home area in relation to possession with intent to supply of a Class A drug, and three suspects (YS45–47) were arrested in relation to a violent disorder in the street which had involved an alleged stabbing. However, the vast majority of the young suspects that I tracked on observation had been arrested for extremely low-level offences. Minor dishonesty allegations, low-level assaults (where no or minimal injury was caused), minor public order offences, and low-value criminal damage allegations predominated. For example, ten of the forty-seven young suspects that I tracked had been arrested for simple theft (often shoplift) or taking a vehicle without consent. Young participants described a similar spread of allegations, a very small minority recounting arrests for serious matters which might realistically require urgent detention, but the vast majority were detained for what appeared to be very minor offending. It could rarely be said that the pain and distress experienced by young participants was a proportionate response to the threat they posed to the public or to the needs of the investigation, given the nature of their alleged offending.

Indeed, quite apart from imposing the 'minimum burdens' on child suspects, in many cases, the custody process only served to magnify their burdens and the disadvantage and adversity that they experience in their wider lives. As identified in Chapter 2, those children finding themselves in police custody tend to have experienced multiple and intersecting disadvantage. Such adversities expose them to criminality, exploitation, and arrest. Once in police custody, it is those adversities which tend to trigger longer detention periods and more problematic responses to those deprivations, which themselves set in motion a vicious cycle of ever harsher treatment and more problematic behaviour in retaliation. The idea of subjecting these children to the trauma of detention in a cell as a safeguarding option, as was often the case, is revealed to be, frankly, perverse.

These punitive experiences of child suspects highlight strikingly the importance of child friendly protections and their full and effective implementation for those few children who must be detained for investigation. In almost every instance, the features which trigger particularly painful experiences (eg the length of the detention episode and the use of the adult cell without adjustment) are features which should have been substantially mitigated by a comprehensive and properly implemented framework of protections. The analysis makes plain that the legal framework which aims to render police custody 'child friendly' is wholly inadequate. The protections which should be in place are rarely implemented in full, and when they are, they prove ineffective in addressing the child's difficulties. The analysis has identified a range of factors, including resourcing, risk management, and third-party engagement, which challenge better implementation. But at the heart of this problem lies the intractable collision of adversity with the adversarial approach of officers and staff behind the closed doors of the custody block. Until this Gordian knot is, in some way, cut, punitive experiences will inevitably persist.

This chapter has explored the impact of such punitive experiences on young participants' general attitudes towards the police and their estimations of police legitimacy. Alienated and angered by treatment they considered to be unjust, young participants described a reduction in their trust in the police and in their willingness to cooperate with them or to rely on them for help. In Chapter 6, the final empirical chapter, I consider the more immediate and specific impact of unduly harsh and protracted detention experiences on the child's ability to engage with the key moment in the custody process, the investigative interview.

6
Police Interview

A Counterproductive Process?

> I was just completely out of it and just didn't want anything to make it longer. I just wanted to get through everything as quickly and as smoothly as possible and just leave.
>
> (Sandor)

Introduction

This final empirical chapter considers police interview, the culmination of the custody process and, generally, the primary purpose of the child's many hours in the cell. 'Obtaining evidence by questioning' is frequently the principal ground for the authorisation of detention.[1] The stated aim of investigative interview is to obtain an 'accurate and reliable' account from the suspect, approaching them 'fairly' and without 'prejudice'.[2] This is essential since the evidence generated in interview is often of 'fundamental importance for the development and the outcome of the case';[3] indeed, frequently, it is determinative of it.[4] However, research into the investigation and interrogation of adult suspects has long observed a police emphasis, rather, on obtaining a confession.[5] Indeed, McConville and colleagues identified

---

[1] Police and Criminal Evidence Act 1984 (PACE), s 37(3).
[2] College of Policing, Authorised Professional Practice (Investigation)(Investigative Interviewing) (APP(I)(II)) (first published 23 October 2013, last modified 26 October 2022) 3–4 <https://www.college.police.uk/app/investigation/investigative-interviewing/investigative-interviewing> accessed 18 August 2023 (Principles 1 & 2). (Any variance between the current APP versions and versions in force at the time of the fieldwork will be noted as it arises.)
[3] Edward Cape, Jacqueline Hodgson, and Taru Spronken, *Suspects in Europe* (Intersentia 2007) 19.
[4] Frank P Belloni, *Criminal Injustice: An Evaluation of the Criminal Justice Process in Britain* (Macmillan 2000).
[5] Barry Irving and Linden Hilgendorf, 'Police Interrogation: A Case Study of Current Practice', Royal Commission on Criminal Procedure Research Study 2 (HMSO 1980); Michael

Introduction 259

this as the primary investigative strategy of the police.[6] This is understandable in an adversarial system where the easiest way to achieve victory is to avoid the contest by securing the 'surrender' of the other party, by way of confession, and ultimately by guilty plea.[7] Whilst there is reason to believe that the introduction of the PEACE (Preparation and planning; Engage and explain; Account, clarification, challenge; Closure; Evaluation) model of interviewing[8] has reduced the use of more oppressive interviewing techniques,[9] there continue to be indications that the police act as 'agents of the prosecution' in interview rather than playing an 'inquisitorial, fact-finding' role.[10]

Miscarriage of justice cases—particularly the *Confait* case[11] and, in the United States, the *Central Park Jogger* case[12]—reveal how dangerous coercive or confession-seeking tactics can be when the suspect is a child. There are three particular factors which might be said to increase the risk of unfairness for child suspects in interview in England and Wales. First, psychological research has demonstrated (and, indeed, the Police and Criminal Evidence Act 1984 (PACE) *Code C* acknowledges)[13] that young suspects are especially vulnerable to providing unreliable answers in interview. In particular, young suspects are more susceptible to interrogative pressure because of a range of factors, including that they may recall fewer details of their experiences, be confused by unfamiliar and complex questions, and are typically more suggestible.[14] They are thus disproportionately more

McConville, Andrew Sanders, and Robert Leng, *The Case for the Prosecution* (Routledge 1991); Belloni (n 4).

[6] McConville, Sanders, and Leng (n 5).
[7] Belloni (n 4).
[8] Ray Bull, 'Police Investigative Interviewing' in Amina Memon and Ray Bull (eds), Handbook of the Psychology of Interviewing (Wiley 1999); Colin Clarke and Rebecca Milne, 'National Evaluation of the PEACE Investigative Interviewing Course' (Home Office 2001).
[9] Stavroula Soukara and others, 'What Really Happens in Police Interviews of Suspects? Tactics and Confessions' (2009) 15 Psychology, Crime & Law 493.
[10] Hannah Quirk, *The Rise and Fall of the Right of Silence* (Routledge 2017) 53.
[11] Sir Henry Fisher, 'Report of an Inquiry by the Hon. Sir Henry Fisher into the Circumstances Leading to the Trial of Three Persons on Charges Arising Out of the Death of Maxwell Confait and the Fire at 27 Doggett Road, London SE6' (HMSO 1977).
[12] Barry C Feld, 'Police Interrogation of Juveniles: An Empirical Study of Policy and Practice' (2006) 97 Journal of Criminal Law & Criminology 219.
[13] *Code C: Revised Code of Practice for the Detention, Treatment and Questioning of Persons by Police Officers* (updated 4 November 2020) (In force at time of writing), 'Notes for Guidance' (NFG), 11C. (Any relevant variance with the version in force at time of fieldwork, published May 2014, will be noted as it arises.)
[14] See for discussion Michael Lamb and others, 'Developmental Factors Affecting Children in Legal Contexts' (2013) 13 Youth Justice 131.

likely to confess, and to confess falsely,[15] and, as discussed in Chapter 1, are more likely to engage in compromised decision-making.[16] Second, where the suspect is a child, there is an emphasis on using out-of-court disposals, particularly cautions and conditional cautions, where that is appropriate.[17] Such disposals dramatically reduce the workload of the investigating officer and are widely favoured, including by solicitors[18] and parents, since they avoid prosecution. However, they most commonly require the young suspect to have made admissions to an offence,[19] potentially prioritizing that outcome in the interview.[20]

This is compounded by a third feature, which is that the only legal protection against undue interrogative pressure (namely, the exclusion of evidence from the interview at trial)[21] is much less likely to be available to children than to adults. As Evans observes, the prevalence of out-of-court disposals means that the majority of children are 'dealt with without recourse to the courts … Since pre-court decisions by the police take place behind closed doors there is little or no opportunity to ascertain how the interview has been conducted or to test the reliability of any confession.'[22] Of almost 53,000 child arrests in the year to March 2022, only 17,200 children were proceeded with at court.[23] Even for those who are prosecuted,

---

[15] Gisli H Gudjonsson and others, 'Custodial Interrogation, False Confession and Individual Differences: A National Study among Icelandic Youth' (2006) 41 Personality & Individual Differences 49; Allison D Redlich and others, 'The Police Interrogation of Children and Adolescents' in G Daniel Lassiter (ed), *Interrogations, Confessions and Entrapment* (Kluwer Academic 2004); Saul Kassin and others, 'Police-Induced Confessions: Risk Factors and Recommendations' (2010) 34 Law & Human Behavior 3.

[16] Alexandra O Cohen and others, 'When Is an Adolescent an Adult? Assessing Cognitive Control in Emotional and Nonemotional Contexts' (2016) 27 Psychological Science 549.

[17] Crime and Disorder Act 1998, ss 66ZA(1)(b) and 66B(3). See Ministry of Justice/Youth Justice Board (MoJ/YJB), 'Youth Cautions: Guidance for Police and Youth Offending Teams' (2013) <www.gov.uk/government/publications/youth-cautions-guidance-for-police-and-youth-offending-teams> accessed 18 August 2023>; Crown Prosecution Service, 'Conditional Cautions: Youths—DPP Guidance' (updated 5 November 2019) <https://www.cps.gov.uk/legal-guidance/conditional-cautioning-youths-dpp-guidance> accessed 18 August 2023.

[18] Simon Holdaway, *Inside the British Police: A Force at Work* (Blackwell 1983).

[19] There has been a welcome rise in point-of-arrest diversion or triage schemes, some of which do not require admissions. However, provision is patchy, and such schemes are not a statutory duty of youth offending teams (YOTs): Carmen Robin-D'Cruz and Eleo Tibbs, *Mapping Youth Diversion in England and Wales* (Centre for Justice Innovation 2019).

[20] Barry Goldson, 'Wither Diversion? Interventionism and the New Youth Justice' in Barry Goldson (ed), *The New Youth Justice* (Russell House Publishing 2000).

[21] PACE, ss 76–78.

[22] Roger Evans, 'Police Interrogations and the Royal Commission on Criminal Justice' (1994) 4 Policing & Society 73 74.

[23] YJB/MoJ, *Youth Justice Statistics 2022–23, England and Wales* (National Statistics 2023) <https://www.gov.uk/government/statistics/youth-justice-statistics-2021-to-2022> accessed 26 January 2023.

the availability of a referral order for a first guilty plea,[24] with its advantageous disposal arrangements, means that significantly fewer cases proceed to trial in the youth court. Even where there is a trial, the courts place heavy reliance on records of taped interview,[25] which are often incomplete[26] and unlikely to reveal undue pressure being imposed.

These three features, in combination, place the child suspect at a substantial disadvantage in interview in comparison to adult suspects. Arguably, they should prompt a greater watchfulness of the process for young suspects, more significant expertise engaged to avoid unfair outcomes, and greater scrutiny of the process. The evidence contained within this chapter reveals that this is not, in fact, what occurs and underlines why these failures should be so critically concerning. The empirical sections of this chapter open with a consideration of how the child's fitness to be interviewed is assessed and the measures that are available to support their effective participation. I then turn to young participants' experiences of questioning and the efficacy of the primary protections provided for them: the presence of the solicitor (where requested) and the appropriate adult (AA). In closing, I consider, applying the evaluative framework set out in Chapter 1,[27] whether police interview procedures, as implemented, are fair and protective of the child's rights and whether, in turn, they foster the production of reliable evidence capable of founding accurate determinations in the later criminal justice process. Sadly, as Sandor's recollection in the epigraph reveals, the toll of the process severely challenges the child's ability to give a good account of themselves in interview, threatening the effective fulfilment of those twin aims of the process.

---

[24] Powers of Criminal Courts (Sentencing) Act 2000, ss 16–28.
[25] Fiona Brookman and Harriet Pierpoint, 'Access to Legal Advice for Young Suspects and Remand Prisoners' (2003) 42 Howard Journal of Criminal Justice 452; John Baldwin, 'Preparing Records of Taped Interview' and 'The Role of Legal Representatives at the Police Station' and 'Supervision of Police Investigation in Serious Criminal Cases', Royal Commission on Criminal Justice Research Study Nos 2–4 (HMSO 1992); Michael Zander and Paul Henderson, 'Crown Court Study', Royal Commission on Criminal Justice Research Study No 19 (HMSO 1993).
[26] John Baldwin, 'Summarising Tape Recordings of Police Interviews' (1991) Criminal Law Review 671.
[27] Andrew Ashworth, *The Criminal Process: An Evaluative Study* (1st edn, OUP 1994); Liz Campbell, Andrew Ashworth, and Mike Redmayne, *The Criminal Process* (5th edn, OUP 2019).

Fitness to Be Interviewed: Procedure and Existing Literature

Ensuring that the child suspect is fit to be interviewed (FI) and able to participate effectively in the process is critical. This is not just in consideration of their young age and the prevalence of conditions likely to give rise to participation difficulties but also because of the protracted and exhausting periods in the cell many will have experienced, as related in Chapter 5. Psychological research has identified a particular risk of false confession by those who have been deprived of sleep and detained in isolation.[28] A fair and rights-focused system might be expected to include a clear statement of what would amount to unfitness for interview and appropriate arrangements for assessing fitness, including expert input where required. Where any risks to the reliability of the interview are identified, such a system ought to have effective mechanisms to address those risks and to support the child's well-being and ability to participate effectively in questioning. A consideration of the current procedure suggests that it may fall short in protecting young suspects.

A Clear Statement of Fitness to Be Interviewed?

In the first instance, the definition of FI is somewhat confused and disjointed. The FI assessment is set out in PACE, *Code C*, paragraph 12.3 as 'determining and considering the risks to the detainee's physical and mental state if the interview took place and determining what safeguards are needed to allow the interview to take place'. Where the custody officer (CO) considers that 'significant harm' would be caused to the suspect's physical or mental state, interview should not be allowed.[29] The same limitation of FI to risk to the well-being of the suspect should the interview proceed is reflected in the College of Policing's 'Authorised Professional Practice' (APP).[30]

---

[28] Mark Blagrove, 'Effects of Length of Sleep Deprivation on Interrogative Suggestibility' (1996) 2 Journal of Experimental Psychology: Applied 48; Yvonne Harrison and James A Horne, 'The Impact of Sleep Deprivation on Decision Making: A Review' (2000) 6 Journal of Experimental Psychology: Applied 236.
[29] *Code C* (n 13), para 12.3.
[30] APP (Detention and Custody)(Response, Arrest and Detention) (first published 23 October 2013, updated 28 October 2022) 16 <https://www.college.police.uk/app/detention-and-custody/response-arrest-and-detention> accessed 18 August 2023.

Consideration of whether the individual can give reliable evidence is confined to Annex G of *Code C*. Annex G, paragraph 2 considerably expands the concept of FI, identifying that a detainee may be 'at risk in interview' not only where 'significant harm to their physical or mental state' could result but also where anything they may say in interview about the allegation 'might be considered unreliable in subsequent court proceedings because of their physical or mental state'. Paragraph 3 requires the assessment of FI to consider how the detainee's physical or mental state may affect their ability to 'understand the nature and purpose of the interview, comprehend what is being asked and appreciate the significance of any answers given and make rational decisions about whether they want to say anything', as well as whether their replies may be 'affected by their physical or mental condition (rather than representing a rational and accurate explanation of their involvement in the offence)'.[31] This formulation of the assessment captures much of the language of effective participation, as set out in *Panovits v Cyprus*.[32] Introduced in 2003, it addresses, to a considerable degree, earlier concerns raised by commentators about the narrow conceptualization of the legal test.[33] However, although it is signposted in *Code C*, paragraph 12.3 and technically part of the *Codes*,[34] it is not only contained within a separate section of the *Codes* but also framed as providing only 'general guidance to help' with assessment.[35]

Appropriate Arrangements for Conducting the Assessment?

In addition, several concerns arise in relation to the conducting of the assessment. First, the assessment is a matter for the CO, who is only required to consult with health-care professionals (HCPs) if he or she deems that 'necessary'.[36] However, assessing a suspect's reliability, and particularly

---

[31] *Code C* (n 13), Annex G, paras 2–3.
[32] *Panovits v Cyprus* App no 4268/04, 11 March 2009, (2008) 27 BHRC 464, [67].
[33] See eg Guy A Norfolk, "Fitness to Be Interviewed'—A Proposed Definition and Scheme of Examination' (1997) 37 Medicine, Science & Law 228; Gisli Gudjonsson, 'Fitness for Interview during Police Detention: A Conceptual Framework for Forensic Assessment' (1995) Journal of Forensic Psychology 185; Gisli H Gudjonsson, Gwilym D Hayes, and Paul Rowlands, 'Fitness to Be Interviewed and Psychological Vulnerability: The Views of Doctors, Lawyers and Police Officers' (2000) 11 Journal of Forensic Psychology 74.
[34] See *Code C* (n 13), para 1.3.
[35] ibid, Annex G, para 1.
[36] ibid, para 12.3.

their ability to make 'rational decisions', will require careful consideration of factors such as their suggestibility, compliance, and acquiescence, those features that have been particularly associated with false confessions.[37] Research has identified that it may be challenging, even for specialist clinicians in a health-care setting, to identify conditions which may give rise to unfitness,[38] let alone a police officer in the pressurized and fast-moving circumstances of police custody. Nor is there any guidance for COs on when to seek expert input.

Second, whilst there is practical commentary,[39] there is no formal clinical guidance as to how HCPs should approach a FI assessment, nor are there any tailored instruments for the purpose. This may be because of the substantial range of conditions and circumstances which might give rise to unfitness for interview.[40] Annex G simply indicates that the 'functional ability' of the suspect should be considered rather than placing reliance on a medical diagnosis[41] and that an identification and quantification of any risks of interview should be provided to the CO.[42] However, HCPs operating in custody suites are drawn from a wide range of medical backgrounds and may not have skills appropriate to the assessment required. Indeed, research has raised concerns about the quality of clinical forensic medical training and the consistency with which minimum standards set by the General Medical Council are met.[43] Third, there is no guidance in *Code C* on when the assessment should be conducted and how likely fluctuations in the child's FI as a result of their detention might be accommodated, save that assessment

---

[37] Gisli H Gudjonsson, *The Psychology of Interrogations and Confessions: A Handbook* (Wiley 2003).

[38] Gisli H Gudjonsson, 'Confession Evidence, Psychological Vulnerability and Expert Testimony' (1993) 3 Community & Applied Social Psychology 117; Allison Edwards and others, 'Fitness to Be Interviewed: Decision-Making in the Mental Health In-Patient Setting' (2021) 27 British Journal of Psychological Advances 115. For difficulties in an Australian context, see Bobbie Clugston and others, 'Interviewing Persons with Mental Illness Charged with Murder or Attempted Murder: A Retrospective Review of Police Interviews' (2019) 26 Psychiatry, Psychology, & Law 904.

[39] See eg Margaret M Stark and Keith J B Rix, 'Fitness to Be Interviewed and Fitness to Be charged' in Margaret M Stark (ed), *Clinical Forensic Medicine: A Physician's Guide* (Springer Nature 2020).

[40] See (and for a discussion of the case law) Michael A Ventress, Keith JB Rix, and John H Kent, 'Keeping PACE: Fitness to Be Interviewed by the Police' (2008) 14 Advances in Psychiatric Treatment 369.

[41] *Code C* (n 13), Annex G, para 4.

[42] ibid, Annex G, para 6.

[43] Margaret M. Stark and Guy A. Norfolk, 'Training in Clinical Forensic Medicine in the UK—Perceptions of Current Regulatory Standards' (2011) 18 Journal of Forensic & Legal Medicine 264.

should occur before interview.[44] Despite the complexity of the test, and the challenges of identification, there has been no previous significant empirical consideration of how the question of FI in respect of young suspects is approached by COs and assessed by HCPs.

Effective Mechanisms to Address Identified Risks?

Reviewing the existing literature, there is good reason to consider that the available safeguards to address risks in interview, where identified, may also be inadequate or function to mask unmet needs. The primary safeguard for an adult identified as being at risk in interview (and, indeed, generally for an adult deemed to be 'vulnerable')[45] is the provision of an AA.[46] However, as Bath has noted, the automatic requirement of an AA for a child suspect may mean that COs do not 'have a prompt which requires them to consider whether a child has any additional needs that make them particularly vulnerable'.[47] In any event, the ability of a lay AA, without clinical skills or specialist communication training, to insulate a young suspect experiencing mental health issues, mood disorder, or neurodivergence from giving unreliable answers or making a false confession has not been the focus of substantive clinical research and may be overestimated by police officers.[48] Whilst Annex G, paragraph 8 allows for additional safeguards to be adopted, such as having an HCP present to monitor the impact of the interview on the suspect's condition, there is no framework to facilitate the use of more specialist support, such as an intermediary.[49] Nor does *Code C* provide any guidance as to the procedure to be followed where unfitness for interview is identified and is considered irremediable, even with the provision of the available safeguards.

---

[44] *Code C* (n 13), para 12.3.
[45] ibid, 1.13(d).
[46] ibid, Annex G, para 5.
[47] All Party Parliamentary Group for Children (APPGC), '"It's All about Trust": Building Good Relationships between Children and the Police. Report of the Inquiry Held by the All Party Parliamentary Group for Children, 2013–2014' (National Children's Bureau 2014) 38.
[48] ibid.
[49] An intermediary is a communication specialist, often a qualified speech and language therapist or a psychologist, specially trained to facilitate communication within a criminal justice setting.

Fitness to Be Interviewed: Child Suspect Experiences

Young participant accounts raise significant concerns about the effectiveness of FI assessments and the range of measures used to address the risk of unreliability in interview. Every young participant had undergone interview during a detention episode, and none, as far as could be identified, had ever been assessed as unfit for interview. Nor had any experienced substantive support in interview beyond the presence of their AA and a solicitor, where requested. Significantly, none had been interviewed in the presence of an HCP or an intermediary. Yet, whilst a significant proportion were very capable communicators, just over one-quarter volunteered, in discussion, a learning disability or a diagnosed mental health condition (such as post-traumatic stress disorder) or a developmental disorder (such as attention deficit hyperactivity disorder (ADHD)), and it is likely that a good number more had similar issues to which they did not refer.

Feeling Up to It: 'I was just completely out of it'

Even where they did not reveal an identifiable condition, young participant accounts raise real concerns about their ability to 'make rational decisions' about how to respond (Annex G, 3(a)) and to give a 'rational and accurate' account of their involvement in an offence (Annex G, 3(b)) as a result of their lengthy detention experiences. As noted in Chapter 5, ten or more hours of isolation in the cell, refusal of food, and disturbance to sleep were commonly complained of by young participants. Aidan described feeling, as a result, 'like a walking zombie' in interview:

> Like now I'm speaking good aren't I? I know what I'm saying, but say if I've had no water or no food, I don't know what to say, like you can't think, you can't function properly, you know what I mean? And that's when you do slip up 'cause you don't know what to say to 'em, know what I mean like?

FAA3 provided a vivid example of how this might affect the accuracy of a child's responses. Her son, in providing his alibi in interview, had, she explained, got his 'times all mixed up' and she had intervened to allow him time to think. The officer had challenged her son, who had responded, ' "Well I'm just tired at the minute, hang on a minute while I get my bearings"' (FAA3). He had gone on to correct his mistake, and eventually no further action was taken against him. Yemi similarly described, in interview, that he had 'lost it' because he 'hadn't eaten anything that day'. Reflecting on long delays and their detrimental effect, Hussain wondered whether lengthy periods in the cell were used by the police 'for psychological purpose, to mess you up' so that 'when you go into the interview room you'll feel a bit different'.

The dangerous effects of detention on reliability have been observed in psychological research. Kassin and colleagues found that prolonged isolation can increase distress levels and act as an incentive for a suspect to remove themselves from the situation by acquiescing to demands in interview.[50] Additionally, sleep deprivation can reduce the ability to maintain attention, think flexibly, and can increase suggestibility in the face of leading questions[51]—a technique commonly complained of by young participants. Such difficulties tended to compound other challenges for child suspects in interview. As discussed in Chapter 3, young participants often struggled to understand more complex legal issues, such as the right of silence or joint enterprise and the significance of the interview, but did not feel up to engaging with the issues—'I'd just try and think about something else' (Jayden).

Several solicitors raised similar concerns about lengthy detention impairing fitness for interview (Sol6), particularly where the police wanted to interview very late at night (Sol4) or where the detention had been particularly problematic.[52] Such issues are not always raised with the CO. Young suspects may not be represented, or their solicitor, or AA, may be unaware of their physical and emotional state. Worryingly, those who described such ill effects tended not to draw attention to their compromised state before the interview for fear of delaying their release. Sandor explained his failure to raise his state: 'I was just completely out of it and just didn't want anything to make it longer. I just wanted to get through everything as quickly and as smoothly as possible and just leave.' Alternatively, some young participants felt that it was better to make no comment in such a

---

[50] Kassin and others (n 15). See also Saul M Kassin and Gisli H Gudjonsson, 'The Psychology of Confessions: A Review of the Literature and Issues' (2004) 5 Psychological Science in the Public Interest 33.
[51] Harrison and Horne (n 28); Blagrove (n 28).
[52] See for similar concerns raised by professionals Vicky Kemp and Jacqueline Hodgson, 'Chapter 4. England and Wales Empirical Findings' in Miet Vanderhallen and others (eds), *Interrogating Young Suspects: Procedural Safeguards from an Empirical Perspective*, Vol 2 (Intersentia 2016).

situation, sometimes against advice, preferring to waive their right to participate rather than undergo interview when exhausted or delay their release. Both approaches should be a cause for concern.

CO and HCP Approaches: 'They have an AA already'

How, then, is the FI assessment undertaken by COs? By contrast to the difficulties described by young participants, although there was some variation, the overriding view of COs was that young suspects are rarely unfit for interview. Some COs primarily associated unfitness with intoxication, others with acute mental ill health, and both groups identified that, since young suspects rarely presented with such conditions, unfitness was rarely an issue. Most strikingly, as Bath had raised, a number of both COs and HCPs across the fieldwork sites suggested that FI is not addressed as an issue for young suspects because, as one psychiatric nurse typically observed, 'they have an AA already' (L&D7). Automatic presence of the AA for a young suspect is considered, in effect, to satisfy any concerns without further assessment being required: 'fitness for interview is not frequently an issue for juveniles. They have an AA in place—I might get a CPN [community psychiatric nurse] to review first but that is a rarity' (CO20).

HCPs confirmed that they were infrequently engaged in fitness assessments for children. To a degree, this results from time pressures. Several HCPs identified the emphasis on swift release for children as a reason why they were not asked to assess: 'We tend not to see them (children) for fitness to detain or fitness for interview. The intent is to get them in and out ASAP' (FNP6). The emphasis on reducing delay for child suspects, whilst otherwise desirable, may have the unintended effect of reducing assessment for child suspects still further than for vulnerable adults. Given the lack of health-care resource, it is easy to see how this comes about. In F3 (FNP6's area), for example, where, at the time of observations, no Liaison and Diversion services (L&D) were in place, there were very considerable delays accessing HCP assessment: 'You can wait eight to nine hours to see the nurse' (Ins2). Understandably, as CO41 related, 'it's not often I send a juvenile to the nurse'.

Across the fieldwork sites, COs and HCPs recognized the high frequency with which young suspects presented with developmental and behavioural disorders (in line with prevalence research).[53] ADHD and autism spectrum

---

[53] See eg Nathan Hughes, *Nobody Made the Connection: The Prevalence of Neurodisability in Young People Who Offend* (Office of the Children's Commissioner 2012).

condition (ASC) in particular were commonly raised by young suspects during risk assessment on fieldwork. Such conditions can have a significant impact on the young suspect's ability to provide reliable answers in interview, according to the factors set out in Annex G,[54] but were rarely identified by COs as an issue in respect of FI. Indeed, with the exception of cases of intoxication and acute mental disturbance, issues of comprehension and reliability were not often raised by COs, and, notably, no CO volunteered a reference to Annex G at all when asked about their approach to FI. Generally, the threshold for unfitness to be interviewed appeared to be set at a very high level.

This is unsurprising. HM Inspectorate of Constabulary (HMIC) identified that COs appeared to be overlooked or not always able to access child specialist training,[55] despite the lack of awareness training for COs in respect of mental health conditions, learning disability, and developmental disorders having been repeatedly identified as problematic.[56] COs during fieldwork tended to confirm this deficit, commonly stating that they had had no specific training on communicating with young people or on health issues relating to young people. CO7 typically observed, 'I have had no youth specific training as a custody sergeant. [You] use your life experience, experience of your own children and everything.' CO31, who had undergone CO training six months previously, described, 'half a day input on mental health issues, alcohol withdrawal and mental health—we don't get much insight on ADHD, autism etc. you pick it up as you go along.' Some COs and IOs alluded to ad hoc, often online, training on particular mental health issues: 'I believe there is NCAL[57] training on autism.' But several acknowledged that this was not a satisfactory approach: 'We have an over-reliance on this—on-screen training—a few clicks. We click boxes and read

---

[54] For discussion see Susan J Young and others, 'The Identification and Management of ADHD Offenders within the Criminal Justice System: A Consensus Statement from the UK Adult ADHD Network and Criminal Justice Agencies' (2011) 11 BioMed Centre Psychiatry 32; National Autistic Society, 'Autism: A Guide for Police Officers and Staff' (2020) <www.autism.org.uk/shop/products/books-and-resources/autism-a-guide-for-police-officers-and-staff> accessed 18 August 2023.

[55] HMIC, *The Welfare of Vulnerable People in Police Custody* (HMIC 2015) (now His Majesty's Inspectorate of Constabulary, Fire and Rescue Services, HMICFRS).

[56] Criminal Justice Joint Inspection (CJJI), 'Who's Looking Out for the Children? A Joint Inspection of Appropriate Adult Provision and Children in Detention after Charge (CJJI 2011); Jessica Jacobson, 'No One Knows: Police Responses to Suspects Learning Disabilities and Learning Difficulties, A Review of Policy and Practice' (Prison Reform Trust 2008) <https://prisonreformtrust.org.uk/publication/no-one-knows-police-responses-to-suspects-with-learning-disabilities-and-learning-difficulties> accessed 18 August 2023.

[57] Digital 'click-through' training packages.

a case study and then the force says we've been trained' (IO2). As CO26 observed, 'Online training packages are informative. But ... you feel if it were important, they'd train me how to do that.'

Timing: Risk Assessment or Later?

The evidence of young participants above suggests that the timing of the assessment of FI could be of critical importance. In F3, COs stated that they considered FI as part of the risk assessment (RA) when the child arrived in custody. Although a CO would typically see a young suspect several times again prior to interview, concentrating this decision on arrival meant that any deterioration during detention would not necessarily be considered as part of the substantive FI assessment and may not be identified before questioning. By contrast, in F2, in addition to the general RA on booking in, each suspect underwent an FI 'assessment' immediately before being taken into interview. The custody record was stamped with a checklist which was completed in the presence of the detainee and their solicitor, if they had one. The checklist required the CO to ask the suspect whether their AA/solicitor/interpreter was present (according to their identified requirements) to confirm that they had had sufficient rest and felt fit to be interviewed and that there were no medical issues preventing interview. However, on observation, this process was often completed in a perfunctory, administrative manner, unlikely to identify, or encourage disclosure of, difficulties arising from prolonged detention. As intimated by young participants above, given the desire of everyone involved at that stage to proceed with the interview, in anticipation of release soon after, there was little prospect that a young suspect, or even those in support (as observed re YS28 in Chapter 4) would pursue an issue at that stage.

Expert Assessment? 'I always try to avoid fitness for interview'

Referral to an HCP for expert assessment, as *Code C*, paragraph 12.3 proposes, may not, even when it occurs, ensure that unfitness is adequately identified in a young suspect. First, no clinician spoken to during fieldwork had specific child or adolescent training, although some, especially those who had worked as nurses in accident and emergency departments, had completed paediatric modules in their core training. Some were quite conscious of this lack of expertise: 'In all our team most of us are a little "eek" about juveniles' (L&D6). Lay experience was again often invoked: 'If it counts for something, I have children myself' (FNP1). Enquiries about ASC and learning disability (LD) specialisms met similar responses: 'no-one on my team (F1) is an LD specialist' (L&D4); 'I have attended the odd day's training on autism' (L&D5). Additionally, apart from occasional reference to the use of a screening questionnaire interview for adolescents (SQIFA) (a youth-specific mental-health needs assessment tool), generally, clinicians described using adult assessment tools for young suspects. Second, despite the specific role of HCPs in FI assessments delineated in Annex G, a number of HCPs expressed reluctance to engage with the question of FI for young suspects in any depth. Those nurses who did not have a mental health specialism generally suggested that such issues should be considered by specialist nurses, or by L&D practitioners, where there was such provision. But these more specialist practitioners were often equally reluctant. L&D6 observed, for example: 'I always try to avoid fitness for interview. I would say, "In my view there is no evidence of acute mental ill health" or "X has capacity" but nothing more. I would never say "X is fit for interview".'

Additionally, many HCPs complained of a lack of access to the information about young suspects required for better identification of unfitness issues. In F1, for example, HCPs had no access to notes from Community Adolescent Mental Health Services or details relating to psychological intervention through the youth offending team (YOT), whilst, in F2, no medical notes were available for children since they were held by a different trust to that which provided health-care services. This lack of information further burdens the child with yet more questions and potentially painful disclosures. Although some found talking to an HCP helpful, others would not necessarily answer accurately ('I just chat rubbish' (Avery)) or may refuse to engage at all: 'I just say fuck off, don't wanna talk to you. They say alright then. They can't force you to talk to them' (Luke).

The hope, expressed in the Bradley Report, that L&D schemes might lead to all young suspects being screened by forensic mental-health practitioners was not necessarily being realized.[58] In F2, for example, where the intention was that all young suspects should be seen by an L&D

---

[58] Lord Keith Bradley, 'The Bradley Report, Lord Bradley's Review of People with Mental Health Problems or Learning Disabilities in the Criminal Justice System' (Department of Health 2009).

practitioner, L&D staff were plain that this is not always manageable: 'We should see all juveniles and we try our best to get through them but it's highly pressurized in here, and acutely unwell people need to come above them in the list' (L&D6). In addition, although assessing ability to participate, recommending reasonable adjustments, and supporting FI assessments were tasks included in the initial L&D service specification, and remain in the current version,[59] they were not a prominent feature during fieldwork. From a L&D perspective, where participation difficulties were identified, the focus tended to be on onward referral rather than measures within custody generally or within the interview specifically. Forensic nurse specialists were, similarly, not focused on the interview. As FNP6 observed, 'More than anything, it's about their release—to make sure they are safe to be released.' As a result, even where young suspects were seen by HCPs, this might not be in time to address FI: 'Sometimes they'll see the CPN, but it's not a barrier for them being interviewed first' (CO20).

The Impact of Solicitors and AAs: 'I couldn't be bothered telling them nothing'

The ability of the solicitor (where requested) and the AA to contribute meaningfully to the identification of FI concerns is inevitably restricted by the timing of their attendance. Their arrival shortly before interview, as previously identified, substantially reduced their capacity to identify any issues that had been overlooked. Additionally, a young suspect who has endured detention for several hours is less likely to raise with an AA or solicitor arriving late in the detention episode an issue which they perceive may delay their release. As Malik explained of his solicitor, 'They don't give a fuck. I couldn't be bothered telling them nothing. I just wanted to get out of there.'

As discussed in Chapter 4, the AA, especially a familial AA, may be aware of participation difficulties or have access to information about the young suspect. However, non-familial AAs and solicitors may attend without prior knowledge of the young person or immediate access to third-party information. Indeed, even where a young suspect has raised a medical or

---

[59] NHS England and NHS Improvement, 'Liaison and Diversion Standard Service Specification' (2019), 2.7.1 and 2.7.2 <https://www.england.nhs.uk/wp-content/uploads/2019/12/national-liaison-and-diversion-service-specification-2019.pdf> accessed 18 August 2023.

participation issue at RA, unless the condition identified may endanger the AA or solicitor, they will not routinely receive disclosure of that information.[60] In the absence of reliable information, the ability of a solicitor or non-familial AA to identify any but the most glaring unfitness issues in a brief consultation is very doubtful considering how challenging identification can be in that setting, even for psychologists.[61]

Where solicitors or non-familial AAs did have concerns, most felt, as Sol5 put it, that 'if we say something it gets taken quite seriously'. In particular, officers might accede to a request to bail rather than interview late at night, where fitness concerns arising from exhaustion were raised. COs themselves generally suggested that they would seek HCP input if challenged in this way. However, some solicitors complained that sergeants could be 'really difficult' and insist on interviewing, sometimes where the effects of prolonged detention were a concern (Sol4). Equally, some solicitors were concerned that HCP assessment did not always result in identification of unfitness where it appeared to be indicated. Sol6, for example, was very critical of responses to fitness concerns:

> there is very little you can do ... It's so rare for a custody sergeant to say that they [young suspects] are not fit for interview. They put them before a medic, a nurse and they always say they're fit for interview. I've never had anyone not fit for interview. But the next day ... the mental health team at court will say they are not fit for court when the custody nurse says he was fit for interview.

Likewise, RHAA1 expressed her frustration at the lack of adjustment for a young suspect with Asperger's whose interview was subsequently challenged at court: 'at the time (in custody) it didn't seem to make a blind bit of difference'.

However, not all AAs suggested that they would raise an issue, even where they were aware of a participation difficulty. This was particularly the case for familial AAs, in large part because they felt they would not be listened to. FAA7 complained that, even though she had shown the CO a report on her son's medical condition, he had still refused to allow her to bring

---

[60] *Code C* (n 13), para 3.8A.
[61] Isabel CH Clare and Gisli H Gudjonsson, 'Interrogative Suggestibility, Confabulation, and Acquiescence in People with Mild Learning Disabilities (Mental Handicap): Implications for Reliability during Police Interrogations' (1993) 32 British Journal of Clinical Psychology 295.

necessary food and drink for him. Even those with training may not be effective in ensuring that FI concerns are attended to. VAA3, for example, explained that on the rare occasion that she has concerns about a young suspect's FI, 'I leave it down to the police officers to carry on ... I would just let the interview continue and it would be sorted out.' Given the prevalence of out-of-court disposals and referral orders, the chances of such an issue being 'sorted out' later are slim.

Inadequate Mechanisms to Address Unfitness: 'We're not equipped to deal with that'

Even where a CO identifies that a young suspect might be 'at risk in an interview', I encountered no meaningful consideration of safeguards 'in addition to those required under the Code' as provided for in Annex G, paragraph 8. No CO identified any specific adjustment, beyond reliance on the AA, to address risk in interview in respect of a young suspect. Sol10, who specializes in representing young people with dispositional vulnerabilities, spoke of her 'frustration' with COs who were unable to identify the vulnerability of young suspects and adjust processes accordingly: 'it's quite rare to find an enlightened one'. The only reference to the possibility of support beyond the use of an AA came from CO26, and his suggestion involved bailing the young person for help to be obtained outside the custody suite.

Nor did any clinician that I spoke to identify any specific adjustments for a young person in interview beyond reliance on the AA. None that I spoke to had ever been asked to, or advised, that they sit in on an interview (as envisaged in Annex G, paragraph 8). Nor did I encounter any professional, AA, or officer who had experienced an interview involving intermediary assistance for a young suspect. There seemed to be a degree of hopelessness in respect of developmental issues in particular, as L&D7 tellingly observed: 'Developmental issues, autism, aspergers ... we're not equipped to deal with that in this sort of place.'

Ultimately, if the CO considers that the suspect is fit but the solicitor or AA disagrees, the options are fairly limited. Both solicitor and AA can repeat their concerns about fitness during the interview itself so that they are captured on the recording. This can, as Sol4 observed, leave an investigating officer feeling 'very awkward' but is not always an effective remedy, given that the contents of the recording are unlikely to be scrutinized at court (as discussed in Chapter 1), and airing those concerns will not necessarily prevent a child opting for an out-of-court disposal or entering a guilty plea on the basis of admissions unfairly extracted. Alternatively, solicitors suggested that they would be likely to advise 'no comment', perhaps following the making of a prepared statement, or may suggest that their client simply refuse to cooperate with interview entirely (Sol9, Sol6, Code C, paragraph 12.5). Whilst this protects the child from having to face questioning which they may be unable to withstand, it has the unfortunate effect of narrowing the child's options since it removes the prospect of an out-of-court disposal and renders formal prosecution more likely.

In those few cases where the CO concludes that, even taking into account available safeguards, the young suspect is unfit and the interview cannot go ahead, the options then are even more heavily constrained. If the CO rules out bailing the suspect for enquiries into obtaining further help, the only option, where 'no further action' is inappropriate and there is sufficient evidence, is to forego the interview entirely and to 'charge and get rid' (CO32). The child's fair trial rights, under Article 6 of the European Convention on Human Rights, are thus protected but at the expense of their right to be heard under Article 12 of the UN Convention on the Rights of the Child (UNCRC)[62] and the option of a less coercive resolution.

In short, the evidence suggests that the assessment of fitness to be interviewed, and the provision of adjustments to mitigate risk in interview, frequently function inadequately for child suspects. As a result, young suspects may commonly be undergoing interview when they are unfit to do so, and those who need extra assistance may not be adequately supported. Additionally, young participant accounts reveal that prolonged detention can significantly undermine the fitness of those who might otherwise function adequately in interview. It appears that the support of the AA is widely considered to address any participation needs raised and that their automatic presence operates to discourage more detailed consideration of functional difficulties. The evidence of HCPs and L&D practitioners themselves reveals that they, too, may not be responding to requests for assessment as Annex G envisages and are not commonly effective in ensuring that adequate adjustments are made to support those 'at risk' in interview.

These shortcomings are exacerbated by the impact of detention and its adversarial context, which can disincline children to raise issues for fear

---

[62] Ratified by the United Kingdom and entered into force September 1990.

of delayed release and to engage with support which is associated with the police and prosecution. At the same time, the ticking PACE clock and the emphasis on speedy release—provisions intended to protect children—can inadvertently result in hurried assessments by COs under-equipped to make such judgements, often without good information or without reverting to more expert assessment. In addition, where unfitness is identified, the framework does not offer a clear alternative process to ensure that the unfit child suspect is not disadvantaged by virtue of their participation difficulties.

More recent fieldwork by Kemp and others, conducted in 2021 and 2022, suggests that, by and large, these difficulties remain.[63] Their findings further illustrate how the time constraints of the custody process and a lack of reliable information undermine effective FI assessment. The perception that the AA can be relied upon to raise and then mitigate fitness issues continues, whilst at the same time, AAs, and some solicitors, complained of difficulties challenging FI assessments with which they did not agree. Finally, there continued to be concerns about CO expertise in making FI assessments and how effectively HCPs were able to contribute to their decision-making.[64] In November 2021, the College of Policing issued new 'Vulnerability-related risks guidelines' which are designed to support better identification of vulnerability and place particular emphasis on professional development in this area.[65] These will, it is hoped, improve the understanding and identification of vulnerability in police custody but, without more fundamental changes to the fitness to be interviewed framework itself, it is likely that the problems identified here will persist.

Questioning in Interview: Procedure and Existing Literature

I turn now to consider how the interview itself is conducted, how young people experienced that process, and the extent to which they felt able to

---

[63] Vicky Kemp and others, *Examining the Impact of PACE on the Detention and Questioning of Child Suspects by the Police in England and Wales* (Nuffield Foundation, 25 May 2023) <https://www.nuffieldfoundation.org/project/impact-of-pace-on-the-detention-and-questioning-of-young-suspects> accessed 3 October 2023, 69–72.
[64] ibid.
[65] College of Policing, 'Vulnerability-Related Risks Guidelines (2021) <https://www.college.police.uk/guidance/vulnerability-related-risks> accessed 18 August 2023.

participate effectively. As identified in Chapter 1, the UNCRC, and related instruments, stress the importance of 'child friendly' approaches to children involved in criminal processes, including in police interview.[66] The Committee on the Rights of the Child (the UNCRC Committee) has noted risk factors associated with false confession, in particular, 'the child's age and development, lack of understanding, and fear of unknown consequences, including a suggested possibility of imprisonment, as well as by the length and circumstances of the questioning'.[67] The UNCRC Committee calls for, in addition to the presence of an AA, the use of child friendly language and interviewing spaces and for officers to be 'well-trained to avoid questioning techniques and practices that result in coerced or unreliable confessions'.[68]

The legal framework domestically falls far short of these aspirations. There is no requirement for officers interviewing child suspects to have specific training in child friendly questioning techniques, as would be the case in relation to child witnesses for the prosecution.[69] Indeed, research based on material elicited through Freedom of Information Act requests to all forces in England and Wales identified that none of the forces responding had separate policies or guidance covering interviews with child suspects.[70] *Code C* itself provides very limited guidance on the interviewing of child suspects. The most significant adjustment is that, save in the case of urgent interviews, a young suspect may not be interviewed unless their AA is present.[71] The AA should be informed of their role in the interview: that they are not to act 'simply as an observer' and that the purpose of their presence

---

[66] See in particular the UN Standard Minimum Rules for the Administration of Juvenile Justice (adopted on 10 December 1985 at the 40th Session of the General Assembly) (Beijing Rules); the Guidelines of the Committee of Ministers of the Council of Europe on child friendly justice (adopted by the Committee of Ministers on 17 November 2010 at the 1098th meeting of the Ministers' Deputies).

[67] General Comment No 24 (2019) on children's rights in the child justice system (CRC/C/GC/24), para 59. (General Comment No 24 replaces General Comment No 10 (2007) (CRC/C/GC/10) extant at the time of fieldwork. Any relevant variance will be noted as it arises).

[68] ibid 46. Echoed in *Principles on Effective Interviewing for Investigations and Information Gathering* (The Méndez Principles), adopted in May 2021 by a Steering Committee of Experts with the support of the Anti-Torture Initiative, the Association for the Prevention of Torture, and the Norwegian Centre for Human Rights <www.apt.ch/sites/default/files/publications/apt_PoEI_EN_11.pdf> accessed 18 August 2023.

[69] Ministry of Justice, 'Achieving Best Evidence in Criminal Proceedings' (Ministry of Justice/National Police Chiefs' Council 2022) <www.gov.uk/government/publications/achieving-best-evidence-in-criminal-proceedings> accessed 29 June 2022>.

[70] Kate Gooch and Piers von Berg, 'What Happens in the Beginning, Matters in the End: Achieving Best Evidence with Child Suspects in the Police Station' (2019) 19 Youth Justice 85.

[71] *Code C* (n 13), para 11.15.

is to advise the interviewee, to observe whether the interview is being conducted 'fairly and properly', and to facilitate communication with the interviewee.[72] Tellingly, the arrangements for removing an AA from interview are rather more detailed.[73] Otherwise, *Code C*, NFG 11C contains the only other guidance. This warns that 'juveniles' (and vulnerable adults) may be 'particularly prone' to providing information which may be 'unreliable, misleading or self-incriminating' and requires 'special care' be taken in questioning such a person, counselling that the AA 'should be involved' if there is any doubt about the individual's age, mental state, or capacity. APP provides no more specific guidance about the interviewing of children.[74] In line with *Code C*, it notes: 'People with clear or perceived vulnerabilities should be treated with particular care, and extra safeguards should be put in place.'[75] Likewise, APP acknowledges that children 'may be more suggestible and require special protection.'[76] However, again, no more specific arrangements are stipulated. There is no requirement for child friendly language or interview spaces adjusted to accommodate the needs of child suspects.

In England and Wales, the PEACE model of interviewing should be employed for all suspects, including children. Introduced nationally in 1992, in response to mounting evidence of the role played by adversarial interviewing approaches in the major miscarriages of justice in the 1970s and '80s,[77] it recast police interrogation as 'investigative interviewing'.[78] The model is designed to encourage the elicitation of truthful, reliable evidence rather than focusing on confession, beginning with the use of open questions to assist suspects to provide their own account, followed by an exploration of inconsistencies or contradictions within that account, which is then challenged by comparison with police evidence that counters the suspect's position.[79] However, as O'Mahony, Milne, and Grant have observed, 'there is no guidance available to police officers about how to effectively challenge

---

[72] ibid, para 11.17.
[73] ibid, para 11.17A.
[74] APP(I)(II) (n 2).
[75] ibid 4 (Principle 2).
[76] ibid 2.
[77] Thomas M Williamson, 'From Interrogation to Investigative Interviewing; Strategic Trends in Police Questioning' (1993) 3 Journal of Community & Applied Social Psychology 89.
[78] Bull, 'Police Investigative Interviewing' (n 8); Colin Clarke, Rebecca Milne, and Ray Bull, 'Interviewing Suspects of Crime: The Impact of PEACE Training, Supervision and the Presence of a Legal Advisor' (2011) 8 Journal of Investigative Psychology & Offender Profiling 149.
[79] Soukara and others (n 9).

Questioning in Interview: Procedure and Existing Literature 279

a vulnerable suspect who has intellectual disabilities or any other mental disorder'.[80] Nor, as reviews have noted,[81] is there more detailed guidance on interviewing child suspects of the sort that is available for the interviewing of child witnesses.[82] This contrasts with the approach taken in the courts, where expertise in acting for young witnesses or defendants is increasingly considered essential and 'radical' adjustment of questioning processes to 'adapt to the witness not the other way round' is expected (*R v Lubemba*[83] at [45], also *R v Grant-Murray*).[84]

Despite the critical importance of the interview, it is concerning that there is also a limited amount of research evidence about the conduct of interviews with child suspects. The Royal Commission on Criminal Justice had to be persuaded that research into the conduct of interviews with 'juveniles' would be a 'useful contribution' to the programme of research in relation to police powers.[85] However, what is available suggests that, in the decade following the introduction of PACE, oppressive interrogation tactics continued to be widely used in interviews of young suspects. Evans's review of 164 juvenile interviews revealed the use of persuasive tactics in 23% of cases and that such techniques were 'more likely to be used where the suspect does not readily confess'. In particular, leading questions were used in 19.5% of cases and legal closure questions in 12.2% of cases.[86] The findings reflected the widespread use of similar questioning techniques in adult interviews.[87]

These studies predate the era of PEACE interviewing. Although evaluations of PEACE have been somewhat mixed,[88] all-ages research suggests that PEACE has led to a reduction in the use of more problematic

---

[80] Brendan M O'Mahony, Becky Milne, and Tim Grant, 'To Challenge, or Not to Challenge? Best Practice When Interviewing Vulnerable Suspects' (2012) 6 Policing: Journal of Policy & Practice 301, 307.
[81] CJJI (n 56); APPGC (n 47).
[82] Ray Bull, 'The Investigative Interviewing of Children and Other Vulnerable Witnesses: Psychological Research and Working/Professional Practice' (2010) 15 Legal & Criminological Psychology 5.
[83] [2014] EWCA Crim 2064, [2015] 1 WLR 1579.
[84] [2017] EWCA Crim 1228, [2018] Crim LR 71, [226].
[85] Evans, 'Police Interrogations' (n 22) 74.
[86] Roger Evans, 'The Conduct of Police Interviews with Juveniles', Royal Commission on Criminal Justice, Research Study No 8 (HMSO 1993).
[87] McConville, Sanders, and Leng (n 5); Michael McConville and Jacqueline Hodgson, 'Custodial Legal Advice and the Right to Silence', Royal Commission on Criminal Justice Research Study No 16 (HMSO 1993).
[88] See eg Clarke and Milne (n 8).

techniques such as intimidation, minimization,[89] and maximization,[90] although the continued overuse of leading questions was noted.[91] However, the picture in respect of children is more worrying. Medford and others' examination of the efficacy of the AA safeguard involved analysis of 136 juvenile interviews.[92] This revealed that the total number of 'interrogation tactics' (including the use of leading questions and mid-sentence interruptions) deployed by interviewing officers was greater for child interviews than for those conducted with adults with an AA. Additionally, officers achieved the lowest ratings for interviewing skills and competence, measured in accordance with the PEACE model, in interviews with children, in comparison with adults.[93]

More recently, a review of twelve juvenile interviews identified coercive techniques employed by officers in six interviews, including maximization, minimization, and the use of 'hypothetical evidence' to encourage admissions.[94] Police participants said that there 'tended to be no difference in the way they interrogated juveniles based on their age', although there was some suggestion that less formal approaches may be taken in interviews for less serious allegations.[95] The CJJI's review similarly found that 'Investigating officers made little adjustment in interviews for difficulties in communication.[96] Likewise, a study of the transcripts of police interviews with mentally disordered suspects revealed that best practice approaches, such as the use of open questions, were 'not being entirely adhered too [sic]', and, concerningly, vulnerable suspects were 'subjected to significantly increased levels of minimization when compared with their non-mentally disordered counterparts'.[97] The use of minimization techniques has been found to increase the rate of false confessions as well as true confessions,[98] whilst there

---

[89] Where the questioner underplays the seriousness of the offence or the consequences, should the suspect confess, in order to encourage an admission.
[90] Where the questioner seeks to increase the anxiety of a suspect who makes no admissions by emphasizing the seriousness of the offence or the consequences of maintaining denials.
[91] Soukara and others (n 9).
[92] Sarah Medford, Gisli H Gudjonsson, and John Pearse, 'The Efficacy of the Appropriate Adult Safeguard during Police Interviewing' (2003) 8 Law & Criminological Psychology 253.
[93] ibid.
[94] Kemp and Hodgson (n 52) 161.
[95] ibid 152.
[96] CJJI (n 56) 8.
[97] Laura Farrugia and Fiona Gabbert, 'Vulnerable Suspects in Police Interviews: Exploring Current Practice in England and Wales' (2020) 17 Journal of Investigative Psychology and Offender Profiling 17, 25.
[98] Melissa B Russano and others, 'Investigating True and False Confessions within a Novel Experimental Paradigm' (2005) 16 Psychological Science 481.

is also ample psychological evidence that misinformation can make suspects vulnerable to manipulation,[99] particularly younger and more suggestible suspects.[100] There may, however, be some cause for optimism. Kemp and others' review of a small sample of recorded police interviews with children in 2021 and 2022 identified an increase in interviewing officers displaying 'active listening' skills when questioning child suspects,[101] in comparison with Kemp and Hodgson's similar review in 2016.[102]

However, there has been no substantial qualitative study focusing on young suspects' experiences of interview, particularly how they respond to questioning techniques. Young people in Hazel and others' research into experiences of the justice system more generally complained of 'rapid and confusing questions',[103] of officers 'twisting' their words, or feeling that the interviewers, as one young participant put it, 'were just putting words into my mouth'.[104] Young people made similar complaints to HMIC of 'unfair' questioning techniques, such as continually challenging their account and repetitive questioning[105]—an approach found, in younger children, to have a significant effect on consistency and accuracy of response.[106] Young participants in Kemp and Hodgson's study also complained of officers trying to 'twist their words' or 'trip them up'.[107]

The power imbalance in the interview room is also a prevalent theme in the literature. Hazel and colleagues' participants spoke of verbal aggression and threats of lengthy custodial terms in interview, which could lead to feelings of isolation and distress, particularly where parental AAs were unsupportive.[108] Commentators have noted that young suspects tend to be 'undemanding and even passive in their resignation to police control'[109] and that all the pressures on the suspect are to capitulate to police

---

[99] Kassin and others (n 15).
[100] Allison Redlich and Gail Goodman, 'Taking Responsibility for an Act Not Committed: The Influence of Age and Suggestibility' (2003) 27 Law & Human Behavior 141.
[101] Kemp and others (n 63) 83.
[102] Kemp and Hodgson (n 52) 161.
[103] Neal Hazel, Ann Hagell, and Laura Brazier, *Young Offenders' Perceptions of Their Experiences in the Criminal Justice System* (Economic and Social Research Council 2003) 12.
[104] Neal Hazel, 'Young Offenders' Perceptions of Their Experiences under Police Arrest' (British Society of Criminology Conference, Glasgow July 2006) 20.
[105] HMIC (n 55) 184.
[106] Sarah Krähenbühl, Mark Blades, and Christine Eiser, 'The Effect of Repeated Questioning on Children's Accuracy and Consistency in Eyewitness Testimony' (2009) 14 Legal and Criminological Psychology 263.
[107] Kemp and Hodgson (n 52) 141.
[108] Hazel (n 104).
[109] McConville and Hodgson (n 87) 51.

expectations.[110] Research has consistently identified disengagement in young suspects' and young defendants' responses to police power,[111] a 'tuning out' rather than 'tuning in' to criminal justice processes.[112]

Questioning in Interview: Child Suspect Experiences

Of those who answered questions in interview, several young participants described feeling that they had been able to give a good account of themselves on at least one occasion. Jackson, for example, explained, '100 per cent—I make sure that I get my position across.' However, this group, who were positive about at least one interview and felt that they had been able to participate effectively in it, were a very small minority. It is not possible to evaluate their interviews or to exclude the possibility that others who did not speak in detail about, or recall much of, their interview were also able to engage positively in that process. However, the very low number expressing satisfaction in the interview process is troubling.[113] Those who found the interview process challenging on one or more occasions described a range of reasons, which broadly fall into three categories: issues arising from the interview process itself, issues relating to the manner of the interviewer, and, closely linked, objections to the nature of the questioning.

Issues Arising from the Interview Process Itself: 'It's just really uncomfortable'

Some young people were simply pleased to be going into interview because this meant that they were progressing towards release: 'to be honest it's actually a relief' (Hussain). But others were 'edgy' (Zayn) or nervous about

---

[110] Jacqueline Hodgson, 'Adding Injury to Injustice: The Suspect at the Police Station' (1994) 21 Journal of Law & Society 85.
[111] Hazel, Hagell, and Brazier (n 103).
[112] Joyce Plotnikoff and Richard Woolfson, 'Young Defendants Pack: Scoping Study' (YJB 2002) 26 <https://vdocuments.site/young-defendants-pack-scoping-study-lexicon-limited-young-defendants-pack-scoping.html> accessed 19 August.
[113] Although the numbers are small, it is interesting to note that those with more positive interview experiences tended to be young participants who did not go on to be charged so were either making admissions, resulting in a caution, or giving an account which ended in no further action. There was no notable disproportionality in terms of ethnicity, gender, or relative youth in the group.

the interview occurring in police custody, 'Just really just being in the police station—them asking all them questions I don't really like' (Kyle). Whilst one might expect any interview with the police to be a nerve-inducing experience, several accounts revealed particular discomfort in interview arising from the detention context and their desperation to leave ('you don't really wanna talk in the interview, you wanna go innit' (Hudson). Others found it difficult to manage their emotions when questioned by those whom they considered responsible for their harsh experiences in detention. Kate, for example, found it difficult being taken from her cell to 'speak to the people that are winding me up'.

For other young people, the power imbalance of the detention experience, and the adversarial context of custody, induced a feeling of helplessness and futility at the outset. Sandor explained, 'It's just really uncomfortable and you just feel like it doesn't matter what you say, it's wrong and it's going to be used against you.' It was notable that no young participant described interview occurring in a setting which could be described as being 'child friendly', and certainly all interviews on fieldwork occurred for children in the same setting as for adults. These experiences reflect similar observations made by McConville and Hodgson in the early 1990s,[114] suggesting that the emphasis on reducing feelings of intimidation in the effective participation jurisprudence[115] has not had a marked effect. This power imbalance, coupled with the unfamiliar demands of the interview, could severely hamper a child's ability to give a good account of themselves. Kyle described how it was more difficult to speak when 'under pressure': 'I get a bit like nervous in speaking so I don't really like saying everything I just say what I say ... you're not used to having to explain yourself to tell a story about what happened—so it can sometimes not be very easy to give all the info.' Whilst, for Tom, the very protections in place for him in interview, the presence of the AA and solicitor, contributed to the challenges for him: 'just so many people looking at you at once, chatting away'.

---

[114] McConville and Hodgson (n 87).
[115] See *Panovits v Cyprus* (n 32).

Issues Relating to the Manner of the Interviewer: 'It's like you've done it, so what's the point?'

Those who were positive about an interview presented a fairly consistent view of what made a good interviewing officer. They focused on officers who established rapport, did not rush or pressurize them, and explained what was happening throughout. Yemi, for example, described one interviewing officer:

> He was really friendly. He was really calm. It was a really chilled interview... Before we started the interview he just told me everything about what's going to happen ... He was clear ... at the end he went through everything that he wrote down just to tell me, am I sure this is what I want to say?

AAs similarly approved of officers who were 'professional' (FAA6), asked 'straightforward questions' (FAA5), and were 'understandable and understanding' (VAA3).

Negative assessments were more marked, with a number of young people complaining that officers did not listen to what they said or made it clear that they disbelieved their account. The idea of the interview as the suspect's opportunity to advance an account which will be meaningfully considered was wholly at odds with the experience some young people recounted. Tom explained, 'if I answered a question, even if it was truthfully, he'd look at me as if I'm lying'. Evan encapsulated the frustration and powerlessness that several young participants experienced in this regard: 'Even when you get interviewed, it's like you've done it, so what's the point?' Some young participants found that interviewing officers could be 'really intimidating' (Simon)—a complaint also made by children in evidence to the APPGC.[116] As Michael described, 'They ask you questions quite rudely—like they're looking for a certain moment to catch you out.' However, more friendly overtures could also be rejected out of hand, particularly where a young participant had had previous negative contact with the police. Luke, a regular in police custody explained:

---

[116] APPGC (n 47).

Some of them look at you funny—like give you looks like trying, like trying to be nice, nice to you like they're your pal, trying to talk to you like. 'Oh yeah, alright then mate...' No, that's—nah, you don't, I've never really spoke to police. I don't really like 'em if that makes sense.

Objections to the Nature of the Questioning

Echoing post-PEACE research findings,[117] a significant number of young participants complained of questioning methods which they felt were designed to 'get you mixed up' (Rezar), 'catch you out' (Aidan, Dexter), 'trip' (Kyle, Sadie, Riley), 'trick' (Carter, Avery, Sadie, Nathan), and 'twist' your words (Kate, Evan, Avery). A number of problematic techniques were complained of by young participants.

'Tripping'

Most prominent, raised by fourteen young participants, was the persistent repetition of questions: 'They will ask you same question over, like, five times' (Rezar). Persistent or repetitive questioning is not outlawed under the PEACE model and can be acceptable as long as it is 'careful and consistent but not unfair or oppressive'.[118] However, young participants' descriptions of the use of this technique suggest that, in some cases, it moved beyond the acceptable. Carter describes how the technique was adopted with him: 'they try to trick you and try to say something, and then say something else, and then go back to the exact same thing, and try and get you to say something different or something like that'. A number of participants complained that the questions would be slightly adjusted each time: 'you say one answer and then they change the question like they've just asked to try and trick you out. Ask it like, word it in another way and that' (Avery). Research findings underline that it is dangerous to adopt such techniques with children, particularly younger children, since they tend to change their response, assuming that the repetition results because their initial answer was not correct.[119] For those with a learning disability, repetitive questioning could be really problematic, as one such young participant explained:

---

[117] Medford, Gudjonsson, and Pearse (n 92); Hazel (n 104); Kemp and Hodgson (n 52).
[118] APP(I)(II) (n 2) 6.
[119] Stephen Ceci and others, 'Children's Suggestibility Research: Implications for the Courtroom and the Forensic Interview' in Helen Westcott, Graham Davies, and Ray Bull (eds), *Children's Testimony: A Handbook of Psychological Research and Forensic Practice* (Wiley 2002); Krähenbühl, Blades, and Eiser (n 106).

> if I'm asking you a simple question like, 'What day is it?' then five minutes after, after somethin' else, so your mind—so you've lost everything—they'll ask you again, 'What day is it?' Then, ten minutes after. So, you're completely—you can't remember—I couldn't remember what the first thing they said to me, so then they ask you again. Then again and again until they get what you [sic] want. But if you don't give 'em what you [sic] want, like—I've been there with my dad and we've been in an interview for about three hours.
>
> (Evan)

Professionals also recognized this technique:

> the questions they ask—confession cases in particular—go on and on. It's quite oppressive actually—I have stopped people being questioned. They ask the same thing in a slightly different way over and over again.
>
> (Sol6)

For some young participants, many desperate for release, the relentless repetition was hard to withstand. Far from eliciting a reliable account, it tended to induce frustration and a loss of focus. Avery, for example, described becoming 'bored' and 'annoyed' and that she 'started not thinking before I say anything'. Likewise, Aaron's response, in the interests of getting out 'quicker', was to 'just answer 'em short, innit, I'm just not arsed'. Evan found containing his frustration more difficult: 'it just really winds me up ... I snapped'.

A significant number of young participants explained that they took the approach of making no comment because of previous experiences undergoing this sort of questioning. Carter explained:

> The questions, they try to trick you and try to say something, and then say something else, and then go back to the exact same thing, and try and get you to say something different or something like that. That's why I just go with, 'No comment' because they've caught me out a couple of times.

Of course, having no answer which 'would withstand questioning' can properly found an adverse inference.[120] However, what young participants

---

[120] See eg R v Petkar [2003] EWCA Crim 2668, [2004] 1 Cr App R 22.

described in some cases appeared to go beyond avoiding being caught out in a lie but rather suggested that they were instead responding to what were felt to be unfair tactics, which might trap them even where they were telling the truth. Alex, for example, explained in this regard, 'I wouldn't say I'm weak-minded, but it's just, they're extremely clever ... Even when I haven't done anything, I do a "No Comment" thing.'

'Twisting'

Allied to these concerns, young participants frequently complained that officers 'twist' what they say in interview, echoing objections in the same terms in Kemp and Hodgson's research.[121] What they seem to be describing is the use of legal closure questions, identified as a prominent tool for case construction by McConville and colleagues thirty years ago,[122] or the drawing of unfair inference from responses to (often leading) questions. Simon, for example, recounted: 'And they go, "Do you know the bike shop, this place?" and I'm like, "Yeah, I know of it. It's in town. Um" and they go, "So you admit that you're selling bikes, you've been selling stolen bikes?" And I'm like, "No mate".' Harper explained how it felt to experience this tactic:

> even if you do say something they will try and twist it into thinking that you've said something completely different. And they will read it back to you but they will say it completely different to how you said it and it's like 'I didn't say that.' And it's like then they try and make out like it's your fault. And then they try and make you think it's your fault and then you slip up and say 'Yeah, it's my fault', kind of thing.

Kaiden's experience, interviewed at thirteen years of age, provides some insight into how dangerous such questioning tactics can be when combined with the powerlessness many felt:

KAIDEN: Sometimes they'll ask me 'Why did you rob that boy, did you say that you'd done this, did you say that you done that?' But I never.
MB: OK and do you feel you can say 'Hey, I never did that?'
KAIDEN: No, 'cos they won't believe it anyway. 'Cos obviously, if they're asking me if I done it, they're thinking it's me.

---

[121] Kemp and Hodgson (n 52) 141.
[122] Where a question appears to force information supplied by the suspect into a legally significant category. See for discussion McConville, Sanders, and Leng (n 5) 70.

MB: OK. And is it not your chance to say—'Hey, this wasn't me'?
KAIDEN: No 'cos they don't deal that.

Evan describes two alternatives for coping with such a technique: either he would not provide full detail ('you won't wanna say exactly, 'cause you know they'll twist it into gettin' what they want) or safer still, he suggested making no comment: 'there's been times where I just feel like saying, "No comment" all the way. 'Cos, no matter what you say, it's gonna get twisted in one way or another.' Again, this questioning tactic is revealed to be wholly counterproductive, jeopardizing the reliability of the account provided or driving the young suspect into a 'no comment' position.

'Tricking'

Six young participants complained specifically about being misled or deceived by officers. Elijah explained, 'They was like, "Your mate has already told us that you was talkin' to him about stabbin' your enemy" ... I knew they was lyin' 'cause my mate got away ... I was like, "Listen, don't try to lie to me." I hate it when the officers lie. I hate it.' However, not everyone recounted having been able to identify the deception at the time of the interview. Nathan described his experience:

> I grassed one of my mates up when I was, when I first got done for something as a young 'un. They told me that two of my mates have said it's me. So I've said 'Nah, nah I'll tell you the truth innit.' But nothing like that happened, they just trickin' us out innit.

Such a tactic can, as Nathan's account reveals, yield results. However, the product may not necessarily be reliable—Abigail explained that her response to deceit is to 'just do it back'. But perhaps more concerning is the damage done to police legitimacy by such tactics. Carter, who felt deceived in interview, reflected of the police, 'they're just as untrustworthy as the criminals ... Who lies to someone to catch them out?' Such an experience could lead to more confrontational exchanges. Alex, for example, described how feeling manipulated on previous occasions had led him to be more 'vocal' on arrest. Although the numbers are small, those complaining of deliberate deceit by officers were disproportionately Black, Asian, or minority ethnic young people and tended also to be those who were regular attendees in custody or had had at least three previous custodial arrests. In no other area of complaint about interviewing approaches was there any other marked disproportionality in respect of ethnicity, gender, or relative youth.

They 'put words in your mouth'

Another common complaint from young participants was that officers 'put words in your mouth' (Simon). One method young participants often referred to was the use of leading questions: 'they weren't like asking me questions, they were telling me questions, like telling me the answers to the question' (Simon). This was particularly difficult when asked as part of a multiple question format. Elijah, for example, described, 'Like, when I got arrested for the knife, they was like, "You was in school with a knife, tryin' to stab someone, correct?" I was like, "No. I was in school with a knife, 'cause I'd been told my life was at threat."' Riley similarly recounted:

> They ask you stupid shit, don't they? Say you 'ad a fight or somethin', it was like, 'Right, well what time did you throw the first punch?' ... They just ask it to you, and that's what fucks with your 'ead and then you end up just blurtin' out random shit and getting yourself in more trouble.

Such an approach goes against APP guidance, which makes clear that questions should be 'as short and simple as possible', 'multiple questions' should be avoided due to the risk of 'confusion', and leading questions should be used 'only as a last resort'.[123]

The combination of repetitive and leading questions could be particularly dangerous. Sol9 was concerned about the use of 'pressure' in combination with leading questions: 'children are more easy to lead. With a younger juvenile it is concerning because they start agreeing to things and that's not what their instructions were.' Logan demonstrates how this sort of questioning can prompt unreliable answers: 'Some questions that they ask, they'll pressure you and you'll be that pressured that you might 'ave to lie and say, "Yeah, fair enough, I did do it" ... Just to get it over with, 'cause they'll just keep pressuring you and asking you.' Such observations correspond with psychological research which identifies children's raised propensity to confess falsely.[124]

---

[123] APP(I)(II) (n 2) 14.
[124] Gudjonsson and others, 'Custodial Interrogation' (n 15); Kassin and others (n 15).

Offering Inducements: 'It's like holding somebody hostage'

There were several young people who objected to the use of what they considered to be inducements by interviewing officers to elicit admissions. Alex felt that his interviewer had been 'manipulative' by telling him, 'if I'm just honest with them, in my reasoning of why I have, why I had the knife, then I think they said that I will get less charges and stuff and ... I've told 'em why I had it, and I still had the same charges, so'. Zayn had similar objections: 'they [the officers] act as if they're the ones that decide if you're going to jail or not sometimes, they don't really think of court and it's just you, if you're new to the system, you've never been arrested, so they manipulate you'. It is illustrative of the lack of progress in improving interviewing techniques for child suspects that similar complaints were noted by Hazel in research conducted fifteen years before the current study.[125]

Several young participants described feeling under pressure to make admissions so that they could receive a caution or, later, a referral order. Whilst the option of diversion where admissions are made is desirable, in the absence of legal advice, the evidence suggests that this can easily be experienced as coercion, especially when combined with the promise of swift release. Avery, for example, without legal advice, had felt that she had no option but to make admissions in relation to a public order offence which she was adamant she had not committed. Her reasoning had been 'if I admit it in interview they would give me a caution and then they would take me home', otherwise the officer had told her 'they would have taken it further'. Sadie, likewise, described asking, 'When can I go home?' and that the officers responded, 'Well it depends what you say'. Similarly, Luke felt strongly that being put in the cell was a tactic to get information from him:

> they want you to feel scared ... it's like holding somebody hostage, like torturing them. 'Right, tell me this or I'm taking your 'and off', that's what they do. 'Tell me, just tell me and we'll let you go. Soon as you tell me you're on your way.'

It is important not to underestimate how powerful such inducements could be, given the distressing experiences of detention recounted in Chapter 5 and combined with normal adolescent impulsivity and deficits in future orientation.[126] The psychological pressure of the detention experience on

---
[125] Hazel, Hagell, and Brazier (n 103).
[126] Elizabeth Cauffman and Laurence Steinberg, 'Emerging Findings from Research on Adolescent Development and Juvenile Justice' (2012) 7 Victims & Offenders 428.

young suspects and defendants has been consistently raised as a feature in false confessions and guilty pleas.[127]

Subject Matter Objections: 'It's not even relevant'
Several young participants objected to being asked what they felt were irrelevant questions in interview. Two particular issues were raised. First, young participants complained of what were considered to be unnecessary and intrusive questions about their general circumstances. Kyle explained how police, 'Wanna know everything really ... Some things that they ask as well, they don't really need to know about ... They aren't necessary for the subject.' For young people with difficult life circumstances or traumatic histories, this could be distracting and difficult to deal with. Kyle, who was unrepresented, described how he responded: 'You can't really have a bad reaction in there, can you? It's just got you thinking in your head really.' He reflected, 'you couldn't really do anything could you? It's police ... I just let it go.'

Second, young participants objected to questions about previous convictions which had no relevance to the allegation. Logan, for example, recounted:

> Winds me up. It could be for burglary and you've got a criminal record for assault or summat. They bring that up even though it's not even relevant.

In his case, his legal representative would advise him, 'No, don't answer it', but as we see with Kyle, without professional support, such a response may not seem like an option.

Lack of Specialist Interview Training

Such shortcomings are unsurprising. At no fieldwork site was there a requirement for specific training for those interviewing young suspects (beyond the Tier 1 PEACE training delivered to all officers). IO1, for example, explained, 'Any officer can interview a juvenile in custody', in contrast to

---

[127] See eg Royal Commission on Criminal Justice, 'Report (Cmnd 2263)' (HMSO 1991) and more recently Rebecca K Helm, 'Conviction by Consent? Vulnerability, Autonomy and Conviction by Guilty Plea' (2019) 83 Journal of Criminological Law (Hertford) 161.

the interview of a child witness, which would be done, 'on ABE [Achieving Best Evidence] and it would not be in custody'. Some investigating officers spoken to, such as IO1, explained that they had done ABE training and drew on those skills in interviewing young suspects. Whilst this is, to an extent, encouraging, the emphasis of the ABE approach is different to that required in an adversarial interview under caution. In F3, budget reductions had led to a force restructure, resulting in officers who had not been required to interview for many years now routinely interviewing suspects, including children. COs and local solicitors had concerns about the quality of interviews as a result.

Without sight of young participants' interviews, one must be circumspect about drawing too many firm conclusions about police interview techniques more generally for child suspects. Nonetheless, as we have seen, young participant accounts correspond strikingly with other research and analysis, suggesting that their experiences may not be uncommon. What is particularly concerning is that these coercive techniques have long been identified[128] and that they persist despite the PEACE model. At the same time, since the early 1990s, psychological research has provided compelling evidence of their damaging impact on the ability of children to provide reliable and accurate testimony.[129] It is plain that the exhortations in *Code C* and APP(I)(II) operate ineffectively, and the lack of specific guidance on the investigative interviewing of child suspects is revealed to be a significant oversight. Such a blind spot for child suspects is hard to justify, given that, since 1992, child witnesses have had the benefit of interview by officers trained to elicit their best evidence.[130]

Such failures threaten a whole host of rights which should be enjoyed by the child, particularly their right to voice (UNCRC, Article 12), age-appropriate treatment, and fair trial (UNCRC, Article 40). But more substantively, they undermine the whole purpose of the process—the obtaining of reliable evidence. Indeed, unnecessarily adult tactics used by police in interview have the effect of driving some young suspects into a blanket position: 'I don't sit there and explain myself any more' (Harper); 'I just knew with my experience with these bastards—I just know you don't talk in there (the interview room)' (Malik). For these children, the interview process has

---

[128] See eg Medford, Gudjonsson, and Pearse (n 92).
[129] See for discussion Ceci and others (n 119).
[130] Home Office/Department of Health, 'Memorandum of Good Practice on Video Recorded Interviews with Child Witnesses for Criminal Proceedings' (HMSO 1992).

become wholly counterproductive—they do not participate effectively in the process and do not engage their right to give their account, whilst at the same time, the police do not obtain useful evidence by questioning. The drawing of an adverse inference in such circumstances is arguably the final flourish of unfairness.

Maintaining 'No Comment': Procedure and Existing Literature

What of those who have decided to exercise their right of silence in interview? Officers are entitled to continue to question a person making no comment. Indeed, APP makes plain that the officer has a 'responsibility' to do so as long as this is done in an 'effective and acceptable way'.[131] Research suggests that most officers do continue to question suspects exercising their right of silence so that the adverse inference can be drawn.[132]

Maintaining 'no comment' in the face of questioning has long been recognized to be challenging, requiring an 'abnormal exercise of will'.[133] This is not least because it violates conversational turn-taking.[134] Writing in the early 1990s, Moston and Engelberg[135] and McConville and Hodgson,[136] building on typologies developed previously by Moston,[137] identified a range of techniques used by the police to attempt to break the silence of suspects. These included 'downgrading' (asking about banal matters, such as personal habits or lifestyle, unconnected to the allegation) and 'upgrading' (questioning which underlines the seriousness of the offence or the suspect's involvement in it). Other techniques identified included persistence, 'rationalization' (commenting on the suspect's exercise of their right of silence in an attempt to rationalize against it), and interpreting non-verbal behaviour by the suspect, such as smiling. There are indications that these techniques have persisted following the introduction of the PEACE

---

[131] APP(I)(II) (n 2) 35.
[132] Quirk (n 10).
[133] Barrie Irving, 'Police Interrogation: The Psychological Approach', Royal Commission on Criminal Procedure Research Study Nos 1–2 (HMSO 1980) 153. See also Quirk (n 10).
[134] Elisabeth Carter, *Analysing Police Interviews: Laughter, Confessions and the Tape* (Bloomsbury 2011).
[135] Stephen Moston and Terry Engelberg, 'Police Questioning Techniques in Tape Recorded Interviews with Criminal Suspects' (1993) 3 Policing & Society 223.
[136] McConville and Hodgson (n 88) 141ff.
[137] Stephen Moston, 'The Ever-So-Gentle Art of Police Interrogation' (British Psychological Society Annual Conference, Swansea 1990).

method, including in interviewing children. Kemp and Hodgson's study revealed the use of some of these tactics with child suspects, particularly 'downgrading' and the interpretation of non-verbal behaviour.[138]

Maintaining 'No Comment': Child Suspect Experiences

Some young participants found maintaining 'no comment' to present few difficulties; for some it was even 'easy' (Nathan). These tended to be young people who had had several, often regular, experiences in custody. RHAA1 explained,

> They know exactly what ticks. When they get into an interview room they're not phased by it. You have to prove I'm guilty so I'm not gonna incriminate myself, I'll leave that for you and the investigation. So yeah, some are just really clued up.

But for others this was more of a challenge. In line with Kemp and Hodgson's findings,[139] young participant accounts suggest that several of the tactics long identified as being used in adult interviews are also adopted where children make no comment. In particular, young participants complained of questioning approaches identifiable as 'downgrading'. Aidan had quite clearly spotted the tactic: 'they ask you questions that you'd know, you know what I mean, that you know, and you know you can answer, but you don't, you do not want to slip up'. Kate offered examples of the sort of banal questions she was asked: 'Have you got a grey hoodie on? Have you got Facebook? Have you got a phone?' She described her response:

> They're trying to slip me up ... they were trying to provoke me and they were trying to get into my mind and like, 'Well, we'll play you. We'll reverse it on you, make you spit sommat out, say something.'

Several solicitors stated that they would interject to remind their client of their advice in such circumstances but often relayed that the child would return to 'no comment' only to find that the officer would 'do it again' (Sol12).

---

[138] Kemp and Hodgson (n 52). See also Quirk (n 10) 80.
[139] Kemp and Hodgson (n 52).

Several young participants felt that officers had deliberately tried to provoke them into answering a question by using tactics that are identifiable as a form of 'upgrading'. Zayn described being made to feel uncomfortable making no comment: 'when they're shouting, they're trying to make you feel bad about something and they think they're smart'. Alex described feeling provoked: 'they will say something that they know will aggravate you, so they like to get a reaction out of you, so it is hard, yeah . . . Sometimes, I feel I just wanna answer.' He and Zayn had resisted the temptation to respond, but Malik, for example, described being caught out when the interviewer asked him about how he 'felt about' the complainants in respect of a serious assault allegation. He recounted, 'This was the only question that hit me. I go "No comment", but I go, "Are they alright?" Do you get me? I don't wanna talk to you, but if I could say sorry, I'm sorry to [them].'

Azade identified another tactic familiar from adult interviews: the interpretation of non-verbal behaviour. She was incensed that, during a 'no comment' interview, the officer had tried to suggest that she was smiling, putting her, she felt, in a very difficult position: 'so obviously when I don't actually say, "I'm not smiling", the judge is gonna think or like have a picture in her head, saying, "Oh, (Azade)'s smiling, she taking this as a joke fam."' She also complained of persistence, describing an interviewing officer in a 'no comment' interview asking, ' "Why didn't you say sorry?" She asked me that about ten times.' She explained that the interview became very confrontational as she struggled to control her feelings. Indeed, a number of young participants related how hard they found it to stick to 'no comment' in the face of persistent questioning because of the twin challenges of containing their emotions and maintaining focus. Kate was worried that she would 'slip up a bit . . . snap and get annoyed and [say], "No that never happened" or sommat' but had been able to maintain her stance. Michael had more difficulty: 'Like for the first couple of questions like I was like "No comment" and then I was like "In my house", then "No comment", "In my house", you know what I mean?' These difficulties might be said to reflect the 'abnormal exercise of will' required of a silent suspect of any age.[140] However, for young suspects, such self-control can be developmentally more challenging; their capacity for self-regulation increasing gradually over adolescence.[141]

---

[140] Irving (n 133) 153.
[141] Sarah-Jayne Blakemore, 'Avoiding Social Risk in Adolescence' (2018) 27 Current Directions in Psychological Science 116.

Solicitors generally took the view that maintaining silence was more challenging for children than adults. Several referred in particular to the natural difficulties for a child of not answering questions asked by an adult; the power differential between the adult in authority and the child exacerbating the difficulty of breaching turn-taking. Sandor described the pressure to defer to an adult officer: 'I just feel like if I say, "No comment" then I'd be holding them back, not working with them, not being polite.' Some solicitors described specifically preparing their younger clients for a 'no comment' interview with this in mind:

> I say, 'Look, you're going to find this difficult because this officer is a grown up and he's asking you questions and you're going to think, "Oh I should be polite, I'll get into trouble if I don't answer grown ups' questions."' I say, 'You know he's not your family, he's not your friend—I'm your only friend. He's out to get you.'
>
> (Sol8)

VAA2 also picked up on the difficulty of resisting the temptation to defer to adults: 'I say about 'no comment', "The officer won't mind—he's used to no comment."' Another solicitor noted the challenge for suspects, but particularly children, of the interview format itself, moving from the preliminary part of the interview, where questions had to be answered (the client's name, date of birth, and understanding of the caution) to the body of the interview, where they were able to choose to reply. She felt it helped to draw this out in a visual diagram to assist her clients (Sol12).

Far from approaching the silence of a young suspect in a child friendly manner, young participant and solicitor accounts suggest that some officers engage in exactly the sort of tactics that they might use in challenging an adult. It seems that neither PEACE interview training nor the exhortation for special care to be taken with child interviewing have eradicated such practices in child interviewing. Whilst often 'effective' in terms of eliciting a response, such tactics can hardly be described as 'acceptable'[142] where they exploit the power differential between interviewer and child and fail to accommodate—indeed, even exploit—the child's natural developmental immaturity. Not only does this undermine the child's right to silence, but it

---

[142] APP(I)(II) (n 2) 35.

also tends to add to young participants' views that the police are operating in an underhand, unfair way, attempting to 'trip' and 'twist' them, rather than being engaged in a fair exchange.

Interview Protections: Procedure and Existing Literature

The prevalence of concerning and coercive interview tactics brings to the fore the question of support in interview: the contribution of the solicitor and the AA. Previous research into the effect of the presence of a solicitor in interview, although much now of some age, generally paints a fairly mixed picture. Evans, in his 1993 study, found that solicitors attended interviews in 11% of the 164 cases that he reviewed; in half of these, police used oppressive tactics and obtained a confession, and in only one interview did a solicitor intervene. Ten years later, Medford and others' study identified more positively that suspects were significantly more likely to make admissions when no legal representative was present.[143] More recently, in Kemp and Hodgson's examination of nine young suspect interviews involving a solicitor, the solicitor intervened in eight cases, including providing advice and requiring a break for consultation, as well as intervening to object to a line of questioning, although the researchers did not conclude, in every case, that the intervention had been appropriate or effective.[144] We have less information about how young suspects themselves experienced legal support in the interrogation itself. The five-strong focus group of young participants in Kemp and Hodgson's study are reported as being complimentary about solicitors' support in interview, especially where police were trying to 'twist their words' or 'trip them up',[145] whilst Hazel and colleagues uncovered a 'heavy reliance' on the solicitor when present, although they do not provide further detail of how this manifested itself.[146]

The AA role in interview has several aspects, according to *Code C*. They are not expected simply to observe but to advise the child, observe whether the interview is being conducted 'properly and fairly', and facilitate communication between child and officer.[147] However, the inefficacy of AAs in

---

[143] Medford, Gudjonsson, and Pearse (n 92).
[144] Kemp and Hodgson (n 52).
[145] ibid 141.
[146] Hazel (n 104).
[147] *Code C* (n 13), para 11.17.

the interviews of young suspects has long been a subject of concern, not least because their presence bestows a 'degree of respectability' on what may otherwise be an unfair interview.[148] It can be challenging for a lawyer to identify inappropriate questioning,[149] let alone an AA. Indeed, Canadian research has called into question, in particular, parents' ability to insulate young suspects in interview from the negative effects of their knowledge deficits and vulnerability to coercion.[150]

Interview analysis research has consistently revealed that AAs rarely intervene in interview,[151] although familial or untrained AAs tend to contribute more frequently than trained or professional AAs.[152] Even where they do intervene, AAs have been found to do so both appropriately and inappropriately, whether trained or untrained,[153] and, unsurprisingly, their presence has not been found to have a significant effect on the rate of admissions.[154] Indeed, Evans's study found that, in 62% of cases where a professional AA (at that time, generally a residential or specialist social worker) attended, the police obtained a confession using persuasive tactics.[155] Nonetheless, Medford and colleagues found that the AA's presence alone in interview appeared to have a 'decisive effect on the behaviour of the police and the legal representative'.[156] There is very little existing literature examining the views of young suspects themselves in relation to the assistance of AAs in interview. Hazel and colleagues' research suggests that young suspects felt significant pressure as a result of the presence of parents in interview,[157] whilst the young participants in Kemp and Hodgson's research seemed to view the AA as not contributing significantly to the interview.[158]

---

[148] Medford, Gudjonsson, and Pearse (n 92) 263.
[149] Kemp and Hodgson (n 52).
[150] Jennifer Woolard and others, 'Examining Adolescents' and Their Parents' Conceptual and Practical Knowledge of Police Interrogation: A Family Dyad Approach' (2008) 37 Journal of Youth and Adolescence 685.
[151] Evans, 'The Conduct of Police Interviews' (n 86); Medford, Gudjonsson, and Pearse (n 92); Megan Sim, 'Appropriate Adults' Contributions during Police Interviews with Juveniles (23rd Conference of the European Association of Psychology and Law, Coventry 2013).
[152] Evans, 'The Conduct of Police Interviews' (n 86); Sim (n 151).
[153] Sim (n 151).
[154] Medford, Gudjonsson, and Pearse (n 92).
[155] Evans, 'The Conduct of Police Interviews' (n 86).
[156] Medford, Gudjonsson, and Pearse (n 92) 262.
[157] Hazel (n 104).
[158] Kemp and Hodgson (n 52).

Interview Protections: Child Suspect Experiences

Solicitors

Not all young participants in the current study opted for legal advice and certainly not on every occasion. Nonetheless, their accounts provide some evidence of the positive effect of having a solicitor in interview, and in which respects they found them most helpful. A significant number of the young participants who had requested a solicitor commented positively on their support in interview. Simon, for example, related how effectively a solicitor could prevent officers using manipulative tactics: 'with a solicitor there they can't say anything, they can't push the things they wanna do and you know, bad things they can't do that, so it excludes them, you know, not abusing their position'. Several young participants described solicitors preventing officers asking repetitive questions, in particular, asking the interviewer to 'move on' in the questioning (Alex, Jo). Young participants also referred to solicitors identifying, and putting a stop to, the asking of irrelevant (particularly personal) questions. Some others appreciated solicitors helping them to avoid incriminating themselves unduly in interview, even where this was done forcefully. Avery, for example, described approvingly having received 'a proper kick under the table' from her solicitor when she was being 'cheeky' in interview or allowing her frustration to take over. Solicitors could also be useful when the young person could not understand a question. Hussain reported, 'when I had a solicitor near me... I would just ask him "What's he talking about?"... and then they fully explained it to me.' Solicitors who could balance the power differential to a degree, or enable agency, were especially welcomed. Dexter, for example, particularly appreciated that his solicitor would just 'tell 'em [the officers] straight' when he was not happy with the questioning, whilst Jo described with approval a solicitor who had suggested a mechanism which gave him a sense of control, tapping on the table to indicate that he wanted to have a break in the interview.

However, there were also indications in the data that the solicitor was not always an effective protection from oppressive interview tactics. A significant proportion of those who experienced coercive tactics reported having solicitors in interview who, it is plain, did not prevent inappropriate questioning. Logan, for example, recounted feeling so pressurized that he was tempted to provide false admissions: 'I felt like lying once and saying, "Yeah,

I did do it." But I just asked to speak to me solicitor and then I just said to 'im and 'e just went in and said … "Don't answer questions." ' It is fortunate that the solicitor drew the interview to a close but concerning that he or she left it to Logan to ask for a break when he was plainly feeling extremely pressurized. Sometimes, the AA was left to take the initiative. Kate, for example, described an interview where officers made lengthy and repeated attempts to break her silence. The solicitor did not object and the interview only ended after the AA intervened saying, 'This is getting ridiculous now.'

Non-familial AAs

The picture of AA engagement and support in interview is similarly mixed. In line with these findings, non-familial AAs in this study suggested that they rarely intervened in police interviews. VAA4's observation was fairly typical: 'I've not had much call to intervene in all honesty in police interviews—they're not kindly but they're not confrontational.' PAA5, a very experienced AA, reflected similarly: 'it's not very often you have to intervene. Very occasionally I would—when the juvenile doesn't understand, only two or three in all the time I've been doing it.' No young participant volunteered an example of a non-familial AA spontaneously intervening. Indeed, in contrast to reflections on familial AA interventions, there did not seem to be any assumption on the part of young participants that non-familial AAs would, or should, intervene on their behalf. Tom, for example, felt that their non-familial AA was 'just sitting there 'cause I needed someone there 'cause I was under eighteen … I think he was just there for the legal side of it.'

Two features emerge from the data which may provide some explanation as to why there is so little intervention by non-familial AAs. The first relates to their understanding of appropriate interviewing and the point at which they should intervene. YOTAA, for example, explained that his role was ensuring

> that the interview goes how it should go, and there's no intimidation, there's no violence, no force, no threats involved. It's gonna be a police interview, which means they're trying to catch somebody out so they will ask repeat questions, and they will ask some questions that you may not think are relevant but they have other information that you're not aware of.

His threshold for intervention was plainly extremely high, and his inclination seemed to be more supportive of police objectives than of the young person.

The second issue arises from the relationship between the role of solicitor and the AA. Commentators have previously identified some overlap between the two roles in terms of monitoring appropriate questioning,[159] and there are indications in the data that deference to the solicitor's expertise may lead to hesitance, even passivity, on the part of the non-familial AA. PAA1, for example, explained that when officers 'ask the same question three to four times in a different way', the solicitor will intervene; she continued, 'I have the right to step in and say something too, *if the solicitor doesn't*' (my emphasis). Likewise, with supporting comprehension, non-familial AAs tended to describe leaving it to officers or solicitors in the first instance.

Familial AAs

Young participants were more likely to comment spontaneously on the intervention of familial AAs. A number recounted very positively their familial AA's intervention in interview, with some suggesting that they always got involved. For example, Aidan explained of his Mum, 'If she didn't like a question that they ask me, she'd step up on it, and like she'd stop the recording ... and we'd go for a talk.' Familial AAs themselves also commented on intervening. This tended to be, they suggested, where the young person did not appear to understand.

Yet, the very closeness which makes the familial AA a welcome support for many young suspects, and an engaged observer of the process, can nevertheless result in an intervention which is problematic in tone, misguided, or unhelpful to the defence position. Several participants described interventions which, whilst triggered by apparent improper pressure, were couched in emotive terms liable to be problematic. Elijah, for example, described his Mum intervening by saying, ' "Because, if you are accusin' my son of doin' somethin' that he isn't, then I'm takin' you to court, 'cause that's offensive. You're pinnin' it on my son that he's a drug dealer before he can even answer." ' Whilst appreciating the emotional situation for the parent,

---

[159] See eg Gudjonsson, *Psychology of Interrogations* (n 37).

one can see how such interventions might raise the tension of the interview and trigger an officer to seek to curtail entirely the AA's involvement. Kaiden described having stopped a particular family member acting as AA because he was 'just too feisty'. Familial AAs could also, because of their lack of appreciation of the adversarial nature of the process, intervene in a way which was unhelpful in terms of the young person's legal interests. Sol2 recounted, 'They can interject in interview—say, "Don't forget to tell the officer about X" and that can be a problem.' IO3 made a similar observation: 'It can be the case that the juvenile says nothing and then the mother uses a couple of expletives and then says his life is over and he may as well tell the truth, and then she comes up with all of it.' Neither solicitors nor interviewing officers displayed much patience when they recalled their dealings with familial AAs in interview, nor appeared to value their contributions.[160]

However, what is most striking in the findings is not so much the challenge of intervening appropriately but rather the familial AA's inability to hold the officers to account where they had identified a problem. The adversarial nature of the interview means that, for some, their lack of professional expertise, and their alignment with the suspect in the eyes of the officer, makes them liable to coercion themselves, as observed in Canadian research.[161] Several young participants and familial AAs complained of officers preventing the AA's involvement, in some instances apparently inappropriately curtailing the exercise of proper support. Riley, for example, described his grandfather 'objecting to the way they was just puttin' pressure on me constantly', but he had been stopped by the officer. Riley noted, 'They said he can get involved if they say anything he doesn't like, but then when he got involved, they said he was answering questions for me.' Likewise FAA1, for example, described interjecting to support her son's understanding: 'therefore I just step in and I interpret it my way... then [he] understands it straight away. And then I'm told to be quiet.' Although the officer had explained her role at the beginning of the interview, on intervening, she had been told that she was there 'as an appropriate adult only' and that it was not her place to get involved in questioning. FAA1 reflected, 'So they do contradict themselves quite a lot.' These findings tend to support previous observations in Kemp and Hodgson's research of officers responding negatively to interventions by AAs.[162]

---

[160] As also observed in APPGC (n 47).
[161] Woolard and others (n 150).
[162] Kemp and Hodgson (n 52).

A solicitor, independent custody visitor (ICV), or even non-familial AA, who found their legitimate role curtailed, might feel empowered to object. By contrast, as explored in Chapter 4, a familial AA is not always aware that they have been inappropriately silenced, and even less likely to feel able to challenge the officer or to pursue a complaint. As with other aspects of the custody process, the power imbalance between family member and officer, the unfamiliar demands of the process, and the fraught nature of the interrogation coalesce to undermine the effectiveness of the protection.

Conclusion

Reviewing the findings of this analysis in light of the theoretical framework set out in Chapter 1, I consider, in closing, whether the police interview process and related protections operate effectively to ensure that the evidence obtained is as reliable and accurate as possible. I ask, in particular, whether the protections are effective in safeguarding against unreliable forms of evidence and in regulating the investigation. I also reflect on whether the procedures operate fairly in practice so that children feel treated with dignity and enabled to exercise their rights, here in particular, their right to participate effectively in their questioning and to maintain silence if that is their choice. Although there is some evidence of good practice, of young participants treated in an age-appropriate way who felt able to advance their account effectively, such positive interactions are few and far between. The majority of young participants describe the experience of interview in extremely negative terms and provide compelling evidence that their effective participation was severely challenged by their physical and emotional state and by the very adult, and often oppressive, interviewing techniques that many encountered.

In terms of safeguarding against unreliable forms of evidence, the data raises concerns that FFI processes may be failing to identify all those who are unfit and to ensure suitable adjustments for those who may be at risk of giving unreliable answers in interview. A number of different challenges arise. In particular, although *Code C*, Annex G sets out in some detail what aspects the CO should consider, the evidence suggests that the full test is not always applied and that an assessment of fitness to be interviewed is rarely fully engaged in the case of a young child, particularly in light of the ubiquitous presence of the AA. Mandatory training in child development and prevalent conditions giving rise to participation difficulties would undoubtedly support COs to make better decisions around FI. However, a significant proportion of the problems revealed by this study stem from, or are significantly exacerbated by, the fact that the assessment of the child, and the provision of appropriate support, occurs in the resource- and time-constrained setting of the custody block. The young suspect is not in a state of mind, or an environment, conducive to engaging with meaningful assessment of their functional capacity, whilst those conducting the assessment lack child and adolescent expertise. The necessary background information is hard to obtain in time, and where specific support is required (an intermediary, for example), it will often be impracticable to arrange it within a time frame that is manageable for a child being detained in a cell and the CO watching the PACE clock.

Despite the promise of PEACE interviewing, the accounts of young participants suggest that case construction, and in particular the obtaining of a confession, remain prominent police objectives in child suspect interviews. The overwhelming thrust of the accounts in this study suggest that the legal framework does not effectively regulate this aspect of the investigation such that many interviewing officers fail to show the 'special care' required in Code C, NFG 11C, or to question child suspects in a 'child friendly' manner. This is disappointing, given that the requirement for adjustment to the needs of young suspects could not be more clearly or more frequently restated—in domestic legislation,[163] guidance,[164] National Police Chiefs' Council strategies,[165] domestic and European case law,[166] and international conventions and guidelines.[167] However, it is, at the same time, entirely unsurprising since there is no general requirement for interviewing officers to have specific training in techniques for interviewing children. The fact that this is the case, despite the guidance for vulnerable (prosecution) witness interviewing having been in place for almost thirty years,[168] illustrates that the indifference to the child suspect's difficulties in interview does not stem from individual officers but reflects an institutionalized, adversarial

---

[163] See eg Equality Act 2010, s 19.
[164] See eg APP(I)(II) (n 2).
[165] See eg National Police Chiefs' Council, 'National Strategy for the Policing of Children and Young People' (NPCC 2016) 8 <https://www.npcc.police.uk/SysSiteAssets/media/downloads/publications/publications-log/local-policing-coordination-committee/national-strategy-for-the-policing-of-children-young-people.pdf> accessed 19 August 2023.
[166] *R on the Application of HC (a child by his litigation friend CC) v Secretary of State for the Home Department* [2013] EWHC 982 (Admin), [2014] 1 WLR 1234 [63]; *Panovits v Cyprus* (n 32).
[167] See eg the Beijing Rules (n 66) and General Comment No 24 (n 67).
[168] Since the Home Office/Department of Health (n 130).

approach to child suspects. It is difficult to conclude that the child suspect is approached in interview with dignity and respect for them as rights holders when the protections for them fall so far short of those available to child witnesses. The lack of comparable adjustment for child suspects undermines the aspiration for fairness and lack of prejudice in the interview process set out in APP.[169]

Young participants' reflections on the contributions of their solicitors during interview suggest that a good solicitor can provide significant and vital assistance to a child in interview: curtailing oppressive questioning techniques, supporting communication, and providing young suspects with some sense of control. However, in the first instance, as discussed in Chapter 3, too many young suspects refuse legal advice. Even for those who do engage that support, the prevalence of coercive techniques in young participant accounts of police interview suggest that not every solicitor is as engaged, or perhaps as skilled, as they need to be to protect their young clients. The findings underline the importance of legal representation for every young suspect sufficiently resourced to ensure expert and timely support.

As with other aspects of the custody process, the evidence in respect of the contribution of the AA to interview is mixed. It is concerning to have received so little positive material about non-familial AAs in interview. It may be that their engagement recedes in the memory of a young participant more quickly than more emotive recollections of the officer's questioning or parental intervention. Nonetheless, it is clear that further research is required to understand whether the non-familial AA's efficacy is undermined by the overlapping of their role with that of the solicitor. Additionally, their apparent difficulties in identifying oppressive techniques do call into question whether it is realistic to require a lay person, even one with training, to monitor whether the interview is being conducted 'fairly and properly'.[170] By contrast, the familial AA's contribution in interview reveals, as elsewhere in the process, the tension between the substantial support they can often provide by virtue of their emotional connection with the young suspect and the challenge of fulfilling that role without training or professional standing. The protection provided by the AA is, at best, highly variable, and at worst, their presence is liable to mask difficulties and legitimize unfair processes.

---

[169] APP(I)(II) (n 2) 4 (Principle 2).
[170] *Code C* (n 13), para 11.17.

In light of the limited impact of the protections, young participants' accounts indicate that adversarial and coercive approaches in interview are liable to cause confusion and frustration rather than to elicit reliable evidence. They may lead to the child exercising their right to silence, or worse, making false admissions to bring the process to an end. Indeed, as discussed in the introduction, these techniques have been associated in psychological research with false confessions, especially where used against children.[171] The wrongful convictions of the young suspects in the *Confait* case,[172] and miscarriages of justice in other jurisdictions, such as the *Central Park Jogger* case,[173] illustrate all too clearly the danger of eliciting evidence from a child suspect using age-inappropriate questioning techniques. Those dangers are likely to be exacerbated where the child has endured many hours in effective solitary confinement, when they are exhausted, hungry, and desperate to leave custody. Indeed, a number of young participants suggest that, having endured such questioning once, they tended to make no comment on later occasions. It seems that solicitors, too, may, in light of such approaches, be inclined to advise no comment unless a caution is the likely outcome. Quantitative research is needed to examine the rate at which young suspects make no comment in police custody and the frequency with which young people answer questions in full in interview to matters which are not resolvable by caution. However, this study suggests that the rate at which child suspects opt for silence is likely to be considerably higher than that of adult suspects. The findings indicate clearly that coercive techniques have the capacity to undermine the whole purpose of the interview and, indeed, the entire detention process by compromising the reliability of answers, when given, or pushing the child and their representative into exercising their right to silence.

Turning to whether the procedures operate fairly in practice, it is plain that the approaches described by young participants often severely compromised their right to participate effectively in the process and could hardly be described as treating them with dignity and due regard for their needs. As with their accounts of detention in the cell, their reflections on police interview pulsated with resentment and negative characterizations of a process which was commonly perceived to be unfair. Young participants described variously how, in interview, they felt targeted (Alex),

---

[171] See eg Redlich and Goodman (n 100).
[172] Fisher (n 11).
[173] Feld (n 12).

manipulated (Zayn), lied to (Elijah), wound up (Logan), provoked (Kate), tripped up (Kyle), tricked (Sadie), mixed up (Rezar), caught out (Abigail), intimidated (Simon), patronized (Harper), pressurized (Riley), baited (Luke), and egged on (Nathan). The stifling of the child's voice, and an apparent refusal to listen to their side of the story, was particularly resented.

In short, the interview process as currently implemented is liable to be thoroughly counterproductive, both in failing to guard adequately against unreliable evidence, or cornering the child into silence, and by alienating the young suspect and undermining, in their eyes, the legitimacy of the police. It is clear that, to a considerable degree, the shortcomings of the interview process and protections arise because the interview is undergone, and the protections engaged with, in the custody environment. The idea that the investigation, and the wider purposes of the youth justice process, are best served by custodial interview is revealed to be a misconception. Much more is lost by custodial interviewing than is likely to be gained. In all but the most serious cases, there is a compelling argument that child suspects should be bailed to attend for interview or invited to attend voluntarily at an appointed time, enabling, in the interim, their fitness for interview to be suitably assessed and for additional support to be arranged, where that is required. Ideally, where the young suspect is previously unknown to the youth justice system, a screening appointment with L&D in the community could be arranged in advance of interview to identify if there are any pre-existing dispositional difficulties which give rise to fitness concerns. For those without such difficulties, interview by arrangement would allow them to attend for questioning in a physical and emotional state which is more conducive to giving a good account of themselves in interview. It would enable them to receive legal advice at a time when they are able to appreciate their options and make the decisions required of them, and when they can be accompanied by an AA who is better placed to support them during the process. Such an approach would treat the child as a 'child first' and would enable them to engage with the process of giving their account as a child witness does. Fairness and equity, intended to be central principles in investigative interviewing,[174] demand nothing less.

---

[174] APP(I)(II) (n 2) 4 (Principle 2).

7
Conclusion
Rethinking the Use of Police Custody for Children

> There has to be a different way. Why don't we have a different system?
>
> (CO40)

How Far Have We Really Come Since *Confait*?

I return, in closing, to the question posed in the preface: how far have we really come in the fifty years since the *Confait* suspects were in police detention? To answer the question meaningfully, we need first to place it in context. The fifty years since the *Confait* suspects were arrested have seen the ratification and adoption of the UN Convention on the Rights of the Child (UNCRC) and the incorporation into domestic law of the European Convention on Human Rights by means of the Human Rights Act 1998. We have seen the development of the concept of effective participation[1] and the introduction of adjustments for vulnerable defendants within the trial process,[2] albeit still lagging behind the protections now available for young and vulnerable witnesses. Since the late 1970s, clinical research has revolutionized our understanding of child development and the impact of various dispositional vulnerabilities and psycho-social adversities on children's experiences of, and engagement with, legal processes.[3] At the same time, social psychologists have developed the concept of procedural justice, and its

---

[1] *SC v United Kingdom* App no 60958/00, 10 November 2004 (2005) 40 EHRR 10; example *T v United Kingdom* App no 24724/94, 16 December 1999 and *V v United Kingdom* App no 24888/94, 16 December 1999, reported as a joint decision in (2000) 30 EHRR 121.

[2] See eg Criminal Procedure Rules October 2020 as amended February 2021 and April 2021, Part 18 Criminal Practice Directions—October 2015 as amended April 2016, November 2016, January 2017, April 2018, October 2018, April 2019, October 2019, May 2020 and October 2020 (Crim PD), 3D.2; *R v Lubemba* [2014] EWCA Crim 2064, [2015] 1 WLR 1579, [45].

[3] See for discussion Lamb and others, 'Developmental Factors Affecting Children in Legal Contexts' (2013) 13 Youth Justice 131.

importance for policing is now widely understood.[4] In short, the landscape of criminal justice has changed profoundly. We understand much better why effective engagement in criminal justice processes is so important for children, how that becomes challenged, and what the ramifications of falling short might be, as well as having domestic and international standards to light the way in terms of fair trial and participation rights.

It is disappointing, therefore, to find that, although the *Confait* case, and the ensuing Fisher Report,[5] were instrumental in triggering the Royal Commission on Criminal Procedure[6] and the subsequent Police and Criminal Evidence Act 1984 (PACE), the position of children in police custody has, in practice, only minimally improved. No research can capture the whole picture, and, inevitably, there will be substantial variations across force areas and different custody episodes, even between the approaches taken on different shifts. Nonetheless, this study indicates that we cannot comfort ourselves that the police custody process now functions in a way which reliably insulates young suspects against the sort of unfairness experienced by the *Confait* suspects. Nor does it appear that there has been wholesale improvement in practice in the years since the fieldwork for this study was conducted. Findings from Kemp and others' more recent fieldwork indicate a similarly bleak picture.[7]

The examination of the early stages of custody in Chapter 2 suggests that today's young suspects, in contrast to the *Confait* suspects, will almost certainly be informed of their 'continuing rights' and, in particular, their right to legal advice.[8] However, young participant accounts suggest that the child suspect is rarely in a state of mind conducive to absorbing the volume of new information delivered at this stage. Often reeling from an arrest process

---

[4] Tom R Tyler, Jeffrey Fagan, and Amanda Geller, 'Street Stops and Police Legitimacy: Teachable Moments in Young Urban Men's Legal Socialization: Street Stops and Police Legitimacy' (2014) 11 Journal of Empirical Legal Studies 751.

[5] Sir Henry Fisher, 'Report of an Inquiry by the Hon. Sir Henry Fisher into the Circumstances Leading to the Trial of Three Persons on Charges Arising Out of the Death of Maxwell Confait and the Fire at 27 Doggett Road, London SE6' (HMSO 1977).

[6] Royal Commission on Criminal Procedure (RCCP), 'Report (Cmnd 8092)' (HMSO 1981).

[7] Vicky Kemp and others, *Examining the Impact of PACE on the Detention and Questioning of Child Suspects by the Police in England and Wales* (Nuffield Foundation, 25 May 2023) <https://www.nuffieldfoundation.org/project/impact-of-pace-on-the-detention-and-questioning-of-young-suspects> accessed 10 October 2023.

[8] *Code C: Revised Code of Practice for the Detention, Treatment and Questioning of Persons by Police Officers* (updated 4 November 2020), para 3.1 (In force at time of writing. Any relevant variance with the version in force at time of fieldwork, published May 2014, will be noted as it arises.)

itself untailored to accommodate their needs, they undergo a lengthy and intrusive booking-in and risk assessment process, commonly in the presence or earshot of other suspects and officers unconnected to their arrest. The requirements in the College of Policing's Authorised Professional Practice (APP) that child suspects be prioritized[9] are infrequently met, and children could be exhausted before these initial stages had been completed. Young participants made plain that a custody officer (CO) who was friendly and non-judgemental could make all the difference. However, too many related treatment that they experienced as disrespectful or antagonistic. In short, the reduction, as far as possible, of 'feelings of intimidation and inhibition', the initial step to fostering effective participation, is rarely achieved, with significant impact on the child's ability to appreciate and exercise their rights.

The ramifications of these untailored early processes are evident in the challenges young participants related in engaging their legal rights. Whilst today, the offer of legal advice is routinely made, we see, in Chapter 3, that the requirement for the child to request legal advice results in many young people declining a solicitor, frequently because of their lack of appreciation of the need for, and benefit of, legal advice, or through desperation to get out of police custody as soon as possible, or both. The findings illustrate that the emphasis on the child's autonomy as a legal actor is inadequately supported by age-appropriate explanation of the child's legal jeopardy and the ramifications of their various options. As a result, too often, child suspects, especially those like Ahmet Saleh and Ronald Leighton, who had previous experience in police custody, are today likely to decline legal advice. Even where they do request a solicitor, young participant accounts reveal that frequently, by the time the solicitor arrives, often many hours into a detention episode, their willingness to provide full instructions and their capacity to weigh complex advice is fundamentally undermined by their exhaustion and the adversarial context of the process. Whilst, on paper, today's young suspects appear to be advantaged by a statutory right to be informed of, and request, legal advice, in practice, many are not able to engage effectively with, and benefit from, this key right.

---

[9] APP (Detention and Custody) (Response, Arrest and Detention) (first published 23 October 2013, last modified 28 June 2022) 6 <https://www.college.police.uk/app/detention-and-custody/response-arrest-and-detention> accessed 20 August 2023. (Any variance between current APP versions and those in force at the time of the fieldwork will be noted as it arises.)

Of course, the major change for child suspects achieved by PACE and *Code C* is the mandatory provision of an appropriate adult (AA) to protect the interests of the child in police custody and during interview. As identified in Chapter 4, the role, as currently formulated, correctly identifies the key areas of assistance that children in police custody require: welfare support and reassurance, help with understanding and exercising rights, oversight of due process on their behalf, and support with communication. However, it is clear, from this study, that very rarely will a single individual be able to fulfil all the required functions and that the protection is undermined by the inherent contradictions and conflicts which arise from combining welfare and due process responsibilities within a single role. Additionally, the fact that this extraordinarily demanding role is required to be fulfilled by a lay person, often without any experience of police process or, conversely, with some training in the procedure but no knowledge of the child, makes a mockery of the protection. To undermine the position still further, the needs which the AA is intended to address plainly arise as soon as the child finds themselves in custody and persist until release. However, the AA's arrival is commonly significantly delayed and their access to the child severely curtailed. As a result, as I conclude in Chapter 4, too often, the role serves more to legitimize the process than to protect and enable the child suspect. As with legal rights, whilst, on paper, today's child suspect appears to enjoy much greater protection than the *Confait* suspects, in practice, the AA is rarely able to render the envisaged support. Indeed, as young participant accounts reveal, the presence of a parent or close relative can serve rather to stifle their voice, inhibit their legal agency, and distort the evidence obtained.

Whilst the major miscarriages of justice of the 1970s and '80s prompted the introduction of the PEACE interviewing approach,[10] the special risks involved in interviewing child suspects, raised so starkly by the *Confait* case, on the evidence of this and related research, have been barely addressed. A child facing a murder allegation would likely be interviewed today by an officer with high-level PEACE training by virtue of the nature of the allegation. Additionally, there is specific training for the interviewing

---

[10] Ray Bull, 'Police Investigative Interviewing' in Amina Memon and Ray Bull (eds), *Handbook of the Psychology of Interviewing* (Wiley 1999). The Acronym PEACE reflects the stages of the interviewing process: Perception and planning; Engage and explain; Account, clarification, challenge; Closure; Evaluation.

of child witnesses, which many officers have undertaken.[11] However, there still exists no training specific to the investigative interviewing of child suspects, nor is there any requirement for an officer interviewing a child to have had anything beyond the minimum level of PEACE training.[12] As a result, many child suspects, including those facing indictable-only and serious allegations, are highly likely to be interviewed by officers with no training tailored to ensure age-appropriate interviewing techniques. The interview will be audio recorded, but transcripts of it will very rarely be scrutinized in court. The accounts of young participants in this study indicate that the use of techniques associated with the eliciting of unreliable evidence persist; indeed, they might be described as commonplace. It seems that little progress has been made in light of the experiences of the *Confait* suspects in the intervening fifty years since the case, despite the advances in our understanding of communication difficulties[13] and the protections now afforded to child witnesses.

Perhaps more worrying still, although a test for assessing fitness to be interviewed now exists,[14] the evidence of this study suggests that it is not rigorously applied in light of the blanket presence of the AA, that risk assessment processes are not adjusted to identify such difficulties in child suspects, and that support for children with cognitive or communication difficulties in interview is woefully inadequate. A child with cognitive difficulties comparable to those experienced by Colin Lattimore would most likely be supported in interview by a parent or carer acting as AA or a trained AA but one lacking specific leaning disability expertise. Unlike a child witness, his or her chances of receiving specialist intermediary support, or more expert AA assistance,[15] to enable their effective participation in the interview are extremely slim. A child's ability, in those circumstances, to participate effectively in the interview—to be able to understand the 'broad thrust' of what is said in interview and to make decisions about how to answer questions based on a meaningful understanding of the ramifications

---

[11] Ministry of Justice (MoJ), 'Achieving Best Evidence in Criminal Proceedings' (MoJ/National Police Chiefs' Council 2022) <www.gov.uk/government/publications/achieving-best-evidence-in-criminal-proceedings> accessed 20 August 2023.

[12] Kate Gooch and Piers von Berg, 'What Happens in the Beginning, Matters in the End: Achieving Best Evidence with Child Suspects in the Police Station' (2019) 19 Youth Justice 85.

[13] Karen Bryan, Jackie Freer, and Cheryl Furlong, 'Language and Communication Difficulties in Juvenile Offenders' (2007) 42 International Journal of Language & Communication Disorders 505.

[14] *Code C* (n 8), Annex G.

[15] ibid; Notes for Guidance (NFG), 1D.

of their position and the options available to them—is severely challenged.[16] Sadly, liaison and diversion (L&D) practitioners, where present, do not seem to play an active role in fitness for interview (FI) assessment or the provision of assistance in interview. As one observed, 'Developmental issues, autism, Asperger's ... we're not equipped to deal with that in this sort of place' (L&D7).

To exacerbate matters, there is good evidence that the average time spent in police custody by child suspects has increased significantly in the past fifty years—from an average of seven hours when arriving without an AA in the late 1990s[17] to just under eleven hours in 2015,[18] to approximately eleven-and-a-half hours in 2019–21.[19] This study, with an average detention time of eleven-and-a-half hours on observation, suggests no improvement in those timescales. Granted, delays may often arise from the challenges of obtaining the required support or failures in other third-party services. However, the impact of lengthy detention periods has been brought to the fore in this study. In this regard, the modern suspect is commonly in a worse position at interview than their contemporary of the late 1970s, having spent many hours in the harsh, and sometimes distressing, confines of a cell. Young participant accounts in Chapter 6 reveal just how damaging such an experience can be to the child's later capacity to participate effectively in the interview process.

In short, despite the apparent improvements on paper, this study suggests that, in practice, the child suspect's position has improved very little in the fifty years since the *Confait* arrests. Whilst there appear to be some areas where better practice is pursued, the overwhelming thrust of young participants' accounts reveal that rarely will the three key elements for effective participation in proceedings be routinely achieved—adjusted treatment to cater for the child's particular needs and situational adversity, the fostering of understanding to enable informed exercise of legal rights, and the enabling of broad comprehension in interview to allow meaningful engagement. Set against our increased appreciation of the adversities they experience, and the presence of international and domestic obligations to ensure child friendly procedures which prioritize children's welfare,

---

[16] See *Panovits v Cyprus* App no 4268/04, 11 March 2009 (2008) 27 BHRC 464, [67].
[17] Coretta Phillips and David C Brown, 'Entry into the Criminal Justice System: A Survey of Police Arrests and Their Outcomes', Home Office Research Study 185 (Home Office 1998) 110.
[18] HM Inspectorate of Constabulary (HMIC), *The Welfare of Vulnerable People in Police Custody* (HMIC 2015) 83.
[19] Kemp and others (n 7) 39.

the lack of effective support for child suspects is, in my view, little short of scandalous.

In the following sections of this concluding chapter, I consider the effect of this lack of progress in the operation of the police custody process for children and then ask, as CO41 does in the epigraph, why it is that we have not made more progress. In the final sections, I consider what a 'different system', in the words of CO41, might look like. I close with some brief observations about the ramifications of the findings of this study for the youth justice process more widely.

Turning Youth Justice on Its Head: The 'Pains' of Police Custody

Evaluated in light of the theoretical framework set out in Chapter 1, the custody process falls far short of the twin aspirations for criminal procedure identified by Ashworth and colleagues: fair processes, protective of fundamental rights, which enable accurate determinations.[20] Police detention is arguably the high point of a child's legal jeopardy in criminal proceedings and their moment of greatest need for protection and support to exercise their rights effectively. However, as the foregoing summary outlines, police custody processes too often fail to protect children's fundamental rights, particularly their rights under UNCRC, Article 37 to be detained only as a 'last resort' and 'for the shortest appropriate period' and to be treated 'with humanity and respect' in an age-appropriate manner. The pre-charge process should impose the 'minimum burdens' on the suspect.[21] Indeed, arguably, where the suspect is a child, there should be an even greater watchfulness that their rights are not avoidably infringed or their future development tainted. This study reveals a process which, far from imposing the 'minimum burdens' on the child suspect, is often experienced as deeply punitive. As we saw in Chapters 2 and 5, rarely were the deprivations experienced by the child a necessary and proportionate response to the demands of the investigation and the need to protect the public. Too often, young participants felt that their treatment had been unduly harsh and disrespectful,

---

[20] Andrew Ashworth, *The Criminal Process: An Evaluative Study* (1st edn, OUP 1994)); Liz Campbell, Andrew Ashworth, and Mike Redmayne, *The Criminal Process* (5th edn, OUP 2019).
[21] Ashworth (n 20) 31.

and they reported a lack of understanding of their rights or that their efforts to exercise them had been frustrated. Despite the police's statutory duty to safeguard and promote the welfare of children in their care,[22] detention experiences tended to exacerbate and entrench disadvantage.

In this regard, the custody process stands in stark contrast to the wider youth justice system, which aims to take a 'child first' approach, prioritizing preventing offending through processes focused on rehabilitation and adjusted to accommodate the needs of children.[23] The police custody experience compares unfavourably, as young participants were keen to explain, with the youth justice system's most severe punishment, a custodial term; a punishment rightly reserved for those convicted of the most serious or repeated offending. Although, of course, much briefer, young participant accounts of the deprivations they experienced in police custody find clear correspondences with the deprivations or 'pains' experienced by sentenced prisoners, as developed in Sykes' classic work,[24] and by later commentators.[25] In particular, the fear triggered for young participants by the presence of adult suspects, and the anxiety arising from their uncertainty about the procedures and their likely impact on their lives, recalled the 'deprivation of security' complained of by Sykes's inmates.[26] Similarly, the removal of all personal belongings, and their distress at the lack of support provided to them in the cell, reflects the pain occasioned to sentenced prisoners through the 'deprivation of goods and services'.[27]

In purely temporal terms, a detention episode bears little comparison to even a short-term sentence. Nonetheless, the sudden and total nature of the 'deprivation of liberty' experienced in the cell was, for many young participants, deeply painful.[28] Indeed, their accounts recall in their intensity,

---

[22] See eg the Children Act 2004, s 11.
[23] Crime and Disorder Act 1998, Part III; see Youth Justice Board (YJB), 'Standards for Children in the Youth Justice System' (2019) 6 <https://assets.publishing.service.gov.uk/government/uploads/system/uploads/attachment_data/file/957697/Standards_for_children_in_youth_justice_services_2019.doc.pdf> accessed 20 August 2023.
[24] Gresham M Sykes, *The Society of Captives: A Study of a Maximum Security Prison* (OUP 1958) 64.
[25] See in relation to children and young people Mark Halsey, 'On Confinement: Resident and Inmate Perspectives of Secure Care and Imprisonment' (2007) 54 Probation Journal 338; Alexandra Cox, 'Doing the Programme or Doing Me? The Pains of Youth Imprisonment' (2011) 13 Punishment & Society 592; Kate Gooch, 'A Childhood Cut Short: Child Deaths in Penal Custody and the Pains of Child Imprisonment' (2016) 55 Howard Journal of Criminal Justice 278.
[26] Sykes (n 24) 76–78.
[27] ibid 67–70.
[28] ibid 65–67.

and often in the specific terminology used, those of children experiencing much longer periods of solitary confinement.[29] Finally, the profound sense of helplessness experienced by young participants, triggered by the extreme imbalance of power between child detainee and adult officer, recalls the 'deprivation of autonomy' so painful to Sykes's inmates.[30] In short, the punitive nature of the custody process in a sense turns the youth justice system on its head. Those who should experience its lightest touch, children as yet uncharged and presumed innocent, in fact endure, albeit briefly, its harshest treatment, otherwise retained only for the most serious of offenders.

However, yet more problematic is that the child suspect, in contrast to the sentenced prisoner, at the same time as experiencing these deprivations is expected to engage with a key phase of the justice process—investigative interview. As a result, far from being a process which supports the production of accurate determinations, young participant experiences explored in Chapters 3 and 6 reveal that the police custody and interview process too often risks the eliciting of unreliable evidence. Exhausted by their detention and desperate to go home, young participants commonly described refusing legal advice in the hope of swift release. Even where they did opt for assistance, they were often not in a state of mind to engage with their solicitor and to make reasoned decisions about any advice they received. Participating effectively in interview was, similarly, extremely difficult in light of lengthy periods in the cell. At the same time, confession-seeking tactics frustrated and confused young participants, rendering false confession more likely. Or such approaches simply drove some children to turn to no comment, even where they had an explanation to give. Thus, not infrequently, the deeply traumatic custody process, in fact, yielded no evidence at all. As a result, in addition to the pains experienced as a result of the deprivations of detention, the custody process, as currently implemented, runs the risk of adding the prospective pain of wrongful conviction to the immediate pains of the custody process for children.[31]

In addition, the disrespectful and disproportionately harsh treatment complained of by many young participants could have a significant and

---

[29] See eg Bronx Defenders, 'Voices from the Box: Solitary Confinement at Rikers Island' (Bronx Defenders 2014) <www.bronxdefenders.org/wp-content/uploads/2014/09/Voices-From-the-Box.pdf> accessed 20 August 2023.
[30] Sykes (n 24) 73–76.
[31] For discussion see Miranda Bevan, 'The Pains of Police Custody: A Recipe for Injustice and Exclusion?' (2022) 62 British Journal of Criminology 805, 815–16.

lasting wider impact. As I explored in Chapter 5, custody processes experienced as unfair and disrespectful could have a negative impact on young participants' views of the legitimacy of the police. Resentful and alienated by what they considered to be unjust treatment, young participants variously described a reduction in their trust in the police and in their willingness to cooperate with them or to rely on them for help. Such exclusionary impacts were not limited to young participants but were also reflected in the attitudes of parents involved as AAs and in the expectations of those entering police custody for the first time. For Sykes's prisoners, the pains of imprisonment tended to invoke feelings of 'personal inadequacy'.[32] By contrast, for young participants, the pains of police custody conveyed to them and their communities that they were not morally acceptable, were not persons of value in the eyes of the police. Thus, harsh detention experiences might be said to add the prospective pain of exclusion to the other pains of police custody.

In this study, such feelings of alienation were not disproportionately expressed by Black, Asian, or minority ethnic young participants (although the numbers are small). Nonetheless, the over-representation in police custody of children from these communities means that they are more likely to be exposed to such alienating experiences.[33] In light of the depleted levels of trust in the police and criminal justice process already experienced by these communities,[34] this outcome should be of particular concern. In essence, as currently implemented, police custody is, for children, too often a thoroughly counterproductive process, risking unjust outcomes and serving to alienate a cohort of the most disadvantaged children. Far from preventing offending, it is liable to interfere with efforts to engage with a child whose behaviour is of concern.

---

[32] Sykes (n 24) 79.

[33] Home Office, 'Police Powers and Procedures: Other PACE Powers, England and Wales, Year Ending 31 March 2022' (National Statistics 2022) <https://www.gov.uk/government/statistics/police-powers-and-procedures-other-pace-powers-england-and-wales-year-ending-31-march-2022/police-powers-and-procedures-other-pace-powers-england-and-wales-year-ending-31-march-2022> accessed 20 August 2023.

[34] David Lammy, 'The Lammy Review. An Independent Review into the Treatment of, and Outcomes for, Black, Asian and Minority Ethnic Individuals in the Criminal Justice System (MoJ 2017).

Why Has So Little Progress Been Made?

This worrying conclusion prompts an obvious question: why has so little progress been made for child suspects over the past fifty years? Why are the protections available to them so scant, so minimally implemented, and even where enacted, so ineffective? Undeniably, resourcing issues clearly contribute to the undermining of welfare and due process efforts. The lack of multi-agency support in the community was a factor in a number of avoidable detentions observed in this study.[35] Cuts to police funding were also felt, not only in terms of longer investigation times, which extended detention periods, but also in terms of the staffing of the block. With bigger, busier blocks, lower staffing levels, and more paperwork, the sheer pressure of the job was liable to overwhelm the effective implementation of protections. COs and custody assistants (CAs) were frequently doing their very best but without the resources to achieve positive outcomes. Under such pressures, PACE protections could easily be reduced to tick-box requirements as physical safety concerns, and institutional risks, were prioritized over the emotional well-being of the child suspect.

Limited resources also affected the capacity of other supportive adults, particularly solicitors and AAs, to fulfil their roles. Contractual arrangements and fixed fees for solicitors were widely acknowledged to have reduced their capacity to support child suspects beyond the immediate requirements of the interview. Their late arrival and swift departure, as identified in Chapter 3, means that they have little, if any, purchase on police decision-making in respect of authorisation or review of detention and very limited scope to enable young suspects' wider engagement with their rights or to support their understanding of the later stages of the process. Likewise, the contractual arrangements of scheme AAs were raised as a factor in their reduced presence in the custody suite and the limited hours of scheme operation, as seen in Chapter 4.

Finally, the physical facilities available to custody staff also played a part in exacerbating detention experiences. Even were a CO or CA to appreciate the ramifications of a particular developmental disorder, for example, there would be little scope for them to adjust the conditions of detention for a young suspect. In all blocks, there was a shortage of 'non-cell' accommodation and space for an AA to sit out with a child, and little means of adjusting

---

[35] See also observations about the lack of support from third-party agencies in Howard League for Penal Reform, *Child Arrests in England and Wales 2020* (Howard League 2021) 3.

the detention space itself. Coupled with this, the brief period which a custody episode spans brings its own difficulties. As we saw in Chapter 4, the brevity of an AA's time with a young suspect is problematic in terms of building rapport and identifying vulnerability. Likewise, in Chapter 6, we saw how the ticking PACE clock provides little scope for a fuller assessment of a young suspect's fitness for interview and that the arranging of an intermediary would be exceptionally difficult within such a short time span.

However, this study as a whole indicates that, even were these funding and facilities issues to be addressed, substantial difficulties would remain. This is because what lies at the heart of failures to protect young suspects are three inter-related issues which, in combination, obstruct progress: the adversity experienced by the child, the adversarial context of their detention, and the closed nature of the custody process. In short, the very issues which make protections for child suspects so vital are also those issues which challenge their effective implementation.

Adversity

As discussed in Chapter 1, in addition to their natural developmental immaturity and the situational adversity in which they find themselves, a child suspect is likely to be significantly disadvantaged on a number of measures in comparison to a child in the general population. Young participant accounts reveal how the custody process, as currently implemented, tends to magnify those disadvantages and hamper the effective functioning of the protections. Unadjusted booking-in processes meant that children with communication or cognitive difficulties were less likely to be aware of, and to be able to engage fully, the adjustments that would have supported their participation. Those who revealed a history of self-harm were likely to be subject to humiliating and traumatizing strip search. Those who had dispositional vulnerabilities, such as an autism spectrum condition or attention deficit hyperactivity disorder (ADHD), were more likely to experience detention in the cell as distressing and destabilizing and to respond in a problematic way. This, in turn, tended to trigger harsher responses, exhausting the child for the demands of solicitor consultation and interview.

Although the group of Black, Asian, and minority ethnic young participants in the study is small, and despite their sense, with the exception of the young Irish traveller, that ethnicity had no particular bearing on their treatment in police custody, there are indications throughout the analysis that ethnicity does also play a part in harsher custody experiences. Black, Asian, and minority ethnic participants were more likely to feel the need to assert themselves during heavy-handed arrests and were thus more likely to experience less accommodating treatment on arrival in the custody block. They were more likely to refuse legal advice and to hold back information in legal conference, and there are indications that they might struggle to engage with unfamiliar AAs of a different ethnicity. They were also more likely to be amongst those who considered that interviewing officers had deliberately deceived them during questioning. Finally, in line with Home Office experimental data, Black, Asian, and minority ethnic young participants were more likely, in this study, to experience longer detention times in comparison to their White peers.[36] Whilst this data is not generalizable, it indicates the complex processes by which discriminatory experiences, both prior to and during an arrest and detention episode, can interact to reproduce and entrench disadvantage in ways not immediately apparent to those experiencing it.

Even for those without additional difficulties to navigate, the situational adversity experienced by young suspects in the cell, resulting from the extreme power imbalance between child and adult officer in total control of that environment, tended to undermine children's faith in, and ability to engage, their rights. As explored in Chapter 5, where staff failed to respond, or respond consistently, to requests for help or information, child suspects, like the suspects in Choongh's study, displayed 'extreme scepticism about the utility of rights'.[37] Many experienced a pervasive sense of disempowerment and utter helplessness in custody, which had really profound implications for their understanding and engagement of their rights. At the same time, the child's natural developmental immaturity was, for some COs and staff, a particular reason for maintaining oppressive and unadjusted treatment, on the basis that a harsh detention episode could have a positive effect on a child. In particular, there was the sense that custody operated as a form of 'naughty step' (CO12), that a period might 'do the trick' (CA10) and set the young person 'on the right path' (CO34). Allied to this was the view expressed by some that custody has a role in teaching young people 'what is done when you have done something wrong' (CA21). We see, in this study, how such a view gives rise to an embedded sense of 'less eligibility',[38] where

---

[36] Home Office, 'Police Powers and Procedures' (n 33), table 2.4.
[37] Satnam Choongh, *Policing as Social Discipline* (Clarendon Press 1997) 177.
[38] Georg Rusche, *Punishment and Social Structure* (Columbia University Press 1939).

the affording of comforts and support, being too 'warm and fluffy' (CO12), is considered to undermine the power and purpose of the custodial episode. As Kyle observed, 'That's what they're trying to do like, make you feel it's a bad, bad place, so you don't ever come back.' In this thinking, a rights violation is understood as a 'courtesy to the child'.[39]

Adversariality and Adversity in Collision

However, it is the combination of this adversity with the adversariality of the custody process which is revealed to be so inimical to the effective functioning of protections for children in police custody. As introduced in Chapter 2, when referring to the 'adversariality' of police custody, I have in mind both the custody process's place as part of the wider adversary system of justice in England and Wales and as a broader, more loosely oppositional relationship between child and officer, which might be said to be a feature of police/suspect interactions in any legal system. In respect of the former aspect, doubts about the suitability of fully adversarial processes for child defendants have long been raised.[40] This study reveals fundamental difficulties with the adversarial system in the investigative stage as well. In court, the adversarial process functions effectively, in so far as it does, because of the presence of the judge (or magistrates), the referee for the contest,[41] who decides whether one side needs additional supports and when questioning has overstepped the mark in some way. In the custody block, there is no neutral referee. In the absence of one, it is perhaps unsurprising that the rules of the game are not, as the evidence demonstrates, scrupulously observed. It is inherently problematic to ascribe oversight of the game to one of the players.

This study underlines the fundamental conflict within the role of the CO. He or she is required by PACE to act as an independent guardian of the welfare and rights of the young suspect, to oversee and enable the adjustments required in *Code C*.[42] Yet, this position is at odds with the institutional

---

[39] Barry Goldson, 'New Labour, Social Justice and Children: Political Calculation and the Deserving Undeserving Schism' (2002) 32 British Journal of Social Work 683.
[40] See eg Lord Carlile, 'Independent Parliamentarians' Inquiry into the Operation and Effectiveness of the Youth Court' (2014) 54 <http://michaelsieff-foundation.org.uk/content/inquiry_into_the_operation_and_effectiveness_of_the_youth_court-uk-carlile-inquiry.pdf> accessed 20 August 2023.
[41] *R v Gunning* (1980) 98 Cr App R 303, 306.
[42] PACE, ss 36–37.

objectives of the police generally and the CO's investigating colleagues in particular. As the National Police Chiefs' Council's (NPCC's) National Strategy for Police Custody makes plain, from a police perspective, the 'primary purpose' of police custody is to render the suspect 'amenable to the investigation of an offence'.[43] Formally, the police remit in investigation is to pursue evidence which both leads towards and away from the suspect—it should be an exercise in unbiased enquiry. However, it appears, from young participant experiences, that the police interview is more commonly approached as an exercise in securing admissions rather than an exercise in securing reliable evidence by facilitating the effective participation of the child in interview. Throughout the process, the evidence indicates COs honouring child suspects' rights in so far as that is required to render any evidence admissible—so that the box on the custody record can be ticked—but not so as to ensure the meaningful exercise of those rights. Thus, legal advice was offered but rarely explained. The AA's presence was secured for interview but not earlier in the process when their support is urgently required, and their role was infrequently enabled by full explanation. The child was kept physically safe, but their treatment could not often sensibly be described as age-appropriate or adjusted to 'promote their sense of dignity and worth',[44] whilst entitlements which could ameliorate the process (eg a phone call,[45] a family visit,[46] and time in an exercise yard)[47] were rarely explicitly identified for the child. Nor was their fitness to be interviewed, in the sense required in *Code C*, Annex G, meaningfully considered following lengthy detention in the cell.

There was an inevitable and observable collegiality between COs and investigating officers, and COs identified their role as part of the wider prosecution process. One can well understand, in those circumstances, how dissonant it might seem to refuse to authorize detention or to encourage a child to take up legal advice, conscious that this might prompt a 'no comment' interview. Unsurprisingly, COs tended, especially where time and resource were scarce, to prioritize institutional objectives over suspects' rights. To return to Packer's models outlined in Chapter 1, officers pursuing these institutional motivations might be understood to prioritize a 'crime

---

[43] NPCC, National Custody Strategy (NPCC 2017) 3 <www.npcc.police.uk/documents/NPCC%20Custody%20Strategy.pdf> accessed 20 August 2023.
[44] UNCRC, Art 40(1).
[45] *Code C* (n 8), para 5.6.
[46] ibid, para 5.5.
[47] ibid, para 8.7.

control' approach.[48] The 'due process' concerns of PACE, *Code C* and APP are acknowledged in so far as they are required to legitimize the process and the evidence which may be obtained but are otherwise drowned out. Consequently, *Code C* and APP, tend to function, in practice, more as a 'fig leaf', legitimizing what is, in many cases, disproportionately harsh and sometimes unfair treatment. In the custody block, due process thus functions more 'for crime control' than as a brake on it, to echo the observations of McBarnet.[49] The custody process remains a key site of 'case construction', as McConville and others identified more than thirty years ago,[50] with the COs working to 'achieve police goals' rather than operating as 'guardians of suspects' rights'.[51] Functioning in this way, the protections in *Code C* create a sort of 'ideological façade', which enables the agencies of the criminal justice system engaged post-charge to turn a blind eye to failings at the pre-charge stage.[52]

Conscious that they are in the 'house' of the prosecution (Rezar), young suspects, in turn, took an adversarial approach to the CO and custody staff, which undermined their engagement with the protections. This is unsurprising against the backdrop of arrest experiences, which were often heavy-handed, and because young participants generally did not appreciate the separation of the CO role from that of the investigating officers. As Waddington has noted, the police–child relationship might be considered 'inevitably ... structurally adversarial'.[53] In those circumstances, it is understandably difficult for the child to appreciate that the CO offers independent help from lawyers, health-care practitioners (HCPs), and AAs when the CO's position is, self-evidently, in opposition to the child. Additionally, young participants reported a reluctance to provide information to COs and HCPs about conditions relevant to their care in detention or their fitness to be interviewed because of doubts as to how the information would be used. The fact that they are in a justice process, in which the police are engaged in gathering evidence against them, entrenches an oppositional approach to the police in the mind of the child, which stifles their

---

[48] Herbert L Packer, 'Two Models of the Criminal Process' (1964) 113 University of Pennsylvania Law Review 1, 9–10.
[49] Doreen J. McBarnet, *Conviction: Law, the State and the Construction of Justice* (Macmillan 1981).
[50] Michael McConville, Andrew Sanders, and Robert Leng, *The Case for the Prosecution* (Routledge 1991).
[51] Choongh (n 37) 179.
[52] Robert Reiner, *The Politics of the Police* (4th edn, OUP 2010) 117.
[53] Peter AJ Waddington, *Policing Citizens: Authority and Rights* (UCL Press 1999) 47.

engagement with assessment and undermines their willingness to take up offers of help and support.

The Challenge of Recognizing Vulnerability in a Justice Context

However, reviewing the process as a whole, it appears that perhaps more fundamental in challenging the effective operation of PACE protections is the more generalized oppositional approach taken by officers to child suspects in police custody, and vice versa. The fact that the child comes into the custody block as an arrestee is revealed, in this study, to be fundamentally problematic for the identification of them as deserving of adjusted, child friendly treatment or, put another way, their identification as 'vulnerable', to use the shorthand of the custody block. The justice context of the encounter, that the child is identified as a potential 'perpetrator'—'here for a reason' (CA3)—positions the child, from a police perspective, in opposition to the victim and/or the community. Recent policing research has observed a growing public service ethos amongst officers whereby 'getting a result' involves achieving a 'meaningful outcome for the general public'.[54] Officers in this study, in the context of discussing child suspects, commonly alluded to the importance of 'doing our best by the victim' (CO7) and of keeping the community 'safe' (CO34). Welcome as this increased focus on the victim is, it has had a chilling effect on concern for 'offenders' and a willingness to protect their rights, as Garland has observed.[55] This polarization of the victim and the suspect tends to undermine the child suspect's claim to specialized support, to be treated as 'vulnerable', since the concept is closely associated with victimhood, as I explore in Chapter 2. On observation, 'vulnerable' was rarely a term ascribed to children in police custody. As CO30 memorably observed, 'some of them [child suspects] are not vulnerable, they're preying on the vulnerable'. Many child suspects, and particularly those who behaved problematically had, in effect, lost the right in officers' minds to adjusted treatment. As one CA observed, with some

---

[54] Nick Caveney and others, 'Police Reform, Austerity and "Cop Culture": Time to Change the Record?' (2020) 30 Policing & Society 1210, 1221. See also Sarah Charman, 'Making Sense of Policing Identities: The "Deserving" and the "Undeserving" in Policing Accounts of Victimisation' (2020) 30 Policing & Society 81; Dale Spencer and others, '"I Think It's Re-victimizing Victims Almost Every Time": Police Perceptions of Criminal Justice Responses to Sexual Violence' (2018) 26 Critical Criminology (Richmond, BC) 189, 205.
[55] David Garland, *The Culture of Control: Crime and Social Order in Contemporary Society* (Clarendon Press 2001) 143.

resentment, 'we have to treat them [child suspects] *as if* they were vulnerable' (CA18; my emphasis).[56]

At the same time, police approaches to those identified as potential victims provide perhaps some indication of why there is such difficulty in identifying child suspects' and, indeed, child defendants' 'vulnerability', their need for 'child first' treatment. In his conceptualization of the 'ideal victim', a victim who is readily given 'the complete and legitimate status of victim',[57] Nils Christie identified a number of attributes. Christie's 'ideal victim' is weak (very old, or very young, for example); engaged in a 'respectable project' at the time of their victimization; unconnected to the perpetrator; and blameless in relation to the incident. Additionally, the offending perpetrator is, by contrast, 'big and bad' and unknown or unconnected to the victim personally.[58] But, critically, the 'ideal victim' must also be powerful enough to successfully lay claim to the status of victim—'strong enough to be listened to'.[59] As Christie notes, such an 'ideal victim' may not suffer a greater harm or loss than the 'far-from-ideal' or undeserving victim.

Charman's research with new police recruits suggests that this conception of the 'ideal victim' retains relevance for the approach taken to victims by police in England and Wales.[60] Police participants identified certain neighbourhoods and individuals as 'underserving' and 'ingenuine' on the basis of particular individual attributes which diminished their status as a victim, particularly their perceived lack of respectability and blamelessness for their situation and their inability to lay claim to their status as victim by virtue of their marginalized status.[61] Charman, and Caveney and others, have added to this concept of the 'ideal victim' in the policing context in identifying the importance of job satisfaction in the ascription of victim status. Caveney and others note the influence of officers' 'frustration' in being unable to resolve the situation for 'repeat' victims, exacerbated by a perceived lack of sufficient resources, which leads to their classification of these individuals as not 'proper victims'.[62]

---

[56] Echoing findings in Roxanna Dehaghani, 'Custody Officers, Code C and Constructing Vulnerability: Implications for Policy and Practice' (2017) 11 Policing 74.

[57] Nils Christie, 'The Ideal Victim' in Ezza A Fattah (ed), *From Crime Policy to Victim Policy, Reorienting the Justice System* (Macmillan 1986) 18.

[58] ibid 19.

[59] ibid 21.

[60] Charman (n 54).

[61] ibid 93.

[62] Caveney and others (n 54) 1220.

Reviewing the evidence in this study, it appears that the police response to child suspects' vulnerability may be understood as operating in a similar fashion to their response to victimhood, functioning, or failing by virtue of the presence of certain corresponding attributes and the ability of the officer to make a difference for the particular suspect. Like victimhood, vulnerability in police custody appears to have similar presentational aspects. As Dehaghani has previously observed of adults, only those who 'manifest' their vulnerability are likely to be treated accordingly.[63] We saw, in Chapters 2 and 5, how aspects of this played out for children as well, in CO observations that one can identify by sight those who are vulnerable and need child friendly approaches by their extreme youth, their observable fear, or their shocked and subdued behaviour, whereas those who might behave problematically, or present in a hostile fashion, are liable to forfeit the right to be treated as a child, despite the fact that their problematic presentation may be the result of fear, distress, a dispositional vulnerability, or the effects of trauma. As CO21 identified, 'the problem is they [young suspects] are rude to the staff here and so they can be overlooked—their vulnerability'.

Also identifiable in officers' ascription of the status of vulnerability was an implicit requirement for some indication of respectability or blamelessness on the part of the child suspect, just as in the identification of the 'ideal victim'. For example, CO36 contrasted the more adjusted treatment likely to be ascribed to 'The schoolkid in uniform who's never been here before' with that of 'someone who is twelve, thirteen, fourteen, a PYO [persistent young offender] with no respect for the system'. As identified in Chapter 2, the pejorative descriptions of child suspects tended to be applied to those young suspects who were frequent attendees, and there was a marked lack of urgency in addressing the needs of those who had been arrested repeatedly, who faced serious allegations, or were considered a nuisance to the community. Plainly, any child arrested on suspicion of an offence is poorly positioned to lay claim to respectability in the eyes of the police.

Additionally, it was possible to identify in some officers' approaches a strong sense of frustration, of the futility of making extra effort in relation to child suspects who were likely to return the following week and who experienced such adversity outside the custody block that their efforts within

---

[63] Roxanna Dehaghani, 'He's Just Not That Vulnerable: Exploring the Implementation of the Appropriate Adult Safeguard in Police Custody' (2016) 55 Howard Journal of Criminal Justice 396.

were unlikely to bear fruit. Like the approach to domestic violence taken by the officers in Caveney and others' study, COs and staff recognized the importance of turning around the lives of many of these young suspects. But sometimes, their inability to do so, the lack of input from third-party agencies whose failings had led to the child's presence in the custody block, and the child's own apparent disinterest in disengaging from troubling behaviour tended to further diminish the child's status as vulnerable in their eyes.

Finally, the child in police custody is highly unlikely to lay claim to their vulnerability. Frequently, the child's voice is silenced by the power imbalance they encounter in the custody block. Equally, in the 'them-against-us' (Avery) context of their detention, revealing weakness and need was commonly avoided. As Alex explained, 'I feel like, police officers, if they think you're weak they will try and like, I don't know, target you.' At the same time, those who had endured adversity in custody and outside tended to be disinclined to consider themselves, and even more to identify themselves, as vulnerable. In short, studies of why some victims are unable to lay claim to that status provide a window onto the challenges for children laying claim to their 'vulnerability', their right to child first treatment, in police custody and the wider youth justice process. The very adversity they experience, and the adversarial context of police custody and the criminal process, operate against their needs being acknowledged and addressed.

Similar challenges in identifying vulnerability have long been documented in responses to child trafficking. Commentators have noted the need for children to display 'incapacity and immaturity' to be identified as trafficked[64] and to pierce the 'culture of disbelief' that could restrict agency responses.[65] At the same time, children's resilience and reluctance to speak, the 'wall of silence' identified by Pearce and others,[66] have tended to mask their exploitation.[67] However, the development of policing responses to 'county-lines' activity in particular presents a positive trajectory and offers some learnings for the policing of child suspects more generally and the

---

[64] Jo Boyden and Jason Hart, 'Editorial Introduction: The Statelessness of the World's Children' (2007) 21 Children & Society 237, 245

[65] Jenny J Pearce, 'Working with Trafficked Children and Young People: Complexities in Practice' (2011) 41 British Journal of Social Work 1424, 1429.

[66] Jenny J Pearce, Patricia Hynes, and Silvie Bovarnick, *Trafficked Young People: Breaking the Wall of Silence* (Routledge 2013).

[67] Patricia Hynes, 'Understanding the "Vulnerabilities", "Resilience" and Processes of the Trafficking of Children and Young People into, within and out of the UK' (2010) 104 Youth & Policy 97, 103–05.

identification of their vulnerability.[68] In the current study, no child was specifically identified in the custody block as the subject of criminal exploitation in a county-lines context, although several were likely candidates,[69] policing awareness and responses being less well developed at the time of fieldwork than at the time of writing. Indeed, since 2017, there have been rapid and substantial increases in the number of children being referred, in the context of county-lines exploitation, for identification and support as victims of modern slavery, through the National Referral Mechanism.[70] Increased awareness training and guidance is enabling officers to recognize children arrested as participants in the drugs trade as victims in need of support and onward referral rather than perpetrators to be prosecuted.[71] It is to be hoped that this growing appreciation of the complex factors bringing children to the attention of the police, the importance of building rapport with children encountered in that context, and the recognition of the key role third-party agencies can play will, in time, have an impact on the approach taken to all child suspects. There is undeniably much more work to be done, but this developing understanding within forces of the adversity experienced by child suspects, and the importance of 'looking beyond the obvious', is invaluable for the proper recognition of child suspects' vulnerability more widely.[72]

---

[68] 'County lines' activity involves drug supply groups from major urban conurbations expanding their reach to regional urban centres, frequently using exploited children to transport and distribute the drugs. See for discussion Jack Spicer, '"That's Their Brand, Their Business": How Police Officers Are Interpreting County Lines' (2019) 29(8) Policing & Society 873.

[69] For instance, YS32 and 33.

[70] Home Office, 'Modern Slavery: National Referral Mechanism and Duty to Notify Statistics UK, Quarter 3 2022—July to September' (3 November 2022) <https://www.gov.uk/government/statistics/national-referral-mechanism-and-duty-to-notify-statistics-uk-july-to-september-2022/modern-slavery-national-referral-mechanism-and-duty-to-notify-statistics-uk-quarter-3-2022-july-to-september> accessed 20 August 2023.

[71] Home Office, 'Criminal Exploitation of Children and Vulnerable Adults: County Lines, (2017, last updated 7 February 2020) <https://www.gov.uk/government/publications/criminal-exploitation-of-children-and-vulnerable-adults-county-lines/criminal-exploitation-of-children-and-vulnerable-adults-county-lines> accessed 20 August 2023.

[72] Michael Blakeburn and Richard Smith, 'Exploring the Role of the British Transport Police in Responding to "County Lines" Drug Markets: Enforcement and Safeguarding Perspectives' (2021) 94(2) Police Journal: Theory, Practice and Principles 239, 251.

Behind Closed Doors

The damaging combination of adversity and adversariality persists in part because it occurs behind the closed doors of the custody block. As I outlined in Chapter 1, the child suspect is invisible in various critical respects. In the first instance, young participant experiences in this study illustrate vividly how problematic, in practice, the invisibility of the child suspect in legislation is. Children in police custody are critically under-protected by scant statutory protections and limited accompanying guidance. Permissive drafting undermines the few statutory protections that there are, as we have seen in the case of separation from adult suspects and female care. What guidance *Code C* and APP provide lacks detail and specificity, as in the case of the provision of non-cell accommodation[73] and the adjustments for particular conditions and adverse childhood experiences.[74] As a result, COs and staff have no consistent, positive conception of what child first treatment in custody might consist of, and there is no clear framework to operate within.

This is magnified by the lack of oversight of the detention process in the criminal courts and the ineffectiveness of accountability mechanisms. As explored in Chapter 5, detention conditions in breach of provisions and guidance are allowed to persist in part because criminal and civil courts are rarely called upon to scrutinize custody conditions for children. Indeed, the greater threat, as perceived by COs and staff, lay in the scrutiny of the coroner's court should a death occur in custody or following detention. Although fear of such an investigation motivated close attention to physical risk of harm, this was sometimes at the expense of considering the child's wider welfare in detention. There are no effective and accessible remedies for the child whose rights have been violated. The extreme power imbalance of the custody process meant that children considered making a complaint a fruitless endeavour, whilst few children and their families are likely to have the resources to pursue litigation. At the same time, as we saw in Chapter 5, those tasked with overseeing conditions—independent custody visitors and His Majesty's Inspectorate of Constabulary (HMIC)/ His Majesty's Inspectorate of Constabulary, Fire and Rescue Services

---

[73] *Code C* (n 8), para 8.8.
[74] Authorised Professional Practice (Detention and Custody)(Children and Young Persons) (first published 23 October 2013, updated 2 May 2023) 3–4 <https://www.college.police.uk/app/detention-and-custody/detainee-care/children-and-young-persons> accessed 20 August 2023 (APP(DC)(CYP)).

(HMICFRS)—have proved ineffective in ensuring child first custody provision,[75] not least because of the limited data which is available in relation to custody episodes, despite HMIC's recommendations.[76] The ability of AAs to oversee welfare and ensure due process is routinely heavily curtailed by COs restricting their access to the block and, once present, to the child suspect. Lawyers also have the potential to improve conditions and motivate change, but their working practices and fee structure mean that their presence, and thus purchase on the issues, is substantially reduced. Whilst the introduction of Liaison and Diversion practitioners, and, in some blocks, specialist diversion workers, has, to a degree, opened the door into the custody world, the monopoly of police control in custody continues effectively unchallenged.

The fact that the academic community has largely overlooked the experiences of the child suspect in England and Wales until quite recently means that opportunities have been lost to identify this challenging combination of adversity and adversariality and to advocate for change. As I outlined in Chapter 1, in relating the challenges of accessing young participants for the study, this may be, in part, because of the substantial requirements put in place to protect children as research participants. Whilst such protections are generally entirely appropriate, they can have the unintended effect of silencing children's voices. The balance between securing appropriate protection and enabling children to be heard is a difficult one to strike. Ethics committees must give substantial weight to the importance of hearing from young people on issues that affect them in considering applications for ethical approval. This can be a complex task, particularly where the protections for children in the environment being studied are, as in this case, surprisingly limited and substantially less robust than those imposed on the research. Indeed, the careful approach taken in such applications, and by reviewing committees, might be instructive for those reviewing PACE protections. The focus on ensuring child friendly methods are adopted to enable the child to participate effectively in the research, the minimization of the power imbalance between researcher and young participant, and the scrupulous care taken in terms of the environment to ensure that the child can give their account in comfort and privacy might be instructive for those seeking to reform the legal framework in custody.

---

[75] John Kendall, *Regulating Police Detention, Voices behind Closed Doors* (Policy Press 2018).
[76] HMIC (n 18). For discussion about the ongoing lack of data see HC Deb 28 June 2022, vol 717, cols 55WH–65WH.

Reform: Retrenchment

The voices of young participants in this study demand that we look afresh at police custody in light of their experiences. As CO41 observes in the epigraph, 'There has to be a different way.' There is an urgent need for wholesale reform to ensure that pre-charge processes are in line with the rest of the youth justice process and its guiding principles. Spending time in custody blocks, there is a strong sense that detaining children in cells whilst they await interview is just how investigation is done. Legislators and policymakers have tinkered at the edge of the process, tweaking guidance, but they have rarely stood back to consider what is being achieved when a child is brought into police custody and, perhaps more importantly, what is being lost. Space here allows only a brief consideration of these reform options. Undoubtedly, further research is required to pilot potential reform arrangements and to review their practicality and effectiveness.

In setting out these proposals, I adopt the language of the 'child first' approach now championed by the Youth Justice Board,[77] drawing on the principle of 'Children First, Offenders Second' initially conceptualized in a Welsh context by Kevin Haines and Mark Drakeford.[78] The child first principle encompasses four tenets. First, children must be seen as children. This requires the prioritization of their best interests and the recognition of their rights, needs, and capacity. Second, the approach seeks to build the child's pro-social identity, focusing on establishing supportive relationships and empowering the child to fulfil their potential. The third tenet emphasizes collaboration with children, the fostering of their effective participation and engagement in all work done with them. Finally, the fourth tenet promotes diversion and a childhood removed from the justice system.[79] The child first approach, in effect, represents a blueprint for operationalizing, and expanding on, the principles that have guided the analysis in this book: the treatment of the child with dignity and respect for them as rational rights-holders, the pursuit of child friendly and supportive processes which impose the 'minimum burdens' on the child, and the focus on their effective participation in all stages of the process.

---

[77] See eg YJB, 'A Guide to Child First' (YJB 2023) <http://PowerPoint Presentation (yjresourcehub.uk) > accessed 20 August 2023.
[78] Kevin R Haines and Mark Drakeford, *Young People and Youth Justice* (Palgrave 1998).
[79] See for discussion Stephen Case and Ann Browning, *Child First Justice: The Research Evidence-Base* (Loughborough University 2021).

Addressing Adversity: A Presumption against Detention for Children

The central proposal for reform is for the widescale retrenchment of police custody. The overwhelming finding from this study, in light of the problematic interplay between adversariality and adversity behind the closed doors of the custody block, is that children should be kept out of police custody as far as that can safely be achieved. Recent years have shown an impressive reduction in child arrests and, as a result, numbers of children in police custody, but the figures remain stubbornly high. Over 50,000 children are still being arrested and detained, on average, each year.[80] There is a need to decouple criminal investigation of youth offending from the detaining of the child in a police cell. The findings explored in Chapters 3 and 6 reveal that detention in police custody is fundamentally incompatible with many children participating effectively in the investigative process and engaging their legal rights, especially younger children. As such, it is not an effective method of obtaining reliable evidence and enabling accurate determinations. Nor does it conform with the emphasis on diversion and minimizing contact with the justice system in the UNCRC and the fourth tenet of the child first approach.

Aside from the process of establishing responsibility, the identification of a child as a suspect for a criminal offence is a moment at which positive interventions can, and should, occur to address the circumstances that may have given rise to any offending. However, it is important to avoid the assumption that this 'reachable', 'teachable moment', as described by prevention strategies borrowed from public health initiatives,[81] requires, or can best be exploited in, police custody. Whilst some such schemes (especially those involving dedicated youth workers) have shown successful outcomes,[82] the evidence of this study suggests that the adversarial context is liable to inhibit engagement and frustrate efforts for many. There is a danger that focusing support services on the custody setting rather than in the community is likely to encourage continued high levels of custodial arrests and to reduce the availability of such support in the community, where children and young people are better equipped to engage with the help offered.

---

[80] YJB/MoJ, *Youth Justice Statistics 2022–23, England and Wales* (National Statistics 2023).
[81] Gillian Holdsworth and others, 'Maximizing the Role of Emergency Departments in the Prevention of Violence: Developing an Approach in South London' (2012) 126 Public Health (London) 394.
[82] See DIVERT, <https://www.tvvru.co.uk/project/divert/> accessed 20 August 2023.

A blanket ban on the use of police detention for children would plainly not be appropriate. There will, sadly, always be some children for whom detention in police custody will be necessary. The offence(s) they are alleged to have committed may be so serious and either the obtaining of forensic evidence is so urgent or the threat posed to the investigation (or the public) were the child to be at liberty so great as to demand immediate detention.[83] However, as discussed in Chapter 5, such circumstances are, and were in this study, rare. In the first instance, therefore, this research indicates that the 'authorisation of detention' test should be amended to include an explicit presumption against the detention of a child in police custody. Police detention should only be authorized for a child, of any age, in the most exceptional of circumstances.

Of course, authorisation of detention already requires the application of a 'necessity' test under PACE, section 37(3). However, as this study illustrates, that test is not always robustly applied. To ensure that the presumption is effective, what might amount to exceptional circumstances should be clearly delineated. Such circumstances could specify a gravity threshold as one of the 'exceptional detention' criteria. Options for such a threshold could include, for example, offences scored as '4' on the Association of Chief Police Officers (ACPO) Gravity Matrix (used for the consideration of youth diversion)[84] or indictable-only offences, coupled with either-way offences specified by the Secretary of State.[85] There should also be more stringent requirements for the detention of younger children. The numbers of younger children (those aged under fourteen) encountered in this research were small, but their experiences, coupled with the developmental literature,[86] make a strong case for their exclusion from police custody entirely. In the extremely rare circumstance that secure interview of a ten- to-thirteen-year-old is required, this research would strongly suggest that alternative arrangements should be made with local authority children's

---

[83] It is hard to see how seriousness of the offence alone could ever be sufficient justification for custodial interview. The more serious the offence, arguably, the greater the need for the child to participate effectively in the interview and the stronger the argument for the child to attend for interview on bail to maximize their ability to participate effectively, with any required adjustments. Victims and the wider public have no interest in unfair trials.

[84] ACPO, 'Youth Offender Case Disposal Gravity Factor Matrix' (March 2013) <https://yjlc.uk/sites/default/files/ACPO%20Youth%20Gravity%20Matrix.pdf> accessed 20 August 2023.

[85] As in the restrictions on the use of cautions, Criminal Justice and Courts Act 2015, s 17(3).

[86] See Chapter 1 for discussion.

services or youth offending teams (YOTs) to supervise the child until the interview can be conducted.

Any provisions could also be strengthened by an explicit acknowledgement in PACE of the different responsibilities that the police have in respect of a child under domestic legislation.[87] In Scotland, for example, primary legislation requires that, when deciding whether to 'hold a child in police custody', a constable 'must treat the need to safeguard and promote the well-being of the child as a primary consideration'.[88] Indeed, this approach is emphasized in the recent High Court case of *ST v Chief Constable of Nottinghamshire Police*, in which Cotter J observed,

> Proper recognition by those engaged within the criminal justice system of the need to consider the best interests, safeguarding and promotion of the welfare of children must begin with the first interaction, which, as regards a suspected offender, is usually within the investigation stage. Relevant to the current case, before any arrest, an officer should, as directed by guidance in Code G paragraph 2.8, consider the broader circumstances and whether arrest is necessary. Within that assessment process the fact that the person to be arrested is a child requires specific consideration due to the need to have regard to the duty to safeguard and promote the welfare of children. Indeed it should be front and centre of the consideration of relevant circumstances and requires an assessment of whether a less intrusive step than arrest or detention is a practical alternative.[89]

Updated provisions in England and Wales could go further and make explicit reference not only to the police's domestic safeguarding duties but also to the child's rights under the UNCRC to be detained as a 'last resort' and 'for the shortest appropriate period'.[90] In New Zealand, for example, Oranga Tamariki 1989 requires decision-makers to be guided by the principle that a young person's rights include those set out in the UNCRC (and, indeed, the UN Convention on the Rights of Person with Disabilities).[91] Such a provision is unusual, if not unique, but academic commentators have been

---

[87] See under the Children Act 2004, s 11.
[88] Criminal Justice (Scotland) Act 2016, s 51(2).
[89] [2022] EWHC 1280 (QB), [99].
[90] UNCRC, Art 37(b). Reference to the UNCRC in general terms appears in the APP(DC)(CYP) (n 74) 1 but not in *Code C* (n 8).
[91] Oranga Tamariki Act 1989, s 5(1)(b)(i).

cautiously optimistic about its positive effect, including in relation to the pre-trial detention of children.[92] Would such a reference prove effective in the context of England and Wales? This is difficult to assess, given its novel nature. This study suggests that the reference to the UNCRC in the College of Policing's non-statutory guidance, APP(DC)(CYP), is insufficient to ensure its observation,[93] and commentators have lamented the challenge of securing UNCRC rights at other stages of the youth justice process.[94] Whilst statutory wording alone may not be effective, the mounting evidence of failure, on the part of the government and youth justice agencies, to give proper effect to children's rights under the UNCRC suggests that all reasonable mechanisms to promote their visibility should be considered.

It is important to note that keeping children out of police custody wherever possible would not prevent the conduct of investigations and the interview of child suspects where that is required. The police have ample powers to search and seize items from the child and their home address on arrest, as discussed in Chapter 2; to bail a child to attend for police interview when arrangements can be made for their proper support; or to invite the child to attend for a voluntary interview without arresting them. Undoubtedly, however, as previously discussed, there is a need to clarify the processes and access to protections for a child invited for voluntary interview so that their access to their rights and entitlements can be properly secured.[95]

This proposed presumption could only function effectively, and without unduly hampering the needs of the investigation, if the police were able to engage third-party support in the community, particularly out of hours. This is no small ask. This study suggests that children are often detained, effectively, for safeguarding purposes because there is no one suitable, and available, into whose care they can be released. Indeed, the Custody Concordat, introduced to reduce the numbers of children being detained overnight, has not resulted in substantial improvement, in large part, it seems, because of lack of resource in the community.[96] Nonetheless, the

---

[92] For discussion see Sam Bookman and Andrew Becroft, 'CROCodile Tears or Provisions with Bite?' (2019) New Zealand Law Journal 267.
[93] APP(DC)(CYP) (n 74) 1.
[94] See eg Laura Janes, 'Thirty Years On: On-Going Challenges in Securing the Rights of Children in Custody in England and Wales' [2019] European Human Rights Law Review 577.
[95] Harriet Pierpoint, 'The Risks of Voluntary Interviews' (2020) 9 Criminal Law Review 818.
[96] Augusta Itua, '"It's Horrible When They Keep You in There at Night." Ending the Overnight Detention of Children in Police Custody (Just for Kids Law 2022) <https://www.justforkidslaw.org/sites/default/files/fields/download/J4KL_Detention%20briefing%202022_0.pdf> accessed 20 August 2023.'

challenge is not insurmountable. In some areas, closer working with local authorities is already bearing fruit, reducing the need for children to be detained and cutting detention times where that cannot be avoided.[97]

Mitigating the Adversarial Approach: Increased Oversight

This research has revealed that the decision to authorize detention is arguably the most important moment in the custody process. At present, it occurs generally when the child is alone, without the support of the lawyer or the AA and without the child appreciating the significance of the decision or being able to address any practical concerns the CO may have which might obviate the conclusion that detention is 'necessary' in the circumstances. At the same time, as identified in Chapter 2, there are police cultural and institutional motivations which feed into what I have argued is an overly permissive approach to authorizing detention. Mitigating these issues is not straightforward. In the first instance, there is a strong argument for the child to be supported for this part of the process, ideally by a lawyer who can make representations as to the application of the test and the suitability of alternative arrangements for interview. Equally, there are good arguments for the input of a suitably trained AA or similar supporting adult, both to assist in identifying arrangements, short of custodial detention, to facilitate the investigation process and to ensure that the child understands the decision being made, their rights, and that they are able to communicate effectively with the CO. It was evident during observations that attendance by supporting adults many hours after the event rendered challenge to the 'authorisation of detention' decision effectively obsolete.

The conflicted nature of the CO role, the routinized nature of authorisation of detention on observation, and the often adversarial approach taken to young suspects suggest that there is good reason to look to dilute the CO's monopoly over this decision. How, exactly, that might best be achieved would require further research. However, several options present themselves for consideration. Approval by a more senior officer (eg an inspector)

---

[97] See eg the Northamptonshire Police TICTAC initiative, Northamptonshire Police, 'Northamptonshire Police Introduce "Trauma-Informed Custody" for Retained Children' (5 April 2022) <www.northants.police.uk/news/northants/news/news/2022/april/northamptonshire-police-introduce-trauma-informed-custody-for-detained-children> accessed 20 August 2023.

would be the least onerous measure practically and has precedent in other provisions in PACE, such as the review of detention. However, given the concerns raised in this study in respect of the routinized nature of detention reviews, this might not be considered a sufficiently robust approach. Alternatively, the decision could require approval by a representative of children's services. Such an approach is adopted in New Zealand whenever a decision to detain in the police station is taken.[98] Were additional funding to be provided to local authorities, as suggested above, this might be a workable option. Otherwise, there is a danger that such a requirement might be rendered as toothless as the statutory protection to provide alternative accommodation under PACE, section 38(6). Most onerous, but arguably likely to be most effective, would be oversight of any decision to detain by a magistrate (lay or district judge), engaging remotely by phone or through video facility such as Microsoft Teams. This has the option of introducing a judicial element to referee the adversarial process but would require primary legislation and, potentially, significant out-of-hours engagement by the judiciary.

Reform: Achieving Child First Police Custody

For those few children who must be detained, this discussion draws together avenues for reform of the custody process explored in the text and considers, in light of the approach taken in other jurisdictions, a package of potential measures to foster the full realization of children's rights in investigative detention. As with the retrenchment proposals above, further research is plainly required, and there is only space to sketch the outline of such a process here. However, the findings of this research indicate the contours of what child first detention should look like. The proposals assume a very significant reduction in the numbers of children being detained, on the basis of the presumption against detention, enabling more substantial protective and age-appropriate measures to be put in place for each detained child.

---

[98] Oranga Tamariki Act 1989, s 236.

Training

The central issue in achieving child first treatment is ensuring that officers and staff not only appreciate the multifaceted adversity every child experiences in police custody, but that they are also motivated to respond to their particular needs and capacities. Training, therefore, must address why a child first approach is necessary, and likely to be effective, as well as how police custody can be adapted to accommodate the child suspect. It is important to dispel any lingering notions that punitive processes pre-conviction are in the child's 'best interests' or will set them 'on the right path' (CO34) and to provide both an introduction to children's rights under the UNCRC and to the evidence base illustrating the efficacy of supportive and collaborative approaches which empower, rather than exclude, children.

All those working with child suspects should receive training on child development (including adolescent brain development), on dispositional conditions prevalent amongst children, on the impact of trauma, and on effective communication with children. The aim of such training is not to achieve significant expertise but to establish a developmentally informed level of understanding sufficient for staff to engage effectively with children and to adapt the environment to support their particular needs and capacities.[99] The training should provide practical guidance, for example, on use of language, methods of checking understanding, and the importance of providing additional explanation about the process and timely information about progress in the investigation. All officers should also receive child-specific restraint training, as provided to those working in the youth secure estate. Most pressingly, the interview experiences recounted in Chapter 6 underline the importance of specific guidance and training for officers conducting investigative interviews with child suspects (and, indeed, with vulnerable adult suspects), akin to the 'Achieving Best Evidence' provisions for child and vulnerable witnesses.[100]

---

[99] See eg in relation to autism spectrum conditions discussion Chloe Alice Holloway and others, 'Exploring the Autistic and Police Perspectives of the Custody Process through a Participative Walkthrough' (2020) 97 Research in Developmental Disabilities 103545.

[100] MoJ (n 11). See for discussion Gooch and von Berg (n 12) and for a similar recommendation Kemp and others (n 7).

Supporting Adults

As I argue in the conclusion to Chapter 4, the findings of this study suggest that a wholesale review of the AA function for children is required and a separation of the due process and rights facilitation role from that of overseeing the child's welfare and providing more general reassurance and emotional support. Whilst the due process role could be situated more squarely within the legal representative's remit, legal aid funding and the availability of solicitors for extended periods in detention may rule out such an option. The proposal that I advance in Chapter 4 is for the creation of a paid and specifically trained youth-specialist AA role, a custody 'navigator', for children. This individual would be present from the earliest point in the custody process to ensure that the child's rights are respected and their exercise facilitated. Ideally, this 'navigator' would be able to liaise with children's services and have access to any records held in relation to the child. Trained in communicating with young people, and familiar with common dispositional vulnerabilities, they would be able to support effective participation and to identify adjustments to mitigate the detention conditions for the child whilst waiting to be interviewed.

The findings also underline the benefit of the child having a trusted adult present, where they are available, to fulfil the more general welfare and reassurance role. This should be an individual chosen by the child (subject to the usual issues of non-involvement in the offence), and their presence in legal consultation and interview should remain a choice for the child rather than the adult. This individual might be the parent or guardian. Where they are not, the provisions for informing those with parental responsibility should remain, and they should have the right to attend and visit the child if they wish.

Mandatory Legal Advice

The case for mandatory legal advice for children is compelling. Too often, the opt-in requirement[101] leads to children waiving legal advice, and the AA's right to request is highly variable in its effectiveness.[102] The depth of young participants' desperation to avoid delay suggests that an opt-out

---

[101] *Code C* (n 8), para 3.1.
[102] ibid, para 6.5A.

provision, as proposed in the Taylor Review of the Youth Justice System,[103] would be likely to be ineffective. As explored in detail in Chapter 3, the difficulties associated with waiver, and assessing competence to waive, in North American jurisdictions also render such an option less desirable. Whilst the autonomy of the child would be restricted by a mandatory provision, alternatives tend to leave the child under-protected—promoting their autonomy in relation to whether to have legal advice whilst undermining their ability to make autonomous decisions about the more important issue of whether, and how, to answer questions in interview.

Reduced Timescales

The experiences of young participants in this study suggest that reducing the time periods during which a child may be detained and interviewed is also of critical importance. This is both in light of the child's right to be detained for the 'shortest appropriate period' under Article 37(b) of the UNCRC but also in consideration of the likely impact of lengthy detention on the child's ability to engage with legal advice, make key decisions required of them, and participate effectively in interview. Additionally, the failure of exhortations to 'prioritize' child suspects in pre-existing guidance suggests that a clearer, reduced timescale is required to effect change. Such a differentiation would be in keeping with the distinctive and tailored approach taken for children and young people elsewhere in the youth justice process (as discussed in Chapter 1).

A halving of the maximum initial time period to twelve hours for children (extendable, where justifiable, with the authorization of a senior officer) would represent a significant reduction without imposing unreasonable demands, falling as it does just outside the average period spent in detention for children in this study. Indeed, in Scotland, following recommendations in the Carloway Review,[104] the Criminal Justice (Scotland) Act 2016 section 9 sets a general twelve-hour initial time limit on detention in police custody for all suspects, extendable by an officer of at least inspector rank by a further twelve hours (and by an officer of at least chief inspector rank for someone under eighteen years).[105] However, it would be

---

[103] Charlie Taylor, *Review of the Youth Justice System in England and Wales* (MoJ 2016) 22.
[104] Colin Sutherland, Lord Carloway, 'The Carloway Review, Report and Recommendations' (Carloway Review 2011).
[105] Criminal Justice (Scotland) Act 2016, s 11(2)(a)(ii).

desirable for an even shorter time period to be considered. Charlie Taylor, in his review of the youth justice system, proposed a six-hour time limit for children.[106] Whether a further reduced time period could be achieved in England and Wales would require additional research, but a pilot scheme being conducted at the time of writing by the Metropolitan Police has had success in reducing very substantially detention periods for child suspects in certain Greater London areas.[107]

Differentiation and Separation

In addition to different timescales, there is a need for a tailored approach to children in certain key functions. In particular, a specifically tailored risk assessment for children is plainly required so that questioning focuses on supporting their welfare and is reduced to what is relevant for children but includes additional questions relating to pertinent issues such as developmental and mood disorders common in the adolescent population; whether they have had support in school; whether they have an education and health-care plan; and whether they are, or have been, in the care of the local authority. The experiences of young participants recounted in Chapter 2 also reveal the importance of achieving full and effective separation from adult arrestees throughout the custody process, from their arrival in the police station. As the All Party Parliamentary Group for Children have previously observed, it is important to separate adults and children not just for holding and booking in, but also in detention accommodation so that adults in detention cannot be heard by children.[108]

Detention Conditions

Finally, in terms of physical facilities, the distress experienced by young participants in the cell (or cell-like accommodation) illustrates the need for more explicit requirements in *Code C* concerning non-cell provision for children and making available child appropriate waiting facilities, including

---

[106] Taylor (n 103) 20.
[107] As identified in HC Deb 28 June 2022, vol 717, col 49WH.
[108] All Party Parliamentary Group for Children, '"It's All about Trust": Building Good Relationships between Children and the Police. Report of the Inquiry Held by the All Party Parliamentary Group for Children, 2013–2014' (National Children's Bureau 2014).

spaces where a child could wait with a supporting adult without being exposed to other detainees. The desperation generated by boredom and uncertainty in the cell raises the importance of more tailored risk assessment being conducted so that children can be allowed to retain more personal items (eg watches) and be provided more regularly with distraction items and age-appropriate reading materials. HMICFRS reports reveal that increasingly good selections of distraction items are available, although, too often, inspectors identify that children are not routinely provided with those supports.[109] Such provision ought not to be restricted to those obviously showing signs of distress, but rather it should be the norm, subject to specific risk assessment to withhold. Ensuring that children are aware of, and are afforded, their incommunicado rights[110] and their entitlement to exercise and washing facilities is also important in terms of responding humanely to children's needs in detention.

Implications for the Wider Youth Justice System

The voices of the children and young people involved in this research do not just have relevance for reform to the custody process. Although police custody obviously imposes particular demands on the child, young participant experiences provide important insights into children's wider abilities to engage with criminal justice processes more generally, especially where that process is adversarial in nature. Young participant accounts reveal the fundamental importance of hearing children's voices on the extent to which they are able to understand and engage with criminal justice processes. There is little existing literature drawing on children's accounts of their experiences in the post-charge process.[111] Studies of court user experiences

---

[109] See eg HMICFRS, 'Report on an Unannounced Inspection Visit to Police Custody Suites in Surrey (HMICFRS 2022) <www.justiceinspectorates.gov.uk/hmicfrs/wp-content/uploads/report-on-an-unannounced-inspection-visit-to-police-custody-suites-in-surrey.pdf> 28.

[110] *Code C* (n 8), part 5.

[111] See for notable, but now quite dated, exceptions Joyce Plotnikoff and Richard Woolfson, 'Young Defendants Pack: Scoping Study' (YJB 2002) <https://vdocuments.site/young-defendants-pack-scoping-study-lexicon-limited-young-defendants-pack-scoping.html > accessed 20 August 2023; Neal Hazel, Ann Hagell, and Laura Brazier, *Young Offenders' Perceptions of Their Experiences in the Criminal Justice System* (Economic and Social Research Council 2003).

have often excluded the experiences of children, most likely because of access difficulties.[112]

The challenges for children in this study in engaging with protections in an adversarial process also underline the importance of expert professional support for children undergoing criminal justice processes more generally. This project provides compelling evidence of the need for advocates with youth-specialist training who are capable of explaining the court process, and available adjustments to it, in a manner accessible to the child and are able to check on their understanding in a meaningful fashion. It also illustrates the importance of those making decisions in relation to the conduct of the process, particularly prosecutors and judges, having child specialist training. Although youth court magistrates are specially trained, there is no requirement at present for judges in the Crown Court hearing cases involving youths to have such specialism.

In particular, young participant accounts provide fresh perspectives on the debate surrounding the minimum age of criminal responsibility (MACR) in England and Wales but also in adversarial jurisdictions more widely. As discussed in Chapter 1, the MACR in England and Wales of ten years[113] is amongst the very lowest in Europe and internationally, and substantially below the minimum age of 'at least 14 years of age' urged by the UNCRC Committee.[114] The rationale for maintaining a MACR is predominantly founded upon what Nicola Lacey has described as 'capacities of cognition' and 'capacities of volition', that it is only fair to punish someone if they understood what they were doing (its nature and its consequences) and were able to act on that understanding in a deliberative fashion.[115] The focus of this justification for a MACR is on the child's capacities at the time of the alleged act. In England and Wales, the now abolished presumption of *doli incapax*,[116] which required the prosecution to prove that a child under fourteen understood that what they did, or did not do, was seriously wrong,

---

[112] See eg Jessica Jacobson, Gillian Hunter, and Amy Kirby, *Inside Crown Court: Personal Experiences and Questions of Legitimacy* (Policy Press 2015); Phil Bowen, *Building Trust: How Our Courts Can Improve the Criminal Court Experience for Black, Asian, and Minority Ethnic Defendants* (Centre for Justice Innovation 2017).

[113] Children and Young Persons Act 1933, s 53.

[114] General Comment No 24 (2019) on children's rights in the child justice system (CRC/C/GC/24), para 22. (General Comment No 24 replaces General Comment No 10 (2007) (CRC/C/GC/10) extant at the time of fieldwork. Any relevant variance will be noted as it arises).

[115] Nicola Lacey, 'In Search of the Responsible Subject: History, Philosophy and Social Sciences in Criminal Law Theory' (2001) 64 Modern Law Review 350, 353; see also Thomas Crofts, 'Catching Up with Europe: Taking the Age of Criminal Responsibility Seriously in England' (2009) 17 European Journal of Crime, Criminal Law, and Criminal Justice 267.

[116] Abolished by the Crime and Disorder Act 1998, s 34.

is firmly rooted in this justification.[117] There is, however, a second strand of justification for maintaining a MACR founded upon the child's need for protection from the full criminal process as applied to an adult suspect or defendant.[118] This conceptualization focuses on the capacities of the child at the time of their participation in the criminal process and their engagement with its outcomes. It takes account of the need for children to be dealt with by way of adjusted procedures and to undergo alternative measures, such as welfare-orientated—rather than punitive—responses. This strand recognizes, in the words of Maher, that 'age is important in the criminal justice system because it poses problems for the methods and processes the system uses to achieve its goals'.[119]

The arguments for raising the minimum age of criminal responsibility hardly need further elaboration. They have been repeatedly and effectively marshalled.[120] Nonetheless, young participant accounts in this study provide a fresh perspective on the importance of raising the MACR in England and Wales, drawing loosely on this second strand of justification. The point is a simple one. This study illustrates how counterproductive criminal procedures are when they do not enable the child to engage the rights which should be afforded to them—those rights which are necessary to balance the responsibility ascribed to them. In making this argument, I do not assert that child suspects towards the lower end of the age spectrum (ten-to-thirteen-year-olds) inevitably lack the capacity to engage those rights due to their young age. Such an assertion undermines their entitlement to legal agency and would be dangerous from a wider rights-realization perspective, as other commentators have observed.[121] Rather, as this research reveals starkly, adversarial criminal processes, in the context of a striking imbalance of power between the child and the authorities, fundamentally

---

[117] *C v DPP* (1996) AC 1; see for discussion Kate Fitz-Gibbon, 'Protections for Children before the Law: An Empirical Analysis of the Age of Criminal Responsibility, the Abolition of Doli Incapax and the Merits of a Developmental Immaturity Defence in England and Wales' (2016) 16 Criminology & Criminal Justice 391.

[118] See for discussion Barry Goldson, '"Unsafe, Unjust and Harmful to Wider Society": Grounds for Raising the Minimum Age of Criminal Responsibility in England and Wales' (2013) 13 Youth Justice 111; Crofts (n 115).

[119] Gerry Maher, 'Age and Criminal Responsibility' (2005) 2 Ohio State Journal of Criminal Law 493, 512.

[120] Elly Farmer and Rod Morgan, 'The Age of Criminal Responsibility: Developmental Science and Human Rights Perspectives' (2011) 6 Journal of Children's Services 86; Goldson, 'Unsafe, Unjust' (n 118).

[121] See eg Don Cipriani, *Children's rights and the Minimum Age of Criminal Responsibility: A Global Perspective* (Ashgate 2009).

Implications for the Wider Youth Justice System 345

undermine the protections which should support the child to exercise their rights and militate against children, particularly younger children, engaging them. So, for example, a ten-year-old may not lack the capacity, in terms of cognitive ability, to exercise their right of silence; to decide whether to answer questions in interview; or, indeed, to give evidence at trial. However, in the context of a justice process, particularly an adversarial one, the emotional and physical toll of the process may disincline the child to raise comprehension difficulties or reduce their ability to reason logically about their options. Uncertainty about the process, about who can be trusted, may disincline them to provide a full account to legal advisers or to place reliance on their advice. Thus, whilst the child may have the capacity to be held responsible for their offending, an adversarial justice process prevents them from fully exercising the rights which render such responsibilization fair.

Equally, the distrust and hostility towards support shown by some young participants in this study indicates how problematic an adversarial justice approach can be in seeking to fulfil the aims of the youth justice system. A process that begins with, and retains, the positioning of the child in opposition to the authorities which seek to support them is liable to stifle the child's willingness to participate in an exploration of the issues leading to their offending and to engage with any support offered. Young participant reflections provide further illustration of the dissonance at the heart of the youth justice system in England and Wales—that uneasy tension between welfare and justice approaches.[122] In particular, they reveal how counterproductive it is to the welfare aims of the process for its gateway, the police custody process, to be characterized by a particularly harsh and punitive justice approach. The continuation of that approach into the youth court is liable to entrench that opposition and further alienate the child at a time when their engagement and cooperation is vital.

Thus, young participant voices lend weight to arguments that younger children should be immune from full criminal prosecution, particularly where that is adversarial in nature.[123] However, despite the emergence of a consensus on the acceptable MACR in continental Europe,[124] there is sadly little political appetite for reform in England and Wales. In the circumstances, it is all the more important that appropriate restrictions on the use of police custody for children are introduced as a matter of urgency.

---

[122] Barry Goldson, 'Children, Crime, Policy and Practice: Neither Welfare Nor Justice' (1997) 11 Children & Society 77.
[123] See eg Goldson, 'Unsafe, Unjust' (n 118) 117.
[124] Crofts (n 115).

APPENDIX A

Schedule of Young Participant Interviews

Column Headings

Pseudonym—name used for young participant to maintain anonymity.

Age at i/v—details of the age of the young participant (YP) at the time of the research interview, unless the individual was over eighteen at the time of interview.

Gender—indicates self-identified gender.

BAME—'N' indicates that the YP did not identify themselves as Black, Asian, or ethnic minority. 'Y' indicates that the YP identified themselves as Black, Asian, or ethnic minority.

Legal advice—'N' alone indicates that the YP has always waived legal advice. 'Y' alone indicates that the YP has always requested legal advice. 'Y and N' indicates that the YP has separate experiences of both waiving and requesting legal advice. N/K indicates that the YP does not know whether they have had legal advice or not.

Frequency—'Once' indicates a single police custody experience. 'Several' indicates accounts of between two and four police custody experiences. 'Repeated' indicates accounts of five or more police custody experiences.

Obs. area?—indicates if YP has had a custody experience in one of the force areas observed during fieldwork (F1, F2, F3).

Charged?—indicates whether the YP reported being charged following a custody episode.

Age at exp.—details the age of the YP at the time of their police custody experience(s). (Some YPs could not recall the exact age they were for each police custody experience).

I/v length—indicates length of the research interview following completion of the consent process and preliminaries.

	Pseudonym	Age at i/v	Gender	BAME	Legal advice	Frequency	Obs. area?	Charged?	Age at exp.	I/v length (mins)
1	Simon	23	M	N	Y and N	Repeated	N	Y	14–17	83.04
2	Avery	24	F	N	Y and N	Repeated	N	Y	17	63.31
3	Yemi	16	M	Y	Y	Several	N	N	14–16	51.45
4	Harper	18	F	N	Y and N	Repeated	N	Y	14–18	74.06
5	Jackson	16	M	N	N	Once	F2	N	15	31.16
6	Jamal	16	M	Y	Y and N	Several	N	Y	15–16	44.09
7	Jake	14	M	N	Y	Once	N	N	13	47.00
8	Will	17	M	N	Y	Repeated	F2	Y	15/16	46.16
9	Tom	18	M	N	Y	Several	F2	Y	17	51.25
10	Luke	17	M	N	Y and N	Repeated	N	Y	11–17	57.03
11	Carter	18	M	Y	Y	Repeated	N	Y	12/13–17	38.05
12	Alex	18	M	Y	Y and N	Repeated	N	Y	16–17	57.53
13	Elijah	15	M	Y	Y and N	Repeated	N	Y	9–14	64.58
14	Malik	16	M	Y	Y and N	Several	F3	Y	16	37.39
15	Cole	15	M	N	Y	Several	F3	Y	12/13, 14	42.40
16	Nathan	15	M	N	Y and N	Several	F3	Y	12–15	37.02

	Name									
17	Robert	17	M	N	Y	Several	F3	Y	14–17	21.33
18	Megan	15	F	N	N	Several	F3	Y	14–15	c. 25 mins (only 19.31 recorded)
19	Hudson	17	M	N	Y	Several	F3	Y	13–16	33.05
20	Abigail	17	F	N	N	Several	F3	Y		14.17
21	Kate	16	F	N	Y	Once	F3	N	16	31.07
22	Dexter	16	M	N	Y	Repeated	F3	Y	15–16	33.20
23	Aaron	16	M	N	Y and N	Repeated	F3	Y	13/14–16	32.09
24	Sadie	17	F	N	Y	Repeated	F3	Y	14–17	41.25
25	Aidan	16	M	N	Y and N	Repeated	F3	Y	15–16	39.46
26	Evan	16	M	N	Y	Repeated	F3	Y	9–15	37.41
27	Kyle	15	M	N	Y	Once	F3	N	15	28.16
28	Logan	18	M	N	Y and N	Repeated	F3	Y	15	48.30
29	Riley	16	M	N	Y	Several	F3	Y	16	34.27
30	Jo	17	M	Y	Y and N	Repeated	F2	Y	15–17	57.39
31	Zoe	15	F	N	N/K	Several	N	Y	14–15	30.37

(*continued*)

	Pseudonym	Age at i/v	Gender	BAME	Legal advice	Frequency	Obs. area?	Charged?	Age at exp.	I/v length (mins)
32	Edison	16	M	Y	Y	Several	N	Y	12–16	41.17
33	Sandor	18	M	N	Y	Once	N	Y	17	68.38
34	Rezar	15	M	N	Y and N	Several	N	Y	13–15	43.28
35	Hussain	17	M	Y	Y and N	Several	N	Y	14/15–17	65.20
36	Zayn	17	M	Y	Y	Repeated	N	Y	15/16	51.06
37	Jayden	16	M	Y	Y	Repeated	N	Y	13/14–16	48.30
38	Tyler	12	M	Y	Y	Once	N	N	12	23.48
39	Michael	14	M	Y	Y	Several	N	Y	13	27.06
40	Kaiden	13	M	Y	Y and N	Several	N	Y	12–13	39.00
41	Azade	14	F	N	and N	Several	N	Y	13–14	42.50

APPENDIX B

Schedule of Police Station Observations

Key

AA—appropriate adult
CA—custody assistant
FAA—familial appropriate adult
FME—forensic medical examiner (doctor, commonly a general practitioner)
FMHP—forensic mental health practitioner
FNP—forensic nurse practitioner
JDR—juvenile detention room
L&D—Liaison and Diversion Service (NHS England)
PCC—Police and Crime Commissioner
PFI—private finance initiative
YOT—Youth Offending Team

Note: Cell capacity is given as a range to preserve the anonymity of the suite/force.

Force area	Custody suite and Youth Service (YS) tracked	Cell capacity	Child detention facilities	Building	Custody staff	Dates and hours (total)	Health-care provision	AA provision (where FAA unavailable)
Force 1 (County force, suites serving both urban and rural areas)	Suite 1 (YS 1–5)	20–29 (CCTV in all)	3–5 JDRs in a separate section. Doors have hatches. CCTV in all	Modern building, PFI.	CAs provided by external contractor	Aug 2016 (62 hours)	FNP embedded 24/7 in each suite (private contractor) L&D service in place (8am–8pm) (one support worker, one FMHP (shared across suites 1 and 2) Single FME on call serving county	Pre 10pm: YOT co-ordinated volunteer AAs Post 10pm: paid AAs from private provider
	Suite 2 (YS 6–12)	10–19 (CCTV in all)	1–2 JDRs. Doors have hatches. CCTV in all	Older building, police owned.				

	Suite	Cells (YS numbers)	Building	Staff	Date observed	Healthcare	Appropriate Adults
Force 2 (County force, suite in an urban area of high deprivation)	Suite 3	40–49 (CCTV in all)	No designated JDRs. Separate 'Vulnerable wing'. Doors have glass panels floor to ceiling. All CCTV	Modern building, PFI	CAs are police employees	Sept 2016 (57 hours)	FNP embedded in custody suite 24/7 (police employees). FME on telephone but no call-out. L&D service in place 8am–8pm (one FMHP)	Volunteer AAs from a private provider
Force 3 (Regional Metropolitan force)	Suite 4 (YS 34)	30–39 (all CCTV)	3–5 JDRs, gated off from adult cells. Doors have hatches. All CCTV	Modern building, PFI	CAs are police employees	November 2016 (73 hours)	No healthcare practitioner embedded. FNP, FMHP, or FME available on request (private contractor). No L&D service	Varies according to timing of request, suspect's circumstances and home local authority, and location of suite. Combination of paid AAs from a private provider until 12 am. Volunteer AAs provided by PCC scheme. YOT workers.
	Suite 5 (YS 35, 38, 39)	60–69 (not all CCTV)	6–10 JDRs, separated by gender. No hatches in doors. CCTV in some male JDRs.	Older building, police owned				
	Suite 6 (YS 36, 37, 40–47)	30–39 (not all CCTV)	3–5 JDRs. Separated by gender. No hatches in doors. No CCTV	Modern building, PFI				

Bibliography

Adams C, 'Suspect Data: Arresting Research' in RD King and E Wincup (eds), *Doing Research on Crime and Justice* (OUP 2000).

All-Party Parliamentary Group for Children (APPGC), 'Children and the Police Inquiry: Oral Evidence Session 2: The Detention of Young People in Police Custody' (National Children's Bureau 2014).

APPGC, ' "It's All about Trust": Building Good Relationships between Children and the Police. Report of the Inquiry Held by the All-Party Parliamentary Group for Children, 2013–2014' (National Children's Bureau 2014).

Amnesty International, *Trapped in the Matrix: Secrecy, Stigma and Bias in the Met's Gangs Database* (Amnesty International 2018).

Anckarsäter H and others, 'Prevalences and Configurations of Mental Disorders among Institutionalized Adolescents' (2007) 10 Developmental Neurorehabilitation 57.

Anckarsäter H and others, 'Autism Spectrum Disorders in Institutionalized Subjects' (2008) 62 Nordic Journal of Psychiatry 160.

Annan LG and others, 'What Makes Young People Get Involved with Street Gangs in London? A Study of the Perceived Risk Factors' (2021) 50(5) Journal of Community Psychology 2198.

Ashworth A, *The Criminal Process: An Evaluative Study* (1st edn, OUP 1994).

Back L, *The Art of Listening* (Berg 2007).

Baldwin J, 'Summarising Tape Recordings of Police Interviews' [1991] Criminal Law Review 671.

Baldwin J, 'Preparing Records of Taped Interview' and 'The Role of Legal Representatives at the Police Station' and 'Supervision of Police Investigation in Serious Criminal Cases', Royal Commission on Criminal Justice Research Study Nos 2–4 (His Majesty's Stationery Office (HMSO) 1992).

Barnes K and Wilson JC, 'Young People's Knowledge of the UK Criminal Justice System and Their Human Rights' (2008) 10 International Journal of Police Science & Management 214.

Bateman T, 'A Night in the Cells: Children in Police Custody and the Provision of Non Familial Appropriate Adults' (Office of the Children's Commissioner 2017) <www.childrenscommissioner.gov.uk/wp-content/uploads/2018/06/A-Night-in-the-Cells.pdf> accessed 16 August 2023.

Bateman T, 'The State of Youth Justice' (National Association for Youth Justice 2020) <https://thenayj.org.uk/cmsAdmin/uploads/state-of-youth-justice-2020-final-sep20.pdf> accessed 11 August 2023.

Bath C, 'Legal Privilege and Appropriate Adults' (2014) 178 Criminal Law & Justice Weekly 404.

Bath C, *Police Searches of People—A Review of PACE Powers* (National Appropriate Adult Network 2022).

Bath C and others, *There to Help: Ensuring Provision of Appropriate Adults for Mentally Vulnerable Adults Detained or Interviewed by the Police* (National Appropriate Adult Network 2015).

Beck U, *World at Risk* (English edn, Polity Press 2009).

Beckett H and Warrington C, 'Making Justice Work: Experiences of Criminal Justice for Children and Young People Affected by Sexual Exploitation as Victims and Witnesses' (University of Bedfordshire 2015).

Bellamy Sir C, Independent Review of Criminal Legal Aid (29 November 2021) <www.gov.uk/government/groups/independent-review-of-criminal-legal-aid> accessed 11 August 2023.

Belloni FP, *Criminal Injustice: An Evaluation of the Criminal Justice Process in Britain* (Macmillan 2000).

Bernuz Beneitez MJ and Dumortier E, 'Why Children Obey the Law: Rethinking Juvenile Justice and Children's Rights in Europe through Procedural Justice' (2018) 18 Youth Justice 34.

Bevan M, 'Effective Participation in the Youth Court', Howard League What Is Justice? Working Papers 21/2016 <https://howardleague.org/wp-content/uploads/2016/04/HLWP_21_16.pdf#:~:text=Effective%20participation%20in%20the%20youth%20court%20Miranda%20Bevan,than%20adults%20when%20they%20face%20a%20criminal%20allegation> accessed 11 August 2023.

Bevan M, 'Investigating Young People's Awareness and Understanding of the Criminal Justice System: An Exploratory Study' (Howard League for Penal Reform 2016) <https://howardleague.org/wp-content/uploads/2016/06/Investigating-young-people%E2%80%99s-awareness-and-understanding-of-the-criminal-justice-system.pdf> accessed 15 August 2023.

Bevan M, 'Vulnerable Suspects: The Investigation Stage' in P Cooper and HH Norton (eds), *Vulnerable People and the Criminal Justice System* (1st edn, OUP 2017).

Bevan M, 'Young Suspect Perspectives: An Exploration of the Factors Affecting the Uptake of Legal Advice by Children in Police Custody' (2020) 8 Criminal Law Review 686.

Bevan M, 'The Pains of Police Custody: A Recipe for Injustice and Exclusion?' (2022) 62 British Journal of Criminology 805.

Bevan M and Ormerod D, 'Chapter 4: Reforming the Law of Unfitness to Plead in England and Wales: A Recent History' in R Mackay and W Brookbanks (eds), *Fitness to Plead: International and Comparative Perspectives* (OUP 2018).

Blackstock J and others, *Inside Police Custody: An Empirical Account of Suspects' Rights in Four Jurisdictions* (Intersentia 2013).

Blagrove M, 'Effects of Length of Sleep Deprivation on Interrogative Suggestibility' (1996) 2 Journal of Experimental Psychology: Applied 48.

Blakeburn M and Smith M, 'Exploring the Role of the British Transport Police in Responding to "County Lines" Drug Markets: Enforcement and Safeguarding Perspectives' (2021) 94(2) Police Journal: Theory, Practice and Principles 239.

Blakemore S-J, 'Avoiding Social Risk in Adolescence' (2018) 27 Current Directions in Psychological Science 116.

Bonnie RJ, 'The Competence of Criminal Defendants: A Theoretical Reformulation' (1992) 10 Behavioral Sciences & Law 291.

Bonnie RJ, 'Fitness for Criminal Adjudication: The Emerging Significance of Decisional Competence in the United States' in R Mackay and W Brookbanks (eds), *Fitness to Plead: International and Comparative Perspectives* (OUP 2018).

Bonnie RJ and Scott ES, 'The Teenage Brain: Adolescent Brain Research and the Law' (2013) 22 Current Directions in Psychological Science 158.

Bookman S and Becroft A, 'CROCodile Tears or Provisions with Bite?' [2019] New Zealand Law Journal 267.

Bowen P, *Building Trust: How Our Courts Can Improve the Criminal Court Experience for Black, Asian, and Minority Ethnic Defendants* (Centre for Justice Innovation 2017).

Bowling B and Phillips C, 'Policing Ethnic Minority Communities' in T Newburn (ed), *Handbook of Policing* (Willan 2003).

Bowling B, Reiner R, and Sheptycki J, *The Politics of the Police* (5th edn, OUP 2019).

Boyatzis RE, *Transforming Qualitative Information: Thematic Analysis and Code Development* (Sage 1998).

Boyden J and Hart J, 'Editorial Introduction: The Statelessness of the World's Children' (2007) 21 Children & Society 237.

Bradford B, 'Policing and Social Identity: Procedural Justice, Inclusion and Cooperation between Police and Public' (2014) 24 Policing & Society 22.

Bradley Lord K, 'The Bradley Report, Lord Bradley's Review of People with Mental Health Problems or Learning Disabilities in the Criminal Justice System' (Department of Health 2009).

Braun V and Clarke V, 'Using Thematic Analysis in Psychology' (2006) 3 Qualitative Research in Psychology 77.

Bridges L and Sanders A, 'Access to Legal Advice and Police Malpractice' [1990] Criminal Law Review 494.

British Medical Association, Royal College of Paediatrics and Child Health, and Royal College of Psychiatrists, 'Joint Position Statement on Solitary Confinement of Children and Young People' (2018) <www.rcpch.ac.uk/sites/default/files/2018-04/solitary_confinement_position_statement.pdf> accessed 17 August 2023.

Britton NJ, 'Race and Policing: A Study of Police Custody' (2000) 40 British Journal of Criminology 639.

Broeking JMC, 'Parents' Involvement in Youth Justice Proceedings from the Perspective of Youth: A Pilot Study' (University of Toronto 2003).

Bronx Defenders, 'Voices from the Box: Solitary Confinement at Rikers Island' (Bronx Defenders September 2014) <www.bronxdefenders.org/wp-content/uploads/2014/09/Voices-From-the-Box.pdf> accessed 11 August 2023.

Brookman F and Pierpoint H, 'Access to Legal Advice for Young Suspects and Remand Prisoners' (2003) 42 Howard Journal of Criminal Justice 452.

Brown DC, 'PACE Ten Years On: A Review of the Research', Home Office Research Study 155 (Home Office 1997).

Brown DC, Ellis T, and Larcombe K, 'Changing the Code: Police Detention under the Revised PACE Codes of Practice', Home Office Research Study No 129 (HMSO 1992).

Brown K, 'Re-moralising "Vulnerability"' (2012) 6 People, Place & Policy Online 41.

Brown K, 'Questioning the Vulnerability Zeitgeist: Care and Control Practices with "Vulnerable" Young People' (2014) 13 Social Policy & Society 371.

Brown K, *Vulnerability and Young People: Care and Social Control in Policy and Practice* (Policy Press 2015).

Brunson RK and Weitzer R, 'Police Relations with Black and White Youths in Different Urban Neighborhoods' (2009) 44 Urban Affairs Review 858.

Bryan K, Freer J, and Furlong C, 'Language and Communication Difficulties in Juvenile Offenders' (2007) 42 International Journal of Language & Communication Disorders 505.

Bucke T and Brown D, 'In Police Custody: Police Powers and Suspects' Rights under the Revised PACE Codes of Practice', Home Office Research Study 174 (Home Office 1997).

Buckingham D, 'What Are Words Worth? Interpreting Children's Talk about Television' (1991) 5 Cultural Studies 228.

Bull R, 'Police Investigative Interviewing' in A Memon and R Bull (eds), *Handbook of the Psychology of Interviewing* (Wiley 1999).

Bull R, 'The Investigative Interviewing of Children and Other Vulnerable Witnesses: Psychological Research and Working/Professional Practice' (2010) 15 Law & Criminological Psychology 5.

Campbell L, Ashworth A, and Redmayne M, *The Criminal Process* (5th edn, OUP 2019).

Cant R and Standen P, 'What Professionals Think about Offenders with Learning Disabilities in the Criminal Justice System' (2007) 35 British Journal of Learning Disabilities 174.

Cape E, Hodgson J, and Spronken T, *Suspects in Europe* (Intersentia 2007).

Carlile Lord A, 'An Independent Inquiry into the Use of Physical Restraint, Solitary Confinement and Forcible Strip Searching of Children in Prisons, Secure Training Centres and Local Authority Secure Children's Homes' (Howard League for Penal Reform 2006).

Carlile Lord A, 'Independent Parliamentarians' Inquiry into the Operation and Effectiveness of the Youth Court' (June 2014) <http://michaelsieff-foundation.org.uk/content/inquiry_into_the_operation_and_effectiveness_of_the_youth_court-uk-carlile-inquiry.pdf> accessed 11 August 2023.

Carter E, *Analysing Police Interviews: Laughter, Confessions and the Tape* (Bloomsbury 2011).

Case S and Browning A, *Child First Justice: The Research Evidence-Base* (Loughborough University 2021).

Casey BJ, Getz S, and Galvan A, 'The Adolescent Brain' (2008) 28 Developmental Review 62.

Cauffman E and Steinberg L, 'Emerging Findings from Research on Adolescent Development and Juvenile Justice' (2012) 7 Victims & Offenders 428.

Cavadino M, *Penal Systems: A Comparative Approach* (Sage 2006).

Caveney N and others, 'Police Reform, Austerity and "Cop Culture": Time to Change the Record?' (2020) 30 Policing & Society 1210.

Ceci S and others, 'Children's Suggestibility Research: Implications for the Courtroom and the Forensic Interview' in H Westcott, G Davies, and R Bull (eds), *Children's Testimony: A Handbook of Psychological Research and Forensic Practice* (Wiley 2002).

Charman S, *Police Socialisation, Identity and Culture: Becoming Blue* (Palgrave Macmillan 2017).

Charman S, 'Making Sense of Policing Identities: The "Deserving" and the "Undeserving: in Policing Accounts of Victimisation' (2020) 30 Policing & Society 81.

Children's Commissioner, 'Strip Search of Children in England and Wales—Analysis by the Children's Commissioner for England' (Children's Commissioner 2023).

Chitsabesan P and others, 'Learning Disabilities and Educational Needs of Juvenile Offenders' (2007) 2 Journal of Children's Services 4.

Chitsabesan P and others, 'Traumatic Brain Injury in Juvenile Offenders' (2015) 30(2) Journal of Head Trauma Rehabilitation 106.

Choongh S, *Policing as Social Discipline* (Clarendon Press 1997).

Choongh S, 'Policing the Dross: A Social Disciplinary Model of Policing' (1998) 38 British Journal of Criminology 623.

Chown N, '"Do You Have Any Difficulties That I May Not Be Aware Of?" A Study of Autism Awareness and Understanding in the UK Police Service' (2010) 12 International Journal of Police Science & Management 256.

Christie N, 'The Ideal Victim' in EA Fattah (eds), *From Crime Policy to Victim Policy: Reorienting the Justice System* (Macmillan 1986).

Church II, WT and others, '"What Do You Mean My Child Is in Custody?" A Qualitative Study of Parental Response to the Detention of Their Child' (2009) 12 Journal of Family Social Work 9.

Cipriani D, *Children's Rights and the Minimum Age of Criminal Responsibility: A Global Perspective* (Ashgate 2009).

Clare ICH, 'Devising and Piloting an Experimental Version of the "Notice to Detained Persons"', Royal Commission on Criminal Justice Research Study No 7 (HMSO 1992).

Clare ICH and Gudjonsson GH, 'Interrogative Suggestibility, Confabulation, and Acquiescence in People with Mild Learning Disabilities (Mental Handicap): Implications for Reliability during Police Interrogations' (1993) 32 British Journal of Clinical Psychology 295.

Clare ICH, Gudjonsson GH, and Harari PM, 'Understanding of the Current Police Caution (England and Wales)' (1998) 8 Journal of Community & Applied Social Psychology 323.

Clarke C and Milne R, *National Evaluation of the PEACE Investigative Interviewing Course: Police Research Award Scheme* (Home Office 2001).

Clarke C, Milne R, and Bull R, 'Interviewing Suspects of Crime: The Impact of PEACE Training, Supervision and the Presence of a Legal Advisor' (2011) 8 Journal of Investigative Psychology and Offender Profiling 149.

Clugston B and others, 'Interviewing Persons with Mental Illness Charged with Murder or Attempted Murder: A Retrospective Review of Police Interviews' (2019) 26 Psychiatry, Psychology & Law 904.

Cohen AO and others, 'When Is an Adolescent an Adult? Assessing Cognitive Control in Emotional and Nonemotional Contexts' (2016) 27 Psychological Science 549.

Cohen L, *Research Methods in Education* (5th edn, RoutledgeFalmer 2000).

College of Policing, 'Vulnerability-Related Risks Guidelines' (2021) <https://www.college.police.uk/guidance/vulnerability-related-risks> accessed 18 August 2023.

Connolly P, 'Race, Gender and Critical Reflexivity in Research with Young Children' in PM Christensen and A James (eds), *Research with Children: Perspectives and Practices* (2nd edn, Routledge 2008).

Cooper P and Wurtzel D, 'A Day Late and a Dollar Short: In Search of an Intermediary Scheme for Vulnerable Defendants in England and Wales' (2013) Criminal Law Review 4.

Coudert C and others, 'Adolescent Arrestees Detained in Police Cells: An Observational Study in the Paris, France, Area' (2019) 133 International Journal of Legal Medicine 1251.

Counihan CM and Kaplan SL, *Food and Gender: Identity and Power* (Harwood Academic Publishers 1998).

Cox A, 'Doing the Programme or Doing Me? The Pains of Youth Imprisonment' (2011) 13 Punishment & Society 592.

Crabtree BF and Miller WF, 'A Template Approach to Text Analysis: Developing and Using Codebooks' in D Silverman (ed), *Doing Qualitative Research* (Sage 1992).

Craig JM and others, 'A Little Early Risk Goes a Long Bad Way: Adverse Childhood Experiences and Life-Course Offending in the Cambridge Study' (2017) 53 Journal of Criminal Justice 34.

Crewe B, *The Prisoner Society: Power, Adaptation, and Social Life in an English Prison* (OUP 2009).

Criminal Justice Joint Inspection (CJJI), 'Who's Looking Out for the Children? A Joint Inspection of Appropriate Adult Provision and Children in Detention after Charge' (CJJI 2011).

Croall H, 'Criminal Justice in Post-Devolutionary Scotland' (2006) 26 Critical Social Policy 587.

Crofts T, 'Catching Up with Europe: Taking the Age of Criminal Responsibility Seriously in England' (2009) 17 European Journal of Crime, Criminal Law, and Criminal Justice 267.

Crown Prosecution Service, 'Conditional Cautions: Youths—DPP Guidance' (updated 5 November 2019) <https://www.cps.gov.uk/legal-guidance/conditional-cautioning-youths-dpp-guidance> accessed 18 August 2023.

Cummins I, 'A Path Not Taken? Mentally Disordered Offenders and the Criminal Justice System' (2007) 28 Journal of Social Welfare & Family Law 267.

Cummins I, 'A Place of Safety? Self-Harming Behaviour in Police Custody' (2008) 10(1) Journal of Adult Protection 36.

Cummins I, '"The Other Side of Silence": The Role of the Appropriate Adult Post-Bradley' (2011) 5 Ethics and Social Welfare 306.
Damaška MR, 'Evidentiary Barriers to Conviction and Two Models of Criminal Procedure: A Comparative Study' (1973) 121 Pennsylvania University Law Review 506.
Damaška MR, *Evidence Law Adrift* (Yale UP 1997).
Davis J and Marsh N, 'Boys to Men: The Cost of "Adultification"' in Safeguarding Responses to Black Boys' (2020) 8 Critical & Radical Social Work 255.
Defence for Children, Belgium, 'Mapping of Youth Lawyers Systems in the European Union, Country Overviews of 18 European Member States 2017 <https://lachild.eu/wp-content/uploads/2016/05/Country-Cards-Rapport.pdf> accessed 11 August 2023.
Dehaghani R, 'He's Just Not That Vulnerable: Exploring the Implementation of the Appropriate Adult Safeguard in Police Custody' (2016) 55 Howard Journal of Crime and Justice 396.
Dehaghani R, 'Automatic Authorisation: An Exploration of the Decision to Detain in Police Custody' (2017) Criminal Law Review 187.
Dehaghani R, 'Custody Officers, Code C and Constructing Vulnerability: Implications for Policy and Practice' (2017) 11 Policing 74.
Dehaghani R, '"Vulnerable by Law (But Not by Nature)": Examining Perceptions of Youth and Childhood "Vulnerability" in the Context of Police Custody' (2017) 39 Journal of Social Welfare & Family Law 454.
Dehaghani R, *Vulnerability in Police Custody: Police Decision-Making and the Appropriate Adult Safeguard* (Routledge 2019).
Dehaghani R, 'Interpreting and Reframing the Appropriate Adult Safeguard' (2022) 42(1) Oxford Journal of Legal Studies 187.
Densley JA, *How Gangs Work : An Ethnography of Youth Violence* (Palgrave Macmillan in association with St Antony's College, Oxford 2013).
Dent N and O'Beirne S, 'Inappropriate Adults? A Review of the Current Use of Appropriate Adults in the Criminal Justice System' (2021) 85 Journal of Criminal Law (Hertford) 44.
Department of Justice, 'Northern Ireland registered Intermediaries Schemes Pilot Project Phase II Review' (July 2016) <www.justice-ni.gov.uk/publications/northern-ireland-registered-intermediaries-schemes-pilot-project> accessed 17 August 2023.
Devlin PD, *The Judge* (OUP 1979).
Dixon D, 'Juvenile Suspects and the Police and Criminal Evidence Act' in DAC Freestone and HK Bevan (eds), *Children and the Law: Essays in Honour of Professor HK Bevan* (Hull UP 1990).
Dixon D, 'Legal Regulation and Policing Practice' (1992) 1 Social & Legal Studies 515.
Dixon D and Travis G, *Interrogating Images: Audio-Visually Recorded Police Questioning of Suspects* (University of Sydney 1990).
Drake KE, Bull R, and Boon JCW, 'Interrogative Suggestibility, Self-Esteem, and the Influence of Negative Life-Events' (2008) 13 Legal & Criminological Psychology 299.

Duff A, Farmer L, Marshall S, and Tadros V, *The Trial on Trial. Vol 3, Towards a Normative Theory of the Criminal Trial* (Hart Publishing 2007).

Dunkel F, 'Juvenile Justice Systems in Europe—Reform Developments between Justice, Welfare and "New Punitiveness"' (2014) 1 Kriminologijos Studijos 31.

Durocher E and others, 'Understanding and Addressing Vulnerability Following the 2010 Haiti Earthquake: Applying a Feminist Lens to Examine Perspectives of Haitian and Expatriate Health Care Providers and Decision-Makers' (2016) 8 Journal of Human Rights Practice 219.

Edström J, 'Time to Call the Bluff: (De)-constructing 'Women's Vulnerability' (2010) 53 HIV and Sexual Health Development 215.

Edwards A and others, 'Fitness to Be Interviewed: Decision-Making in the Mental Health In-Patient Setting' (2021) 27 British Journal of Psychological Advances 115.

Ellis K, 'Contested Vulnerability: A Case Study of Girls in Secure Care' (2018) 88 Children & Youth Services Review 156.

Emerson E and Hatton C, 'The Mental Health of Children and Adolescents with Learning Disabilities in Britain' (2007) 1(3) Advances in Mental Health and Learning Disabilities 62.

Equality and Human Rights Commission, 'Protecting Human Rights: Key Challenges for the UK's Third Universal Periodic Review' (EHRC 2016) <www.equalityhumanrights.com/sites/default/files/protecting-human-rights-uk-third-universal-periodic-review-december-2016.pdf>, accessed 17 August 2023.

Evans R, 'The Conduct of Police Interviews with Juveniles', Royal Commission on Criminal Justice, Research Study No 8 (HMSO 1993).

Evans R, 'Police Interrogations and the Royal Commission on Criminal Justice' (1994) 4 Policing & Society 73.

Fagan J and Piquero AR, 'Rational Choice and Developmental Influences on Recidivism among Adolescent Felony Offenders' (2007) 4 Journal of Empirical Legal Studies 715.

Fagan J and Tyler TR, 'Legal Socialization of Children and Adolescents' (2005) 18 Social Justice Research 217.

Farber HB, 'The Role of the Parent/Guardian in Juvenile Custodial Interrogations: Friend or Foe?' (2004) 41 American Criminal Law Review 1277.

Farmer E and Morgan R, 'The Age of Criminal Responsibility: Developmental Science and Human Rights Perspectives' (2011) 6 Journal of Children's Services 86.

Farrugia L and Gabbert F, 'Vulnerable Suspects in Police Interviews: Exploring Current Practice in England and Wales' (2020) 17 Journal of Investigative Psychology & Offender Profiling 17.

Fassin D, *Enforcing Order: An Ethnography of Urban Policing* (English edn, Polity 2013).

Feeley MM, 'Two Models of the Criminal Justice System: An Organizational Perspective' (1973) 7 Law & Society Review 407.

Feeley MM, *The Process Is the Punishment: Handling Cases in a Lower Criminal Court* (1st pbk edn, Russell Sage Foundation 1979).

Feld BC, 'Juveniles' Waiver of Legal Rights: Confessions, *Miranda*, and the Right to Counsel' in T Grisso and RG Schwartz (eds), *Youth on Trial: A Developmental Perspective on Juvenile Justice* (University of Chicago Press 2000).

Feld BC, 'Juveniles' Competence to Exercise Miranda Rights: An Empirical Study of Policy and Practice' (2006) 91 Minnesota Law Review 26.

Feld BC, 'Police Interrogation of Juveniles: An Empirical Study of Policy and Practice' (2006) 97 Journal of Criminal Law & Criminology 219.

Fenner S, Gudjonsson GH, and Clare ICH, 'Understanding of the Current Police Caution (England and Wales) among Suspects in Police Detention' (2002) 12 Journal of Community & Applied Social Psychology 83.

Fereday J and Muir-Cochrane E, 'Demonstrating Rigor Using Thematic Analysis: A Hybrid Approach of Inductive and Deductive Coding and Theme Development' (2006) 5 International Journal of Qualitative Methods 80.

Fisher Sir H, 'Report of an Inquiry by the Hon. Sir Henry Fisher into the Circumstances Leading to the Trial of Three Persons on Charges Arising Out of the Death of Maxwell Confait and the Fire at 27 Doggett Road, London SE6' (HMSO 1977).

Fitz-Gibbon K, 'Protections for Children before the Law: An Empirical Analysis of the Age of Criminal Responsibility, the Abolition of Doli Incapax and the Merits of a Developmental Immaturity Defence in England and Wales' (2016) 16 Criminology & Criminal Justice 391.

Forde L, 'Realising the Right of the Child to Participate in the Criminal Process' (2018) 18 Youth Justice 265.

Fox BH and others, 'Trauma Changes Everything: Examining the Relationship between Adverse Childhood Experiences and Serious, Violent and Chronic Juvenile Offenders' (2015) 46 Child Abuse & Neglect 163.

Fram SM, 'The Constant Comparative Analysis Method Outside of Grounded Theory' (2013) 18 Qualitative Report 1.

France A, 'Young People' in S Fraser and others (eds), *Doing Research with Children and Young People* (Sage 2007).

Freeman S and Seymour M, '"Just Waiting": The Nature and Effect of Uncertainty on Young People in Remand Custody in Ireland' (2010) 10 Youth Justice 126.

Gamble J and McCallum R, 'Local Child Safeguarding Practice Review: Child Q' (City & Hackney Safeguarding Children Partnership March 2022) <https://chscp.org.uk/wp-content/uploads/2022/03/Child-Q-PUBLISHED-14-March-22.pdf> accessed 13 August 2023.

Garcia A, 'Is Miranda Dead, Was It Overruled, or Is It Irrelevant?' (1998) 10 St Thomas Law Review 461.

Garland D, *The Culture of Control: Crime and Social Order in Contemporary Society* (Clarendon Press 2001).

Gau JM and Brunson RK, 'Procedural Injustice, Lost Legitimacy, and Self-Help: Young Males 19 Adaptations to Perceived Unfairness in Urban Policing Tactics' (2015) 31 Journal of Contemporary Criminal Justice 132.

Geluk CAML and others, 'Autistic Symptoms in Childhood Arrestees: Longitudinal Association with Delinquent Behavior' (2012) 53 Journal of Child Psychology & Psychiatry 160.

Gendle K and Woodhams J, 'Suspects Who Have a Learning Disability: Police Perceptions toward the Client Group and Their Knowledge about Learning Disabilities' (2005) 9 Journal of Intellectual Disabilities 70.

Gilligan R, 'Adversity, Resilience and Young People: The Protective Value of Positive School and Spare Time Experiences' (2000) 14 Children & Society 37.

Goff PA and others, 'The Essence of Innocence: Consequences of Dehumanizing Black Children' (2014) 106 Journal of Personality & Social Psychology 526.

Goffman E, *Asylums: Essays on the Social Situation of Mental Patients and Other Inmates* (Penguin Books 1968).

Goldsmith C, '"It Just Feels Like It's Always Us": Young People, Safety and Community' (DPhil thesis, University of Brighton 2011).

Goldsmith C, '"It Just Feels Like It's Always Us": Young People, Peer Bereavement and Community Safety' (2012) 15 Journal of Youth Studies 657.

Goldson B, 'Children, Crime, Policy and Practice: Neither Welfare Nor Justice' (1997) 11 Children & Society 77.

Goldson B, 'Children in Need or Young Offenders? Hardening Ideology, Organizational Change and New Challenges for Social Work with Children in Trouble' (2000) 5 Child & Family Social Work 255.

Goldson B, 'Wither Diversion? Interventionism and the New Youth Justice' in B Goldson (ed), *The New Youth Justice* (Russell House Publishing 2000).

Goldson B, 'New Labour, Social Justice and Children: Political Calculation and the Deserving–Undeserving Schism' (2002) 32 British Journal of Social Work 683.

Goldson B, '"COUNTERBLAST: Difficult to Understand or Defend": A Reasoned Case for Raising the Age of Criminal Responsibility' (2009) 48 Howard Journal of Criminal Justice 514.

Goldson B, '"Unsafe, Unjust and Harmful to Wider Society": Grounds for Raising the Minimum Age of Criminal Responsibility in England and Wales' (2013) 13 Youth Justice 111.

Goldson B and Muncie J, *Youth, Crime and Justice: Critical Issues* (Sage 2006).

Goldstein J, 'Police Discretion Not to Invoke the Criminal Process: Low-Visibility Decisions in the Administration of Justice' (1960) 69 Yale Law Journal 543.

Goldweber A and others, 'The Development of Criminal Style in Adolescence and Young Adulthood: Separating the Lemmings from the Loners' (2011) 40 Journal of Youth & Adolescence 332.

Gooch K, 'A Childhood Cut Short: Child Deaths in Penal Custody and the Pains of Child Imprisonment' (2016) 55 Howard Journal of Crime and Justice 278.

Gooch K and von Berg P, 'What Happens in the Beginning, Matters in the End: Achieving Best Evidence with Child Suspects in the Police Station' (2019) 19 Youth Justice 85.

Goodin REE, *Protecting the Vulnerable: A Re-analysis of our Social Responsibilities* (University of Chicago Press 1985).

Goodwin-De Faria C and Marinos V, 'Youth Understanding & Assertion of Legal Rights: Examining the Roles of Age and Power' (2012) 20 International Journal of Children's Rights 343.

Graham L, '"Fair Trial" (Case Commentary)' (2020) 5 Criminal Law Review 453.

Gray P, '"I Hate Talking about It": Identifying and Supporting Traumatised Young People in Custody' (2015) 54 Howard Journal of Criminal Justice 434.
Gregory J and Bryan K, 'Speech and Language Therapy Intervention with a Group of Persistent and Prolific Young Offenders in a Non-Custodial Setting with Previously Un-diagnosed Speech, Language and Communication Difficulties' (2011) 46(2) International Journal of Language & Communication Disorders 202.
Griffiths J, 'Ideology in Criminal Procedure or A Third "Model" of the Criminal Process' (1970) 79 Yale Law Journal 359.
Grisso T, 'Juveniles' Capacities to Waive Miranda Rights: An Empirical Analysis' (1980) 68 California Law Review 1134.
Grisso T, *Juveniles' Waiver of Rights: Legal and Psychological Competence* (Plenum Press 1981).
Grisso T, 'The Competence of Adolescents as Trial Defendants' (1997) 3 Psychology, Public Policy, & Law 3.
Grisso T and others, 'Juveniles' Competence to Stand Trial: A Comparison of Adolescents' and Adults' Capacities as Trial Defendants' (2003) 27 Law & Human Behaviour 333.
Grodin M and Glantz L, *Children as Research Subjects: Science, Ethics and Law* (OUP 1994).
Gudjonsson GH, 'Confession Evidence, Psychological Vulnerability and Expert Testimony' (1993) 3 Journal of Community & Applied Social Psychology 117.
Gudjonsson GH, 'Fitness for Interview during Police Detention: A Conceptual Framework for Forensic Assessment' (1995) Journal of Forensic Psychology 185.
Gudjonsson GH, *The Psychology of Interrogations and Confessions: A Handbook* (Wiley 2003).
Gudjonsson GH, Hayes GD, and Rowlands P, 'Fitness to Be Interviewed and Psychological Vulnerability: The Views of Doctors, Lawyers and Police Officers' (2000) 11 Journal of Forensic Psychology 74.
Gudjonsson GH and others, 'Custodial Interrogation, False Confession and Individual Differences: A National Study among Icelandic Youth' (2006) 41 Personality & Individual Differences 49.
Gwynedd Parry R, 'Protecting the Juvenile Suspect: What Exactly Is the Appropriate Adult Supposed to Do?' (2006) 18 Child & Family Law Quarterly 373.
Haas NE, de Keijser JW, and Bruinsma GJN, 'Public Support for Vigilantism, Confidence in Police and Police Responsiveness' (2014) 24 Policing & Society 224.
Haines KR and Drakeford M, *Young People and Youth Justice* (Palgrave 1998).
Hall M, 'Young Advocates for Youth Justice: A Youth-Led Report from Children and Young People with Experience of the System' (Alliance for Youth Justice/Leaders Unlocked 2022) <www.ayj.org.uk/news-content/young-advocates-report-publication> accessed 13 August 2023.
Halsey M, 'On Confinement: Resident and Inmate Perspectives of Secure Care and Imprisonment' (2007) 54 Probation Journal 338.
Harrington R and Bailey S, *Mental Health Needs and Effectiveness of Provision for Young Offenders in Custody and in the Community* (Youth Justice Board 2005).
Harrison Y and Horne JA, 'The Impact of Sleep Deprivation on Decision Making: A Review' (2000) 6 Journal of Experimental Psychology: Applied 236.

Harvey J, *Young Men in Prison: Surviving and Adapting to Life Inside* (Willan Publishing 2007).

Harvey J, 'Crossing the Boundary: The Transition of Young Adults into Prison' in A Liebling and S Maruna (eds), *The Effects of Imprisonment* (Willan 2013).

Haydon D, McAlister S, and Scraton P, 'Young People, Conflict and Regulation' (2012) 51 Howard Journal of Criminal Justice 503.

Hazel N, Hagell A, and Brazier L, *Young Offenders' Perceptions of Their Experiences in the Criminal Justice System* (Economic and Social Research Council 2003).

Hazel N, 'Young Offenders' Perceptions of Their Experiences under Police Arrest' (British Society of Criminology Conference, Glasgow July 2006).

Hazel N, *Cross-National Comparison of Youth Justice* (Youth Justice Board 2008).

Helm RK, 'Conviction by Consent? Vulnerability, Autonomy and Conviction by Guilty Plea' (2019) 83 Journal of Criminal Law (Hertford) 161.

Hendrick H, 'Constructions and Reconstructions of Childhood: An Interpretative Survey, 1800 to the Present' in A James and A Prout (eds), *Constructing and Reconstructing Childhood: Contemporary Issues in the Sociological Study of Childhood* (Taylor and Francis 2003).

HM Inspectorate of Constabulary (HMIC), *The Welfare of Vulnerable People in Police Custody* (HMIC 2015).

HM Inspectorate of Constabulary, Fire and Rescue Services (HMICFRS), 'Report on an Unannounced Inspection Visit to Police Custody Suites in Metropolitan Police Service, 9–20 July 2018' (HMICFRS 2018) <www.justiceinspectorates.gov.uk/hmicfrs/publications/metropolitan-joint-inspection-of-police-custody> accessed 16 August 2023.

HMICFRS, 'Report on an Unannounced Inspection Visit to Police Custody Suites in Gloucestershire' (1 June 2022) <www.justiceinspectorates.gov.uk/hmicfrs/publication-html/report-on-an-unannounced-inspection-visit-to-police-custody-suites-in-gloucestershire> accessed 15 August 2023.

HMICFRS, 'Report on an Unannounced Inspection Visit to Police Custody Suites in Surrey' (HMICFRS 2022).

Hodgson J, 'Adding Injury to Injustice: The Suspect at the Police Station' (1994) 21 Journal of Law & Society 85.

Hodgson J, 'Vulnerable Suspects and the Appropriate Adult' (1997) (11) Criminal Law Review 785.

Hodgson J, *The Metamorphosis of Criminal Justice: A Comparative Account* (OUP 2020).

Hoeve M and others, 'A Meta-Analysis of Attachment to Parents and Delinquency' (2012) 40 Journal of Abnormal Child Psychology 771.

Holdaway S, *Inside the British Police: A Force at Work* (Blackwell 1983).

Holdsworth G and others, 'Maximizing the Role of Emergency Departments in the Prevention of Violence: Developing an Approach in South London' (2012) 126 Public Health (London) 394.

Holloway CA and others, 'Exploring the Autistic and Police Perspectives of the Custody Process through a Participative Walkthrough' (2020) 97 Research in Developmental Disabilities 103545.

Home Office, 'Judges' Rules and Administrative Directions to the Police' (HMSO 1964).

Home Office, 'Appropriate Adults: Report of Review Group' (Home Office 1995).

Home Office, 'Concordat on Children in Custody' (Home Office 2017) <www.gov.uk/government/publications/concordat-on-children-in-custody> accessed 13 August 2023.

Home Office, 'Criminal Exploitation of Children and Vulnerable Adults: County Lines' (2017) <http://Criminal exploitation of children and vulnerable adults: county lines-GOV.UK (www.gov.uk)> accessed 13 August 2023.

Home Office, 'Modern Slavery: National Referral Mechanism and Duty to Notify statistics UK, Quarter 3 2022–July to September' (3 November 2022) <https://www.gov.uk/government/statistics/national-referral-mechanism-and-duty-to-notify-statistics-uk-july-to-september-2022/modern-slavery-national-referral-mechanism-and-duty-to-notify-statistics-uk-quarter-3-2022-july-to-september> accessed 13 August 2023.

Home Office, 'Police Powers and Procedures: Other PACE Powers, England and Wales, Year Ending 31 March 2022' (National Statistics 2022) <https://www.gov.uk/government/statistics/police-powers-and-procedures-other-pace-powers-england-and-wales-year-ending-31-march-2022/police-powers-and-procedures-other-pace-powers-england-and-wales-year-ending-31-march-2022> accessed 13 August 2023.

Home Office/Department of Health, 'Memorandum of Good Practice on Video Recorded Interviews with Child Witnesses for Criminal Proceedings' (HMSO 1992).

Home Office and the National Appropriate Adults Network, 'Guide for Appropriate Adults' (2011) <https://assets.publishing.service.gov.uk/government/uploads/system/uploads/attachment_data/file/117682/appropriate-adults-guide.pdf> accessed 17 August 2023.

House of Commons, 'Health Committee, Children's and Adolescents' Mental Health and CAMHS, Third Report of Session 2014–15' (HMSO 2014), <https://publications.parliament.uk/pa/cm201415/cmselect/cmhealth/342/342.pdf> accessed 16 August 2023.

Howard League for Penal Reform, *Criminal Care: Children's Homes and Criminalising Children* (Howard League 2016).

Howard League for Penal Reform, *The Carlile Inquiry 10 Years On: The Use of Restraint, Solitary Confinement and Strip-Searching on Children* (Howard League 2016).

Howard League for Penal Reform, 'Ending the Criminalisation of Children in Residential Care. Briefing One' (Howard League 2017).

Howard League for Penal Reform, 'Howard League Legal Challenge Brings an End to the Routine Use of Adult Restraint Techniques on Children at Feltham Prison' (5 September 2018) <https://howardleague.org/news/howard-league-legal-challenge-brings-an-end-to-the-routine-use-of-adult-restraint-techniques-on-children-at-feltham-prison> accessed 15 August 2023.

Howard League for Penal Reform, 'Child Arrests in England and Wales 2020' (Howard League 2021) <https://howardleague.org/publications/child-arrests-in-england-and-wales-2020> accessed 16 August 2023.

Hoyano LCH, 'Coroners and Justice Act 2009—Special Measures Directions Take Two: Entrenching Unequal Access to Justice?' (2010) Criminal Law Review 345.

Hughes N, *Nobody Made the Connection: The Prevalence of Neurodisability in Young People Who Offend* (Office of the Children's Commissioner 2012).

Hunter G and others, 'Time to Get It Right: Enhancing Problem-Solving Practice in the Youth Court' (Centre for Justice Innovation 2020) <https://justiceinnovation.org/publications/time-get-it-right-enhancing-problem-solving-practice-youth-court> accessed 13 August 2023.

Hynes P, 'Understanding the "Vulnerabilities", "Resilience" and Processes of the Trafficking of Children and Young People into, within and out of the UK' (2010) 104 Youth & Policy 97.

Inch H, Rowlands P, and Soliman A, 'Deliberate Self-Harm in a Young Offenders' Institution' (1995) Journal of Forensic Psychiatry & Psychology 161.

Independent Office for Police Conduct, 'Police Complaints: Statistics for England and Wales 2021/22' <https://www.policeconduct.gov.uk/publications/police-complaints-statistics-england-and-wales-report-202122> accessed 13 August 2023.

Irving B, 'Police Interrogation: The Psychological Approach', Royal Commission on Criminal Procedure Research Study Nos 1–2 (HMSO 1980).

Irving B and Hilgendorf L, 'Police Interrogation: A Case Study of Current Practice', Royal Commission on Criminal Procedure Research Study 2 (HMSO 1980).

Irwin-Rogers K, Muthoo A, and Billingham L, 'Youth Violence Commission: Final Report' (London Youth 16 July 2020) <https://londonyouth.org/youth-violence-commission-final-report> accessed 13 August 2023.

Itua A, ' "It's Horrible When They Keep You in There at Night." Ending the Overnight Detention of Children in Police Custody' (Just for Kids Law 2022) <https://www.justforkidslaw.org/sites/default/files/upload/J4KL_Detention%20briefing%202022_0.pdf> accessed 17 August 2023.

Jackson J and others, 'Monopolizing Force? Police Legitimacy and Public Attitudes toward the Acceptability of Violence' (2013) 19 Psychology, Public Policy, & Law 479.

Jacobson J, 'No One Knows: Police Responses to Suspects Learning Disabilities and Learning Difficulties, a Review of Policy and Practice' (Prison Reform Trust 2008) <https://prisonreformtrust.org.uk/publication/no-one-knows-police-responses-to-suspects-with-learning-disabilities-and-learning-difficulties> accessed 18 August 2023.

Jacobson J and Cooper P, *Participation in Courts and Tribunals: Concepts, Realities and Aspirations* (Bristol UP 2020).

Jacobson J and Talbot J, *Vulnerable Defendants in the Criminal Courts: A Review of Provision for Adults and Children* (Prison Reform Trust 2009).

Jacobson J and others, *Punishing Disadvantage: A Profile of Children in Custody* (Prison Reform Trust 2010).

Bibliography 369

Jacobson J, Hunter G, and Kirby A, *Inside Crown Court: Personal Experiences and Questions of Legitimacy* (Policy Press 2015).

Janes L, 'Thirty Years On: On-Going Challenges in Securing the Rights of Children in Custody in England and Wales' [2019] European Human Rights Law Review 577.

Jennings WG, Piquero AR, and Reingle JM, 'On the Overlap between Victimization and Offending: A Review of the Literature' (2011) 17 Aggression & Violent Behavior 16.

Jessiman T and Cameron A, 'The Role of the Appropriate Adult in Supporting Vulnerable Adults in Custody: Comparing the Perspectives of Service Users and Service Providers' (2017) 45 British Journal of Learning Disabilities 246.

Johnston K and others, 'Assessing Effective Participation in Vulnerable Juvenile Defendants' (2016) 27 Journal of Forensic Psychiatry & Psychology 802.

Jones HL, 'The Pains of Custody: Young Men's Experiences of Pre-Prison Custodial Settings' (2011) Prison Service Journal 20.

Jones HL, 'The Pains of Custody: How Young Men Cope through the Criminal Justice System' (DPhil thesis, University of Hull 2007).

Justice B and Meares TL, 'How the Criminal Justice System Educates Citizens' (2014) 651 Annals of the American Academy of Political & Social Science 159.

Kassin SM, 'On the Psychology of Confessions: Does *Innocence* Put *Innocents* at Risk?' [2005] American Psychologist 215.

Kassin SM and Gudjonsson GH, 'The Psychology of Confessions: A Review of the Literature and Issues' (2004) 5 Psychological Science in the Public Interest 33.

Kassin SM and others, 'Police-Induced Confessions: Risk Factors and Recommendations' (2010) 34 Law and Human Behavior 3.

Katz J, *Seductions of Crime* (Basic Books 1988).

Kazdin AE, 'Adolescent Development, Mental Disorders, and Decision Making of Delinquent Youths' in T Grisso and RG Schwartz (eds), *Youth on Trial: A Developmental Perspective on Juvenile Justice* (University of Chicago Press 2000).

Kemp V, *Transforming Legal Aid: Access to Criminal Defence Services* (Legal Services Commission 2010).

Kemp V, '"No Time for a Solicitor": Implications for Delays on the Take-Up of Legal Advice' 2013 (3) Criminal Law Review 184.

Kemp V, 'Effective Police Station Legal Advice, Country Report 2: England and Wales' (University of Nottingham 2018).

Kemp V, 'Digital Legal Rights: Exploring Detainees' Understanding of the Right to a Lawyer and Potential Barriers to Accessing Legal Advice' (2020) (2) Criminal Law Review 129.

Kemp V and Balmer NJ, 'Criminal Defence Services: Users' Perspectives: Interim Report' (Legal Services Research Centre 2008).

Kemp V and Hodgson J, 'Chapter 4. England and Wales Empirical Findings' in M Vanderhallen and others (eds), *Interrogating Young Suspects: Procedural Safeguards from an Empirical Perspective*, Vol 2 (Intersentia 2016).

Kemp V and Watkins D, 'Exploring Children's Understanding of the Legal Rights of Suspects in England and Wales' (2022) 22(3) Youth Justice 320.

Kemp V, Pleasence P, and Balmer NJ, 'Children, Young People and Requests for Police Station Legal Advice: 25 Years On from PACE' (2011) 11 Youth Justice 28.

Kemp V, Balmer N, and Pleasence P, '"Whose Time Is It Anyway?" Factors Associated with Duration in Police Custody' (2012) (10) Criminal Law Review 736.

Kemp V and others, *Examining the Impact of PACE on the Detention and Questioning of Child Suspects by the Police in England and Wales* (Nuffield Foundation forthcoming).

Kendall J, *Regulating Police Detention, Voices behind Closed Doors* (Policy Press 2018).

Kent H and Williams H, *Traumatic Brain Injury* (His Majesty's Inspectorate of Prisons (HMI Probation) 2021).

Kent R, 'Four Models of the Criminal Process' (1999) 89 Journal of Criminal Law & Criminology 671.

Kessler R and others, 'Lifetime Prevalence and Age-of-Onset Distributions of DSM-IV Disorders in the National Comorbidity Survey Replication' [2005] Archives of General Psychiatry 593.

Kidd DA, *Collins Gem Latin Dictionary* (Collins 1957).

King P, 'The Rise of Juvenile Delinquency in England 1780–1840: Changing Patterns of Perception and Prosecution' (1998) 160(1) Past & Present 116.

Kirby A, *Neurodiversity—A Whole-Child Approach for Youth Justice* (HMIP 2021).

Klockars CB, 'The Dirty Harry Problem' (1980) 452 Annals of the American Academy of Political & Social Science 33.

Knapp M and others, *Youth Mental Health: New Economic Evidence* (London School of Economics and Political Science 2016).

Krähenbühl S, Blades M, and Eiser C, 'The Effect of Repeated Questioning on Children's Accuracy and Consistency in Eyewitness Testimony' (2009) 14 Legal & Criminological Psychology 263.

Kroll L and others, 'Mental Health Needs of Boys in Secure Care for Serious or Persistent Offending: A Prospective, Longitudinal Study' (2002) 359 The Lancet 1975.

Kurzon D, 'The Right of Silence: A Socio-Pragmatic Model of Interpretation' (1995) 23(1) Journal of Pragmatics 55.

Kushner M, 'Betrayal Trauma and Gender: An Examination of the Victim–Offender Overlap' (2022) 37(7–8) Journal of Interpersonal Violence NP3750.

Lacey N, 'In Search of the Responsible Subject: History, Philosophy and Social Sciences in Criminal Law Theory' (2001) 64 Modern Law Review 350.

Lamb ME and Sim MPY, 'Developmental Factors Affecting Children in Legal Contexts' (2013) 13(2) Youth Justice 131.

Lammy D, 'The Lammy Review. An Independent Review into the Treatment of, and Outcomes for, Black, Asian and Minority Ethnic Individuals in the Criminal Justice System' (Ministry of Justice 2017).

Lee J, 'Some Structural Aspects of Police Deviance in Relations with Minority Groups' in C Shearing (ed), *Organizational Police Deviance* (Butterworth 1981).

Leese M and Russell S, 'Mental Health, Vulnerability and Risk in Police Custody' (2017) 19 Journal of Adult Protection 274.

Lewis S and Holt A, 'Constituting Child-to-Parent Violence: Lessons from England and Wales' (2021) 61(3) British Journal of Criminology 792.

Liamputtong P, *Researching the Vulnerable: A Guide to Sensitive Research Methods* (Sage 2007).

Liddle M and others, *Trauma and Young Offenders: A Review of the Research and Practice Literature* (Beyond Youth Custody 2016).

Liebling, A, 'Moral Performance, Inhuman and Degrading Treatment and Prison Pain' (2011) 13 Punishment & Society 530.

Liefaard T and van den Brink Y, 'Juveniles' Right to Counsel during Police Interrogations: An Interdisciplinary Analysis of a Youth-Specific Approach, with a Particular Focus on the Netherlands' (2014) 7 Erasmus Law Review 206.

Littlechild B, 'Reassessing the Role of the "Appropriate Adult"' [1995] Criminal Law Review 540.

Littlechild B, 'An End to "Inappropriate Adults"?' (1998) Childright 8.

Loader I, *Youth, Policing and Democracy* (Macmillan 1996).

Loftus B, 'Policing the "Irrelevant": Class, Diversity and Contemporary Police Culture' in M O'Neill, M Marks, and A-M Singh (eds), *Police Occupational Cultures* (JAI Press 2007).

Loucks N, *No One Knows: Offenders with Learning Difficulties and Learning Disabilities—A Review of Prevalence and Associated Needs* (Prison Reform Trust 2007).

Luna B and others, 'The Teenage Brain: Cognitive Control and Motivation' (2013) 22 Current Directions in Psychological Science 94.

Lyon J, Dennison C, and Wilson A, '"Tell Them So They Listen": Messages from Young People in Custody', Home Office Research Study 201 (Home Office 2000).

Magarey S, 'The Invention of Juvenile Delinquency in Early Nineteenth-Century England' (1978) 34 Labour History (Canberra) 11.

Maguire M, 'Effects of the "P.A.C.E." Provisions on Detention and Questioning' (1988) 28 British Journal of Criminology, Delinquency and Deviant Social Behaviour 19.

Maher G, 'Age and Criminal Responsibility' (2005) 2 Ohio State Journal of Criminal Law 493.

Mayall B, 'Conversations with Children: Working with Generational Issues' in PM Christensen and A James (eds), *Research with Children: Perspectives and Practices* (2nd edn, Routledge 2008).

McAra L, 'Models of Youth Justice' in DJ Smith (ed), *A New Response to Youth Crime* (Willian 2010).

McAra L and McVie S, 'The Usual Suspects?: Street-Life, Young People and the Police' (2005) 5 Criminal Justice 5.

McAra L and McVie S, 'Youth Crime and Justice: Key Messages from the Edinburgh Study of Youth Transitions and Crime' (2010) 10 Criminology & Criminal Justice 179.

McAuley R, *Out of Sight: Crime, Youth and Exclusion* (Willan 2007).

McBarnet DJ, 'Pre-Trial Procedures and the Construction of Conviction' (1975) 23 Sociological Review (Keele) 172.

McBarnet DJ, *Conviction: Law, the State and the Construction of Justice* (Macmillan 1981).

McConville M, *Standing Accused the Organisation and Practices of Criminal Defence Lawyers in Britain* (Clarendon Press 1994).

McConville M and Hodgson J, 'Custodial Legal Advice and the Right to Silence', Royal Commission on Criminal Justice Research Study No 16 (HMSO 1993).

McConville M, Sanders A, and Leng R, *The Case for the Prosecution* (Routledge 1991).

McCrory E and Viding E, 'The Neurobiology of Maltreatment and Adolescent Violence' (2010) 375 The Lancet 1856.

McEwen CA and McEwen BS, 'Social Structure, Adversity, Toxic Stress, and Intergenerational Poverty: An Early Childhood Model' (2017) 43 Annual Review of Sociology 445.

McKenzie IK, 'Helping the Police with Their Inquiries: The Necessity Principle and Voluntary Attendance at the Police Station' [1990] Criminal Law Review 22.

McKinnon IG and Finch T, 'Contextualising Health Screening Risk Assessments in Police Custody Suites—Qualitative Evaluation from the HELP-PC Study in London, UK' (2018) 18 BioMed Central Public Health 393.

McKinnon IG and Grubin D, 'Health Screening in Police Custody' (2010) 17 Journal of Forensic & Legal Medicine 209.

McKinnon IG and Grubin, D, 'Health Screening of People in Police Custody—Evaluation of Current Police Screening Procedures in London, UK' (2013) 23 European Journal of Public Health 399.

McKinnon IG, Thorp J, and Grubin, D, 'Improving the Detection of Detainees with Suspected Intellectual Disability in Police Custody' (2015) 9 Advances in Mental Health & Intellectual Disabilities 174.

McKinnon IG and others, 'Police Custody Health Care: A Review of Health Morbidity, Models of Care and Innovations within Police Custody in the UK, with International Comparisons' (2016) 9 Risk Management & Healthcare Policy 213.

Medford S, Gudjonsson GH, and Pearse J, 'The Efficacy of the Appropriate Adult Safeguard during Police Interviewing' (2003) 8 Legal & Criminological Psychology 253.

Medlicott D, *Surviving the Prison Place: Narratives of Suicidal Prisoners* (Ashgate 2001).

Merikangas K and others, 'Lifetime Prevalence of Mental Disorders in U.S. Adolescents: Results from the National Comorbidity Survey Replication—Adolescent Supplement (NCS—A)' (2010) Journal of American Academic Child & Adolescent Psychiatry 980.

Mills KL and others, 'Developmental Changes in the Structure of the Social Brain in Late Childhood and Adolescence' (2014) 9 Social Cognitive & Affective Neuroscience 123.

Milne R, Clare ICH, and Bull R, 'Using the Cognitive Interview with Adults with Mild Learning Disabilities' (1999) 5 Psychology, Crime & Law 81.

Ministry of Justice, 'Achieving Best Evidence in Criminal Proceedings (Ministry of Justice/National Police Chiefs' Council 31 January 2022) <www.gov.uk/government/publications/achieving-best-evidence-in-criminal-proceedings> accessed 14 August 2023.

Ministry of Justice/Youth Justice Board, 'Youth Cautions: Guidance for Police and Youth Offending Teams' (2013) <www.gov.uk/government/publications/youth-cautions-guidance-for-police-and-youth-offending-teams> accessed 18 August 2023.

Morrow V and Richards M, 'The Ethics of Social Research with Children: An Overview' (1996) 10 Children & Society 90.

Moston S, 'The Ever-So-Gentle Art of Police Interrogation' (British Psychological Society Annual Conference, Swansea 1990).

Moston S and Engelberg T, 'Police Questioning Techniques in Tape Recorded Interviews with Criminal Suspects' (1993) 3 Policing & Society 223.

Mou Y, 'The Transplanted Appropriate Adult Scheme in China' (2021) 60 Howard Journal of Crime and Justice 25.

Muncie J, 'Institutionalized Intolerance: Youth Justice and the 1998 Crime and Disorder Act' (1999) 19 Critical Social Policy 147.

Muncie J, 'The Globalization of Crime Control—The Case of Youth and Juvenile Justice: Neo-liberalism, Policy Convergence and International Conventions' (2005) 9 Theoretical Criminology 35.

Muncie J, 'The "Punitive Turn" in Juvenile Justice: Cultures of Control and Rights Compliance in Western Europe and the USA' (2008) 8 Youth Justice 107.

National Autistic Society, 'Autism: A Guide for Police Officers and Staff' (2020) <www.autism.org.uk/shop/products/books-and-resources/autism-a-guide-for-police-officers-and-staff> accessed 18 August 2023.

National County Lines Coordination Centre, 'Rights and Entitlements in Police Custody Video—England and Wales' <https://www.youtube.com/watch?v=3oKMWe-_fXc&t=42s> accessed 16 August 2023.

National Crime Agency, 'County Lines Drugs Supply, Vulnerability and Harm 2018', NAC(19)095 (2019) <https://nationalcrimeagency.gov.uk/who-we-are/publications/257-county-lines-drug-supply-vulnerability-and-harm-2018/file> accessed 14 August 2023.

National Police Chiefs' Council (NPCC), 'National Strategy for the Policing of Children and Young People' (NPCC 2016) <https://www.npcc.police.uk/SysSiteAssets/media/downloads/publications/publications-log/local-policing-coordination-committee/national-strategy-for-the-policing-of-children-young-people.pdf> accessed 16 August 2023.

NPCC, 'National Custody Strategy' (NPCC 2017) <www.npcc.police.uk/documents/NPCC%20Custody%20Strategy.pdf> accessed 16 August 2023.

NPCC and others, 'COVID Joint Interim Interview Protocol Version 2' (NPCC in force to 1 May 2021) <https://www.cps.gov.uk/sites/default/files/documents/publications/National-Interview-Protocol-COVID19-Version-4-4-Oct-2021.pdf> accessed 16 August 2023.

NPCC and others, 'COVID Joint Interim Interview Protocol Version 4—October 2021' <www.cps.gov.uk/sites/default/files/documents/publications/National-Interview-Protocol-COVID19-Version-4-4-Oct-2021.pdf> accessed 16 August 2023.

Nemitz T and Bean P, 'The Effectiveness of a Volunteer Appropriate Adult Scheme' (1998) 38 Medicine, Science & the Law 251.

Nemitz T and Bean P, 'Protecting the Rights of the Mentally Disordered in Police Stations: The Use of the Appropriate Adult in England and Wales' (2001) 24 International Journal of Law & Psychiatry 595.

Newburn T and Hayman S, *Policing, Surveillance and Social Control: CCTV and Police Monitoring of Suspects* (Willan Publishing 2002).

Newburn T, Shiner M, and Hayman S, 'Race, Crime and Injustice? Strip Search and the Treatment of Suspects in Custody' (2004) 44 British Journal of Criminology 677.

NHS England and NHS Improvement, 'Liaison and Diversion Standard Service' (2019) <Unabbreviated link is https://www.england.nhs.uk/wp-content/uploads/2019/12/national-liaison-and-diversion-service-specification-2019.pdf> accessed 18 August 2023.

Norfolk GA, '"Fitness to Be Interviewed"—A Proposed Definition and Scheme of Examination' (1997) 37 Medicine, Science & the Law 228.

Northamptonshire Police, 'Northamptonshire Police Introduce "Trauma-Informed Custody" for Retained Children' (5 April 2022) <www.northants.police.uk/news/northants/news/news/2022/april/northamptonshire-police-introduce-trauma-informed-custody-for-detained-children> accessed 20 August 2023.

O'Mahony BM, Milne B, and Grant T, 'To Challenge, or Not to Challenge? Best Practice When Interviewing Vulnerable Suspects' (2012) 6 Policing 301.

O'Malley P and Mugford S, 'Crime, Excitement and Modernity' in G Barak (ed), *Varieties of Criminology* (Praeger 1994).

Obsuth I and others, 'Violent Poly-Victimization: The Longitudinal Patterns of Physical and Emotional Victimization throughout Adolescence (11–17 Years)' (2018) 28 Journal of Research on Adolescence 786.

Owusu-Bempah A, 'Understanding the Barriers to Defendant Participation in Criminal Proceedings in England and Wales' (2020) 40 Legal Studies 1.

Packer HL, 'Two Models of the Criminal Process' (1964) 113 University of Pennsylvania Law Review 1.

Palmer C, 'The Appropriate Adult' (1996) Legal Action 6.

Parsons S and Sherwood G, 'Vulnerability in Custody: Perceptions and Practices of Police Officers and Criminal Justice Professionals in Meeting the Communication Needs of Offenders with Learning Disabilities and Learning Difficulties' (2016) 31 Disability & Society 553.

Payne-James JJ and others, 'Healthcare Issues of Detainees in Police Custody in London, UK' (2010) 17 Journal of Forensic & Legal Medicine 11.

Pearce JJ, 'Working with Trafficked Children and Young People: Complexities in Practice' (2011) 41 British Journal of Social Work 1424.

Pearce JJ, Hynes P, and Bovarnick, S, *Trafficked Young People: Breaking the Wall of Silence* (Routledge 2013).

Pearse J and Gudjonsson GH, 'Police Interviewing Techniques at Two South London Police Stations' (1997) 3 Psychology, Crime & Law 63.

Pemberton S, 'A Theory of Moral Indifference: Understanding the Production of Harm by Capitalist Society' in P Hillyard and others (eds), *Beyond Criminology: Taking Harm Seriously* (Pluto Press 2004).

Peterson-Badali M and Abramovitch R, 'Children's Knowledge of the Legal System: Are They Competent to Instruct Legal Counsel?' (1992) Canadian Journal of Criminology 130.

Peterson-Badali M and others, 'Young People's Experience of the Canadian Youth Justice System: Interacting with Police and Legal Counsel' (1999) 17 Behavioral Sciences & the Law 455.

Phillips C and Brown DC, 'Entry into the Criminal Justice System: A Survey of Police Arrests and Their Outcomes', Home Office Research Study 185, (Home Office 1998).

Phillips C and Earle R, 'Reading Difference Differently?' (2010) 50 British Journal of Criminology 360.

Pierce CS and Brodsky SL, 'Trust and Understanding in the Attorney–Juvenile Relationship' (2002) 20 Behavioral Sciences & Law 89.

Pierpoint H, 'How Appropriate Are Volunteers as "Appropriate Adults" for Young Suspects? The "Appropriate Adult" System and Human Rights' (2000) 22 Journal of Social Welfare & Family Law 383.

Pierpoint H, 'A Survey of Volunteer Appropriate Adult Services in England and Wales' (2004) 4 Youth Justice 32.

Pierpoint H, 'Reconstructing the Role of the Appropriate Adult in England and Wales' (2006) 6 Criminology and Criminal Justice 219.

Pierpoint H, 'Quickening the PACE? The Use of Volunteers as Appropriate Adults in England and Wales' (2008) 18 International Journal of Research & Policy 397.

Pierpoint H, 'Extending and Professionalising the Role of the Appropriate Adult' (2011) 33 Journal of Social Welfare & Family Law 139.

Pierpoint H, 'The Risks of Voluntary Interviews' (2020) 9 Criminal Law Review 818.

Plotnikoff J and Woolfson R, 'Young Defendants Pack: Scoping Study' (Youth Justice Board 2002) <https://vdocuments.site/young-defendants-pack-scoping-study-lexicon-limited-young-defendants-pack-scoping.html> accessed 14 August 2023.

Powers M and Faden R, *Social Justice: The Moral Foundations of Public Health and Health Policy* (OUP 2006).

Presdee M, *Cultural Criminology and the Carnival of Crime* (Routledge 2000).

Price C and Caplan J, *The Confait Confessions* (Marion Boyars 1977).

Quinn K and Jackson J, 'The Detention and Questioning of Young Persons by the Police in Northern Ireland', Northern Ireland Office Research & Statistical Series: Report No. 9 (Northern Ireland Office 2003).

Quinn K and Jackson J, 'Of Rights and Roles' (2007) 47 British Journal of Criminology 234.

Quirk H, *The Rise and Fall of the Right of Silence* (Routledge 2017).

Qvortrup J, *Childhood Matters: Social Theory, Practice and Politics* (Avebury 1994).

Redlich A and Goodman G, 'Taking Responsibility for an Act Not Committed: The Influence of Age and Suggestibility' (2003) 27 Law & Human Behavior 141.

Redlich AD and others, 'The Police Interrogation of Children and Adolescents' in GD Lassiter (ed), *Interrogations, Confessions and Entrapment* (Kluwer Academic 2004).

Reiner R, *The Politics of the Police* (4th edn, OUP 2010).

Rivara FP and others, 'Victim as Offender in Youth Violence' (1995) 26 Annals of Emergency Medicine 609.

Robin-D'Cruz C and Tibbs E, *Mapping Youth Diversion in England and Wales* (Centre for Justice Innovation 2019).

Rogers R and others, 'Juvenile Miranda Warnings: Perfunctory Rituals or Procedural Safeguards?' (2012) 39 Criminal Justice & Behavior 229.

Rogowski S, 'Young Offenders: Their Experience of Offending and the Youth Justice System' (2000) 70 Youth & Policy 52.

Royal Commission on Criminal Justice, 'Report (Cmnd 2263)' (HMSO 1991).

Royal Commission on Criminal Procedure, 'Report (Cmnd 8092)' (HMSO 1981).

Rumgay J, 'Scripts for Safer Survival: Pathways Out of Female Crime' (2004) 43 Howard Journal of Criminal Justice 405.

Rusche G, *Punishment and Social Structure* (Columbia UP 1939).

Russano MB and others, 'Investigating True and False Confessions within a Novel Experimental Paradigm' (2005) 16 Psychological Science 481.

Samele C and others, 'The Prevalence of Mental Illness and Unmet Needs of Police Custody Detainees' (2021) 31(2) Criminal Behaviour & Mental Health 80.

Sampson RJ, *Crime in the Making: Pathways and Turning Points through Life* (Harvard UP 1993).

Sampson RJ and Bartusch DJ, 'Legal Cynicism and (Subcultural?) Tolerance of Deviance: The Neighborhood Context of Racial Differences' (1998) 32 Law & Society Review 777.

Sanders A, *Criminal Justice* (2nd edn, OUP 2000).

Sanders A, *Criminal Justice* (4th edn, OUP 2010).

Sanders A, Bridges L, and Mulvaney A, *Advice and Assistance at Police Stations and the 24 Hour Duty Solicitor Scheme* (Lord Chancellor's Department 1989).

Santo A, ' "Sometimes You Gotta Go in the Shower and Go Knife-to-Knife, Right?" ' (The Marshall Project & New York Magazine 2015) <www.themarshallproject.org/2015/06/28/this-is-rikers> accessed 14 August 2023.

Saywitz K and Jaenicke C, 'Children's Understanding of Legal Terminology' (Annual Meeting of the Society for Research on Child Development, Baltimore 1987).

Saywitz K, Jaenicke C, and Camparo L, 'Children's Knowledge of Legal Terminology' (1990) 14 Law and Human Behavior 523.

Schoovaerts H, Vanderhallen M, and McIntyre S-J, 'Lawyers and Children: Is There a Need for Mandatory Legal Assistance in Suspect Interviews?' (2021) 23 International Journal of Police Science & Management 55.

Scott E and Grisso T, 'The Evolution of Adolescence: A Developmental Perspective on Juvenile Justice Reform' (1997) 88 Journal of Criminal Law & Criminology 137.

Shalhoub-Kevorkian N and Kovner B, 'Child Arrest, Settler Colonialism, and the Israeli Juvenile System: A Case Study of Occupied East Jerusalem' (2018) 58 British Journal of Criminology 709.

Sherman LW, 'Defiance, Deterrence, and Irrelevance: A Theory of the Criminal Sanction' (1993) 30 Journal of Research in Crime & Delinquency 445.

Sim MPY, 'Appropriate Adults' Contributions during Police Interviews with Juveniles' (23rd Conference of the European Association of Psychology and Law, Coventry 2013).

Sim MPY and Lamb ME, 'An Analysis of How the Police "Caution" Is Presented to Juvenile Suspects in England' (2018) 24(8) Psychology, Crime & Law 1.

Simmons M and others, 'Sixty Years of Child-to-Parent Abuse Research: What We Know and Where to Go' (2018) 38 Aggression and Violent Behavior 31.

Skinns L, '"I'm a Detainee; Get Me Out of Here": Predictors of Access to Custodial Legal Advice in Public and Privatized Police Custody Areas in England and Wales' (2009) 49 British Journal of Criminology 399.

Skinns L, ' "Let's Get It Over With": Early Findings on the Factors Affecting Detainees' Access to Custodial Legal Advice' (2009) 19 Policing & Society 58.

Skinns L, 'Stop the Clock? Predictors of Detention without Charge in Police Custody Areas' (2010) 10 Criminology & Criminal Justice 303.

Skinns L, *Overnight Detention of Children in Police Cells* (Howard League 2011).

Skinns L, *Police Custody: Governance, Legitimacy and Reform in the Criminal Justice Process* (Willan Publishing 2011).

Skinns, L, *Police Powers and Citizens' Rights: Discretionary Decision-Making in Police Detention* (Routledge 2019).

Skinns L and Wooff A, 'Pain in Police Detention: A Critical Point in the "Penal Painscape"?' (2020) 31(3) Policing & Society 245.

Skinns L, Sorsby A, and Rice L, '"Treat Them as a Human Being": Dignity in Police Detention and Its Implications for "Good" Police Custody' (2020) 60(6) British Journal of Criminology 1667.

Skinns L, Wooff A, and Sprawson A, 'Preliminary Findings on Police Custody Delivery in the Twenty-First Century: Is It "Good" Enough?' (2017) 27 Policing & Society 358.

Skolnick JH, *Justice without Trial: Law Enforcement in Democratic Society* (Wiley 1966).

Smith DJ and Ecob R, 'An Investigation into Causal Links between Victimization and Offending in Adolescents' (2007) 58 British Journal of Sociology 633.

Smith DJ and Gray J, 'Police and People in London: The Police in Action' (PSI Study 1983).

Snow PC, 'Speech–Language Pathology and the Youth Offender: Epidemiological Overview and Roadmap for Future Speech–Language Pathology Research and Scope of Practice' (2019) 50 Language, Speech & Hearing Services in Schools 324.

Softley P and others, 'Police Interrogation: An Observational Study in Four Police Stations', Home Office Research Study No 4 (HMSO 1980).

Soukara S and others, 'What Really Happens in Police Interviews of Suspects? Tactics and Confessions' (2009) 15 Psychology, Crime & Law 493.

Spencer D and others, ' "I Think It's Re-victimizing Victims Almost Every Time": Police Perceptions of Criminal Justice Responses to Sexual Violence' (2018) 26 Critical Criminology (Richmond, BC) 189.

Spicer J, ' "That's Their Brand, Their Business": How Police Officers Are Interpreting County Lines' (2019) 29(8) Policing & Society 873.

Spivak GC, 'Can the Subaltern Speak?' in C Nelson and L Grossberg (eds), *Marxism and the Interpretation of Culture* (University of Illinois Press 1988).

Staines J, *Risk, Adverse Influence and Criminalisation. Understanding the Over-Representation of Looked After Children in the Youth Justice System* (Prison Reform Trust 2016).

Stark MM and Norfolk GA, 'Training in Clinical Forensic Medicine in the UK—Perceptions of Current Regulatory Standards' (2011) 18 Journal of Forensic & Legal Medicine 264.

Stark MM and Rix KJB, 'Fitness to Be Interviewed and Fitness to Be Charged' in MM Stark (ed), *Clinical Forensic Medicine: A Physician's Guide* (Springer Nature 2020).

Steinberg L and others, 'Around the World, Adolescence Is a Time of Heightened Sensation Seeking and Immature Self-Regulation' (2018) 21 Developmental Science 12532.

Steiner H, Garcia IG, and Mathews Z, 'Post Traumatic Stress Disorder in Incarcerated Juvenile Delinquents' (1997) Journal of the American Academy of Child Psychology & Psychiatry 357.

Stoneman M-J and others, 'Variation in Detainee Risk Assessment within Police Custody across England and Wales' (2018) 29 Policing & Society 951.

Stuart M and Baines C, *Safeguards for Vulnerable Children: Three Studies on Abusers, Disabled Children and Children in Prison* (Joseph Rowntree Foundation 2004).

Sutherland C and Lord Carloway, 'The Carloway Review, Report and Recommendations' (Carloway Review 2011).

Sykes GM, *The Society of Captives: A Study of a Maximum Security Prison* (OUP 1958).

Taggart J, '"I Am Not Beholden to Anyone … I Consider Myself to Be an Officer of the Court": A Comparison of the Intermediary Role in England and Wales and Northern Ireland' (2021) 25 International Journal of Evidence & Proof 141.

Taylor C, *Review of the Youth Justice System in England and Wales* (Ministry of Justice 2016).

Thomson LDG, Galt V, and Darjee R, 'Professionalizing the Role of Appropriate Adults' (2007) 18 Journal of Forensic Psychiatry & Psychology 99.

Tobey A, Grisso T, and Schwartz R, 'Youth's Trial Participation as Seen by Youths and Their Attorneys: An Exploration of Competence-Based Issues' in T Grisso and R Schwartz (eds), *Youth on Trial: A Developmental Perspective on Juvenile Justice* (University of Chicago Press 2000).

Transform Justice, 'National Appropriate Adult and Fair Trials, Not Remotely Fair? Access to a Lawyer in the Police Station during the COVID-19 Pandemic' <https://www.transformjustice.org.uk/publication/not-remotely-fair-access-to-a-lawyer-in-the-police-station-during-the-covid-19-pandemic/> accessed 14 August 2023.

Turner A, Belcher L, and Pona I, *Counting Lives: Responding to Children Who Are Criminally Exploited* (Children's Society 2019).

Tyler TR, *Why People Obey the Law* (Yale UP 1990).

Tyler TR, 'Procedural Justice, Legitimacy, and the Effective Rule of Law' (2003) 30 Crime & Justice 283.

Tyler TR and Huo YJ, *Trust in the Law: Encouraging Public Cooperation with the Police and Courts* (Russell Sage Foundation 2002).

Tyler TR, Fagan J, and Geller A, 'Street Stops and Police Legitimacy: Teachable Moments in Young Urban Men's Legal Socialization: Street Stops and Police Legitimacy' (2014) 11 Journal of Empirical Legal Studies 751.

Ugelvik T, 'The Hidden Food: Mealtime Resistance and Identity Work in a Norwegian Prison' (2011) 13 Punishment & Society 47.

van Oosterhout M and de Vocht D, 'Chapter 5: Protecting Juvenile Suspects in a Pedagogical But Punitive Context. Country Report the Netherlands' in M Panzavolta and others (eds), *Interrogating Young Suspects: Procedural Safeguards from a Legal Perspective* (Intersentia 2015).

Vaswani N, 'The Ripples of Death: Exploring the Bereavement Experiences and Mental Health of Young Men in Custody' (2014) 53 Howard Journal of Criminal Justice 341.

Ventress MA, Rix KJB, and Kent JH, 'Keeping PACE: Fitness to Be Interviewed by the Police' (2008) 14 Advances in Psychiatric Treatment 369.

Viding E, Fontaine NMG, and McCrory EJ, 'Antisocial Behaviour in Children With and Without Callous-Unemotional Traits' (2012) 105 Journal of Royal Society of Medicine 195.

Viljoen JL, Klaver J, and Roesch R, 'Legal Decisions of Preadolescent and Adolescent Defendants: Predictors of Confessions, Pleas, Communication with Attorneys, and Appeals' (2005) 29 Law & Human Behavior 253.

Vizard E, 'Child Defendants: Occasional Paper 56' (Royal College of Psychiatrists 2006).

Wacquant L, 'From "Public Criminology" to the Reflexive Sociology of Criminological Production and Consumption' (2011) 51 British Journal of Criminology 438.

Waddington PAJ, *Policing Citizens: Authority and Rights* (UCL Press 1999).

Wainwright A and Mojtahedi D, 'An Examination of Stigmatising Attributions about Mental Illness amongst Police Custody Staff' (2020) 68 International Journal of Law & Psychiatry 101522.

Weaver VM and Lerman AE, 'Political Consequences of the Carceral State' (2010) 104 American Political Science Review 817.

Weisselberg CD, 'Mourning Miranda' (2008) 96 California Law Review 1519.

West Midlands Violence Reduction Partnership, 'Trauma Informed' <https://westmidlands-vrp.org/about/trauma-informed> accessed 18 August 2023.

White C, 'Re-assessing the Social Worker's Role as an Appropriate Adult' (2002) 24 Journal of Social Welfare & Family Law 55.

Wigzell A, Kirby A, and Jacobson J, 'Youth Proceedings Advocacy Review: Final Report' (Institute for Criminal Policy Research 19 November 2015) <https://cilexregulation.org.uk/wp-content/uploads/2019/02/Youth-proceedings-advocacy-review-report.pdf> accessed 14 August 2023.

Williams J, 'The Inappropriate Adult' (2000) 22 Journal of Social Welfare & Family Law 43.

Williamson TM, 'From Interrogation to Investigative Interviewing; Strategic Trends in Police Questioning' (1993) 3 Journal of Community & Applied Social Psychology 89.

Windle J, Moyle L, and Coomber R, '"Vulnerable" Kids Going Country: Children and Young People's Involvement in County Lines Drug Dealing' (2020) 20 Youth Justice 64.

Wishart H, 'Young Minds, Old Legal Problems: Can Neuroscience Fill the Void? Young Offenders and the Age of Criminal Responsibility Bill—Promise and Perils' (2018) 82(4) Journal of Criminal Law 311.

Woodbury-Smith M, 'Conceptualising Social and Communication Vulnerabilities among Detainees in the Criminal Justice System' (2020) 100 Research in Developmental Disabilities 103611.

Woodhead M and Faulkner D, 'Subjects, Objects or Participants? Dilemmas of Psychological Research with Children' in PM Christensen and A James (eds), *Research with Children: Perspectives and Practices* (2nd edn, Routledge 2008).

Wooff A and Skinns L, 'The Role of Emotion, Space and Place in Police Custody in England: Towards a Geography of Police Custody' (2018) 20 Punishment & Society 562.

Woolard J and others, 'Examining Adolescents' and Their Parents' Conceptual and Practical Knowledge of Police Interrogation: A Family Dyad Approach' (2008) 37 Journal of Youth and Adolescence 685.

Woolard JL, Harvell MPPS, and Graham PDS, 'Anticipatory Injustice among Adolescents: Age and Racial/Ethnic Differences in Perceived Unfairness of the Justice System' (2008) 26 Behavioral Sciences & Law 207.

Youth Justice Board (YJB), 'Case Management Guidance 2014' (YJB 2014).

YJB, 'Standards for Children in the Youth Justice System' (2019) <https://assets.publishing.service.gov.uk/government/uploads/system/uploads/attachment_data/file/957697/Standards_for_children_in_youth_justice_services_2019.doc.pdf> accessed 20 August 2023.

YJB, 'A Guide to Child First' (2023) <https://yjresourcehub.uk/images/YJB/Child_First_Overview_and_Guide_April_2022_YJB.pdf#:~:text=Child%20First%20is%20the%20guiding%20principle%20for%20the,children%2C%20to%20recognise%20the%20potential%20they%20each%20bring> accessed 20 August 2023.

YJB/Ministry of Justice (MoJ), *Youth Justice Statistics 2018–19, England and Wales* (National Statistics 2020).

YJB/MoJ, *Youth Justice Statistics 2020–21, England and Wales* (National Statistics 2022).

YJB/MoJ, *Youth Justice Statistics 2021–22, England and Wales* (National Statistics 2023).

Young SJ and others, 'The Identification and Management of ADHD Offenders within the Criminal Justice System: A Consensus Statement from the UK Adult ADHD Network and Criminal Justice Agencies' (2011) 11 BioMed Centre Psychiatry 32.

Young SJ and others, 'The Effectiveness of Police Custody Assessments in Identifying Suspects with Intellectual Disabilities and Attention Deficit Hyperactivity Disorder' (2013) 11 BioMed Centre Medicine 248.

Zander M and Henderson P, 'Crown Court Study', Royal Commission on Criminal Justice Research Study No 19 (HMSO 1993).

Zelle H, Riggs Romaine CL, and Goldstein NES, 'Juveniles' Miranda Comprehension: Understanding, Appreciation, and Totality of Circumstances Factors' (2015) 39 Law & Human Behavior 281.

Index

For the benefit of digital users, indexed terms that span two pages (e.g., 52-53) may, on occasion, appear on only one of those pages.

abuse 9-10
  strip searches, history of abuse, and 89
ADHD 134
  appropriate adults, and 190-91
  buzzer usage 239
  custody officers' training, and 269-70
  decision-making, and 102
  detention, and 78, 220-21, 239, 319
    detention as safeguarding 77-78
  disclosure about 80-81
  'easyread' notices 110-11
  fitness to be interviewed 266, 268-69
  medication 232
  prevalence among child suspects 7-9
  risk assessments, and 80-81
adversities in childhood 10-12
  immediate situational adversity 13
  nature of 10-11
  physical effects on developing brain 11-12
  police scrutiny, and 11
  structural disadvantage, and 10-12
All Party Parliamentary Group for Children (APPGC) 23, 117-18, 205-6, 210-11, 220, 248-49, 284
appropriate adult viii-x, 16-17, 153-203, 311
  ADHD, and 190-91
  booking in process, and 103, 158-59
  Children's Commissioner 23, 160
  communication, assisting with
    familial appropriate adults 188-90
    non-familial appropriate adults 190-91
    young suspect experiences 188-91
  custody officer control
    conflicts of interest 174
    enabling the appropriate adult 174-76
    fundamental problem with 198-99
    limited information given to appropriate adult 174, 175-76
    limited information given to child suspect 174-75
    suitability of appropriate adult for role 172-74
    young suspect experiences 172-77
  delays in attending 157, 160-61
    absence for much of detention episode 168
    concerns about 160
    deliberate delay to coincide with interview 153, 169-70, 171
    effects of 161, 168-72, 182
    false confessions, and 161, 171-72
    overnight delays 170
    reasons for 160, 168-69
    rights of child suspects, impact on knowledge of 108-9
    undermining appropriate adult's ability to support child suspect 171-72
    young suspect experiences 168-72
  'easyread' notices 110-11
  false confessions, and *see under* false confessions
  family members as 159
    aggression or hostility towards child suspect 173
    booking in, and 159
    burden to family members, child suspect feeling 180
    communication, assisting with 188-90
    communication difficulties of child 188
    communication with solicitors and officers, inhibiting 189-90
    facilitating rights of child suspect 183-84, 185-86
    guardian of due process 191-94

appropriate adult (*cont.*)
  inability to attend as appropriate adult 107, 180
  ill-equipped to perform role 153–54
  lack of training and knowledge of role 165
  legal advice, and 128–30
  limited information given to 174, 175–76
  linguistic difficulties 188–89
  majority of child suspects supported by 163–64
  no systematic method of assessing suitability for role 197–98
  parental distress 180
  parental/familial anger 179–80
  parents or guardians as 16–17
  predominant reliance on familial support 157
  reassurance, providing 177–79
  role usually fulfilled by 153–54
  suitability and effectiveness, concerns about 163–66
  support and welfare, young suspect experiences 177–80
  undue compliance 165–66
  guardian of due process
    familial appropriate adults 191–94
    non-familial appropriate adults 194–95
    young suspect experiences 191–95
  HMICFRS 85, 157, 160, 168, 194
  issues raised in existing literature 160–67
    complexity of role 161–62
    delays 160–61
    lack of legal privilege 162–63
    suitability and effectiveness of familial appropriate adults 163–66
  learning disability, and 190–91
  legal advice, and 128–30
    appropriate adult overriding refusal of advice 114, 128–30
    familial appropriate adults lacking knowledge 129
    familial appropriate adults, refusal of advice and 115–16, 128–29
    non-familial appropriate adults, concerns of 129–30
    remote legal representation, concerns about 144–45
  legal privilege, lack of 157, 162–63, 178–79
    capable of undermining role of appropriate adult 198

  concerns over 163, 198
  reform of 202
looked after children 159
non-familial appropriate adults 159
  communication, assisting with 190–91
  conflicts of interest 174, 181
  facilitating rights of child suspect 184–85, 187
  guardian of due process 194–95
  identification of communication needs 190–91
  obstacles to building rapport 181–82
  passivity 194–95
  personal questions, burden of 183
  problematic behaviour of child suspect 182
  suitability and effectiveness, concerns about 166–67
  support and welfare, young suspect experiences 181–83
  trained lay adults as 159
  trust issues 182–83
police interviews, and *see* police interviews
RCCP 156–57, 161–62, 164
reform, avenues for 199–203
  advisory and facilitation role of trained specialist 201
  intermediary support for child with communication needs 202–3
  lack of legal privilege, reform of 202
  separation of welfare support from other functions 199–200
reviews of operation of 157
rights of child suspects
  awareness of role of appropriate adult 104, 106–7
  continuing rights delivered in presence of appropriate adult 104
  delays in appropriate adult attending 108–9
  facilitating rights 183–87
  repetition of rights in presence of appropriate adult 108–9
  right to consult privately with appropriate adult 103, 106–7, 111–12, 174–75
  see also child as legal actor
rights of child suspects: supporting child to exercise legal rights
  familial appropriate adults 185–86

non-familial appropriate adults 187
young suspect experiences 185–87
rights of child suspects: understanding
 familial appropriate adults 183–84
 non-familial appropriate
  adults 184–85
 young suspect experiences 183–85
role and duties of 16–17, 24–25, 93–94,
 157–67
 booking in process, role and 103,
  158–59
 child suspect's awareness of 104, 106–7
 complexity of role 161–62
 composite and conflicted role 195–203
 critical nature of role 153–54
 current formulation of role 157–59
 definition of role in legislation 157–58
 lack of clarity in inception of
  role 156–57
 making good 'imbalance' between
  child and prosecution in police
  custody 153–54
 multifaceted nature of role 153–54,
  161–62
 procedure and existing
  literature 157–67
 role ill understood and variably
  exercised 153–54
 role in practice: young suspect
  experiences 168–77
 safeguarding role, concerns
  about 24–25
 shortcomings in the way role is
  conceived 197–99
 welfare aspects and ensuring due
  process, tension between 161–62
role in practice: young suspect
 experiences 168–77
 assisting with communication 188–91
 custody officer control 172–77
 delay 168–72
 facilitating rights 183–87
 guardian of due process 191–95
 support and welfare 177–83
scope of empirical data 167
statutory duty on local authorities to
 provide 159, 160
strip searches and intimate searches *see*
 strip searches
support and welfare
 familial appropriate adults 177–80

non-familial appropriate adults 181–83
young suspect experiences 177–83
arrest
 assumption that arrest lawful 72
 Black, Asian and minority ethnic
  children 55–57, 91–92
 coercive nature of 97
 dispositional vulnerabilities, and 91–92
 family members informed 170
 handcuffs, use of 49–50, 54–55, 95
 heavy-handed arrests 54, 57
 impact of 54–58
 inappropriate use of force 55
 lack of knowledge of what follows
  arrest 57–58
 mental health issues 55
 problematic behaviour on arrest, effects
  of 57
 profound feelings, engendering 56–57, 91
authorisation of detention
 automatic approach to 95–96
 child suspect experiences 73–78
  changing approach to detaining
   children 73–74
  detention as safeguarding 77–78
  extra-PACE objectives 76–78
  incapacitative or social disciplinary
   aspect of detention 76–78, 95–96
  independence of custody officers 74–75
  investigative convenience 75–76
  refusal to authorise detention 73–75
  self-harm, and 74
 dispositional vulnerabilities, and 91–92
 procedure and existing literature 71–72
  assumption that arrest lawful 72
  concerns about unnecessary detention
   of arrestees 71–72
  duty to consider best interests of
   child 72
  reasons for authorizing detention/
   necessity grounds 71, 73
autism 7–9, 232
 custody officers' training, and 269–70
 detention, and 319
  detention as safeguarding 77–78
  rights of child suspects, knowledge
   of 108–9
 'easyread' notices 110–11
 fitness to be interviewed 274, 312–13
 healthcare professionals, and 270–71
 risk assessment, and 268–69, 274, 312–13

Index

bereavement 10–11, 50
Black, Asian and minority ethnic
    children xi–xii, 12
  appropriate adult, and 199
  arrest, and 55–57
  booking in, problematic behaviour at 67
  detention
    longer detention periods 217–18
    overnight detention 215–16
  legal advisers
    declining legal advice 118
    lack of trust in 29–30, 117, 134
    withholding of information 135
  strip searches 85–86
booking in 60–63
  adversarial nature of custody process 94
  appropriate adult, and *see* appropriate adult
  at the desk 64–68, 91
    acting up, acting tough 66–68
    child suspects behaving problematically 66–67, 95–96
    child suspects moderating behaviour 65–66
    coercive nature of setting 65, 67
    humiliating and demeaning treatment 92
    physical arrangements 64
    punitive nature of, child suspects perception as 92–93
    staying calm, challenges of 65–66
  authorisation of detention *see* authorisation of detention
  child suspect experiences 60–70
    at the desk 64–68
    waiting to be booked in 60–63
  contingent nature of custody process, effects of 91
  custody officers *see under* custody officers and child suspects
  oppositional nature of custody process 95–96
  rights communication *see* child suspect as legal actor
  risk assessments *see* risk assessments
  search and seizure of belongings *see* search and seizure of belongings
  waiting to be booked in 60–63
    contact with arrested adults 61–63
    conversations with adult detainees 63
    effect of lengthy delays 61
    holding child suspects in suitable, safe place 59–60
    lack of prioritization 60–61, 93–94
    lengthy waits to be booked in 60
    physical confrontations with adult detainees 62–63
    separation practically achievable 63, 95
Bulger, Jamie 3–4, 33–34

Child and Adolescent Mental Health Services (CAMHS) 77–78
child as legal actor 98–152, 310
  benefiting from legal rights 132–45
    deciding whether to answer questions in police interview 138–44
    engaging with the solicitor 133–38
  communicating legal rights: child suspect experiences 105–12
    comprehension difficulties 106
    limited awareness of rights 111–12
    need for tailored delivery 105–6
    notice of rights and entitlements 103–4, 109–12
    pared-down approach 106–7, 111, 130–31
    presumed familiarity 107–8
    previous arrests, and 107–8
    repetition of rights in presence of appropriate adult 108–9
    right to complain 104, 106–7
  communicating legal rights: procedure and existing literature 103–5
    appropriate adult, and *see* appropriate adult
    continuing rights 103–4, 111–12, 128
  doubts whether child suspects able to appreciate their rights 104–5
    incommunicado rights 103–4, 106–7, 220, 227–28, 240, 341–42
    rights communication at end of booking in process 103–4
    written notice of rights 103–4
  deciding whether to answer questions in police interview 138–44
    coercion, child suspect's feelings of 143–44
    factual understanding and appreciation of consequences of silence 139–41
    rational decision-making, frequent absence of 141–42, 147

Index 385

declining/waiving legal advice 114,
116–17, 118, 120–23, 147–50
  competence to waive, requirement to
    establish 148–49
  presumption of legal advice, proposal
    for 147–48
  striking right balance between
    autonomy and protection 150–52
  US approaches to competence to
    waive 148–50
engaging with the solicitor 133–38
  ability to trust solicitor, importance
    of 133–35
  competence and engagement 135–36
  custody record, right to review 138
  delay in solicitor attending, effects
    of 137–38
  delay in solicitor attending, reasons
    for 136–37
  independence of solicitor, lack of belief
    in 127, 133–34, 147–48
  lack of trust, effects of 117, 127, 133–35
  low solicitor fees, effects of 137
  withholding of information 134–35
exercising right to legal advice: child
    suspect experiences 118–32, 145–46
  ability to reason logically about options:
    impact of the process 123
  adversarial approaches, effects of 126–28
  choice free from coercion 123–28
  consequences of waiving legal advice,
    appreciation of 121–23
  inability to engage with meaning of
    rights and entitlements 119
  legal advice not enabled in
    practice 130–32
  limited appreciation of nature and
    purpose of legal advice 120–21
  natural developmental immaturity,
    understanding legal rights
    and 119–20
  protections against poor
    decision-making 128–30
  steering child suspect to/from taking
    legal advice 124–26
  understanding the right 118–20
exercising right to legal advice: procedure
    and existing literature 112–18
  admissions 113–14
  appropriate adult requesting legal
    advice 114

coercion, and 113–14, 123–28
continuing right, legal advice as 128
declining/waiving legal advice 114,
  116–17, 118, 120–23
emphasis on diversion and community
  resolutions, and 113–14
ethnicity, legal advisers and 117
free legal advice, right to 113–14
information about engaging legal
  advice 114, 117–18
legal assistance, right to 112–13
limited understanding of value of legal
  advice 116–17
low uptake of legal advice, reasons
  for 115–18
need to request legal advice 113–14
provision of sufficient information to
  solicitor 114–15
solicitors viewed as unwelcome
  'challengers' 117–18, 136–37
unrepresented child suspects 114–15
expert, appropriately resourced, and
  in-person legal advice, importance
  of 144–45
good quality representation, vital
  importance of 144
wider use of remote legal
  representation, concerns
  about 144–45
fundamental reform, need for 145–52
importance of legal representation 305
legal autonomy in police custody:
  essential but challenged 100–2
  ability to participate as an autonomous
    legal actor, importance of 100
  autonomous decision-making
    challenging for child suspects 102
  fitness-for-interview assessment,
    approach in 101
  individual's competence to make
    decisions 100–1
  lack of appreciation of nature and
    content of rights 99
  notice of rights and entitlements 109–12
    accessibility, concerns around 109–11
    booking in, available at 103–4, 109
    child friendly approaches, features
      preventing 111
    'easyread' formulations of 110–11
    including all required
      information 109–10

children
  abuse 10–11
  adversity, and *see* adversities in childhood
  Black, Asian and minority ethnic children *see* Black, Asian and minority ethnic children
  child suspects *see* children in police custody
  courts, and *see* Youth Justice System (YJS)
  custody, in *see* children in police custody
  dispositional vulnerabilities *see under* children in police custody
  immaturity *see* immaturity of children
  legal actor, as *see* child as legal actor
  meaning of 'child' in youth justice system and policing 1–4
  mental health *see* mental health
  social and emotional capacities 5
  statistics on arrest of xi–xii
  UNCRC 4
children in police custody
  age-related protections, end of 4
  children in police custody, knowledge about 6–13
    childhood adversities and structural disadvantage 10–12
    dispositional vulnerabilities 7–10, 50, 79–80, 91–92
    immediate situational adversity 13, 50
  custody officers *see* custody officers
  detention *see* detention
  false confessions *see* false confessions
  HMICFRS *see* His Majesty's Inspectorate of Constabulary, Fore and Rescue Services (HMICFRS formerly HMIC)
  interviews *see* police interviews
  invisibility of child suspects *see* invisibility of child suspects
  'juveniles', use of term 1–2
  meaning of 'child' 1–4
  natural developmental immaturity in custody 5–6
  oversight mechanisms, concerns about 19–20
  risk assessments *see* risk assessments
  strip searches *see* strip searches
  vulnerability *see* vulnerability
  welfare principle 13
  see also College of Policing

Children's Commissioner
  appropriate adults 23, 160
  strip searches 85–86
College of Policing
  'Authorised Professional Practice (Detention and Custody)' 16–17
  detention of child suspects 71, 220–21
  girl suspects 220–21
  prioritization of child suspects 59–60
  right to complain 104, 106–7
  right to legal advice 114, 124–26, 131
  rights of child suspects, tailored communication of 104, 105–7
  'children and young persons', use of 1–2
  guidance 19–20
conclusions 308–45
  custody process, failings in 314–17
  implications for wider youth justice system 342–45
  progress since *Confait* case 308–14
  reasons for so little progress 318–30
    adversariality and adversity in collision 321–28
    adversity 319–21
    challenge of recognizing vulnerability in a justice context 324–28
    invisibility of child suspect 329–30
  reform: achieving child first police custody 337–42
    detention conditions 341–42
    differentiation and separation 341
    mandatory legal advice 339–40
    reduced timescales 340–41
    supporting adults 339
    training 338
  reform: retrenchment 331–37
    addressing adversity: presumption against detention for children 332–36
    mitigating adversarial approach: increased oversight 336–37
Confait cases vii–xi
  emotional reassurance and support, children's need for 156–57, 199
  false confessions vii, 7–9, 156–57
  Fisher Report, and 199, 309
  miscarriage of justice, as 28, 45, 98, 199, 259–60, 306
  integrity of pre-charge procedures, and 120–21, 130–31, 156–57, 199
  progress since decision 308–14

Royal Commission on Criminal
        Procedure, triggering vii–viii, 309
confessions
    coercive or confession-seeking
        tactics 259–60, 316
    Confait case *see Confait* case
    excluding confessions at trial 148
    fallibility of 28
    false confessions *see* false confessions
    minimization techniques increasing rate
        of 280–81
    oppressive tactics, police use of 297
    persuasive tactics, police us of 298
    police emphasis on obtaining 258–59,
        278–79, 304–5
    repetition of questions 286
    testing reliability of 18–19, 260–61
'county-lines' drug supply 11
custody, children in *see* children in police
    custody
custody officers viii–x, 17–18, 68–70
    ADHD, and 269–70
    adversarial nature of custody process 94
    appropriate adult, and *see under*
        appropriate adult
    autism, and 269–70
    booking in
        advice, giving 70
        human approaches 70
        humour, use of 69
        respectful treatment 69–70
    conflicted position of 46–47, 126, 131,
        147, 321–22, 336–37
    fitness to be interviewed
        assessments 268–70
    see also police interviews
    HMICFRS 269–70
    independence of 74–75, 95–96, 126
    intersecting perspectives, and 45
    learning disability, and 269–70
    resource pressures 95
    role 17
        prioritization of child suspects 59–60
        rights communication *see* child suspect
            as legal actor
        risk assessments *see* risk assessments
        safety and welfare of detainees 78–79,
            95

detention
    ADHD, and *see under* ADHD

adjustments to detention conditions *see*
    detention conditions, adjustments to
autism, and *see under* autism
barriers to child friendly detention 235–47
    constraints imposed by lack of police
        resources 235–36
    extraordinary imbalance of
        power 239–41
    low visibility of detention
        conditions 244–47
    pedagogical and social disciplinary
        approaches 237–38
    resignation and resistance 241–44
child suspects' experiences of *see*
    detention, child suspects'
    experiences of
custody officers *see* custody officers
custody process magnifying child's
    burdens and disadvantages 256
detention in isolation, false confessions
    and 262
detention times 214–15
    opting for legal advice, and 125
    early stages *see* detention, initial stages of
false confessions, and *see under* false
    confessions
HMICFRS 214–15, 245–46, 329–30
impacts of punitive detention
    experiences 247–54
    compliance and cooperation, impact
        on 251–52
    detention experienced as
        punishment 204–5, 247
    procedural injustice undermining
        perceptions of police
        legitimacy 248–51
    reporting crime and seeking help,
        impact on 252–53
    vicarious effects 253–54
learning disability, and *see* learning
    disability
limiting detention period *see* detention,
    limiting periods of
proportionality, and 255–56
detention, child suspects' experiences
    of 23–24, 60–70, 73–78, 207–13, 255
    conditions in detention 207–10
        food as central focus of
            complaint 207–8
        harsh cell conditions 207
        toilet issues 208–9

detention, child suspects' experiences of (*cont.*)
  confinement 209–10
  isolation 209
  sense of containment 209
  importance of child friendly protections 256–57
  lack of stimulation, coping with 210–12, 229–30
    boredom 210–11, 229–30
    distress 212
    reading 229–30
  managing uncertainty 212–13
detention conditions, adjustments to additional adversities, adapting for 231–33
  healthcare professionals, use of 232–34
  increased surveillance 231
  limited alternative accommodation 231–32
  reasons for lack of adjustments 231–32
  self-harm 233–35
  very few adjustments 231
  child suspect experiences 222–35
    adapting for additional adversities 231–33
    adult distress, enduring 223–25
    general welfare support 229–30
    minimal contact with appropriate adult and family members 226–28
    routine use of adult cells 222–23
    support for girls 228–29
    visits and checks 225–26
  procedure and existing literature 220–21
    adjustments for particular groups of children 220–21
    characteristics increasing risk to safety 220–21
    children held separately from detained adults 59–60, 61–62, 220, 223–24
    girl suspects under care of female officer 220–21, 228–29
    recording reasons for detention in a cell 220
    right to speak to appropriate adult 'at any time' 220
    scant protections not consistently implemented 221
    visits to child suspects 220

detention, initial stages of 46, 49–97, 204–5, 309–10
  adversariality in police custody 93–97
    adversarial nature of custody process 94
    institutional constraints 93–94
    structural factors 93–94
  adversity and vulnerability 50–53
    child's rights, ensuring observance of 50
    vulnerability of child suspects *see* vulnerability
  authorisation of detention *see* authorisation of detention
  booking in *see* booking in
  custody officers and staff *see* custody officers
  immediate situational adversity 13, 53–58
    impact of arrest 54–58
    lack of knowledge 57–58
  impact of failures to respond to adversity 91–93
  importance of initial period 49–50
  length of initial stages 49–50, 60–61
  procedure and existing literature 59–60
    need for adjusted treatment 59
    oppositional nature of custody process 95–96
    process largely unadjusted to young suspects 90–91
  risk assessments *see* risk assessments
  routinized risk aversion 79, 80–81, 88, 89–90, 95, 96–97
  search and seizure of belongings *see* search and seizure of belongings
  victim-orientated focus, and 95–96
detention, limiting periods of 213–16
  average child suspect detention periods 214–15, 313
  child suspect experiences 216–19
    detention for extremely long periods, reasons for 216–17
    detention reviews 217–18
    longer detention for those experiencing greater adversity 218–19
    overnight detention 215–16
  time limits on detention 214
doli incapax provisions 2–3

effective participation, right of
  adjusted treatment of child suspects not frequently achieved 92–93

Beijing Rules 33–34
child suspect at the centre of investigatory
process 99
development of 308–9
ECHR Art 6, and 33–36
key elements of 35–36
ethnicity *see* Black, Asian and minority
ethnic children
European Convention on Human Rights
(ECHR) 32–34
Human Rights Act, incorporation
into 308–9
right of effective participation *see* effective
participation, right of
right to legal assistance 112–13
exclusion from school 10–11
county-lines' drug supply, and 11

false confessions 7–9
adversarial and coercive interview
approaches 259–60, 306, 316
appropriate adult, and
delay in attending 161, 171–72
lay appropriate adult, mental health
issues and 265
detention
detention in isolation 262
psychological pressure of 290–91
difficulty of detecting at trial 28
features associated with 263–64
minimization techniques increasing rate
of 280–81
risk factors associated with 276–77
sleep deprivation 262
see also confessions
fitness to be interviewed 312–13
ADHD, and 266, 268–69
approach of 101
autism, and 274, 312–13
child suspect perspectives 266–76
ability of solicitor or appropriate adult
to contribute meaningfully 272–74
concerns about ability to make rational
decisions 266–68
custody officer and healthcare
professional approaches 268–70
expert assessment 270–72
inadequate mechanisms to address
unfitness 274–76
timing of assessment, importance
of 270

custody block setting, problems stemming
from 303–4
custody officer approach 268–70
dangerous effects of detention on
reliability 266–68
definition of 262
detainee's physical and mental state, risks
to 262
focus on ability to answer
questions 100–1
healthcare professionals, role of 263–65,
268–72
learning disability, and 266
mandatory training in child development,
importance of 303–4
not identifying all those unfit or ensuring
suitable adjustments 303–4
reliable evidence, ability to give 263
sleep deprivation 267
solicitor's assessment of 138
procedure and existing literature 262–65
appropriate arrangements for
conducting assessment 263–65
clear statement of fitness to be
interviewed 262–63
effective mechanisms to address
identified risks 265
food 207–8

girl suspects 15–16, 220–21
physical restraint to avoid self-harm 229,
234
strip searches 88–89
support for 228–29
under care of female officer 220–21,
228–29

healthcare professionals
detention conditions, adjustments
to 232–34
fitness to be interviewed
assessments 263–65, 268–72
lack of access to information 271
lack of specific child training 270–71
self-harm, preventing 233–34
His Majesty's Inspectorate of Constabulary,
Fire and Rescue Services (HMICFRS
formerly HMIC) 210–11
appropriate adults 85, 157, 160, 168, 194
complaints about questioning
techniques 281

His Majesty's Inspectorate of Constabulary, Fire and Rescue Services (HMICFRS formerly HMIC) (*cont.*)
  custody officers 269–70
  detention conditions 245–46, 329–30
  detention times 214–15
  key measures for child suspects 20–21
  lack of management information about child suspects 19–20
  monitoring and data collection, recommendations for 20–21
  risk assessments 79–80
  strip searches 85
  thematic inspection 23

immaturity *see* natural developmental immaturity
incommunicado rights 103–4, 106–7, 220, 227–28, 240, 341–42
intimate searches *see* strip searches
invisibility of child suspects x–xi, xii
  courts and other accountability mechanisms 18–21
    complaints about police conduct 19–20
    official data on child suspects 20–21
    out-of-court disposals 18–19
    police interviews 19
  legislation and policy, in 13–18
    appropriate adult *see* appropriate adult
    child defendants, treatment of 13–15
    child-specific protections 17
    children in police detention, treatment of 15–16
    custody officers *see* custody officers
    girl suspects 15–16
    questioning children 17
    transfer of child remandees 15–16
  previous research, invisibility in 21–25

Judge's Rules and Administrative Directions v, 156–57
juveniles
  definition and meaning of 'juvenile' 1–2, 4
  PACE *Code C* 1–2

learning disability 7–9, 50, 134, 232
  appropriate adults, and 190–91
  comprehension difficulties 106
  custody officers' training, and 269–70
  decision-making, and 131–32
  detention, and 77–78
  'easyread' notices 110–11
  fitness to be interviewed 266
  healthcare professionals, and 270–71
  questioning 285–86
  risk assessments, and 79, 80–81
legal rights of child suspects *see* rights of child suspects
looked after children 10–11, 78, 80–81, 209–10
  appropriate adult 159, 177–78
  county-lines' drug supply, and 11
  detention, and 78
  inadequacy of residential care provision 235–36

mental health 7–10
  anxiety and mood disorders 9–10
  arrest, and 55
  mental illnesses 9–10
  risk assessments, and 79
  violent behaviour, and 67–68
  vulnerability, and 52–53
minimum age of criminal responsibility (MACR) 2–3, 98
  doli incapax provisions, and 2–3
  inadequacy of arguments supporting low MACR 146–47
  low in comparison with other countries 2–3
  powers to raise 3–4
  punitive turn in youth justice, and 3–4, 93–94
  Scotland, in 3–4

National Police Chiefs' Council (NPCC)
  children treated as children 32–33
  'National Strategy for Police Custody' 94–95, 321–22
natural developmental immaturity
  booking in, problematic behaviour during 67
  children's ability to engage in legal processes 5–6
  natural developmental immaturity in custody 5–6, 50–51
  physical maturity 6
  social and emotional 6

Index

neuro and cognitive disability and developmental disorders 7–9, 11
no comment interviews *see under* police interviews

out of court disposals 18–19
　diversion and community resolutions, emphasis on 113–14
　preference for 259–60
　prevalence of 260–61

PACE viii–x, 16–17
　Code C 16–17
　　appropriate adult 156–59, 161–63, 170, 172–73, 174, 175–76, 193, 197–98, 297–98
　　breaches of 18–19
　　checking on child suspects in cells 17
　　'child', definition of 4
　　child specific protections 17
　　custody officer, and *see* custody officers
　　custody record, right to review 138
　　detention of child suspects 71, 73
　　fitness-for-interview assessment 101, 262, 264–65, 270–71, 303–4
　　intimate searches 84
　　invisibility of child suspects in PACE 15–16
　　'juvenile' to describe a child, use of 1–2
　　police interviews 263, 274–75, 277–78, 292, 297–98, 304–5
　　revision in 2013 4
　　rights of child suspects 103–5, 106–7, 125–26, 128–30
　　seizing personal belongings 87
　　separate cells for child suspects and adults 59–60, 61–62, 220, 223–24
　　strip searches 89
　　vulnerability 52–53
　conflicted position of custody officer 131
parents
　accompanying child suspects 156–57, 163–64
　see also appropriate adult
　not always supportive 156–57
　right to be notified 144, 199–200
　see also appropriate adult
police interviews 19, 258–307
　aim of investigative interview 258–59
　appropriate adult 312–13
　　ability to contribute meaningfully to fitness assessment 272–74
　　concerns about the effectiveness of safeguard 24–25
　　decisive effect on behaviour of police and legal representative 298
　　familial appropriate adult, interviewing protections and 301–3
　　inefficacy in interviews, concerns about 297–98
　　mechanism to address risk in interview, as 265
　　non-familial appropriate adult, interviewing protections and 300–1, 305
　　passivity of 24–25
　　rarely intervening in interview 298
　　required to be present at interview 277–78
　　role at interview 277–78, 297–98
　autism, and 274, 312–13
　confessions, and *see* confessions; false confessions
　counter-productive nature of current interview process 307
　deciding whether to answer questions in *see under* child as legal actor
　factors increasing risk of unfairness for child suspects 259–61
　　exclusion of evidence less likely to be available 260–61
　　out of court disposals, preference for 259–61
　　vulnerable to providing unreliable answers in interview 259–60
　fitness to be interviewed *see* fitness to be interviewed
　free legal advice, and *see under* child as legal actor
　inadequacy of current arrangements 147
　interviewing protections: child suspect perspectives 299–303
　　familial appropriate adults 301–3
　　non-familial appropriate adults 300–1, 305
　　solicitors 299–300
　interviewing protections: procedure and existing literature 297–98
　　research into effect of presence of a solicitor 297
　　role of appropriate adult 297–98

police interviews *(cont.)*
  interviews in custody, concerns about 147
  lack of specialist interview training 277–78, 291–93
    obtaining reliable evidence, undermining 292–93
    threatening rights of child suspect 292–93
  learning disability, and 266
  questioning 285–86
  maintaining no comment: child suspect perspectives 294–97, 306
    challenging to maintain 293–94, 295–96
    'downgrading' questioning approach 294
    exploiting power differential between interviewer and child 296–97
    interpretation of non-verbal behaviour 295
    persistent questioning 295
    right to silence, unfair tactics undermining 296–97
    'upgrading' questioning approach 294
  maintaining no comment: procedure and existing literature 293–94
    adverse inferences, and 293
    challenging nature of 293–94
  night time questioning, undesirability of 216–17
  questioning in interview: child suspect perspectives 282–93
    issues arising from interview process itself 282–83
    issues relating to the manner of interviewer 284–85
    power imbalance of the detention experience 283
  questioning in interview: objections to nature of questioning 285–91
    offering inducements 290–91
    'putting words in child suspect's mouth' 289
    subject-matter objections/relevance 291
    'tricking' 288–89
    'tripping' 285–87
    'twisting' 287–88

  questioning in interview: procedure and existing literature 276–82
    'active listening' skills, increase in use of 280–81
    appropriate adult required to be present 277–78
    'child-friendly' approaches, importance of 276–77
    coercive techniques, use of 280–81, 305
    disengagement in child suspects 281–82
    'interrogation tactics', use of 279–80
    limited research evidence on conducting interviews with child suspects 279
    no requirement for child friendly language or interview spaces 277–78
    no specific training in child friendly questioning techniques 277–78, 304–5
    PEACE model of interviewing, evaluation of 279–80
    PEACE model of interviewing, use of 258–59, 278–79, 296–97, 311–12
    power imbalance in interview room 281–82
    'unfair' questioning techniques, complaints about 281
  role of police 258–59
  summarized records of interview, courts' reliance on 19, 260–61
police legitimacy, perceptions of 248–51

racial discrimination/racism 45
  strip searches 85–86
  see also Black, Asian and minority ethnic children
referral orders viii–x, 18–19, 113–14, 201, 260–61, 273–74, 290
reform *see under* conclusions
reporting crime 252–53
research methods 37–45
  methodological reflections 40–45
    autonomy and compromise 42–44
    consent and stamina 41–42
    reflexive approach
    visibility and protection 40–41
  methods overview 38–40
    interviews 38, 39–41

observations in police custody blocks 39
theoretical framework for evaluating process for child suspects 36–37
   fair procedures 37
   production of accurate determinations 36–37
research methods, theoretical underpinning of 25–37
   Campbell, Ashworth, and Redmayne framework 27
   fair implementation of procedures 29–31
   fair procedures 28–31
   integrity of officers, importance of 30–31
   internal values 27–31
   obtaining of reliable evidence/rectitude 27–28
   special protection for children 29–30
   systems of accountability 31
   'crime control' and 'due process' models 25–26
   critiques of 26–27
   lay fact-finders and adversarialism 36
rights of child suspects 32–36
   appropriate adult, and *see* appropriate adult
   Beijing Rules 33–34
   domestic legal rights *see* child as legal actor
   ECHR *see* European Convention on Human Rights (ECHR)
   ensuring observance of 50
   right of effective participation 33–36
   UNCRC *see* United Nations Convention on the Rights of the Child (UNCRC)
risk assessments
   ADHD, and 80–81
   autism, and 268–69, 274, 312–13
   child suspect experiences 80–83
      assessments not tailored to young suspects 80–81
      length of risk assessments 81–82
      purpose of risk assessments, explanation of 81
      questions focusing on physical health and risk of self-harm 80–81, 82
      response to positive disclosures, limited nature of 82–83

   risk assessments as source of distress 82–83
   HMICFRS 79–80
   learning disability, and 79, 80–81
   not generally required to be shown to solicitor 138
   privacy and dignity, and 93–94
   procedure and existing literature 78–80
      content of risk assessment, variation in 78–79
      efficacy of risk assessment processes 79–80
      factors undermining effective assessments 79
      importance of risk assessments 79–80
      purpose of risk assessments 78–80, 82–83
      role of custody officer 78–80
      training of custody officers 79–80
   risk aversion 79, 80–81, 95, 96–97
      linkage of vulnerability with risk 96–97
      risk of child coming to physical harm in the cells 96–97
   self-harm *see* self-harm
   stigmatizing experience of 95–96
Royal Commission on Criminal Procedure (RCCP)
   appropriate adult, role of 161–62, 164
   parents
      accompanying child suspects 156–57, 163–64
      right to be notified 199–200
   searches of child suspects 83–84

safeguarding
   detention as 77–78
   risk assessments, and 79–80
   see also risk assessments
   strip searches 96–97
   see also strip searches
search and seizure of belongings
   child suspect experiences 87–90
      harassment and upset, searches causing 87
      initial search and seizure 87–88
      laces and cords, removal of 88
   custodial arrest not required 71, 76
   initial search and seizure 87–88
   intimate searches *see* strip searches

search and seizure of belongings (*cont.*)
  pat-down searching 87
  procedure and existing literature 83–86
    conduct of search 83
    humiliating and upsetting nature of searches 83–84
    purpose of search 83
  recording seized property 87
  risk, and 96–97
    physical risk as overriding consideration 87
  stigmatizing experience of 95–96
  strip searches *see* strip searches
self-harm 78, 212, 233–35
  authorising detention, and 74
  preventing 84, 233–35
    clothing removal 233–34
    constant watch 234
    handcuffs, use of 89–90
    healthcare professionals, use of 233–34
    laces and cords, removal of 88
    no possessions/distraction items in cells 230
    physical restraint 229, 234–35
  response to custody, as 233
  risk assessments, and 80–81, 82, 96–97
  strip searches and intimate searches, and 84, 88–90, 91–92
sleep deprivation 267
solicitors
  appropriate adult inhibiting communication with 189–90
  child suspect engaging with *see* child as legal actor
  fitness to be interviewed assessments
    ability to contribute meaningfully 272–74
    solicitor's assessment 138
  interviewing protections, and 299–300
    balancing power differential 299
    not always effective protection from oppressive interview tactics 299–300
    positive effect of having solicitor in interview 299, 305
    relationship between role of solicitor and appropriate adult 301, 305
    research into effect of presence of solicitor 297
  no comment interviews 294, 296, 306
  risk assessments, and 138

strip searches
  appropriate adult, in presence of 84–85
  Black, Asian, and minority ethnic children 85–86, 88–89
  child suspect experiences 88–89
    removal of all clothes at once 89
    repeat strip searches 89
    traumatizing effect of 85, 89–90
    violating nature of 88–89
  Children's Commissioner 85–86
  communicative power of 86
  constant watch as alternative 89–90
  data on 20–21
  HMICFRS 85
  intimate searches
    appropriate adult, in presence of 84–85
    nature of 84
  markers triggering future strip searches 87, 89–90
  predominantly involving girl suspects 88–89
  racism, and 85–86
  reasons for 84
  safeguarding, as 96–97
  self-harm, and 84, 88–90, 91–92
  undignified, degrading and traumatic nature of 84–85

Taylor Review of the Youth Justice System 147–48

United Nations Convention on the Rights of the Child (UNCRC)
  adjusted conditions for particular needs 255
  adoption of 308–9
  arrest of child suspects 71
  'best interests of the child' as primary consideration 32–33
  'child', definition of 4
  child's right to be heard and listened to 32–33
    legal assistance, right to 112–13
    overridden 90–91
  United Nations Committee on the Rights of the Child
    'child-friendly' provision, importance of 32–33, 276–77
    effective participation 99
    fair trial rights 32–33
    false confessions 276–77

legal assistance, right to 112–13, 114–15
minimum age of criminal
  responsibility 2–3
nature of proceedings involving
  children 59
police detention 32–33, 204–5

victims
  arrested children as 11–12
  empathy for 183
  victim-orientated focus in police
    culture 95–96
  vulnerability, victimhood and 50–51, 90–91
violence
  arrest, during 54
  custody block, and 64–65, 224
  domestic violence 326–27
  family violence 10–11
  mental health issues, and 67–68
  physical restraint to avoid harm 229, 234–35
  research, and 41–42, 252–53
  youth violence 252–53
vulnerability 50–53
  child suspects not explicitly identified as
    vulnerable 52–53
  contested concept, as 50–51
  downplaying structural adversity 51–52
  problematic behaviour, and 67–68, 95–96
  risk of harm to and by the child, and 51–52
  shifting nature of concept 52–53
  victim-orientation intersecting with
    concept of 95–96
  vulnerable person in police custody,
    definition of 52–53
  weakness and frailty, and 50–51, 90–91,
    95–96
  police reliance on outward signs of 68

welfare principle 13

youth cautions 18–19
youth court
  adultification and responsibilization of
    child defendants 14–15
  adversarial proceedings in 2–3
  child witnesses 14–15
  children appearing in 2–3, 15–16
  excluding confessions at trial 148, 164–65
  nature and practice of 13–14
  participation of young and vulnerable
    defendants 13–14
  prosecution disclosure 19
  questioning children 13–14
  shortcomings of 14–15
  summarized records of interview, reliance
    on 19, 260–61
  training of judges and
    magistrates 13–15
  welfare principle 13
Youth Justice System (YJS)
  adversarial nature of custody
    process 94–95
  Black, Asian and minority ethnic
    backgrounds overrepresented
    in 12
  'child', definition of 1–2, 4
  diversion and community resolutions,
    emphasis on 113–14
  'juveniles', move from use of 1–2
  out-of-court disposals 18–19, 259–61
  police interviews *see* police interviews
  primary aim of 13–14
  punitive turn in 3–4, 93–94
  referral orders viii–x, 18–19, 113–14,
    201, 260–61, 273–74, 290
  reform: implications for wider youth
    justice system 342–45
  youth cautions 18–19
youth offending teams 13–14